Union Public Library

Made In Italy
Food & Stories

Giorgio Locatelli

with Sheila Keating

Photographs by
Dan Lepard

Union Public Library

ecco
An Imprint of HarperCollinsPublishers

To Plaxy

Contents

14

Soup

Risotto

Ravioli di patate e menta con peperoni
360 Potato and mint ravioli with pepper sauce

Ravioli di erbe con salsa di noci
362 Herb ravioli with walnut sauce

Ravioli di patate e funghi selvatici
363 New potato ravioli with
wild mushrooms

Tordelli di cipolla rossa e salsa al Chianti
364 Red onion tortelli with Chianti sauce

Tordelli di zucca agli amaretti
366 Tortelli with pumpkin
and amaretti

Tordelli di melanzane e mozzarella
367 Eggplant and mozzarella tortelli

Malfatti di ricotta, melanzane e noci
368 Ricotta pockets with eggplant
and walnuts

Ravioli di gamberi
372 Prawn ravioli

Ravioli all'osso buco
374 Veal shank ravioli

Ravioli di coda di manzo
376 Oxtail ravioli

Ravioli di fagiano
379 Pheasant ravioli

Strozzapreti alle tre cipolle
380 Pasta twists with onion

Spaghetti alla chitarra con polpettine
di tonno
382 Handmade spaghetti with balls of tuna

Gnocchi di patate al pepe nero
e salsa al caprino
388 Potato gnocchi with black pepper
and goat cheese sauce

Gnocchi di patate pomodoro e rucola
390 Potato dumplings with tomato and arugula

Gnocchi di patate al pesto
390 Potato gnocchi with pesto

Gnocchi di patate ai funghi porcini
392 Potato gnocchi with porcini

Gnocchi di patate con carciofi
e Murazzano
393 Potato gnocchi with artichokes
and Murazzano cheese

Gnocchetti di funghi al burro
e salvia e tartufo nero
394 Small mushroom dumplings with butter,
sage and truffles

Pesce

Fish

Branzino alla Vernaccia in crosta
di pomodoro
408 Sea bass with tomato crust and
Vernaccia wine

Branzino in crosta di sale e erbe
410 Sea bass in sea salt and herbs

Branzino al basilico
414 Sea bass with basil potato puree

Trancio di tonno alla griglia
415 Chargrilled tuna

Nasello in scabeccio
417 Steamed hake with parsley and garlic

Sgombro alla griglia con crosta di erbe
418 Chargrilled mackerel with herb crust

Trancio di merluzzo con lenticchie
423 Cod with lentils

San Pietro con patate e olive
424 Fillet of John Dory with potato and olives

Coda di rospo in salsa di noci
e agrodolce di capperi
426 Monkfish with walnut and agrodolce

Trancio di rombo ai funghi porcini
con purè di patate
428 Roasted turbot (or brill) with porcini
and potato puree

Sogliola arrosto con patate,
fagiolini e pesto
429 Roast Dover sole with potatoes,
beans and pesto sauce

Orata al balsamico
431 Pan-fried sea bream with
balsamic vinegar

Trancio di rombo liscio all'acquapazza
432 Roast brill with green olives and
cherry tomatoes

Filetti di passera al basilico con
patate e olive
434 Plaice with basil, potatoes and olives

Filetti di passera con castelfranco
finocchi e bagna càôda
437 Roast fillet of plaice with fennel and
anchovy sauce

Sardine con panzanella
438 Sardines with bread salad

Carne

Meat

Agnello primaverile alla griglia
con peperonata e melanzane
456 Chargrilled lamb with peppers
and eggplant puree

Stufato di agnello con peperoni
459 Lamb stew with peppers

Filetto di manzo, spugnole e patate
466 Beef chops with morels and potatoes

Sottofiletto di manzo alla griglia con
radicchio trevisano tardivo e polenta
467 Chargrilled beef sirloin with trevisano
radicchio and polenta

Filetto di cervo, porcini e crema fritta
470 Loin of venison, porcini and fried
pastry cream

Costoletta di vitello con carciofi
e patate novelle
472 Veal chop with artichokes
and new potatoes

Paillard di pollo con spinaci
474 Chargrilled chicken breast
with spinach

Pollastra bollita al tartufo nero
di norcia, vegetali bolliti e salsa verde
476 Poached chicken stuffed with
black truffle, with boiled vegetables
and salsa verde

Filetti di maiale con cavolo nero
e fagioli
477 Pork chops with black cabbage
and cannellini beans

Filetti di maiale con crosta di
mostarda e borlotti
479 Pork chops with mustard crust
and borlotti beans

Fegato di vitello al balsamico
484 Calves' liver with balsamic vinegar

Rognone di vitello con lenticchie
e carciofi
487 Veal kidney with lentils
and artichoke

Anatra con broccoli
488 Duck breast with broccoli

Pernice con lenticchie e purè di patate
491 Partridge with lentils and potato puree

Piccione, tartufo nero e purè d'aglio
493 Roast pigeon, black truffle
and garlic puree

Animelle di vitello in agrodolce
495 Veal sweetbreads with
sweet-and-sour sauce

Dolci

Desserts

Sorbetto di melone, fragole selvatiche,
salsa all'arancio
520 Wild strawberries with melon sorbet
and orange sauce

Lasagne di fragole e mango
521 Strawberry and mango lasagne

Pere cotte al vino rosso e bianco
524 Poached pears in red and white wine

Pere cotte e crude con zabaione a moscato
526 Muscat zabaglione with confit and
fresh pears

Pesche sciroppate, semifreddo di menta
e gelatina d'Amaretto
530 Poached peaches with fresh mint
nougat glace and Amaretto jelly

Macedonia di nespole e sanguinelle,
gelatina di violetta e schiuma allo yogurt
532 Blood orange and fresh loquat salad with
violet jelly and yogurt foam

534 Catalan cream foam with berries

Sorbetto di menta, frutta della passione
e schiuma di cocco
535 Mint sorbet, passion fruit jelly and
coconut foam

Torta di ciliege
536 Cherry tart

Torta di pesche all'amaretto
538 Peach and amaretto tart

Torta di mele
540 Apple tart

Torta di limone e mascarpone
541 Lemon and mascarpone tart

Torta di ricotta
544 Ricotta tart

545 Cannoli di ricotta

Pastiera Napoletana
548 Easter tart

549 Rusumada

Zuppa di pomodoro dolce, gelatina
di balsamica e sorbetto al basilico
550 Sweet tomato soup, balsamic jelly
and basil sorbet

Soufflé di riso carnaroli al limone
552 Carnaroli rice and lemon soufflé

554 Tiramisù with banana and
licorice ice cream

Sorbetto di melone
560 Melon sorbet

Sorbetto di menta
560 Mint sorbet

Sorbetto di basilico
560 Basil sorbet

Gelato alla vaniglia
561 Vanilla ice cream

Gelato al latte
561 Milk ice cream

Gelato di crema Catalana
561 Crème Catalan ice cream

Gelato al mascarpone
562 Mascarpone ice cream

Gelato al timo limonato
562 Lemon thyme ice cream

Gelato all'Amaretto
564 Amaretto ice cream

Gelato al mirto
564 Myrtle ice cream

Gelato al Limoncello
565 Limoncello ice cream

La Convivialità

I wanted to call this book *Made of Italy*, because that is what I am – but I could as easily have called it *La Convivialità* – because that is the word I use most to explain the way Italians feel about food. For us the sign of welcome is to feed people. At the heart of all cooking, whether you are rich or poor, is the spirit of conviviality, the pleasure that comes from sharing a meal with others. And there is no enjoyment of food without quality.

The way I think about food is entirely in tune with the Slow Food movement, started in Italy back in 1986 by Carlo Petrini in defiance of the opening of a McDonald's outlet in the Piazza di Spagna in Roma. Now a worldwide force, Slow Food champions local, traditional produce with real flavor, made by caring people with skill and wisdom, which is celebrated every two years – with wonderful conviviality – at the Salone del Gusto, the famous food fair in Torino.

In the U.S. it is easy to blame supermarkets for chalking up air miles, for persuading us that we want fruit and vegetables that look perfect but often have little flavor; for luring us on to diets of things that are salty, fatty, sugary and easy to eat; for packaging everything into convenient parcels so that we almost forget where our food comes from; and conditioning us to think that as long as our food is cheap, we are satisfied. But *we* have responsibilities too, and we have the power to change things. Of course I understand when you have kids you want to go to the supermarket, not traipse for miles trying to find a good butcher and fishmonger and green-grocer, and I'm not sitting here in my restaurant saying you must do this and that, only remember that every time you pick up food in a supermarket, you are making a choice that has consequences. Where do you want to invest your money? In the profits of a supermarket, or in a farm rearing fantastic old breeds of pigs, or a small dairy making beautiful cheese?

You will see the letters DOP (PDO in the UK) and IGP (PGI in the UK) throughout the book. DOP represents Denominazione di Origine Protetta or Protected Designation of Origin (PDO), and it appears alongside the specific name of a product such as Parmigiano-Reggiano or prosciutto di Parma. What it tells you is that in order to earn the stamp of the DOP and be allowed to use this name, the food must be produced in a designated area, using particular methods. IGP represents Indicazione Geografica Protetta, or Protected Geographical Indication (PGI), which is similar, but states that at least one stage of production must occur in the traditional region, and doesn't place as much emphasis on the method of production. Whenever you buy Italian produce, look for these symbols.

Salt should ideally be natural sea salt, and pepper freshly ground and black. Spend a little extra on good extra virgin olive oil and vinegar, and it will repay you a thousand times. And whenever possible buy whole chickens, and meat and fish on the bone, not portioned and wrapped in plastic.

All recipes serve 4, unless otherwise stated.

"You'll never be a chef, Locatelli!"

"Pass the prawns … the prawns … where are they … are they ready?" I had been helping with the cooking in my uncle's restaurant since I was five years old, but now, at sixteen, and a few months into my first real job, I used to get picked on all the time by the head chef. Now he wanted the prawns and they weren't ready. The water in the pan was almost boiling. It needed to be boiling before I put in the prawns, but I panicked and put them in anyway. He saw it and shouted at me, "You will never be a chef, Locatelli. You are an idiot," and he sent me to clean the French beans.

I couldn't forget those words: "You will never be a chef." By the end of the day, I wanted to cry like a baby. I went home and my grandmother was waiting. "What does he know?" she said. "Who is he?" "He is The Chef!" I told her. I would have run away, but as always my grandmother put everything into perspective, and she told me I had to go back and show him. So I went back. And I did show him.

Food, love and life…

My first feelings for cooking came from my grandmother Vincenzina. But my first understanding of the relationship among food, sex, wine and the excitement of life came together for me very early on, when I was growing up in the village of Corgeno on the shores of Lake Comabbio in Lombardia in the north of Italy – long before I was suspended from cooking school for kissing girls on the college steps.

My uncle Alfio and my auntie Louisa, with the help of my granddad, built our hotel and restaurant, La Cinzianella – named after my cousin Cinzia – on the shores of the lake, on the edge of the village of Corgeno in 1963.

There were eight founding families in the village. The Caletti family, on my mother's side, was one of them; and on my grandmother's side, the Tamborini family, along with the Gnocchi family, who are our cousins, and who have a pastry shop in Gallarate, near Milano, in the hinterland, before the scenery changes from city to green and beautiful space, and where the specialty is gorgeous soft amaretti cookies.

The shop gave me my first taste of an industrial kitchen. I used to love going in there as a kid, because the ovens were so big you could walk into them. In the season running up to Christmas, over and above the other confectionery, they would make around 10,000 panettoni (our Italian Christmas cake). It was fascinating to watch the people take the panettoni from the ovens, and then, while they were still warm, hang them upside down in rows on big ladders in the finishing room, so that the dough could stretch and take on that characteristic light, airy texture. Years later, when I first started in the kitchens at the Savoy, I felt at home immediately, because I recognized that same sense of busy, busy people, working away in total concentration.

Of course, everyone in Corgeno seems to be some sort of cousin, though none of us can remember exactly how we are related. Six generations of our families are buried in the village graveyard, and the names are etched many times into the war memorial outside the church with the two Roman towers, above the makeshift football pitch where we kids played every day after we had (or hadn't) done our homework.

Life in the north of Italy is very different from the way it is in the pretty Italy of the south – the idyllic Italy, still a little wild, that you always see in movies. The south fulfills the Mediterranean expectation, whereas the north is the real heart of Europe. Historically we have been under many influences: Spanish, French, Austrian…at home we are only around 12 and a half miles from Switzerland, and Milano is the most cosmopolitan city in Italy. In the north I don't know anyone who hasn't got a job and everyone comes to the north to find work – the reverse of the way it is in England.

The industrial north of Ferrari and Alessi can be more stark; but somehow I think it has a tougher, more impressive and real kind of beauty than the regions that have been written about so much, like Toscano and Umbria. You might not think they are very far down the boot of Italy, but where I come from anything below Bologna is south. In the north, we are famous for designing and making things, things that work properly. Northern Italians always tell jokes against southern Italians, and vice versa. We like to say that in Roma, if you have to dig a hole in the road it will take eight months; in the north everything will be fixed and running like clockwork in a day. And while most of Italy used to stop for a big break at lunchtime – especially in the south, where it was too hot to work – in Milano and around Lombardia it would be one hour only. The factory whistles would go at 12 noon – the signal for the wives and mothers at home to put in the pasta – and then the road would be full of bicycles and scooters and motorcycles, as everyone shot home to eat and then straight back to work.

In the south, they are used to delicate foods like mozzarella and tomatoes and seafood. In the north, we are proud of our Parmigiano-Reggiano and prosciutto di Parma and big, warming dishes like polenta and risotto. And if we haven't used our food to promote our area around the world as strongly as other regions, it is not because it is less important to us, but that we haven't needed to, because we are known for other things.

Corgeno is a place steeped in history, first because of its twin Roman towers and more recently because of its pocket resistance to fascism. On one of the old walls you can see the faded words of one of Mussolini's slogans that still makes me angry every time I see it, with its call to the youth of Italy to put down their picks and shovels and take up arms. There are many stories in our village of the local men of the resistance who used to hide in the woods, where the women would bring them food. One of them, my father's brother, Nino, was shot on one of his trips, trying to help 40 Jewish people escape over the border into Switzerland.

Below the village is La Cinzianella, only a few steps to the edge of the lake, which I love, especially in autumn, my favorite time of year. Almost tragic, isn't it, autumn? But so beautiful. Early in the morning, you can't see the lake because it is hiding in a mauve mist, but when it rises the sky is bright blue and the trees around the lake, with their red and gold leaves, stand out clearly against it. And it is so quiet: all you can hear are the birds calling and scudding over the water – and across the lake the faint buzz of motorcycles going a hundred miles an hour across the *superstrada*, the straight toward Mercallo, and into the turn, as if they were on a racetrack.

We are only 45 minutes' drive from the center of Milano, and right next to the bigger and more famous Lago Maggiore, so now a lot of people from the city come for weekends; they have bought houses, and the village has grown. But when I was growing up, there were only about 2,000 people and everyone knew everyone else: who was just born, who died; it was all-important to our lives.

I remember one of the first new families to move into Corgeno, from Sicilia – the wife worked at La Cinzianella, and we nicknamed one of the kids

Mandarino after the oranges that came from Sicilia. They spoke a dialect that sounded foreign to us, and the father was loud and dramatic when he talked; tragic, comical…so different from my father, who never raised his voice.

Almost everything we ate and drank was produced locally. We even picked up the milk every evening from the window of the house of Napoleone, who kept a few cows. Each family had its own bottles and he would fill them up and leave them for us to collect – in winter outside the window, in summer in the courtyard under a fountain. Later, when I was a young boy and I was working in restaurants abroad, when I came home for the holidays, people would always open their windows to lean out and say hello. They still do. Whenever we go to Corgeno, my wife, Plaxy, complains that it takes an hour to walk through the village, because someone will always shout, "Hey, Giorgio" – and it always seems to be an ex-girlfriend.

I remember coming back home after one summer when I was a teenager. I stopped in at the tobacconist to buy cigarettes, and by the time I got to our house, my grandmother already knew that I had changed from Camel to Marlboro. That is how small our village was.

My auntie and uncle and my father and mother all worked in the hotel and my uncle ran the restaurant where I worked, too, as soon I was big enough. Later we had a Michelin star, but then we just served good, honest Italian food and on Saturdays we did banqueting and wedding receptions in a big beautiful room at the top of the hotel, looking out over the lake. We used to feed around 180 people and when we were at our busiest, we would make 45 pounds of dough for the gnocchi and everyone, from the waiters to the women who did the rooms, would come into the kitchen to help shape them. In summer, our guests could sit out on the terrace under big umbrellas. If it was raining they gathered inside around a big table in the corridor, and no one ever complained.

There are ten rooms in La Cinzianella, and we would send food to the rooms, too. Every Sunday a well-known gentleman from the village, Luciano, would come to the hotel in his Mercedes, with a woman named Rosetta. Everyone knew that his wife had been ill for a long time and that Rosetta was his mistress. So on Sundays his room would be ready for him from about two o'clock, and by six, six-thirty, he would call us and order a bottle of champagne. I remember my mother would put it on a tray and, of course, somebody had to take it up – all of us young boys wanted to do it, because we wanted to catch a glimpse of Rosetta.

I still remember her – warm and round and womanly, like my auntie Maria Luisa, who was beautiful too, the nearest thing to royalty. Maria Luisa was the only one who had any power over me when I was wayward, and could tell me off without ever losing her temper, unlike my mother, who is quite a nervous woman. When my granddad died, we sat down for our first meal all together without him, and we all expected that my father would take his place at the head of the table, but Maria Luisa came in and sat down in the place of my granddad and she has been there ever since.

My auntie and Rosetta – for me they represented sexuality, but all bound up with good food and wine and generosity, because by seven-thirty, showered and beautifully dressed, Rosetta and her gentleman friend would come down to eat dinner and we would welcome them warmly; we were part of their lives, and they were part of ours. There was a complicity between restaurateur and guest, which is one of the things I have tried to create in my own restaurant.

Even in the heart of London, I feel we have a special bond with our customers. Eating is not just about fueling up to get through the day; it is about conviviality, friendship and celebration. I like the fact that people come to us again and again for an anniversary or a birthday. I want them to bring their kids, so I can take them into the kitchen, and they can help prepare the dessert for their mums and dads. I like to feel that I can come and sit down and chat with them in between cooking; and if I see them on the street one morning, I can invite them into the restaurant for coffee. Sometimes people who have eaten at Locanda, and before that at Zafferano, whom we have known for many years, come to see us after a husband or wife has died, or they have split up, because in a strange, poignant way, we have become part of their lives. For my wife, Plaxy, and for me that is so special; because this is *our* restaurant, an extension of our family; and everything that happens in it is personal to us. I know how important it is to have that intimacy, because the memories of our relationship with the local gentleman and Rosetta at La Cinzianella have stayed with me all my life.

Antipasti

Starters

"It is true that man does not live by bread alone;
   he must eat something with it."

Pellegrino Artusi

Italians are very impatient people. We can't sit for more than a minute
in traffic and we hate to wait for our food. That is why we invented antipasti, which literally means "before the meal [*pasto*]." When I first
came to England, I thought it so strange to see people at parties and
weddings standing around having drinks before they ate. Italians just
want to get to the table as soon as possible, so the bread can arrive. Not
just bread – we also want salami, prosciutto, maybe some marinated artichokes, some olives… We want to enjoy a glass of wine, to talk and argue, because everything we do in a day is a small drama and everyone
has an opinion on it – but we need to eat while we are discussing it. Once
the antipasti are on the table, that is the signal to relax, get into the
mood and interact, because you have to pass the plates and everyone is
saying, "Oh, what is this?" and "Can I have some of that?" It is all
about conviviality and sharing and generosity.

A few miles from my home in Corgeno, in Lombardia, on the way to
nowhere, is the village of Cuirone, with its pale, yellow-washed houses;
a place that has hardly changed since I was a child. In the middle of the
village is the Società Mutuo Soccorso, the cooperative shop and restaurant with a bakery attached, where they make fantastic chestnut and
pumpkin bread, as well as the big *pane bianco*, which is the everyday
bread. Inside the bakery, they have a basket full of drawstring bags,
some gingham, some flowery. Each family makes its own bag, and the
bakers know which bread they have, so in the morning when the loaves
come out of the oven, the bags get filled up and delivered by scooter.

At one time in our region of Italy, most of the villages had a *cooperativa*,
run by the locals, where everyone could bring their produce to sell and
where you could get a simple lunch for not much money. Everything
you ate would be produced locally. You have to remember that Italy has
been a united country for not much more than a hundred years. Before
that it was made up of different kingdoms, dukedoms, republics, and
so on, each influenced by different neighbors and invading armies
throughout its history.

Also in Italy you have a massive geographical change, from mountains
to coastlines, from the colder north with its plains full of cows giving
beef and milk for cheese, to the hot south, on the same parallel as
Africa, where they grow a profusion of lemons, tomatoes, capers and
peppers. So in every region, town and village, they have their own particular ingredients and style of cooking, which of course they will insist
is absolutely the right way – and that what everyone else does is wrong.

In Corgeno, the *cooperativa* was next to my uncle's restaurant, La
Cinzianella, overlooking the lake, and when you turned twenty years

old, you were asked to run it for the summer (the year my friends and I took charge we had a fantastic time). But now the space is rented out as a café and restaurant. In Cuirone, though, the *cooperativa* is still thriving, and sometimes, especially when I come home to visit, my mum and dad and my aunts, uncles and cousins all meet up there for lunch at the weekend. Lunch is at 12:30, and 12:30 is what they mean, so you don't dare be late.

It's a very simple place: a large room with a long bar down one side and wooden tables and chairs where the farmers and the old men of the village drink red wine and play cards. But the moment you sit down, big baskets of bread from the bakery arrive with bottles of local wine, and then the plates of antipasti: salami, prosciutto, lardo, carpaccio, local cheeses, artichokes, porcini. As one plate is taken away, more arrive, and so it goes on and on. Then, just when my wife, Plaxy, especially, is thinking that there can't be any more food, out comes a pasta dish – maybe a baked lasagne – and then a fruit dessert.

The antipasti are based around simple produce, just like in people's homes and most small restaurants. The members of the *cooperativa* bring whatever they have that is fresh that day, along with ingredients such as artichokes and mushrooms, prepared when they were in season, then preserved in big jars under vinegar or oil, or *salamoia* (brine). In Italy, things are done differently from in the UK, especially London, where you buy your food, eat it, and then buy some more. Most people in Italy still behave like they did in the old days, when you would always have a store cupboard full of dried or preserved foods because you never knew when there would be a war or some other disaster.

In smarter restaurants, the kitchen would have the chance to show off a little more with the antipasti. In my uncle's kitchen at La Cinzianella we really worked at our antipasti, bringing out some fantastic flavors, because we knew that this prelude to the meal said a lot about what we were trying to achieve with our food, and about the dishes that would follow. The slicing machine was right in the middle of the big dining room, so everyone could see the cured meats being freshly cut, and we would prepare seafood salads and roasted vegetables. Imagine how I reacted the first time I went to a French restaurant and they sent out some canapés before the meal – those tiny, bite-sized things. I was shocked. I thought, If this is what the rest of the food is going to be like, forget it! Italians don't like to fiddle about with fancy morsels, they just want to welcome people by sharing what they have, however simple, in abundance. An Italian's role in life is to feed people. A lot. We can't help it.

The traditional Italian meal

In Italy the concept of the "starter" – individually plated dishes that you eat by yourself, just *you* – is quite a modern thing. Only in the last twenty years or so have restaurants started putting them on the menu. Traditionally, after the antipasti the real "starter" was the pasta course, or first plate *(i primi piatti)*. Then came the second plate *(i secondi piatti)*, which would be meat or fish, and, to finish, fruit or a dessert *(i dolci)*.

When I look at the books I have of old regional recipes, no mention is made of "starters" as we think of them today. One of the books I love most is *La Scienza in Cucina e l'Arte di Mangiar Bene (Science in the Kitchen and the Art of Eating Well)* by Pellegrino Artusi. All Italian cooks know about Artusi – he was a great gourmet and one of the first writers to gather together recipes from all over Italy. He published the book himself back in 1891, in the days when Italian food was considered a bit vulgar in "smart" society because the food of the royal courts was French.

Artusi spent twenty years traveling around Italy and his knowledge of regional produce and cooking was remarkable. His stories are full of beautiful descriptions and witty comments, sometimes using old Italian words that I have to look up. I keep his book in my office in the kitchen at Locanda to research ingredients and old recipes. But even Artusi has only a short section on "appetizers," which is really just an acknowledgment of the moment before the meal when you show off your capacity to bring out food of a high quality. (Interestingly, he says that in Toscana they did things differently from other regions and served these "delicious trifles" *after* the pasta, not before.) Artusi talks about various cured meats, caviar and *mosciame* (salted and air-dried tuna), but the only "recipes" he gives for appetizers are a selection of crostini: fried bread topped with ingredients such as capers, chicken livers and sage, or woodcock and anchovies.

Traditionally, the kind of antipasti you ate was determined by where you lived. Around the coast there would obviously be more seafood, while inland there were cured meats. Every region would have different breads to serve with the antipasti: light, airy breads in the north, white unsalted bread in Toscana and enormous country loaves made with harder flour in the south – fantastic for bruschetta, which these days has become rather elevated in restaurants, but is really just chargrilled stale bread with a bit of garlic and tomato rubbed over it and some oil drizzled on top.

Even now, food in Italy is very regional, but after the Second World War, when everything became more abundant and people began to travel more, some chefs started to be a little inventive and borrow ideas for their antipasti from other regions, and from the street food you see cooked in cities such as Napoli by vendors with gas burners on trolleys: *arancini* (rice balls), *crocchette* (mashed potato croquettes), *panzerotti* (little pasties filled with meat, cheese, tomatoes or anchovies, then deep-fried), *mozzarella in carrozza* (mozzarella "in a carriage" – deep-fried between slices of bread), and *frittelle* (fritters filled with artichokes, mushrooms or prawns).

Italian food today

Nowadays in Italy – in the cities at least – like everywhere else in the world, the way people want to eat is changing, though perhaps a little more slowly than everywhere else. Not everyone wants a meal of several courses anymore. They want to be more relaxed, so you can order just a bowl of pasta and nobody thinks anything of it. And there are now city bars serving only antipasti, where you make yourself up a plate of whatever you want, and that's all you have. Then there are the newer, smarter restaurants, which try really hard to make their starters more imaginative than a plate of carpaccio or an *insalata caprese* (tomatoes and mozzarella).

As for me, I am an Italian chef who has cooked in Paris and come of age in London, and inventive starters are what people expect from me. I might have in the kitchen a salami that is so beautiful it makes you cry, but I can't just slice it and put it out with some artichokes and bread. I have to present it in a more sophisticated way. We must include such starters in the restaurant, but we can't lose the pasta course, so the modern Italian menu usually has four sections: starters, pasta, main courses and dessert, which I know can seem daunting. Sometimes customers say, "What should I do? Do I have to have a starter, then pasta and a main course after that? Or can I have just pasta and a dessert?" Of course, you can do what you like; we just try to give a selection of everything an Italian would want to be offered, so you can eat as few or as many courses as you want.

However sophisticated our menu may be at Locanda, it always has its roots in classic regional Italian cooking. Sure, some of our favorite starters have come about, like all good dishes, from getting excited about a particular ingredient that comes into the kitchen, but many of them are simply our interpretation of the traditional elements of the *antipasti misti* – the artichokes, porcini and cured meats with which I and most of my kitchen staff have grown up. We look at them, rethink them and work at representing them in more imaginative or surprising ways.

The key is always to concentrate on just a few flavors. I think it is terrible to eat out in a restaurant and not remember afterward what you had because there were too many tastes happening at once on your plate. It is better to buy primary ingredients that have their own fantastic flavor and then you have to do less with them.

One of the great things that has happened since I came to this country is the revolution in the quality of ingredients. When the first Italian immigrants came to the UK and set up their restaurants, they brought what they could over from Italy and created a limited Italian kitchen, making Anglo-Italian dishes that catered to British tastes. Then when people began to be more interested in the genuine food of Italy, and were prepared to pay for real Parmigiano Reggiano and prosciutto di Parma and mozzarella di bufala, the best-quality food began to be imported, and producers in this country began to think, "We can do this, too." So now there is a wonderful mix of high-quality Italian and British produce that you can use in your antipasti.

Reinterpreting the classics

Very little of the traditional *antipasti misti* involves hot food – just a few deep-fried dishes, such as zucchini blossoms or squid, or the *panzerotti* and *frittelle* I mentioned earlier. Personally, I don't like to eat too many fried foods at the start of a meal. So, instead, for our hot starters at the restaurant we look to the kind of main dishes that every Italian knows – great classics with brilliant flavors, such as sardines baked in bread crumbs, or pig's feet – then we refine them and scale them down into starters. We play a bit of a game with the presentation, or make them easier for people to eat in a restaurant environment. Sometimes, when I see some of our famous customers thoroughly enjoying an appetizer of *gnocchi fritti* with *culatello*, it makes me smile to see something that you would find in any antipasti bar in Italy being celebrated in such a way, when I am only playing around with an idea that was worked out hundreds of years ago in Mantova. But perhaps that is the magic of a restaurant like Locanda – with a little imagination, the essential flavors and combinations of ingredients that have stayed in people's hearts and minds for centuries can be elevated into something glamorous.

What we do in the restaurant and what we do at home, however, are two different things. At home, the idea is to keep things simple. But if you can approach cooking for family and friends with a little of the organization we need in a professional kitchen, *you* will enjoy a good meal as well, instead of being in the kitchen with smoke everywhere and your hair standing on end, so when someone comes in and says, "How are you?," you want to scream. Use this chapter more as a source of inspiration than as a series of recipes. You don't have to serve the dishes as individual starters, as we do in the restaurant. If you are having friends over, use the idea of shared antipasti to your advantage. Buy some good prosciutto, salami or mozzarella, which need nothing done to them, then choose a few of the recipes and dedicate your time to working on them, doubling the quantities if necessary, so you can serve everything on big plates to hand around. You can make your dessert in advance too, so you have only a main course to cook, which can be as simple as you like. It is *my* job to stay in the kitchen and cook for people. Your job is to make life as easy as possible, so when your friends arrive you can just put everything down on the table and sit and have a drink and talk with them.

Insalate e condimenti

Salads and dressings

At home in Corgeno I don't remember my grandmother ever making a salad that was a dish in its own right, or had any sophistication, but salads have become an important part of the way we eat now. As with all our dishes in the restaurant, we look to classic Italian combinations of ingredients and flavors for our inspiration. What is exciting is to play with whatever is in season and what is good from the market: porcini mushrooms in autumn, root vegetables in winter, asparagus in spring, tomatoes in summer.

Like any other dish, a good salad needs structure – different textures, such as something soft, something with a little crunch. Throw in some pomegranate seeds and people think you have done something fantastic. Italians often find it difficult to put fruit in salad, but a chef who has been a real inspiration to me is David Thompson at Nahm, such a clever man – I really like what he does with Thai food. I came up with the idea of putting pomegranate into a winter salad after eating at Nahm, and having a brilliant salty-sweet warm salad, layered with leaves and peanuts and fruit such as mango and papaya – almost like a lasagne.

When we eat, we experience taste sensations in different parts of the mouth: sweet, sour, salty, bitter – and the most recently recognized, umami. Think about balancing ingredients that satisfy all these tastes, so that when you eat the salad it fills your whole mouth with flavor. A tomato can give sweetness; maybe you want something peppery, like arugula, or something aniseed, like raw fennel, which is so underused in salads in the UK. And remember that salad leaves all have different flavors and textures, so it is good to include a mixture.

I don't like to see ready-prepared salads and vegetables in supermarkets, though – all those bags of mixed leaves, looking perfect thanks to a little cocktail of pesticides and kept going in their "modified-atmosphere" bags, alongside packets of shelled peas, and beans with their tops and tails cut off. Vegetables and leaves begin to lose some of their nutrients, especially vitamin C, the moment they are plucked or cut up, so who knows what value is left in prepackaged ones by the time they reach your plate?

I know not many of us are lucky enough to do what my grandmother did and just go out into the garden and pick a few heads of this and a head of that, depending on what my granddad had planted. But I would far rather buy a variety of different salads in their entirety at a farmers' market, from someone I know doesn't use chemicals, and mix them myself. What I get especially mad about are those bags of romaine lettuce with their little packets of ingredients ready to make Caesar salad. If you simply buy a head of lettuce, make up a vinaigrette and grate in some cheese, you achieve double the quality at half the price.

If you are serving salad leaves with hot ingredients – for example, seared scallops or grilled porcini mushrooms – try to use the more robust leaves, such as wild arugula, which will not "cook" and wilt too quickly. And if you are serving your salad on individual plates and want it to look good, arrange the heavier ingredients on the plates first, then the lighter ones, such as leaves, on top.

Finally, you need careful seasoning and a good vinaigrette or other dressing to pull all the different elements together. Again, I love the way Thai people make dressings out of crushed peanuts, fish sauce and lime juice to bring everything together. That is what we are aiming at – to transform an assembly of ingredients into something exciting.

Olio d'oliva

Olive oil

"Liquid gold"

In Italy, olive oil is still considered something you buy from someone you know, either direct from a small local producer, or via a shop that will probably only stock a few oils, mostly local. The bigger national companies often export more of their oil around the world than they sell at home in Italy. Margherita, my daughter, asked me one day why, when Noah sent one of the doves out from the ark, it flew back with an olive branch in its beak; and I explained to her that the olive – and the oil that is pressed from it – has always been seen as the fruit of peace, and often prosperity.

Olive oil has been made since around 5000 B.C., first in ancient Greece and then in countries like Israel and Egypt, eventually being introduced to Italy by the Greeks around the eighth century B.C. The Romans planted olive trees everywhere throughout their empire. It seems strange that something that has been made and used since ancient times should almost have been reinvented, at least outside the Mediterranean countries, over the last twenty years or so, since everyone started talking about its health-giving properties. Good extra virgin olive oil is rich in antioxidants that can help fight bad cholesterol and prevent heart attacks and cancer. Even in ancient times, however, people understood that olive oil had special properties, that it was good for the body, and in some cultures it has an almost mythical significance. Homer called it "liquid gold"; and it was considered so precious that champion athletes at the Olympic games were presented with it instead of medals. Olive branches were even found in Tutankhamun's tomb, and Roman gladiators used oil on their wounded bodies. And as far back as A.D 70, the Roman historian Pliny the Elder wrote that "olive oil and wine are two liquids good for the human body."

The highest grade of oil, extra virgin, means first that it is "virgin" olive oil, that is, the liquid from the fruit is extracted purely by cold pressing – with no heat or chemicals used. Then, to be "extra virgin" and therefore the best quality, the oil must have less than 1 percent oleic acidity – a higher percentage than this would suggest that the acids had been released because the fruit was damaged or had been roughly handled. If an oil is labeled just "olive oil," it will be a blend of inferior oil that has been refined, probably using chemical treatment, and virgin oil.

When I was growing up in Lombardia we used very little olive oil, except in salads and minestrone, and what we had was the light gold, fruity, quite delicate oil from Liguria, made from Taggiasca olives, which I still love. There is also a beautiful, sophisticated oil from the Lombardia shores of Lago di Garda, which we use in Locanda. It is made right on the northern limits of where olives can grow and now has its own DOP (Denominazione di Origine Protetta, or Protected Designation of Origin, and any producers who want to use its symbol must meet strict criteria).

In our house in Corgeno, if an olive oil was peppery it was considered a defect, whereas in Britain, since everyone fell in love with Toscana, the deep green, peppery, often prickly oils that characterize that region are more fashionable. When I first came to London, Antony Worrall Thompson was *the* man at Ménage à Trois – and one of the first to serve little bowls of olive oil with the bread, instead of butter. His idea of oil was the more peppery, the better. Then, when the River Café opened in London, Tuscan oil became even more popular. I remember when I was working at the Savoy; I took a bottle of River Café oil home to Corgeno. My dad tasted it and said, "Take it back to England!" Peppery oil has its place, of course, but not for everything: if you steam a delicate fish, like sole, the sweetness of the fish juices can make a strong oil taste almost rancid. And if you use a peppery oil with an equally hot leaf, the two will just clash.

When I cook a dish from a particular area, I like to try the oil that comes from there too; as with all Italian food, local produce – even the oil – determines the flavors. In general, olives that have had more exposure to the sun and more dramatic variation in temperature between day and night give more peppery oils; whereas in more temperate areas, the oil is lighter. Even within a region, though, the character can vary dramatically, and from producer to producer, as so much depends on the variety of the fruit, the altitude at which it is grown, the time of harvest and the care taken in handling the olives. For example, Tuscan oils made from olives grown around the coast, which really soak in the sun, have a different character from those grown in the Chianti hills, which are picked when only just ripe, before the frost, and so can produce young, herbaceous, almost prickly oils. Umbria can make oil that is sweet and fruity, or spicy; Marche and Abruzzo tend to make oils that are similar to Tuscan ones, whereas the ones from Puglia (the biggest production area), Calabria and Sicilia are mostly intense, but they might be almondy or very green and grassy. In Sicilia there is also a rare and beautiful oil made from the Minuta olive, which is unusual for the island in that it is delicate and fruity.

I'm not suggesting you have a kitchen full of bottles sitting around waiting to turn rancid, but it is good to taste a few different good-quality oils from various regions and get to know the flavors that you like. Read the labels carefully first. Just because an oil is bottled in Italy doesn't mean that the olives have been grown there, too. It hurts my heart to say it, but there is a big scam where olive oil is concerned. We sell millions of liters a year, but we don't grow nearly enough olives for that. Instead, a poor farmer in somewhere like Spain or North Africa sends his olives to Italy, because the oil is worth more if it says on the bottle that it was "produced" in Italy. That, to me, is completely wrong, because I believe first of all that an oil should have something of the character of the region it comes from, just as a wine should represent its "terroir." And second, how much quality of the olives is lost in transportation? If the farmer had pressed his olives there and then in his own country, I believe it would be better oil. Because of such problems, scientists are developing amazing tests that use infrared spectroscopy to detect the geographic origin of the oil and could be used in the future to prevent cheating, and the European Commission has tightened up the laws, so that if the olives are not grown in Italy, this should be declared on the label. Also, if a producer wants to say that his oil comes from a particular region, he must meet the strict criteria of the DOP or Indicazione Geografica Protetta (Protected Geographical Indication or PGI), which is awarded to food where at least one stage of production occurs in the traditional region, but doesn't specify particular production methods.

However, if you want to be sure what you are buying is good quality, look for bottles that state that the oil has been made from olives grown, and preferably handpicked, pressed and bottled on the same estate. Such oils are now being regarded almost like fine wines and, on the best estates, the olives will have been picked at just the right moment, to give the maximum flavor and the optimum level of health-giving polyphenols. They may cost you $30 a bottle, but what is that really – 40 cents per tablespoon? Not that much to pay for something so good for you, that gives so much pleasure and adds so much flavor to a dish. Think how much we pay for some bottled waters, when very little has been proved about their health-giving properties in comparison with olive oil.

When you taste an oil, do so like wine: pour some into a spoon or glass and check the aroma first; there should be a connection with the fruit there, rather than just an oiliness. Then taste, holding the oil in your mouth until you really experience the flavors.

What happens to the fruit on the tree and during the pressing is only part of the story. Just as important is the way it is bottled, and the way we the consumers store the oil, which must be away from heat, light and air, otherwise it will quickly lose its particularity, and its health-giving properties will begin to deteriorate. I only fully understood this from talking to Armando Manni, who makes the most expensive but probably most healthy oil in the world, high up on Mount Amiata in Toscana. His oil has levels of polyphenols that can reach 450mg per liter, compared to 100 to 250mg in other high-quality oils. It is truly beautiful, but most special because, in order to keep the oil as "alive" and valuable to the health as the day it was bottled, instead of using clear glass to show off the color of the oil he uses dark ultraviolet-resistant glass, and only tiny 100ml bottles. So when they are opened the oil won't deteriorate as quickly as it would in big bottles. He also treats the oil like wine in that he puts in a layer of inert gas to help prevent oxidization, before corking the bottles with a synthetic stopper, rather than cork, which he believes can contaminate the oil.

Cooking with olive oil

The last thing to know about the best extra virgin olive oil is not to use it for frying. For a start, when it is heated to a high temperature it burns easily, changes flavor and the polyphenols begin to lose their properties. Use a lesser olive oil, or even a vegetable, sunflower, or other interesting oil, and keep your extra virgin oil for making dressings, or drizzling over fish or pasta, so that it has the maximum impact.

Aceto

Vinegar

"A big, big difference to every salad you eat"

As with olive oil, the flavor of vinegar and how much you use of it is quite a subjective thing – if you were to eat a salad dressed the way my mother likes it, you might spit it out, because she loves the flavor of vinegar to come through really strongly. At home in Italy, there will always be one bowl of salad on the table just for her, and a big one for everyone else.

I use very little white wine vinegar; I prefer red wine vinegar, and what I actually like most of all is not officially classed as vinegar in Italy (which by law must have 6 percent alcohol per volume) but is known as *condimento morbido* (*morbido* means "soft"). This is brewed in the same way as vinegar but is filtered through wood chips, which smooths it out and takes away some of the sharpness, leaving a "condiment" with lower acidity and alcohol – only 3 percent.

When we talk about good wine, we often think of there being great merit if the production is small and intimate, but with wine *vinegar*, providing you begin with good grapes, there is no such advantage. You can make millions of liters and still have the same quality; it is like brewing beer. However, you can usually be sure that if you buy vinegar from a producer who makes good wine, the vinegar will also be good quality. People tend to think that it isn't worth spending a few more pounds on a bottle of good vinegar. But, as I always say when people complain about the price of good olive oil, if you think about how little you use at a time, you are only talking about a few cents, which will make a big, big difference to every salad you eat. And the vinegar isn't going to go bad, unless you actually put it in the sun with the top off and let it evaporate.

Balsamic vinegar, which comes from Modena and the surrounding region of Reggio Emilia, is something completely different, which I use only occasionally and sparingly. As far back as 1046, a visiting German emperor, Henry II, wrote about a special vinegar that "flowed in the most perfect manner," and it has been eulogized ever since as a mysterious, precious elixir. Originally, it was taken as a tonic as much as it was used in cooking – *balsamic* actually means "health-giving." However, it remained something of a local secret, made in small quantities that you used when a guest came to visit, or at Christmas, but not every day. In Lombardia, I never saw balsamic vinegar until I was about sixteen and started working in restaurants. We didn't even have any in the kitchen at La Cinzianella. Then, like sun-dried tomatoes, balsamic vinegar suddenly became fashionable all over the world, and people fell in love with it, using it for everything. Because the traditional production in and around Modena was so small, people began manufacturing it commercially to meet the demand – so now there is great confusion about what is the authentic vinegar and what is just an industrial product that resembles it. In America, especially, there are even balsamic "sauces," "glazes" and "creams" that you can buy in squeezy bottles, like ketchup.

Unlike other vinegars, true balsamic vinegar is made not from wine but from the must of the Trebbiano grape that has been cooked slowly to concentrate it. This is blended with aged wine vinegar, then matured for at least twelve years in a series or family *(acetaia)* of barrels, which range downward in size, and are made from different woods (typically oak, cherry, chestnut, mulberry, ash and juniper), so that each adds its own character. Each year, as some of the vinegar evaporates, the smallest barrel is topped up with liquid decanted from the next smallest one, and so on, until finally, the last and largest barrel is topped up with freshly cooked must from the new grape harvest. It is a continuous, complex, serious art, which produces a naturally thick, syrupy vinegar with a taste that should have a perfect balance of sweetness and acidity. (The barrels are traditionally stored in attics under the rooftops, where the heat of summer and then the cold of winter are intensified, as this naturally prompts the processes of fermentation and oxidization.)

In 1980 a controlled denomination of origin for the vinegar was set up, and by law, for a vinegar to be called *aceto balsamico tradizionale*, it has to be produced according to these methods and approved by the Consortium of Producers of Traditional Balsamic Vinegar (Consorzio fra Produttori di Aceto Balsamico Tradizionale di Reggio Emilia). If you are a producer, you must send your vinegar to them; they taste it blind and, if it is good enough quality and meets all the requirements, they bottle it in their special tulip-shaped bottles. They then mark it with different-colored stamps: red for up to 50 years, silver for a minimum of 50 years, and gold for a minimum of 75 years. Production of this balsamic vinegar is very limited, and for some of the people who supply their vinegar to the *consorzio* it is almost more of a hobby than a business: some will only make 100 or so bottles a year. We are talking about vinegars that cost up to $200 a bottle, but when you taste the real thing, the experience is extraordinary.

There is another category of balsamic vinegar that is either produced outside the designated region of Reggio Emilia, and so cannot be called "tradizionale," or is made by people who don't want to deal with the consorzio – maybe they have such a small production that it isn't worth their while. Or sometimes, producers of "tradizionale" also make other, high-quality vinegars that haven't been aged for so long. Such vinegars must be labeled *condimento* balsamic vinegar and although they can't be called "tradizionale" they are made using identical methods, so they can be fantastic quality, and are usually cheaper. I have stayed near Modena and seen people go to the local producers with their own bottles, which the guys fill up for them – and it is beautiful vinegar – but, of course, you have to rely on local knowledge to find out where to go.

The big difficulty is over bottles that are just labeled "aceto balsamico di Modena." Ever since the world "discovered" balsamic vinegar there has been a huge industrial production, which bears no relation to the true artisanal product. The legal definition of this vinegar is very loose. Much of it is only white wine vinegar with caramel added. I could make it for you in a pot in the kitchen in 15 minutes – but what an insult to the people who have been making beautiful vinegar in the proper way for hundreds of years. Some of it, though, has been made in a way that is similar to the traditional methods, using at least some cooked grape must, and aged in wood for at least a few years. So how to tell? Often "aceto balsamico" vinegar comes in elegant bottles, sealed with wax, with beautiful labels that suggest ancient traditions, but it is important not to be distracted by the lyrical descriptions that the producers tend to use, and go straight to the ingredients list. The first thing to be listed should be the must of the grape, and there should be no mention of caramel, or any added flavorings. Look for a vinegar that says it has been aged in wooden *barrels* – as "aged in wood" can sometimes mean that wood chips have been added as the vinegar ages.

There is yet another type of vinegar, called *vincotto* ("cooked wine"), which is similar to balsamic, made in a serious way but without the aging and complexity. They say vincotto has its roots in the old Roman tradition of pressing grapes that had been partly dried, then fermenting them to make raisin wine. It became something farmers would make as a sweet dressing for festivals, or as a tonic, but is now being produced commercially, using the Trebbiano grape in the north. As you move further south it is more likely to be made with the Negroamaro and the Black Malvasia, which are left to dry on the vine or on wooden frames before being "cooked" and reduced for 24 hours. The syrup goes into small oak barrels with some of the "mother" or "starter" vinegar from their wine vinegar production, and it is then aged for four years.

In the kitchen at Locanda we use various different balsamic vinegars, and also sometimes vincotto, but for the table we use only the "tradizionale," which we often dispense with great ceremony, using a syringe. It is very expensive, but used sparingly it will last you a long time. I would say that if you can afford to buy only one bottle of it in your life, it is worth it, because only by tasting the true traditional vinegar can you begin to understand what balsamic vinegar is about. It is something I would like everyone around the world to experience, because then it can be used as a benchmark by which to judge other, less expensive, balsamic vinegars.

Almost everyone likes the taste of a true balsamic vinegar, kids especially. At one time, the only way we could get my daughter, Margherita, to eat a green bean salad was to toss it in balsamic vinegar. It is like a natural flavor enhancer. Good balsamic vinegar needs to be used very simply, though, with specific ingredients. Its combination of sweetness and acidity is at its best with salty, fatty things: so a few drops are perfect with Parmesan, especially the concentrated flavor of an aged cheese. A lovely thing to serve before dinner with an aperitif is just a sliver of Parmesan on a spoon with a drop of vinegar on top. Or sometimes, when we have held parties at Locanda, we have put out half a wheel of Grana Padano cheese, which is similar to Parmesan (see page 209), so that people can pick up small pieces, drizzle some vinegar over it and eat it with a glass of Prosecco. I always keep a good bottle of balsamic vinegar at home and sometimes, if I go home late at night from the kitchen, that is all I have – a big wedge of Parmesan with a little vinegar. Since both the cheese and the vinegar originate in the same region of Italy, there is an affinity there that comes with produce of the same land, and so the combination is very satisfying.

Sometimes we make agnolotti with Parmesan, tossed in a little butter, with a couple of drops of balsamic vinegar added; and I love to serve balsamic vinegar with pork belly, or with calves' liver, in a simple sauce made with golden raisins and nuts (see page 484). A little drop is amazing with plainly cooked wild salmon, and balsamic vinegar and strawberries is another famous combination.

I don't think balsamic vinegar works with bland food. With a cheese like mozzarella, the effect is wasted, and I wouldn't usually use it to dress a leaf salad, as it loses its impact, unless you are using strongly flavored leaves like chicory, radicchio or arugula. And I completely disapprove of serving bread with a bowl each of oil and balsamic vinegar – oil yes, but if you dip good bread into balsamic vinegar, you ruin both things. For me it doesn't work with complicated dishes either. If you were to spoon balsamic vinegar over an elaborate fish dish with lots of different elements, yes, it would add another level of flavor, but again it would be a waste of something special that deserves to be treated with respect.

Dressings

There is no real Italian equivalent for the word *vinaigrette* because traditionally, when you went into a restaurant and ordered a salad, they would bring the oil and vinegar and some salt to the table – or if you wanted oil and lemon, you would just ask for *olio e limone*. Nowadays, if a salad comes ready-dressed, we just borrow the French term. Or we might use the word *condimento*, which can mean any kind of seasoning or flavoring as well as a dressing; or even *aspretto* – from *aspro*, meaning "sour." We usually use this term when we create a dressing in which there is an element that we have made ourselves – such as our saffron "vinaigrette," which we would call aspretto di zafferano.

When my brother, Roberto, and I were kids, we were sometimes taken to a local restaurant where dressing the salad was considered a bit of an art. Usually we didn't want to eat salad at all; we just wanted to watch the waiter perform his ceremony at the table. He would take a silver spoon, put some salt into it, then pour in the vinegar and let the salt dissolve in it. Then he would drizzle a line of oil into the salad bowl and pour in the seasoned vinegar at the same time, so the two met in a stream. Finally, he would put in the leaves and toss everything together in front of us.

The point is that dressing salad leaves should be done at the very last moment before serving, to preserve some crunchiness. Wash the leaves well, trying not to squeeze them, let them drain naturally in a colander, then finish off in a salad spinner. Dress the leaves very lightly so that the dressing just coats them without drowning them and when you toss everything together, really lift up the leaves so that the dressing coats every single one.

If you are dressing a more complex salad that includes other ingredients besides leafy greens, think about their consistency before you add the dressing. It is only the delicate leaves that need to be dressed at the last minute, so if, for example, you are making an arugula and tomato salad, the heavier, denser tomato will need more seasoning – earlier – than the arugula. What I would do is put the tomatoes in the salad bowl with some dressing, season them and leave them for ten minutes or so to soak up the flavors and release the juices that the salt will bring out. Then, at the last minute, I would throw in the arugula and toss everything together, adding a little more vinaigrette if necessary – a lovely thing to do at the table.

I will never understand why people buy ready-made vinaigrette in a bottle when there can hardly be anything simpler than mixing together some good oil and vinegar, seasoning it with a little salt (I also add some water, just to soften the dressing), putting it into a bottle with a cork in it and storing it in the fridge. That's it. My children make vinaigrette at home without even thinking about it. So how can commercial manufacturers tell us that what they put in a bottle is better? Some of them seem to have invented a machine that leaves the dressing in a state of permanent emulsion, which people think must be a good thing. But all you have to do to emulsify a dressing is shake your bottle of oil and vinegar.

There is, of course, no rule that says you must use olive oil for everything – not even in an Italian kitchen would we be that partisan. Sometimes we use other oils, including walnut and hazelnut, to give a different taste to a salad. Just think about your flavors before you add a very distinctive-tasting oil, so that your ingredients and your dressing complement each other and you have no violent clashes.

Giorgio's vinaigrette

The reason this is called Giorgio's vinaigrette is not that I am doing anything special – millions of people around the world make exactly the same thing. It just happened that when I was at Zafferano there was a young Algerian chef who could never remember which dressing was which, because we used several in our kitchen. We would shout to him, "Vinaigrette!" and he would say, "What does it look like?" Eventually he stuck a label on each bottle and he called this basic vinaigrette, with oil and vinegar, "Giorgio's vinaigrette" – so the name has stuck.

I like to mix the vinegar and oil in the ratio of one part to six, but the flavor of vinaigrette is a very subjective thing and everyone has their own ideas. Personally, I don't like to use a strong Tuscan oil, nothing too peppery and strong for vinaigrette, and you might prefer to add more or less vinegar. It also depends on the quality of the vinegar and its alcohol level. Make up some vinaigrette, taste it and adjust it as you like. The important thing to remember is that if you try it alone, it will taste more powerful than when you mix it with a salad. So, either test it with some greens, or do what I suggest to my chefs: take a little of the dressing on a spoon, put it into your mouth, then suck it in quickly – it should be sharp enough to make you cough slightly, but not so strong that it really catches in your throat.

Buy the best-quality oil and vinegar you can afford, because you can't put in flavor that isn't already there. And make up a big bottle, so that you use it all the time. I would be a very happy man if every British family had a bottle of Giorgio's homemade vinaigrette in the fridge.

Put the salt into a bowl, then add the vinegar and leave for a minute so the salt dissolves.

Whisk in the olive oil and the water until the vinaigrette emulsifies and thickens.

Pour into a bottle, seal and store in the fridge, where it will keep for up to 6 months. It will separate out again into oil and vinegar, so before you use it, just shake the bottle.

Makes about 1½ cups
½ teaspoon sea salt
3 tablespoons red wine vinegar
1¼ cup extra virgin olive oil
2 tablespoons water

Aspretto di zafferano

Saffron vinaigrette

Makes about 3¼ cups
2 cups plus 2 tablespoons
white wine
⅔ cup white wine vinegar
1 level teaspoon saffron strands
1 tablespoon superfine sugar
about ½ cup extra virgin
olive oil

Put the white wine, vinegar and saffron into a pan over low heat and bring to a boil. Simmer until reduced by three-quarters, then remove from the heat, stir in the sugar until dissolved and leave to cool. Whisk in the oil.

Store the vinaigrette in the fridge, where it will keep for up to 6 months in a screw-top jar or bottle – or a plastic squeeze bottle. Take it out of the fridge half an hour or so before you need it, and shake to emulsify before use.

Condimento allo scalogno

Shallot vinaigrette

Makes about 1 cup
2 banana shallots or
4 ordinary shallots
⅓ cup red wine vinegar
⅔ cup extra virgin olive oil
salt and pepper

Finely chop the shallots, then put them in a bowl and season with salt and pepper.

Add the vinegar and leave to stand for 30 minutes.

Whisk in the oil and use right away.

Condimento all'aceto balsamico

Balsamic vinaigrette

Makes about 1½ cups
1 teaspoon salt
1 cup plus 2 teaspoons
balsamic vinegar
about ½ cup extra virgin
olive oil

Put the salt into a bowl, then add the vinegar and leave for a minute so the salt dissolves. Whisk the oil into the vinegar.

This will keep in the fridge for up to 6 months in a screw-top jar or bottle – or a plastic squeeze bottle. Take it out of the fridge half an hour or so before you need it, and shake to emulsify before use.

Olio e limone

Oil and lemon dressing

Makes about ¾ cup
pinch of salt
3 tablespoons lemon juice
⅔ cup extra virgin olive oil

Put the salt into a screw-top bottle or jar, then add the lemon juice and leave for a minute so the salt dissolves.

Add the oil, put the top on, and shake well to emulsify. It is best to use this dressing immediately.

Maionese

Mayonnaise

Put the egg yolk in a mixing bowl and break it up a bit.

Add the salt and mustard with half of the vinegar and whisk together for a couple of minutes (this is very important as it helps the mayonnaise to emulsify once you start to put in the oil).

Slowly start to add the oil, whisking continuously, until it is completely incorporated. If it starts to get too thick, add the rest of the vinegar; and if is still too thick add a tablespoon of hot water – just enough to loosen it.

When the oil is completely incorporated, add the lemon juice and adjust the seasoning to your taste – add a little more vinegar or lemon juice if you like it a little sharper.

Makes about 2½ cups
1 egg yolk
pinch of salt
1 teaspoon dry mustard
2 tablespoons
    white wine vinegar
2 cups plus 2 tablespoons
    vegetable oil
juice of ½ lemon

Seasoning

"All about balance"

At home, when I cook something that Plaxy regularly makes, my kids often say my version tastes different – the reason, I think, is the seasoning. I was shocked the first time I saw chefs using salt in a restaurant kitchen because the proportions seemed enormous: handfuls were going into every pot, over meat, fish, vegetables. I remember going home to my grandmother and saying: "They use so much more salt than you."

As a chef, you are taught to see salt in a different way. You have to think about how we taste our food, receiving different sensations in different parts of the mouth. If you underseason, you are taking away a whole layer of flavor; if you overseason, you block out all the other sensations. Salt can also help you experience sweet flavors in a more pronounced way. Heston Blumenthal of the Fat Duck in Bray does an experiment with a glass of tonic water – if you keep adding salt a little at a time, it gets to the point where it tastes sweeter; then obviously if you carry on, the saltiness takes over. At Locanda, we do a tomato "soup" for a dessert with basil ice cream. When we first made it, we served it with sweet sablé biscuits, then we tried it with slightly salty biscuits, and the difference was amazing.

Seasoning is all about balance, so you must be constantly tasting and adjusting. Of course, it is also true that taste is a subjective thing, and I would never be so fussy as to get angry with anyone in the restaurant who wanted to add extra seasoning to their food, as some chefs famously have. I only hope that people taste first.

These days everyone is rightly concerned about the quantity of salt that children, in particular, are eating, but most of the damage is done not when we cook fresh food, but by the salt we often unconsciously eat in processed food. Also, if you taste and season carefully as you are cooking, allowing the salt time to dissolve and do its job of flavoring properly, you will end up using far less than if you taste at the end, panic because everything is bland, and start seasoning crazily.

Most chefs have cut back the quantity of salt in cooking over the years, and looked for different ways of amplifying tastes, for example bubbling up juices and sauces in the pan, so that they reduce and thicken and the flavor intensifies. Also, we are constantly trying to find producers and farmers who value traditional methods and believe that flavor is more important than fast-grown, perfect-looking homogeneous products that will please the supermarkets. So, when you have a carefully and slowly reared, properly hung piece of meat, a terrific vegetable that has not been forced under glass, or a fish straight from the boat, you don't need to season heavily, or you will distort the essential flavors.

On the other hand, everyone is crying, "Salt, salt, salt!" as if it were a demon, but we all need a certain amount of it for our bodies to function

properly. We can take a lesson from the behavior of animals in the wild, whose trails will often lead to natural sources of salt, because it is essential for them to stay alive. I remember reading about the big apes, the ones that are so human that they look like us and have a "spouse" and family – at certain times of the year they will head toward mountains which they know form natural rock salt and lick the salt.

Because we are so used to refrigeration, we underestimate the importance that salt has played in our civilization and politics. As well as keeping the body healthy, and flavoring food, when it was first discovered that you could use it to extract moisture from meat or fish, and therefore cure and preserve foods so you had something to eat year-round, it must have seemed a magical thing. No wonder whole communities were built around the production and trade of something so precious. In Italy, Venezia owes much of its splendor to its position at the center of the salt trade (along with Genova). Roads were built especially to transport salt; wars were fought over it, taxes raised on it – all of which Mark Kurlansky brings together in his brilliant book called *Salt: A World History*.

The first proper saltworks date back to 640 B.C., when one of the early Roman kings, Ancus Martius, built an enclosed basin at Ostia and let in seawater, which evaporated under the sun, leaving behind sea salt. The road that the salt traveled in order to be sold was called the Via Salaria, and the soldiers who protected it were often paid in salt, which is where the word *salary* comes from. If someone didn't do his job properly he was considered "not worth his salt." The word *salami* (pork preserved with salt) comes from the Latin *sal* for salt, as does salad (it was used to describe the Roman way of adding salt to greens and herbs, perhaps to draw out bitter juices in the way that we do with eggplant, then dressing it with oil and vinegar).

We have Parma ham because people in the region needed to preserve meat, and salt could be brought in from Venezia, with payment in either money or hams. Of course, there was a massive trade in smuggling in order to avoid paying the taxes that were levied on salt. The route the smugglers used is called La Via del Sale (the road of salt) and runs all the way from the Appeninos to Liguria. Nowadays part of the route is used for a fantastic endurance motorbike race, also called La Via del Sale.

What we are talking about is natural sea or rock salt, very different from "table salt," which is bleached and refined, often has chemicals added and has a harshly salty flavor. I always thought what a great job it would be to spend your days skimming off the perfect little crystals at some natural salt pan, somewhere wild and beautiful. This is the kind of salt you can pack around a piece of meat or fish for baking in the way that has been done for thousands of years. (Originally, you would have dug a pit in the ground, put in the fish or meat in its salt crust, covered it over and built a fire over the top.) As it cooks, the salt crust becomes rock hard, sealing in all the moisture and juices, and gently seasoning at the same time, but without making the cooked meat or fish taste "salty."

When Thomas Keller, the inspirational chef of The French Laundry in California, came to Locanda to eat, we got talking and he told me about the way he served foie gras with five different salts, including Dead Sea salt and Jurassic salt. When he went back to America he sent me some of the Jurassic salt, which is mined in Utah. It is incredible to think that it comes from a geological layer underneath that of the dinosaurs. At one time most of North America lay below a shallow sea, which evaporated over millions of years, leaving behind the salt, then in the Jurassic era volcanoes erupted around the old seabed and sealed the salt inside volcanic ash. The salt comes in a pinkish block that you have to grate, and it has a flavor that is amazing; it almost has an almost fizzy quality. We sprinkled it over some carpaccio and served it with nothing else but a piece of lemon and it was beautiful.

When you are seasoning, it is important to remember that salt has the function of extracting moisture as well as flavoring. You need to season meat or fish before you start to cook it, because once the outside has been sealed, your salt and pepper won't penetrate in the same way. However, once you season a piece of meat or fish with salt, it will start to "sweat" out its juices, so if you do this too far ahead of cooking it the flesh will become tougher. The trick is to season your meat or fish with salt and pepper *just* before you cook it – then, especially if you are cooking it over a high heat, the meat will be properly seasoned, and the salt and pepper will help form a nice "crust" around the outside of the meat, while the juices will be sealed inside.

With some dishes you also need to consider how much salt is contained in the ingredients you are cooking before you add any extra. I will taste and season a risotto, for example, only right at the end, because you are working with a lightly seasoned stock all the way through, which will intensify in flavor as it reduces, and then it will be finished with pecorino or Parmesan, which is also quite salty.

And remember that when you cook beans or pulses in water, unlike other vegetables, they should be seasoned only at the end of cooking, as the salt will draw the moisture from their skins and toughen them up if you put it in at the beginning.

At home, we always have a pot of sea salt crystals in the kitchen, which we keep away from the heat and moisture from the steam around the cooker, so that it keeps dry. Then we put a little of it into the grinder at a time.

Always also use freshly ground black pepper, which has much more warmth and aroma and a cleaner taste than white pepper. As with all spices, the flavor is held in the volatile oils inside the peppercorns, which are quickly lost once they are released; so ready-ground pepper, especially if it is exposed to warmth or sunlight, will lose its potency very quickly. I hate big pepper grinders, not only because they remind me of the way many "Italian" restaurants were when I first came to England, but because everyone fills them up and leaves them for years. I prefer small ones that you can fill with a couple of teaspoonfuls of freshly bought peppercorns on a regular basis.

Prezzemolo e aglio

Parsley and garlic

"Such an Italian flavor"

Parsley and garlic … the mixture has such an Italian flavor. It has become a joke in our house that whenever I am wondering what to cook – "Shall I do this? Shall I do that?" – Plaxy always tells me, "Just do your parsley and garlic!" She knows that whatever I do, I will use them, and also that by the time I have stopped talking and finished chopping, I will have decided what I am going to cook.

Every morning in the restaurant kitchen, one of our jobs is to chop parsley and garlic, ready to sprinkle into dishes whenever needed. We put the garlic cloves on a chopping board and squash them to a rough paste with the back of a knife. Then we put the parsley on top and chop it quite fine, so that the crushed garlic is chopped too. That way the garlic becomes almost a pulp, and it releases its flavors into the parsley and vice versa.

By parsley, I mean flat-leaf parsley, not the curly sort that was once the only kind available in the UK and the U.S. The first time I saw curly parsley, I thought it looked beautiful – but then it was the *nouvelle cuisine* era.

Now I can't imagine cooking with anything else but the flat-leaf variety, which has a much more refined flavor – though I have had a few discussions about the merits of curly parsley with Fergus Henderson of St. John restaurant. A big champion of English food, and one of the few chefs I know who loves to use the curly variety, he persuaded me to try it chopped in a salad, and it wasn't bad. Not bad at all.

Caponata

Caponata is a Sicilian dish of eggplant and other vegetables, cut into cubes and deep-fried, then mixed with golden raisins and pine nuts, and marinated in an *agrodolce* (sweet-and-sour) sauce. In some parts of Sicilia, it is traditional to mix in little pieces of dark bitter chocolate. Because it is such a southern dish, I had never even tasted it until I started cooking at Olivo. Then, one day when we were looking for something sweet-and-sour as an accompaniment, I found the recipe in a book and I remember thinking: "This will never work!" But we made

it, the explosion of flavor was incredible, and it has become one of my favorite things. You can pile caponata on chunks of bread, or serve it with mozzarella or fried artichokes (see page 70). Because it is vinegary, it is fantastic with roast meat, as it cuts through the fattiness, particularly of lamb. Traditionally it is also served with seafood – perhaps grilled or fried scallops (see page 108), prawns or red mullet. With red mullet, I like to add a little more tomato to the caponata.

We often cut some fresh tuna into 1½-inch dice and either sauté it in olive oil or grill it until it is golden on the outside but still rare inside (to test whether it is ready, cut open a piece and it should be a nice rose color in the center). Then we add the tuna to the caponata just before serving and toss everything together well.

If you don't like fennel or celery, leave them out and increase all the other ingredients slightly. Keep in mind that this is not a fixed recipe; it is something that is done according to taste and you can change it as you like.

1 large eggplant
olive oil for frying
1 onion, cut into ¾-inch dice
vegetable oil for deep-frying
2 celery stalks, cut into
    ¾-inch dice
½ fennel bulb, cut into
    ¾-inch dice
1 zucchini, cut into ¾-inch dice
3 fresh plum tomatoes,
    cut into ¾-inch dice
bunch of basil
⅓ cup plus 1 tablespoon golden
    raisins
⅓ cup plus 1 tablespoon
    pine nuts
about ½ cup extra virgin
    olive oil
5 tablespoons good-quality
    red wine vinegar
1 tablespoon tomato passata
1 tablespoon superfine sugar
salt and pepper

Cut the eggplant into ¾-inch cubes, sprinkle with salt and leave to drain in a colander for at least 2 hours. Squeeze lightly to get rid of excess liquid.

Heat a little olive oil in a pan and gently sauté the onion until soft but not colored. Transfer to a large bowl.

Put the vegetable oil in a deep-fat fryer or a large, deep saucepan (no more than one-third full) and heat to 350°F. Add the celery and deep-fry for 1 to 2 minutes, until tender and golden. Drain on kitchen paper.

Wait until the oil comes back up to the right temperature, then put in the fennel. Cook and drain in the same way, then repeat with the eggplant and zucchini.

Add all the deep-fried vegetables to the bowl containing the onion, together with the diced tomatoes.

Tear the basil leaves and add them to the bowl with all the rest of the ingredients, seasoning well. Cover the bowl with plastic wrap while the vegetables are still warm and leave to infuse for at least 2 hours before serving at room temperature. Don't put it in the fridge or you will dull the flavors. It is this process of "steaming" inside the plastic wrap and cooling down very slowly that changes caponata from a kind of fried vegetable salad, with lots of different tastes, to something with a more unified, distinctive flavor.

Deep-frying

People think deep-frying is easy, but it isn't at all, and it can be danger-ous. If you shallow-fry something you can touch and turn it easily, but with deep-frying you enter into a contract with the oil in which you have no control. Little home fryers are brilliant because they have safety mechanisms and you can set the temperature, which is so impor-tant, to avoid having something that is burnt on the outside and raw on the inside, or vice versa. If you *must* use a pan, never put more than 6 cups in a 1-gallon pot because not only will the level rise when you add your ingredients, but oxygen is released and so the expansion will be even greater. And use a thermometer.

Insalata di radicchio, prataioli e gorgonzola piccante/dolce

Radicchio salad with button mushrooms and Gorgonzola dressing

In Lombardia, we call Gorgonzola *erborinato*, after the "parsley green" color of the mold. In the old days, it was made in damp caves around the Lombardia town of Gorgonzola, where it was left for up to a year so the mold developed naturally. Nowadays the mold is introduced by piercing the cheese with steel or copper needles when it is around a month old. In the restaurant, we use 90-day-old Gorgonzola, which is harder and saltier *(piccante)*, instead of the young creamy one *(dolce)*, but you could use either.

2 small round heads of radicchio
2 tablespoons olive oil
4 handfuls of button mushrooms, sliced
½ wineglass of white wine
2¼ ounces (about ⅓ cup) mature Gorgonzola cheese
2 to 3 tablespoons mayonnaise (see page 53)
1 garlic clove
handful of flat-leaf parsley
3 tablespoons extra virgin olive oil
salt and pepper

Clean the radicchio, removing all the white parts from the base and keeping the small red leaves whole. Tear the larger leaves into halves or quarters.

Heat the olive oil in a pan, add the mushrooms and sauté until golden. Add the wine and stir until that has evaporated. Season, remove from the heat and keep warm.

Break up the Gorgonzola and melt it gently in a bowl placed over a pan of simmering water until it is creamy. Allow to cool slightly and mix into the mayonnaise to make a dressing.

Squash the garlic to a paste with the back of a knife, put the parsley leaves on top and chop it, so that the two combine.

Season the radicchio and toss with the extra virgin olive oil. Arrange the radicchio in nests on 4 serving plates, so the whole leaves are around the outside. Mix the parsley and garlic with the mushrooms and spoon into the middle. Drizzle with the Gor-gonzola dressing and serve.

Insalata di porcini alla griglia

Chargrilled porcini salad

This is a dish for those times when you go shopping and just happen to see fantastic fresh porcini (see page 232). Whenever I find them, I buy 2 pounds, use some for a risotto, put some in a veal stew and keep back the most beautiful ones to grill for this salad. In the restaurant, we serve quite a smart porcini salad with reduced veal stock and *beurre fondu* drizzled around the plate. This is too complicated to do at home, but it is just as good simply to grill the mushrooms, dusted with chopped garlic and parsley, as suggested below, and then rub your plates with a cut lemon before you put the porcini on them.

½ garlic clove
2 handfuls of flat-leaf parsley
10½ ounces small porcini
    mushrooms (ceps) (see
    page 239 for preparation)
a little extra virgin olive oil
½ lemon
2 handfuls of mixed
    green salad leaves
5 celery stalks,
    cut into matchsticks
1¾ ounces Parmesan
4 tablespoons Oil and lemon
    dressing (see page 52)
small bunch of chives,
    cut into batons
salt and pepper

Preheat the grill or, preferably, a ridged griddle pan. Squash the garlic to a paste with the back of a knife, then put the parsley on top and chop it so that the two mix together well.

Cut the mushrooms lengthways into slices about ¼ inch thick (cutting through the stem, too) and reserve any trimmings. Season the slices and brush with extra virgin olive oil, then dust with the parsley and garlic mixture.

Grill the porcini slices, turning them over to cook the other side as soon as they start to brown. Rub the serving plate or plates with the halved lemon and arrange the porcini on top.

Slice any reserved porcini trimmings very fine and mix with the salad leaves and celery strips. Grate about 2 tablespoons of the Parmesan, season the salad and mix with the grated cheese.

Toss the salad with the dressing, then pile it on top of the porcini and scatter with the chives. Shave the rest of the Parmesan and sprinkle it over the top.

Acciughe

Anchovies

"A fish that deserves respect"

Sometimes it seems to me that people in the United States and Britain don't think of the anchovy as a fish at all but as something in a category all of its own, something that goes on top of pizza or into a salade niçoise. In Italy, though, we have great respect for anchovies. The ancient Romans ate them fresh and it is thought that, together with sardines and mackerel, they also saturated them in salt and let them ferment in the sun, sometimes adding herbs and wine, to make a sauce called *liquamen* for seasoning food – rather like Thai fish sauce. In the north, they sometimes add anchovies to *osso buco*. In Sicilia, they like to cook them *al beccafico* – boned, sprinkled with a little vinegar, covered in bread crumbs and herbs and grilled or baked. In Trentino–Alto Adige, they specialize in *speck* (the hind leg of the pig, cured in salt, pepper, juniper and bay, then smoked over wood and juniper berries), which they serve with anchovies mashed into butter. In the south, anchovies are used in a sauce for pasta.

When I was a child, at Christmas and on special occasions, such as my granddad's birthday, we used to have anchovies in *salsa piccante* (the only time I ever tasted chile pepper when I was growing up), which came in small gold tins decorated with three little dwarves, like the ones in *Snow White*, wearing yellow, red and green hats. They were made by a company called Rizzoli in Parma, which still produces them, in a sauce it has been making to a secret recipe for a hundred years. Whenever I go to Italy and see the gold tins in a delicatessen, I still can't resist them.

Another thing I adore is dissolved or "melted" *(sciolte)* anchovies. You put some anchovies into a pan with some olive oil, turn on the heat and warm gently to "melt" the anchovies, rather than fry them, or they will lose their flavor. If you buy a pound of salted anchovies, rinse off the salt, dry them, then "melt" them like this, you can transfer the paste to a sterilized jar and cover it with a layer of olive oil. It will keep for six months in the fridge, so you can take it out and spoon some over pasta whenever you want. "Melted-down" anchovies are the basis of the famous Piemonte autumn dish *bagna càôda*, which literally means "warm bath" (see page 146). Like so many Piemontese recipes, it is a dish that needs lots of people to gather round the table with a bottle of good Barolo and share big plates of vegetables, usually raw but sometimes boiled, which you dip into the *bagna càôda*. It is made with anchovies, garlic (soaked first in milk), oil and butter, and is kept warm in an earthenware pot over a spirit flame in the middle of the table. Sometimes, when only a little of the sauce is left, people break in some eggs and scramble them. Such a fantastic, convivial thing to do.

It is a funny thing that Piemonte, one of the only regions of Italy that doesn't touch the sea, has a dish based on anchovies as one of its specialties. The reason is historical. About 300 years ago, the Piemontese people harvested salt and made butter in the mountains. These were traded along the ancient salt routes in return for anchovies from Liguria. A traditional thing that many Piemonte bars do in the early evening is to put out little sandwiches made with butter and anchovies, which you can eat with a glass of wine. Even now, there are still associations of *anciue* (anchovy sellers) in and around the old trading town of Val Maira that hold dinners to celebrate the relationship between salt, anchovies and butter.

In British fish markets, you rarely find the blue-green and silver fresh anchovies. So you usually have to buy them either still on the bone and preserved in salt (the fish are layered with sea salt in small barrels), or filleted and preserved in olive oil. Frequently, though, the oil is cheap and tastes rancid, and if the fillets are in upright jars they are squashed in so tightly that the ones in the center become mashed and broken (the fillets laid flat in tins are better), so I always prefer to buy the ones in salt. I have to admit that I buy Spanish ones, because the quality is so good. You have to soak them first in water to get rid of excess salt, then take out the bones and pat the fish dry. Then you can either marinate them in good olive oil, a little vinegar and some chopped herbs and serve them as part of an antipasto, or use them in whatever recipe you want.

Insalata di puntarelle, capperi e acciughe

Puntarelle salad with capers and anchovies

Puntarelle (Catalogna chicory) is difficult to get in this country, but beautiful, especially raw, rinsed and kept in a bowl of ice cubes to get rid of the bitterness. It's a real thirst-quencher. When people ask me what puntarelle is like, I usually compare it to fennel, because they share very similar characteristics, apart from the aniseed flavor of fennel. The puntarelle season runs from October to January or February, but as time goes on it can become more bitter and woody, so you need to wash it much more, and also eventually discard the tougher parts. Otherwise, the closest you can get is regular chicory, cut into strips, but don't put these in ice.

When we make this dish, we usually discard the outer leaves of the puntarelle, but, if you like, you can keep them to serve as an accompaniment to fish or meat, especially barbecued meat. Blanch the leaves briefly in boiling salted water, then drain, chop and sauté in a little olive oil. Mix with some toasted pine nuts and some golden raisins that have been soaked in water for half an hour or so to plump them up. You could even add the mixture to this salad – spoon it onto your plates first, then arrange the salad on top.

2 tomatoes
2 heads of puntarelle
    (or chicory)
8 anchovy fillets
2 tablespoons baby capers (or
    3 tablespoons larger capers)
small bunch of chives,
    cut into batons
4 tablespoons Oil and lemon
    dressing (see page 52)
3 tablespoons
    extra virgin olive oil
salt and pepper

Blanch the tomatoes, skin, quarter and deseed (see page 304).

Discard the outer green leaves of the puntarelle, slice the hearts very thin lengthways, then wash well under cold running water until the water is clear – the puntarelle will turn the water green at first – to take away some of the bitterness. When you serve the puntarelle it needs to be really crisp, so put it into a bowl with some ice cubes and leave in the fridge for a couple of hours, adding more ice if necessary, and it will curl up beautifully.

Drain the puntarelle well and pat dry. In a bowl, mix together the tomatoes, anchovies, capers, chives and finally the puntarelle. Season, but be careful with the salt, as the anchovies and capers will add quite a lot of saltiness. Toss with the oil and lemon dressing and serve as quickly as possible, drizzled with the olive oil.

Capperi

Capers

"Unique and pungent"

Capers are beautiful things, with a unique pungent flavor, which we use a lot in Italy, especially with antipasti, but also with meat and fish. When Prince Charles talked about boiled mutton with caper sauce at a celebration of English mutton and they said this was an old English sauce, I was amazed. Of course you see capers in jars all over the world these days, but I had always thought of fresh capers as Italian. Then I did some research, and found out that in the 1700s there were merchants who brought Marsala wine and capers over to England from Italy.

The best capers come from the islands of Salina and Pantelleria off Sicilia, with their volcanic soil and hot climate. The capers, which are not seedpods, as many people think, but tiny tight flower buds of the shrub *Capparis spinosa*, grow everywhere. The shrubs are planted in special trenches which are dug to hold them firm and protect them from the sirocco wind. And of course, the people of each island say that their capers are the best.

Like saffron, capers are harvested by hand, in the late spring to early summer, before they begin to open. It is only if you pick them at just the right time that you get the proper, stratified texture. If the bud hasn't developed enough, they are too compact. Like olives, they must be cured, as they are too bitter to eat as they are. The best are laid down on canvas outside, to get the sun for a couple of days, then layered with salt in wooden barrels, though they can also be put into brine or wine vinegar.

We use them in tartar sauces, hot caper sauces, sweet-and-sour sauces and salsa verde, and serve them with any kind of dish where you want their saltiness and special flavor to cut through a fatty ingredient. Sometimes, also, we soak them for 24 hours, then crush them, and fry them as a garnish for fish dishes. It is always best to add capers to dishes at the end if you are using them in cooking, or they will be too strong.

If the buds are allowed to stay on the bushes, they open into beautiful white flowers that seem to turn the whole island into a sea of white, before developing into fruit, which we call the caper berry, or *cucunci*. They look a little like green olives on stalks, but when you cut them in half they are full of tiny seeds. They have a flavor similar to capers but are less intense. Sometimes we combine capers and caper berries in the same dish, as in Monkfish with walnut and caper sauce (agrodolce, see page 426) in which the caper berries go into an arugula salad.

Insalata di endivia e Ovinfort

Chicory with Ovinfort cheese

Ovinfort is a fantastic Sardinian blue cheese that didn't exist ten years ago. Now I think it beats any French Roquefort – though I would say that, wouldn't I? In the north of Italy we are more used to blue cheeses made from cow's milk, but this is made from very high-quality sheep's milk and matured for 90 days, so it has quite a strong spicy flavor. People sometimes forget that cheeses have seasons – like every other natural product – and this one is available most of the year except between September and mid-December, when the ewes need their milk for their lambs. If you can't find Ovinfort, you could use a hard Gorgonzola, or even Roquefort – just don't tell me.

If you want to serve this dish for a party, you could use each chicory leaf to hold the pear and cheese. Drizzle a little mayonnaise into each leaf, put a slice of pear on top, followed by a slice of cheese, and let everyone help themselves.

Peel, quarter and core the pears, then slice them thin lengthways.

Cut the base off each head of chicory, so that the leaves come away. Mix the mayonnaise with the mustard and add 2 to 3 tablespoons of hot water to loosen it up enough to be able to drizzle over the salad.

Put the chicory leaves in a bowl, season and toss with the vinaigrette.

Put a layer of chicory on each serving plate, followed by a layer of pear, then more chicory. Drizzle with the mayonnaise and, using a potato peeler, shave the Ovinfort over the top.

2 ripe pears, such as Comice
2 heads of yellow chicory and
    2 of red chicory (if
    possible, otherwise
    4 yellow)
2 tablespoons mayonnaise
    (see page 53)
1 teaspoon dry mustard
salt and pepper
2 tablespoons Giorgio's
    vinaigrette (see page 51)
5¼ ounces Ovinfort cheese
    (or mature Gorgonzola)

Carciofi

Globe artichokes

"Beautiful, purple, perfect…"

In the restaurant kitchen we get through one box of baby globe artichokes a day when they are in season in the spring – usually *carciofi spinosi* from Sicilia or the purple *violetta di chioggia*. They are such beautiful things, less intensely iron-flavored than the bigger ones, so they make a perfect raw salad. Slice them very thin, mix with some salad leaves, season with salt and pepper, and dress with a little lemon juice or vinegar and oil mixed with a tablespoon of grated Parmesan. Finish with a handful of chopped chives and some shavings of Parmesan over the top – beautiful.

First, of course, you have to prepare them, which isn't as complicated as you might think. Start by taking the artichoke in one hand and, leaving the stalk on (because it makes the artichoke look more elegant), snap off and discard each outside leaf in turn, stopping when you get down to the tender, pale green-yellow leaves. Next, with a small sharp paring knife, peel off the stringy outside of the stalk and work around the top of the stalk at the base of the artichoke, trimming and scraping away the base and turning the artichoke as you go. Finally, trim off the pointed tops of the remaining leaves, then cut each artichoke in half lengthwise and use a spoon to scoop out and discard the hairy choke from each half (it will be very small, as the artichokes are not fully developed). To prevent the artichokes from discoloring, rub them with a halved lemon, then keep them submerged in a bowl of water with a squeeze of lemon juice added (or vitamin C, which you can buy from health food shops) until you are ready to use them.

Something we like to do with baby artichokes is to make *carciofi fritti*. We prepare the artichokes as described above, dust them with hard durum wheat flour, then deep-fry them in moderately hot oil (325°F) until crisp, season and serve right away.

Another of our favorite starters is Artichoke salad with Parmesan (see overleaf), which uses both raw and marinated blanched artichokes, prepared in the same way my grandmother used to do them. In our kitchen at home in Corgeno, we always had a jar of preserved artichokes on a cool shelf, ready to use in the winter months when fresh ones were out of season. Homemade marinated artichokes are so much tastier than store-bought ones that I suggest whenever you are making a recipe that calls for artichokes, you prepare four or five times the quantity you need and preserve the rest (see page 84). Then you will always have some on hand, not only for this salad but also just to serve with prosciutto or salami, or as part of an antipasto.

Insalata di carciofi alla Parmigiana

Artichoke salad with Parmesan

The combination of marinated and raw artichokes gives a fantastic contrast of flavor and texture in this salad. If you like, you can add some split chile peppers (with or without seeds, depending on how spicy you like them) to the marinade to give it an extra kick. The boys in the kitchen always do this for my wife, Plaxy, because it is her favorite way of eating artichokes. In winter, when you don't have any fresh artichokes, you can make the salad with ones that have been kept under oil.

Sometimes, if you are lucky, you can find *really* tiny artichokes, the size of golf balls. When we get these in the kitchen, we leave them whole and just trim the tops, remove the outer leaves and clean what there is of the stalk. You don't need to worry about the choke, because there will be nothing there. We blanch them as described in the recipe below, then brush them with olive oil and chargrill them on a hot griddle until they are well marked, to give them a roasted flavor, before marinating them.

10 baby artichokes
¾ cup white wine
¾ cup white wine vinegar
juice of ½ lemon
a little olive oil
a good wedge of Parmesan
2 tablespoons Shallot
        vinaigrette (see page 52)
4 handfuls of mixed green salad
2 tablespoons Giorgio's
        vinaigrette (see page 51)
small bunch of chives,
        cut into batons
salt and pepper

    For the marinade:
2 cups plus 2 tablespoons
        extra virgin olive oil
2 black peppercorns
2 juniper berries
2 bay leaves
5 sage leaves
sprig of rosemary
2 garlic cloves, lightly crushed
⅓ cup white wine vinegar

Prepare the artichokes and cut in half as described on page 70, and keep 2 of them to one side. Blanch the remaining artichokes in a mixture of the white wine, white wine vinegar, ¾ cup water and 2 teaspoons of salt for 3 to 4 minutes. They should still be quite firm. Drain and leave to cool.

To make the marinade, pour the olive oil into a pan and add all the remaining marinade ingredients except the vinegar. Place over medium heat (the oil shouldn't be too hot – just enough to cook the herbs gently). As soon as the herbs start to fry and the garlic starts to turn lightly golden, turn down the heat and stir in the vinegar.

Cut the blanched artichoke halves in half again and put them into the pan. Bring back to the boil, turn off the heat and cool completely.

Slice the 2 reserved artichokes, toss with the lemon juice and a little olive oil, and season with salt and pepper. Keep to one side. Grate about 2 tablespoons of Parmesan and set this aside, too.

Spoon the blanched artichokes from their pan (you can save the marinade for next time). Dress with Shallot vinaigrette and arrange on 4 serving plates.

Season the mixed green salad, toss with the grated Parmesan and Giorgio's vinaigrette, and arrange it on top of the artichokes. Sprinkle the raw artichokes over the top. Shave the rest of the Parmesan and sprinkle that and the chives over the salad to serve.

Insalata di fagiolini, cipolle rosse e Parmigiano

Green bean salad with roasted red onion and Parmesan

You can prepare the onions for this salad a few hours before you need them – or even the day before – to improve the flavor. It is important that they be quite soft, not crunchy.

Preheat the oven to 425°F. Leave their skins on and wrap the onions in foil and bake in the oven for about 1 hour until soft.

While the onions are cooking, put the vinegar into a small pan and boil until reduced by about a third. Remove from the heat, stir in the sugar until dissolved, then stir in the extra virgin olive oil to make a vinaigrette.

When the onions are cooked, unwrap them and peel off the skin. While they are still warm, cut them in half, separate the layers and season with salt and pepper, then put them into the vinaigrette.

Blanch the green beans in plenty of boiling salted water for about 5 minutes, then drain. Place in a bowl, sprinkle with the grated Parmesan and season with salt and pepper. Toss with the Shallot vinaigrette and sprinkle over the chives.

Arrange the onion layers on your serving plates. Place the beans on top and shave some more Parmesan on top.

2 large red onions
1¼ cups red wine vinegar
1 tablespoon sugar
⅓ cup plus 1 tablespoon extra virgin olive oil
8–9 ounces fine green beans
2 tablespoons freshly grated Parmesan, plus extra for shavings
3 tablespoons Shallot vinaigrette (see page 52)
small bunch of chives, chopped
salt and pepper

Insalata di fagiolini gialli, patate e tartufo

Yellow bean, potato and black truffle salad

One day some lovely yellow beans came into the kitchen, fresh from the market, and I remembered something my grandmother used to make for me and my brother, Roberto, when we came home from school after the summer holidays. My granddad grew yellow beans in our garden and he would leave them as long as possible over the summer, so they developed proper little *fagioli*, tiny beans, inside. The flavor was fantastic.

Each summer Roberto and I used to go away to a children's holiday camp, then our parents would come and get us and we would go to Emilia-Romagna or, later, Liguria for another few weeks. By the time we came home to Corgeno, three things were certain: we would have to go back to school, the maize would have grown as tall as Roberto and me, and the yellow beans would be ready. My grandmother used to boil them – not until al dente, like green beans, but for longer, so they were soft. Then she would boil some potatoes and break them down into a chunky mash – what has since been fashionably called "crushed" potatoes. When we came in from school, she would heat up some butter in a pan, put in the potatoes and beans and cook them until the potatoes were a little crusty and burned. Then she would break two eggs into the pan, to make a kind of frittata. I remember we would look for the little *fagioli* inside and pounce on them like prizes. So much of the food we ate when we were children seemed to be associated with little games.

So when, many years later, the yellow beans came into the kitchen at Locanda, that combination of beans and potatoes kept coming to mind. Of course we had to come up with something a little more refined, so we decided to bring in some black truffles – partly because they are in season at the same time as yellow beans and partly because the starchiness and sweetness of potato really support the flavor of black truffle, which is milder than the white truffle. To highlight the flavor of the truffle even more, and balance the sweet/sour/starchy elements, the salad also needs to be more vinegary than usual, so the vinegar has a real presence in the mouth. If you don't have any truffles, you can still make a lovely salad – or, if you can find some good-quality black truffle and mushroom paste in an Italian deli, add a tablespoon of it to the vinaigrette. In Italy, I would use the yellow Piacentine potatoes, which come from very sandy ground. They have a similar quality to the baby Jersey Royals that we use in London for this salad when they are in season.

Cook the potatoes in their skins in boiling salted water until soft, then drain (it is always best to cook potatoes in their skins, to keep in as much flavor as possible). Peel them if you like (we do this in the restaurant, purely for the look of the salad, but at home I might not bother).

In a separate pan, cook the beans in boiling salted water for about 7 to 9 minutes, until they are slightly overcooked (both the beans and the potatoes should be warm for this salad, so try to make sure they are ready at around the same time). Drain and set aside.

Cut each potato into quarters lengthwise and put them in a bowl with the beans and chives. Season, sprinkle with the Parmesan and toss first with the Shallot vinaigrette, then with Giorgio's vinaigrette. The dressing should be quite sharp to bring out the flavor of the truffle, so add a little more vinegar if necessary.

Arrange the potatoes and beans on serving plates and, at the table at the last minute before serving, grate the black truffle over the top.

8 medium-sized new potatoes
8–9 ounces yellow beans
small bunch of chives,
    cut into batons
    about 1½ inches long
1 tablespoon freshly
    grated Parmesan
2 tablespoons Shallot
    vinaigrette (see page 52)
3 tablespoons Giorgio's
    vinaigrette (see page 51)
2–2½ ounces fresh black truffle
salt and pepper

Insalata di asparagi e Parmigiano

Asparagus salad with Parmesan

For one month of the year only – April – we get wonderful, early, thick white asparagus from Friuli in the northeast of Italy, but otherwise we make this dish only when the green asparagus is in season from late April to mid-June. Such a short time, but an exciting one, especially in Italy. For ten months of the year you have no asparagus at all, then suddenly millions of kilos, then none again, so during this precious period there are large fairs in all the growing regions, with every restaurant serving asparagus. It is no good eating tasteless asparagus all year round, flown hundreds of miles from other countries – where is the magic in that?

Sometimes, especially in London hotels, I see restaurants using little asparagus tips to decorate a dish of something else entirely, such as meat or fish. I consider that an insult – a great misuse of a fantastic flavor. Asparagus should be the entire dish – a large portion served with eggs, Parmesan, butter, or a savory zabaglione made with white wine. That's the way to eat asparagus.

Good, fresh asparagus should be firm. If you bend a spear in the shop or at the market when no one is looking, it should snap in the natural place just below halfway – if it simply bends and doesn't snap, then it isn't fresh. Some people also say that only really fresh asparagus will squeak if you rub the spears together.

It is best to use a griddle pan for this recipe – or you could grill the spears on a barbecue. However, if you prefer to blanch your asparagus, divide it into bunches of five or six spears and tie with string, to prevent the tips from getting bashed and broken. Then stand the bundles in a tall pan of boiling salted water, keeping the tips above the water so they will steam gently thanks to the heat below and the flavor will be stronger.

Often people say that once the asparagus is cooked you should plunge it into ice water to stop it cooking further, but I think it is better to take the spears out of the water about a minute before they are ready (after about 4 to 6 minutes, depending on thickness).

Untie them, wrap them in a wet cloth and then let them finish cooking as they cool down naturally at room temperature – the color might not be quite so bright but the flavor will be better, as the spears won't soak up the cold water, which would dull the flavor. If you like, you can cook the asparagus a few hours in advance, but make sure you leave it at room temperature. If you put it into the fridge, again you will deaden the taste.

Trim off the woody bases from the asparagus spears. Preheat a ridged griddle pan and grate the Parmesan.

Lay the spears in a row with the tips level and divide them into groups of 3 or 4 – however many you can get a toothpick through easily – then very gently secure them with the toothpicks (this makes it easier to turn them).

Brush the asparagus with some of the olive oil, season with salt and pepper, then put the spears on the hot griddle for a couple of minutes on each side, until they are tender but still slightly crunchy. If you think they are not cooked enough but might become too charred, take the pan off the heat and cover with foil – then they will continue to cook gently for a little longer.

While the asparagus is still warm, transfer to a plate, drizzle with the remaining oil and sprinkle with about 2 tablespoons of the grated Parmesan. Cover with plastic wrap and leave for about an hour for the flavors to meld.

Boil the eggs for 6 to 7 minutes, cool under running water, then peel and push through a fine sieve. Keep on one side.

Season the salad leaves and sprinkle with another 2 tablespoons of the grated Parmesan. Toss with 2 tablespoons of the Shallot vinaigrette and Giorgio's vinaigrette.

Arrange the asparagus spears on serving plates. Sprinkle the sieved eggs on top, together with the remaining Shallot vinaigrette. Pile the salad on top, sprinkle the rest of the Parmesan over and finish with the chopped chives.

20–24 medium-sized
    asparagus spears
about 3½–4 ounces grated
    Parmesan
⅓ cup plus 1 tablespoon
    extra virgin olive oil
4 eggs
2 handfuls of
    mixed salad greens
4 tablespoons Shallot
    vinaigrette (see page 52)
2 tablespoons Giorgio's
    vinaigrette (see page 51)
small bunch of chives, chopped
salt and pepper

Insalata di cardi alla Fontina

Swiss chard envelopes with Fontina

The idea here is to make little "sandwiches" of chard stalks, filled with Fontina cheese, and deep-fry them.

2 large Swiss chard stalks
2 thin slices of Fontina cheese
1 cup all-purpose flour
2 eggs
3 tablespoons freshly
    grated Parmesan
¾ cup dried bread crumbs
2¼ cups vegetable oil for frying
3 tablespoons Shallot
    vinaigrette (see page 52)
small bunch of chives,
    cut into batons
salt and pepper

Remove the leaves from the chard stalks. Blanch the stalks in boiling salted water for 3–4 minutes, until just tender, then drain and pat dry (this is important for later). Put the chard leaves into the boiling water for about a minute, then drain and pat dry.

The chard stalks will be pointed at the top where the leaf was attached. Trim off this pointed part and cut it into thin batons, then set aside. Cut the rest of the stalk into an equal number of pieces each about 2¾ to 3¼ inches long. Then slice each of these pieces horizontally through the middle, so you are left with pairs of identical pieces.

Cut the cheese into slices just a little smaller than the pairs of Swiss chard. Keep the chard slices in their pairs, cut side up. Place a slice of Fontina on one of the slices of chard, then put the other one on top, cut side down. As long as the pieces of chard are dry when you start to fill them with the Fontina, they will stay together in a sandwich – you don't need to secure them.

Place the flour on a large plate. Put the eggs into a bowl and beat lightly. Mix 1 tablespoon of Parmesan with the bread crumbs on another plate. Take each "sandwich" and dust each end and side in turn in the flour – leave the larger surfaces for now. Shake off excess flour. Do the same with the egg, making sure the sides and ends are covered and shaking off the excess. Finally, dip the chard into the bread crumbs – again cover the ends and sides – and shake off the excess.

Repeat the whole process, this time dipping the larger surfaces first into the flour, then the egg and then the bread crumbs. At the end every surface should be completely covered, and you can press each surface with a spatula, to make sure the bread crumbs stick really well.

Heat the oil in a large, deep pan (no more than one-third full). Meanwhile, mix the reserved little chard batons with the leaves. Season with salt, pepper and 1 tablespoon of the remaining Parmesan. Toss with the Shallot vinaigrette, then arrange on serving plates.

When the oil is hot enough to sizzle when you sprinkle in a few bread crumbs, put in the "sandwiches" and fry for about 2 minutes, until golden. Move around with a spoon or a spatula, taking care not to puncture them or the cheese will start to leak out. When they are ready, remove and drain on kitchen paper. Season with salt and arrange on top of the salad. Sprinkle the rest of the Parmesan and the chives on top.

Olive

Olives

"A taste so good it makes you cry"

A beautiful, slightly salty, bitter olive can be so good it makes you cry, but a bland olive that tastes of nothing, or that has been pitted and drowned in marinade in a supermarket tub is a disaster that makes you want to cry for a different reason. If I go into a restaurant and they serve an aperitif with a bowl of tasteless olives, I think, "Forget it" – what a terrible start to a meal. What upsets me most are the insipid olives you find on most takeout pizzas. Often they are not even true black olives, because the really jet-black varieties, as opposed to violet-black or brownish black, are quite rare. Mostly they are green olives that have been dyed black by putting them in a water bath and running oxygen through them. Then they are treated with ferrous gluconate, a colorant, to give them their shiny, bright black appearance. How unnatural is that?

You can't eat an olive straight from the tree, whether it is unripe (green) or ripe (purplish black), because it will be far too bitter. They all have to go through a salt-curing process first before they are edible. One of my favorite olives is the small, black and quite delicate Taggiasca, the variety grown in Liguria that was first planted by the Romans. Liguria is a beautiful place, high up in the mountains that stretch all the way to Monaco. You drive there from Milano on a gray day and suddenly you are in the sunshine. They say that Caesar's armies fell in love with Liguria. After thirty-seven years of conquering Turkey and having the Ottoman Empire at their feet, they found this paradise, almost like a spa – where it is never too cold, even in winter, and never too hot, even in summer; where there is hardly any rain, and the Alps protect the countryside from the storms that blow in from France, pushing them on toward the East. So they defeated the resistance of the Ligurians and decided to stay there.

The olives are grown on terraces and the silvery trees are beautifully twisted like no other olive tree, pruned low so they can be harvested easily by hand. Some of the trees are extremely old (they can bear fruit for around six hundred years) but so strong that even when they have been hit by frost and some of the roots have died, you will find that four more little trees have sprung up on top. Traditionally, the olives are cured by soaking them for forty days in fresh water, which is changed daily, then putting them into a brine of water and sea salt scented with thyme, rosemary and bay.

This is the way we buy them in the restaurant – in their brine, never ready-marinated. Then, if we want to, we can rinse and dry them, and mix them with olive oil, crushed chiles and garlic. I always buy unpitted olives, because the bitter flavour that is so important is concentrated in the stone.

It is ironic that in the UK and the United States olives are so, so popular now – yet many people have never tasted a really good one. Let us not forget that olives are a fruit. If you go shopping for peaches, you are careful to choose ones that are ripe and unblemished. Yet, when people buy olives, they are often content to buy cheap ones that have been pasteurized (which dulls the flavor) and commercially pitted and stuffed – not with fresh anchovies or capers, in the way that people in Italy might do at home, but with strips of synthetically flavored paste. The artificial flavorings are pushed in by machines that can pit and stuff a thousand olives an hour, no doubt in factories run by the sort of people who get excited about making extra money from packing one less olive into each jar.

The best olives, the kind that you can find in good delicatessens, cost a little more because they have been freshly imported from the region where they were grown, with the stones left in. If they are pitted, this will have been done at the last minute, and if they are marinated and stuffed, it will have been done by hand, with fresh ingredients. Sometimes you can even find a Greek or Italian delicatessen that will sell fresh (uncured) unpitted olives in season, which you can cure yourself. If you come across them, buy 2 pounds and put them into a sterilized jar with about 1 cup of sea salt. Seal it tightly and store for 12 to 15 days, turning the jar upside down one day and then upright the next, until enough brine is made to completely cover the olives. Then you can leave the jar upright. Beware, though – home-cured olives have a really powerful, pungent bite.

Accompaniments for salumi

Zucchine all'olio

Grilled zucchini in olive oil

We serve these with *culatello* (cured meat made from the fillet of the pig's thigh), but they are also lovely with slices of ricotta salata cheese. To serve 4, you need 2 zucchini, sliced at an angle to give long pieces about ¼ inch thick. Season them with a little salt, put in a colander and let them drain for 10 minutes, then squeeze lightly to get rid of excess liquid. Brush them with olive oil and griddle or grill them until they just begin to mark on both sides. Remove from the heat, then drizzle with extra virgin oil and sprinkle with some rosemary. You can do this an hour or so ahead of serving and keep them at room temperature – but not in the fridge because they will dry out and the flavor will be suppressed.

Sottaceti

Pickled vegetables

In Italy there is a ritual that goes on throughout the year of picking or buying vegetables, such as peppers, artichokes and mushrooms, when they are at their best, eating some, then preserving the rest for another time. If you have a jar of peppers, a jar of artichokes, and a salami hanging up somewhere cool, you have the makings of a feast.

If you add garlic to any of these vegetables, blanch it briefly first and then make sure that it stays under the oil all the time, to prevent it from becoming rancid. Keep the jars in a cool place, where the temperature is consistent, and always spoon out the vegetables with a clean spoon or tongs – never fingers – so you don't introduce any bacteria into the jar.

Cipolline all'aceto balsamico

Baby onions in balsamic vinegar

You can triple or quadruple the quantity given here and store some of these onions for a month in a cool place (the longer you keep them, the better the flavor), but make sure they are always completely covered with the vinegar. Sometimes for this recipe we also use vincotto (see page 48).

Peel 3 or 4 (1 pound) pickling onions but keep the root intact. Bring 2¼ cups white wine and 2¼ cups white wine vinegar to the boil in a pan, add the onions and blanch for about 3 minutes, until just soft. Remove the onions from the wine and vinegar, peel off the outer membrane and leave to cool.

Put ¼ cup light, soft brown sugar into a small pan and melt until it darkens slightly. Just before it starts to bubble, put in the onions and toss around to coat.

Add 1 cup balsamic vinegar and cook gently for about 2 minutes. Remove from the heat and cool. The onions are ready to eat, but if you want to keep them, put them into sterilized jars and make sure the vinegar completely covers the onions (add a little more if necessary).

You can serve the onions with salumi, such as ham or cured pork, or, if you like, mix them into a salad. Chop the onions, then season a handful of rocket and toss with a little Balsamic vinaigrette (see page 52). Arrange the salad on the center of a plate with the slices of cured meats around the outside.

Carciofi

Artichokes

Prepare about 20 artichokes as for the recipe on page 70, blanching them in a big pan with 1¾ cups each of water, white wine and white wine vinegar and 2 tablespoons of salt. Make the marinade (doubling the quantities) and cook briefly (see page 72). When the artichokes have cooled down in their marinade, spoon them into a sterilized jar, strain the marinade and then pour it over the top, making sure the artichokes are completely covered. Seal the jar tightly. The artichokes will keep in a cool place for 3 months (the longer you keep them, the more vinegary they will taste). Serve them with whatever you like – in salads or with prosciutto or salami.

Peperoni

Peppers

Halve and deseed 5 red or yellow peppers, then blanch in 2¼ cups each of white wine and white wine vinegar, plus 2 tablespoons of salt, for 3 to 4 minutes. They should still be quite firm. Take the peppers out (you can cool the cooking liquid and keep it in the fridge for next time). Put them in a bowl, cover with plastic wrap and leave them to steam for about

10 minutes, after which time you should be able to peel them easily. Leave them to cool completely, then put them into a sterilized jar. Cover with light olive oil and, if you like, a few sprigs of rosemary and bay and some blanched whole peeled garlic cloves. Make sure everything is completely covered and seal. Store in a cool place for up to 3 months.

Barbabietole

Beets

Use baby beets if possible – golden or red. If they are very small, blanch them whole and unpeeled (just washed) in 2¼ cups each of white wine and white wine vinegar and 2 tablespoons of salt for about 10 minutes, until just soft. Drain and, while still warm, peel and cut into halves, quarters or cubes, as you like. Put into sterilized jars and cover with light extra virgin olive oil. Make sure the oil covers the beets completely and seal. Keep for up to 3 months in the fridge.

If you can find only large beets, cook them whole and unpeeled in salted water until just soft (don't add any vinegar to the water at this point, as the beets will take a couple of hours to cook and during that time the vinegar would flavor it too strongly). Keep topping up the water level as necessary. When the beets are cooked, let them cool, then peel and cut into cubes, etc. Because larger beets can taste blander than small ones, you need to work a bit harder at bringing out their flavor. So, put the pieces into a bowl and cover with white wine vinegar, then leave in the fridge for a couple of days. Lift them out of the vinegar and place in a sterilized jar. Top up with enough extra virgin olive oil to cover and seal. Store as before.

Melanzane

Eggplant

The best eggplants for preserving are the pale purple, melon-shaped ones, as they are firmer and a little sweeter. Cut them into slices about ¾ inch thick, place in a colander and sprinkle with salt. Leave for at least half an hour, preferably overnight. Drain them, brush with olive oil and grill or cook in a ridged griddle pan until they mark (a couple of minutes on each side). Don't overcook them or they will become too soft and disintegrate after being in the oil for a while. Remove them, lay them out on a tray and sprinkle with whole peppercorns, blanched peeled whole cloves of garlic, sprigs of rosemary and, if you like, some large chiles, deseeded and split lengthwise (or with the seeds, if you prefer them spicier). Layer in sterilized jars, then cover completely with light extra virgin olive oil and seal. Keep in a cool place for up to 3 months.

There is another typical *sottaceto* with eggplant, which is originally from Napoli, and is often served with antipasti in bars in Italy – my wife, Plaxy, calls the little strips "worms." What makes them very special is that the eggplant pieces, which are blanched in vinegar, retain a slight crunch, and if you eat them with a salami that is very generous with the fat, they really help to cut through the richness.

To make a jarful, take 2 eggplants, peel them, and, using a mandoline grater, cut into thin slices and then into strips. Sprinkle with salt, leave to drain for an hour, then squeeze gently. Rinse under cold running water, then squeeze again. Get a pan with a measured amount of water boiling, and for every quart of water add ½ cup red wine vinegar. Bring to the boil again, then add the eggplant and keep boiling for about 3 to 5 minutes, depending on the thickness. They should still be quite firm. Lift out with a slotted spoon onto a clean tea towel. Move them around until completely cold and dried, then put into a sterilized jar along with some big chiles that have been deseeded and split lengthwise. Cover with light extra virgin olive oil and seal.

Serve with bread and salami, or maybe some anchovies (if you like, you can scatter the eggplant with chopped garlic and parsley).

Finferli

Chanterelle mushrooms

Clean 2 pounds small to medium chanterelle mushrooms and blanch them very briefly in 2¼ cups each of white wine and white wine vinegar with 2 tablespoons of salt – they should cook for less than a minute. Drain and lay them on a clean tea towel to dry. This is very important or the mushrooms will release their water into the jar (in Italy we leave them out in the sun to dry – but in the United States you might have to pick your day). When they are dry to the touch, put them in a sterilized jar with some blanched peeled whole garlic cloves, bay leaves and enough light extra virgin olive oil to cover. Seal the jar and keep in a cool place for up to 6 months. Serve with salumi – if you like, you can mix them with balsamic onions (see page 82).

Mozzarella and Burrata

"Pearly-white treasure"

In Britain and America, people seem to be convinced that mozzarella is something rubbery and bland, after years of having only a version of this cheese that was made of cow's milk (Fior di Latte), sold in packets and looked like Ping-Pong balls. This is the mozzarella that you could buy in every supermarket twenty years ago, when every neighbourhood Italian restaurant had salad *caprese* on the menu: mozzarella and tomatoes, sometimes turned into a *tricolore* with slices of avocado.

Real, fresh, hand-made unpasteurized mozzarella, made from pure buffalo milk in Campania, close to Napoli, is a beautiful pearly white treasure that keeps for only a few days – something sensual and soft, full of the sweaty, mossy flavors of the buffalo milk. When you have a large ball of this mozzarella, which drips buttermilk when you cut into it, you don't want to do anything other than drizzle over some peppery olive oil, grind some black pepper over it and serve it as a starter, just as it is.

To make the cheese, whole fresh buffalo milk is inoculated with a "starter culture" of whey from the previous day's cheese making, which is left to sour naturally. This is mixed with rennet and, after about half an hour, it coagulates into soft curds, which are broken up into pieces and left to ripen in warm whey for 4 or 5 hours, until the curd becomes stretchy. Then the curds are put into wooden vats of boiling water and stretched by drawing them out continuously with a wooden stick. Finally the *mozzatore*, the cheese maker in charge of the final stages of the process, judges just the right moment for the hot elastic cheese to be cut into pieces (the name *mozzarella* comes from the Italian *mozzare*, "to cut"). Then it is gently shaped into large balls, *trecce* (plaits) or *bocconcini* (tiny balls weighing just 1½ ounces) and dipped into a brine bath to let the cheese relax and soften.

Like so many Italian specialties, buffalo mozzarella started off as a poor man's food, made from the buffalo that were brought into Italy through trade with India and used as beasts of burden, grazing on the marshes of Campania. You had to milk the animals, so people made the milk into cheese. Now, of course, the whole world wants to eat mozzarella. But how many buffalo do people think we have in Italy? Where are they all? Do you get off the plane in Napoli and say to the kids, "Look at all the buffalo"?

The reality is that there are only about 600,000 buffalo in Italy and each one will give you around 4 to 6 quarts of milk a day, enough to make about twenty mozzarella. You would need about a million buffalo just to satisfy the demand from the UK alone, so a lot of the cheese has to be made with cow's milk, or a mixture of buffalo and cow's milk. If you buy cheese labeled buffalo mozzarella, or *mozzarella tradizionale*, it might be made with either buffalo milk or a mixture of buffalo and cow's milk – and there is as yet no law that says the producer must tell you which.

So the way to be sure that the mozzarella you buy is made with 100 percent buffalo milk is to look for one that carries the mark of the DOP (Protected Designation of Origin) and is labeled *mozzarella di bufala Campana*. This tells you that the cheese has been made by one of the *consorzio* of producers within a specific area with unique microclimatic conditions, who have to make their cheese according to very strict laws.

Confusingly, there is another label, *mozzarella di latte di bufala* (which must also carry the name or registered trademark of the producer between the words *mozzarella* and *di latte)*. This means that the mozzarella must be 100 percent buffalo milk. However, it can be made anywhere in Italy and, of course, true aficionados of *mozzarella di bufala Campana* will say its unique taste is all to do with the particular quality and characteristics of the terrain where the buffalo graze.

Because real, traditionally made unpasteurized buffalo mozzarella is at its best for only a day or so, if we want to buy it in London the producer has to drive it to the airport just hours after it has been made, put it on a plane overnight, then have it collected and sent out to customers in the morning. So, of course, it is expensive and not always easy to find. However, there is another version allowed under DOP rules, which says that the whey in which the mozzarella is kept (in little packets or pots) can be pasteurized, so that the cheese will last longer. This is the one you are most likely to find in delicatessens, and at least you know it has been made traditionally in Campania, from pure buffalo milk.

Burrata

Another beautiful cheese is burrata, which is made in a way similar to mozzarella, but with cow's milk. The stretched curd is made to form a little "pouch" which is filled with mozzarella-like strings of curd, mixed with cream from the whey, and the pouches are knotted and dipped in brine. Traditionally they are wrapped in bright green asphodel (lily) leaves, which look beautiful against the milky white cheese.

Burrata is brilliant as part of an antipasto with salami or prosciutto – put it in the middle of the table and let everyone scoop out a little of the rich creamy cheese with a spoon.

Seafood antipasti

In England and America, people love big fish, like salmon or sea bass, with no bones left in to negotiate. But Italians have a bit of a love affair not only with octopus, squid and cuttlefish but also with little fish, cooked whole, head and bones included. I have always loved those cheap little fish like mackerel and sardines, which are so full of flavor yet so underrated because they don't have any snob value. We always have one or two of these oily "bluefish" on the menu, and they are a very healthy option. Sardines and mackerel contain the fatty acids called omega-3, which are thought to protect the heart, and help the working of our brains and immune systems. Again, we go back to the idea that good-quality food doesn't have to be expensive. I believe you are being more generous to someone if you give them cheap and healthy sardines than if you spend a lot of money on farmed salmon, which is so controversial in terms of the health of the fish and our environment.

At home in Italy we would prepare these fish really simply, perhaps whole under a marinade. In the restaurant, of course, it is crucial that we don't serve things that are too fiddly to eat, or that will cause people to end up with food splashed down their clothes. So I'm afraid that some of these recipes require you to fillet the fish first – or, if you don't want to do it yourself, ask your fishmonger to do it for you.

Sgombro all'aspretto di zafferano

Mackerel with saffron vinaigrette

This is the dish that Tony Blair ate when he came to the restaurant – I was impressed by his choice of healthy proletarian food. Where I come from in Lombardia, we are quite close to the Ligurian Sea but for some reason we get more fish from the Adriatic – mackerel is one that we used to have all the time when I was little – in addition to our usual diet of fish from the local lakes. Fat and flavorsome, mackerel actually have a better flavor when they are well cooked (unlike most fish) and, because they are very oily, the flesh won't dry out the way other fish do.

Sometimes I make this dish without the pancetta but with a little saffron instead. You brush the mackerel fillets with oil and a few saffron threads, then season them with salt. Heat a pan and add a little oil. When it is hot, put in the fish, skin side down, pressing it down so that all the skin comes into contact with the pan. Don't fiddle with it, just leave it for three or four minutes, until the skin turns golden, and you will see the flesh starting to turn white, rather than translucent. Once the flesh has turned white almost to the top, turn the fillets over and finish them off very briefly on the other side for about a minute. This is a dish of hot fish with a cold salad, which is why you need to choose fairly robust leaves, such as arugula. Note: if you are using saffron vinaigrette that you have made earlier and kept in the fridge, warm it up in a pan (but don't let it boil) before using it, to bring out the flavor.

2 large mackerel
　　(each about 3 ounces)
8 thin slices of pancetta
　　or Parma ham
4 handfuls of mixed
　　green salad leaves
2 tablespoons Giorgio's
　　vinaigrette (see page 51)
3 tablespoons Saffron
　　vinaigrette (see page 52)
bunch of chives,
　　cut into short lengths
salt and pepper

Take one of the mackerel and cut down either side of the central bone, so that you can remove this "panel" completely, leaving you with 2 small, boneless fillets. Repeat with the other mackerel. You don't need to season the fish, as there will be enough saltiness from the pancetta. (See page 95.)

Wrap each fillet completely in pancetta, without overlapping it. Cut each fillet crosswise, at an angle, into 2 or 3 pieces depending on the size of the fillet.

Place a nonstick frying pan on the burner until it is moderately hot, but don't add any oil. Put in the fish "parcels" and cook until the pancetta is crisp and golden on each side (about 3 to 4 minutes in all).

While the fish is cooking, quickly season the salad leaves, toss with Giorgio's vinaigrette and arrange in the center of your serving plates.

Carefully remove the fish "parcels" from the pan, then dip them into the Saffron vinaigrette and toss them around gently, and arrange them around the salad. Drizzle over the rest of the Saffron vinaigrette and sprinkle with the chives.

Sardine alla rivierasca

Fried stuffed sardines

Sardines are my favorite of all the oily fish, with an amazingly rich flavor. My grandmother used to fry sardines in really hot oil, then take them off the heat and keep them on one side. She would put some sliced onions into a big pot with plenty of oil (enough to cover the sardines later), add a splash of white wine and vinegar and let everything warm up to make an infusion. Then she would pour this over the sardines and leave them for 12 hours. Finally, she would take out the sardines, break them up and serve them with pasta. Or sometimes she would just put the pot on the table and let everyone take a bit of fish and eat it with some bread. This is a little more complicated, and a dish to make in the summer, when fresh sardines are plentiful, but make sure the ones you buy have really silvery skins. If they are being sold from a stall and the sun is out, or they are under the lights in a fishmonger's, you should be able to see the skin shining from far away. If not, don't buy them, because they are old. In Italy, we get smaller sardines than the ones in the U.S.; no matter – the bigger ones just look a little less precious.

There is a really famous Italian dish from Sicilia that I love, called *sardine al beccafico*, which is sardines split open and stuffed with bread crumbs, olive oil and tomato, then rolled up and baked for 5 or 6 minutes. The story is that the little rolls with their tails sticking out look like the beccafico, a small, greedy bird who loves to eat figs, and so is considered to be a great judge of good food. I really wanted to have this dish on the menu, but it isn't easy to serve in a way that is right for the restaurant. I knew I would have to take out all the small bones – it is very important for a London restaurant to clean fish. So we came up with this way of filleting the fish and then wrapping the fillets around little balls of stuffing, made of bread crumbs, herbs, olive oil and Parmesan. I have to confess, though – and whisper this – that it breaks one of the fundamental rules of Italian cooking: never put cheese and fish together.

Because sardines are so generously fatty, we cut through the richness by serving them with a little salad of tomatoes (seasoned with salt and vinegar to bring out their acidity), some leaves, black olives and plenty of chives – a really big handful. I hate to use any herb just sprinkled on a dish for decoration; I use them for their texture and taste, and I really like the oniony flavor of chives, especially in this recipe.

Whenever we can, we use the fantastic sweet San Marzano tomatoes that come in from Italy, because they have thick flesh and very few seeds, so they absorb the vinegar well. And we use wild salad greens, predominantly arugula but also red chard, mizuna and mustard – the more aromatic and peppery the salad, the better. Again, remember you are putting hot fish on soft leaves, so you don't want any leaves that are too delicate or they will "cook" and wilt immediately. That is why we favor arugula so much, because it has real tenacity and a lovely pepperiness.

8 small, vine-ripened tomatoes,
    blanched, skinned, cut into
    quarters and deseeded
    (see page 304)
10 tablespoons Giorgio's
    vinaigrette (see page 51)
12 small or 8 large sardines
about 20 black olives,
    pitted and halved
2 tablespoons olive oil
3 handfuls of arugula
small bunch of chives,
    cut into batons
salt and pepper

    For the stuffing:
2 slices of soft white bread,
    crusts cut off
a little milk
good handful of basil
good handful of
    flat-leaf parsley
1 tablespoon
    extra virgin olive oil
2 tablespoons breadcrumbs
3 tablespoons freshly grated
    Parmesan
1 garlic clove, chopped

Start making the stuffing well ahead. Put the slices of bread into a bowl and pour over enough milk to wet them all the way through. Transfer to a fine sieve and leave to drain for 4 or 5 hours, but preferably overnight, until the bread is moist but not wet (this step isn't essential, but it is best if you can do it).

Toward the end of the bread soaking time, sprinkle the tomatoes with 4 tablespoons of the vinaigrette and leave to marinate.

Put the basil and parsley into a food processor with the olive oil and whiz until finely chopped. Then add the bread crumbs, soaked bread (first squeezing out any excess milk, if necessary), Parmesan and garlic. Pulse until all the ingredients come together into a paste. Taste for seasoning and add some pepper and salt if necessary (there will already be some saltiness from the Parmesan).

Under running water, scale the sardines and then open them out, leaving the heads attached. To do this, insert a sharp filleting knife at the tail end, next to the backbone, and cut upward, until you reach the belly of the fish. Turn the sardine over, then cut in the same way to the same point on the other side of the bone. Starting at the tail end, take the backbone between your forefinger and thumb and run them along the length of the bone up to the head. Cut across the bone at the tail end and head end and the bone should lift out, leaving the fillets still attached at the opposite side, so you can open them out like a book. At the outside of each fillet, you will see a black area with some fine bones. Just take your knife under these parts, and remove them. Then, with a pair of tweezers, take out any pin bones that may have remained in the fillets.

Take a little of the stuffing and work it into a ball. Then place a filleted sardine on a board, put the stuffing inside, as close to the head as possible, and wrap the fillets around it. Smooth the stuffing that is still visible at the top and bottom, then secure with toothpicks.

Alternate the tomato and olives around the edge of 4 serving plates.

Cook the sardines in 2 batches. Heat half the olive oil in a large, nonstick frying pan. Season the sardines with a little salt and, when the oil is hot, put in half of them and brown on one side for about 1 to 2 minutes. Turn over and cook for 2 minutes on the other side. To make sure the stuffing is heated through, insert a sharp knife into the center and then put the knife to your lips to check that it is hot. Remove the sardines and keep hot while you cook the remainder in the rest of the oil.

Take the toothpicks out of the sardines. Toss the arugula with 2 tablespoons of the vinaigrette and put it in the middle of the serving plates. Place the sardines on top of the arugula, then sprinkle with the chives and spoon the rest of the vinaigrette over.

Carpione di pesce persico

Escabèche of perch

Where I come from in northern Italy, the local fish is all lake fish – especially perch – which we would cook and put under vinegar with vegetables, to bring to the table cold as part of the antipasti. The idea here is that you don't completely cook the fish in the pan but finish it off in the oven, still in the vinegar mixture. We serve it hot, but you can also leave it to cool, cut it into smaller pieces and serve at room temperature, with more antipasti. If you do this, don't reduce the juices at the end, as you will need enough to cover the fish completely. You can also serve this as a main course with some fregola (see page 166) or couscous – use 12 onions, double the quantities of carrots, white wine, vinegar, rosemary and leek, and choose fillets of fish around ½ pound. Then cook 4 tablespoons of fregola or couscous in plenty of salted water for 7 to 8 minutes, and sauté with some diced cucumber and tomato.

8 baby onions
1 carrot
about 3 tablespoons sunflower
    or vegetable oil
4 perch fillets or steaks, each
    about ¼ pound
2 tablespoons white wine
5 tablespoons
    white wine vinegar
4 bay leaves
2 small sprigs of rosemary
white part of 1 small leek
4 juniper berries
4 black peppercorns
small handful of
    flat-leaf parsley
3 tablespoons olive oil
salt and pepper

Preheat the oven to 425°F. Blanch the onions in boiling salted water for about a minute, then remove them with a slotted spoon and cut them in half. Blanch the carrot for 1 to 2 minutes (you can use the same water), then drain and slice thin. Set aside.

Heat the sunflower or vegetable oil in a large, ovenproof frying pan (or 2 small ones). Season the fish, put it in the pan, skin side down, and fry until golden; this will take about 2 to 3 minutes.

Turn the fish over, add the white wine and leave for that to evaporate for a minute or so, then add the vinegar, blanched vegetables and all of the remaining ingredients except the parsley and olive oil. Bring to a boil, then transfer to the oven for 2 minutes, until the fish is cooked through (larger fish may need 3 to 4 minutes).

Remove from the oven and transfer a fillet to each serving plate. Put the pan on the heat, and simmer until the cooking juices have reduced and thickened slightly. Check the seasoning, then spoon the juices over the fish and finish with the parsley and oil.

Insalata di polpo e patate novelle

Octopus salad with new potatoes

For years, I always boiled octopus in water, the way I was taught when I first started cooking. Then one day I was with my good friend Vincenzo Borgonzolo, who used to own Al San Vincenzo, which was one of my favorite family-run Italian restaurants in London. Vincenzo grew up a true *scugnizzo napoletano*, one of the street urchins who give the city so much of its color. For some reason we were talking about octopus. He asked me how I cooked it and when I told him, he said, "But you don't have to cook it in water – it has enough water of its own." He showed me how he cooked his octopus for 40 minutes with no water, just simmering it gently in oil so that it released its juices and moisture into the pan, braising itself in its own liquid. You end up with a fantastic concentration of flavor and an incredibly tender octopus. After it is cut up and cooled a little, it becomes rich, sticky and gelatinous and really meaty in the mouth, with a huge flavor of the sea. When I saw the octopus done this way, I couldn't believe it. Brilliant, brilliant. How could it be that I never knew about it before? It seems this method of braising is the way they cook octopus in Napoli, with the addition of tomatoes, where it is eaten with bread – but in the north I had never seen it done. (By the way, in the north we call octopus *polpo*, in the south it is *polipo*.) I can honestly say I had been wrong for 20 years. Except for certain recipes, like the Octopus carpaccio on page 99, boiling is completely the wrong way to cook an octopus.

Ask your fishmonger to clean and prepare the octopus. If you can't find a fresh one, use frozen, which comes already cleaned and works almost as well. It will already be tenderized, as the freezing process breaks down the cell structure. If you use a fresh octopus you will need to pound it before cooking.

Wrap the octopus in a cloth and pound it with a meat hammer for 3 to 4 minutes to tenderize it. Rinse well under cold running water for 10 to 15 minutes, to take out any excess salt.

Put the chile, one handful of parsley, 3 whole garlic cloves and 3 tablespoons of the olive oil in a large casserole. Add the octopus (don't season it, or it will toughen up), cover with a lid and simmer gently for about 1½ hours, until tender. Leave to cool.

Meanwhile, boil the potatoes until tender, then drain. When cool enough to handle, remove the skins.

Heat a couple of tablespoons of the remaining oil in a small casserole dish, add the onion and sweat until soft but not colored. Add the white wine vinegar and let it bubble until completely evaporated. Remove from the heat. Cut the potatoes into quarters, mix with the onion and season to taste.

1 large octopus, cleaned
1 large chile, split in half
2 handfuls of flat-leaf parsley
4 garlic cloves
6 tablespoons
    extra virgin olive oil
8 small new potatoes, scrubbed
1 onion, chopped
3 tablespoons white wine vinegar
juice of 1 lemon
2 celery stalks
small bunch of chives
2 handfuls of mixed salad
    greens (optional)
2 tablespoons Giorgio's vinaigrette
    (see page 51, optional)
salt and pepper

Squash the remaining garlic clove to a paste with the back of a knife, then put the rest of the parsley on top and chop it so that the two mix together well.

When the octopus has cooled enough for you to handle it, remove any big suckers and discard, then cut the rest into small chunks and put into a bowl. Add the parsley and garlic, and the lemon juice. Season if necessary and mix in the rest of the olive oil. (At this point, you can keep it in the fridge for 2 to 3 hours and finish it just before serving.)

Cut the celery into julienne strips, and the chives into batons. Combine the potatoes with the octopus mixture and add the chives. If using the salad, dress it with Giorgio's vinaigrette and some salt and pepper. Arrange on serving plates and put the octopus and potato mixture on top. Garnish with the celery.

Carpaccio di polpo

Octopus carpaccio

This is the exception to the rule of not boiling octopus, because in this case you need to keep as much gelatin as possible inside the octopus (rather than letting it come out as the octopus cooks in its own juices). It is this gelatin that will hold the pieces of octopus together in the carpaccio.

When you slice and serve the carpaccio, it looks beautiful: the perfect pearly white flesh of the octopus, with its purple streaks, against the bright red of the tomato and the green of the basil. We serve it as a starter, but it would also be fantastic as part of an antipasto.

The trick here is not to boil the octopus too fast. Just bring the water to a boil, then turn down the heat and keep it simmering very slowly. Also, put a couple of corks into the pot – don't ask me why. I don't know if there is anything scientific about it, but Corrado Sirroni taught me to do it in my first job and I have done it ever since.

Put the octopus in a large pan and cover with cold water. Add the lemon halves, whole onion, carrot and celery stalk, plus the bay leaves, peppercorns and wine. Put in a couple of clean wine corks at this point if you like. Bring to a boil, reduce the heat and keep at a very slow simmer for about 15 minutes. Remove from the heat.

When the octopus is still warm, take it out of the water. Cut off the head and put it inside the body, close up the tentacles and lay the octopus on a large sheet of plastic wrap. Take the edge of the plastic wrap, pull it over the top of the octopus and roll it up very tightly, twisting the ends. It is important to compress the carpaccio firmly, otherwise it will fall apart when you try to slice it.

Wrap the roll of octopus in a clean cloth, let it cool slightly, then put it in the freezer.

When the octopus is completely hard, use a very sharp knife to cut it into thin slices – as thin as you can manage – being careful not to let it warm up or it will be too soft to cut and will break up. If it starts to soften, put it back in the freezer. Lay the pieces, not overlapping, on a tray covered with plastic wrap, then lay another sheet of plastic wrap on top and keep in the fridge until required (it needs a couple of hours).

Mix the tomatoes with Giorgio's vinaigrette, season and set aside.

When ready to serve, arrange the tomatoes on a serving plate with basil leaves around and put the octopus on top. Drizzle with the olive oil and sprinkle with a little sea salt.

1 large octopus (about
    2–3 pounds)
1 lemon, cut in half
1 onion
1 carrot
1 celery stalk
2–3 bay leaves
3 black peppercorns
wineglass of white wine

    To garnish:
3 tomatoes, deseeded
    and finely diced
2 tablespoons Giorgio's
    vinaigrette (see page 51)
small bunch of basil
3 tablespoons
    extra virgin olive oil
salt and pepper

Calamari

Squid

"The flavor of the sea"

If I could have one really good *calamari fritti* a week, I would be a very happy man. It is one of those favorite childhood memories – like the little gold tins of anchovies in *salsa piccante*, or the bread with five faces that I used to buy with my granddad – that have lodged in my brain and make me feel good whenever I think about them.

In the summer, when I was a boy, we used to go and eat in a local pizzeria run by six brothers, all of them short and fat. They came to our restaurant; we went to theirs. It was a great place. All you had to do was decide what kind of pizza you wanted and then before it arrived the brothers would bring out a long tray piled with fried prawns and rings of calamari. The Spanish slice their calamari rings quite thick but Italians cut them very thin, like wedding rings, and dust them only in flour or semolina – not batter – before frying.

Incidentally, on restaurant menus in some parts of Italy, around the coast of Liguria and also in Sardegna and Toscana, you might come across *totano*, also called "flying" squid, because it shoots out of the water and "flies" over the waves. *Totani* are longer than squid and they hunt different prey, so the flavor is slightly different and they are a little tougher, but they are cooked in similar ways. The smaller ones are often served in a *fritto misto*.

Cooking squid at home is easy in one way, because it is very quick, but hard in another, because there is about 40 seconds' difference between squid that is beautiful and squid that is as tough as a shoe sole. Like octopus, squid contains a lot of water, so you have to chargrill or sauté it extremely fast (1 to 1½ minutes on each side, that's all) over a very high heat. Otherwise it will just boil in its own liquid, losing flavor and toughening up at the same time. People always tend to worry that it might not be cooked, so they leave it a little bit longer and then – disaster – it is too late.

Many people say that frozen calamari is as good as fresh, but I can tell the difference from a long way off – really I can. For me, when you blast-chill something as delicate as squid, unlike octopus, it sanitizes all those unique flavors and the smells of the sea. So, when you buy squid, look for a pearly white membrane, which shows that it is fresh.

Cleaning squid isn't the nicest job in the world – I recommend you teach your children to do it as soon as possible, then they can take over. Usually when you buy squid, the head – with its tentacles attached – will be tucked inside the body pocket. So pull out the head, detach it from the body and set it aside. Discard the intestines, which will come out too,

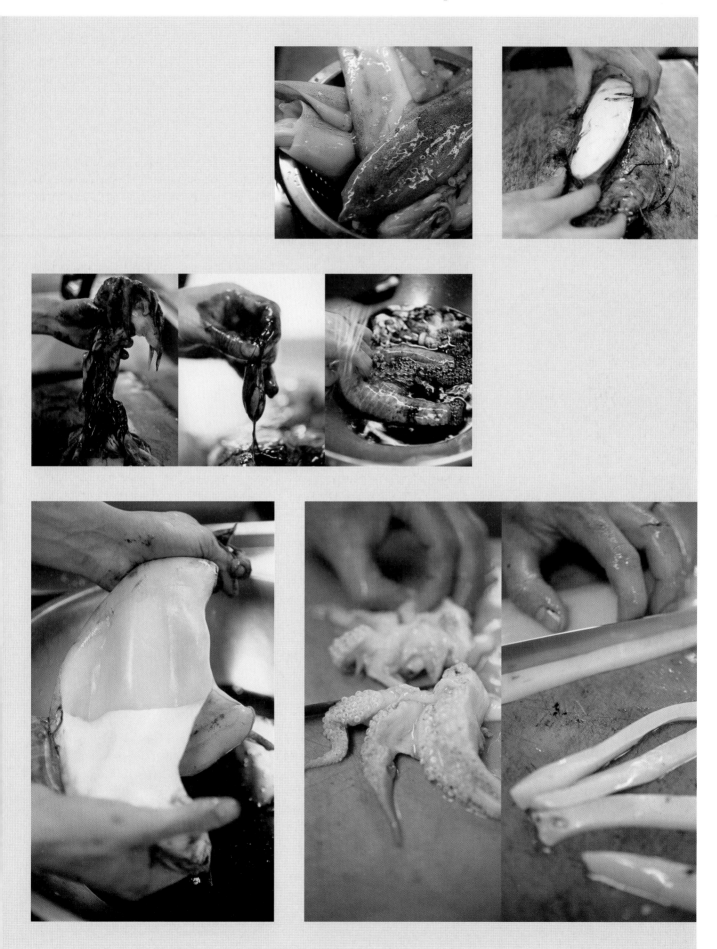

then reach inside the body with your fingers and pull out any other innards, including the plastic-looking quill. Throw all of these away. Next, you have to take off the fins. Pull them downward so that you pull off the purplish skin at the same time. Throw away the skin and the fins. Then you need to wash the body "pocket" inside and out. I always make my chefs turn the pocket inside out to wash it because it may contain a bit of sand or other debris – who knows? But it is very important to turn it back again – you can tell immediately when somebody has left it inside out, because the outside of the squid has a different, shinier texture. Finally, you should take the head, cut away the tentacles in front of the eyes and squeeze out and discard the beak. Keep only the tentacles.

To grill (or barbecue) squid, slash the pockets down one side, then open them out so that the whole area will touch the grill and pick up the charred flavor. If the squid are thick, pound them out a bit, or slash them on the inside crisscross fashion with a sharp knife (but not cutting all the way through). If the squid is thin, though, there is no need to do any of this. Chop some garlic, mix it with some olive oil, season it with salt and pepper and then brush it over the squid (including the tentacles) and grill as quickly as possible.

Calamari ripieni alla griglia

Chargrilled stuffed squid with tomato

This is a lovely, quite rustic dish. It is simple to make, but relies on very good-quality ingredients, so it is another one to do in the summer, when tomatoes and basil are at their best.

The dish dates back to the days when I was cooking at Olivo and each week we used to get three large boxes of calamari arriving in the kitchen, full of squid of all different sizes.

Because I hate waste – all Italians do – I came up with this recipe using all the squid, big or small, tentacles and all, and it tastes fantastic – despite the fact that this is yet another case of breaking the cardinal Italian rule of never putting cheese with fish.

The finished dish is something between a starter and a soup, almost like squid in a broth of warm tomato salsa. Serve with a knife, fork and spoon and let people dip bruschetta into it.

Make the stuffing by putting the anchovies, oil, garlic and herbs into a food processor and processing until finely chopped, then adding the chopped tentacles and extra squid bodies, together with the bread crumbs and Parmesan. Do not add any seasoning at this point. Pulse until the mixture will come together in your hands without being too sticky.

Since both the squid and the Parmesan are quite salty, you need to check whether any extra salt is needed, so take a small amount of the stuffing mixture and cook it quickly in a nonstick pan; taste and season with salt if necessary. Otherwise, just add a twist of black pepper.

Stuff the squid pockets with the mixture – not too full, or they will burst during cooking – then close up and secure the openings with toothpicks.

Put the olive oil, diced tomatoes and basil into a pan with a large base set over a low heat and warm through without boiling. Season to taste.

Brush the squid with a little oil, then heat a griddle pan or heavy frying pan until smoking. (If the pan isn't hot enough, the squid will boil, leaching out its liquid, which will make it tough and flavorless.) Don't overcrowd the pan or griddle – cook no more than 4 squid at a time. You need enough space around each one to enable you to turn it over onto a spare hot space, so that once again you can make sure it sears rather than boils. Grill quickly (about a minute on each side), until the squid begin to mark if on a griddle or take on a bit of color if in a frying pan.

Remove the toothpicks and add the squid pockets to the pan of sauce. Move them around gently, taking care not to break them. Really, you just need to leave the squid in the sauce long enough to release some of the juices from the stuffing that will have gathered inside the pockets, so they can blend with the tomato, basil and oil – but don't leave the squid in for too long, or it will become rubbery.

Grill or sauté the slices of ciabatta on both sides until crisp, then rub with the garlic clove and drizzle with oil.

Serve the squid in its sauce in bowls, garnished with basil leaves and with the bread on the side.

enough squid (including tentacles) to give you 16 small, intact bodies, plus 2 or 3 extra for the stuffing, prepared as above
4 tablespoons light extra virgin olive oil, plus a little extra for brushing
2 very ripe large tomatoes, diced
handful of basil
salt and pepper

For the stuffing:
2 anchovy fillets
4 tablespoons light extra virgin olive oil
2 garlic cloves
handful of flat-leaf parsley
handful of basil
bread crumbs made from stale bread (a quantity equal to the chopped-up squid tentacles and reserved bodies – so for a handful of squid, you need a handful of bread crumbs)
2 tablespoons freshly grated Parmesan cheese

To serve:
8 slices of ciabatta bread
1 garlic clove, halved
a little extra virgin olive oil
a few basil leaves

Insalata di seppia alla griglia

Chargrilled cuttlefish salad

Cuttlefish are bigger than squid and have larger "bones" that often get made into earrings. They also have a little sac inside the body containing a sweet-tasting black ink, which they squirt at enemies in self-defense, and which we use in this recipe. Clean the cuttlefish in the same way as squid (see page 100), being very careful not to puncture the ink sac – just pull it out whole. Sometimes the sac will have emptied when the cuttlefish was caught, so it is best to buy a little packet or jar of ink, which your fishmonger will sell separately, just in case you find no ink inside.

With this sauce, we try to bring out the sweetness and full flavors of both the ink and the onion. To do this you need to cook the onion very slowly and gently, because if it burns, the sauce will taste bitter. Also, when you finish off the sauce after straining it, use a straight-sided pan because you need to keep a low flame just underneath the base. It is very important that the heat doesn't spread around the sides of the pan because, again, if you overheat it the sauce will turn bitter. The sauce can also be used for risotto and pasta.

2¼ pounds cuttlefish, cleaned
　　(see above), heads reserved
olive oil, for brushing
1 garlic clove
handful of flat-leaf parsley
4 handfuls of mixed peppery
　　salad greens (or just
　　mizuna, if you can get it)
3 tablespoons Oil and lemon
　　dressing (see page 52)
salt and pepper

　　For the cuttlefish sauce:
5 tablespoons extra virgin olive
　　oil, plus extra for drizzling
4 onions, sliced
about 1 tablespoon cuttlefish
　　ink
1 quart fish stock
salt and pepper

To make the sauce, heat 3 tablespoons of the oil very gently in a small, straight-sided pan, add the onions, then cover and sweat slowly for about 15 minutes until softened but not colored.

Add the cuttlefish heads and cook uncovered, still very gently, until the juices released by the cuttlefish have completely evaporated.

Add the ink and fish stock, stir until well mixed and bring to the boil. Reduce the heat and simmer for 20 minutes. Pass through a fine sieve into a clean small, straight-sided pan, pressing and squeezing the onions and heads to extract all the juices.

Bring the sieved liquid to a boil, then reduce the heat and simmer until the sauce thickens and becomes very syrupy. Cover and keep warm.

Cut the cuttlefish into pieces roughly 3¼ x 4 inches, score diagonally each way to make a diamond pattern and season with salt and pepper. Brush with a little olive oil.

Crush the garlic with the back of a knife, put the parsley on top and chop it all together, to mix well.

Cook the cuttlefish in 2 batches. Preheat a dry griddle pan or a heavy frying pan until hot and smoking (otherwise the fish will just boil in its own juices). Sprinkle the cuttlefish with the garlic and parsley mixture, put it into the pan and cook for about 30 seconds on one side, then 30 seconds on the other. As with squid, be very careful not to overcook it, or it will become tough.

Season the salad with salt and pepper, toss with the Oil and lemon dressing and arrange it in the center of 4 serving plates. Quickly beat the rest of the oil into the sauce and spoon it around the salad. Place the grilled cuttlefish on top of the salad and drizzle with extra virgin olive oil.

Gamberi e borlotti

Prawns with fresh borlotti beans

This is based on the dish my grandmother used to make with *gamberi rossi*, the beautiful pink prawns that come in from Liguria. Sometimes, if we are lucky, we can get them in London, but otherwise we use large Mediterranean prawns, or you could use tiger prawns. Of course, cooking in a restaurant is different from the way my grandmother worked at home, boiling up the beans while we waited, and then dipping the prawns into the pot at the last minute. So we have adapted the dish so that everything can be ready in advance and you have only to sauté the prawns and bring everything together in five minutes.

The fresh sweet chiles that we use are quite large – long, thin and not too spicy – not the tiny ones used in Thai cooking. This is a brilliant recipe to glorify good olive oil and demonstrate how it can enhance simple flavors. In this case, the one we use for drizzling over the finished salad is the peppery Manni Per Me.

Remember that when you are cooking a large number of prawns, you need enough space in the pan for them all to touch the bottom, so that they all sear quickly. If some of the prawns are not in direct contact with the pan, and therefore don't get hot enough, they will release their juices and boil in them rather than frying. So, no overcrowding. In the recipe directions, I have suggested that you cook the prawns in two batches to avoid this problem.

I have also suggested that you use some of the liquid from cooking the beans to make a little "sauce." However, in our kitchen we never waste anything, so before we start this dish we make a stock from the shells of the prawns, which we use instead of the bean water.

We sauté the shells in a little olive oil with a splash of white wine, some chopped chile and garlic (for about 6 ounces prawn shells, we would use half a chile and two garlic cloves), plus a tablespoon of our homemade tomato sauce (you could use tomato passata). Then we add enough water to cover (no more, as we want to concentrate the flavor), boil everything for 10 minutes and strain the stock, really squeezing the shells against the sieve.

1 pound fresh borlotti
      (cranberry) beans in their
      pods (about 9 ounces
      shelled) or
   ¼ pound dried
      borlotti beans, soaked
      for 24 hours
½ head of garlic (unpeeled),
      plus 3 extra cloves,
      finely chopped
1 celery stalk, chopped
bunch of sage
6 tablespoons
      extra virgin olive oil
12 large fresh prawns, shell on
4 tablespoons olive oil
2 teaspoons sliced sweet
      chile pepper
½ wineglass of white wine
2 tablespoons tomato passata
salt and pepper

   To serve:
1 garlic clove
handful of flat-leaf parsley
extra virgin olive oil,
      preferably Tuscan

First cook the beans: put them into a large pot with the ½ head of garlic, the celery, sage and 2 tablespoons of the olive oil (don't add salt until the beans are completely cooked, otherwise they will harden). Cover with plenty of cold water (about double the volume of the beans), put a lid on the pan and bring to the boil. Remove the lid, skim the foam from the top and reduce the heat to a gentle simmer. Cook until the beans are soft to the bite (45 minutes to 1 hour), stirring every 5 to 10 minutes, then leave to cool in their cooking water.

When the beans are almost ready, peel the prawns, leaving only the heads on. Run a sharp knife along the back as far as the tail and remove the black thread that runs down it. Then open out the prawns as far as you can.

Cook the prawns in 2 batches. Heat a large, heavy-bottomed frying pan and add 2 tablespoons of the olive oil. Add half the chopped garlic and half the sliced chile, and cook for a few seconds over a medium heat, without allowing to color. Season the prawns, then put them into the pan, back downward. Once they have seared and caramelized a little, press the heads to release some of their juices. This not only helps the flavor but will reduce the temperature of the oil and prevent the garlic from burning and turning bitter. If there still isn't enough liquid and the garlic begins to color too much, add a little more oil. Sauté the prawns for a couple of minutes, until they turn pink or dark red (depending on the type of prawn), then flip them over. Transfer to a warm plate.

Wipe out the pan with some paper towel. Add the rest of the oil, garlic and chile and cook the rest of the prawns in the same way.

Return the first batch of prawns to the pan, then add the wine and let it evaporate. Remove the prawns and set aside in a warm place.

With a slotted spoon, take the beans from their cooking liquid (reserving the liquid) and put them into the pan in which you cooked the prawns. Season and bring to the boil, then add the tomato passata and a ladleful of the cooking water from the beans – you need to add enough liquid to create a little sauce around the beans. Adjust the seasoning if necessary. Let the beans heat through for a couple of minutes so they take on the garlic and chile flavors. As they do so, crush a few of them with a wooden spoon to thicken the sauce. Return the prawns to the pan and toss everything together.

Quickly crush the garlic to a paste with the blade of a knife, chop the parsley on top and mix together.

Serve the beans and prawns drizzled liberally with extra virgin olive oil. Season with lots of freshly ground black pepper and finish with the chopped parsley and garlic.

Capesante all'aspretto di zafferano

Pan-fried scallops with saffron vinaigrette

Sautéed scallops are fantastic just with salad, if you don't feel like making the celeriac puree with which we serve them in the restaurant. Scallops were a great revelation for me when I came to London, because in the UK they have the best in the world. In the Mediterranean we have what are known as "queenies," which are much smaller, and don't have the same milky sweetness.

8 large fresh scallops or 12 small
    ones, cleaned but with any
    corals (roe) still attached
4–5 celery stalks
4 tablespoons Saffron
    vinaigrette (see page 52)
2 tablespoons lemon juice
3 tablespoons
    extra virgin olive oil
2 tablespoons vegetable oil
salt and pepper

For the celeriac puree:
½ celeriac, diced
1 tablespoon olive oil
2 garlic cloves
1 sprig of rosemary
3 tablespoons heavy cream
1½ tablespoons butter

If the scallops have been in the fridge, bring them to room temperature before cooking.

To make the celeriac puree, preheat the oven to 350°F, put the celeriac in an ovenproof dish with ½ wineglass of water, a pinch of salt and the olive oil, garlic and rosemary, seal completely with foil and then bake for about 30 minutes, until soft.

Transfer to a food processor and blend, adding the cream as you go. Then push through a fine sieve, so you have a smooth puree (it is important to process the celeriac while it is still hot, as it makes the puree smoother and it will pass through the sieve more easily). Keep the puree to one side.

Cut the celery into julienne strips and leave in a bowl with a handful of ice cubes to crisp them. Have the Saffron vinaigrette ready in a large, shallow bowl. Mix the lemon juice and extra virgin olive oil.

Turn the oven up to 375°F. Heat a large ovenproof frying pan – or 2 if you have 12 scallops (see my note about overcrowding the pan on page 105). When the pan is good and hot, but not smoking (or the scallops will burn), pour in the vegetable oil, then add the scallops. Don't season them at this stage, or the salt will make them leach out their moisture and they will become dry.

Let the scallops turn nice and golden on their undersides (about 1½ minutes for large scallops, less for smaller ones), then turn them over and place the pan in the oven for 1 minute. This just makes sure that after frying them hard on the outside they are cooked through. Season and transfer them to the bowl of Saffron vinaigrette.

Warm up the celeriac puree in a small pan and season if necessary. Remove from the heat and beat in the butter.

Spoon the puree onto 4 serving plates and arrange the scallops on top. Drain the celery from the ice, season with the lemon oil and arrange on top of the scallops. Drizzle the remaining Saffron vinaigrette around.

Razza al balsamico

Skate wing with aged balsamic vinegar

Skate is a great, great fish, with a fantastic flavor, and it's in season most of the year. In winter, I love it cooked this way, served with balsamic vinegar and pomegranate seeds; or in the summer, simply with a tomato salad.

Sadly, as with so many of our favorite fish, we have taken too much of it from the sea, so it is an endangered species, but I am including this recipe in the hope that stocks will recover and we can enjoy it in good conscience again.

2 tablespoons golden raisins
1¾ cups white wine
1 cup white wine vinegar
1 shallot, coarsely chopped
1 carrot, coarsely chopped
1 bay leaf
2 parsley stalks (no leaves)
3 black peppercorns
2 tablespoons salt
2 medium-sized skate wings, cleaned and trimmed (ask the fishmonger to trim off the thin part of the skate wings for you)
4 tablespoons extra virgin olive oil
½ pomegranate
2 tablespoons pine nuts
2 bunches of arugula, coarsely chopped
2 tablespoons Giorgio's vinaigrette (see page 51)
4 teaspoons aged balsamic vinegar

Soak the golden raisins in water for about 30 minutes, until they plump up.

Put the wine, ¾ cup of the vinegar and 1 quart of water into a large pan, wide enough to hold the skate wings side by side. Add the shallot, carrot, herbs, peppercorns and salt. Bring to a boil and put in the skate wings, thickest side downward. Turn the heat down to a simmer and cook for about 3 to 4 minutes, depending on size, until the flesh will come away from the bone if you insert a knife. Remove the pan from the heat and leave the skate in the cooking liquid for a couple of minutes.

Take the skate out of the pan, then put it on a tray and drizzle it with 2 tablespoons of the olive oil and the rest of the white wine vinegar. Cover with plastic wrap, so that the fish "steams" in the marinade and keeps moist.

Meanwhile, deseed the pomegranate, reserving the seeds. Toast the pine nuts in a dry pan until golden.

Take the skate wings from the marinade and cut each one in half, through the bone (it will be soft and easy to cut through).

Toss the arugula with the vinaigrette, arrange on 4 serving plates and place the skate on top. Scatter over equal quantities of pomegranate seeds, golden raisins and pine nuts. Drizzle the rest of the olive oil and the balsamic vinegar over the skate.

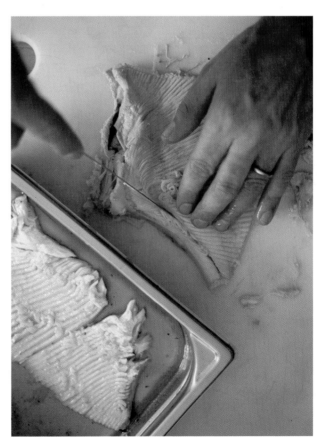

Insalata di borlotti, tonno e cipolle rosse

Tuna salad with borlotti beans and red onion

This is good when fresh borlotti beans are in season, from June to September; otherwise use dried ones. Just remember to soak these in water for 24 hours, without putting them in the fridge, and change the water as close to every 5 or 6 hours as you can. You can cook the beans well in advance. They will keep in their cooking water in the fridge for 4 or 5 days, but don't put your fingers into the water or you will introduce bacteria. When the beans become cold, they harden a little, so take them out of the fridge an hour or so before using, or warm them up in a pan, and they will soften again.

1 pound fresh borlotti
    (cranberry) beans
    (about ½ pound shelled), or
    ¼ pound dried borlotti
    beans, soaked for 24 hours
    (see page 183)
1 tablespoon extra virgin olive
    oil, plus extra for drizzling
1 celery stalk, chopped
2 garlic cloves, unpeeled
bunch of sage
1 red onion
about 2¼ cups vegetable oil
    for frying
10½ ounces fresh tuna,
    cut into 16 cubes
    (about 2 x 2 x 2 inches)
4 bunches of arugula
2 tablespoons Giorgio's
    vinaigrette (see page 51)
salt and pepper

Put the beans in a large pan with plenty of water, plus the olive oil, celery, garlic and sage (no salt, or the beans will toughen). Cover and bring to a boil, then reduce the heat and simmer for about 45 minutes to 1 hour. Try a bean: they are cooked when the skin, and not just the bean inside, feels soft in the mouth. At this point, you can add salt to taste, then leave the beans to cool in their cooking liquid.

Slice the red onion into very thin rings. Rinse under cold running water to remove some of their sharpness, then put them in a bowl with some ice cubes.

Take out 2 tablespoons of the beans and pulse to a puree in a food processor. Keep on one side.

Heat the vegetable oil in a deep-fat fryer or a deep saucepan (no more than one-third full) to about 350°F. Season the tuna with salt and pepper, then put about 3 to 4 cubes at a time (so as not to lower the temperature of the oil) on a skimmer (see photograph, below left) or in a fine sieve. Dip them into the oil and cook for about a minute, moving the cubes around, until the outside of the tuna turns crisp but the inside stays rose-colored. Remove and drain on kitchen paper, then put in the next batch and continue until all the tuna is cooked.

Season the arugula with salt and dress with the vinaigrette. Squeeze the red onion rings to remove any excess water and mix with the arugula. Finally, remove the beans from their cooking water with a slotted spoon and mix with the arugula and onions. Season to taste.

Spoon the bean puree onto 4 serving plates, then arrange the arugula, onion and bean mixture on top, with the tuna on top of that. Drizzle with extra virgin olive oil.

Bottarga

There are two kinds of bottarga, which is the salted, pressed and sun-dried roe of either gray mullet *(muggine)* or tuna *(tonno)*. You should be able to find it in blocks of 1¾ ounces or 3½ ounces in good Italian deli-catessens, or on-line, usually two roe per package. Most of it comes from Sardegna and, since it is such a regional speciality, many Italians have never eaten it – my father never tasted it in his life, until I served it to him. Nowadays it has become something of a luxury, but I guess orig-inally it was just another way for the fishermen to feed their families. They fished the gray mullet or tuna, cleaned them, took out the egg sac, sold the fish and then salted and dried the roe to eat at home.

If you visit the south of Sardegna they will tell you, categorically, that the amber-colored gray mullet bottarga is best – partly because it is rarer, and because it takes two mullet to make one *baffa* (the commer-cial unit), whereas tuna are much bigger and the roe much more plenti-ful. Also, when the gray mullet roe is completely dry it becomes powdery, with a texture similar to Parmesan, and less powerful and salty-tasting. In other parts of the island and in Sicilia, though, they will insist that the tuna bottarga (which looks dark browny gray and is slightly saltier and stronger and richer-tasting) is best.

Personally, I can't say I like one better than the other; I love them both. For me, the best time to buy bottarga is in the spring; it is available year-round but early in the year the flavor is fantastic and the color of the gray mullet roe is a brilliant yellow-orange. When the new batches of spring bottarga come into the kitchen, I have to stop myself from just sitting there, slicing it and eating it then and there – it is beautiful on toasted bread, with some quite strong olive oil (as with Parmesan, never buy bottarga ready-grated, as all the flavor will be lost. Buy it in a piece and grate it yourself just before you need it). It is a curious flavor, a lit-tle like caviar, that opens up in your mouth and then you are hooked.

In Sardegna, gray mullet bottarga is usually served sliced, as part of the antipasto, with lots of olive oil and lemon juice. In Cagliari, in the south of the island, they serve it in a very pure way, just shaved, like a truffle, over pasta, with only a pat of butter and some pepper (no salt because the bottarga is salty enough). Butter seems to help the flavor of the bot-targa, though it can also make it a little heavy, and because it has such a high fat content it needs plenty of seasoning with pepper or lemon juice – or something fresh like shavings of fennel – to cut through it.

Tuna bottarga is also produced in Sicilia, where you will sometimes find it served in a pasta sauce made with olive oil, chile, garlic and parsley. Either way, it is an acquired taste, with such an intense flavor that when you serve it as a starter you set a very high note at the beginning of the meal, which you have to follow with powerful flavors.

Insalata di ravanelli e bottarga di muggine

Gray mullet roe and radish salad

Near our house in London is a small Sardinian restaurant, a family affair, very local, offering simple things – the kind of place I used to know when I was growing up. We would often take Margherita there for a pizza, and the owner, who is also the chef, would always bring us out a plate of beautiful bottarga with *carasau*, the famous crispbread of Sardegna. After a while, I got talking to him, and he told me he brings in the bottarga himself from Sardegna, where his brother still lives. So we started to buy some from him. I liked the way he served just a little of it before the meal, with a drink, and so we began experimenting with something you could serve to people in a Chinese spoon – one mouthful of flavor. In spring, when I believe the bottarga is at its best, English radishes are also in season, and the two are just brilliant together. There is something about the heat that comes at the end of the radish that complements the salty bottarga experience, which carries on in your nose and mouth in the same way as truffles. Remember, though, that the radish and celery need be only very lightly seasoned with lemon juice, as the bottarga is very salty.

As a variation, instead of the radish (which incidentally in my region of Lombardia we call rapanelli, not ravanelli), we often serve the bottarga grated over a salad made with two large fennel bulbs, sliced thin, seasoned lightly and tossed with the lemon juice and half the olive oil. Then we deseed and quarter two tomatoes, again lightly season them, and arrange them in the center of each plate. We mix the fennel with a bunch of chives, cut into batons, and pile it on top, scatter the grated bottarga on top, and drizzle with the rest of the oil. Or sometimes we do it in exactly the same way, but with green beans instead of the fennel. Just blanch the beans for a minute or so in boiling water, then drain and refresh under cold running water.

Thinly slice the radishes, using a mandoline or knife, then cut into matchsticks and put in a bowl. Cut the celery into similarly sized strips and add to the radishes. Toss with the lemon juice and half the olive oil.

Make a mound of radish and celery on each plate and finely slice or grate the bottarga on top.

Season with black pepper and drizzle with the rest of the olive oil.

24 radishes
2 celery stalks
juice of 2 lemons
4 tablespoons extra virgin olive oil, plus a little extra for drizzling
1¾ ounces bottarga
salt and pepper

Salumi

Cured meats

"The voice of the people"

I am a great believer in the idea that – as much as art or literature or poetry – cured meats are truly representative of the cultural background of society; they are the voice of the people, and have been over hundreds of years. You have to remember that Italy was traditionally an agricultural country; so at one time most families would have kept a pig and used every part of it. In our region a typical dish was *cazzola*, made with a whole pig's head, feet and ribs, and Savoy cabbage. What wasn't eaten fresh would be cured to feed the family for the next year. In every larder there would have been hams and salami hanging from hooks in the ceiling, each representing the taste, produce and microclimate – the real rural roots – of a particular community. In some villages, on the feast of St. Anthony Abate, they still run a lottery to win a pig that runs around the village for a year before being slaughtered to feed the winning family.

In the northeast around Trentino – Alto Adige, where it is more rainy and often cold, you are not going to cure anything in salt alone as easily as in Parma, so you tend to have salumi that are also lightly smoked, such as speck (smoked prosciutto). Or you first marinate the meat in wine to speed the curing process, as in bresaola, the specialty of Valtellina, in my region of Lombardia. Though the majority of salumi is made with pork, in northern Lombardia we have more cattle than pigs, so the bresaola is made with beef, first marinated in red wine, and then air-dried. Sometimes, too, they make bresaola with horse meat or venison. And in the mountains, the leg of a kid goat is often cured, like a ham *(violino di capra)*, or made into salami.

In Colonnata in the mountains above Carrara in the northwest of Toscana, they traditionally make lardo, which is hard pig fat from under the skin of the animal's back, covered with salt, garlic, peppercorns, spices and herbs like rosemary, then matured in a closed container for six months, so that the oils in the seasoning impregnate the snowy white fat. (In ancient times, it was packed in tubs made using marble from the local mines, and known as "white marble.") Unpromising as it might sound, lardo is beautiful when sliced very thin and served on toasted bread.

Never underestimate how local such foods still are in many parts of Italy – even though you might see a selection from every region in an Italian deli. In Bologna, for example, they make the famous mortadella, the biggest of Italian sausages, which is steamed or poached, rather than cured, and has a texture so fine it is almost a paste. It is made with pork, but sometimes with beef added, together with spices, and often pistachio nuts, coriander seeds, wine and sugar. I remember talking to a guy I met in the army, about how we used to go into Bologna and have a focaccia with mortadella, and he said he had never had mortadella, because he came from Napoli.

Salami

Salami really began their life as the food of the poor. The lean cuts of the animal would be sold to the rich, and whatever was left over would go into salami, along with whatever herbs and spices you had locally. Originally, everything would have been chopped by hand, and in many places it still is. In Toscana, for example, the typical *coppa di testa* is made with practically the whole head of the pig: the tongue, cheek, skin, ear, everything.

To make salami, you need lard, or hard fat, which is cut into pieces, like nuggets of white marble, which won't go rancid in the way that soft fat can; and the best salame achieves the perfect balance between meat and fat. The mixture is forced into the casing or skin of the salami *(i budelli)*, which is traditionally the intestine of the pig, but may be synthetic. Once the salami has been forced into its "sock" or skin, and tied with string, it is hung up in carefully controlled conditions for two to four months, to cure and dry. During this time it forms *le muffe* (mold), which should be uniform all the way over the surface of the salame (and all the same color), leaving no gaps to allow air in, as this could cause the salami to become rancid. This aging process, which contributes so much to the final character, is called *la stagionatura*.

For a simple family lunch, I like nothing better than a good salame with some bread, a little salad and some balsamic onions or other *sottaceti* (pickled vegetables). You can serve salami at dinner and then that is one course you don't have to think about. I would always choose salame over prosciutto, perhaps because I still have a special memory of going up into the mountains with my granddad when I was small. We would buy some bread and a *salame cacciatore* – these are the little ones from my region of Lombardia that are not much bigger than a plump sausage and that hunters would carry in their rucksacks – which he would slice with his knife; and it was the best taste out in the open air. On a picnic, even now, I can't think of anything better.

If you were to ask me now which is my favorite salame, I guess I would have to say *salame di felino*, the long one made in Emilia-Romagna, which is a very straightforward salame, the first one you are given to have in your *panino* when you are very young. It is made with coarsely minced pork, seasoned only with salt and peppercorns and, usually, no garlic, so it is quite sweet-tasting and still moist in the middle. But there is no salame I don't like; and there are so many to choose from, varying in texture: some are soft; some are like dry sticks of meat. In the south, you often find less salty salame, made with more chile peppers; peppercorns and, occasionally, light smoking are favored in the north. In Toscana, they like to flavor their salame with fennel seeds *(salame toscano finocchiona* or *sbriciolona)*.

They say this salame was first made by the farmers in order to sell their wine that wasn't so good. The fennel seeds have an anesthetic power over your taste buds, so when you came to the farm to taste the wine, they would first offer you a slice of the finocchiona, so that the flavor would disguise the poor quality of the wine.

On holiday in Calabria I tasted *'nduja* from Spilinga for the first time (strangely, the name *'nduja* comes from the French *andouille*). It is a soft *(morbido)*, almost spreadable, salame: a mixture of pork and offal, chopped with a knife, with a lot of chile, which goes inside the pig's intestine and is lightly smoked over wood, then matured. You spoon it out and mix it with some pasta, or have it on bread. My son, Jack, would come back from swimming in the sea all afternoon and tuck into it as if it were peanut butter or chocolate spread.

Prosciutto

Prosciutto crudo is famous all over the world and the word may be an amalgamation of two Latin verbs, one meaning to burn, the other to draw out or strip (as in drawing out the moisture of the meat). Of course the best known is prosciutto di Parma (Parma ham), which – like Parmesan cheese, from the same region of Italy – has traveled the world. Just as you could roll your wheel of cheese onto a boat, you could pack your ham and a knife in your knapsack and go off on your travels.

Meat has been cured since ancient times, so why is Parma so important? Partly because there was an abundance of salt passing through the area from the trading port of Venezia as far back as Roman times, and partly because the dry, aromatic breezes that circulate through the Appeninos create the perfect environment for curing hams. Italian pigs, salt, air and time – those four ingredients, they say, give Parma ham its special sweetness (no sugar, spices, water, nitrites or smoking are allowed).

Prosciutto di Parma has become so synonymous with prosciutto crudo, I often think people don't even know that there are many, many more styles of cured ham being made in regions around Italy. All the time at Locanda, we are being brought new ones to taste, from small producers reviving old methods, and I am always fascinated by the subtle differences that come not only from the various breeds of pigs that are used but from the diet of the animals and the environment and conditions in which the ham is cured and dried.

After the Second World War, when there was not enough food for everyone, many people went into intensive breeding of pigs, but now there is much more attention being paid to traditional breeds and the way they are raised. Remember, we are talking about raw cured ham, so the quality of the meat is the most important thing. What you put in at the beginning, you get back at the end.

Parma's fame has also brought it close to a disaster, because, until the rules tightened to protect the product, who was going to say: "No, we can produce only 150,000 hams a year," when the demand around the world might be 150 million? It was easier to bring in pigs from outside the region – even from Poland and Romania – and have them slaughtered and cured in the locality, in order to get the Parma certification. Imagine vans of several hundred animals, banging around inside trucks, kicking each other as pigs do, and getting crushed. Of course, the first thing that would be damaged would be the legs (only the hind legs are cured to make Parma ham), so the flesh becomes soft. Why do you think prosciutto without the bone became so popular? Because, if the bone was taken out and the flesh squeezed together, it was a way of selling second-quality meat, and still calling it Parma ham, so that a truckful of pigs that left Spain worth $40,000 was now worth $80,000.

So gradually Parma ham has come under much stricter controls. Since 1970 it has been awarded a Protected Designation of Origin and production is controlled by the Consorzio del Prosciutto di Parma (CPP).

Now the law says that you must produce your ham from Italian pigs, either pure-breed or cross-breeds derived from Italian Large White, Landrance and Duroc animals, that must be born and raised in one of eleven specified regions of central-northern Italy. To be certified by the Istituto Parma Qualità (IPQ) the hind legs of the pig must also carry an indelible tattoo put on within 30 days of being born, which shows the date and place of birth and the breeder's code. The pigs are raised in huts, which increases their fat, and fed on a diet of grain and whey from the production of Parmesan cheese. The idea is similar to the "West Country cycle" that used to be followed in Somerset, which you have to chant, like a nursery rhyme: "The cows eat the grass, then give the milk that makes the cheese, that gives the whey, that is fed to the pigs, who make the muck to grow the grass that the cows eat."

When a pig is slaughtered (at a minimum of nine months, and weighing at least 300 pounds), the code of the abattoir in which it is slaughtered will be fire-branded onto its skin. It will be kept in cold rooms to harden, then pressed and cleaned and trimmed of some of its fat to give the characteristic "chicken drumstick" shape. Then, at the salting stage, it will have a metal seal attached to the ham that bears the initials (CPP) of the Consortium and the date that curing began. The salt master (maestro salatore) controls the salt levels, temperature and humidity, so that the flesh absorbs only enough salt to keep the meat tasting sweet. Next, the hams hang for 70 days in refrigerated rooms, before being washed and brushed to remove excess salt, and then hung for three months in well-ventilated rooms with large windows that are opened to let the famous aromatic breezes through. After this, they are greased with minced lard and salt, and then finished in dark, cellar-like rooms for at least a year, but sometimes up to 30 months.

At last, at the end of curing, the ham must meet certain taste and appearance requirements. Its color can be from pale to deep rose, and the fat should be white or rosy, but not yellow. The flavor should be rich and sweet, and the texture velvety but slightly chewy. Only if it satisfies all these criteria is it awarded the five-pointed ducal crown of Parma, which is branded into the skin, together with the producer's identification code. So, in theory, it should be traceable every step of the way – though the Consorzio continues to prosecute the makers of the hundreds of imitations it tracks down around the world.

In the region of the Po valley, near Parma, they also produce the famous culatello di Zibello, which is made from the filet of the pig's thigh. This is the pear-shaped ham that you see encased in mesh, which is aged for at least 11 months and owes its intense aroma and sweet flavor to the special climate around the river Po, with its humidity, fogs and hot summers.

Some people prefer San Daniele ham, which is made in the same fashion as in Parma, but only in very small quantities in the Friuli region – where the microclimate is different and the pigs roam free, feeding on acorns in the woods. Unlike Parma ham, in which the feet of the pig are taken from the leg, on a San Daniele ham the feet are left on and the meat tends to be lean, with a stronger flavor, as the pigs develop more muscle from their exercise.

Despite all the noise about Parma, my ultimate ham is prosciutto di Cinta Senese from Umbria. The Cinta Senese are a smallish breed of pig, dating back to the Middle Ages, that you sometimes see depicted in old paintings. They are very beautiful—dark brown with a white stripe or "belt" *(cinta)*—and are very agile because they were bred to live in the wild, and if they run at you, you have to move fast, because they really are quite scary. They are reared around Siena and, before the fifties, most people would have kept one in the backyard, but when everyone began intensively producing bigger pigs to satisfy the lust for Parma ham, they almost became extinct. Now, because of the revival of interest, they have been saved. Because they are allowed to wander freely around the woods, picking up acorns or chestnuts, they produce lean, deep red hams, with a quite hard surrounding of fat, which I think give the perfect balance of long-lasting sweet-savory flavor and aroma.

Slicing and serving salumi

I always buy whole salami and hams, and slice them at home, because so much of the magic comes with the release of the aroma as it is cut – but then I am so dedicated to salumi that I have a slicing machine at home as well as at Locanda. Otherwise, I recommend you buy your prosciutto crudo from a good delicatessen and ask them to slice it for you, because slicing is a skilled thing. You want it to be cut very thin to show off its delicacy of texture and flavor – but not so thinly that it ends up in shreds. The pig has been killed once – you don't want to kill it again with terrible slicing.

Salame is easier to slice yourself at home, provided you have a very sharp knife, but, again, if you prefer, have them slice it for you at a delicatessen. Personally, I would never buy any salame or ham that was sliced and prepackaged, because so much flavor is lost – and anyway I never buy anything I can't smell beforehand.

Remember that cured meats were being made long before refrigerators – that is precisely why they were invented, because there was no other way to keep meat without its going bad – so they would have been kept in a cool cellar or pantry. In the fridge the cold temporarily deadens the aromas and flavors, so always bring your salame or ham out of the fridge a while before serving, so that you enjoy it at its very best.

Prosciutto e fichi

Parma ham and figs

Figs are so sexy, aren't they? When you open them up they have that beautiful latticework between the flesh and they seem almost alive. With their sweetness and the sweet fattiness of the ham you have a combination that has entered our taste code and one that we will always love – it is the same with ham served with the best, sweetest melon. Even in a restaurant such as Locanda, when either fruit comes into season and we offer it with a plate of ham, that is all people want to eat. And don't say it's a simple dish: because first someone has to produce that brilliant ham.

This is barely even a recipe. Just peel the figs – or you can leave the skin on – and cut them into quarters, then arrange on plates with slices of Parma ham. Mediterranean figs, in season from the end of August until the end of September, are the best, as they are picked from the tree when they are ripe and then transported quickly. This means they are juicier than ones that come from further away, which tend to be harvested while they are still green.

Bresaola di cervo e sedano di Verona

Cured venison with celeriac and black truffle

Cured venison is made from a whole loin. You'll find it in good Italian delis, and they should slice it for you. If the loin is small, you will need around thirty slices; if it is larger, use less. You only need half the head of celeriac for this recipe, so you can use the rest for another dish – perhaps the celeriac puree on page 108. The mayonnaise is a little sharper than usual in order to cut through the richness of the venison. If you can't find fresh black truffles, make the dish without any truffle at all rather than using truffles from jars or truffle oil, which is usually chemically flavored.

½ head of celeriac
1 teaspoon dry mustard
2 tablespoons white wine vinegar
2 tablespoons mayonnaise
    (see page 53)
¾ ounce fresh black truffle
    (optional)
30 slices of cured venison
2 tablespoons extra virgin
    olive oil
salt

Slice the celeriac very thin, then cut the slices into matchsticks. Mix with a pinch of salt and leave to drain in a colander for about 1 hour to allow it to soften up.

Add the mustard and vinegar to the mayonnaise and grate in the fresh truffle, if using. Mix the celeriac sticks with the mayonnaise mixture.

Spoon the mixture into the center of your serving plates and arrange the venison around or on top, as you like. Drizzle with the extra virgin olive oil.

Bresaola di manzo al caprino

Thinly sliced cured beef
with goat cheese dressing

Bresaola of beef is another of our Lombardia specialities from the Valtellina valley. It is raw filet that has been salted, marinated in wine and
herbs, and then air-dried to give it a lovely, delicate flavor. It is sliced
very thin to serve as an antipasto, traditionally with oil, lemon juice and
black pepper. At the restaurant, we like to be a little different…

Put the cheese into a bowl and mash with a fork until it becomes a
little smoother. Slowly mix in the vinegar and 5 tablespoons of the
oil. The mixture should still be a little coarse.

Mix the lemon juice with the rest of the oil and use to dress the
arugula lightly. Season to taste.

Put a small bunch of arugula in the center of each slice of bresaola
(roll up if you like). Arrange on serving plates and drizzle with the
goat cheese dressing. Finish with a good grinding of black pepper.

3½ ounces soft fresh goat cheese
3 tablespoons white wine vinegar
6 tablespoons
    extra virgin olive oil
juice of ½ lemon
4 handfuls of arugula
7 ounces thinly sliced bresaola
salt and pepper

Carpaccio di manzo

Beef carpaccio

I suppose everyone these days knows the story of how beef carpaccio was invented, but just in case…It happened in Harry's Bar in Venezia in 1950, when a regular customer, the Contessa Amalia Nani Mocenigo, came to dine. Her doctor had put her on a special diet, which meant she couldn't eat cooked meat. In a moment of inspiration, Giuseppe Cipriani, the father of the current owner of Harry's Bar, Arrigo Cipriani, suggested to his chef that he cut up some raw beef into wafer-thin slices, and they then decorated it crisscross fashion with a sauce made from mayonnaise mixed with Worcestershire sauce, lemon juice and milk. Giuseppe called the creation carpaccio, after the Italian painter Vittore Carpaccio, who was famous for his use of brilliant reds and whites.

Of course, now every Italian restaurant has come up with its own version of beef carpaccio. At Locanda we often serve it with our own mayonnaise (as in the recipe below), perhaps with some fresh black truffle grated over it. Or we dress some arugula in a little olive oil and lemon juice and serve it with the carpaccio, with Parmesan shavings over the top. At other times we cook some finely diced broccoli stalks and florets until they are soft (i.e., slightly overcooked), then whiz them to a puree in a food processor and season. Then we season the carpaccio, brush with lemon and oil and serve with the broccoli puree drizzled on top.

Once one of our suppliers sent a box of *persicelle* (probably from *persicum*, which is the Latin for peach), or baby peaches, to Locanda. In Italy, when there are too many peaches on the tree the farmer snips off the smaller green ones, like little fat green almonds, which are mostly thrown away, but are sometimes kept and put into syrup or, as in this case, sent out as a specialty to kitchens. We blanched them, made some truffle oil, which we put over them, and served them with the carpaccio. They were beautiful – but sadly we have never had a box since.

Remember, you are showing off raw beef, so it must be the best quality.

10½ ounces beef filet
2 tablespoons mayonnaise
    (see page 53)
2 tablespoons salted capers,
    rinsed and drained
    (optional)
salt and pepper

Trim the fat from the filet and chill the beef in the fridge to firm it up and make it easier to cut into thin slices. Place three or four slices at a time (side by side) on a sheet of plastic wrap, cover with another sheet of plastic wrap, then pound with a meat hammer or rolling pin until the meat is paper-thin. Season the carpaccio and serve drizzled with the mayonnaise and, if you like, sprinkled with capers.

Sformato di patate, pancetta e Taleggio

Layered potatoes and pancetta with cheese sauce

Sformato is a kind of savory pudding cooked in the oven. Traditionally it was made in a ring mold so it could be turned out and the center filled with sauce. This one isn't traditional at all. It is one of my mixtures of French technique and Italian ingredients. Potatoes, cheese, pancetta, these ingredients are as old as time. For me, they are the flavors of cold weather. They have been used in a million ways, but I wanted to try to find a way of my own and this idea first came to me when I was cooking in Paris at Le Laurent. One of my jobs was to prepare the potatoes for a special fish dish. I used to peel the potatoes without washing them, so that the starch stayed inside, then "turn" them into perfect cylinder shapes and finally slice them into thin rounds with a mandoline. Then I had to lay them out on a tray, sprinkle them with a little salt and bake them until golden. When they came out of the oven, I would lay them out again, overlapping slightly this time, so that when they cooled down, the starch in the potatoes would stick them together in a sheet.

When the order for the fish came in, I would take a fillet, place it on top of the sheet of potatoes and cut around it. Then I would cook the fish in a frying pan, skin side up, turn it over, skin down, lay the sheet of potato on top and put the pan in the oven, so the fish would roast with the potatoes "melting" over the top.

The dish was served with crème fraîche and caviar, which was too fussy and complicated an idea for my taste, but I loved the idea of the potato sheet and it stayed in my mind. I used to experiment with wrapping other ingredients inside, and then one day, when I had a potato sheet left over, I dropped it into a cup that happened to be nearby. After a while, I noticed it had set in the shape of the cup, and when I turned it out it stayed that way. That gave me the idea of making a container with the potatoes, which would be like a crust but also add another layer of flavor. I started trying out different fillings enclosed in potato and then fried – eventually I came up with this one.

I think of this as a winter dish, and sometimes when porcini mushrooms are in season I like to use them instead of the pancetta – just sliced and sautéed with a little chopped garlic and then mixed with the Taleggio cheese, as in the recipe that follows.

This is a little bit complicated, but the important thing is to have really starchy potatoes for this dish, so that they will stick together well. You also need some small round ovenproof flan dishes or ramekins, about 3 inches in diameter. If you want to serve the *sformati* more simply, you could just make a salad instead of the sauce.

Peel the potatoes and slice them about $\frac{1}{16}$ inch thick, using a mandoline grater or a large, sharp knife. Put them on a baking tray and season with sea salt to draw out some of their water.

Heat the sunflower oil in a large, deep pan to about 250°F. To test, dip in one of the slices of potato; it should just fry very gently. Put the potatoes into the oil to "blanch" them – i.e., so they soften without crisping or coloring. Cook them in batches of 3 or 4 slices at a time, keeping them well away from each other so that they don't stick together. Remove them with a slotted spoon and place on paper towels to drain very briefly – again, keep them separate from each other. Don't leave them longer than a few minutes or the paper will blot away all the starch, which you will need to stick the layers together.

Line each small ovenproof dish with overlapping slices of potato, covering the entire base and sides and making sure there are no gaps (this is where the starch in the potatoes will stick the slices together). The potatoes around the sides need to come about $1\frac{1}{4}$ to $1\frac{1}{2}$ inches above the top of the dish or enough to fold over and completely enclose the filling.

Heat a dry frying pan, add the pancetta strips and fry quickly to release excess fat but not enough to color them. Remove and drain on paper towels.

Mix the diced Taleggio cheese with the pancetta, and scatter over the base of each potato-lined dish. Pull the overhanging slices of potato over the top, making sure there are no gaps, and press down lightly so the potatoes seal the top completely. Put in the fridge for at least an hour or overnight to firm up.

Preheat the oven to 425°F. Meanwhile, make the sauce. Bring the milk just to the boil and then take off the heat. Melt the butter in a pan, add the flour and cook, stirring, for a couple of minutes. Slowly pour in the milk, mixing well, then add the nutmeg. Bring to a boil, then reduce the heat and simmer for 3 to 4 minutes, stirring all the time, until the sauce thickens. Keep in a warm place covered with plastic wrap to prevent a skin from forming.

Heat a film of sunflower oil in an ovenproof nonstick frying pan and turn the *sformati* out of the dishes into the pan (2 at a time if you have a small pan). Cook gently for 3 to 4 minutes, until golden (be careful not to cook too fast, in case the cheese melts too quickly and begins to bubble through the potato). Turn over carefully with a spatula, add the butter to the pan and transfer to the oven for 2 to 3 minutes to finish off.

Mix the grated Fontina into the sauce and spoon it onto 4 serving plates (preferably deep ones). Remove the *sformati* from the oven, rest each one briefly on a paper towel to blot off any excess butter, and place on top of the sauce.

2 large starchy potatoes,
    such as Desiree
$2\frac{1}{4}$ cups sunflower oil, for frying
$5\frac{1}{4}$ ounces pancetta,
    cut into strips
$5\frac{1}{4}$ ounces Taleggio cheese,
    cut into small dice
$1\frac{1}{2}$–2 tablespoons butter
sea salt

For the sauce:
1 cup milk
$1\frac{1}{2}$ tablespoons butter
$2\frac{1}{2}$ tablespoons flour
pinch of freshly grated nutmeg
$\frac{2}{3}$ cup grated Fontina cheese

Mondeghini
Stuffed cabbage

Around Milano, there are a few recipes that break with the tradition of serving pasta or risotto followed by a meat course by bringing the two together. Many reasons are given, but the main one is that when the men came home from the factories they had only one hour to eat, so it was seen as a quick way of having your meat and carbohydrate together – the same principle as the American hamburger.

The most famous of these dishes is risotto Milanese (saffron risotto) with *osso buco*, but stuffed cabbage is another that I have always loved. When my grandmother made this dish, the smell would fill the whole house. When I came home from school, I knew what was cooking as soon as I opened the door, and I couldn't wait to eat it.

My grandmother served it in the traditional way: a big dish of risotto alla Lodigiano (made with grana cheese) with a portion of the *mondeghini* – cabbage stuffed with meat – on top. Let's not forget that, forty years ago, to eat meat twice a week was a luxury – whereas now it is almost a luxury not to. So you would share what meat there was, cooked inside the cabbage, which was a way of stretching whatever food you had.

Now, because I am cooking in a London restaurant and because we all live in a more affluent society, we have played with the old idea a little. So meat (in this case sausage) and cabbage have become the main ingredients, and the risotto is now the garnish.

½ recipe quantity of Saffron
    risotto (see page 226)
1 large Savoy cabbage
12 slices white bread,
    crusts cut off
¾ cup milk
14 ounces good-quality plain
    pork sausages, skins
    removed
1 small garlic clove,
    finely chopped
sprig of sage, finely chopped
sprig of rosemary,
    finely chopped
1 tablespoon freshly grated
    Parmesan cheese
2 tablespoons olive oil
2 tablespoons vegetable oil
½ wineglass of white wine
1½ tablespoons butter
salt and pepper

If you are making fresh risotto, follow the recipe on page 226 but keep cooking it until it is "overcooked" – about 25 to 30 minutes, so it is really sticky and dry. Don't finish with any butter, just the Parmesan. If you are using leftover risotto, put it back on the heat, add a little hot water or, better still, hot stock, and cook it for about 10 minutes, until it reaches this "overcooked" stage. Keep on one side.

Discard the outer leaves of the cabbage and choose 8 fairly large inner ones. Blanch them in boiling salted water until just soft, then drain, rinse under cold running water and pat dry.

Soak the bread in the milk. Put the skinned sausages in a separate bowl and mix with the garlic, sage, rosemary and Parmesan. Squeeze the bread and add to the sausage mixture. Season and roll into 8 balls, each about the size of a golf ball.

Lay the cabbage leaves out flat and cut out the stalks with a sharp knife. Now you need to make little balls of cabbage-wrapped sausage meat – to do this, hold a cloth in one hand, put a cabbage leaf on top, and then a ball of the sausage mixture in the center. Close your hand so that the cabbage wraps itself around the sausage meat. Turn your hand over and, with the other hand, twist the bottom of the cloth so that it squeezes the cabbage into a tight ball. Unwrap the cloth and trim the cabbage of any excess, leaving enough to enclose the sausage meat completely. Repeat with the rest of the sausage meat and cabbage leaves. If not using right away, keep in the fridge.

Heat a sauté pan on the burner, add the olive oil, spoon in the risotto and press into a "cake." Cook until crisp and golden underneath, then place a plate over the top and turn over the pan, so the risotto cake lands on the plate. Slide it back into the pan to crisp up on the other side.

While the risotto is crisping up, heat another flat pan large enough to hold all the cabbage balls. Put in the vegetable oil and add the cabbage balls, smooth side down. Cook over medium heat for 2 to 3 minutes, turn them over, then add the white wine. Cover with a lid and cook for another 15 minutes, very slowly, adding a little water (or chicken stock if you have it) if the liquid evaporates. Remove the cabbage balls from the pan and keep warm. Let the liquid in the pan reduce a little, then add the butter to make a slightly creamy sauce. Take the pan from the heat.

Slice the risotto into whatever shapes you like and place on 4 serving plates, with the cabbage balls on top. Drizzle the sauce over.

Lingua di manzo in salsa verde

Ox tongue with green sauce

In Italy we traditionally serve *salsa verde*, our famous green sauce, with anything that is boiled – *bollito misto* (mixed meats), boiled chicken or ox tongue. If you go into a butcher's to buy ox tongue, they will usually sell you a little pot of green sauce to go with it.

I prefer to make salsa verde with a mortar and pestle, the way it was made for centuries before modern kitchen gadgets came along. You can, of course, use a food processor, but it tends to warm up the sauce and darken the fantastic bright green color, whereas in a mortar you don't crush out any of the flavor or color.

The tongue can be served hot or cold. If you like it cold, you can cook it the day before you want to serve it. Just make sure you peel the skin off while it is still warm (it will be impossible to do it later) and keep the tongue in the cooking water in the fridge, to preserve it and keep its color. The cooking liquid will solidify because it will be full of gelatin from the tongue.

By rinsing the tongue well before cooking, you should draw out the excess salt but if, when it is cooked, you taste the cooking liquid and it still seems too salty, you can cover it with sparkling water – the gas helps to draw out the salt – and leave it overnight in the fridge. Take it out a few hours before you need it so that it is not too cold, or keep back the cooking liquid (keep it in the fridge as well) and warm the tongue up in it, in a pan.

1 salted ox tongue
1 carrot, cut in half
1 shallot, cut in half
1 wineglass of white wine
3–4 black peppercorns
1 bay leaf
3 tablespoons all-purpose flour
2 tablespoons white wine vinegar

    For the salsa verde:
6 salted anchovy fillets, rinsed
1 garlic clove
leaves from 1 bunch
    flat-leaf parsley
yolks of 2 hard-boiled eggs,
    plus a few extra for garnish,
    if you like
1 tablespoon white wine vinegar
2½ tablespoons dried bread
    crumbs
¾ cup plus 1 tablespoon
    extra virgin olive oil

Rinse the tongue under gently running cold water for an hour to remove the excess salt.

Put the carrot, shallot, wine, peppercorns and bay leaf in a large pan of water. Bring to a boil and add the ox tongue. Once it is boiling, taste the water and, if it is salty, bring another pan to the boil and transfer the vegetables, herbs and tongue from the first pan.

Mix the flour with the vinegar to make a thin paste, add it to the pan and whisk in. It will make the water appear cloudy, but it will help to keep the color and bring out the flavor of the tongue. Turn down the heat and simmer for about 2½ hours. The tongue is cooked when you can easily peel off the skin. Peel, then leave to cool in the cooking liquid. If it still tastes a little salty, leave it to cool down more, as the salt will be less apparent when the tongue is cold.

Make the sauce, preferably using a mortar and pestle. First crush the anchovies and the garlic, then put in the parsley leaves and egg yolks and work to a fine paste. Mix in the vinegar and bread crumbs, then add the olive oil a little at a time. If you prefer the sauce a little sharper, add a touch more vinegar; if you like it firmer, put in more bread crumbs. (To make the sauce in a food processor, put everything except the oil in together, then add the oil a little at a time. Pulse very quickly, as the longer you let it go on, the darker green it will get as the food processor warms up.)

Slice the tongue quite thin, drizzle the green sauce over it and, if you like, grate some more hard-boiled egg yolks over the top.

Testina di vitello

Calf's head salad

Until thirty or forty years ago, when the market for veal began to decline, veal farming thrived in northern Italy, especially in my region of Lombardia and Piemonte. Small farmers reared calves along with chickens and other animals, and sold the prime meat to rich people or Milanese restaurants, so they were left with the cheaper cuts and the heads and feet, which would be eaten at home or sold to poorer people. Cooking these parts of the animal requires much more work, but because they are full of gelatinous tissue they become meltingly tender, with long-lasting flavors that make some of the most memorable and tasty dishes.

I understand that people these days find offal a harsh reality to deal with at home, and even in the restaurant I know it can take a bit of courage to try. One of the reasons we have become wary of eating certain parts of animals is the prevalence of problems such as BSE, which is why you have to find a responsible butcher and trust him. But, you know, sometimes I think that if people saw what goes into the processed foods they eat every day they might think differently about some of the food they buy without question. The foot of an animal is far more wholesome than the chemicals, additives and processed fats many people consume regularly, most of the time without even knowing it. Think about it: we happily buy anything in friendly sanitized commercial packaging because we are convinced it must be okay, when the guy who set up the company is probably already in Bermuda with a big house and a private jet. He doesn't give a damn if we die after twenty years from eating all the additives his factory has put into our food.

But if you buy a calf's head that has been carefully boned and rolled up and tied with string, a process that takes a lot of time and care, you know you are being given something that has been prepared by someone who doesn't cut corners. And if you go into a restaurant where calf's head is on the menu, you know that the cook is someone who cares about sharing fantastic flavors – because it would be much easier just to do a burger and fries. Again, it brings us back to the idea that good food doesn't have to be expensive.

The problem, I know, is finding prepared calves' heads. Supermarkets? Forget it. Even the few high-end butchers that are left rarely sell them, but if you ask, they may be able to get them for you. And if enough people ask, maybe we can make them fashionable, the way the humble lamb shank became something "smart" in the nineties.

If you like, you can do a variation on this dish by cooking the calf's head in the same way, then slicing it about ⅓ inch thick, dipping it in flour, then egg yolk, then bread crumbs and deep-frying the slices until they are golden. Serve the slices with pickled red and yellow peppers (see page 84) mixed with capers.

Cook the calf's head with the onion, celery, carrot, bay leaf, flour and glass of vinegar in the same way as the ox tongue (see page 132). Leave it to cool completely in the liquid, then put it in the fridge until it sets to make a jelly.

Slice through the calf's head, including the jelly, as thin as you can.

Sharpen up the Shallot vinaigrette by adding the 3 tablespoons of white wine vinegar and a few twists of freshly ground black pepper.

Mix the spring onions with 2 tablespoons of the Shallot vinaigrette and arrange on serving plates. Lay the thinly sliced calf's head on top and finish with the rest of the vinaigrette and the chopped chives.

1 prepared calf's head
    (i.e., boned, shaped
    and rolled)
1 onion, cut in half
1 celery stalk, cut in half
1 carrot, cut in half
1 bay leaf
3½ tablespoons all-purpose flour
1 wineglass of white wine
    vinegar, plus 3 tablespoons
5 tablespoons Shallot vinai-
    grette (see page 52)
3 bunches of large spring
    onions, thinly sliced
    lengthwise
bunch of chives, finely chopped
pepper

Insalata di piedino di vitello

Calves' feet salad

This can be made with pigs' feet as well. If you buy whole feet, you will need to open them out once they are blanched. Alternatively, you can sometimes buy feet that have already been boned and opened up.

If you don't have a deep-fat fryer, use a deep saucepan no more than one-third full of oil – and don't turn away and forget about it while it is heating up. If necessary, cook the calves' feet in batches: preheat the oven before you start the preparation, then switch it off, and as you cook each batch, put them into the oven to keep warm.

If you wanted to serve this for a party, then rather than make the salad you could just serve the deep-fried strips with the mustard fruits (see page 482) in a pot, for people to dip the fritters into.

4 whole calves' feet
1¾ cups white wine vinegar
1 lemon
3 tablespoons
    extra virgin olive oil
2 eggs
7 tablespoons all-purpose flour
7 tablespoons bread crumbs
    (made from bread that is
    2 to 3 days old)
2¼ cups sunflower oil for frying
2½ tablespoons mostarda
    di Cremona (mustard
    fruits, see page 482),
    finely diced if large
2 handfuls of
    mixed salad greens
salt and pepper

Put the calves' feet into a large pan of cold water, bring to a boil, then drain. Put them into fresh cold water and bring to a boil again. Reduce the heat and simmer for about 2 hours, until tender. The meat will start to come away from the bone, but not completely. Leave to cool down in the water for about half an hour, to let the meat firm up a little.

Peel off the skin and remove any small hairs that might have been left behind. Take the meat off the bone with a knife, open it out and lay it flat on a tray. Cover it completely with the vinegar. Put another tray on top and weight it down, so the meat is pressed flat; that way it will be easier to cook and will look more attractive. Leave overnight in the fridge – up to 2 days if you want a more pronounced vinegary flavor.

With a vegetable peeler, remove the zest from the lemon, taking care to leave the bitter white pith behind. Then cut the zest into julienne strips. Squeeze the lemon, mix the juice with the olive oil and set aside.

Bring a small pan of water to a boil, put in the strips of lemon zest, then remove immediately with a slotted spoon. Bring the water back up to a boil, put the zest back in and remove it again immediately – this will soften it and take away a little of the bitterness.

Cut the meat from the calves' feet into strips or squares, whichever you prefer.

Lightly beat the eggs in a bowl and season them. Put the flour on a plate and the bread crumbs on another, then dip each piece of meat first in the flour, then into the eggs, then into the bread crumbs. Do this carefully, because the meat needs to be completely coated with flour before dipping it into the egg, but any excess flour should be shaken off, otherwise the egg will stick only in patches. Then make sure you dip the meat completely into the egg, again shaking off any excess – so when you dip it into the bread crumbs you get a nice even coating. (Don't be tempted to do another coating of egg and bread crumbs as it will be too thick, and all you will taste is bread crumbs.)

Preheat the sunflower oil to about 360°F (to the point where if you put in a little morsel of bread it will start to fry). Put in the pieces of breaded calves' feet and fry for 2 to 3 minutes, moving them around with a fork or metal spoon, until golden all over. Remove, drain on kitchen paper and season with a little salt.

Drizzle your serving plates with the mustard fruits. Mix the salad leaves with the lemon zest, season with salt and pepper and toss with the reserved lemon oil. Pile the salad up on the plates and arrange the pieces of calves' feet around.

Pane

Bread

My father goes 4 miles to buy the bread every day. In our house, like most houses in Italy, bread is the first thing that goes on the table. It is such a big part of the meal – at one time, in poor families, it *was* the meal, supplemented by whatever else you had on hand.

When I was in Sicilia I learned a new expression, *il conpanatico*. I was out in the olive groves at the Planeta estate near Menfi, tasting the oils we buy from Alessio Planeta and his family, and they had some agricultural students from Roma working there. At about eleven o'clock, one of them asked, *"Che cosa c'è per il conpanatico?"* "What are you talking about?" I asked them. Of course the word *conpanatico* must mean "with the bread" – but I had never heard the expression before. In this area, they told me, bread is considered so important that you don't ask "What is for lunch?" but "What are we going to have with the bread?"

I thought it was a brilliant expression that really shows the way that Italians, like most Europeans, value bread. It is something that is difficult for many people in Britain and America to understand, because, despite there being a new wave of artisanal bakeries and a big interest in different kinds of bread, the best-selling loaf is still the commercially made white square one that goes in the toaster, and is eaten only at breakfast time, or in sandwiches. When my father first came to London, it drove him crazy that if you went out to eat there was no bread on the table as soon as you sat down. He even asked for bread in a Chinese restaurant.

In Italy, people don't bake at home that much, because they don't need to. Virtually every village still has a bakery and every region has its own style of baking. In the very north, close to Austria, they make a lot of rye bread, and often use spices. In Lombardia, we still make *castagnaccio*, chestnut bread, which was a staple during the war, and *pane de mais*, made with polenta, but most of our breads are quite light, and, like the French, we buy some every day.

In Toscana and further south you have the bigger breads. In Toscana they are also often unsalted, perhaps because they use a lot of salt in the local salami and prosciutto, which is traditionally eaten with it. In Sardegna they like to use semolina in their bread and they also have the wonderful crispy *pane carasau*, or *carta di musica*: thin, thin sheets that are so-called because they resemble music parchment paper, which you buy stacked up like Indian papadams, then sprinkle with olive oil and rosemary, and put into the oven for a few minutes to serve with olives and drinks before you eat.

It makes me laugh that one of the first Italian breads to become fashionable in Britain was the ciabatta, when at home it was originally the

bread of the poor people. After the war, there was a shortage of grain, and white dough was considered to be the privilege of the rich, but when there were scraps of the dough left over, they were stretched into long "slipper" shapes for everyone else.

The bread that really brings back nostalgic memories for me is the *michetta* (or rosetta), which is almost a symbol of Lombardia. When I used to go mushroom hunting with my granddad, we would go to the *salumificio* and buy the mortadella, and then to the baker for the panini (bread rolls), usually the michetta, then sit down on the wall and eat it. Michetta is the bread with "five faces," which is made using a special stamp, a little like a rose (which is why it is also called rosetta) that is pressed down into the dough. When it goes into the oven, the air is forced into each of the five "faces" or "petals," which puff up until they are virtually hollow.

At Locanda we are very proud of our breadbasket, because, when it comes to the table as soon as you sit down, with some long Parmesan grissini, it gives you a taste of what is to come. We have our own dedicated bakery area in the kitchen and we are always developing new breads. At Zafferano, and when we opened Locanda, we worked with our good friend Dan Lepard to create the kinds of breads that we were looking for. Now we have our own baker, "little Federico" Turri (as opposed to "big Federico," our sous chef) who, like me, is from Lombardia and used to work at the gnocchi bakery of my cousins in Gallarate.

Baking is a beautiful thing to do. The dough is soft and warm and gorgeous and the smell of the yeast is fantastic – but you need to have some patience, and when you work with dough constantly, you begin to learn to judge instinctively how to adapt your bread to the conditions of the kitchen, which can be different every day. So you might use more or less water, according to whether the kitchen is drier or more humid, and when it is summer, and hotter, you see that the bread proofs faster, so you might use less yeast the next time you bake.

However, the recipes that follow are some of our more straightforward ones, which you should be able to make successfully at home even if you haven't made bread before – and, of course, you have the satisfaction of knowing that you are putting only pure ingredients into your bread to feed your family, and none of the commercial additives and "improvers" that the big companies use in order that your bread can stay on the supermarket shelves for weeks.

The flour

The flour we use for all our breads is Italian extra-strong (W300 P/L 0.55 on the bag), which has a good elasticity and the power to absorb water well. It isn't easily available outside Italy, but to create a similar flour you can mix equal parts of Italian 00 (doppio zero) flour with strong white bread flour.

The colomba

Instead of kneading, most of our breads involve a technique of "folding," the Italian way of incorporating air into the dough, to help and speed the fermentation and lighten the finished bread. We call it the *colomba*, which means "dove," because it is as if we are folding the "wings" of the dough. We spread out the dough into a rough rectangle by pressing down with the fingers (hold them vertically, not at an angle), stretching and dimpling the dough at the same time, to create pockets in which the air can be trapped. Then we fold the top third of the dough into the center, and dimple it lightly again. Next we fold the bottom third of the dough over the top and dimple again. Then we turn the dough 45 degrees and repeat.

Baking

It is a good idea to check the temperature of your oven using an oven thermometer – as you might find that it isn't actually as hot as your controls tell you it is. When you put the bread into the oven, put a metal bowl half full of water into the bottom of the oven, and when it comes to a simmer, this is the time to put the bread in. This puts some humidity into the oven, which will help the dough stay moist enough to expand properly at the beginning of baking. For the focaccia, if you make a salamoia (see page 148), you don't need the water.

Yeast

We like to use fresh yeast because it has a subtle flavor and, as it is a living thing, it works as soon as you mix it in, so you can do it at a cooler temperature; dried yeast, on the other hand, needs warmth. More and more health food shops and delis are stocking fresh yeast, or you could ask your local baker for some – if you are lucky enough still to have one.

Water

It is best to use bottled water rather than tap water, to ensure there are no chemicals that can slow down the fermentation. Have it at room temperature (around 68°F) because, if it is too cold, the dough will take longer to rise, and if you don't give it enough time the bread will be heavy and dense. In our baking recipes we measure water by weight as it is more accurate.

Parmesan grissini

They say that Napoleon loved grissini, which he called *le petit baton de pain de Torino* – and that he was eating it at Waterloo when he lost the battle. I would always make a big batch of these, because if you have any left over you can keep them in an airtight container for about a week – also they make fantastic crunchy bread crumbs, with a special flavor from the Parmesan. Just put the breadsticks in a clean plastic bag and crush them with a rolling pin. Kids especially love chicken breasts dipped in some flour, a little beaten egg, then into the bread crumbs and sautéed.

Makes about 25 grissini
(10 inches long)
3½ tablespoons unsalted butter
¾ cup plus 1 tablespoon
    whole milk
.35 ounce fresh yeast (10 grams)
13¼ ounces strong white bread
    flour (see page 140) or
    Italian 00 (doppio zero)
    flour
3 generous tablespoons
    grated Parmesan
1 tablespoon fine salt

Preheat the oven to 450°F.

Melt the butter in a pan, add the milk and heat it gently until it just feels warm to the fingertips (about body temperature). Whisk in the yeast.

Put the flour, Parmesan and salt in a bowl, then add a little of the milk mixture at a time, mixing it in well with your hands until it forms a dough. Alternatively, use a mixer with a dough hook, for 3 minutes on the first speed, then 6 minutes on the next speed.

Turn the dough out on a clean work surface (you don't need any flour or oil), and dimple and fold as described on the previous page. Cover with a damp tea towel and leave for 30 minutes.

Repeat the dimpling and folding process and leave for another 30 minutes, again covered with the tea towel.

Cut the dough in half lengthwise, flour your work surface and roll each piece out into a big rectangle.

Cut the dough across its width into strips about ⅓ inch wide – you can use a sharp knife against a clean plastic ruler.

Roll each strip with your fingertips, starting at the center and moving outward in three movements, stretching the dough slightly as you roll. Press each end lightly with your thumb, to make an "ear" shape. Lay on a nonstick baking sheet and leave to rest for 10 minutes.

Turn the oven down to 350°F and bake for 10 to 15 minutes, until crisp and lightly golden. Remove from the oven and let cool on a wire rack.

Pizzette

I was making a journey across London in a cab one day and the driver asked me, "What do you do?" I made the big mistake of saying, "I have an Italian restaurant." "So," he started, "what is it about pizza, anyway? It's just tomatoes on toast, isn't it? With a bit of cheese on top…" and off he went. Well, all right; he had a point – probably the guy had never eaten the real thing.

In Italy, though, everyone understands that a proper Italian pizza (not what we call *pizza al taglio* – the thicker-based one that has come in from America) has to have the perfect balance between a thin crisp base and a softer garnish, which means that you have to eat it within 5 to 6 minutes of its coming out of the oven, or it will be soggy and ruined. So you buy pizza in the baker's shop, or from the guys who sell slices of it on the streets, straight from big wood-fired ovens – not from the freezer section of the supermarket or delivered from a takeout. In Italy, we don't think of pizza as something cheap that can be packed into boxes and driven around town. Not even if you were threatened with six years in prison would you eat a takeout pizza delivered on a motorbike!

The perfect pizza oven is a work of art, heated to 500° Fahrenheit, designed to give a combination of air rolling over the top of the pizza, while the bricks underneath seal the base immediately and it becomes so crisp that when it comes out of the oven and you cut a slice, it will be completely firm. I'm not saying anything that has a thick base of dough topped with tomato and cheese is bad – in fact, the kids love it—it's just not pizza.

I am very proud of the pizza we introduced to London when I worked at the Red Pepper, and later during the time I was at Zafferano, when we launched Spiga and Spighetta, and though we don't serve pizza at Locanda, we often serve these little pizzette to our guests with aperitifs, while they are waiting for their table. If you want to make big pizza instead of little ones, this recipe will make three – just bake them for about 10 minutes.

Bagna càôda (anchovy sauce) is a very typical sauce in the north of Italy. Not everyone likes anchovies, I know (in which case, serve the pizzette without the sauce); but, if you do, you can make up bigger quantities of it and store it in a squeeze bottle in the fridge, then just shake it up before you use it and drizzle it over pasta or on toasted bread rubbed with garlic, whatever you like… Though I would normally say buy anchovies in salt, this is one recipe that is traditionally made with anchovies in oil.

Makes around 24 small
  pizzette for serving with
  drinks, or 12 larger ones
3 cups strong white bread flour
  (see page 140)
¾ cup plus 1 tablespoon
  water at 68°F
about 4 tablespoons
  extra virgin olive oil
.35 ounce (10 grams) fresh yeast
1 tablespoon fine salt

For the bagna càôda:
3 garlic cloves
3 tablespoons milk
1 small tin of good anchovies,
  drained
a little extra virgin olive oil
pat of butter

For the topping:
15–20 cherry tomatoes, sliced
a handful of good olives,
  pitted and sliced

Put all the ingredients for the pizzette, except the salt, into a mixer with a dough hook. Mix for 3 minutes on the first speed, then add the salt and mix for 6 more minutes on the second speed. The dough should be very soft and sticky. If working by hand, mix with a wooden spoon, rotating the bowl as you do so for about 5 minutes, then work it for another 5 minutes with your hands until the dough is smooth.

Turn the dough out on a work surface (you don't need any flour), dimple with your fingers and fold (see page 140) and leave to rest for 20 minutes.

Lightly flour your work surface and roll out the rested dough till thin. Have ready 2 upturned baking trays.

With a 2- to 2½-inch diameter biscuit cutter, cut the dough into rounds. Lay them on the baking trays and put into the fridge for at least 4 hours – but no longer than 8. If you like, you can roll the trimmings of dough into rough grissini and bake them (see page 142).

A good hour or so before you are ready to bake, preheat the oven as high as it will go. If you have a baking stone, put it into the oven as soon as you turn it on; if you don't have a stone, use a baking tray.

To make the bagna càôda: put the garlic in a small pan with the milk, bring to the boil and then turn down to a simmer and cook until the garlic is soft, about 10 minutes.

While the garlic is cooking, put the anchovies with a little olive oil and butter into a small bowl over the top of the pan and stir to "melt" them – it will take only a few minutes. (Alternatively, what I often do is just put the closed tin of anchovies into boiling water for 8 to 10 minutes, then take it out carefully, open it up and discard the oil.) Push through a fine sieve. Crush the garlic with a little of the cooking milk and mix into the anchovies. Loosen, if necessary, with a little more extra virgin olive oil.

Remove the dough from the fridge and, with your fingers, prod each circle of dough, starting from the center and working out and around in a circle, then back to the middle again. Prick the tops with a fork, and add your tomatoes, sprinkled with a little sea salt, and the olives.

Slide onto your hot baking stone or baking tray in the oven and cook in batches for 7 to 10 minutes, depending on the thickness, until golden brown and shiny. Drizzle with a little bagna càôda and serve.

Schiaccata di San Zenone

These are named after the patron saint of Crenna di Gallarate in Lombardia, where my cousins have their bakery, and where Federico, our restaurant baker, used to work. They make fantastic wafer-like canapés so thin they practically dissolve in your mouth, which we serve with drinks at the restaurant along with the pizzette – much better than any chips. You need to make the dough 24 hours in advance and leave it in the fridge. We use strutto for this, which is pure pork fat – but a good alternative would be goose fat.

Put the onion and fat into a small pan and sauté gently for 10 to 15 minutes until the onions are soft. Leave to cool to room temperature.

Transfer to a large mixing bowl, add the flour and water, and mix until you have a sticky, greasy, soft dough. Form it into a rough square, about 3 fingers deep. Oil a deep container, put in your dough, put into the fridge and leave for 24 hours.

When ready to bake, preheat the oven to 425°F (or up to 500°F, if possible). Cut the dough into 4 squares. Lightly oil a sheet of non-stick parchment paper. Put your first square of dough on top and rub the top with a little oil.

Roll out the dough until it is paper thin, then transfer it, together with the parchment paper, on to a baking tray. Put in the oven for 6 minutes until golden, crisp and just singed at the edges (if you can get the oven as high as 500°F, this will take only 2 to 3 minutes). Repeat with the other 3 squares.

When the schiaccata come out of the oven, drizzle them with olive oil, season and top with the grated Parmesan – as much as you like. As they begin to cool, the schiaccata will crisp up, and they will stay crisp for hours.

Makes around 20
1 tablespoon finely chopped onion
½ cup strutto or rendered goose fat
1⅔ cups strong white bread flour (see page 140)
⅓ cup plus 1 tablespoon water at 68°F
a little olive oil

To finish:
a little extra virgin olive oil
freshly grated Parmesan
salt and pepper

Focaccia classica

This is Federico Turri's fantastic foolproof focaccia, ready to bake in just over an hour. The dough is very soft, like a sponge, so that when you brush it with good extra virgin olive oil, it absorbs it.

If you like, you can replace ⅓ cup of the quantity of flour with chestnut, chickpea or rice flour. Sometimes we roast the rice flour to give a darker color and slightly more intense flavor. We just put it in a dry pan and heat it in an oven preheated to 400°F or in a frying pan on top of a burner until it colors: whether you let it turn golden or a darker brown is up to you, though obviously don't let it burn.

Makes 1 loaf
3⅔ cups strong white bread flour (see page 140 and above)
.53 ounce (15 grams) fresh yeast
1 cup water at 68°F
2 tablespoons extra virgin olive oil, plus more for greasing
1 tablespoon salt

For the salamoia:
¼ cup water at 68°F
¼ cup extra virgin olive oil
2½ tablespoons salt

For the topping:
small handful of rosemary sprigs or handful of good pitted olives

To make the salamoia, whisk all the ingredients together so they emulsify and the color changes to light green.

Preheat the oven to 425°F. In a bowl, mix together all the ingredients (except the topping) until they form a dough. Rub the surface with a little oil and leave to rest for 10 minutes, covered with a damp cloth.

Oil a baking tray and transfer the dough to it, then rub a little more oil on the top of the dough (preferably spray on the oil, using a clean plant mister). Leave for another 10 minutes.

Using a rolling pin and, starting at the center of the dough, roll it very lightly upward, once only, to the top of the dough. You need a light touch, so as not to break the bubbles in the dough. Go back to the center of the dough and, this time, lightly roll downward to the bottom of the dough, once only. Leave for 20 minutes, during which time the dough will double in size.

With your fingertips, make deep dimples in the dough, taking care not to go all the way through. Whisk the salamoia, then pour it over the surface and into all of the holes. Leave for 20 minutes more.

Either press the rosemary into the dough or push the olives into the holes. Bake for 25 to 30 minutes or until golden, then let cool on a wire rack.

A more complex focaccia

This is the bread Dan Lepard developed for us using 10g malt extract and ⅔ cup of "biga" (see page 153), and only half the amount of yeast shown in the classic recipe on page 148, which we mix with the rest of the ingredients to form the dough. Instead of leaving it to rest for 10 minutes, we leave it for an hour. Then, instead of rolling with a rolling pin, we dimple and fold it (see page 140) and leave it for 20 minutes, fold it again and leave it for another 20 minutes before pressing it out into a rectangle, making the dimples, oiling the surface or using a salamoia (see previous page), sprinkling with salt and pressing in sprigs of rosemary or olives as described on the previous page. Then we bake it in the same way.

Flavored bread

We use focaccia dough to make garlic, eggplant, and sun-dried tomato and sage bread, or cabbage, potato and buckwheat bread (see page 152 for the recipes).

Make the dough as in the previous recipe, oil it and leave to rest for 20 minutes. Then turn the dough over, dimple it and spread the filling over two-thirds of the dough. Fold the short side, covered with the filling, into the center. Fold the other short side (without filling) over the top. Then fold in the sides in the same way. Press down very gently with your fingertips and flatten out. Handle the dough as carefully as you can, as the filling mixture makes it quite fragile. Turn the dough over and rest for another 20 minutes. Turn it back again and repeat the turning and folding twice more.

So that you get three lines of filling running through the bread, it is important to fold always in the same order, so make a mark with some flour on your work surface and also make a mark with the top of a knife on your piece of dough. Then you can match these up and start folding from the same place each time.

Leave to rest for 30 minutes, no longer, otherwise the weight of the filling will knock out the bubbles (especially if it is quite moist) and you will have a line of unbaked dough. Sprinkle well with flour and place on a large baking sheet or nonstick tray. With a long knife, cut in half across the width. Turn each half over onto one end and stretch each half lengthwise. Rest for 10 minutes to let the dough relax.

Bake as in the previous recipe, opening the door slightly for the last 10 minutes. This is because the wet filling will introduce humidity into the middle of the bread and you need to help it dry out a bit.

Flavorings

All'aglio

Garlic confit

1 head of garlic, broken into
    cloves and peeled
1 tablespoon superfine sugar
enough milk to cover
pinch of salt

Rinse the garlic under cold running water, to reduce some of the strong aroma. Put in a pan with the sugar, milk and salt. Bring to a boil, turn down the heat and cook gently for 15 minutes, until the garlic is pink. Take off the heat and cool to room temperature. The mixture will be quite sticky and will cling to the dough as you spread it.

Alle melanzane

Eggplant

1 large eggplant
2 tablespoons olive oil
2 garlic cloves, thinly sliced
2–3 tablespoons finely chopped
    herbs (e.g., rosemary,
    oregano, parsley and basil)
1 teaspoon sea salt

Cut the eggplant into medium-thick slices and put it into a bowl with a little sea salt and a little water. Place a plate on top to weight it down and leave for 20 minutes until the water turns violet. Squeeze the eggplant gently to get rid of the excess moisture and pat dry.

Heat the oil in a pan, add the garlic and the eggplant and cook for 5 to 10 minutes. Take the pan from the heat, add the herbs, cover and leave to cool down and infuse for about 30 minutes.

Al pomodoro secco e salvia

Sun-dried tomato and sage

4½ ounces (1 heaping cup)
    sun-dried tomatoes
1 small sprig of sage, leaves only

Drain the oil from the tomatoes and halve them, then combine with the sage leaves.

Al grano saraceno, patate e verze

Cabbage, potato and buckwheat

This is inspired by pizzocheri, a typical pasta of the north.

1 cup buckwheat
1 pound Savoy cabbage
3½ tablespoons unsalted butter
1 large potato, cubed and boiled
    until soft
a little extra virgin olive oil
salt and pepper

Preheat the oven to 400°F. Scatter the buckwheat on a baking tray and put into the oven for 25 minutes until toasted and golden.

Cut the cabbage into ½-inch chunks and blanch in boiling salted water for about a minute. Drain.

Heat the butter in a pan and cook the cabbage until soft and melting.

Add the buckwheat and 2 tablespoons of water and cook for about a minute until the buckwheat just begins to soften.

Remove from the heat, stir in the potato and leave until cold.

Season and drizzle with a little olive oil before using.

The biga

Most of the breads we make in the restaurant are done with a biga, which in other countries is called a "starter," "ferment" or "mother" – this is the way bread has been made for thousands of years, making use of the wild yeast spores that are found on the surface of starchy or sugary ingredients.

The biga is made using flour, water and something sweet, such as fruit – grapes are classic, but we like to use pear. The idea is to introduce simple sugars, which the wild yeast spores and natural bacteria can ferment easily, so they bubble quicker. When you build a dough on this biga, the acid provided by the lactic bacteria helps to strengthen the elastic gluten and intensifies the flavor of the finished bread. The first time you make your biga, you need to be patient, though, as you will need to refresh it every day, and it will take a few weeks until it's bubbling happily and smells sweetly acidic.

1 pear, grated
1 cup water at 68°F
1¾ cups strong white bread
    flour (see page 140)

Then each day until the
    biga is ready:
¾ cup plus 1 tablespoon
    water at 68°F
2¾ cups strong white
    bread flour

Grate the pear and leave in the water for 24 hours in a loosely covered container.

Strain the mixture through a fine sieve, reserving the pear water. Whisk in the flour. Pour into a tall 2-liter jar or clean plastic container that will allow plenty of room for expansion and put a mark on the outside to indicate the level of the mixture.

Leave for around 3 to 4 weeks at room temperature (70–75°F). Every day you need to take away about three-quarters (1½ cups) of the mixture (discard the rest), put it in a bowl and whisk it for 5 minutes. Then mix in ¾ cup plus 1 tablespoon water and 2¾ cups flour as if you were making a dough. Wash and dry your glass or plastic container each time and don't allow anything to touch it that might contaminate the biga before you put it back. After a while you will see it begin to bubble up.

The biga is ready when, in the space of 8 hours, it triples in size – this could take 3 weeks or more, but eventually the mixture will ferment. After refreshing it for the last time you can put it in the freezer, then take it out the day before using. Any that is left over, refresh as before and return to the freezer in a large clean container for using next time (you need a large container because as it defrosts it will again triple in volume).

Pane di mais

Polenta bread

Makes 2 large loaves
3 cups water at 68°F
2 heaping cups polenta
4¼ cups strong white bread
    flour (see page 140)
.53 ounce(15 grams) fresh yeast
¾ cup plus 1 tablespoon biga
    (see previous page),
    active and still bubbling
1½ tablespoons fine salt
a little olive oil

Preheat the oven to 425°F (or up to 500°F if possible).

Bring 1⅔ cups of the water to a boil and slowly beat in the polenta, stirring well, so that you have a smooth, lump-free mixture. Cook for a few minutes, then remove from the heat and spread on a tray to cool.

Put the flour, remaining water, yeast and the biga into a food mixer with a dough hook for 3 to 4 minutes. Let the dough rest for 10 to 15 minutes, then add the salt and polenta mixture, and mix for another 8 to 10 minutes on the second speed. The dough should feel barely warm after mixing.

Oil a deep container and turn the dough into it. Dimple and fold the dough (see page 140) and leave to rest for 20 minutes.

Repeat the folding and leave for 20 more minutes. Spray or spread a little oil over the top. Turn out the dough onto an oiled work surface. Press out into a large rectangle and cut in half. Fold as above and leave for another 20 minutes.

Shape each piece of dough into a ball by bringing each "corner" to the center, stretching slightly as you do so, then pressing it down, turning the dough as you go, until you have a completely smooth ball.

Place on oiled trays and leave for 40 minutes until the dough almost doubles in size.

With a sharp blade, either cut a cross in the top of the dough, or make a cut about ½ inch deep all around the circumference. The bread will expand in the oven, and if you don't cut it, it will burst open.

Bake for 40 minutes (or as little as 30 minutes at 500°F), then leave to cool on a wire rack.

Pane di zucca e uva

Pumpkin and raisin bread

Makes 2 large loaves
1 pound pumpkin, cut into
    wedges and left unpeeled,
    but deseeded
1¼ cups biga (see page 153),
    active and still bubbling
⅔ cup warm water
1 teaspoon malt extract
    (or honey)
1 teaspoon fresh yeast
3¾ to 4 cups strong white
    bread flour (see page 140)
2½ cups raisins
a little olive oil
a little flour for dusting
2 level teaspoons salt

The night before, preheat the oven to 350°F. Wrap the pumpkin in foil and bake on a tray for 1 hour or until you can pierce it easily with a knife. Leave to cool, then separate the flesh from the skin and cut into small chunks. Set a small sieve over a bowl, line it with a damp kitchen towel and let the pumpkin drain in it overnight in the fridge to get rid of the excess moisture.

The next day, put the drained pumpkin, biga, warm water, malt extract and yeast into a mixer with a whisk attachment and whisk gently on a low speed until you have a smoothish orange batter.

Change to the dough hook, add the flour and mix for 2 minutes on the slowest speed until a dough forms, then turn the machine off and leave for 20 minutes.

Then add the salt and raisins, increase the speed and continue to mix for 4 to 5 minutes. The dough should feel barely warm after mixing.

Oil a deep container, then rub a little oil over your hands and the top of the dough to stop it sticking to the bowl before turning it out into the container. Oil the top of the dough, cover and leave for 15 minutes.

Dimple and fold (see page 140) and leave to rest for 20 minutes.

Turn the dough out onto an oiled work surface and press out into a large square about 8 x 8 inches. Then cut in half so each piece is about 4 x 8 inches.

Roll each piece of dough lengthwise to about 15 inches, then dimple the dough vigorously to flatten.

Line a large tray (12 x 16) with a dry tea towel and dust heavily with white flour. Lay the pieces of dough side by side on top, seam side upward. Cover with another dry tea towel and leave the dough to rise for 4 hours, or until puffy and doubled in height.

Meanwhile, preheat the oven to 425°F and have an 8 x 12-inch baking sheet ready. Carefully flip the pieces of dough onto the sheet, spray the upper surface with water and bake for 40 to 50 minutes, or until the crust is dark golden brown and the loaves feel light in weight. Remove from the oven and let cool on a wire rack.

Pan tramvai

Raisin bread

Makes 2 small loaves
3⅓ cups extra-strong flour
    (see page 140)
.35 ounce (10 grams) fresh yeast
⅔ cup biga (see page 153),
    active and still bubbling
1⅓ cups water at
    room temperature
4 cups raisins or golden raisins
vegetable oil, for brushing
1 tablespoon salt

Preheat the oven to 450°F.

Mix the flour, yeast, biga and water in a mixer with the dough hook attachment for 3 to 4 minutes. Let the dough rest for 10 to 15 minutes, then add the salt and raisins.

Mix for another 5 minutes on the second (quicker) speed. The dough should feel wet, sticky and warm after mixing.

Oil a deep container and turn the dough into it without folding it. Leave it for 20 minutes.

Turn out the dough on an oiled work surface. Press it out into a large rectangle and cut in half. Turn each half over and place on an oiled baking tray. Bake for 40 minutes until golden. Remove from the oven and leave to cool on a wire rack.

Pane al farro

Spelt bread

We began making this because the British people seem to like brown bread, whereas Italians still associate brown bread with poverty. The bread looks like whole meal, and I love the flavor. We serve it with crab salad.

Makes 1 small loaf
.18 ounce (5 grams) fresh yeast
3 cups plus 2 tablespoons
    water at room temperature
¾ cup spelt (faro) (see page 184)
1½ cups spelt (faro) flour
    (see page 184)
1 teaspoon salt

Dissolve the yeast in half the water.

Soak the spelt in enough water to cover generously for 10 to 15 minutes, skim the bits of husk from the surface of the water and drain. Put into a pan with the rest of the water, bring to the boil, then turn down the heat and simmer until all the water has virtually disappeared and the spelt is the consistency of risotto.

While it is hot, transfer the spelt to a large mixing bowl and mix in the flour and salt. Add the yeast mixture gradually, working it in with a wooden spoon until it is all incorporated. The dough will be very soft and sticky. Ladle it into a large loaf pan and leave for 1 to 1½ hours until doubled in size.

Meanwhile, preheat the oven to 500°F or to its highest heat. Put the bread in the oven and bake for 40 minutes. It is good to open the door very slightly for the last 10 minutes to help crisp up the crust.

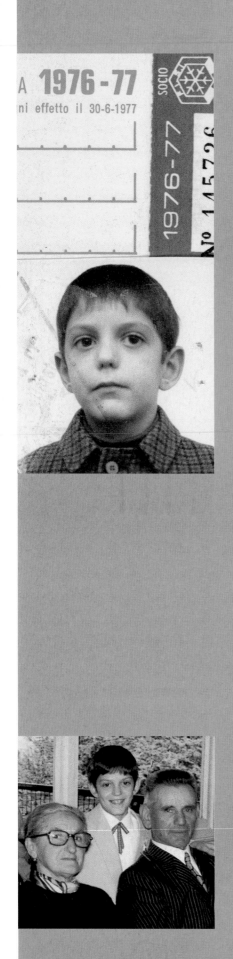

Like grandmother, like grandson

I was the little one of the Locatelli family, two years younger than my brother, Roberto, and my grandmother was the one who brought us up, because we all lived together in the new house my granddad built at the top of the village. At first, everyone thought he was completely mad, because at that time the house was in the middle of the woods. Since then, the village has grown and now a road runs right through the land and past our house, but that didn't exist until I was seven years old. Once the house was built, though, it was considered the most beautiful one in the village, and my granddad planted two cherry trees, which are still there – one for me and one for Roberto.

My granddad Mario Caletti and my grandmother Vincenzina Tamborini were of a generation who had seen enough of hard times and war, and making do. And while the world around them was changing so much, they never stopped being grateful for the fact that they had enough food to cook and enjoy. Every time we sat down to eat, they would thank God – not a formal prayer, just an acknowledgment that to have this food was a joy.

They were extremely honest people, and the way they looked at life, you didn't become rich by making a lot of money but by saving. Nothing was ever wasted. For my granddad to throw away a rubber band was considered a disaster, and the guilt I feel whenever I see food wasted comes from my grandmother.

Vincenzina was brought up in the house next to the square in Corgeno and her father, Nonno Stefano, used to sing the vespers in church. When the fascists came around and the priest was not available, they would talk to him. My granddad had married Vincenzina's sister, Giuseppina, but then he was sent off to fight in Africa in 1935, before the Second World War. In all, he was away for around six years and in the meantime, Giuseppina had died. When my granddad came home, Nonno Stefano said, "Come and stay with us, and why don't you marry Vincenzina?" Of course, she didn't want to marry Mario. She had an education, she wanted to be a teacher, and she was courting a man who had a hat shop in Milano, who drove out to Corgeno at weekends at a time when nobody local had a car, and brought her presents of swanky hats. In comparison, my granddad must have seemed like a peasant. But Nonno Stefano said she must get married.

The story goes that one day my granddad, who kept chickens, was running around trying to find something to protect some newborn chicks from the rain, when my grandmother went and found her smart hats and gave them to him to put the chicks in. It was the day she finally gave up her idea of being a smart lady living in Milano. When my mother was born, they called her Giuseppina, in memory of her sister, and by the time my granddad died, my grandmother loved him so much, she collapsed, because she couldn't think of living without him.

My granddad was a very emotional man, and a great gourmet, who hardly ever ate out in restaurants because he believed that the simple flavors of my grandmother's cooking were the best. We found an old faded black-and-white film of the celebration of their fiftieth anniversary in the sixties, when the whole family hired a coach and went to a hotel in Portofino for a special lunch. There is a brilliant moment when Roberto and I stood up in our short trousers and recited some poetry. You could see the tears in my granddad's eyes, then out came a big handkerchief, and my grandmother gave him a big kiss on the cheek.

She was a strong woman, very active, and she ran our house in quite a military way (three sponges in the bathroom: one for the face, one for the body, and a green one like a Brillo pad for the knees) and we loved her to pieces. She did all the cooking while my granddad raised his rabbits and chickens, and grew vegetables and herbs for the family and the restaurant, especially potatoes – 50 to 100 sacks in a season – along with onions, which he hung up in strings in the shed, and beans and maize, which the chickens were fed on. I remember helping to pick the potatoes as a kid – it always seemed like a miracle to find these treasures under the earth, and when we went to market, I could never understand why there were people buying potatoes. I wanted to tell them, "We make them ourselves! It's easy!"

My granddad never used chemicals or insecticides; I doubt if he even knew what such things were. But every now and again in the summer the plants would be attacked by hordes of beautiful beetles, like Egyptian scarabs, with yellow and black stripes. The job of picking off the beetles was always given to Roberto and me, and we would put them in a bowl of water to drown. We loved it, because it meant that we ended up with a big box of beetles, which we could throw at our cousins or the girls in the village.

We used to get up at seven each day and, after breakfast, we biked to school through the little streets, then back home again for lunch. Every morning my grandmother would come into our bedroom and say, "Wake up! You know I've got macaroni with cheese and tomato for lunch when you come back from school" or "I've got risotto cake – but what would you like for dinner?" She was always planning the next meal. That was how it was in our house. While we were having breakfast, she would be preparing the chicken for lunch or dinner, and she would say, "Run to the garden and get some rosemary" or "Quickly, go and pick me some chard." Other kids would go home from school and have a yogurt as a snack, but we would have chicken legs with salt, pepper and olive oil, and a big potato from the garden. She would cook the unpeeled potato in stock, and then give half to me and half to Roberto.

On weekends everyone was always busy working in the hotel and restaurant. I don't remember a single Sunday with my father sitting reading the newspaper or eating with the family. He is an electrical

engineer and he looked after the electrical system at the hotel, but on Saturday and Sunday he would put on a waiter's jacket and a bow tie – though he was a terrible waiter apparently – and my mother and aunt would serve in the bar.

On Tuesday, though, when the restaurant was closed, that was the big day, when everyone came to eat lunch at our house on the top of the hill. My brother and I would be picked up from school so we could be home on time – because everyone knew how important it was for the young and old to sit down together and eat.

So, once a week my grandmother would cook for twenty people. And if rabbit was on the menu, on the previous Friday or Saturday she would have taken us with her to choose which ones to kill. My granddad used to kill them with an iron bar to the back of the head and then hang them for a few days, which seemed quite natural to us children. We weren't sadistic; we had respect for animals. You knew you were going to eat those rabbits, so it was normal. On Tuesday morning, even before seven o'clock, we would be woken by the sound of my grandmother chopping the rabbits – bang, bang, bang on the kitchen table, with the big machete we still have at home.

It was the same with the chickens. You saw them running around, and then one would get chosen and killed for dinner. And when the cow came to Corgeno once a week, we would come back from school at lunchtime and see the butcher shoot it, with the vet beside him to make sure everything was done properly. Then he would hang it up in the *mattatoio* (abattoir) and butcher it so cleverly, then take away the insides in a wheelbarrow. Nobody ever said, "I am going to be vegetarian because we can't kill the cow," because that cow would feed everyone in Corgeno.

We weren't like my kids, who are incredibly squeamish. One Christmas holiday I brought home a live crab that was left over from Zafferano. I showed it to Jack and Margherita and they said, "Aah, lovely crab," and walked it around the house on a piece of string, trying to give it some food. Then Plaxy took them out for a while, and after they had gone I chopped the crab in half, cooked it and made it into a sauce for pasta. When they came home a few hours later – tragedy. "You are an assassin!" they told me. I felt terrible, but worse, I couldn't believe how far away my children were from understanding where their food comes from.

In Corgeno on a Wednesday, the fishmonger would set up his stall in the little village market, and we would buy *gamberi di San Remo*, the beautiful prawns from Liguria. Usually Mediterranean prawns are gray, turning red when cooked, but in the waters of San Remo bay, they are a wonderful orange/pink color, and after cooking they become an even darker red. They are thin, elegant creatures, with beautiful mustaches. Their tails are not as big as those of northern European prawns or the ones from the Far East, but they have longer fins, because they are good swimmers from so much battling against the tide, and they have the sweetest taste.

On Wednesdays, we would make our entire evening meal from the *gamberi*. My grandmother would let the fire go down and chargrill them for a main dish, or she would make spaghetti or a risotto. If she was making a risotto, first she peeled the prawns and put the shells into a pan with cold water, vegetables and herbs, which she simmered for about forty minutes to make the broth for cooking the rice. Then, to begin the meal, she would make a salad of prawns with the dried borlotti (cranberry) beans she always kept in big jars. She would have started the beans earlier in the day, first putting some garlic and onions, cut very thin, in some olive oil in a big pot, then adding some herbs and the soaked beans. She would cover the lot with water, put on the lid and let the beans cook. When they were ready, she ladled them out onto plates and dressed them with pepper and olive oil, then she would take a few of the peeled prawns by their mustaches and dip them into the boiling risotto broth very quickly, just long enough to cook them through. Finally, she put them on top of the beans, and that was her *insalata di borlotti e gamberi*. I still make a version of it now when I can get the *gamberi* from Liguria (see page 105). Whenever I taste those prawns, I remember, as if it were yesterday, sitting with my brother and everyone else around the table, eating my grandmother's salad and waiting for the risotto to follow.

In all the years I watched my grandmother cook for so many people, I never once saw a recipe in the kitchen. I couldn't say she had a philosophy of cooking – the way she prepared food was just part of the way things were in our house, and in most of the houses in the village – but her feeling for food has stayed with me all my life. Even now, I find it difficult to think in terms of menus and recipes planned in advance, with everything thought through before you even see your ingredients for the day. When I first came to London and worked in the kitchens of the Savoy, it was a shock to see everything written in stone, but ever since I have run my own kitchens, nothing is decided until we have seen the meat, the fish, the vegetables – what is fresh, what is good. That way, we cook from the heart, from instinct, and with respect for the food we have. My grandmother's way.

Zuppa

Soup

"Sette cose fa la zuppa, cava fame e sete attuta, empie il ventre, Snetta il dente, fa dormire, fa smaltire, e la guancia fa arrossire."

"Soup does seven things, it takes away hunger and thirst, fills the stomach, cleans the teeth, makes you sleep, makes you slim, and puts color in your cheeks."

Old Italian proverb

We have beautiful soups in Italy that have made names for themselves around the world, like *la ribollita* (Tuscan bean soup) and the king of all soups, minestrone, which in Italy is not actually classed under the heading of *zuppa* at all, as that name refers to a thick soup, ladled over bread, but not creamed, or containing pasta or rice, as minestrone often does. Instead, such dishes are known as *minestre*.

I notice that at home in Italy people, especially those of my parents' generation, don't like to eat soup if they go out to a restaurant. I think it reminds them of harder times, maybe after the war, when soup represented the national diet of the country; a miracle food that stretched a little of something a long way to feed everyone. You boiled a black-legged chicken and ate the breast, and then you boiled up the carcass to make the *brodo*, and extended it with beans or whatever vegetables or herbs you had in the garden or could afford at the market. In times of plenty, though, I think there is nothing better than a good soup bubbling away in the kitchen. Sometimes food can be exciting, sometimes it is chic; but a soup is always warm and inviting and convivial.

English or French soups seem to me to be about big bowlfuls of liquid with a few pieces of vegetables or meat swimming around in them, which you stumble across every now and then. In Italy, what we call a soup is really more like a deep plate of borlotti beans, or perhaps prawns, or tiny ravioli, with only a ladle or two of broth spooned over, more like a sauce, finished with peppery olive oil and black pepper. Also, in Italy, we have no truly creamy soups – any creaminess comes from the addition of a grain, such as rice, not from dairy products. When I first began cooking in Paris, I was amazed to see how the chefs would add butter and cream to finish off almost all their soups.

Sometimes chunks of bread would be used to thicken soup, but in the rice-growing north of Italy, we naturally used rice for that purpose. Every week I remember my grandmother used to make her *riso e prezzemolo*. She would boil up the chicken broth, then add the rice and let it cook until it thickened up, then she would chop a big handful of fresh parsley from the garden, using an old-fashioned machine with a handle, and throw it in, before she ladled the soup into bowls and grated Parmesan over the top. At other times, she made minestrone, also adding rice to the vegetables, which changed throughout the year according to the season.

Sometimes my grandmother made *pastina in brodo* – broth with tiny pasta stars and other shapes (*pastina* means "little dough") – which I love now, but hated then. Or she made onion soup, thickened with flour that she browned first in the oven and that gave the finished soup a slightly burned taste. And when she put down the bowls for us kids to eat, she used to quote bits of the old proverb about the reasons why soup was good for us, and, especially, she would tell us that it would put color into our cheeks.

In central Italy, where the land and the climate are better suited to growing more diverse grains and legumes, they add *farro* (spelt) or *ceci* (chickpeas), or the famous lentils from Casteluccio in Umbria. In Lazio and Marche, they traditionally make *stracciatella*, with meat stock and eggs, beaten with nutmeg or lemon zest and a little semolina and added to the soup with a fork so that the strands look "torn" or *stracciata* – we have a saying in our kitchen at the restaurant that if someone comes into work with a big hangover, they look "*stracciata.*" In Roma, they make *stracciatella* with Parmesan added to the egg. And in the south, they add fish or seafood to almost every soup they make.

You know, I don't think I ever had soup from a can in my life. Sometimes Plaxy buys cartons of fresh soup – maybe carrot and coriander or leek and potato – which are not too bad at all, but I love the whole magic of putting together a soup and filling the house with the smell of it cooking. I like to put in whatever I have, and enjoy never quite knowing what the soup will be like in the end. Not that the soup pot should be a wastebasket. Making a new soup is a good exercise for a cook; it tests your capacity to imagine flavors and textures in your head and then bring them together, balance them and play them off against each other, so that the finished soup has as much interest as any other dish. That often means you have to add something to give it a little unexpected punch – I remember trying out a new soup with cannellini beans in the restaurant; it tasted lovely, sweet and delicate in the pot, but when we poured it into bowls, it seemed so boring. So we made some ravioli filled with salty, pungent bottarga, dropped them in and it came to life.

Zuppa di cannolicchi e fregola

Razor clam and fregola soup

As with all Italian soups, this is more a dish of clams with a little liquid than soup as it is thought of in England, but if you really prefer it more "soupy," then double the quantity of stock. The stock here is similar to the one we use to make Clam risotto (see page 250), so if you like you can make double the quantity required for the soup and put the rest in the freezer ready to make a risotto another time.

Razor clams have a more intense flavor than other varieties – they are strange creatures that are difficult to catch, because they bury themselves in the sand. They say that when the weather is cooler they come to the surface more and are quite slow to burrow away again, whereas in hot weather they become very speedy and race down into the sand (especially if it is wet and soft). When they are cut into long pieces, razor clams also look quite elegant, but you could use *vongole veraci* (*palourdes* or carpet-shell clams), or a mixture of these and mussels instead if you prefer – but leave them whole.

If you do use mussels, scrub them well under running water, removing any barnacles and beards. Discard any that are open or won't close when tapped. Then when you cook them discard any that fail to open.

When you buy razor clams, as with all bivalves, it is very important to ensure that they are still alive, so make sure the shells are tightly closed – if they are open and the meat is pushing its way out, forget it. Once they are dead, they lose their juices and flavor, and the flesh becomes floppy. Fregola, the grain used in this soup, is a kind of yellow wheat couscous, dried in the sun or the oven, which comes from Sardegna and is also served with stews. If you can't find it, you could use coarse couscous instead, or *pastina* (pasta shapes) like risoni or stellini.

8 razor clams
⅓ cup fregola or coarse couscous
    (see page 167)
3 tablespoons
    extra virgin olive oil
2 garlic cloves, chopped
2 long red chiles,
    deseeded and chopped
5 tablespoons white wine
2 tablespoons tomato paste
2 tablespoons chopped parsley
salt and pepper

    To serve:
about 8 slices of ciabatta or
    similar white bread
a little extra virgin olive oil
    (to brush the toasted bread)

    For the stock:
4½ pounds cherrystone clams
3 tablespoons
    extra virgin olive oil
2 garlic cloves, chopped
2 long red chiles,
    deseeded and chopped
5 tablespoons white wine
1 tablespoon tomato paste

Keep the razor clams and the cherrystone clams for the stock separate. Put each into a bowl of cold water with some salt to re-create their natural environment. As they breathe, they filter the water and push out any sand trapped inside the shells. Lift them out, scrub the shells really well with a brush and wash them three times in running water. Check and discard any that are still open. Sometimes there is too much sand to come out into the water, and the weight of it can keep the shell of a dead clam closed. To be sure, drop each clam into a bowl, and if the clam is dead the impact should make the shell open.

To make the stock, heat the oil in a large, heavy-bottomed pan, add the garlic and chile and cook gently without coloring. Add the cherrystone clams, shake them around for another few minutes, then add the wine. Cover and cook for a few more minutes, until the clams open and release their juices. Add the tomato paste and about 2¼ cups water (or a little more if necessary – enough to cover the clams). Bring to a boil, then turn down the heat and simmer for about 20 minutes.

While the stock is cooking, cook the fregola in plenty of boiling water (no salt) for 8 minutes, until al dente. Drain and cool on a tray or plate. As it cools, toss with a little olive oil to keep the grains separate.

Strain the stock through a fine sieve and keep to one side.

Open the razor clams by running a sharp knife down the length of the shell, so that the two sides open out like a book. Remove the black vein with a knife, but leave the clams in their shells.

Heat 3 tablespoons olive oil in a saucepan with a base wide enough to take the clams without bunching. Add the garlic and chile, and cook gently for a few minutes, without allowing them to color.

Put in the clams, meat side down (i.e., shells facing upward) and cook for a minute. (Keep an eye on the garlic; if it starts to turn brown, add a little more oil to keep it from burning and tasting bitter.) Add the wine and cook for one more minute, until the alcohol evaporates.

Turn the heat down, then take out the clams. Lay them on a cutting board, pull the clams from their shells and discard the shells. Lay the clams side by side on the cutting board, and cut through them all at the same time into small pieces.

Add the reserved stock to the pan, stir in the tomato paste, then add the fregola. Bring to a boil and continue to cook for a few minutes, until the soup thickens up. Season, then take the pan off the heat and add the pieces of razor clam (it is important not to boil the clam meat or it will toughen). Stir for a minute or so, and add the parsley.

Toast the bread until golden and brush with extra virgin olive oil. Pour the soup into bowls, and serve with the toasted bread on the side.

Minestrone alla genovese

Minestrone verde with pesto

For me minestrone is the best soup in the world, the one that represents the whole of Italy, and yet everyone makes it differently, with whatever vegetables they have that are in season. My grandmother and my mother both made fabulous minestrone. In spring and summer, there would be fresh peas and baby fava beans, and plenty of green vegetables. In autumn and winter, the minestrone would be made mainly with onions, carrots, potatoes, spinach or sometimes Swiss chard (in the restaurant in winter, we often add raw artichokes, prepared as described on page 70 and then chopped up). The only vegetable we tend not to put into winter minestrone is pumpkin, because it is so big and dominant – if you are not careful, what do you have…pumpkin soup.

No matter what the season, there would be an argument. My dad would want minestrone with more peas; my granddad loved it with beans and pesto. And white beans – we all used to fight over the white beans: "I've got five!" "I've got six!" Whatever went into the soup, though, there would always be a drizzle of olive oil to finish. We weren't a family big on olive oil – at that time, olive oil wasn't much used in the north – but you couldn't have minestrone without olive oil over the top.

I like to make minestrone the way my grandmother did it, adding rice *(minestrone con riso)* – which made it so thick that you could stick your spoon into it upright and watch it fall down slowly (Margherita loves to do that now, just as I did). However, I have never done it this way in the restaurant – it's a little too rustic. When I am at home, though, I often make my minestrone, then let it cool down (that is important, so you can see how thick it is), pass it through a sieve and then put it back on the heat, with enough stock to loosen it up. Then I add some arborio rice, which I wouldn't use in a risotto as the grains tend to break, but in a soup this is an advantage, as it thickens it up better. I bring the soup to a boil and cook gently for 20 minutes so the starch from the rice makes it really creamy, and serve it with olive oil and some good twists of black pepper. Whatever ingredients you use, a good minestrone has to have the right balance between the starchy element (potato or rice) and the vegetables.

This is the recipe we make in the restaurant during spring, going into summer. We finish it with a little fresh pesto – but, if you prefer, you can just drizzle on some good peppery extra virgin olive oil. Obviously, when you make minestrone, you can cook all the vegetables together if you are in a hurry, but the proper way to do it is slowly, adding the vegetables separately in stages, so that they are all cooked to the same consistency and keep their own identity, with the potatoes only just soft. It's up to you.

Also, if you don't have any vegetable stock, you could just use water – or make a quick stock from all the vegetable trimmings, apart from the fava bean skins (they turn the stock dark green), and add a couple

handfuls of peas, to give an extra sweetness. Cook them all gently in a little olive oil until they start to become soft and mushy, then pour in about 8½ cups of water, simmer for about 20 minutes, pour through a fine sieve, and you are ready to make your minestrone. We use just a tablespoon each of cooked borlotti (cranberry) beans and chickpeas. Normally I would say cook these yourself, but since we are talking about such a small quantity, on this occasion if you don't happen to have any already cooked, use good-quality canned beans and chickpeas – but rinse them very well first.

Blanch the tomato, skin, quarter, deseed (see page 304) and dice.

Peel and dice the carrots and onions, and dice the leek, celery, chard and zucchini, reserving any flowers for garnish. (Reserve the trimmings of everything except the fava beans, if you are going to make a vegetable stock as above.)

Heat the olive oil in a large saucepan, then add the onion, cover with a lid and cook for 3 to 4 minutes on low heat, checking that the onion isn't coloring. Then add the rest of the vegetables in this order: carrots, celery, chard and Tuscan kale if using it, zucchini, leek, peas and fava beans, and spinach. The idea is to put in the vegetables one at a time, starting with the ones that take the longest to cook and letting each one cook briefly, just long enough to release its juices, before adding the next. Then, at the end, the vegetables should all be cooked equally. As you add each vegetable, put in a little sprinkling of salt.

When the last vegetable has been in the pan for a few minutes, add the stock and the whole potato, followed by the borlotti beans and chickpeas. Bring to a boil, turn down to a simmer and cook gently until all the vegetables are quite soft.

Once the minestrone is cooked, adjust the seasoning if necessary and add the tomato. With a slotted spoon, lift out the potato, smash it lightly with a fork, then put back into the soup to give it some thickness. Spoon into bowls and garnish with some strips of zucchini blossom (if you have them) and/or the basil, and drizzle with the pesto or olive oil.

2 carrots
2 white onions
1 leek
2 celery stalks
1 small bunch of Swiss chard
2 zucchini
 (with blossoms if possible)
3 tablespoons
 extra virgin olive oil
1 small bunch cavolo nero
 (Tuscan kale), roughly
 chopped (optional)
1 handful of fresh peas
1 handful of fresh fava beans,
 blanched and
 skin taken off
1 handful of spinach,
 roughly chopped
8½ cups good vegetable stock
 (see page 268 and above)
1 medium potato, peeled
1 tablespoon cooked borlotti
 (cranberry) beans
1 tablespoon cooked chickpeas
1 tomato
some basil leaves, to garnish
4 teaspoons pesto (see page 309)
 or about 4 tablespoons
 extra virgin oil (if you
 are not serving the soup
 with pesto)
salt

Minestrone agli scampi

Minestrone with langoustines

At Locanda we sometimes make a much more elaborate variation of this minestrone with langoustines, starting not with vegetable stock but with a langoustine consommé made with all the claws and heads that are left over after we prepare the langoustines for serving with spaghetti.

Making the consommé is quite a complicated process because langoustines are so much more delicate than meat, the traditional ingredient of consommé. I don't really expect many people to try it at home, so you could just make the soup as on the previous page, but finish it using live langoustines. You take off the heads, then split the tails in two lengthwise and sauté them in a very small amount of olive oil (or the delicate flavor of the langoustines will take up too much taste from the oil). Just put them into the soup before you serve it.

If you do want to try making the consommé, what we do is use the langoustine heads and claws (but remove the eyes). We put them into a meat grinder, with carrots, celery, onion, a bay leaf and some peppercorns. When it is all minced together, we add some tomato paste, whip in some egg whites with a little salt and put the mixture into a pan, covered with just over double the volume of water. Then we slowly bring it to the boil, scraping the bottom of the pan for the first half hour, to stop everything from sticking. Slowly a crust will start to form on top, in the traditional way of consommé. Once the crust has formed, you make a hole in the middle and then carry on simmering for another half hour – you will see the impurities bubble up through the hole you have made and add to the crust. Once it is cooked, we take it off the heat and let the crust sink slowly to the bottom of the pan, then we pour off the liquid and pass it through a fine sieve until it is totally clear, ready to use in the minestrone.

Zuppa di pesce

Fish soup

Wherever you go in Italy, provided you are not too far from the sea, there will usually be a fish soup, a staple that, like minestrone, unites Italians but also divides us, because there is so much variation between the regions, and so much disagreement: "Our way is right, yours is wrong…"

In my own village of Corgeno there are no typical recipes because the only local fish comes from the lake, and it has too muddy a taste for soup, but drive toward the Ligurian coast and you will start to find fish soup prepared one way in this village and 12 miles away it will be done completely differently. There are hundreds of recipes, which depend on the type of fish available and what other local ingredients can be used: maybe potatoes or saffron; onions, or tomatoes and chiles, garlic and white wine.

In Genova, they serve fish soup with pesto and the soup is often pureed; in Sardegna, it is dotted with little pieces of pasta. Along the length of the Adriatic coast, they call fish soup *brodetto* (though, confusingly, this is also the name for an Easter dish in Lazio, made with beef and lamb).

In Romagna, vinegar is added to the *brodetto*; in Venezia, they traditionally use no tomato and further down south, in Abruzzo, they use lots of chiles but, strangely, no saffron, even though this is a big area for its production. In Livorno, on Toscana's Mediterranean coast, they claim that they have been making fish soup for longer than anyone else. Instead of *brodetto*, they call their soup – which is actually more of a rich dark stew – *cacciucco* (the Livornesi traded a great deal with the Turks and some say the word is derived from the Turkish *küçük*, meaning "little" as in little fish). Traditionally, five different fish are used in *cacciucco*, one for each of the *c*'s in its name. These often include pieces of cuttlefish or squid, or perhaps some prawns. The soup is spiced up with some chiles and served over unsalted Tuscan bread.

Often this line between soups and stews is blurred. Further north around the Ligurian Mediterranean coast, as well as their soup with pesto they have *buridda*, which is again more like a stew, but they add ingredients like anchovies, pine nuts or walnuts, mushrooms and wine. Then, in Sardegna they have a fish stew spelled almost the same way, *burrida*, which has its roots in the dish the Ligurian people brought with them when they settled in Sardegna. The Sardinians developed their own version of the soup/stew, but instead of using lots of different fish, shellfish and sometimes squid or cuttlefish, they use only one fish, the dogfish, and add garlic.

Sometimes fish soup is thickened with bread crumbs, elsewhere it is not thickened at all, but left loose. Is it really a soup or stew, more like the French bouillabaisse? Somewhere in between, I would say. If I am making fish soup for friends, I would serve it as a main course in a big pot in the middle of the table, with plenty of bread. But it can be a starter, too.

For me, a good variety of fish is important and generally we use a mixture of small fish – *pescato misto* – which in Italy are sold by the kilo at the market, because they have more bone than flesh, and so they release more gelatinous quality as they cook.

One of the best fish soups I ever made came about by chance, when a box of fish came into the kitchen from Barcelona, full of big John Dory, grouper and sole, little sea bass and tiny crabs. We had some scallops in the kitchen already, as well as some langoustines, prawns, *vongole* (clams) from Italy and mussels. There was such a mountain of fish, we hardly knew what to do with it, so we made a stock, and then kept on adding more and more varieties of fish, getting more and more excited about what we were doing, and the finished soup was amazing... just amazing. Note: the stock is best made the day before you need it.

3 tablespoons olive oil
2 garlic cloves, chopped
24 clams, cleaned (see page 168)
24 mussels, cleaned (see page 167)
5 tablespoons white wine
¾ to 1 pound mixture of whole scaled white fish, such as John Dory, monkfish, red mullet, sea robin, sliced
2 medium tomatoes, chopped
8 langoustines or large raw prawns, peeled, deveined, and eyes removed
¾ to 1 pound baby octopus, cleaned, prepared and cut into pieces
8 small squid, cleaned (see page 100) and each cut into four
salt and pepper

For the stock:
2 sea robin, gutted
2¼ cups tomato passata
10 basil leaves

To serve:
4 slices of country bread
1 garlic clove

The day before, make the stock by cutting each sea robin into 2 or 3 pieces, covering these with the passata and basil, and leaving in the fridge to marinate overnight.

Next day, whiz in a food processor (bones and everything), then put in a pan with 2¼ cups water and bring to a boil. Skim, then turn down the heat and simmer for 15 to 20 minutes. Press through a fine sieve and reserve.

To make the soup, heat the olive oil in a large pan, add the chopped garlic, clams, mussels and white wine, and cover. As soon as the shellfish have opened, remove them (discarding any that don't open).

Put the mixed fish into the pan and add the stock. Simmer gently for 2 to 3 minutes, then add the tomatoes. Add the langoustines or prawns, the baby octopus and squid, then put back the clams and mussels (you can discard most or all of the shells as you like). Simmer gently for a couple of minutes. Taste the soup and season as necessary.

To serve: rub the bread with the garlic, place a slice in each of 4 serving bowls, top with the soup and serve.

Zuppa fredda di pomodoro

Chilled tomato soup

This isn't even a recipe, it is just about taking brilliant tomatoes and pureeing them – fantastic in summer. Obviously, the most important thing is that you use the best tomatoes you can find, because the taste is all tomato and you can't put in flavor that you don't have in the first place. We use three different varieties: cherry tomatoes, larger vine tomatoes (which give the fantastic red color) and Cuore di Bue, "heart of the cow," from Sorrento, which look like little ridged pumpkins – not that pretty, but so full of flavor that we even serve them, just as they are, with mozzarella in the summer.

If you have a juicer, put all the tomatoes through that, then take all the trimmings and press them through a fine sieve, pushing as much of the pulpy juice through as possible (this adds even more flavor and will thicken the soup). If you don't have a juicer, use a food processor, but the heat of the motor will cause you to lose a little of the vivid color and flavor. Season the soup with salt to taste, add a little red wine vinegar, if you feel it needs a little extra sharpness, then chill it in the fridge for at least an hour.

In the restaurant, we serve the soup with a little tomato sorbet. If you want to do something similar, keep back some of the juice, sharpened up with a little extra vinegar, pour it into an ice cube tray and freeze while the soup is chilling. When you are ready to serve it, put a cube of sorbet into the center of each bowl of soup. It is even more interesting if you swirl a little bit of tomato paste on top – it gives another dimension to the flavors. Garnish with basil leaves and a swirl of extra virgin olive oil.

Aglio

Garlic

"Ennobles everything it touches"

The food writer and cook Angelo Pellegrini, who left Toscana for America in the early part of the twentieth century, said in his book *The Unprejudiced Palate* that it was his "final, considered judgment that the hardy bulb [garlic] blesses and ennobles everything it touches – with the possible exception of ice cream and pie." Garlic – along with parsley – is something I couldn't imagine my kitchen without. I crush it and then chop it with parsley, to add to dishes at the last minute (crushing it breaks down the membranes of the cells and releases all the flavor and aroma even more powerfully than chopping). Sometimes I add some grated lemon zest, to make *gremolata*, which is typically sprinkled over meat stews. Or I might mix the garlic and parsley with chopped chiles and olive oil, and toss it through spaghetti. At other times, I prefer to roast the cloves. If you leave them whole, the cell membranes stay intact and the cloves just melt into a sweet mild paste. Why would anyone want to buy garlic paste in a tube, when it is so easy to make?

You can trace the use of garlic back to central Asia and the Mediterranean in ancient times, and it was prized by the Greeks, Romans and Egyptians for its health-giving properties (it is rich in minerals, and is thought to strengthen the body against illness and to have antibacterial, antiviral and anticoagulant qualities). And, you know, people worry so much about garlic on the breath, but if it isn't on your breath, then it hasn't worked properly as a tonic all the way through your body – that's what I think.

We have this idea of garlic created for us by the supermarkets, that garlic is garlic, it all tastes the same and it comes in little bags of three heads. Not true: the garlic of Italy is different from that of Spain or France, which is often darker in color and stronger in taste. Some cultivars are snow-white, others rose-colored or streaked with purple, some short and fat, like the Neapolitan garlic, some are more pungent, some keep longer, some tend to have double cloves, some peel more easily. What mainly determines the difference in flavor are the nutrients in the ground. The more sulfurous the soil is, the stronger the garlic, and the heavier on your breath. The garlic you find in supermarkets has been dried, which is why it is available year-round, but what I love most (though it is less easy to find, unless you live near a production area) is new season's garlic *(aglio novello)*, when the bulbs are just pulled from the ground and are at their delicious peak.

Wild garlic is something different again, that you might find in your garden, or near lakes or rivers. It grows rampant, but most people probably walk past it without even knowing what it is. The leaves are beautiful – garlicky of course – pick them before flowering, and use them like sorrel or spinach, in salads or in soups (see page 180).

Zuppa all'aglio novello

New season's garlic soup

This, for me, is the equivalent of chicken noodle soup for Jewish people – full of restorative powers. I first made it when I worked with Corrado Sironi at Il Passatore in Varese, and I always knew when the time had come to make it, because I would ride to the restaurant in the morning on my motorcycle and, when they were pulling up the new garlic on the shores of the Lago di Varese, the air was full of it. I would go in and say, "Hey, Corrado, I smelled the garlic!" And in the afternoon, he would go on his scooter to the farmer and buy two or three boxes, so we could make this soup. You can also use wild garlic (see page 178) – just substitute 12 ounces or so of it for the heads of garlic. We tend to use Grana Padano for this soup because it is a little lighter and sweeter than Parmesan.

3 heads of spring garlic
20 sage leaves
1 tablespoon thyme leaves
3 juniper berries
6 slices of polenta bread or
 country bread
a little butter
3½ ounces Grana Padano
 (or Parmesan), grated
salt and pepper

Put the garlic, herbs and juniper berries into a pan with 6 cups cold water. Bring to a boil, then turn down the heat and simmer for 30 minutes.

Put in two of the slices of bread to thicken and continue to simmer for another 10 minutes.

Taste and season.

Toast the remaining bread, spread with butter and top with cheese.

Put a slice of toasted bread in the bottom of each of 4 serving bowls and pour the garlic soup over the top.

Zuppa di lenticchie

Lentil soup

Lentils are very much an ingredient of central Italy – the climate in the north is too harsh for them to grow, though where I come from we use them occasionally, usually served with *cotechino* (pork boiling sausage). In Italy, we have so many different sizes and types of lentil – many more than you see in Britain or America – all with different properties. The ones we use for this soup are lenticchie di Castelluccio, which are less starchy than the flat brown ones, so the soup doesn't become too thick. If you want to make a vegetarian version of this, leave out the pancetta and use vegetable stock.

Soak the lentils in cold water for half an hour, then drain.

Heat half the olive oil in a pan and add the vegetables and the piece of pancetta. Cook for 5 to 10 minutes, until the vegetables are soft but not colored. It is important that the vegetables are soft, so that they release all their sweetness, flavor and moisture into the lentils.

Add the lentils, then tie the herbs together and add them. Cook for 5 minutes, stirring, until everything is well mixed and the lentils start to stick to the bottom of the pan. Don't season at this point, as salt will make the lentils harden up.

Meanwhile, heat the stock in a pan. Add 4¼ cups of stock to the lentils, bring to a boil, then turn down the heat and simmer for 45 minutes, until the lentils are soft.

At the end of cooking time, take 3 to 4 tablespoons of the lentils from the pan and set aside.

Remove the herbs and pancetta (if you like, you can slice the pancetta and add it to the soup at the end).

Put the contents of the pan into a food processor. Blend until smooth (if you want an even smoother soup, pass it through a fine sieve).

Return to the heat and add the lentils that you have kept aside. Heat through, and if the soup is too thick, add some more hot stock.

Taste and season. Serve in bowls, drizzling over the rest of the extra virgin olive oil, sprinkling with some rosemary leaves and grinding some fresh black pepper on top.

1⅓ cups small brown lentils
  (preferably lenticchie
  di Castelluccio)
6 tablespoons
  extra virgin olive oil
1 onion, finely chopped
1 carrot, finely chopped
1 celery stalk, finely chopped
1 small leek, finely chopped
3½-ounce piece of
  unsmoked pancetta
1 sprig of rosemary
small bunch of sage
2 bay leaves
6 cups vegetable or
  chicken stock
a few rosemary leaves to garnish
salt and pepper

Fagioli

Beans

"The meat of the poor"

I used to have romantic daydreams about running away, just disappearing on my motorcycle. I figured you could fill a backpack with bags of beans and flour to make pasta, and you could live for quite a long time. In Italy, *fagioli* are an essential ingredient, different from *fagiolini* (the French-style long beans that my granddad used to grow). *Fagioli* are the beans, such as borlotti (cranberry beans) and cannellini, which can be used fresh, or dried to store all year. In Italy, the fresh beans are sold loose by the kilo at the market, by the guys who also sell lentils and dried mushrooms, and when they are out of season you buy big bagfuls of dried beans for the pantry. Back in the sixteenth century, *fagioli* were considered so valuable that they were served at court and exchanged by noblemen as gifts. Later, when everyone began to grow them, they became known as *"la carne dei poveri"* (the meat of the poor), because they are full of protein and vitamins, so tasty and yet much cheaper than meat.

The Italian writer Umberto Eco put it very evocatively in an essay he wrote all about beans, in which he says that in the Middle Ages, because the poor were able to eat very little meat, the population was "ill-nourished, thin, sickly, short and incapable of tending the fields. So," he wrote, "when, in the tenth century, the cultivation of legumes (the whole of the family that includes peas, lentils and chickpeas) began to spread, it had a profound effect on Europe. Working people were able to eat more protein; as a result, they became more robust, lived longer, created more children and repopulated a continent. We believe," he went on, "that the inventions and the discoveries that have changed our lives depend on complex machines. But the fact is, we are still here – I mean we Europeans, but also those descendants of the Pilgrim Fathers and the Spanish conquistadors – because of beans."

In the north of Italy, the favorite bean is undoubtedly the borlotti or cranberry bean (which you can buy fresh from June to September): beautiful, pale-pink, streaked or speckled with red, and with a more pronounced flavor than the white beans, such as the cannellini and the smaller toscanelli, which are more associated with Toscana. The Tuscan people are jokingly called *mangia-fagioli* (bean-eaters) because they use beans in so many of their recipes. My granddad also grew fava (broad) beans – in springtime, you can eat the tender baby beans raw with pecorino cheese. In Sicilia, where the big, wide variety of fava called Leonforte are grown, they incorporate the beans into a traditional dish with pasta, called *"ccu' I favi a du' munni"* in dialect. One of the chefs in our kitchen, Rino, who comes from Sicilia, says that it means pasta (in this case fresh tagliatelle) with broad beans "of the two worlds" – the idea is that the beans are first cooked with vegetables (so they start off the dish in the world of vegetables) and then they join the world of meat, because they are mixed with sautéed skin of pork, tossed through the pasta and topped with pecorino. Or they make *frascatula*, a polenta of toasted fava beans and chickpeas, with baby wild fennel. And there are many more varieties of bean that you rarely see outside Italy; such as lamon, from Belluno in the Veneto, and sarconi from the Basilicata region, which now has the PGI. In Sicilia you also find the amazing-looking badda beans from Polizzi, which are two-tone: either half ivory and orange, or half ivory and deep, deep violet, almost black, like the color of an eggplant.

Fresh beans like cranberry beans were once difficult to find, but now you often see them in markets and shops that sell Italian ingredients. If you can't get them, you can use dried beans in exactly the same way – you just need to soak them for 24 hours first. I know it takes a bit more organization, because you have to think about what you are going to cook tomorrow, but the payoff is much greater, because the whole idea of beans is that when you revive them in water, they are not so different from the fresh bean, whereas if you buy them in a can, the chances are you also get things you don't want, like salt or sugar. As a rough guide, 1 pound fresh beans in their shells produce about 1 cup shelled, and this equates to about ½ cup dried beans before soaking. I would also go for frozen beans over canned, because if they are picked and frozen at the right moment, they are as good as fresh. So: fresh first, dried as the next preference, then frozen – and canned as a last resort.

Soaking and Cooking Beans

If you are using dried beans, soak them in water for 24 hours, without putting them in the fridge, and change the water as close to every 5 or 6 hours as you can.

The way we cook beans at Locanda is first to put them into a large pot. For 1 cup of beans, we put in anything from 2 cloves to half a head of garlic (unpeeled), according to taste, or what an individual recipe requires, then we add a chopped celery stalk, a bunch of sage and about 2 tablespoons of olive oil (you should never add salt until the beans are completely cooked, otherwise they will harden). Cover with plenty of cold water (about double the volume of the beans), put a lid on the pan and bring to the boil. Remove the lid, skim the foam from the top and turn down the heat to a gentle simmer. Cook for about 45 minutes to 1 hour, until the beans are soft to the bite. Try one: they are cooked when the skin, and not just the bean inside, feels soft in the mouth. At this point, you can take the pan off the heat, add salt to taste, then leave the beans to cool in their cooking liquid.

You can cook the beans well in advance. They will keep in their cooking water in the fridge for 4 or 5 days, but don't put your fingers into the water or you will introduce bacteria. When the beans become cold, they harden a little, so take them out of the fridge an hour or so before you want to use them, or warm them up in a pan, and they will soften again.

Zuppa di borlotti e farro

Borlotti bean soup with spelt

Farro (spelt) is an ancient grain that is enjoying a big renaissance, and is becoming known around the world. It is very similar to wheat and from the same family as bread wheat and macaroni wheat. (The Latin name for spelt is *Triticum spelta*, while bread wheat is *T. aestivum* and pasta wheat is *T. turgidum*.) Farro was used by the Romans to make flour for bread and pasta, before it was understood how to grow wheat in large quantities – which is why flour is "farina" in Italian. Because it is a strong grain, it grows higher in the mountains and on less good terrain than wheat.

These days, the main production area is Umbria, and also Toscana and Lazio. Besides being used in soups, the cooked grain can be fried, mixed with olive oil and golden raisins, and served with stews. At one time you bought spelt with its husk still on, and every family would have had a little machine, in order to hull the grains. Now it is sold already prepared.

Spelt is traditionally used in food for feasts and festivals because they say it makes you happy when you eat it. Perhaps because it apparently has a lot of healthy properties: more protein even than lentils, a lot of fiber and complex carbohydrates – it is even supposed to be good for the skin and hair. You need to soak it for 24 hours before you use it, and cook it quite gently and slowly to give the grains time to absorb maximum water.

1⅓ cups spelt (farro)
extra virgin olive oil,
　　　plus extra for finishing
1 carrot, finely chopped
1 onion, finely chopped
1 red onion, finely chopped
1 small red pepper, deseeded
　　　and finely chopped
1 celery stalk, finely chopped
1 tablespoon tomato paste
some rosemary and sage leaves,
　　　to garnish
salt and pepper

　For the beans:
1 pound fresh borlotti (cranberry)
　　　beans (around 1 cup shelled),
　　　or ½ cup dried, soaked for
　　　24 hours (see page 183)
1 celery stalk
4 garlic cloves, crushed
small bunch of sage
2 tablespoons olive oil

Soak the spelt in at least double its volume of cold water overnight.

Cook the beans as described on the previous page.

Heat a little oil in a small pan and add the carrot, both onions and the pepper and celery. Cook for 5 to 10 minutes, until the vegetables are soft but not colored, then add the tomato paste and three-quarters of the drained cooked beans (keep the rest on one side). Cook for another 20 minutes. Put into a food processor and process until smooth.

Put back on the heat, add 2¼ cups of the liquid from cooking the beans (make it up with water if necessary) and bring back to a boil.

Drain the spelt and add to the pan. Turn down the heat and cook for about 30 minutes, stirring all the time, as the spelt will tend to stick to the bottom of the pan and thicken the soup; so check and, if necessary, add more water during cooking. When the spelt is cooked, it will have swollen to about twice the size of a grain of risotto rice and be very soft, and the soup should be the consistency of a milk shake.

Add the reserved beans, season the soup and serve drizzled with some more extra virgin olive oil and finished with chopped rosemary and sage leaves, and some freshly ground black pepper.

Zuppa di cannellini

Cannellini bean soup

Cannellini beans have made quite a name for themselves, possibly thanks to that famous Gordon Ramsay recipe, white bean cappuccino. The recipe I give here is for a very gentle, subtle soup that is beautiful just as it is, but it can also serve as a base for any other ingredient that you want to add to make the soup a little more sophisticated. As I mentioned earlier, we often brighten it up by dropping in some tortellini filled with bottarga. The saltiness of the fish roe seems to make a good connection with the subtlety of the beans. Or you could just cook all those little pieces of broken dried tagliatelle that you find in the pasta jar, and add them at the end with a spoonful of pesto.

6 tablespoons
    extra virgin olive oil
1 white onion, finely chopped
1 carrot, finely chopped
1 celery stalk, finely chopped
1 small leek, finely chopped
1 pound cannellini beans,
    preferably fresh
    (if not, ½ cup dried beans,
    soaked overnight)
1 sprig of rosemary, plus a few
    more leaves for garnish
small bunch of sage
2 bay leaves
6 cups vegetable or
    chicken stock
salt and pepper

Heat half the olive oil in a pan and add the vegetables. Cook for 5 to 10 minutes until they are soft but not colored. It is important that the vegetables are soft, so that they release all their sweetness, flavor and moisture into the beans.

Add the beans and the herbs, all tied together, and cook for 2 to 3 minutes, stirring around, until everything is mixed well. Don't season at this point, as salt will make the beans harden up.

Meanwhile, heat the stock in a pan. Add 4¼ cups of stock to the beans and bring to the boil, then turn down the heat and simmer for 30 to 45 minutes until the beans are soft.

At the end of the cooking time, take 3 to 4 tablespoons of the beans from the pan and keep to one side. Put the rest of the contents of the pan into a food processor and process until smooth. (If you want an even smoother soup, pass it through a fine sieve.)

Put back on the heat and add the beans you have kept on one side. Heat through and, if the soup is thicker than you would like, add some more of the hot stock.

Taste and season. Serve in bowls, drizzling over the rest of the extra virgin olive oil, sprinkling with some chopped rosemary leaves and grinding some fresh black pepper on top.

Zuppa di ceci e pancetta

Chickpea soup with pancetta

Chickpeas belong to the same legume family as beans and have been a favorite with Italians since Roman times. Their botanical name is *Cicer arietinum* – *arietinum* means ram-like, and if you look at a chickpea, it really looks like a perfect little ram's head. They are grown mostly in the south, left to dry in the sun in their pods, then harvested at the right moment. Look for chickpeas that are creamy textured, with a delicate thin, shiny, unwrinkled skin, and always soak them overnight, as, especially if they are a little old and dry, they can take a very long time to soften during cooking.

If you like, you can cook some tortellini separately (or tagliatelle cut into short strips after cooking) and add it to the soup just before serving – or you could even add some squid, quickly fried in a little garlic and oil and sprinkled with parsley.

Soak the chickpeas in at least double their volume of cold water, and leave overnight.

Drain the chickpeas and put them in a large pan with the celery and garlic. Add the herbs tied together in a bouquet garni, the extra virgin olive oil and double the quantity of water as that of the chickpeas. Cover and bring to a boil, then turn down the heat and simmer for about 1½ hours, adding more water if necessary. Take off the heat and set aside.

Heat a little more extra virgin olive oil in a small pan and add the carrot, both onions, the celery and half the pancetta. Cook for 5 to 10 minutes until soft but not colored, then add the tomato paste and three-quarters of the cooked chickpeas (keep the rest on one side). Cook for another 10 minutes.

Put into a food processor and process until smooth. Put back on the heat and add a little of the liquid from cooking the chickpeas (make it up with water if necessary) to bring it to a soupy consistency. Bring back to a boil and add the chickpeas you have kept to one side.

Just before serving, heat a small dry frying pan and gently cook the remaining pancetta until golden (or crispy, if you like). Drain on paper towels.

Season the soup and serve drizzled with some more extra virgin olive oil. Finish by adding chopped rosemary and sage leaves, freshly ground black pepper, and a tablespoon or so of pancetta to each bowl.

1 carrot, finely chopped
1 onion, finely chopped
1 red onion, finely chopped
1 celery stalk, finely chopped
5–6 ounces pancetta,
    cut into strips
1 tablespoon tomato paste
rosemary and sage leaves,
    to garnish
salt and pepper

For the chickpeas:
1¼ cups chickpeas
1 celery stalk
4 garlic cloves, crushed
1 sprig of rosemary
small bunch of sage
2 bay leaves
1 tablespoon extra virgin olive
    oil, plus extra for sautéing
    and finishing

Zuppa di broccoli e gnocchetti di ricotta

Broccoli soup with ricotta cheese dumplings

This is a soup we made up in London. It is based on something similar I saw in Paris, served with a spoonful of clotted cream. Broccoli is an amazing vegetable – so full of everything good, including compounds that can help protect against cancer, that they call it a "superfood." I discovered broccoli only late in life – we didn't eat much of it when I was growing up in Italy – but when I started cooking with it I was surprised at the vividness of the flavor and color, something that seems to appeal especially to kids.

Remove the ricotta from its tub or container, and wrap it in a clean tea towel to soak up the excess moisture.

Heat 3 tablespoons of the olive oil in a pan, add the onion, leek and potato, and sweat for 5 minutes, until soft but not colored.

While the vegetables are cooking, take the heads of broccoli and peel the stalks. With a small knife, scrape off the very tops of the florets – so you have a mound that looks like green bread crumbs. Set aside. Finely chop the stalks and add to the vegetables in the pan. Season and sweat for another 5 minutes.

Add the vegetable stock and cook until the vegetables are completely soft (about 20 minutes).

In a separate pan, boil enough water to blanch the "green bread crumbs." Put them in a sieve and dip them into the boiling water for 10 to 15 seconds only, just to soften them up. Drain and, while still warm, either crush them with the back of a knife, or puree in a blender until you have a bright green paste. Add a little water, if necessary, to loosen.

Take the pan containing the vegetables from the heat and put them into a food processor. Process until smooth (the soup will be quite pale).

Put the egg, ricotta and Parmesan into a bowl and mix together well. Keep on one side.

Return the soup to the heat and season if necessary. Turn down the heat to a simmer and whisk in the puree of broccoli flowers, so that the soup turns bright green.

Dip a teaspoon in hot water and scoop out little dumplings of the ricotta mixture. Drop them into the hot soup and let them rise to the surface (about 15 to 20 seconds). Gently ladle the soup into bowls, taking care not to break the ricotta dumplings, which will be quite fragile. Add the blanched florets and drizzle with the rest of the extra virgin olive oil.

⅔ cup ricotta cheese
6 tablespoons
    extra virgin olive oil
2 onions, thinly sliced
1 leek, thinly sliced
2 large potatoes, thinly sliced
3 heads of broccoli, plus
    some florets (blanched),
    to garnish
6 cups vegetable stock
1 egg, beaten
1 tablespoon freshly
    grated Parmesan
salt and pepper

Tortellini in brodo

Chicken tortellini in clear broth

For the best soups you really need to make your own stock – and for this one, especially, it isn't worth falling back on ready-made versions, as the entire taste of the soup comes from the stock, so it needs to be as flavorsome and clear as possible. You can make the stock in advance and keep it in the fridge or freezer. You can also make the tortellini in advance and freeze them. If you have some black truffle, you can shave it over the top of the soup at the end.

4¼ cups chicken stock
    (see page 264)
a little grated Parmesan to serve
    (optional) and/or a little
    black truffle (optional)

For the pasta:
1¾ cups 00 (doppio zero) flour
    (see page 330)
1 egg plus 2 egg yolks, plus extra
    beaten egg for brushing
pinch of salt

For the filling:
1 small chicken breast,
    about ¼ pound
3 tablespoons heavy cream
¼ pound pancetta
¼ pound mortadella
1 tablespoon grated Parmesan
pepper

First make the pasta by following the method for making egg pasta on page 330.

Meanwhile, make the filling: put the chicken breast into a food processor, with a little cream if necessary to loosen, and blend until smooth, then pass through a fine sieve to remove any sinews from the meat.

Put back into the processor and add the pancetta and mortadella with the rest of the cream and some freshly ground black pepper. Process again until completely smooth. Add the Parmesan, and process again to mix in completely. Put the mixture in the fridge until needed.

Cut the rested pasta dough in half and flatten slightly with a rolling pin. Pass the dough through a pasta machine on the widest setting. Fold in half and then put through again. Repeat the process, moving the machine to a thinner setting each time, until the pasta is as thin as possible. Repeat with the rest of the pasta, so you end up with two thin strips.

Lay the pasta strips on a work surface. From each strip cut around 30 squares, about 2 x 2 inches. Fill the center of one set of squares with a little of the chicken mixture (about three-quarters of a teaspoon). Brush the edges of each square with beaten egg and fold over two of the edges to make a triangle, enclosing the mixture. Take each triangle, one point facing upward, bring the two opposite points straight down and underneath, then press the pasta together to seal.

Bring the stock to the boil in a big pan. Put in the tortellini and simmer for 4 to 5 minutes. Taste the stock and season if necessary. Then serve in bowls. If you like, you can grate a little Parmesan and/or black truffle over the top.

The great escapist

There was a waiter at my uncle's restaurant named Giovanni, a real character. He had a picture of himself serving Mussolini, which he kept in his wallet. He had been to America and England, and he had worked at the Cipriani and at Harry's Bar in Venezia. I was too young and too much in awe of him to go up to him and ask him about his travels myself, but I used to listen to him when he talked to my granddad and I loved hearing his stories – I still remember all the dirty ones!

When I was maybe ten, he died, and a few years later, his sister, Elisa, offered the priest in our village some of his things for the church fete. So my brother and I were sent to fetch them. She lived in a scary old farmhouse and she told us there was some old stuff of Giovanni's at the top of the house. We climbed up to the loft. It was very dark, but there was a little shaft of light coming through and I could see an old bed and, among his things, an old leather suitcase. It was covered in beautiful labels from his travels, and right in the middle was one that read "The Savoy, London" with the motto "For excellence we strive." All my life, I have remembered that suitcase, because those words had a big impact on my imagination. I couldn't stop thinking about what it would be like to work at the Savoy; and I was desperate to travel the world.

By the time I was seven, I already wanted to be a chef, because all the chefs I knew in my uncle's restaurant were noisy and temperamental and all the things that appeal to kids. At first, I had wanted to be a waiter, like Giovanni and my brother, my cousin and even my father, who wore white jackets at the weekends and served in the banqueting room. The trouble was that if I got nervous, my hands got sticky, and that was a disaster every time I touched the handles of the silver cutlery. Then one day I pulled on a tablecloth by mistake and I broke forty glasses that were sitting on top of it: a big mess. I was under the table hiding from my uncle, who was shouting: "I've had enough; you're too clumsy, you will have to go and help in the kitchen!" So that is how it started.

One of my first jobs was to watch the béchamel sauce as it thickened. After a while, I could tell if it was too thick or too thin by the size of the bubbles. Then I got to make the fruit salad in big plastic bins – each one big enough to hold fifty portions. They would tell me how many bins we needed, and I used to sit there for hours cutting up the fruit. But at La Cinzianella the windows of the kitchen look out over the lake and the mountains, so peeling and chopping weren't so bad.

When I was nine or ten, the old head chef, Michele, died, and his wife said, "I have got something for you. Michele would have liked you to have these." And she gave me three of his chef's jackets. My first jackets. My grandmother altered them to fit me and I was so proud to wear them. Then the new chef, Silvano, arrived. He had traveled on cruise ships, and he used to tell me fantastic stories. He showed me pictures of some of the elaborate food he had made, like a centerpiece of chicken liver pâté in gelatin, which I thought was a masterpiece, and it fired me up even more to want to see the world and cook.

At home, they called me Houdini, after the great escapist, because I was always disappearing. Once, when I was small, I ran away to the woods, made a fire, and stayed out all night, which almost broke my grandmother's heart. Another time, when I was about twelve, my mother and father gave me money to get my hair cut – it was always long, because I liked it that way – but instead of going to see the barber, I went to the train station and asked the man in the ticket office: "How far can I go for 2,000 lire?" But the village grapevine had reached my father, and before I could buy a ticket, he appeared at the station to take me home.

People used to joke that I took after my great-uncle, my granddad's brother, Enrico, who was something of a legend in the village. Everyone used to call him Enrico Ciaveta – *ciaveta* means "the small key that opens every door" – and there were all kinds of stories about him: that he used to play cards with a knife stuck underneath the table, that once he killed somebody who came and took the most beautiful girl in Corgeno, then ran away and hid from the police in the mountains; that another time, when he was working in the mines in Luxembourg, he jumped off a train and swam across a lake when police came on board the train, because he had no papers to work there. To hear people talk about him you would think he was the desperado of Corgeno. Well, of course, I wasn't really like him – and when the priest's barn caught on fire, it wasn't me, I promise. But I think my mum and dad clamped down on me more because of his reputation, whereas my brother, who grew up to be an engineer, like my father, always got away with everything.

My first real job was at Il Passatore, the best restaurant in Varese, which was then owned by someone who used to work at La Cinzianella, and it had a great reputation not only for its food and wine but for its fantastic wood chargrill. My first few months were hell. I was blamed for everything that went wrong, but then the restaurant was sold to a guy called Giorgio Nizzardo, who brought in a new star chef, the famous Corrado Sironi, *Il Re del Risotto* (the Risotto King). Suddenly I was the one who knew where everything was, the favorite little one. Sironi called me Locatellini and he used to take me with him sometimes when he cooked for people in their houses. Now my job was to be in charge of the chargrill and I was in my element, full of energy, working from eight in the morning to twelve at night and enjoying myself. Sironi was an amazing character, who had broken both his knees racing motorcycles, and he used to drink several bottles of wine a day, but I still think of him and Giorgio as my mentors. I learned so much while I was at Il Passatore, in particular the way to whisk in small cubes of very cold butter at the end of making the risotto. But still I wanted to travel.

First, though, I had to do my year in the army. I didn't tell them I was a chef because, when I saw the enormous pots of horrible-smelling stew, I was horrified. I thought, "This isn't real cooking." But later I wished I had, when I met a couple of guys who did the cooking in the nice little restaurant where the officers ate, as they had a very good life.

When I came out, I took a job over the border in Switzerland before returning to Il Passatore, where Giorgio and his English wife, who knew how much I dreamed of cooking at the Savoy, encouraged me to apply for a position there. The rest of my family seemed content to stay in Corgeno, to work in the hotel as they had always done, and they used to say, "Everyone wants to work in the kitchens at La Cinzianella – but you don't want to? Why?" I could have been the third generation of our family to work at La Cinzianella, along with my cousin Maurizio. I could have parked my Maserati in the drive of a nice big house and had an easier life, but I wanted my own adventures and stories to tell, like Giovanni.

When the letter on the famous letterhead notepaper arrived inviting me to the Savoy for an interview, my mum and dad were very unhappy that I was leaving. For them it seemed like losing a child for good, but even so they were impressed enough to say, "You must go," and, later, every time they came to see me in London, they admitted, "You did well, to do what you wanted to do." I think my dad, and maybe even my mother, understood deep down, that I had to go – because ever since that day when I was ten years old, and I found Giovanni's battered old suitcase, I knew I had to escape. I wanted a hat and a jacket with a motto written on it; I wanted the whole theater of the Savoy.

Risotto

"The Italian *risotto* is a dish of a totally different nature, and unique."

Elizabeth David, *Italian Food*, 1954

My grandmother's sister left Italy in the fifties and went to live in Boston, where she married an Italian. When they came home some thirty years later, she always used to complain, "The risotto isn't good anymore," because in the time she had been in America the way we prepared risotto had changed. She still remembered how, as a child, she would put a fork into the rice and it had to stand upright; if the fork fell down, it wasn't a good risotto. Whereas now, in most regions of Italy and especially in the restaurant world, when we think of risotto we have in mind a dish that has a gorgeous soft, loose texture, so if you tilt the plate, the risotto ripples in waves, which we call *all'onda*.

These days, one of the most important stages of making a risotto is considered to be the *mantecatura*, which comes from the Spanish word for butter, *mantequilla* (the Spanish influence in the north dates from Renaissance times, when Lombardia was ruled by the Spanish). It means the beating in of butter and cheese right at the end of cooking, to give the risotto that fantastic creaminess. In my aunt's day, however, most families couldn't afford to use so much butter and cheese, so the risotto was quite stiff and unyielding.

In Elizabeth David's day, risotto was seen as a warming dish very much of the north, where the main rice crop was cultivated (the word *risotto* comes from the Lombard dialect, even though there are not many rice fields in Lombardia itself; they are in lower Piemonte, on the other side of Lago Maggiore). In *Italian Food*, she wrote that rice is to the northern provinces of Italy (Lombardia, Piemonte and the Veneto) what pasta is to the South. However, after the Second World War, there began to be a fairer sharing of the land that had once been owned by the rich and cultivated by the poor, and more small companies began to produce rice.

Distribution of food was better throughout the country, so pasta spread to the north, and rice to the south, and people started crossing varieties of rice in order to cultivate different shapes and properties, which began to be seen as just as important in Italian cooking as a particular shape of pasta. And, gradually, all over Italy they began to create their own recipes, which, as always with Italian cooking, changed from city to city, village to village, and home to home. So, eventually, from being just a dish of the north, risotto has come to represent a little bit of all Italy. There is a saying where I come from that even the Colosseum in Roma is stuck together with risotto – one of our many northern political jokes, that it is the money of the north that holds the country together.

In some parts of Italy, though, particularly the central regions and the south, where olive oil is used much more than the dairy products that are so abundant in the north, you will still find risotto that resembles the stiff rice dish that my great-auntia remembered. When I was on vacation with the family in Calabria a few years ago, I remember there was a little bar on the beach by our hotel that was run by a woman who cooked risotto that she ladled out into domes on each plate, and that was the shape it stayed until you worked your fork into it.

By contrast, in the coastal areas such as Venezia, for as long as they have made risotto it has been served all'onda, probably because traditionally their recipes use more fish and seafood, and with such delicate ingredients you don't want heavy, starchy rice. Others say, more romantically, that around the coast the risotto ripples to mimic the waves of the sea.

There are very few other ways Italians eat rice than in risotto. We rarely use boiled rice, for example, except *in insalata* (in salad) or in soup – though in Sicilia they traditionally make *arancini* with boiled rice. Arancini are deep-fried rice balls, about the size of a small tennis ball or orange (arancini means "little orange"). Often the rice would be mixed with saffron to give it an "orange" color, then it was molded around traditional fillings of meat or ham and peas, dusted in flour, dipped in beaten egg and finally in fine bread crumbs, and deep-fried until the rice balls were golden. Now arancini are made all over Italy, and very often with saffron risotto, rather than boiled rice, sometimes with pieces of mozzarella mixed in (see page 262). You will see them being fried by sellers on street corners, inevitably the mama doing the cooking and the son taking the money. And, around Napoli, they make a more pear-shaped arancini, which they reckon are more appealing and easier for women to eat delicately.

Occasionally, because of its high starch content, rice is used in other dishes as a thickening agent. In Liguria, they have *torta di verdura*, a pie, or "cake," made with green vegetables. They make a pasta with flour and water, then take whatever green vegetables they have – like zucchini, spinach or borage – chop them up, take two or three handfuls of rice and mix them in. Then they roll out the pasta quite thin, lay one piece on top of the other, put in the vegetables and rice, lay two more sheets of pasta on top, seal the edges with a little beaten egg or water, brush it with beaten egg and bake the "pie" in the oven. As it cooks, the vegetables release their water, which is absorbed into the rice, and the starch binds the filling together.

I never saw rice used in a dessert until I came to England. When I first saw them making rice pudding at the Savoy in London I was shocked, and when I tasted it I reacted with complete amazement: it was such an alien flavor: rice with milk and sugar and vanilla, which they served with quince...very weird. Once I got used to it, though, I thought it was fantastic. It reminded me that even an ingredient you think you know so well can surprise you, and later at Zafferano, for fun we started to make a "pudding risotto" for the dessert menu, a variation of which we still serve now, at Locanda (see page 552).

To most Italians, though, rice means only the savory risotto they have grown up with. What makes a risotto a risotto – and quite different from any other rice dish in the world – is the way it combines the al dente rice (al dente means "firm to the bite") with the starchy creaminess that enfolds it. Even the famous French food writer Escoffier, in one of the few mentions he made of Italian cooking, declared risotto to be a completely Italian affair that could not be compared to anything else he knew, a sentiment with which Elizabeth David obviously agreed.

I could never imagine having a restaurant without serving risotto; it has always been such a big part of my life. In our house in Corgeno, risotto was a part of the cycle of preparing and cooking food that went on all the time. One of the secrets of a good risotto is good stock, so if my grandmother cooked a chicken, she always took the time to use the bones to make the stock for the risotto.

When the wild mushrooms were around, we would have mushroom risotto, or sometimes it would be an even simpler affair. My granddad would come in from the garden with some fennel and a big bunch of parsley, and my grandmother would make a fennel risotto, then chop the parsley with a mezzaluna and add it with the butter at the end – such a wonderful fresh flavor. If there was asparagus she would boil it up, putting the trimmings into the stock, then make a risotto simply with butter and grana cheese and serve the asparagus on the side – not so very different from the way we do asparagus risotto now in the restaurant. And, once a year in the white truffle season, my brother and I would go off to Alba with my granddad to buy a precious truffle. Then, when we came home, there would be a little ritual by the stove: my granddad would hand the truffle to my grandmother as she finished the risotto, she would grate the brown sweaty ball over it like Parmesan, and the fragrance that filled the kitchen would be incredible.

Sometimes for our special Tuesday lunch with the whole family she would make her famous risotto allo zafferano, in the traditional way with powdered saffron, rather than strands, which I never saw until much later. I remember the saffron jar in my grandmother's kitchen. It had a picture of a chef with a big hat on it, and inside were lots of small paper envelopes, which you opened very carefully at one end and then tapped the other, so the rich yellow powder flowed out. My granddad used to say it cost as much as gold, and the flavor and the color were so vivid and fantastic, they have stayed with me all my life. So much so that when I opened my first London restaurant, I could think of only one name for it: Zafferano.

Riso

The rice

Once upon a time in Italy, the main culture of rice was the variety known as arborio, which was the typical rice cultivated in the feudal Lomellina region, the first recognized area to be planted with rice in the eighteenth century. When I was drafted into the army in 1982, I stayed near the plantations: so beautiful, with their light green plants separated into squares surrounded by canals and dykes. These days the harvesting and weeding are done by machine, but once it was all done by *mondine*, women who spent their days with their backs bent double, their bare feet in water, singing traditional communist songs, which we all learned when we were young.

The area around the rice fields was also home to frogs and snails that would find their way into local stews. And now, one of the artisan growers we buy our rice from, Gabriele Ferron in Isola della Scala near Verona, is doing a fantastic thing, raising carp in the flooded fields where the rice grows. The fish eat a lot of the vegetation so they help to keep the weeds down and the water healthy. At the same time the carp grow big and fat. So when the time comes to harvest the rice they also take out the carp and have a big party with risotto and fish.

In a beautiful risotto, within the softness of the finished dish the grains of cooked rice will look like pearls, much as they did when they were raw. This is because risotto rice, which is the type known as japonica, is made up of two different starches. On the surface is a soft starch called amylopectin, which will swell and partly dissolve during cooking – so some of the starch will be absorbed into the rice, making it creamy. Then inside the kernel there is a firmer starch called amylose, which shouldn't break and which will keep the rice al dente.

There are three grades of rice for risotto: *semifino*, which is the smallest; *fino*; and *superfino*, the largest. Then within each grade, there are different varieties. The three major varieties are arborio, carnaroli (both superfino) and vialone nano (nano means "dwarf"), which is a semifino. Increasingly, people are producing new varieties, such as baldo, a superfino that cooks a little quicker, or trying to invent more and more pretreated, precooked and preflavored rice. One of the popular ideas is to temper the rice by bringing it up to a certain temperature to harden the outside, in order to stop the grains from overcooking and help them hold their shape. Personally, I don't believe in any of that stuff. The more you treat a grain of rice, the more you lose the starch that is the whole essence of risotto. And surely, if you have a jarful of pure, good-quality risotto rice in your kitchen and you cook it properly, what could be any better than that?

Each type of rice acts in its own way during cooking – and the quantity of each starch it contains is important. If it is very high in surface

starch, and you are not careful, the risotto can become too sticky; whereas if it is high in the inner starch, each grain can absorb more liquid, helping to keep the risotto creamy rather than heavy. Of course, every region and every cook will tell you that one variety is better than another for their kind of risotto. I grew up with arborio. It was what my grandmother used, and it is still the rice most people use to cook risotto at home. It was only much later that I started using any other sort of rice, when I left college and began working at a local restaurant on the shores of Lago di Varese, called Il Passatore, where the chef was Corrado Sironi. Il Passatore was the only restaurant in the area that had a big brigade, twelve cooks, and it was the first time I saw a head chef who didn't use his own hands, only his knowledge, to teach and direct other people. I never felt that Sironi had just learned his techniques from a piece of paper at college; cooking came naturally to him. Most of all he was famous as the Risotto King, and he was the one who showed me the importance of the grain in a really, really soft, all'onda risotto, which a customer would think quite special.

In the restaurant world, people are looking for more elegance – you don't want to be served something that looks like a rice pudding – and arborio contains the highest level of the surface starch, amylopectin, so it gives out more starch than it absorbs, making a quite sticky, dense risotto in which the grains have a tendency to lose their shape a little. Sironi taught me that it is best to keep it for soup and use either vialone nano or carnaroli, depending on what kind of risotto you are making.

Vialone nano has a quite round, thick grain that contains high levels of the inner starch, amylose, so it is capable of absorbing a lot of liquid. When you cook it, it becomes translucent on the outside, leaving the kernel inside looking like a pearl, but the tips of the grain can smooth out and lose their shape a little. So it is best suited to more starchy risottos that have robust ingredients mixed into it, as the kernel is less likely to break as it is tumbled about.

Carnaroli is a very thin, very long grain rice, which is lighter and starchier than vialone nano, but because it has a good balance of the two starches – amylopectin and amylose – it becomes almost totally translucent and pearly when it is cooked, but also holds its shape really well, and absorbs enough liquid to give the risotto a lovely creaminess. We use it in simpler, more elegant risottos, such as saffron risotto and seafood risottos, in which you have only a few added ingredients, or something delicate that goes in at the last minute.

Brodo

The stock

A good stock is important for risotto, and the flavor of your stock will determine the taste of the finished dish, so it is best to make your own. I know people get nervous about making stock, either because they think it is complicated, or they think they don't have the time, but a stock is a really simple and very rewarding thing to make. You can make a big batch, freeze it in ice cube trays, then transfer the cubes to bags, which you can keep in the freezer to use whenever you need them. See page 264 for recipes.

The technique

So much has been said about risotto. One cook will tell you, "It is easy; what is all the fuss about?" Others will say no two risotti ever come out the same, that risotto is unpredictable, and if you don't take care you end up with either soup or heavy mush. Well, I suppose all those things are true. It is easy for me to say that making risotto is simple, because I have done it all my life. The truth is it does come out slightly differently each time, but that is part of the joy of it, and it is easy, once you understand the way a risotto works.

Perhaps more than any other dish, you need to make risotto a few times to get the feel of the way it is built up through five distinct stages, to achieve that gorgeous mixture of rich creaminess and bite. What happens is this:

First you need to have a pan of hot stock ready on the burner, next to where you are going to make your risotto.

You begin with the *soffritto*, which is the base of the risotto. Making this involves sautéing onions – and sometimes garlic – in butter. Usually this is all, but if you are making a risotto with wild mushrooms, say, you might also add a few soaked dried porcini at this stage to enhance the flavor. Or, if you are making a risotto with robust ingredients, like sausage, you might add this to the base as well – but whatever ingredients you put in at this stage must be able to withstand 20 minutes or so of cooking at a very high temperature.

Next you have the *tostatura*, the "toasting" of the rice in this mixture so that every grain is coated and warmed up and will cook uniformly. At this point, you usually stir in a glass of wine and let it completely evaporate before beginning to add the hot stock.

Now you start adding your stock slowly (a ladleful at a time) and when each addition is almost absorbed, you add the next one, stirring almost continuously so that the heat is distributed through the mixture and you achieve the rubbing away and dissolving of the starch around the outside of the rice, without breaking the grains.

At some point during this time, unless you are making a risotto just with grana cheese, you will add your principal ingredient: seafood, wild mushrooms, asparagus, etc. The exact point at which you add it varies according to how delicate or sturdy the ingredient is, but most keep their flavor better if they are put in around two-thirds of the way through cooking the rice, rather than added to the base.

When the rice is ready, i.e., tender but still al dente, you need to rest the risotto – just for 1 minute – off the heat, and without stirring, to bring the temperature down, ready to accept the addition of cold butter and cheese, at the final stage.

This last step is the *mantecatura*, the beating in of butter, cheese, and so on, which helps gives the modern risotto its unique consistency. Then you are ready to serve – and the sooner it is eaten, the better.

Risotto is something that I do for friends when they turn up unexpectedly – because what do you need for a basic risotto? Rice, stock, Parmesan … and from when you start adding the stock it should take only around 17 to 18 minutes for the rice to be cooked correctly (that is for 4 portions – the rule is the more rice you cook, the less time it takes, because the rice retains more heat). What I do with new chefs when we go through the risotto for the first time is set an alarm clock for 17 minutes, from that point, so that they can get a feel for the timing.

It is quite hard to get the texture right if you cook only a little risotto at a time, because the heat penetrates more strongly, so the rice absorbs the liquid too quickly. If you want to cook a risotto for one person, make enough for three, keep the rest to mold into a cake and bake it in the oven, or form it into little balls and deep-fry them to make arancini (see page 262).

On the other hand, trying to make too much risotto in one go is not a good thing either, because it is harder for the heat to circulate properly through a large quantity and the rice will not cook as evenly. Really, I think that around a kilo of rice (enough for 8 to 10 people) is as much as you can comfortably handle at home. Once, when I was at Zafferano, we made risotto for 280 people at a wedding, but we had 28 pans on the go.

I have seen chefs cook "risotto" for a lot of people in one huge pan, with all the stock added at once, without stirring. If the result tasted good, I would say, "Okay" – but this is not what a true risotto is about. You have to add your stock slowly and stir almost continuously to achieve the right texture at the end. The rule is one ladle of stock at a time, no more, until each addition of liquid is absorbed – no matter how much pressure a chef is under.

All that said, there is one old-style risotto that is magically made without stirring, called Risotto alla Pilota, after the guys who moved the rice around the fields using donkeys and couldn't stop to stir their risotto at lunchtime. They would have minced meat or pancetta in some stock, then the rice went in in a stream through a cone made with paper, the heat was turned up gently, the lid put on, and it was left until the rice was cooked.

The beauty of risotto is that once you understand how it works, you can make it with anything you like, whatever is in season or you happen to have in the kitchen: seafood, asparagus, quail, mushrooms, peas, pumpkin (my granddad used to use leftover rabbit). At home, my son, Jack, loves the risotto we make with sausages and peas. It has become the dish that we do when we come back from vacation, because everything you need is either in the freezer or the pantry. As I have already mentioned, all that really varies is the time when you add this "garnish."

Risotto can be a peasant dish, made with quite inexpensive ingredients, or it can be something quite sexy. And there are very few things you

can't add to it. What wouldn't I put in a risotto? Mussels are possibly the only things. I hate mussels in a risotto; I don't know why – I have had risotto where the mantecatura has been done with a little bit of mussel stock and lemon juice, which I have enjoyed – but for me, the texture of whole mussels in a risotto feels wrong.

Traditionally in Italy, a risotto is served alone, with the two famous Milanese exceptions of saffron risotto served with *osso buco* (veal stew) or *cotolette alla Milanese* (with veal cutlet), but when we used to cater for banquets, and especially weddings, at my uncle's restaurant, La Cinzianella, we would make a centerpiece of veal and risotto. It was my job to do it. I used to take a saddle of veal and roast it lightly. While the meat was roasting, I would make a mushroom and truffle risotto, then put it in a food processor until the mixture became very sticky. When the meat was roasted I would take off the loin and cut it into thin slices; then, slice by slice, I would rebuild the shape of the saddle, using layer after layer of meat, with the gluey rice in between, then glaze it and put it back into the oven. When it came out, it looked and smelled beautiful, and, when you served it, it was full of magical flavors and creamy, sticky textures. I must have made that dish a hundred times during weekends at La Cinzianella, but I still love it.

Sometimes at Locanda, I also like to break free from tradition and serve risotto as an accompaniment; for example, we might serve a mushroom and black truffle risotto alongside roast quail. You can be as adventurous as you like, but it is hard to beat the classic recipe on page 214.

As beautiful as it tastes, I admit that a plain risotto is not a pretty thing, so in restaurants we need to make it appear more exciting. As a rule, I am not a great builder of elaborate dishes, but a chef must leave his mark. There is nothing worse than someone coming to your restaurant and afterward saying, "I don't remember what I ate"; and part of what stays in your memory is the way a dish looks. So we might garnish a seafood risotto with langoustine tails or chargrilled crayfish, or a mushroom or pumpkin risotto with slices of those vegetables dried in the oven.

When we make risotto nero with calamari and its ink, we keep some squid back. Then, at the last minute, we heat some olive oil in a pan, put in the squid very briefly and take it off the heat the moment it turns opaque, so that we have a stark white piece of calamari to put on top of the black rice.

Sometimes, of course, you can get too carried away with trying to be artistic. Once when we were experimenting in the kitchen, I made a walnut and eggplant risotto and I decided to make some eggplant "chips" for a garnish. When I deep-fried the strips of eggplant, I thought they looked fantastic, but the other guys in the kitchen kept shaking their heads and saying they wouldn't work, because there is so much water content in eggplants, they wouldn't stay crisp. Naturally, the moment I put them on the hot risotto, they just drooped sadly – of course, everyone was standing behind me laughing. "Okay, guys, you were right."

Ideal proportions

The easy rule to remember for risotto is to use 2¼ cups stock for each ½ cup of rice – that is enough for a hearty bowlful for one person at home. In the restaurant, we are more likely to use a little less rice, because we will usually serve a more delicate-looking portion with a more elaborate garnish.

The cheese

For the mantecatura, we use grana cheese (grana just means "grainy"), either Parmigiano Reggiano (see next page) or the famous cheese of my region of Lombardia: Grana Padano. Amazingly, though Parmesan is the name everyone knows around the world, Grana Padano is the biggest-selling Italian cheese at home and abroad. Both cheeses belong to the same family of grana cheeses, and look very similar. The difference is that the wheels of Grana Padano are stamped with the diamond mark of the consortium and the number of the dairy and date of production within a four-leaved clover. Grana Padano was first made 1,000 years ago, by Cistercian monks, and originated either in Lodi or Codogno in my region of Lombardia. Now it has its own DOP, but unlike Parmigiano-Reggiano, which can be made only in a very small area, the production stretches over a vast area of the Po Valley, from Piemonte and Lombardia to Veneto, as far as Trento, and production is more industrial in scope.

While the cheeses are made in the same way, there are important differences. The grana cows have a less specialized diet, and though both cheeses are made with milk from two milkings, for Grana Padano the two are simply mixed together, without the evening milk going through the Parmigiano process of separation into cream and skimmed milk first.

Grana Padano is aged less than Parmesan and tends to be softer, moister, subtler and lighter tasting. If I want to eat a piece of cheese with a pear, nothing else, then I would want some aged Parmesan, but in cooking, the two cheeses are almost interchangeable, though I can tell you the difference with my eyes closed. I use Parmesan when I want more salinity, and if I want something a little more sweet-tasting, creamy and clean I choose Grana Padano, for example in a quail or saffron risotto.

Incidentally, there is also a third important cheese in the family, which is also seeking its own DOP: Trentingrana, which at the moment is certified by the Grana Padano Association, but has the word *Trentino* stamped into its rind. It is made high up in Trento, with milk from two collections in the same way as Parmigiano Reggiano, and the farmers still take the cows even further into the mountains to graze in summer, keeping them inside only in winter. The seasonal difference is quite dramatic, and in summer, when the cows produce less milk, production is halved. The cheese is also eaten younger than Parmesan or Grana Padano.

Parmigiano-Reggiano

Parmesan

"The king of Italian cheese"

Parmigiano-Reggiano, our wonderful cheese of the north, has the title of the king of Italian cheese, and it is – no question. You only have to put a few shavings of Parmesan over a dish and people say, "Oh how beautiful!" Not only does a wheel of Parmesan look magnificent but it is the biggest cheese in the world, weighing more than 30 kilograms (66 pounds) – and what other cheese enjoys such international celebrity?

Wherever Italians have settled in the world they have taken Parmesan with them. You could literally roll your Parmesan wheel down the street onto the boat and take it to Australia, because it traveled so well. Long before temperature-controlled trucks, Parmesan would still arrive at its destination in perfect condition. It took a little longer to get to Britain, though. When I first came to London, I was amazed to see that Parmesan came already grated, in little shakers. But the real thing is here now, so I am happy.

In Italy, the cheese is so important, they say that when your wife is pregnant, during the last few months you should give her Parmesan to eat, because it makes the milk for the baby more flavorsome. And in my region, when you eat Parmigiano-Reggiano, you never throw any of it away, so even the pieces of rind are collected, put into a bag, and then grilled for the kids to eat as a snack.

Italian food has been found to be high in umami, the fifth, "mouth-filling," "savory" taste that comes from the amino acid glutamic acid, which is found naturally in ripe or cured, aged and fermented foods, like tomatoes, mushrooms, salami – but most of all Parmesan. Interestingly, the body also produces glutamate, especially in breast milk, so it seems that Italians for centuries have instinctively understood the "wow" factor of Parmesan, and attempted to enhance our appetite for it, even from infancy.

When the Florentine writer and poet Giovanni Boccaccio began his epic collection of medieval Italian tales, *The Decameron*, in 1348, he talked of a place called Bengodi where there was a mountain made entirely of grated Parmesan, and those who lived there did nothing but make gnocchi, or macaroni, and ravioli, which they used to roll down the mountain, dusting them in the cheese as they went, so the people passing by could pick them up and eat them. Can you imagine? What a fantastic place to live.

Parmesan began to be really well known in Italy somewhere between A.D. 800 and 900; and later, as usual, we Italians influenced French cooking when the Duchess of Parma married a grandson of Louis XIV in the seventeenth century and introduced the cheese to French kitchens. In 1951 they first gave the name Parmigiano-Reggiano to the

cheese that is produced by a consortium of small artisanal cheese-makers in Emilia-Romagna; and since 1996 it has been designated as one of thirty DOP (Protected Designation of Origin) Italian cheeses. In order to carry the DOP mark, a cheese must be made in the provinces of Reggio Emilia and Parma (the original production areas), Modena, an area of Bologna on the left bank of the river Reno, or Mantova, on the right bank of the river Po.

There are around 600 of these small producers, called *caselli*. The word is one we also use for a toll that you pay when you enter a different zone on the highway. In Emilia-Romagna, though, it is used to refer to the fact that each producer makes best use of the different natural characteristics of his land to produce a cheese that is classically made, yet, like wine from a particular estate, it will also have its own individual character.

Each wheel of Parmigiano-Reggiano carries its own ID, printed on the rind, showing the code number of the dairy, the mark of the consortium (which guarantees strict standards) and then the month and year of production, so you can track your cheese all the way back to the beginning – who was the farmer? What was the milk like at that time of year? Everything can be found out.

How do you describe a good Parmesan? Well, the slightly oily rind can range in color from golden to brown and should be around ¼ inch thick. Inside, the color of the cheese can also vary from pale ivory to golden straw, but the flavor should always be quite intense, rich and slightly salty, and the texture should be fine-grained and crumbly – slightly moist when the cheese is young and drier when it is aged.

In Reggio-Emilia, where producers are recognized by code numbers under 1,000, and where many believe the finest, most classic cheese is made, you still find very small cheese makers, producing only 8 to 12 wheels of cheese a day, who still take their cows on the traditional climb up through the hills each summer so that they can graze on fresh mountain grasses and herbs (in winter they would eat hay and stay indoors in barns). We call this cheese Parmigiano di montagna.

However, many producers are now following a new feeding system called the *piatto unico*, a sort of "big dish" in which fresh grass and hay are balanced with vitamins, proteins, water, and so on. And instead of grazing outside in summer, most cows spend more time lazing in modern, roomy cowsheds, as the farmers believe that this gentler, more sedentary lifestyle produces richer, creamier milk, though the cheese still retains its seasonal nuances: drier and more crumbly in summer; richer and heavier in winter.

The cows are milked twice a day, in the morning and evening, and each batch of cheese is started off with the milk from the evening's milking. It is put into wide, shallow troughs, and the cream is allowed to rise to the surface. The next morning the cream is taken off and the skimmed milk that is left is mixed with the new whole milk from the morning's milking. Then it is put into vats and in order to start the fermenting process it is inoculated with enzymes, which come from the soured whey left over from making the previous batch of cheese.

Next, the milk is heated and calves' rennet is added. Once it has coagulated, the curd is cut into granules (which give the cheese its grainy texture), then heated again and finally transferred to molds in which it is left to drain for two or three days. After that, the cheese goes into a bath of brine for 24 more days to give it its saltiness.

Then the maturing process begins in huge cellars, with the enormous wheels of cheese stacked on racks high up into the ceiling for at least 12 months (when the cheese is known as *nuovo*), but it can be much longer, according to the quality of each individual cheese. They say that the prime age for Parmesan is at 24 months, when it is known as *vecchio* and is believed to be at the peak of its organoleptic properties (i.e., its appearance, smell, taste, feel, and so on). This is the age of the Parmesan that we use at Locanda for virtually everything in the kitchen. After that, as it matures, its flavors become more sophisticated, but it loses a lot of humidity and the texture becomes drier. Twenty-four months is considered a good age for eating the cheese just as it is (when it is over two years old, it is known as *stravecchio*), but you can keep Parmesan for up to three years, and very exceptionally four.

In Italy, especially in the countryside, where they have more space, a restaurant might buy six wheels of Parmesan at a time, so it can have a selection of cheeses of different ages. And it will serve the most special stravecchio at the end of the meal, with great ceremony at your table, using a special knife to scoop out the cheese from the center of the enormous wheel.

In London, though, the market for aged Parmesan is very small, and many cheese shops and restaurants think it is too expensive to bring in – but I don't care about the price because a fantastic three-year-old Parmigiano-Reggiano is one of the most beautiful things to have after lunch or dinner. We serve ours from the cheese trolley, with a little chutney, or some sliced pears, or just with a touch of 50-year-old balsamic vinegar – for me, these two ingredients, together with a wonderful prosciutto, just sum up the whole idea of what Emilia-Romagna is about.

Risotto alla lodigiana

Classic risotto with grana cheese

Made with a base of onions and chicken or vegetable stock, this is finished with Parmesan or Grana Padano, and butter. In our house, as in most houses in the region, grana was the cheese we used most in cooking, while Parmesan was kept for the table. It is the most straightforward risotto of all – the one that everyone in Italy cooks and that you are given as a child when you are sick. First some tips:

Chop the onions as finely as you can (the size of grains of rice); this is because you don't want the onion to be obvious in the finished risotto, and if you have large pieces, they will not cook through properly.

Grate the grana finely so it is quickly absorbed at the end of the process.

Make sure that your butter is very cold. Cut it into small, even-sized dice before you start cooking and put it into the fridge until you are ready to use it. That way it won't melt too quickly and it will emulsify rather than split the risotto.

Remember, the more rice you cook, the more heat it will retain, so it will take less time to cook.

10 cups good chicken stock
    (see page 264)
3½ tablespoons butter
1 onion, chopped very, very fine
    (see tip above)
2 cups superfino carnaroli rice
½ cup dry white wine
salt and pepper

For the mantecatura:
about 5 tablespoons cold butter,
    cut into small cubes
about 1 cup finely grated
    Grana Padano or
    Parmesan

Put the stock into a pan, bring it to a boil and then reduce the heat so that it is barely simmering.

Making the soffritto

Put a heavy-bottomed pan on the heat next to the one containing the hot stock, and put in the butter to melt. The choice of pan for risotto is important, as a heavy base will distribute heat evenly, preventing burning.

As the butter is melting, add the onion and cook very slowly for about 5 minutes, so that it softens and becomes translucent, losing the pungent onion flavor, but doesn't brown – otherwise it might add some burned flavor to the risotto and could also spoil its appearance with brown flecks.

I don't recommend that you add any salt at this point, because the stock that you will shortly be adding will reduce down, concentrating its flavor and saltiness. You will also be adding some salty grana at the end, so it is best to wait until all these flavors have been absorbed and then decide at the end whether you need any seasoning or not.

The tostatura – "toasting" the rice

Turn up the heat to medium, add the rice and stir, using a wooden spatula, until the grains are well covered in butter and onions, and heated through – again with no color. It is important to get the grains up to a hot temperature before adding the wine.

Add the wine and let it reduce and evaporate, continuing to stir, until the wine has virtually disappeared and the mixture is almost dry – that way you will lose the alcohol and tannins. If you don't let it reduce enough you will get a slightly bitter flavor of wine in the risotto.

Adding the stock

From this point to the end of the cooking, for this quantity of risotto, should take about 17 to 18 minutes (a minute or so less if you are doubling the quantity). Start to add the stock a ladleful at a time (each addition should be just enough to cover, but not drown, the rice), stirring and scraping the base and sides of the pan with your wooden spoon. Let each ladleful be almost absorbed before adding the next.

The idea is to keep the consistency runny at all times, never letting it dry out, and to keep the rice moving so that it cooks evenly (the base of the pan will obviously be the hottest place, and the grains that are there will cook quicker than the rest, unless you keep stirring them around). You will see the rice beginning to swell and become more shiny and translucent as the outer layer gradually releases its starch, beginning to bind the mixture together and make it creamy.

Keep the risotto bubbling steadily all the while as you continue adding stock, stirring and letting it absorb, before adding more again.

After about 15 minutes of doing this, start to test the rice. A word of warning: let it cool before you taste, as risotto retains the heat dramatically, like polenta, and you will burn your mouth if you don't wait for a moment. The rice is ready when it is plump and tender, but the center of the grain still has a slight firmness to the bite.

When you feel you are almost there, reduce the amount of stock you are adding, so that when the rice is ready, the consistency is not too runny but nice and moist, ready to absorb the butter and cheese at the next stage and loosen up some more. If it is too soupy at this point, once you add these ingredients the finished risotto will be sloppy, whereas if it is not quite wet enough, you can always rescue the situation by beating in a little extra hot stock to loosen it up at the end, after the mantecatura.

Resting

Take the pan off the heat and let the risotto rest for a minute without stirring. This slight cooling is important because you are about to add butter and cheese, and if you add these ingredients to piping-hot risotto, they will melt too quickly and the risotto may split. You see this sometimes in restaurants, where the grains of rice, instead of clinging together, seem to stick out, each surrounded by a little pool of oily liquid.

The mantecatura

Quickly beat in the cold butter cubes, then beat in the cheese, getting your whole body behind it, moving your beating hand as fast as you can, and shaking the pan with the other. You should hear a satisfying *thwock, thwock* sound as you work the ingredients in. The result should be a risotto that is creamy, rich and emulsified.

At this point, taste for seasoning and, if you like, add a grind of salt and pepper. Remember, though, that if your stock is strongly flavored, and once you have added the salty cheese, the risotto may not need any seasoning at all.

Serve the risotto as quickly as you can, as it will carry on cooking for a few minutes even as you transfer it to your serving bowls (shallow ones are best), and you want to enjoy it while it is at its creamiest.

If you have achieved the perfect consistency (all'onda), when you tilt the bowls the risotto should ripple like the waves of the sea.

Tartufi bianchi

White truffles

"A smell of people"

Ever since I was little, I have thought of white truffles as exciting and mysterious, and of course expensive. Our family wasn't rich, but every year we went with my granddad to the fair at Alba to buy the truffles and bring them home so my grandmother could cook a special meal from them – we went just for us, not even to buy truffles for the restaurant. It was an annual tradition; and I think a lot of families did the same thing. It was a fantastic place for a young boy to be. The big square was full of stalls, where the *trifolau* (truffle hunters) set out their weighing scales and their truffles, mysteriously wrapped up in cloths. You had to haggle with them and do deals over the price of the truffles, and often they would keep their biggest and most valuable ones hidden away, unveiling them with great ceremony only when they recognized a buyer with serious money to spend.

Now, during the short season (from the end of September to early December), we have customers who come in to the restaurant to eat truffles every day. I have always thought, though, that you shouldn't eat them twenty times, just two or three times in a year, because every time you taste a truffle it should be a special thing, and there should be plenty of it; a big, generous helping. Alexandre Dumas, who was a great lover of truffles (though, being French, he favored the black truffle of Périgord), wrote, "When I eat truffles, I become livelier, happier, I feel refreshed. I feel inside me, especially in my veins, a soft voluptuous heat that quickly reaches my head. My ideas are clearer and easier." He also believed that the first requirement for something to be a luxury is that you are not mean with it; it must be celebrated in abundance. In other words, true luxury is not snobbish, but three mean little slivers of truffle, now *that* is snobbish. I think that is exactly right.

The white truffle from the area around the ancient city of Alba Pompeia in Piemonte has become like the blue-and-white pottery of Delft in Holland: something famous and symbolic not only of its own region but of the entire country. The local name for it is the *trifola*, though its scientific name is *Tuber magnatum pico*, and it has been enthroned in our society since the days when the custom was that the biggest truffle would be presented to the King of Italy. Now we have no more kings, but the tradition in Alba has still been to present important visitors to the region, such as Marilyn Monroe, Mikhail Gorbachev or Gianni Agnelli, the president of Fiat, with a special truffle. The record so far was the one weighing 2 kilos and 520 grams (5½ pounds), which was given to President Truman in 1954.

The first time someone tastes a truffle, they often find it quite disappointing, even off-putting, because usually they have heard so much about them and they expect so much. Sometimes people say to me, "Oh, they smell of feet. Horrible!" It hurts me to hear it, but I understand. If life could be described in a smell, then it is the smell of truffles. They smell of people and sweat. They just remind me so much of human beings; that is why I love them. Also, I think, as you get older, you appreciate truffles more, I don't know why.

Other people have described truffles a bit more delicately than I do, as the perfect marriage between the flavors of garlic and Parmesan, but it is the smell that is released when a truffle is at body temperature, rather than the flavor, that is so powerful; it fills your nose and stays there for a long time. Scientists say that there is a volatile alcohol in truffles that has a very strong musky character related to testosterone, so maybe that is another reason for their attraction. Remember, though, that a truffle is at the peak of its powers for only around fifteen days – after that it begins dramatically to lose its aroma and flavor.

Because the truffle is such a unique thing, it is traditionally used very simply – shaved over a risotto made with grana cheese, or on top of pasta, beef carpaccio or eggs – so no other flavor can try to compete with it. In Piemontese restaurants during the season, they serve the traditional dish of *fonduta*, which was once the meal of local farmers but is now considered a luxury. Fontina cheese from Valle d'Aosta is heated with milk, egg yolks and butter until it is creamy, then some white truffle is shaved over the top, and you eat it with slices of toasted bread to dip in it.

The truffle hunt, like the mushroom hunt, is an exciting thing. For many people, especially city folk, it feels too harsh to go hunting for game – to go out with a gun and hack down an animal or bird and see it die – even fishing is something difficult for some people to accept. But if you go out with the dogs hunting for truffles you have all the same sensations: the waiting, searching, chasing, hiding from other truffle hunters – but without the pain. If you see a truffle, the joy and fulfillment is the same as coming across a deer, but there are no losers; no one has to give their blood or their life. Of course, it is a bit depressing when you spend five hours looking, and you find nothing. But you can always find a good restaurant nearby and have a portion of truffles to eat anyway.

In the old days, they thought that truffles were the result of lightning bolts hitting the ground close to trees, because they were such incredible, inexplicable treasures; and if anyone could find a way of cultivating white truffles they would make a fortune. Being such a profitable business – white truffles from Alba have fetched $125,000 for 1.2 kilos (2⅔ pounds) – it has been studied inside out. They say the last king of Italy, Umberto II, paid people to try to grow truffles, but they just took his money and kept spinning him stories, because nobody has ever come up with the solution.

Truffles are a wild fungus and for them to grow the ground must have certain properties. (What kind of soil the truffles grow in also decides their shape. Smooth truffles grow in soft soil; the lumpy, knotty truffles come from soil that is more compact.) Most of all, though, they need trees, because the way they grow is to absorb water, mineral salts and fibers from

the soil, through the roots of the trees. You can tell whether a truffle has grown close to oak, hazelnut, poplar, lime, willow or cherry – the trees the truffle favors – because each tree gives the fungus a slightly different character. (They say the harder the tree, for example oak, the more intense the smell of the truffle; so those that grow close to lime trees are lighter in aroma.) Really, the difference is incredible. Which is why, when we buy truffles, we examine them one by one, because you can have three collected by the same guy in Italy from the same place, yet one will have grown closer to a particular tree than the other, and each will be completely different: one dark, one light, one very, very pungent, another much softer.

People have tried inoculating the exposed roots of trees with spores from the truffles to try to grow more, with some success for black truffles, but not with the white truffle, which keeps its sense of mystery – where it grows has also to do with the microclimate and the phases of the moon. You can't be in Bournemouth and say, "Okay, I'm going to grow truffles," because if you look at some of the other places where truffles are historically found, like Albania, Romania or Yugoslavia, they are on the same parallel as Alba, with similar microclimates. In Italy, on that same parallel, all along the Appennino mountain range to Acqualagna in the Marche region, you can find fantastic white truffles – but because they don't come from Alba, people think they are not as good and they sell for a third of the price. There is nothing wrong with eastern European truffles, either, they just don't grow as big as the ones from Alba, or have the same mystique.

In the last 50 years, the Piemonte region has also maximized the production of its Barolo and Nebbiolo wines – and some of the original truffle ground is being given up to make space for the vines. So you might have a stretch of wood, then a space, then more wood, which affects the cross-insemination of the truffle spores by animals. So the quantity of truffles (both black and white) has come down, but the demand and the prices have gone up, which is a big problem for the truffle traders of Alba. Every year millions of people arrive from around the world for the truffle fairs, and if there are not enough truffles, the trifolau don't make their money.

So, if there are not enough truffles, what else can you do but bring some in from somewhere else? In one of the biggest stories to come out of Alba in recent years, a family with a 200-year history of dealing in truffles was found with a cache of 24 tons of black truffles from China.

Tartufi neri

Black truffles

If I were French, I might get more excited about black truffles. If you ask someone from Périgord what are the best truffles in the world, I doubt if he would say the white ones from Alba. Of course, I love black truffles too, but they don't have the intensity of flavor and smell of the white ones.

While white truffles smell of all human life, black truffles remind me of damp cellars. However, they are still in season when the white ones are finished (they begin in November and go on until March) and they come again in summer, though the winter ones are usually of a better quality.

Our customers love the magic of white truffles so much that I wouldn't serve black truffles over risotto or pasta, but at home I might. The exception is gnocchi, because black truffles have a particular earthy affinity with potatoes – they seem to bring out the best in each other – and because they are not as crazily expensive as the white ones, they are a way of giving a simple dish a sense of luxury.

Truffle oil

I love truffles, but I hate all the by-products – I would never buy truffles in brine, as they don't have the same flavor, and the thing I detest most is commercial truffle oil, which some people drizzle over everything. It invariably contains a chemical flavoring that messes up your taste buds and repeats on you. Fresh truffles begin to lose their intensity of scent and flavor quite quickly, so they are no good for oil that must be kept for months, which is why most manufacturers resort to artificial means.

At Locanda, we make our own truffle oil (though we don't use it for risotto), which has to be used within two or three days or it will lose its intensity. In the restaurant, it is inevitable that we end up with lots of small pieces of truffle. When someone pays a lot of money for white truffle to be grated over their pasta or risotto, you can't just bring a little piece to the table, it has to be a whole (or at least a half) truffle. So the pieces that are left over each day are chopped, crushed and then put into oil in a bottle, which we keep in a bath of warm water, so that the aroma and flavor stay powerful.

Preparing truffles

If, when you go to buy your truffles, you are allowed to take off a little skin and look at the inside, the truffle should be light to dark brown. If it is white or off-white, it is either not mature enough or it has been found in wet soil and taken in so much water that it has turned white. If you were to keep it in the fridge on a sheet of paper, it would mature a little more – but remember that everything else in the fridge might also smell of truffles, and every day you keep them, they lose moisture and weight.

You can buy truffles already cleaned, but if you need to clean them yourself, put some water into a bowl with an equal quantity of white wine, dip a small, soft brush into it and brush the truffle very lightly, then pat dry.

Risotto al tartufo bianco

White truffle risotto

Make the risotto as for Risotto alla lodigiana (see page 214). You need a white truffle and a teaspoon of white truffle butter, which you can buy at Italian delicatessens. At the final stage of the risotto – the mantecatura – add the truffle butter along with the grana. Serve the risotto in bowls and then shave the cleaned white truffle over it at the table with great ceremony. (See previous page for how to clean a truffle.) For the ultimate truffle risotto, put a truffle into your jar of rice for at least 24 hours before you want to make it, so that its wonderful aroma can infuse the rice.

Zafferano

Saffron

Saffron has been valued as a spice and a dye since Greek and Roman times. According to one legend, we have to thank the Greek god Hermes, the winged messenger, for saffron (he was also in charge of looking after olive trees, so he was a very useful god). One story is that he was throwing his discus when he hit his friend Crocus, who fell down dead on top of some flowers. To honor him, Hermes turned the stigmas of the flowers scarlet, and it is the stigmas of the species *Crocus sativus* that give us saffron.

Although saffron was used in Roman times, it may also have been introduced to my region of Lombardia by the Spanish when they invaded in the sixteenth century. And the Spanish may have been introduced to it through trade with the Arabs, who gave saffron its name of *zaffer*, the root of the Italian *zafferano*.

One of the reasons that saffron is considered so precious, and is so expensive, is that it takes around 50,000 flowers, which must be harvested by hand, and the stigmas dried, to give every pound of saffron. I spent three days in the village of La Mancha in Spain at harvesttime, and it was a beautiful sight: suddenly there were mountains of flowers everywhere – you wanted to jump into them. Seeing the pillows of flowers, and knowing what care and effort went into producing the spice was another reason why I called my first restaurant Zafferano.

However, it is quite fitting that Hermes was also supposed to be the god of thieves and commerce, because the high prices you can ask for saffron have often meant that people have tried to cheat, by mixing other spices into powdered saffron, like the cheaper turmeric, or safflower, which will add color but no flavor; or even by bulking up saffron threads with the dyed fibers of beet or pomegranate.

Risotto allo zafferano

Saffron risotto

The saffron risotto my grandmother used to cook is also known as risotto Milanese, and is famous in Lombardia. It is the only risotto of my region that is traditionally served alongside meat – with *osso buco* or *cotolette alla Milanese* – probably it was designed as a quick lunch for city businesspeople or factory workers who had no time to have first the risotto and then the meat course.

I don't know what it is about saffron and rice that make them work so well together, but they are natural partners that travel together around the world, from paella to risotto to saffron rice in Morocco, Iran and India.

This risotto follows the recipe for Risotto alla lodigiana, but is made richer by putting in some saffron threads with the first addition of stock – threads feel a little more luxurious, and keep better than saffron powder, which was all my grandmother had to use. Buy the best quality you can find – long threads are often an indication of good saffron.

Traditionally you would also add veal marrow to Risotto allo zafferano, which makes it very rich, but if you prefer not to use marrowbone, then you can make it without, as in the recipe that follows.

If you do want to make the risotto with marrowbone, for four people use five marrowbones. Rinse them first in cold running water for about an hour, then push out the marrow from inside. Preheat the oven to 375°F. Put the marrow from one of the bones in the risotto pan with the butter at the beginning of cooking, and smash it up with a fork, before adding the onions.

Lay the rest of the marrow on a baking tray and sprinkle it with a mixture of 4 tablespoons of bread crumbs and 4 tablespoons of grated Parmesan and, while the risotto is cooking on top of the stove, put the tray into the preheated oven for 4 to 5 minutes, until the mixture is golden on top. Drain off any excess fat from the marrow and then slice it and serve on top of the finished risotto.

Note: When we make the chicken stock for this risotto, we add a little tomato paste to the chicken bones when they are roasting (see page 264). This gives the stock a rosy color and will make the finished risotto look more vivid. Italians wouldn't normally do this – they would just boil up a whole chicken or a carcass, so they might just add a teaspoon of tomato passata to the risotto as they start to add the hot stock.

Bring your pot of stock to a boil next to where you are going to make your risotto, then turn down the heat to a bare simmer.

Melt the butter in a heavy-bottomed pan, and add the chopped onion. Cook gently until softened but not colored (about 5 minutes).

Add the rice and stir to coat it in the butter and "toast" the grains. Make sure they are all warm, then add the wine. Let it evaporate completely until the onion and rice are dry, then add the saffron. Start to add the stock, a ladleful or two at a time, stirring and scraping the rice in the pan as you do so. When each addition of stock has almost all evaporated, add the next ladleful.

Carry on cooking for about 15 to 17 minutes, adding stock continuously (if you like, you can add a teaspoon of tomato passata to bring up the color). After about 12 to 14 minutes, slow down the addition of stock, so that the rice doesn't become too wet and soupy, otherwise when you add the butter and Parmesan at the end, it will become sloppy. The risotto is ready when the grains are soft but still al dente. Turn down the heat and allow the risotto to rest for a minute.

For the mantecatura, with a wooden spoon, vigorously beat in the cold butter cubes and finally the cheese, making sure you shake the pan energetically at the same time as you beat. Season to taste and serve.

10 cups good chicken stock
     (see page 264)
3½ tablespoons butter
1 onion, chopped very,
     very finely
2 cups superfino carnaroli rice
½ cup dry white wine
about 40 good-quality saffron
     threads (look for long ones)
1 teaspoon tomato passata
     (optional, see note on
     page 226)

For the mantecatura:
about 5 tablespoons cold butter,
     cut into small cubes
about 1 cup finely grated Grana
     Padano or Parmesan
salt and pepper

Risotto agli asparagi

Asparagus risotto

For this risotto, we use every part of the asparagus – the tender spears go into the risotto itself and the peelings and woody stems are made into the simple stock. There is also more onion than usual because, as well as using it for the base of the risotto, we cook the asparagus stalks separately with onion.

12 asparagus spears
7 tablespoons butter
2 onions, chopped very,
    very fine
2 cups vialone nano rice
½ cup dry white wine
salt and pepper

For the stock:
3 tablespoons olive oil
4 onions, diced

For the mantecatura:
about 5 tablespoons cold butter,
    cut into small cubes
about 1 cup finely grated
    Parmesan

First prepare the asparagus: wash, then peel each spear below the tip and keep the peelings. Cut off the tips, then trim off the woody part of the stem (keep these back also and crush lightly with the back of a kitchen knife). You should now have three different mounds of asparagus: the tips, the tender spears, and the crushed woody ends and peelings.

To make the stock, heat the olive oil in a deep pan, add the diced onions and sweat them until soft but not colored. Add the asparagus trimmings and the crushed woody stems, cover (to keep in the moisture) and cook for another 5 to 6 minutes.

Cover the mixture completely with about 10 cups cold water, bring to a boil, then turn the heat down and simmer for about 20 minutes.

Remove from the heat and put through a fine sieve, squeezing and pressing the vegetables, to get all the flavor into the stock. Reserve for later.

While the stock is cooking, dice the asparagus spears, reserving the tips.

Heat 3½ tablespoons of the butter in a pan, add one of the chopped onions and cook gently until soft but not colored. Add the diced asparagus, cover and cook for 7 to 8 minutes.

Put 2 tablespoons of the cooked asparagus into a food processor and pulse into a puree, then mix in the rest of the cooked asparagus. Season and keep to one side.

Now you are ready to start the risotto. Return the stock to the heat close to where you are going to make your risotto. Bring it to a boil, then turn the heat down to a bare simmer.

Melt the remaining butter in a heavy-bottomed pan and add the other chopped onion. Cook gently until softened but not colored (about 5 minutes). Add the rice and stir around to coat in the butter and "toast" the grains. Make sure all the grains are warm, then

add the wine. Let the wine evaporate completely until the onion and rice are dry.

Start to add the stock, one or two ladlefuls at a time, stirring and scraping the rice in the pan as you do so. When each addition of stock has almost all evaporated, add the next ladleful.

After about 10 minutes, add the reserved asparagus mixture and bring the risotto back up to temperature. Carry on cooking for another 5 to 6 minutes until the grains are soft, but still al dente, adding more stock as necessary. Remember, you don't want the risotto to be soupy when you add the butter and Parmesan, or it will become sloppy.

Blanch the reserved asparagus tips for about a minute in the stock, remove with a slotted spoon, set aside and season.

When the risotto is ready, turn down the heat and allow the risotto to rest for a minute; then, for the mantecatura, using a wooden spoon, vigorously beat in the cold butter cubes and finally the Parmesan, making sure you shake the pan energetically at the same time as you beat. Season to taste and garnish with the asparagus tips.

Risotto alle ortiche

Nettle risotto

This is a spring risotto – for when the nettles are growing everywhere. Food for free. Just remember to handle the nettles with gloves, or avoid touching the stalks, which are the part with the sting. In the restaurant, we garnish this risotto with deep-fried nettle leaves.

2 handfuls of young
    nettle leaves
10 cups good vegetable stock
    (see page 268)
3½ tablespoons butter
1 onion, chopped very, very fine
2 cups vialone nano rice
½ cup dry white wine
salt and pepper

For the mantecatura:
about 5 tablespoons cold butter,
    cut into small cubes
about 1 cup finely grated
    Parmesan

Blanch the nettles in boiling salted water for 30 seconds, drain and put into a food processor. Pulse to a puree, adding a little water if the mixture isn't moist enough.

Bring the pot of stock to a boil close to where you are going to make the risotto, then turn the heat down to a bare simmer.

Melt the butter in a heavy-bottomed pan, and add the chopped onion. Cook gently until softened but not colored (about 5 minutes).

Add the rice and stir it around to coat it in the butter and "toast" the grains. Make sure all the grains are warm, then add the wine. Let the wine evaporate completely until the onion and rice are dry.

Start to add the stock, a ladleful or two at a time, stirring and scraping the rice in the pan as you do so. When each addition of stock has almost evaporated, add the next ladleful.

Carry on cooking for about 15 to 17 minutes, adding the stock continuously in this way. After about 10 minutes, add the nettle puree and bring the risotto back up to temperature. Carry on cooking for another 5 to 6 minutes until the rice grains are soft but still al dente, adding more stock as necessary. The risotto shouldn't be too soupy when you add the butter and Parmesan at the end, or it will become sloppy. The risotto is ready when the grains are soft but still al dente.

Turn down the heat, to allow the risotto to rest for a minute; then, for the mantecatura, using a wooden spoon, vigorously beat in the cold butter cubes and finally the Parmesan, making sure you shake the pan energetically at the same time as you beat. Season to taste and serve.

Porcini

"You never heard a mushroom scream"

For me it is very romantic when the first porcini come into the kitchen. Porcini herald the start of autumn, that season that is so wistful but also so dramatic and operatic in its colors and its mood. In the city, you get so little sense of the influence of the seasons. The weather turns cold so you put on a hat and a scarf, or it gets hot so you wear a T-shirt, and that's it. In the country, the shift of seasons means so much more. In spring and summer, even when you are eating fish and grilling vegetables outside, you are already thinking ahead to preserving vegetables for the autumn and winter; when the tomatoes are plentiful, you make big jars of passata for later. Autumn signals the beginning of the season of warming stews and risotti; it is a time when you smell the fires being lit; a less busy season, when you go through a kind of quietness in preparation for the snow and ice of winter. Above all, it is the time when you get the best food for nothing. Besides the wild mushrooms *(funghi)*, you have chestnuts, and game … but nothing represents that generous idea of free food for everyone more than porcini.

Growing up in Lombardia, you have a kind of mythological admiration for the mountain people and shepherds, who are completely at ease and in tune with nature and always know where to find wild food. There is something a little mystical about these guys. They usually don't talk too much and often seem a little weird, but there is a magic in the way they always know where to find the biggest mushrooms or the best fish. There was a man called Mauro, a woodcutter, who lived near our village, who would check by the moon which were the best days for mushrooms and then he would be up and out at four o'clock in the morning. He knew that the mushrooms that grew near the pine trees, underneath all the needles that the tree had shed, would have dark caps and be white underneath, and the ones that grew near the chestnuts would be solid, with dark brown caps and slightly more yellow underneath. He knew how the flavor would depend on the water and mineral content of the ground – the ones near pine, because they had less water, would have a very concentrated flavor; he knew everything … Sometimes he would let us kids go out with him, which was such a privilege. At ten years old, I wanted to be a man of the mountains, like Mauro.

The joy of finding wild mushrooms, as with finding truffles, is similar to the excitement you feel when you hunt or fish, but without the suffering of any creature. You never heard a mushroom scream. Antonio Carluccio told me that after the former Russian leader Mikhail Gorbachev, who is passionate about mushrooms, ate in his restaurant, he sent him a copy of his book. Gorbachev wrote back to thank him, and he talked about "the quiet hunt," which is the way the Russians describe searching for mushrooms. I love that description.

No one I know ever got rich picking mushrooms, but you could make some kind of living selling them. Near my house, in the season, you would come across women or young girls sitting by the side of the road with a few boxes of porcini, picked that morning – and if you were driving it was fantastic to put them in the car and travel with that beautiful smell wrapping around you. It's not something you can easily describe; let's just say it is a benchmark smell – sweet, strong, distinctive, like woodland.

The name porcini comes from *porcinus*, which means "like a pig" *(porcus)*, perhaps because the mushrooms are fat, like little pigs, though the official Latin name is *Boletus edulis*. In England, porcini were known as penny buns, but these days most people know them by their French name, ceps. Now in northern Italy, like everywhere, they eat lots of different varieties of wild mushroom, and in our kitchen we often serve a mixture, but for me, though other mushrooms can be beautiful, they don't capture that flavor of the wild in quite the same way. When I was young, the only mushrooms anyone hunted for seriously were porcini, though sometimes we would take the tiny *chiodini*, which taste slightly bitter, like chanterelles. (*Chiodo* is the word for nail, and they were shaped like very tiny nails.) My grandmother used to preserve them under vinegar to serve with salami.

If we saw the Milanese arriving from the city to pick field mushrooms, we laughed because none of us locals ever ate them. There were morels too, but we had no interest in them either. I remember when I went to Paris, the chefs in the kitchens became so excited when the first morels of the season arrived, and we sold them in the restaurant for $70 a portion. I looked at them, and thought, "I have been kicking those around the woods for 20 years."

Now the people come from the city to the woods around Corgeno for the porcini too. In the season, the moment the weekend arrives you see the cars with the Milano license plates parked all over the verges and people swarming all over the mountains. Sometimes things can get a bit crazy – it has been known for people to come back to their car and find it gone, or the tires punctured, because they were on someone else's "patch." I don't like the idea of that, because the food of nature is for everybody, and that is what I love about it. The mushrooms are there to be picked – as long as people respect the woods. You mustn't use rakes or instruments, just the naked eye. Although you must be careful when you put your hand down because there are sometimes small vipers in the undergrowth.

That's not to say it isn't a competitive business, just that the local people have a quieter way of doing things. Fishermen will always say: "I caught a fish this big!" and every time they tell the story the fish gets bigger, but the people who hunt mushrooms are completely different. You have to be more secretive. Because the mushroom spores develop underground, porcini usually grow in families. Occasionally it is possible to find just one mushroom, but it is unusual – if you spot one, there will usually be more. As kids, we knew the rule that you never scream out if you see a porcino. You must look around to see that no one else is there, before you say, "I've got one," otherwise someone will come and find the mushrooms next to yours.

Almost every day during the season, my granddad took my brother, Roberto, and me up into the woods to look for mushrooms and he always brought two baskets (you must always use woven baskets when you pick mushrooms, so that they are kept nice and airy and the spores can fall through, back to the earth to reseed). He would put just a few mushrooms into one of the baskets, and the other one would be full. Then, if he saw someone coming, he would hide the full one and say, "Naah, nothing much around here, really bad; look, this is all I have…"

The biggest mushroom we ever found was massive – about 2 pounds. Of course, Roberto and I argued all the way home saying, "I found it!," "No, you didn't – I saw it first!," with my granddad telling us, "Okay, okay! Just don't break the mushroom!" We came hurtling down the mountain and started to shout to my grandmother, "Look at this mushroom!" We got to the road by our house and, I don't remember whose fault it was, but in our huge excitement we fell over each other and this fantastic porcino broke into a hundred pieces.

Now I love to go mushroom hunting with my own kids, just roaming around – such a healthy pastime – and in these days when we are not used to getting anything for nothing, it is good for them to see what nature can offer. Of course, the most important thing is to remind everybody that you don't eat anything if you don't know what it is. There was a story that used to be told in our village about a man who lived not far away from us, who was said to have killed three of his wives with poisonous mushrooms. Whenever anybody came into the bar next to our hotel and said he had had a fight with his wife, the joke used to be "Mushrooms for dinner tonight!"

Mushrooms grow all over Italy, right down to Sicilia, but their flavor is determined by the different types of woodland and the local climate. As always in Italian cooking, recipes grow up around produce that is grown or raised in the same region. So at home in Corgeno we mostly had mushrooms in risotto, or with pasta, though sometimes my grandmother made a beef stew with red wine and mushrooms, which had a flavor I can still taste. We used to eat it with polenta. Polenta, rice, pasta – all these starchy ingredients seem to go really well with the flavor and texture of porcini. One of my favorite dishes that we serve in the restaurant is new potato ravioli with wild mushroom sauce – fantastic.

Sometimes I see mushrooms being served as a side dish for a main course, which always seems strange to me. In Italy, if you have mushrooms, they are a main part of a meal or the antipasto – not an accessory.

For me, one of the best things about porcini is their slightly slimy texture, which amazes me every time – it seems to be a completely new experience for the mouth. How many foods, except for oysters, have that strange texture, and yet eating them is a pleasant experience? Smell and texture, these are what make porcini special. In a strange way, their distinctive nutty flavor, fantastic though it is, is almost secondary.

I always think that when you cook porcini, it is best to keep the flavors really simple – exaggerate the taste of the mushroom, rather than complicate things with too many other ingredients – and be careful not to overseason them, especially with salt, because they are very receptive to flavors and will take in anything you offer them.

Where I come from in Italy, you would never mix sea and mountain, so I don't like to eat mushrooms with fish – mushrooms, cheese and fish are three things that I don't think go well together. However, if you travel not too far away, to Liguria, you find a lot of mushrooms growing up in the mountains close to the sea, and there you do find *mari e monti* (sea and mountain) recipes; and they are also becoming more common in contemporary Italian cooking.

In the north, we cook porcini simply in butter with parsley and garlic and some white wine. Garlic is a great enhancer of the flavor of porcini. I also like to put a little chile pepper with them, or a squeeze of lemon juice, and I prefer to cook mushrooms in butter rather than oil, because, again, I think it brings out their flavor, whereas if you use a flavorful oil, especially a piquant Tuscan one, that is all you taste.

In the south, where tomatoes are so plentiful, they cook mushrooms with tomatoes, which is something we would never do in the north, but, if it is done well, the acidity from the tomato can really help bring out the sweetness of the mushrooms.

I must admit that one of the most beautiful, really simple plates of pasta and mushrooms I ever had was in Val Varaita, in the north of Italy, made for me by some people from the south. They just cooked the mushrooms in a little oil with some wine, let it reduce, then chopped in some wonderful fresh tomatoes, covered the pan and let everything simmer for about 10 to 20 minutes to reduce the sauce some more, then tossed some tagliatelle through it, and it was fantastic.

Until I left Italy, I never saw mushrooms cooked harshly in a sauté pan, so you get that crisp brown caramelized outside that chefs in France and England like. In Italy, we always cooked the porcini gently in the butter and garlic, letting the mushrooms "dissolve," without browning. Porcini don't contain as much water as we think; they have quite a lot of fiber and cooking slowly like this really accentuates the flavor. When I worked for Corrado Sironi, the Risotto King, we used to cook big potfuls of them, with a piece of lemon peel put in as well. In our kitchen now, we use both methods, but I always have to show the new boys in the kitchen how to cook porcini slowly, because it isn't the fashion in most kitchens.

In Italy, most people have a jar of porcini preserved under oil to serve as an antipasto, and a jar of dried porcini to use in risotto. I never saw porcini wasted at home – even the smaller, harder ones that we sometimes found, usually under the pine trees, where the sun couldn't reach and the ground was completely dry. When we brought our baskets

home, the softer, more mature mushrooms would be cooked straight away, and the harder ones would be either preserved or dried.

To preserve them, my grandmother used to bring to a boil a pan of about three parts water to one part vinegar with some salt, then she would put in the mushrooms, blanch them briefly, drain them, let them cool down, dry them, then put them into a sterilized jar and cover them with olive oil. Some people put in juniper berries or bay or rosemary, too. Preserved mushrooms were never used in cooking; just to serve with plates of salami – with chopped garlic and parsley sprinkled over the top. If I put mushrooms under oil now, I usually use chanterelles (see page 86),

which appeal to more people, because porcini done in this way are definitely an acquired taste, a little slimy, like oysters, but I love them. For me, some porcini under oil, with artichokes preserved in a similar way, and cured meats, make a great starter – you don't need anything more.

If you want to dry porcini, just slice them about ½ inch thick, lay them on some cheesecloth, and leave them somewhere warm and dry, turning them quite regularly, until all the moisture has gone. (My granddad used to take some slats of wood, lay them on the floor in some sunlight, with some cheesecloth over them, then put the porcini on top.) When they are completely dry, store them in an airtight jar. Then, if you make a wild mushroom risotto (see page 240), you can use dried porcini in the base and sauté some fresh ones for the garnish. Even if you don't have any fresh porcini, you can still make a fantastic risotto by putting some dried ones in with the onions at the beginning of cooking, then just sauté some field mushrooms with parsley and garlic, and pile them on top.

Sometimes in the restaurant we make a light pasta sauce: a classic beurre blanc with shallots, vinegar and white wine. We reduce it down, then add some sautéed dried porcini (soaked in water for 2 hours) and beat in a little cream and butter – people say it has a very special flavor.

Buying and preparing porcini

When you choose fresh porcini, the *cappella* (the cap) should be firm, not soggy. Never keep porcini in plastic bags or use plastic bags when you are out picking mushrooms because they need air to circulate around them, otherwise they will become sweaty and go off more quickly. I would keep them in a cold place, like a pantry, rather than in the fridge, otherwise they lose their aroma. Sometimes you find perfect mushrooms in the shops, which may have a little bit of *muffa* (mold) on the surface, which you have to take off, but a little is okay. You will know when the mushrooms are no longer usable, because they have a distinctive, horrible, dank smell.

Never wash the porcini – never. The mushrooms will absorb the water and become soggy and lose their flavor. Just take a little flexible knife, if you really want to, and scrape it over the mushrooms, and then just before you cook them, go over the mushrooms with a damp cloth, then dry them. Usually it is best to cut them right through the middle to check that there are no worms. Sometimes also, a spore might have been touching a stone and the mushroom will have grown around it – in our restaurant that could be a big problem, because if someone bites into a mushroom in a risotto and breaks their teeth, we are in court. So be careful – as you slice your mushrooms, just check for any small pieces of stone or grit.

If you think the mushrooms won't last long, just chop them, sauté them in a little olive oil, let them cool down and put them in the freezer. Then, when you need them, you can cook them quickly over really high heat, in a little more oil or butter, with some garlic and parsley, and serve them with pasta.

Risotto ai porcini

Porcini risotto

You can do this with other fresh wild mushrooms if you can't find any fresh porcini – but you will still need the dried ones to give the risotto its depth of flavor. If you want to make the risotto look especially beautiful, you can keep some of the sautéed porcini aside and use them as a garnish at the end.

about 8 slivers of dried porcini
    (ceps), coarsely chopped
½ pound fresh porcini
    (see page 239
    for preparation)
5 tablespoons butter
2 garlic cloves, finely chopped
⅔ cup dry white wine
10 cups good chicken stock
    (see page 264) or vegetable
    stock (see page 268)
1 onion, chopped very, very fine
2 cups vialone nano rice
2 tablespoons chopped parsley
salt and pepper

For the mantecatura:
about 5 tablespoons cold butter,
    cut into small cubes
about 1 cup finely grated
    Parmesan

Soak the dried porcini in a bowl of water for a couple of hours until soft. During this time, any grit will have sunk to the bottom of the bowl. Gently lift the porcini out of the water and squeeze them, as the water will be quite pungent, so you don't want it to go into the risotto. Some people do like to add this to the risotto, but I find it too bitter.

Prepare the fresh porcini (see page 239) and slice them lengthwise.

Heat 2 tablespoons of the butter in a sauté pan over a low heat, add the garlic and cook until soft but not colored (it needs to be soft, or the finished risotto will have pieces of uncooked garlic that will be difficult to digest). Add the sliced fresh porcini with 2 tablespoons of the wine, keeping the heat low, and toss around for about a minute, making sure you "stew" rather than fry the mushrooms, so that they almost "melt" into the risotto and give it its characteristic brownish color. Season, cover with a lid and set aside while you make the risotto.

Bring your stock to a boil close to where you are going to make your risotto, then turn down the heat to a bare simmer.

Melt the rest of the butter in a heavy-bottomed pan and add the onion. Cook gently until soft but not colored (about 5 minutes).

Add the dried porcini, then the rice and stir to coat in the butter and "toast" the grains. Make sure all the grains are warm, add the remaining wine and let it evaporate completely so the onion and rice are dry.

Start to add the stock, a ladleful or two at a time, stirring and scraping the rice in the pan as you do so. When each addition of stock has almost evaporated, add the next ladleful. Carry on cooking for about 15 to 17 minutes, adding stock continuously as above. Remember, you don't want the risotto to be soupy when you add the butter and Parmesan at the end, or it will become sloppy. The risotto is ready when the grains are soft but still al dente.

Turn down the heat and add the reserved fresh porcini and the chopped parsley. Allow the risotto to rest for a minute; then, for the mantecatura, with a wooden spoon, vigorously beat in the cold butter cubes and finally the Parmesan – making sure you shake the pan energetically at the same time as you beat. Season to taste and serve.

Risotto ai carciofi

Artichoke risotto

The best time to make this is from February to April or May, when the Italian spiky baby artichokes with long stalks are in season.

about 10 baby artichokes
10 cups good chicken stock
    (see page 264)
a little lemon juice
3½ tablespoons butter
1 onion, chopped very, very fine
2 cups superfino carnaroli rice
½ cup dry white wine
2 tablespoons chopped parsley
salt and pepper

For the mantecatura:
about 5 tablespoons cold butter,
    cut into small cubes
about 1 cup finely grated
    Parmesan

Cut the stalks from the artichokes, leaving about 1¼ inches below the bulb.

Peel the stalks and crush with the blade of a kitchen knife. Put the stalks into a pan with the chicken stock. Bring to a boil, then turn down the heat and simmer until you are ready to make the risotto – just long enough to infuse the artichoke flavors into the stock.

Snap off the outer leaves of the artichoke until you reach the tender part, then trim about ¾ inch off the tops.

Cut the artichokes in half lengthwise, scoop out the chokes, then chop the hearts quite finely lengthwise. Keep in a bowl of water, with a few drops of lemon juice squeezed into it to preserve the color.

Now you are ready to start the risotto. Make sure your pan of barely simmering stock is close to where you are going to make your risotto. Melt the butter in a heavy-bottomed pan and add the onion. Cook gently until softened but not colored (about 5 minutes).

Add the rice and stir around to coat in the butter and "toast" the grains. Make sure all the grains are warm before adding the wine. Let the wine evaporate completely until the onion and rice are dry.

Start to add the stock, a ladleful or two at a time, stirring and scraping the rice in the pan as you do so. When each addition of stock has almost evaporated, add the next ladleful. Continue cooking for about 15 to 17 minutes, adding stock continuously as above.

After about 11 to 12 minutes, squeeze the artichokes to remove any excess water, season with a little salt and pepper and add to the risotto. Continue adding stock, but slowly toward the end, so that the rice doesn't become too wet. Remember, you don't want it to be soupy at this stage, otherwise when you add the butter and Parmesan at the end, it will become sloppy. The risotto is ready when the grains are soft but still al dente.

Turn down the heat and allow the risotto to rest for a minute; then, for the mantecatura, with a wooden spoon, vigorously beat in the cold butter cubes and finally the Parmesan, making sure you shake the pan energetically at the same time as you beat. Season to taste, mix in the chopped parsley and serve.

Risotto alla zucca e noce moscata

Pumpkin and nutmeg risotto

This reminds me of a rather disastrous night when a bunch of journalists came into the restaurant kitchen to cook pumpkin risotto for the charity Action Against Hunger – hopefully you can do a better job. They managed to overcook the rice, then added too much stock at the end, so the whole thing was too wet. So remember what I always say about cooking the rice until it is just al dente, and then slowing up the addition of the stock toward the end of cooking, because, after the mantecatura, you can always loosen your risotto. If it is too wet, there is nothing you can do to rescue it. Preferably use the big, bright orangey-red pumpkins from Mantova in the northeast (in season between October and January), which are really rich in flavor. If you can't find them, use the sweetest orange ones you can find, or in season butternut squash (September to December). My favourite pumpkin is Rossa Piacentina, which is available in some supermarkets.

Soak the pumpkin in milk for up to 12 hours (somehow the milk seems to act as a catalyst and helps the pumpkin cook better), and drain just before you start making the risotto.

Bring the stock to a boil in a pan next to where you are going to make your risotto, then turn down the heat to a bare simmer.

Melt the butter in a heavy-bottomed pan, and add the onion and half the drained soaked pumpkin. Cook gently until the onions are softened but not colored (about 5 minutes).

Add the rice and stir around to coat in the butter and "toast" the grains. Make sure all the grains are warm before adding the wine. Let the wine evaporate completely until the onions and rice are dry.

Start to add the stock, a ladleful or two at a time, stirring and scraping the rice in the pan as you do so. When each addition of stock has almost evaporated, add the next ladleful. Continue cooking for about 15 to 17 minutes, adding stock continuously as above.

After about 11 to 12 minutes, add the rest of the pumpkin. Continue adding stock, but slowly toward the end, so that the rice doesn't become too wet and soupy, otherwise when you add the butter and Parmesan at the end, it will become sloppy. The risotto is ready when the grains are soft but still al dente.

Turn down the heat and allow the risotto to rest for a minute; then, for the mantecatura, using a wooden spoon, vigorously beat in the cold butter cubes and finally the Parmesan, making sure you shake the pan energetically at the same time as you beat. Season and add nutmeg to taste, then serve.

about 2 cups pumpkin flesh, cubed
about 2 cups milk
10 cups good chicken stock (see page 264)
3½ tablespoons butter
1 onion, chopped very, very fine
2 cups superfino carnaroli rice
½ cup dry white wine
grating of nutmeg to taste
salt and pepper

For the mantecatura:
about 5 tablespoons cold butter, cut into small cubes
about 1 cup finely grated Parmesan

Risotto al Barolo e Castelmagno

Risotto with Barolo wine and Castelmagno cheese

Whenever I go home to Corgeno, they call me up from La Cinzianella, my uncle's restaurant, if the cheese man calls by. This is a man who travels all around the hills in his van, picking up his produce from the small dairies and selling it to the local restaurants. He knows everything about the cheese: who made it and how, the names of the cows that gave the milk and what kind of grasses and herbs they have been eating. Over the years he has shown me all sorts of cheeses, but the one I loved most the first time I tasted it was Castelmagno, which is like a small, young, semihard Parmesan, with a similar texture and a salty flavor. Only a limited number of cheeses are made from a mixture of cow's, goat's and sheep's milk, up in the Cuneo mountains in Piemonte, where they are aged in humid conditions, so they grow thick brown rinds, and sometimes after about six to eight months blue-green veins appear, running through the white cheese.

They have been making Castelmagno since the twelfth century, so it is as old as Gorgonzola, and it is supposed to take its name from a sanctuary dedicated to St. Magnus, a Roman soldier, who was killed in the mountains and became a martyr.

One time I was at the restaurant when the guy who delivers the cheeses brought in the Castelmagno, and the chef made a radicchio risotto, which is an old family favorite. On this occasion, though, instead of adding white wine in the early stages of the risotto, he used some red Barolo wine, from the same region as the Castelmagno; then for the mantecatura at the end, in place of the Parmesan, he added some grated Castelmagno. Finally, when the risotto was made, he took a silver spoon from a pan of boiling water and poured some more of this fantastic aged Barolo into it to warm up a little. When the risotto was on the plate, he balanced the spoon on top, so that you could tip it over the rice, letting the red wine drizzle over the risotto – it was a beautiful dish; truly beautiful, and I brought the idea back with me to London.

For this dish, we use a little more wine than is usual in risotto, because the risotto really depends on the Barolo to flavor and color it, and also we need some extra for the ceremony when we serve it. What we do at Locanda is make a small well in the top of the risotto, then, at the table, one waiter pours in the Barolo, while another shaves the Castelmagno over the top.

The Castelmagno that we buy is made by a family that lives high up in the mountains, where it is so wild it feels as if they are making cheese at the end of the world. Riccardo's father was a shepherd and so poor that from November to April he would leave his family in the mountains and walk to Paris and shine shoes to make some money. Riccardo and his wife don't even speak Italian, only dialect, and when they had their first child, he was the first to be born in the village (an hour's drive down the mountain) for 18 years. When it snows, if his wife has taken the children to school in the village, it is sometimes two days before they can get back home. Theirs is the other side of the story of EC certification of cheese, aimed at safeguarding and promoting regional foods by giving them the DOP (Protected Designation of Origin) and the stamp *(bollino)* of a local *consorzio*, which follows strict rules. Though I am happy that there are such laws, sometimes there are casualties among the smallest families, who have been making cheese in a very small artisanal way for generations but cannot satisfy the demands of the EC for modern milking sheds and updated, sanitized equipment.

Riccardo keeps only 25 cows, which graze on the wild grasses and herbs of the mountains in the summer and, in winter, come into sheds beneath his living room, eating hay from the grass he cuts himself. He is up at four every morning, his family's life is very hard, and, until he found a market selling cheese to people like us, he made very little money. At one point, because he couldn't meet the EC requirements for modern cowsheds, they confiscated his cheese, worth thousands of pounds. So some of us, who applaud what he is doing, grouped together to help him through the difficult times, and now, hopefully, he can earn the DOP cross of Castelmagno and earn a living, and his cheeses will not be lost to the world.

Note: if you want to make this risotto with radicchio as well, you need about one head of radicchio, very finely chopped. Add half of it with the onion at the beginning of cooking, and the rest when you beat in the Castelmagno cheese at the end.

10 cups good chicken stock
    (see page 264)
3½ tablespoons butter
1 onion, chopped very, very fine
2 cups vialone nano rice
¾ cup Barolo wine, plus a little
    extra for serving (optional)
salt and pepper

For the mantecatura:
about 5 tablespoons cold butter,
    cut into small cubes
about 1 cup finely grated
    Castelmagno cheese
    (plus a little extra for
    serving, if you like)

Bring your pot of stock to a boil close to where you are going to make your risotto, then turn down the heat to a bare simmer.

Melt the butter in a heavy-bottomed pan and add the chopped onion. Cook gently until softened but not colored (about 5 minutes).

Add the rice and stir around to coat in the butter and "toast" the rice. Make sure all the grains are warm, then add the Barolo. Let the wine evaporate completely until the onion and rice are dry.

Start to add the stock, a ladleful or two at a time, stirring and scraping the rice in the pan as you do so. When each addition of stock has almost evaporated, add the next ladleful. If the color of the risotto isn't as intensely pinky-red as you would like, add a little more wine.

Carry on cooking for about 15 to 17 minutes, adding stock continuously as above. After about 12 to 14 minutes, slow the addition of stock, so that the rice doesn't become too wet and soupy at this stage, otherwise when you add the butter and Castelmagno at the end, it will become sloppy. The risotto is ready when the grains are soft but still al dente.

Turn down the heat and allow the risotto to rest for a minute; then, for the mantecatura, using a wooden spoon, vigorously beat in the cold butter cubes and finally the Castelmagno, making sure you shake the pan energetically at the same time as you beat. Season to taste.

If you like, have some spoons warming in a pan of boiling water, then pour in a little Barolo and rest a spoon on top of each plate of risotto, so that everyone can pour the warm wine over the rice. Alternatively, do what we do at the restaurant, and make a little well in each plate of risotto; then, at the table, pour in the wine and grate some more Castelmagno over the top.

Seafood risotti

There is a basic pattern to making these risotti, which involves using the seafood shells to make a simple stock. Often when people give recipes for risotto they say to use "fish stock," but we usually prefer to make the stock from the main ingredient; that way if you are making a clam risotto, it will really taste of clams, the same with prawns, etc. You have the shells anyway – otherwise, what are you going to do with them, throw them away? For the sake of 20 minutes or so cooking them with maybe a little garlic and chiles or a few vegetables or herbs in some water, you can make a risotto that will be outstanding.

The other difference between these risotti and the ones that have gone before is that Italians *never* put seafood and cheese together (occasionally, though, a customer will come into the restaurant and ask for Parmesan on a fish dish – and of course we don't throw them out). I have to admit that, for some of our starters, I occasionally break the rule myself – but in a risotto, never. So, for these recipes, the mantecatura is done with just butter, and no cheese.

Sometimes we also use a little garlic oil to bring out the flavor of the seafood even more. (We steep the garlic we are going to use for the risotto in olive oil for a little while before we use it, then the oil is drizzled over the risotto at the end.) And we often finish with a touch of lemon juice and parsley.

More than any other type, seafood risotti should be all'onda – that is, if you tilt the plate, the rice should ripple like the waves of the sea. So just before you serve your risotto, if you think the consistency is too firm, beat in a little more hot stock.

Risotto alle vongole

Clam risotto

For this risotto, we use two types of clam: cherrystones for the stock, because they are the most flavorful but a little too big and tough to put whole into the risotto; and the smaller *vongole veraci* (*palourdes*, or carpet-shell), which have a lighter, more delicate flavor. The stock is the same as we use for Razor clam and fregola soup (see page 166), so if you have any left over, you could freeze it in ice cube trays to make the soup another day.

1¾ pounds *vongole veraci*
    (carpet-shell) clams
6½ pounds cherrystone clams
5 tablespoons
    extra virgin olive oil
6 garlic cloves, chopped and put
    into a little olive oil to
    steep
2 fresh chiles, sliced
1½ cups dry white wine
1 tablespoon tomato paste
3½ tablespoons butter
1 onion, chopped very, very fine
2 cups superfino carnaroli rice
1 tablespoon tomato passata
juice of ½ lemon
2 tablespoons chopped parsley
salt and pepper

For the mantecatura:
about 5 tablespoons cold butter,
    cut into small cubes

If any clams are open, even slightly, don't use them. Keep the carpet-shells and cherrystones separate. Put each into a bowl of cold water, with a handful of salt to recreate their natural environment. This will encourage them to release any sand trapped inside the shells. Brush the shells well, wash three times in running water; then, to be sure no dead clams are being held closed by sand, drop each one into a bowl and throw away any that open.

To make the stock, heat 3 tablespoons of the extra virgin olive oil in a large, heavy-bottomed pan. Take 2 of the garlic cloves out of the oil in which it has been steeping (but reserve the oil) and add to the pan with half the sliced chile. Cook for a minute or so, without allowing them to color, then put in the cherrystone clams and cover with a lid. Shake the pan and, after a minute, add ⅔ cup of the wine. Continue to cook over a high heat, letting the alcohol evaporate. After about 2 to 3 minutes, the clams will have opened. Discard any that haven't opened. Reserve the rest and chop them.

Add the tomato paste and cover with 10 cups water (to cover the clams). Bring to a boil, then turn down the heat and simmer for about 15 minutes.

While the stock is cooking, heat the rest of the oil in another pan, then add the rest of the garlic (again, reserving the oil) and chile. Cook for a minute or so, without allowing them to color, then add the carpet-shell clams and cover with a lid. Shake the pan and, after a minute, add ⅓ cup of the wine. Continue to cook over a high heat for about a minute, letting the alcohol evaporate. As soon as the clams open, take the pan off the heat (the carpet-shells will cook quicker than the cherrystones, as they are smaller). Take out the clams carefully with a slotted spoon (discard any that don't open), and set aside, reserving the cooking liquid.

Take most of the carpet-shell clams out of their shells, keeping back a few in their shells for garnish, and mix with the chopped cherrystone clams.

When the cherrystone clam stock is cooked, add the stock from cooking the carpet-shells, and strain through a fine sieve into a clean pan.

Now you are ready to make the risotto. Have the stock at a bare simmer next to where you are going to make the risotto.

Melt the butter in a heavy-bottomed pan, and add the onion. Cook gently until the onion is softened but not colored (about 5 minutes).

Add the rice and stir around to coat in the butter and "toast" the grains. Make sure all the grains are warm before adding the rest of the wine. Let the wine evaporate completely until the onions and rice are dry.

Start to add the stock, a ladleful or two at a time, stirring and scraping the rice in the pan as you do so. Also add the tomato passata along with the first ladleful of stock. When each addition of stock has almost evaporated, add the next ladleful.

Continue cooking the risotto for about 15 to 17 minutes, adding stock continuously, but slowly toward the end, so that the rice doesn't become too wet and soupy, otherwise when you add the butter at the end, it will become sloppy. The risotto is ready when the grains are soft but still al dente.

Turn down the heat, add the shelled clams, 2 tablespoons of the garlic oil and the lemon juice. Season to taste.

For the mantecatura, with a wooden spoon, vigorously beat in the cold butter cubes, making sure you shake the pan energetically at the same time as you beat.

Just before serving, if the risotto is too firm, beat in a little more hot stock – the risotto should be all'onda (it should move like waves). Add the chopped parsley and serve garnished with the clams in their shells.

Risotto alle code di gamberi

Prawn risotto

In Italy we would make this with Mediterranean prawns, which are pink when they are raw and beautifully sweet and delicate in flavor and texture – but you have to search a little to find very large ones, as they live in warm water, where they tend to grow bigger and have a stronger flavor. In America, however, the easier option is to use the imported gray-blue tiger prawns, which are always large and firm. If you like, you can garnish the risotto with some whole prawns, sautéed in a little oil, together with a little garlic and diced chili. Add them to your pan just before you beat in the butter for the mantecatura.

Peel the prawns, take off the heads and devein them, reserving the shells and heads. Cut the tails into pieces about ¾ inch long.

To make the stock, heat the oil in a large, heavy-bottomed pan. Take the garlic out of the oil (but keep the oil) and add to the pan with the vegetables, parsley and peppercorns. Cook for a minute or so, without allowing them to color, then put in the prawn heads and shells. Crush with a wooden spoon, to release the juices. Shake the pan and, after a minute, add the wine. Continue to cook over a high heat for about 3 minutes, letting the alcohol evaporate.

Add the tomato paste and cover with 8½ cups water (make sure all the shells are covered). Bring to a boil, then turn down the heat and simmer for about 15 minutes.

To make the risotto, strain the stock into a clean pan and have it barely simmering next to where you are going to make the risotto. Melt the butter in a heavy-bottomed pan and add the onion. Cook gently until the onion is softened but not colored (about 5 minutes).

Add the rice and stir around to coat in the butter and "toast" the grains. Make sure all the grains are warm before adding the wine. Let the wine evaporate completely until the onion and rice are dry.

Start to add the stock, a ladleful or two at a time, stirring and scraping the rice in the pan as you do so. Also add the tomato passata with the first ladleful of stock. When each addition of stock has almost evaporated, add the next ladleful.

Continue cooking the risotto for about 14 minutes, adding stock continuously as above, but slowly toward the end, so that the rice doesn't become too wet. Remember, you don't want it to be soupy at this stage, otherwise when you add the butter at the end, it will become sloppy. The risotto is ready when the grains are soft but still al dente.

Season the pieces of prawn, add them to the risotto and continue cooking for another minute. Add 2 tablespoons of the garlic oil and the lemon juice. Season to taste.

Take off the heat and let the risotto rest for a minute without stirring. For the mantecatura, with a wooden spoon, vigorously beat in the cold butter cubes, making sure you shake the pan energetically at the same time as you beat. Just before serving, if the risotto is too firm, beat in a little more hot stock. Add the chopped parsley and serve.

2 pounds large prawns
(Mediterranean or tiger)
3½ tablespoons butter
1 onion, chopped very, very fine
2 cups superfino carnaroli rice
½ cup dry white wine
1 tablespoon tomato passata
juice of ½ lemon
2 tablespoons chopped parsley
salt and pepper

For the stock:
3 tablespoons
extra virgin olive oil
4 garlic cloves, chopped and put
into a little olive oil
1 leek, coarsely chopped
1 onion, coarsely chopped
1 celery stalk, coarsely chopped
1 bay leaf
a few parsley sprigs
a few black peppercorns
⅔ cup dry white wine
1 tablespoon tomato paste

For the mantecatura:
about 5 tablespoons cold butter,
cut into small cubes

Risotto agli scampi

Langoustine risotto

In the restaurant, we buy live langoustines, but these are difficult to find, so I suggest you use very fresh – or even frozen – ones from a good fishmonger. You can also do this recipe with crayfish (Risotto alla certosina) if you can find them. Crayfish are the freshwater version of langoustines – in Italy we call them *gamberi di acqua dolce*, prawns of sweet water.

about 2 pounds medium-sized
    langoustines or crayfish
3½ tablespoons butter
1 onion, chopped very, very fine
2 cups superfino carnaroli rice
½ cup dry white wine
1 tablespoon tomato passata
about 2 tablespoons of olive oil
    (flavored with a chopped
    garlic clove if you like)
juice of ½ lemon
2 tablespoons chopped parsley –
    reserve stalks for the stock
salt and pepper

For the stock:
3 tablespoons
    extra virgin olive oil
1 carrot, coarsely chopped
1 onion, coarsely chopped
1 celery stalk, coarsely chopped
1 bay leaf
a few black peppercorns
1 tablespoon tomato paste
5 tablespoons dry white wine

For the mantecatura:
about 5 tablespoons cold butter,
    cut into small cubes

Take the heads from the langoustines or crayfish, but remove the eyes, then cut the tails through the shell lengthwise, leaving the shell on, and keep in the fridge until ready to use. (If you like, you can keep back a few heads to garnish the risotto.)

To make the stock, heat the oil in a large, heavy-bottomed pan, add the heads and crush them a little with a wooden spoon, so that they start to release their juices. Cook for about 5 minutes, tossing the shells around in the pan, to get all the flavor from them.

Add the vegetables, bay leaf, parsley stalks and peppercorns. Sweat for 3 to 4 minutes, then add the tomato paste and the wine. Allow the alcohol to evaporate, then add 10 cups water (make sure all the shells are covered). Bring to the boil, then turn down the heat and simmer for about 30 minutes. (If you are going to garnish the risotto with langoustine heads, put them into the stock for a few minutes until they change color, then take out and reserve.) Strain the stock through a fine sieve, pressing the shells to get all the flavor out.

To make the risotto, put the stock back on the burner, next to where you are going to make your risotto. Bring to a boil, then turn down the heat to a gentle simmer.

Melt the butter in a heavy-bottomed pan, and add the onion. Cook gently until the onion is softened but not colored (about 5 minutes).

Add the rice and stir around to coat in the butter and "toast" the grains. Make sure all the grains are warm before adding the wine. Let the wine evaporate completely until the onion and rice are dry.

Start to add the stock, a ladleful or two at a time, stirring and scraping the rice in the pan as you do so. Also add the tomato passata with the first ladleful of stock. When each addition of stock has almost evaporated, add the next ladleful.

Continue cooking the risotto for about 14 minutes, adding stock continuously as above. Slow up toward the end, so that the rice doesn't become too soupy, otherwise when you add the butter at the end, it will become sloppy. The risotto is ready when the grains are soft but still al dente.

Take off the heat and let the risotto rest for a minute without stirring, then season the langoustines lightly and add to the risotto, with 2 tablespoons of the garlic-flavored oil, and the lemon juice. Check the seasoning and adjust if necessary.

For the mantecatura, with a wooden spoon, vigorously beat in the cold butter cubes, making sure you shake the pan energetically at the same time as you beat. Just before serving, if the risotto is too firm, beat in a little more hot stock to loosen it.

Add the chopped parsley and garnish with langoustine heads, if using.

Risotto al Prosecco con capesante

Prosecco risotto with scallops

This is the only risotto I can say I invented.

about 10 medium-large scallops,
    with corals (roe)
10 cups fish stock (see page 267)
3½ tablespoons butter
1 onion, chopped very, very fine
2 cups superfino carnaroli rice
⅔ cup Prosecco, plus a little
    extra for finishing
juice of ½ lemon
salt and pepper

For the mantecatura:
about 5 tablespoons cold butter,
    cut into small cubes

You need to cut 12 very thin (about ¹⁄₁₆ inch) slices of scallop to garnish the risotto – so do this first and keep these slices on one side. Dice the rest of the scallops, together with the corals.

To make the risotto, bring the stock to a boil in a pan next to where you are going to make your risotto, turn down the heat and keep at a bare simmer.

Melt the butter in a heavy-bottomed pan and add the onion. Cook gently until the onion is softened but not colored (about 5 minutes).

Add the rice and stir around to coat in the butter and "toast" the grains. Make sure all the grains are warm before adding ½ cup of the Prosecco. Let the alcohol evaporate completely until the onion and rice are dry.

Start to add the stock, a ladleful or two at a time, stirring and scraping the rice in the pan as you do so. When each addition of stock has almost evaporated, add the next ladleful.

Continue cooking the risotto for about 15 to 17 minutes, adding stock continuously as above, but slowly toward the end, so that the rice doesn't become too wet. Remember, you don't want it to be soupy at this stage, otherwise when you add the butter at the end, it will become sloppy. The risotto is ready when the grains are soft but still al dente.

Turn down the heat, add the diced scallop and corals, season and add the lemon juice. Check the seasoning again and adjust it if necessary.

For the mantecatura, with a wooden spoon, vigorously beat in the cold butter cubes, making sure you shake the pan energetically at the same time as you beat. If the risotto is too firm, beat in the rest of the Prosecco (rather than hot stock this time) – so that it is all'onda (rippling like waves).

Just before serving, lightly season the scallop slices with salt and a few grinds of black pepper, and put 3 on top of each dish or plate of risotto – the heat of it will cook the scallops immediately. Drizzle with a little extra Prosecco.

Risotti di carne

Risotti with sausage and game

The idea with these risotti is to add all or some of the main ingredient at the beginning of cooking, to give a strong flavor base and enhance the color. Then, if you like, you can cook some more sausage or game separately, and add it at the end, before the mantecatura, to give an extra kick of flavor.

Risotto luganiga e piselli

Risotto with sausage and peas

Luganiga is a very small, peppery pork sausage from Lombardia – but you can use whatever sausages you prefer, even chorizo if you like. This is my son, Jack's, favorite risotto, which he would eat at any time of the day, every day. What I often do is put half the chopped sausages in at the beginning of the recipe, then sauté the rest in a pan, so that they become crispy and brown, and then stir them in when I put in the peas.

1 cup freshly shelled peas
2 good pork sausages,
     preferably luganiga
10 cups good chicken stock
     (see page 264)
3½ tablespoons butter
1 onion, chopped very, very fine
2 cups superfino carnaroli rice
½ cup dry white wine
2 tablespoons tomato passata
salt and pepper

For the mantecatura:
about 5 tablespoons cold butter,
     cut into small cubes
about 1 cup finely grated
     Parmesan

Blanch the peas in boiling salted water for about 2 minutes and drain. Smash one-third of them with a fork to make a coarse puree.

Chop the sausages into small pieces.

Now you are ready to start the risotto, so bring your pot of stock to a boil next to where you are going to make the risotto. Then turn down the heat and keep it at a bare simmer.

Melt the butter in a heavy-bottomed pan and add the onion and the sausages. Cook gently until the onion is softened but not colored (about 5 minutes).

Add the rice and stir around to coat in the butter and "toast" the grains. Make sure all the grains are warm before adding the wine. Let the wine evaporate completely until the onion and rice are dry.

Start to add the stock, a ladleful or two at a time, stirring and scraping the rice in the pan as you do so. Add the tomato passata with the first ladleful. When each addition of stock has almost evaporated, add the next ladleful.

Continue cooking for about 15 to 17 minutes, adding stock continuously as above. After about 12 to 14 minutes, add the peas. Slow up on the stock toward the end, so that the rice doesn't become too wet and soupy, otherwise when you add the butter and Parmesan at the end, it will become sloppy. The risotto is ready when the grains are soft, but still al dente.

Turn down the heat and allow the risotto to rest for a minute, then, for the mantecatura, with a wooden spoon, vigorously beat in the cold butter cubes and finally the Parmesan, making sure you shake the pan energetically as you beat. Season to taste and serve.

Risotto alle quaglie

Quail risotto

The basis of this is the classic grana risotto, Risotto alla lodigiana (see page 214), which is enriched with a stew of quail. It is a fantastic risotto, though you have to do a little more work than usual. If you don't have the time to follow the full recipe on page 260, there is another way to make a quail risotto – with roasted quail. If you want to do this, to roast the quail, first preheat the oven to 425°F. Lay a sage leaf on each breast, then wrap with pancetta. Tie up the bird with string and season with salt and pepper.

Heat some olive oil in an ovenproof pan, put in the quail and brown on all sides, then turn the quail onto its back and transfer the pan to the oven. Roast for about 4 minutes, then take the quail from the pan and leave it to rest in a warm place for about 8 to 10 minutes, breast downward, so that the juices keep the breast meat moist. Remove the pancetta and discard it, together with the sage leaves.

You can either chop up all the meat, ready to add it to the risotto before beating in the butter, or, if you want to be more elegant about it, break the legs in half and put these, and the wings, into the risotto before adding the butter. Then slice each breast into 4 and use these to garnish each plate of risotto.

While the risotto is cooking, deglaze your roasting pan with a little red wine: put the pan on top of the burner, pour in a little wine and bubble it up, scraping all the bits from the bottom of the pan, until the wine and juices reduce right down. Then add this to your risotto right at the end, before the mantecatura, along with your chopped quail (or the legs and wings).

Note: For the full recipe that follows, ask your butcher to take the breasts and legs off the quail for you, but keep the carcass to add to the chicken stock for extra flavor.

10 cups good chicken stock
    (see page 264)
3½ tablespoons butter
1 onion, chopped very, very fine
2 cups superfino carnaroli rice
½ cup dry white wine
about 12 sage leaves, fried in a
    little olive oil (optional)
salt and pepper

For the mantecatura:
about 5 tablespoons cold butter,
    cut into small cubes
about 1 cup finely grated Grana
    Padano or Parmesan

For the quail stew:
3 tablespoons virgin olive oil
1 small shallot, chopped
1 small carrot, chopped
1 celery stalk, chopped
½ cup chopped pancetta
bouquet garni, made with
    rosemary, sage and a
    bay leaf, tied together
4 quail, breasts and legs
    taken off and separated,
    carcass reserved
1 teaspoon tomato paste

Put the quail carcass into the chicken stock, bring to a boil and then turn down the heat and simmer for about 20 minutes.

To make the quail stew, heat half the olive oil in a large pan, add the vegetables, pancetta and bouquet garni, and cook slowly until the vegetables soften and turn translucent, without coloring (about 4 to 5 minutes).

In a separate frying pan, heat the rest of the oil, then put in the quail breasts and legs, skin side down, and cook for 3 to 4 minutes until golden, seasoning while they cook. Add to the pan containing the vegetables and toss around for 3 to 4 minutes.

Add the tomato paste, cover with 2¼ cups of stock (or just enough to cover the quail) and simmer gently for 30 minutes, adding more stock if the quail starts to dry out.

When the quail is cooked, let it cool down enough to be able to handle the meat, then pull all the meat, including the breast meat, off the bones (make sure you discard all the bones) and flake it with your fingers. Put the meat back into the cooking juices and keep on one side.

To make the risotto, have your pot of stock (with the quail carcass added) barely simmering on the burner next to where you are going to make your risotto. Melt the butter in a heavy-bottomed pan and add the onion. Cook gently until softened but not colored (about 5 minutes).

Add the rice and stir around to coat in the butter and "toast" the grains. Make sure all the grains are warm, then add the wine. Let the wine evaporate completely until the onion and rice are dry.

Start to add the stock, a ladleful or two at a time, stirring and scraping the rice in the pan as you do so. When each addition of stock has almost evaporated, add the next ladleful.

After about 9 to 10 minutes, add the flaked quail meat and juices. Continue cooking for about 7 to 8 minutes, letting the rice absorb the juices, and adding stock if necessary – just remember that you don't want the risotto to be too soupy when you add the butter and Parmesan at the end, or it will become sloppy. The risotto is ready when the grains are soft but still al dente.

Turn down the heat and allow the risotto to rest for a minute; then, for the mantecatura, with a wooden spoon, vigorously beat in the cold butter cubes and finally the cheese, making sure you shake the pan energetically at the same time as you beat. Season to taste and serve. Garnish, if you like, with the fried sage leaves.

Risotto another day

I never saw leftover risotto thrown away in our house. My grandmother would mold it into a *torta* (which means cake or pie), which she baked in the oven until it was brown on top, and when we came home from school we were very happy to tuck into it. You can also fry risotto in a little olive oil, patting it down into a round cake in the pan. Cook it for about 4 to 5 minutes, until it is golden brown underneath, then turn it over and cook it again until golden on the other side. If you like, you can grate some Parmesan over the top.

Another way to use risotto is to make *arancini*, which, as I mentioned at the beginning of this chapter, are deep-fried rice balls (about the size of tennis balls), frequently made with saffron risotto. Traditionally, the risotto is molded around a center of meat ragù (sometimes also with peas – my favorite), so that this filling is completely enclosed. Then the risotto balls are dipped in flour, eggs and bread crumbs before frying. In Italy, they are served at the counter in bars or fried on street corners. We make them often for private parties at the restaurant, for when people are standing around with drinks – and the kids especially love them. If you like, you can simply use mozzarella cheese for the filling, or even anchovies, a little homemade tomato sauce and some basil.

Arancini

Makes around 20
1 preparation of Saffron risotto
(see page 226)
½ preparation of Ragù (see page 349), with some cooked peas added if you like
about 2 balls of buffalo mozzarella, cubed
handful of basil leaves (optional)
3 eggs, beaten
flour, for coating
bread crumbs, for coating
vegetable oil, for deep-frying

Take a small ball of risotto in the palm of your hand (wet your palms first to stop the risotto sticking) and make an indent with your other thumb. Spoon a little ragù into the indent, push in some cubes of mozzarella and a basil leaf, if you like, then close up your hand, so that the risotto encloses the filling in a ball. Smooth the surface so that there are no gaps in the risotto casing, then dip it first into some beaten egg, then into some flour, then back into the egg and finally into some bread crumbs. Repeat until you have used up all the risotto.

Deep-fry the arancini at 340°F (not too many at a time, depending on the size of your fryer or pan – if using a pan fill no more than one-third). Fry for at least 4 to 5 minutes, according to the size, stirring them around all the time until evenly golden all over. To test that they are cooked through and hot in the center, break one open. If you don't want to fry them immediately, you can freeze the arancini on a tray (keep them apart so they don't stick together) and, when they are firm, transfer them to a bag; then you can fry them (for at least 10 to 12 minutes at 285°F) when frozen.

Brodi

Stocks

In Italy, stocks, or broths, are usually light, made purely from bones and/or vegetables simmered in water; or, more often than not, we would put a whole chicken in the pot with a few vegetables (see Chicken stock below).

Roasting the bones in the oven first and adding tomato puree to make a richer, slightly more sophisticated stock is something I learned during my time cooking in Paris, and I have carried on making stocks this way ever since.

However, in the Michelin-starred kitchens I worked in there, we would spend many, many hours clarifying the stock to make consommé, adding egg white, bringing the stock to the boil and creating a crust. You would then make a hole in the middle of that crust and carry on simmering until all the impurities had bubbled up through the hole and added to the crust. Then we would take it off the heat and let the crust sink slowly to the bottom of the pan, so we could take off the liquid and pass it through a fine sieve until it was perfectly clear.

I was happy to learn the technique, and we use it at Locanda sometimes, for example, when we make a special minestrone with langoustines (see page 172). However, for most dishes, although I feel that a nice clear stock makes the best sauce or risotto, you only have to skim it regularly during cooking to take off the scum that rises to the surface – you don't have to go crazy.

You may notice that I never suggest adding salt to a stock, as you may want to reduce the stock down to store it or to make a sauce or glaze, and then it could become far too salty.

Chicken stock

In Italy, no one roasts bones to make stock, as we do in the recipe on page 266. You would simply take a whole chicken, put it in a pan with a whole carrot, a whole onion, cut in half, a couple of celery stalks, a couple of bay leaves, a couple of peppercorns and juniper berries, then cover well with water and bring slowly to just under the boil as in the recipe that follows, and continue cooking in the same way until the chicken was cooked.

The boiled meat would typically be sliced and eaten with either mayonnaise, mustard fruits (see page 482) or green sauce (see page 132), or in a salad, and then the brodo would either be served separately or kept for risotto. Whenever you make stock, remember how important it is to the finished dish – the rule is that a good-quality chicken makes a good-quality stock, so buy the best you can find.

Makes about 5 quarts
2½ pounds chicken carcasses
and/or wings
1 teaspoon tomato paste
1 carrot, halved lengthwise
1 onion, halved
1 celery stalk
2 bay leaves
2 black peppercorns
2 juniper berries

Preheat the oven to 425°F. Put the carcasses and/or wings in a roasting pan and put into the oven for about 15 to 20 minutes until golden.

Brush each carcass with tomato paste, and put back into the oven for 3 to 4 minutes.

Transfer the carcasses to a big pan with the rest of the ingredients, then cover with about 1½ to 2 gallons water. Slowly bring up almost to a boil – but don't let it actually boil or the fat that comes out of the chicken will cook into the stock, and you won't be able to remove it, even if you put the stock through a very fine sieve. It is important to take it slowly, as the longer the stock takes to come to this point, the more the flavors will infuse into the water.

To make a clear stock, it is very important to skim off the impurities. Just before it boils you will see white foam or scum forming. Take this off by skimming the surface with a ladle, bringing all the foam to the sides of the pan, then you can just lift it off. Turn the heat down to a simmer, and continue to take off the foam regularly, until the liquid is clear.

Let the stock simmer for about 3 to 4 hours, then turn off the heat. Leave to cool down slightly. The sediment will sink to the bottom. Slowly pour the stock through a fine sieve, taking care not to tip in the sediment (you will need to leave the last inch or so of stock in the pan, in order to keep the stock clear). Leave to cool completely, then skim off any fat that has solidified on the surface.

Unless using immediately, pour the stock into ice cube trays, cool and freeze. When the cubes are frozen you can transfer them to a bag and keep them in the freezer ready to use whenever needed.

Veal stock

We make this in the same way as for Chicken stock above, replacing the chicken carcasses and/or wings with veal shank bones and trimmings. The only difference is that, as the shank of the veal usually has more nerves around the bone than most meat, we roast it more slowly at a lower temperature (355°F for around 1½ hours), and we let the stock simmer for 12 hours, skimming it regularly.

Pork, lamb and venison stock

We make these in the same way as Chicken stock, simply substituting pork, lamb or venison bones and trimmings for the chicken carcasses and/or wings.

Fish stock

The bones of flatfish, such as the sole family, plaice, halibut and turbot, make the best stock, as they give a good flavor but aren't oily. If you want to give the stock a rosy color or a little more acidity, add a couple of squashed tomatoes.

Put everything into a pan and cover with water by about two fingers (depending on how intense you want the stock to be – the less water you use, the richer it will be).

Bring to just under a boil (the slower you do this, the more flavor the finished stock will have). Skim, turn down the heat and simmer for 20 minutes, skimming as necessary.

Turn off the heat and let the stock settle, then pour through a fine sieve.

Makes about 8½ cups
1 pound flatfish bones, washed
    well to remove any blood
    as this will make the stock
    bitter
1 leek, coarsely chopped
1 onion, coarsely chopped
1 celery stalk, coarsely chopped
1 bay leaf
a few parsley stalks
a few black peppercorns
⅓–½ cup dry white wine

Vegetable stock

When I was growing up, I never heard of vegetable stock. I remember my father coming into Zafferano one time and looking at the big stock-pots bubbling away – veal, beef, chicken. "What's that one?" he asked. "Vegetable? What? You make stock from vegetables for people?"

The vegetables listed below are intended merely as a guide, because when we make a vegetable stock, we use whatever is in season: it could be fennel, asparagus, broccoli, etc. The only vegetables we wouldn't use are beans, eggplant, peppers and beet, as these all have such strong characteristic flavors, they might predominate. If you like, you can add tomatoes and/or a couple of cloves of garlic. Our secret ingredients are peas, which we shell, crush and put in for sweetness. It is an idea I saw a long time ago in Italy. Sometimes when people taste a risotto at Locanda made with vegetable stock they say, "Surely you must have put in some sugar?" But no, it is just the peas. If I don't have any fresh peas, I put in a handful of frozen, which are almost as good, because they are frozen so quickly after they are picked that all the flavor and goodness are sealed in.

Makes about 10 cups
3 tablespoons
    extra virgin olive oil
4 handfuls of fresh or frozen peas
4 carrots
4 white onions
2 leeks
4 celery stalks
2 small bunches of Swiss chard
4 zucchini
2 potatoes
2 handfuls of spinach,
    coarsely chopped

Heat the oil in a big pot, put in the peas, squashing and smashing them as much as you can, then add the rest of the vegetables and let them stew until they start to break up.

Cover with about 13 cups (3 quarts plus 1 cup) cold water. Slowly bring to just under a boil, skim, then turn down the heat and simmer for 20 minutes, skimming again if necessary.

Take off the heat and leave to settle, then pour through a fine sieve.

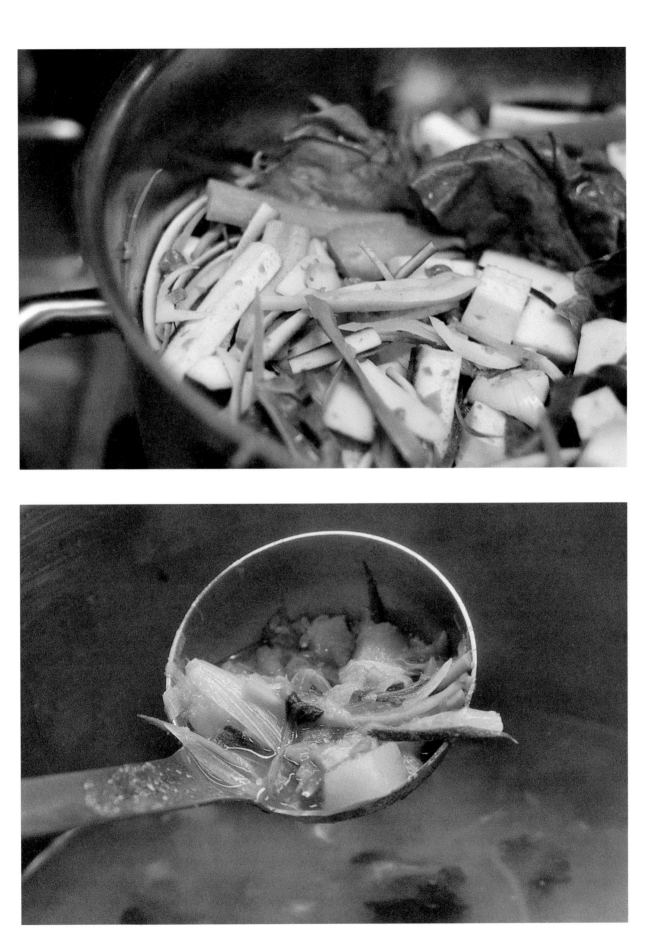

Soho nights

Every Italian who came to London since the fifties seemed to gravitate to Soho. When I arrived in 1986, it was full of Italians. Very charming and bohemian, with lots of markets, bars and risqué clubs, it had a kind of dangerous glamour, so tourists were still quite scared to go there.

I bought a new shirt and went for my interview at the Savoy, a few minutes' walk away in the Strand – the place I had imagined for so long, where Anton Edelmann was the maître chef des cuisines. I was prepared to work every hour, every day, just to be at the Savoy. Naively I thought they would offer me a job right away, but they said, "We'll call you back when something comes up." So there I was in the street, with no money and too much pride to go home.

You have to remember that I was someone who was born in a small village and went from A to B on a bicycle. I spoke hardly any English, and this was my first real taste of metropolitan life. What was I going to do? I called Giorgio back home at Il Passatore, and he put me in touch with a friend of a friend who had an old-style trattoria in Surrey. When I saw the so-called Italian food they served, I was shocked. I had to make dishes with names like "chicken surprise," and all the time I was thinking: "No, no! This is so contrary to everything I have ever cooked in Italy."

I saved every penny I earned, and on every day off, I came up to London, to Soho, and sat in the Italian bars and coffeehouses where the chefs used to go. By chance, on one of these occasions I met a guy I knew from back home in Varese, who was cooking at the Rue St Jacques on Charlotte Street. We agreed to share a place and so as soon as I could escape from Surrey I was in the employment office in Soho, saying: "I'll go anywhere you send me – just not another Italian restaurant. I never want to cook food like that again."

Just as my money was about to run out, a job came up at a restaurant called Bates in Soho, where the people were lovely, and the chef, a great guy named Joe Rayner, was especially impressive to me because he had been a sous chef at the Savoy. Joe had quite a Mediterranean flair, and I was so eager to prove myself I used to make things like champagne risotto, and in every spare minute I taught myself English by reading the newspapers.

At last a letter arrived offering me the job of commis chef at the Savoy. There were three of us who started together: a French chef and a crazy, brilliant Scot, Laurence Robertson – one of those Scots even the Scots are scared of. We called him William Wallace, after the Highland hero, and he became one of my best friends. My job was to be in charge of the mise-en-place, which involved cutting, chopping, preparing everything in advance of the lunchtime and dinner service. Right from the beginning, I felt part of something important. We were like a football team – but one of about a hundred people – all working for one another. Twenty years later, I still keep in touch with many of these guys.

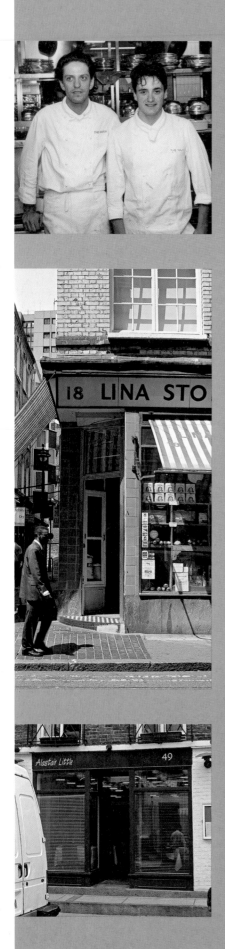

The work was so absorbing that sometimes I didn't leave the Savoy for days – I would just fall asleep in one of the rooms kept back for kitchen staff. And even if I did go home, home changed every two or three months. I had a bag of white T-shirts and a couple of pairs of blue jeans and that was it. Eventually I shared a house above a gallery on Dean Street with another Italian, named Marco, who worked at the Armani shop on Bond Street, and about twenty other people. I was a real bohemian. Everyone used to say, "Giorgio – he never sleeps."

The people I hung out with were all bright young things, like Fergus Henderson (now of St John) who was studying to be an architect then. None of us had actually done anything yet, but we all felt we were destined to be famous. There were lots of artists, especially – and though most of us were completely broke most of the time, we managed to have an amazing time. We used to go to places like the Colony Room Club, where they would usually let us in after we had finished late in the kitchen, and artists like Francis Bacon and Lucian Freud would be sitting at the bar. When my brother, Roberto, came over, I remember, I took him to the legendary Soho gay club Kinky Gerlinky. He looked around at all these guys with no shirts, and I will never forget his face.

We bought our food at the two famous Soho Italian delicatessens, Camisa on Old Compton Street and Lina Stores on the corner of Brewer Street. Marco was a friend of the family at Lina, so if we didn't have any money, they would look after us and say, "Okay, pay us later." The classiest place was the Soho Brasserie, and everyone was trying to copy what Antony Worrall Thompson was doing at Le Ménage à Trois, but the places I wanted to eat at in Soho were Alastair Little, which had just opened, and L'Escargot, where Alastair had cooked for a while. I used to stand outside looking in, wondering when I would be able to afford to eat there. The moment my mum and dad came over from Italy, I took them to both places right away, because they were paying. At Alastair Little, we had a fantastic meal and I remember my father saying: "I can't believe it. I come all the way to London and I eat cotechino!"

The restaurant revolution was beginning, and it was a big time for the English perception of Italian food. People were starting to see that it was about much more than big peppermills and lasagne and, strangely, it was an Englishman who was leading the way. Alastair Little inspired me enormously. It was fascinating to see the way he cooked Italian food, putting it together in his own way, pushing the boundaries further and further. He was very clever, one of a handful of brilliant English intellectual cooks, like Simon Hopkinson at Bibendum and Rowley Leigh at Kensington Place, who really understood good food.

Much later, I remember the first time Plaxy and I went to eat at Rowley's home. It was so relaxed: the food kept on coming, slowly, all day, and everyone would get up and help with something; the kids were around, there was no bullshit, everything was stripped away, except the good food and company. I said to Plaxy, "This is just like being in Italy."

At the Savoy I was involved with a more intricate kind of cooking, though Anton Edelmann had become famous for a modern, lighter way with the classics. I had moved up through the sauce section, and finally I was made sous chef, earning a princely £250 ($500) a week. We cooked for Pavarotti at a big party at the Italian Embassy and, when Anton Edelmann wrote the book to celebrate the centenary of the Savoy, I prepared the food for the photography, and I was so proud when I saw my credit.

Then an artist I knew, Daniel Harvey, told me he had done some work for a film director named Peter Greenaway, who was going to make a film about a restaurant – would I like to help? The film was *The Cook, The Thief, His Wife and Her Lover*, and the backdrop was a grand hotel restaurant. I was in charge of the displays of food. I had a bus set up as a kitchen, and we created huge, decadent sets inspired by the pictures of medieval banquets we found in old books and art galleries. The film is one you either love or hate, but the images are beautiful and working on it was exhilarating. We used to go to Smithfield and Billingsgate markets with guys who had bags of money and they would say: "Anything you want you can buy," so we would spend $12,000 on fish, $1,200 on mushrooms…all paid for in cash. We even called Buckingham Palace to ask if we could have a swan. When I was invited to the premiere at the Venezia Film Festival I spent all the money I had on a suit, and when Sophia Loren walked in I thought, "This must be a dream."

What impressed me most was the collaboration between the people who designed the set, the clothes, the lighting…everyone exchanged and shared information. It seemed such a contrast to the restaurant world, where the different sections are often so separate. I had learned from Anton Edelmann that managing a kitchen is a skill that goes beyond cooking, and the teamwork amongst the chefs was very strong, but outside in the restaurant the waiters were in a separate team. I thought that if I had my own restaurant one day, I would have *one* team, with everyone working for one another.

I had been at the Savoy for nearly four years and now I wanted something more. Despite cooks like Alastair Little and Rowley Leigh making a big impression, the famous names you read about around the world were still mostly French. In London in 1989, all the talk was of a genius and madman named Marco Pierre White who had opened Harveys on Wandsworth Common and threw people out of his restaurant – but he too was inspired by classical French cooking. I didn't want to be just a chef from Lombardia, so the next part of my plan was to work in Paris. I told Anton Edelmann and he said, "I can get you a job at the Laurent." At that time, the Laurent was owned by Sir James Goldsmith, and it was – and still is – one of the city's most prestigious restaurants, an elaborate place with salons and terraces, in its own gardens in Rue Gabriel, near the Elysée Palace. It had two Michelin stars and the consultant chef was one of the new Parisian stars, Joël Robuchon.

Pasta

"Everything you see I owe to spaghetti."

Sophia Loren

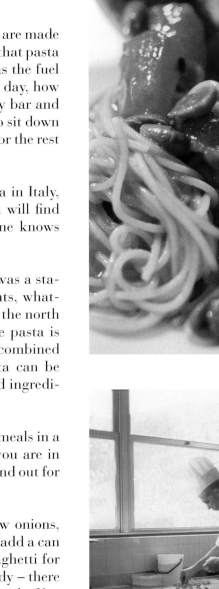

Italians are born and raised on pasta; two-thirds of our bodies are made of pasta! Garibaldi, when he liberated Napoli in 1860, vowed that pasta would be the force that united Italy and I like to think of it as the fuel that runs the country. Imagine, at around ten to twelve every day, how many millions of pounds of pasta are going into pots in every bar and restaurant and in every home all over Italy, ready for people to sit down and have a plate of pasta for their lunch, to give them energy for the rest of the day.

There are hundreds of different shapes and varieties of pasta in Italy, some particular to a region or town, some so local that you will find them only in one village, and some so famous that everyone knows about them all over the world.

Over the centuries, in the poorest areas all over Italy, pasta was a staple that would often only have a few simple, local ingredients, whatever you could grow or afford, to enhance it. For example, in the north one of the most typical pastas was pizzocheri, in which the pasta is made not from durum wheat but with buckwheat and is combined with cabbage and potato. Now, in smart restaurants, pasta can be something delicate, even elegant, but we still draw on the old ingredients and flavors.

Pasta is also our fast food. Of course everyone has to prepare meals in a hurry sometimes, maybe even most of the time, but when you are in Italy and hungry for something in a hurry, what do you do? Send out for a takeout pizza? No way.

Instead, if you want fast food, what you do is chop up a few onions, sauté them in a little bit of olive oil with some chopped garlic, add a can of tomatoes and reduce them down while you cook some spaghetti for around six minutes, during which time your sauce will be ready – there is no shame in using good-quality canned tomatoes; all Italians do. You drain the spaghetti, toss it in the sauce, and if you have some herbs sprinkle them in too. Everything is done in roughly the time it would take you to open up a prepared meal from the supermarket and microwave the packets and trays in their plastic wrap. And you have the satisfaction of eating something you have prepared yourself, with nothing in it that isn't good for you.

I remember at Zafferano we had a customer who came in every day and wanted to eat only spaghetti with tomato sauce. One day I got talking to him, and he told me that when he cooked spaghetti at home, he didn't know how to make a tomato sauce, so he mixed up tomato ketchup and cream – imagine. I told him how to make the sauce in the way I have

just described, and the next day he came in and told me I had changed his life.

Italians are used to having packets of dried pasta in the cupboard, and cans of tomatoes and jars of olives, or anchovies, which can just be melted in a pan to make a quick sauce. Perhaps one of the reasons that in Italy we still haven't been swamped by the likes of McDonald's is that we already have our own tradition of quick food on the streets – slices of good pizza, fried snacks like *panzerotti* or *arancini*, *piadina* (flat, unleavened bread), panini (rolls with maybe some salami or cheese inside). And when we are at home, we don't need to phone for something to be delivered, because we always have pasta.

Marco Polo?

The first thing you need to know about pasta is that Marco Polo didn't bring it to Italy from China. At school, like most kids in Europe, we were taught about Marco Polo. He was one of my heroes. In paintings, he was always good-looking, he had long hair and would be draped in silks, surrounded by beautiful girls and beautiful things, and most exciting of all, he was a traveler. I thought he had the best sort of life; I wanted to be Marco Polo. But as far as pasta is concerned, yes, he brought back different shapes of pasta, and maybe new ideas on how to keep it, but the evidence is that in Italy we already knew about some kind of pasta long before his explorations.

Even as far back as Etruscan times, there is a suggestion that they had a type of sheet pasta. Historians have found frescoes in the ancient tombs at Cerveteri, near Roma, showing people mixing flour and water, and implements such as a rolling pin and a cutting wheel. Of course, like most topics in Italy, there is much dispute about what this really means. Some say this flour-and-water dough might not have been boiled in water, but cooked on a stove to make flatbread or cakes.

Later on, a first-century Roman cook, Apicius, writes of something called *lagane*, which resembles lasagne. And it seems that the Sicilians were making pasta in the twelfth century, according to an Arabian geographer named Al-Idrisi. In 1154 he wrote about a food "made from semolina shaped into strands" that he saw in Trabia, near Palermo, made in such quantities that it met the needs of the people of Sicilia, and was "exported throughout Muslim and Christian lands." Other evidence suggests that it was the Arabs themselves who introduced the concept of pasta to the Mediterranean basin around the eleventh century, and there are Arabic texts that mention *itriyah*, a form of dried pasta.

Certainly by the thirteenth century dried pasta is mentioned in Italian documents. There is a record of dried pasta in Liguria on a medical prescription dated 1244, and in another medieval Italian document, dated 1279, a Genoese notary named Ugolino Scarpa mentions *una bariscela plena de macaronis* (*bariscela* is a medieval word that means "container"), which was part of his dead client's estate and which is thought to be some sort of dried pasta. This is the first time we get a feeling of the value of dried pasta as we know it today, something that you have in your pantry, to feed you at any time. All this was well before Marco Polo is supposed to have brought the idea of noodles from China to Venezia in 1295.

Pasta was mentioned by poets and writers in the fourteenth century, and famously in *The Decameron* (c. 1351) by Giovanni Boccaccio, who talks about the people who lived underneath a mountain of grated Parmesan cheese and "did nothing but make macaroni and ravioli, and boil them in capon broth…"

No one knows for sure about the exact origins of pasta that was boiled as we know it today. After all, what is pasta made of? Flour and water. Such basic ingredients must have been worked into a kind of dough by primitive peoples all over the world since the beginning of time. All we can say with certainty is that no people took to the idea quite like the Italians – and we're the best at cooking it!

More than macaroni

Now we think of macaroni as a specific kind of short, tubular pasta, but originally *macaroni* was used as a generic term for various pasta shapes. The word probably comes from the Latin *macerare*, which means to mix or knead, though there is a nice story told by my good friends Ann and Franco Taruschio, who ran the Walnut Tree Inn near Abergavenny for many years, and who wrote one of the seminal chef's books on Italian cooking, *Leaves from the Walnut Tree*. Their idea is that, in Napoli, a prince heard the cost of making such pasta and declared, *"Si buoni ma caroni!"* (so good, but so expensive). I like that, though it is more likely a comment from Renaissance times, when pasta became known for a while as a rich man's food, because of the cost of milling the wheat before the invention of mechanical mills.

Sometime from the fifteenth century onward, we began to use other names for pasta, which usually say something about the way it is made or the way it looks. Apart from the simple sheets of dough *(sfoglia)*, the first types of pasta were the ones that could be made in a very basic way, with the hands, like gnocchi (potato pasta dumplings), orecchiette ("little ears") from Puglia, trofie (little twisted dumplings) from Recco, *strozzapreti* ("priest stranglers") from Lazio and Umbria, and *malloreddus* from Sardegna, which are made from durum wheat and saffron, and shaped around a special basketlike tool called a *ciuliri*.

Sometimes pieces of pasta were pressed between wooden molds that stamped a pattern into the dough: like *corzetti* from Liguria, which are shaped like the *corazzo*, the ancient coins from Genoa; or *garganelli*, which is made by pressing rectangles of pasta against a grooved stick, or comb, called a *pettine*.

Later we began to have shapes like *farfalle* ("butterflies"), which in Emilia-Romagna are called *strichetti*, describing the way the middle of each shape is pinched together to make the butterfly shape. A lovely little curly pasta is *gramigna*, named after the herb of the same name, which grows everywhere in Italy, like a weed.

There is even a shape called *maltagliati*, which means "badly cut." It can be triangular, which is the way they make it in Mantova, or diamond-shaped in Veneto and Emilia-Romagna. Other pasta shapes are named after a traditional way of serving, like *zite* and *zitoni*, which are typical at weddings and take their name from the word *zita*, which is Neapolitan for "bride." Some commemorate a moment in history; for example, the wavy-edged ribbon pasta called *reginette* or *mafaldine* (the curly edges help it to hold quite delicate sauces) was created for the Princess Mafalda di Savoia, after a royal visit to Napoli.

Then someone made the discovery that you could roll out your pasta dough and cut it into strips, which were given names like tagliatelle, tagliolini and taglierini (all variations on the world *tagliare*, which means "to cut"); or fettuccine and fettuce (from *affettare*, "to slice").

The last big step in the history of pasta, from making simple handmade shapes to producing the commercial tubular pastas that everyone recognizes today, came when it was discovered that you could press your dough through a special mold or dye, full of holes, and make shapes like spaghetti or penne. Even now new shapes of pasta are being produced that reflect the times in which we live. The contemporary equivalent of the quill-shaped penne is a pasta called *chiocciola*, the old word for *snail*, which is now used for the @ sign in e-mails.

A pasta for every sauce

In Italy, every kind of pasta is linked to a particular traditional sauce, depending on what region you are in. All over the country, people have taken this simple commodity and designed it – literally designed it – differently in terms of shape and texture, to suit specific sauces made with local ingredients.

Of course, the whole world now loves pasta, and in other countries they have come up with their own inventions, such as spaghetti bolognese, which is not an Italian dish – traditionally you would never serve a meat ragù with long thin pasta, because it doesn't hold the sauce properly in the way that short tubular pasta or tagliatelle does. And then there is the American idea of spaghetti and meatballs, which again is not an Italian idea (you might have meatballs and spaghetti in separate courses, but how can you eat meatballs with strips of pasta – impossible). I sometimes wonder if the idea for the dish came from the tradition of *lasagne di carnevale*, a special dish served in Napoli just before Lent that was made with meatballs as well as ricotta, eggs and spinach. Hundreds of thousands of Italian emigrants left the Campania region around Napoli to go to America, so perhaps they took with them this tradition, and Americans, having such an abundance of meat, turned it into a staple dish of a different kind.

Italians always look first at what pasta they have, and then decide what to do with it, because the shape of pasta dictates the sauce. If you want to make a garlic and chile pasta, for example, then find you only have penne, it is a waste, because this kind of sauce is more suited to spaghetti. No one in Italy has to think about such decisions; they are just instinctive, something inherited from your mother and your grandmother, something you feel you have always known.

In cooking, however, our ideas are constantly evolving, as the books I have in my office from the last 200 years show. They put a marker in history that says: "In 1891 or 1920 this is what we are doing; this is not the final word; things are going to change, but this is a reference of our times." The world moves on and we have to move with it. I'm not talking about suddenly deciding to make pasta with mango or kumquats – pasta is a pretty sacred thing to Italians, and there are boundaries you can never cross. But what I like to do is look at our heritage and then try to reinterpret, update and fine-tune those ideas a little to suit the way we eat now. For example, at Locanda we make a raviolo stuffed with osso buco. In a restaurant like ours, people would be uncomfortable if we were to give them an enormous bowl of osso buco and then expect them to sit and suck the meat from the bones; but I know that they will love the flavor of the dish, so we came up with this neater, more concentrated way for them to enjoy it. I couldn't claim to have created anything really new; it is just a different way of looking at a classic meat dish with pasta.

The only pasta dish I can truly say I "invented," that I really consider to be 100 percent mine, is pappardelle with fava beans and arugula (see page 338), which came to me in one of those brilliant moments you sometimes have in the kitchen. Of course, pappardelle are hundreds of years old, but the idea of serving the pasta with a puree of fava beans underneath it and the pasta itself tossed in *beurre fondu* to keep it really moist and highlight the flavor of the beans is an idea I admit is influenced by my time cooking in Paris. When I see it copied in other restaurants, sometimes done by guys that I really respect...well, I like that. I consider it a great compliment.

We are all interested in what our contemporaries are doing. For example, the Milanese chef Gualtiero Marchesi, who was the first Italian to be awarded three Michelin stars, is credited as being the great inventor of the modern idea of open raviolo *(raviolo aperto)* which is like a layered lasagne, and many chefs now have a version of it (ours is on page 357). Sometimes you might see it done with a little twist in the tail: perhaps the sheets of pasta will be embellished with saffron or squid ink, or herbs, then layered up with the ragù or vegetables inside a ring, occasionally sauced and glazed under the grill. The first time I saw *raviolo aperto* I thought, "Wow," but then I remembered that years ago my mum and dad used to take my brother and me to a great trattoria where they did something similar, which they called *lasagne luna*. It would take two people to serve it: one holding a strip of pasta and letting it drop into folds like a ribbon, while the other spooned layers of pesto and Parmesan inside each fold. So, though I take my hat off to Marchesi, his idea has roots in dishes that have been made in small villages for decades.

At Locanda, we like to research regional handmade pasta, like spaghetti alla chitarra (see page 382), and play with sauces that will complement that particular texture and shape. At Refettorio, in the City, where I devised the menu, my head chef, Mattia Camorrani, came up with a brilliant way of using octopus with an artisanal fusilli lunghi, the pasta that looks a little like a corkscrew. This handmade one was a little less twisted than the commercial versions you usually see. The cleverness was not just in the way the pasta held the sauce but in the way he used the shape to mimic the ridgy, curling pieces of octopus. You see, in the kitchen you never, ever stop learning. If you lose that capacity to be surprised and excited, you know it is time to find another job.

Fresh or dried

There are two main types of pasta: fresh and dried. If you ask an Italian from almost anywhere in Italy for fresh pasta, he will assume you mean pasta made with eggs *(pasta all'uovo)*, which is used mainly for "filled" pasta, like ravioli or tortellini, and for lasagne. It can also be cut into long strips of pasta, such as tagliatelle and pappardelle. Of course, as always, there are a few regional exceptions, such as orecchiette, little "ear-shaped" pieces, which are typical of Puglia but contain no eggs, and are often sold fresh as well as dried.

Dried pasta is usually made only with durum wheat flour and water, though you can also have dried egg pasta. (In general, I prefer egg pasta to be fresh rather than dried, but occasionally you find a fantastic, carefully made one.) Dried pasta is usually divided into "long" (spaghetti, linguine, vermicelli, etc.) and "short" (penne, rigatoni, farfalle, etc.).

It is important to understand that dried durum wheat pasta and egg pasta are not versions of the same thing; they are completely different. Dried pasta, made without eggs, is something very light, digestible and healthy, whereas egg pasta contains more protein and is heavier to digest.

A plate of pasta...

I can almost tell you whether a pasta was good or not by looking at the plate straight after it has been eaten. Of course, you *really* know it was good if someone has polished their plate with a piece of bread – which we call *scarpetta* ("little shoe"). But if they haven't done that, there should be very little sauce left, because it should have been perfectly amalgamated with the pasta, and what traces there are shouldn't be dry and crusted – this shows that the sauce was too thick. There should also be a little moisture left on the plate, which tells you that the pasta didn't become too dry and sticky during the ten minutes or so it took to eat it.

I don't want to make cooking pasta sound complicated, when really it is one of the simplest things in the world, but, as with all cooking, if you understand a few basic principles, you can appreciate the difference between a plate of something that is okay and something that is truly fantastic, in which the sauce and pasta are no longer two separate things, but become one entity, in which every surface and nook and cranny of pasta is coated and saturated with flavor.

There is a very easy way to achieve this. When you drain your pasta, keep back some of its cooking water to add to the sauce – partly because this adds extra starch to the sauce, emulsifying it and helping it to cling much better to the pasta, and partly because you need to keep the pasta "alive," i.e., moist, until the last mouthful. Be brave: if you are cooking pasta for four, you need to add about ¼ cup of the cooking water. I promise you, it will make a great difference to the way your sauce coats your pasta – and if you find you have accidentally added too much cooking water, you can always drain off the excess. Pasta will carry on absorbing moisture, up to 30 percent of its weight, after it comes out of its cooking water. And whereas one minute too long boiling in the water can kill it by making it too soft, one minute longer in the sauce will let it absorb the flavors, without ruining its bite. The more you appreciate the relationship between your pasta and the sauce, the better a pasta dish will become.

What also influences the finished result is how much pasta you try to cook at a time. If you eat a fantastic plate of pasta in a restaurant, you have to consider that the kitchen was making a portion only for you, and that there were probably two chefs looking after it. At Locanda, we would never cook more than two portions of long pasta – spaghetti, linguine, etc. – at one time, because it is difficult to toss any more through the sauce comfortably. So, if we have an order for a table where everyone wants pasta, we have as many chefs as it takes, looking after it in separate pans. Even at home, I prefer not to cook more than 1 pound of long pasta at a time. Instead, if, say, ten people are coming to our house – always a challenge, because I don't have huge pots at home, and ten people means a couple pounds of pasta and a couple gallons of water – then I would either use two separate pans or avoid long pasta. I would instead either do a baked pasta, which is always appreciated and which you can prepare the day before (see page 352); or I would choose a short, sturdy pasta, like macaroni, *elicoidali* or penne, that is easier to handle and will hold up longer.

Dried pasta

Dried pasta must be made with the hardest variety of wheat: durum wheat (*durus* is Latin for "hard"). When most flours are milled, the endosperm – the heart of the kernel of wheat – breaks down into powdery flour. The endosperm of durum wheat is different – bigger than other varieties, very hard and amber-colored – and, when it is ground, it breaks into tiny chips, or semolina. In Italy, since 1967, the law requires that all dried pasta – including dried egg pasta – must be made with durum wheat. However, in the quest to satisfy the world's insatiable desire for pasta and make a profit at the same time, there is nothing that says that other countries can't use other flours in their dried pasta. But only durum wheat, with its high gluten content, can give pasta its unique texture and "bite" when it is cooked.

Traditionally, durum wheat was grown more in the warm, more arid regions of the south of Italy, especially around Napoli and Puglia. In the cooler, wetter areas of Lombardia, Veneto and Emilia-Romagna, they

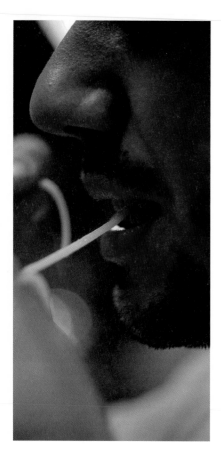

tended to grow more soft wheat for bread, biscuits and cakes. Then, between the two world wars, Mussolini, in his bid to make Italy self-sufficient, ordered that wheat, along with rice, should be grown in the north, especially on the Lombard plain, so these days durum wheat is grown all over Italy. However, the best is grown high above sea level, preferably over 7,200 feet, where the natural climate lets it grow, often without the need for pesticides, as the pests that might otherwise attack the crop can't survive the cold nights. In the mountains, the wheat develops a high level of chlorophyll, the plant's "fat," which strengthens it to cope with the change of temperature from warm day to cold night, and gives it a fuller flavor.

Now pasta is dried in sophisticated temperature-controlled drying rooms, but at one time it had to be done outside, and it could be a tricky business. If it was too hot, the pasta might dry too fast, and crack. If it dried too slowly, it could grow fungus. Napoli was known as the pasta capital of Italy – not only because so much durum wheat was grown in the region around the city but also because it was a perfect place to dry pasta – especially Gragnano, right behind the bay of Napoli. You can be in Napoli and feel you are going to die from the heat, then you move out to Gragnano, and somehow there always seems to be a whirlwind of fresh air up on the "magic hill" of the town. In the cooler north, however, because we couldn't dry pasta in the same way and because there is traditionally more dairy and poultry farming, if we ate pasta at all (rice was originally the northern staple), it became more usual to make fresh pasta with eggs, and cook it right away.

Dried pasta is such a simple, unsophisticated product, and yet there is a huge difference between poor-quality pasta and pasta that has been carefully made and has real flavor – just ask my daughter, Margherita. If Plaxy, my wife, has been in a hurry and bought a cheap package of pasta from the supermarket, Margherita will taste it and say: "What's wrong with the pasta?" Sometimes people forget that dried durum wheat pasta isn't just a vehicle for a sauce; it should have its own, slightly nutty flavor, so you could eat it with just Parmesan and oil and it would be brilliant. And, most important, it must be made and cooked with care, so that it will hold its "bite."

The soul of the pasta

I am often invited to food shows and festivals, and when I cook dried pasta at such events, I talk about the *anima* – the "soul" – of the pasta. People look at me at first as if I am some crazy romantic: "What is he talking about ... the 'soul' of the pasta?" But it is true: there is a "chain," made up of starch and links of protein, that runs down the center of a strand of dried pasta. If the durum wheat is picked at the right time, handled well and dried correctly, and if you cook the pasta for the right length of time, then the outer layer of starch will dissolve and be released into the water, but that "chain" will stay intact in the middle of the pasta. This is its "soul," and this is what gives it that slight crunch to which we refer when we say it is "al dente." The process of the soft outer starch softening, and the inner starch staying firm, is similar to what happens when you cook risotto rice.

For Italians, al dente is more than a cooking term that translates as "firm to the bite," it is an expression that has great meaning and significance for us; in other countries it is something people have heard but don't necessarily understand. If you want to see for yourself where the "bite" comes from, just squash a strand of cooked spaghetti between your thumb and forefinger and you should see this faint yellow, perfectly unbroken line. If the pasta is not made entirely from durum wheat (which is permissible if it is made outside Italy) or if it is of poor quality, or you overcook it, the molecules of starch soften as they get moist, and the links of protein will start to pull away until they break, and at first the line will appear fragmented, and then it will disappear, leaving the pasta pale and flabby. It's an interesting exercise to begin to cook some spaghetti, then take some strands out of the pan after two minutes and smash them with the side of a knife. Do the same after maybe 4, 6, 7 and 8 minutes, and you can see for yourself what happens to the "soul" as the spaghetti cooks, and eventually gets overcooked.

Every pasta is slightly different, but I would always look at the cooking time on the box and take away one minute, and then keep testing the pasta as it cooks, because it will continue to absorb moisture when it is tossed through the sauce – and it is better to have slightly more bite than to let the pasta become soggy and die. I remember once finding in the cupboard at home some long spaghetti in a smart package with a label I didn't know, and one Sunday night I decided to cook it. I made up a little sauce, tossed the pasta through it, and it was ready, but Jack was busy doing something, Margherita was off doing something else – when they came to the table a few minutes later, the pasta was stuck together in one piece. It wasn't my fault – it was the fault of the spaghetti. Good-quality pasta should hold up and stay nice and loose without sticking together, or the "chain" or "soul" inside cracking, for around five minutes.

The color of durum wheat pasta is very important: it must be golden-yellow. Apart from that, however, it is hard to tell its quality simply by looking at it in the package. For me, the price is the best indicator of the quality of the pasta, because it reflects everything that has or hasn't been done to it. I have a problem with cheap supermarket pasta. In Italy there is great competition between the big pasta companies, and Italian people are very careful about price, so how can other countries come in and commission Italian producers to make pasta for them more cheaply without cutting corners? As always with food, you have to ask not "Why is one product so expensive?" but "What has been done, or not done, to the alternative product that makes it so cheap?" Maybe, instead of starting with a pure, beautiful grain, the quality is not so good; maybe the wheat has been bleached; maybe they turned the temperature up a couple of degrees higher in the drying room, which will give you pasta that is ready one week earlier, instead of drying it more slowly at a low temperature, which preserves the molecular structure of the starches and the fragrance of the wheat. Cut all these corners and the cost of production goes down, but so does the quality.

And then the next problem is, despite the packages that say "Produce of Italy" and have Italian flags all over them, how can there be enough wheat grown in Italy to feed the world's greed for pasta? We don't have that quantity of wheat, any more than we have enough buffalo to satisfy the hunger for buffalo mozzarella. Of course wheat has to be imported, from Canada and the United States, and I can see that in the future whoever buys grains from these countries is going to have a big problem, because they are going with genetically modified food in a big way.

In Italy the Slow Food movement is trying to get a law passed that says that in order for something to be labeled 100 percent Italian pasta, it must be made with only Italian durum wheat. Just as we shouldn't be allowing olives from other countries to be pressed in Italy – not because there is anything wrong with them but the oil should not be called Italian olive oil – we should realize how important it is for the image and high quality of Italian pasta that we look after our "*terroir*," that we are proud of and protect what we grow.

The best pasta comes from producers (like Latini) who have their own wheat production areas in Italy and are in total control of the process from the grain to the factory. Maybe that means you have to pay more for a package of pasta, but think about it: a pound of pasta can feed six people really well, so even if it costs 40 cents a portion more, it is still not an expensive food. Even if I were very poor, I would still buy my pasta from such a company, rather than a cheap house-label pasta in the supermarket, because, when it comes to my family, my kids, my customers, I think they deserve something brilliant, not only in terms of taste but something that is ethically better and more healthy for them.

Six minutes of your life...

Something I find completely absurd is "fast cooking" spaghetti. Instead of cooking for six minutes, it takes ... what? Three? What is that all about? Are we all on such fast tracks that those three minutes of our lives are going to be a turning point? What are you going to do with your life to capitalize on your big gain of three minutes?

The way fast-cooking spaghetti works is that instead of having strands of pasta that are completely tubular, each piece has a little channel, which is the point of entrance for the heat. You don't really notice it, because when the pasta swells up it appears round again, but if you look carefully you will see a little mark running the length of the outside of the pasta. The pasta literally has no "soul," because it is made from inferior durum wheat flour, which won't hold its perfect line of protein as the spaghetti cooks.

The other thing I don't really understand is the fashion for colored pasta. In Italy we might occasionally use spinach or tomato pasta, because these ingredients add some flavor, but for the most part less traditional colored pastas are only a gimmick. I'm not saying I haven't experimented – as a chef you do things to show off your ideas sometimes. At Zafferano, for a bit of fun, we used to do a ravioli of white and black pasta stripes, but like most Italians I am interested in the quality of the pasta first; the way it looks is not so important.

There are two schools of thought about dried pasta. Some companies favor the "Teflon" shiny surface that is almost lacquered, like plastic, with no real texture, which is produced by pushing the dough through a stainless steel disk with holes coated with Teflon – this is a technique that was invented by the Barilla pasta company.

Other pastas are extruded through bronze plates, as they would have been done originally, and this gives them a rougher surface, which leaves a little starch on your hand when you handle the pasta, and which allows the juices and flavors of a sauce to be absorbed better.

If you are cooking something like a tomato sauce, that is full-flavored, the shiny-surfaced pasta is perfect, because it keeps the tastes and textures of the sauce and pasta distinct. Sometimes, though, if you are making a dish with a delicately flavored "split" sauce, like linguine with crab, I would rather have a pasta with more texture, which will absorb the flavors of the sauce better and strengthen the overall taste of the dish. By a "split" sauce, I mean one that isn't thick like tomato but quite thin and loose, maybe made with oil, or fish stock and ingredients that stand out, like prawns, or anchovies.

The formula

Someone once told me that when her mother drained cooked spaghetti she rinsed it under the cold tap to get rid of the starch, so that there was no danger of any strands clinging together. Are we talking here about food as a nutrient or art? One of the greatest properties of both rice and pasta is its starch content, so the last thing you want to do is wash it away. Of course some of the starch comes out into the water, and there will be some cloudiness, but a good pasta should retain most of its starch and leave the water relatively clear, whereas a poor-quality pasta will leach out all of its starch into the water, leaving it cloudy and the pasta limp, with very little bite.

The other thing I sometimes read in recipes is that you should add oil to the cooking water to keep the strands or shapes of pasta from sticking together, but I don't know where that idea comes from – I never saw anyone do it in Italy, and apart from anything else it is a waste of good oil. The way to keep the pasta separate and let it cook properly is to give it enough space to swirl and roll around easily and cook evenly. The ratio I always use for cooking dried pasta is 4¼ cups of water to every 14 ounces of pasta.

Once your water is at a rolling boil, put all your pasta in together. If it is long pasta, use a fork to curl the strands gently around the pan, so that they are underwater as quickly as possible. Stir the pasta around quickly when it first hits the water, as this is when the starch first begins to soften, and you want to keep the strands separate, or they will begin to stick together. The pasta swells as it cooks and, if the pieces are crowded in the water, then the pasta trapped at the bottom (if you are using a stainless steel pan, which generates most heat at the base) or at the sides (if you use an aluminum pan, which generates heat all around) will cook quicker than the rest.

Another reason for not trying to cram in too much is that as you put your pasta into the water, which should be at a rolling boil, you want to bring it back to this temperature as soon as possible. If you drop 14 ounces of pasta into a gallon of water, it will come back to a rolling boil very quickly – whereas if you were to drop 4 pounds into the same amount of water it would be a very different story.

For every 14 ounces of pasta and 4¼ cups of water, I add 1 tablespoon of salt. Some people say that rather than seasoning the water before you add your pasta, you should put in the salt just before the pasta is cooked – but for me that is too late. We always do it in the traditional way, by seasoning the water as soon as it starts to boil, so that the salt disperses evenly – always with crystals of rock or sea salt – and then we taste the pasta as it begins to soften (after about 2 to 3 minutes) and add a little more if necessary. You don't want to taste saltiness; you just want to make sure that the pasta is not bland.

Dried pasta: long

Bucatini ("little holes") – Also called perciatelli in Napoli, bucatini is traditional in Roma, and is like spaghetti but bigger, with a larger space in the center – a bit like a drinking straw. Bucatini is good with powerful sauces, like Amatriciana, made with *guanciale* (cured pig's cheek), chiles and tomato, and can hold on well to ragù and sauces made with spicy salami. It is also used to line a timballo (see page 355).

Bucatoni – This is like bucatini but a little fatter; so it is perfect for a big party-size timpano (the southern version of timballo).

Capelli d'angelo ("angel hair") – These are very thin strands, which they call *capelvenere* ("hair of Venus") in Liguria. They are too thin to hold a sauce, so are usually used in soups or broth; if you break up the strands, their starch will thicken the soup slightly.

Capellini ("fine hair") – This, the very thinnest, wispiest pasta, is used in the same way as capelli d'angelo. It is often given to small children, with butter and cheese, or sometimes cooked in milk and served to them with sugar or honey when they aren't feeling good.

Fusilli lunghi – These are curly, like springs. *Lunghi* means "long" (you also have fusilli corti, short fusilli, see page 294). They are best with chunky sauces, made with ingredients like peppers, olives, broccoli, eggplant, etc., that cling to the curves. They are rarely served with fish, though one of my chefs, Mattia Camorrani, makes a wonderful fusilli lunghi with octopus, in which the shapes of the octopus and the pasta mirror one another.

Linguine ("little tongues") – This is made from durum wheat and is very like spaghetti, only flat rather than round – and is more of a southern pasta; not nearly as well known in the rest of Italy. The two types of pasta are quite interchangeable; there are no sauces that really work better with spaghetti or linguine – it is just a matter of choice.

Spaghetti – Everyone knows this, probably the most famous pasta in the world, but not so many people know that it comes in various sizes, so there is no standard cooking time. It is odd, though, that one of the world's most famous dishes is spaghetti bolognese, which doesn't really exist in traditional Italian cooking. In fact, it contradicts every principle of pasta, because a heavy meat ragù would always be paired with wider flatter pasta, such as tagliatelle or pappardelle, or short, chunkier-shaped pasta that will hold the sauce far better than spaghetti. Think about it: you put your fork into a plate of spaghetti and turn it around, and anything chunky that doesn't twist with the pasta gets left on the plate, whereas with penne, every time you put your fork into a piece of pasta you also pick up pieces of meat and vegetable that are trapped inside the tubes.

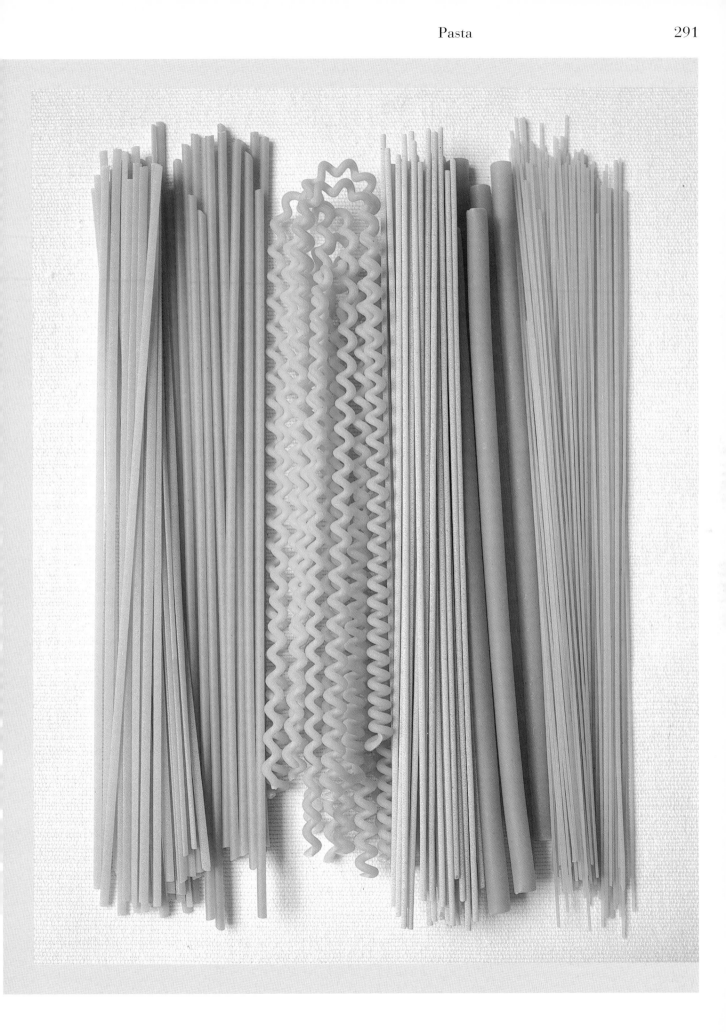

Spaghetti is really best with sauces that are oil- and tomato-based, in which you have nothing too chunky, so the sauce can cling to it – think of the silky egg and bacon mixture in a carbonara, or tomato, olives, capers and melted anchovies in spaghetti alla puttanesca.

Of course, you can make fresh spaghetti, but I wouldn't buy fresh spaghetti in the supermarket as, in my experience, it tends to be much softer than pasta you make yourself at home. It is much better to do as most Italians would do, and buy a good-quality dried durum wheat spaghetti.

Spaghettini ("thin strings") – Anything that has "ini" at the end in Italian means "small," so this is literally a thinner version of spaghetti, used with light herby or spicy sauces, or anything with oil, cheese or tomato, cooked or raw. Remember that everything that goes into your sauce must be cut a little thinner than for spaghetti.

Vermicelli ("little worms") – Smaller versions are vermicellini; larger ones are vermicelloni. Like a thinner spaghetti, this works with the same kind of sauces, but you need to chop everything very fine. If you have any left over, when it is cold you can make it into a frittata: mix it with some beaten egg (and some Parmesan, depending on your sauce), maybe add some finely chopped cooked green beans or potatoes, mix everything together and sauté it, flattening it in the pan, until it is golden, then turn it over and cook the other side until golden and heated through. It will become entwined and gel together and crisp up beautifully, so it looks a bit like a bird's nest. Vermicelli are also good in broth.

Dried pasta: short tubes

Because they are quite strong, and because they have big holes in them, pasta tubes trap chunky rich sauces inside – and those that are ridged *(rigate)* hold them also on the outside. Almost all tubular pasta is dried, apart from garganelli, which can also be fresh. You can have corkscrew ones *(cavatappi)* or straight-edged ones that have ridges curving around them *(elicoidali)*, but the most usual are:

Garganelli – Traditional in Romagna (the southern, coastal area of Emilia-Romagna), it can be fresh as well as dried. It is similar to penne but more rustic, made from a square of pasta rolled up to look like the ridged quill of a pen. This is done using a special "paddle," a little like the one we use for making gnocchi. Also, whereas penne is made with durum wheat, garganelli is made with eggs, and the pasta is thinner and more delicate, so when it is cooked it will squash a little – unlike penne, which keeps its shape.

Maccheroni – This was once the name by which all pasta was known, but it is now used to mean various kinds of short pasta, usually cooked with butter and cheese for children or baked, like penne.

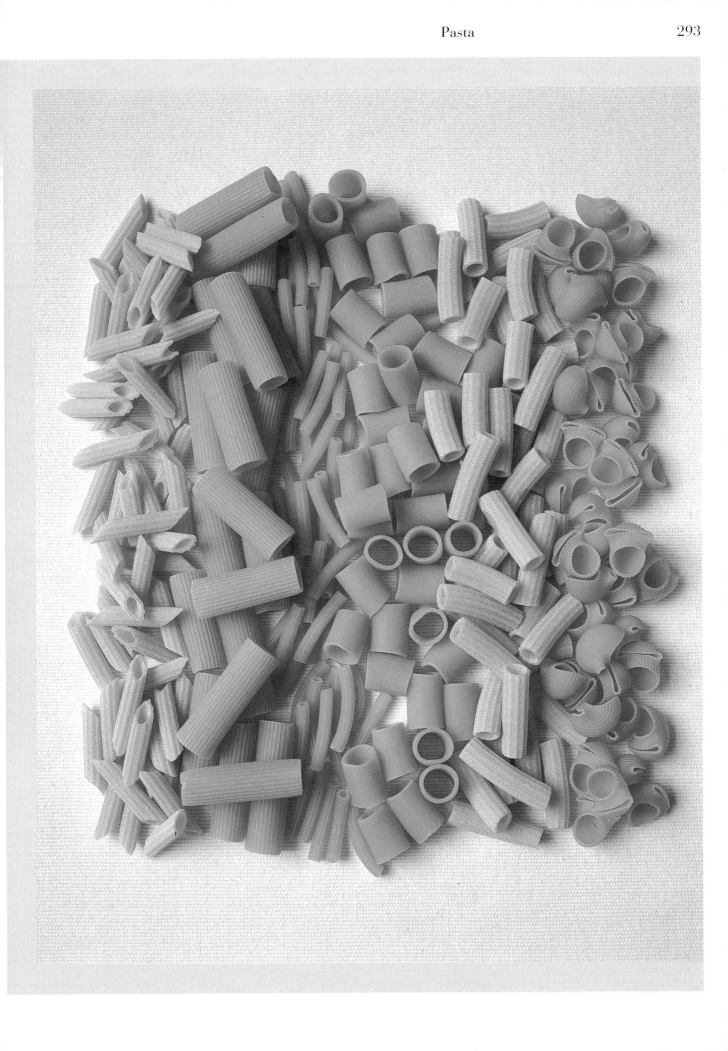

Penne ("pens") – Pointed like pen nibs, and either smooth or ridged, these can take up and hold on to any rich sauce, such as a ragù or the traditional all'arrabbiata. Penne works well with béchamel, which coats the pasta easily, so it is often used with meat sauce (or vegetables) and béchamel and baked in the oven (pasta al forno, see page 352).

Rigatoni – Similar to penne, but without the pointed "quill" ends, these have a big hole through the middle and ridges on the outside. Traditionally they are served with meat sauces, because they can hold on to the sauce inside too, or they might also be baked in the oven in the same way as penne. There are variations called *mezze maniche* ("half sleeves"), or *maniche di frate* ("priest's sleeves") from central and northern Italy.

Ziti – From Napoli, this very big tubular pasta is traditional with meat sauces, often spicy ones.

Dried pasta: shapes

You might think that these are just for fun, but they also have a purpose, because they are able to hold sauces in special ways. They come in all sorts of shapes, like lumache ("snails"), radiatori (ridged like tiny "radiators") and rotelle, from Sicilia, which look like little steering wheels or cartwheels with spokes. The best known include:

Conchiglie rigate – Sea shells with grooves on the outside, these come in all sizes, from the tiniest, which are usually used in soup, to larger ones often served with cheese and speck, to big, fat ones, which resemble the conch shells you might find on the seashore. These pasta shapes are often blanched, stuffed, then put into a sauce and baked.

Farfalle – From Emilia-Romagna, these squares of pasta are pinched in the center, so that they look like butterflies, with a thicker "body" in the center and light wings. They give a large surface area to take up the sauce and usually go with light sauces, made with vegetables and fish. In the mountains, however, they are often served with vegetable sauces, perhaps broad beans and lardo. The idea is to have pieces of vegetable a similar size to the pasta.

Fusilli – Also known as fusilli corti ("short springs"), originally these were rolled on a gadget that looked like a knitting needle to make them spiky. Traditionally they are served with rich meat and cheese sauces or oily sauces with tuna, spices, etc.

Orecchiette – The name means "little ears." Though you can buy them dry, they are traditionally made fresh by hand, using an eggless pasta dough, which is pressed between the thumb and forefinger. Typically they are served with a sauce made with turnip tops or cime di rapa (see page 318) or other vegetables.

Pastina ("little pasta") – These are most often used in soup for children, because they are made into all sorts of shapes. Some of the oldest have been given new names; for example the old *avemarie* or *paternostri*, which were based on rosary beads, are now called *corallini* ("little pieces of coral"); and what we call ditalini rigati ("ridged little fingers") used to be called garibaldini in the nineteenth century (after Garibaldi, the great Italian hero). When I was little we had alfabetini ("letters of the alphabet") and stelline ("stars"), but now there are many more shapes, such as *acini di pepe* ("peppercorns"), *semi di melone* ("melon seeds"), *puntine* ("dots"), *risoni* ("rice grains"), *quadrucci* ("little squares"), *funghetti* ("little mushrooms"), *farfalline* ("little bow ties"), *lumachine* ("little snails") and *anellini* ("little rings"). A bit more grown-up are flat pasta triangles *(maltagliati)*.

Strozzapreti – Confusingly, in some regions potato gnocchi are also sometimes known as strozzapreti, but the ones most people know are little twists of pasta that you can buy dried (though we make our own fresh ones). The name means "priest stranglers" or "priest chokers" – from *strozzare* ("to throttle"). The story is that the shape of the pasta killed a priest who ate too many too quickly. In Marche, they have something similar called *strangolapreti* (from *strangolare*, "to strangle"). All are good with tomato sauces and ingredients that can also be "stringy" like onions and vegetables cut into long, thin strips (julienne).

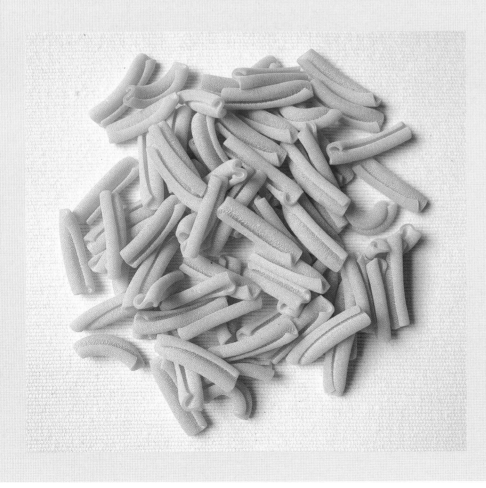

Spaghetti al crudo

Spaghetti with tomatoes, olives, capers and anchovies

Crudo means "raw" – so in this recipe the ingredients for the sauce are uncooked. Look for a spaghetti with a surface that is slightly rough rather than very shiny, because you need everything to cling to the pasta. In Italy, this is usually a dish you make in summer, because it is all about the quality of ingredients like tomatoes and basil. The tomatoes we use are the big ones, Cuore di Bue (see page 300), which are fleshy and juicy, with not too many seeds. On a hot day in Italy, many people will add a can of tuna to spaghetti al crudo, and that is lunch – just one course.

2 tablespoons capers
(baby ones if possible)
4 tablespoons black olives,
preferably Taggiasche,
pitted
5 anchovy fillets, preferably
salted and rinsed,
finely chopped
2 tomatoes (preferably Cuore
di Bue, or 3 smaller ones –
the best quality you can
find), chopped
2 tablespoons tomato passata
14 ounces spaghetti
bunch of basil
5 tablespoons
extra virgin olive oil
salt and pepper

Put all the ingredients except the spaghetti and basil into a sauté pan with half the olive oil and mix together but don't heat. Taste and season.

Bring a large pot of water to a boil, add salt (use a little less than usual, as the anchovies will add salt later) and put the pasta into it, using a fork to curl it around the pan, so that it gets under the water quickly. Cook for about a minute less than the time suggested on the package, until al dente.

While the pasta is cooking, put the sauté pan containing the ingredients for the sauce over the top of the pasta pan, so that the steam can just warm everything up a little, and let the flavors begin to infuse.

When the pasta is cooked, drain, reserving the cooking water.

Add the pasta to the pan containing the sauce ingredients, and toss well, adding some cooking water if necessary, to loosen.

Add the rest of the olive oil and toss again.

Tear the basil leaves, scatter over the top and toss again. Serve immediately.

Spaghetti al polpo

Spaghetti with octopus

This is the way that I learned to cook octopus from my friend Vincenzo Borgonzolo, who used to own Al San Vincenzo in London – cooked very simply, simmering it gently in oil for about half an hour. It is the same way that we cook it for the recipe for Octopus salad with new potatoes (see page 97). As the octopus cooks it releases its own moisture into the pan, so at the end of cooking, you have something very, very tender – much more so than if you had boiled the octopus in water.

Once it is cooked, it is important to cut up the octopus and let it cool in the cooking juices, so that it becomes sticky and gelatinous. You can keep it in the fridge for a couple of days, where it will solidify; then, when you want to make the dish, bring it out and finish it off in the tomato sauce. Because it is so gelatinous, when you eat the octopus the meaty texture combines with this wonderful, rich, sticky sensation in the mouth, to give a special flavor of the sea that people will remember for a long time.

Your fishmonger can clean and prepare the octopus for you. As I mentioned in the recipe for Octopus salad, you can use frozen octopus instead, and because the freezing process breaks down the cell structure and therefore tenderizes the flesh, you don't have to bat it before cooking.

In the restaurant, we make this with fresh Spaghetti alla chitarra (see page 382). You can buy this in Italy but also in the United States. If you don't feel brave enough to make your own, then it is better to use dried spaghetti.

When we make any seafood pasta, we tend to leave it in its sauce a little longer before serving. This is because these "split" seafood sauces won't naturally cling to the pasta as thicker sauces will – so you need to give the pasta more time in the sauce, to allow it to release its starch and thicken it, and also for the pasta to absorb a little more of the delicate flavors.

1 octopus, cleaned
1 large chile, split in half, plus 1 more (optional, to taste)
large handful of parsley (with stalks) plus 2 tablespoons chopped parsley
3 whole garlic cloves
6 tablespoons extra virgin olive oil, plus a little more for finishing
2 tablespoons tomato passata or 2 crushed tomatoes
14 ounces spaghetti
salt and pepper

If the octopus is fresh, beat it with a meat hammer to tenderize, and rinse very well under cold running water, to remove excess saltiness.

Put the chile, the handful of parsley and stalks, the garlic and half the olive oil into a large casserole. Add the octopus (don't season it, as it will be salty enough), cover with a lid and let it simmer for about 1 hour – but stir every 5 minutes.

Remove the octopus from the pan, reserving the cooking liquid, and cut it into little pieces. Put the octopus pieces back into the cooking liquid and let it cool down. Once cool, you can store it in the fridge if you don't want to make the dish immediately.

Heat the rest of the oil in a large sauté pan, add the passata or the tomatoes and extra chile, if using, with the octopus and a little of the cooking liquid (taste it first and, if it is too salty, use plain water). Let the octopus heat through, taste and season only if you need to.

Cook the spaghetti in salted boiling water for about a minute less than the time suggested on the package. Drain, reserving some of the cooking water. Add the spaghetti to the pan containing the octopus. Toss through in the pan for 30 seconds or so, adding a little of the cooking water, if necessary, to thicken the sauce. Add the rest of the parsley, toss through quickly and serve, drizzled with some more of the olive oil.

Pomodori

Tomatoes

"The steak and kidney pie of Italy"

I can't imagine life without tomatoes. Really, I can't. The world would be a completely different place – certainly Italy would be. What other fruit is there that has that texture and bite, that combination of sweetness and acidity? Take a tomato straight from the vine and smell it, and it is like nothing else. In Italy, when you drive south along the road in summer, you have this fantastic aroma all around you and, when it is time to pick, it is an exciting moment, comparable to the grape harvest – suddenly the fields are buzzing with people and everyone is running up and down.

I will never forget one time we were in Italy with one of our waiters and his family, who live in Liguria, where they make olive oil on a small estate. On this particular day, we all went to the seaside, and the father brought out the bread and some Cuore di Bue ("heart of the cow") tomatoes, which they grew in their own garden. He squashed them into the bread, poured over some of the olive oil from their farm, seasoned the tomatoes with salt and pepper, and I tell you it was one of the best things I have ever eaten.

Tomatoes are not associated with the rich or the poor, they are everybody's food, a truly great thing. So it breaks my heart to say it, but the Italians didn't invent the tomato. We think of tomatoes as coming from southern Italy, but the reality is that the big production there didn't really start until the 1800s, when the famous dish of pasta and tomatoes became popular in and around Napoli. (By the way, in this country, I know that when people make spaghetti with tomato sauce, they like to sprinkle it with Parmesan cheese – so does my dad; he is a Parmesan addict – but in Napoli, if you sit in a restaurant and order *spaghetti al pomodoro*, that is what you get – maybe a little basil, and some olive oil, a piece of bread, but no cheese – they won't even suggest it. If you want it, you have to ask.)

If we have to bow to two civilizations to say thank you for the tomato, it is the Aztecs and the Spanish, because tomatoes were brought into Spain from South America, sometime after the Spanish conquered Napoli in 1503 (remember, Italy was still a collection of city-states, and Napoli was ruled by the Spanish kings and later the house of Bourbon). Also, during the era of the Medici, the great multiculturalists of the time, a huge influx of Jewish people came over to Italy from Spain, and were encouraged by Ferdinando I to set up in Livorno, as they were considered a great asset to society, because of their ability to deal and do business. The Jewish community was used to the idea of cooking with tomatoes and many of the traditional dishes from Livorno are tomato-based.

Even now, while Campania, the province around Napoli, and Parma are huge producers of tomatoes, Catalunya in Spain still produces half of the world's supply. Even *bruschetta al pomodoro* has its counterpart in Spanish toasted bread with garlic, tomato and olive oil – the most famous one, as my Catalan pastry chef, Ivan Icra, likes to remind me, is the Catalan version, *pa amb tomaquet*. So I have to acknowledge that the tomato is as important to the Spanish as it is to us.

The tomato is a relation of the pepper, eggplant and potato – and if you think about it, there is a great similarity between the leaf of the potato and the tomato plant. The first tomatoes were brought over to Napoli from Seville purely as decorative plants, with little pea-sized fruit. Imagine, back in the 1600s, how incredible and fascinating it must have been to suddenly see an ornamental hedge covered with these tiny, beautiful bright fruits.

Before we find any mention of tomatoes in cooking, we can find old paintings with tomatoes in them. The Italian word for tomatoes is *pomodoro*, which means "golden apple" (the first tomatoes were probably yellow), and in some countries, like France, they were called "fruit of love" *(pomme d'amour)*, so clearly artists were interested in their romantic image long before the general public knew much about them. One of the earliest mentions of tomatoes in any Italian literature was by a chef, Antonio Latini – who talked about "tomato sauce, Spanish style" in a book on Neapolitan cooking, *Lo Scalco alla Moderna (The Modern Steward)*, in the seventeenth century. Still, it was a while before they reached the dinner table, after the botanical gardens started to distribute seeds around the Vesuvian plain, with a soil that is very high in calcium and phosphate, so the tomato plants grew very well.

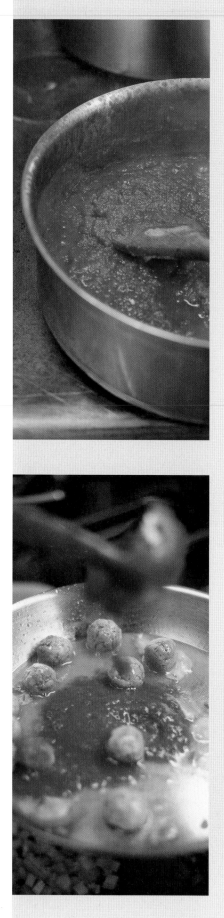

Of course, once the cultivation of tomatoes began in a big way, in the technological north we realized that we had the potential to create an industry from the produce of the south. So near Parma, next to the Ducati factory, they built the first plant for pulping, preserving and canning tomatoes. Every Italian kitchen uses good-quality canned tomatoes – you come home from vacation, you have a couple of cans of tomatoes in the cupboard, some dried pasta, olive oil and a couple of cloves of garlic, and you have dinner. Often the tomatoes used are quite regional, so all over the country you will find different varieties and brands. The important thing to check is that the can says only tomato, and maybe a touch of salt; that's it – no added water, no emulsifiers or thickeners.

For Americans I think tomatoes are often just tomatoes, but Italians have an instinctive understanding of different varieties and the way to use them. In Italy, if you have even a tiny patch of ground for a garden, you grow tomatoes. When I was young, we would grow three different kinds for the salad, including San Marzano, which have thin skins, less water and a higher percentage of pulp than many other types of tomato.

All in all, there are about 5,000 cultivated varieties of tomato in the world, and in America new hybrids are being developed all the time: more disease-resistant, with faster maturation, but, of course, I think there is no substitute for the natural microclimatic conditions you find in southern Italy or Spain. At Locanda, we buy from the different regional markets – maybe 15 to 20 types throughout the year; in summer from Sorrento, in winter from Sardegna – and always on the vine, which isn't just an aesthetic thing. You can tell by the state of the vine how long ago the tomato was picked. I am looking for a beautiful, mature green vine that isn't dry and old, which would tell me that the tomato was picked five days before, or more. Every morning, when the tomatoes come into the kitchen, we see the quality, and then we decide what we can do with them. If you are making something as simple as a salad of chargrilled tuna with arugula and tomato, that tomato has to be fantastic, or you don't make the salad at all.

There is no doubt that for a fresh salad or sauce, the round, ridged Cuore di Bue is the superior tomato: the flavor of Italy in a big half-pound fruit. Chop some and cook them briefly in a little olive oil, with chopped garlic and parsley, black olives and anchovies, and they will give you a fantastic, refreshing sauce. Or you can make a richer, sweeter, longer-cooked sauce by cutting them into big pieces, cooking them lightly in olive oil, then adding some more oil, a little salt and some torn basil leaves, closing up your pot and letting the tomatoes cook gently for about 45 minutes. At the last minute, crush your tomatoes a bit, and toss your cooked pasta through it.

San Marzano are thought to be the best for canning, and in our village, they would traditionally be used to make passata, the sauce that would also be your lifeblood for the winter. Before the technological advances that have given us canned tomato pulp, there was only passata. Even when I was small, our village of Corgeno stopped in the middle of summer, when the blue pulping machine with its big handle was set up in

the courtyard, and everyone – old men, women, children – brought their wheelbarrows full of tomatoes from their gardens to put through the machine. You would put your pots underneath to catch the thick pulp, take it home, boil it up with a little salt, and then put it into sterilized jars, top it with olive oil and keep it in the larder. My granddad used to take the tomato skins, which were separated by the machine, and put them on our vegetable garden, like manure. He said it was good for the soil. As always in our family, nothing was wasted.

In Italy, there are no rules about when to use passata, or when to use canned tomatoes. The two differ in that for passata the skins and seeds are taken away as the tomatoes are pulped, and then the pulp is passed through a sieve ("passed" – that is what the word *passata* means), so that you have something that is quite smooth and dense, and ready to use. If you want to make a quite loose, split, chunky tomato sauce, and you have fresh tomatoes, you might cook them in oil, with some garlic, and then add some passata; whereas if you want something thicker that will coat the pasta quite strongly, you might use canned tomatoes.

If you find yourself with large quantities of overripe tomatoes, you can make your own slightly more sophisticated passata. Sauté a little garlic and onion in oil, then squash your tomatoes, add them to the pan and cook until soft and pulpy. Put them through a sieve to get rid of the skins.

In the old days, tomato paste was also made locally – the passata was boiled up in big cauldrons in the village square and, when it was reduced right down and really thick, everyone had a share to take home. Nowadays, most people buy their paste – oddly, for me, it is something I learned the value of only quite late in my career in Sardegna, watching a chef make clam and tomato soup. He tasted it and clearly wasn't happy with the flavor, so he took a big spoonful of tomato paste and added it, and after two minutes of boiling, the paste had lifted the flavor and acidity of the soup and given it a fantastic tomato sweetness. It is important that you buy a good paste, though, because some of the ones in the supermarket are pretty terrible. Taste it; it should be pleasant enough to eat straight from the can or tube, not too astringent and acidic, but sweet and concentrated, almost like eating a tomato that has dried naturally in the sun.

Sometimes we do a dish of pasta (garganelli) with a mixture of fresh and sun-dried tomatoes (see page 323). Sun-dried tomatoes are something that, coming from the north, I didn't encounter much when I was younger. I would say use them only occasionally and be restrained, as their flavor is quite powerful. They can add a different dimension to a dish, but they have become so fashionable they are dramatically overused and misused.

For me one of the joys of the tomato in all its guises is that it can be thirst-quenching and refreshing, but I also like to think of the tomato as the steak and kidney pie of Italy – warming and comforting. Whenever I came home to Corgeno after being away for a long time, my grandmother cooked spaghetti with tomatoes – my welcome-back dish – and, if tomatoes were out of season, she would have made a tomato sauce from the passata that she had bottled from the tomatoes we grew in our garden in the summer. There is something very special about that.

A practical note: In restaurant kitchens we tend to peel and deseed tomatoes, then chop them, for neatness. Just blanch the tomatoes first in boiling water for about 10 seconds (if you are boiling water for pasta, you can dip the tomatoes into it before you put in the pasta). Take them out with a slotted spoon, put them under cold running water, then they should peel easily. Cut them in half and scoop out the seeds with a teaspoon, then cut each half into two or four, and then into small dice, depending on the recipe.

Linguine al pesto

Linguine with pesto

Linguine with pesto is traditional in some parts of Liguria, whereas in the city of Genova they often prefer pesto with *trofie*, small triangles of pasta, which you can buy fresh in the *pasticceria*, and which were originally made with leftover pieces, rolled up, then flattened, so they look like tiny uncooked croissants – or long, thin maggots. What is beautiful about trofie is that the oily pesto gets inside them and attaches itself to all their twists, but somehow the trofie seem to remain white against the green of the sauce.

Toast the pine nuts: preheat the oven to 355°F, spread the pine nuts on a baking tray and put them in the preheated oven very briefly, just long enough to turn them golden.

Bring some salted water to a boil in a small pan, put in the beans and blanch them quickly, about 2 minutes. Drain and split apart lengthwise (they should just pull apart). Reserve for later.

Peel the potato and cut it into dice about ½ inch. Put into a pan of cold salted water, bring to the boil, turn down the heat and cook until soft. Take the pan off the heat and leave the potato pieces in the water until you need them.

Bring a large pan of water to a boil, add salt, then put in the linguine and cook for about a minute less than the time suggested on the package until al dente.

While the pasta is cooking, put the potatoes into a sauté pan and mix in the beans and pesto with half the olive oil.

When the pasta is cooked, drain, reserving some of the cooking water. Add the pasta to the pan containing the sauce and toss together, without heating. You need to do this quickly, or the pasta will cool and the pesto will darken in color (the heat will start to turn the bright green of the basil black). Add a little of the cooking water, if necessary, to loosen the sauce.

Add the cheese and the rest of the olive oil. The pesto should provide all the seasoning you need, but taste and season if necessary. Toss well to coat, then serve with the pine nuts sprinkled over.

2 tablespoons pine nuts
12 long green beans
1 large potato
14 ounces linguine or dried trofie
4 tablespoons Pesto
    (see page 309)
2 tablespoons
    extra virgin olive oil
2 tablespoons grated Parmesan
    or Pecorino Sardo
salt and pepper

Pesto

"Truly made to go with pasta"

There was a man my father knew in our village named Feruccio, who was a *camionista*, a truck driver. This man traveled all over Italy and seemed to have an amazing knowledge of everything, though my dad used to tell me, "Don't listen, he'll say he's a doctor today, a priest tomorrow." One day Feruccio said to me: "So you want to be a chef? You know how to make pesto?" I started to say, "Yes, like this…" "No, no," he said. "I'll give you some of my pesto to taste and, if you like it, before I die I will tell you my secret recipe." Well, he gave us some of his pesto and it was fantastic; but I never did discover his secret, because one day when I was in London, my father phoned me up, and told me Feruccio was dead. "No!" I said. "He never gave me the recipe!"

There are only half a dozen ingredients that go into pesto – nuts, garlic, salt, sweet basil, olive oil and cheese – but everyone has his own "secret" way of making it. At Olivo one of our chefs worked with the two brothers who make the pesto for the Vatican, and he used to say that all the ingredients would be brought into a special room, and then they would shut the doors and make the pesto by hand. No one else was allowed to know the recipe. All you could hear from outside was the thwock of the marble pestles and mortars being worked.

If there is a secret, for me it has to be the quality of the basil. Out of every box that arrives in our kitchen, only a proportion will be good enough to use for pesto; the rest will be used in other dishes. I love basil – even in a salad, it gives a fantastic lift – and there are more than 50 varieties of basil grown all around the Mediterranean. What I think is most important, though, is the size of the leaf. The perfect sweet basil leaf is tiny and the best is from Liguria, where most of the commercial pesto production in Italy is based, from a particular village called Prà. The reason for this is that during the day, the plants have the full force of the sun, and then at night, the temperature drops dramatically, because of the region's exposure to the winds. To protect it from the cold, the basil builds up more chlorophyll, which is a green plant's lifeblood and gives the leaves their taste. Because the smaller leaves are the most vulnerable, they build up the highest concentration of chlorophyll, and therefore flavor. Also, the smaller leaves are less fibrous than the bigger ones, so the pesto will have a smoother texture.

It sounds crazy, but we have the leaves from Prá flown over specially, with their roots still attached, and wrapped in plastic because they won't last long. As soon as they come into the kitchen, the big process of making them into pesto involves a team of chefs washing the leaves in a big sink to take off the earth, lifting them out with a skimmer, then letting them drain. Then we wrap them very gently in clean cloths to protect them and shake them outside the kitchen door. Finally, they are spread out on the work surfaces, and left to finish drying completely,

ready to make the pesto. It takes us a whole morning to make two big jarfuls, which we cover with three fingers of oil, and then they can be kept in the fridge and ladled out as we need it.

Some people use white almonds or walnuts rather than pine nuts (or a mixture), and there is a great divide between those who favor pecorino and those who prefer Parmesan. Personally I prefer to use pine nuts and pecorino from Sardegna, which is a little less salty than Parmesan. There is a natural connection between Liguria, where the basil grows, and Sardegna. Despite the sea that separates them, there are parts of Sardegna – such as the satellite island of San Pietro, whose main town, Carloforte, was founded by Ligurian fishermen – where they still speak the Ligurian dialect.

I am quite a purist about pesto – I don't like to see anything other than the classical ingredients added (though we do an arugula "pesto" in a similar way, which we serve with chicken). Sometimes you see salads dressed with pesto, but I think pesto needs warmth to bring the flavors to life and arouse that aroma which fills your nose and makes it so special. That is why a spoonful added to minestrone is beautiful – but it was truly made to go with pasta.

If you can make pesto in a mortar, it is the most satisfying way. I remember hearing an Italian actor talking about his passion for pesto and the way the salt and garlic and basil screamed out at you from the bowl. Every time I make it by hand, I think of that, because it is true, the smells are enormous. On a large scale, though, it is easier to do it in a food processor. The important thing is to make sure you have a sharp blade that will chop the basil quickly without its becoming warm, or it will begin to ferment and taste bitter, whereas what you want from pesto is that wonderful freshness of the basil. The same goes for the nuts: if you overwork them, they become sweaty. Also, you don't want an oil that will overpower the basil; I would always choose a light Ligurian one. In Italy, we use very little garlic when we make pesto; and in some regions, like Liguria, they use none at all – and no salt, either. Often I watch chefs making it with so much garlic that the flavor overpowers the light, fragrant taste of the basil.

In England the perception of pesto seems to be based on the kind you find in house-brand jars in the supermarket, which is so garlicky I would call it a green garlic sauce, not a true pesto. Probably it is made this way because garlic is a cheaper ingredient than basil. This is the flavor people have come to know, to the point that they often don't understand a real pesto when they taste it.

Yes, you want some flavor of garlic, but it should be there to sustain the basil, and not be so strong that you will kill half the people in your office if you eat some and then breathe over them.

Pesto

Because pesto relies so much on good-quality basil, make it when the herb is plentiful and you can pick the tastiest small leaves. Buy a few big potfuls rather than little packets of leaves. You can make plenty and keep it in the fridge under a layer of oil for 6 months. If you are making pesto to keep, make sure you don't use late basil that has started to flower, as the leaves will be too mature, and the pesto will go bad quickly, even under oil. Also remember, as you use your pesto, to clean the sides of the jar, because any of the sauce that clings to the sides above the oil will turn black and rancid.

Either in a food processor with a sharp blade or using a mortar and pestle, start with the garlic and salt. Smash the garlic, then add the nuts and crush them, but try not to overwork them.

Drop in the basil leaves only a few at a time and work them in as quickly as you can.

Then add your cheese and finally the oil, until you have a bright green paste (the quicker you bring the whole thing together, the less heat you will generate, and this will keep the bright color; the longer you work it, the darker it will look).

Makes a small jar
2 garlic cloves
2 tablespoons pine kernels, toasted
½ pound fresh basil leaves
2 tablespoons grated pecorino or Parmesan
around 1¼ cups extra virgin olive oil, preferably Ligurian
tiny pinch of salt

Linguine all'aragosta

Linguine with lobster

Lobsters are beautiful creatures. They look so primitive, like something between an animal and a dinosaur, and chefs are constantly fascinated by them – their color, shape, the gorgeous sweetness of the meat. But because they have become a symbol of luxury – if ever there was a social standing in food, lobster comes right at the top, along with truffles and caviar – they have been the victims of overzealous cooks who see them as a culinary challenge. So they have had humiliating things done to them, like being smothered in cheese for lobster thermidor or, worse still, made into mousse.

At the Laurent in Paris, my job was to weigh the lobsters every morning. They had to be 1 kilo (2.2 pounds) precisely – 50 grams under or over and I had to send them back. They used to be really lively too, because they didn't freeze them before their journey from the market. I had to split them, chop up the tails and mix them with an enormous amount of eggs and cream, and make a terrine. What a waste of such a lovely creature. I made a promise to myself that if ever I was in charge of my own kitchen, I would serve lobster chargrilled, with a piece of lemon, nothing else. Nothing!

Then one day, when I was cooking at Olivo, I was talking to someone who had just come back from Posilipo, near Napoli, who told me about this fantastic lobster with spaghetti that he ate by the sea – the best meal, he said, he had ever had in his life. The way he described it, I could taste this lobster… I was there, eating it. So I was torn: do I do a dish that I know everyone loves, or do I stand by my vow and let the lobster be the hero, chargrilled, nothing else? Well, I made the dish, and I still make it and, especially on a sunny day, people still tell me it reminds them of their holiday in Italy.

Some people argue that you shouldn't combine lobster with tomato, as we do here, but I feel that the touch of acidity from the tomato and wine, and the little touch of chile pepper, all help sustain the sweetness of the lobster.

You need a really fresh lobster for this, so buy one from a fishmonger you trust – most important is to make sure the lobster hasn't been blanched, otherwise there will be no flavor left in it by the time you have finished the sauce and combined it with the pasta. The best thing, if you have the courage, is to buy a live lobster. Put it into the fridge for a couple of hours, or the freezer for 15 minutes, to put it into a torpor; then you can dispatch it quickly, accurately and humanely, by holding the claws still and inserting a sharp knife into the head behind the eyes and cutting straight down, between the eyes, so the head is split completely in half.

I know this will upset some people, but we have paid a lot of attention to the research that university biologists have done on killing lobsters painlessly. They concluded that lobsters do feel pain, so plunging them alive into boiling water, which was the custom in many kitchens, is inhumane. There is an electric stun gun that has been developed that makes lobsters and crabs unconscious in seconds and oblivious to pain long enough to be cooked in boiling water. Until that is available commercially, however, it is agreed that the way I described above is the best method of dispatching the lobster. If you think about it, it is no worse than killing a chicken – just that you have to do it yourself. A word of warning, though: the lobster might jump around a bit, even after the head has been split – it is only a reflex; I promise you there is no life left in the lobster.

When you make pasta with seafood such as lobster and langoustines, the cooking of the seafood has to be very quick, or it will end up like shoe leather. Also remember that you need to drain the pasta about a minute before it is going to be al dente, so that it can finish cooking in the sauce, and absorb more of the seafood flavors and let the starch it releases thicken the sauce at the same time. You probably won't need to use all of the stock, so any that is left over, pour into ice cube trays and freeze, and you can use it another time.

1 lobster (about 2¼ pounds),
        either very fresh or live
        (see above)
14 ounces linguine
4 tomatoes
4 tablespoons
        extra virgin olive oil
3 garlic cloves, finely chopped
1 chile pepper, deseeded and
        finely chopped
½ wineglass of white wine
2 tablespoons tomato passata
handful of parsley, finely
        chopped, reserving the
        stalks for the stock
salt and pepper

        For the stock:
1 tablespoon
        extra virgin olive oil
½ carrot, cut into chunks
½ onion, cut into chunks
1 celery stalk, cut into chunks
1 bay leaf
2 black peppercorns
½ wineglass of white wine
½ tablespoon tomato paste

If using a live lobster, kill it first (see previous page); if using a freshly killed one, split the head in half between the eyes. Twist off the head and reserve.

To make the stock, heat the olive oil in a pan and add the vegetables, bay leaf, peppercorns and parsley stalks. Sweat for a couple of minutes to soften but not color.

Add the lobster head and, with a wooden spoon, crush it a little, to release the juices. Add the white wine and cook until the alcohol has evaporated completely. Add the tomato paste and continue cooking over a low heat for another 2 minutes or so, taking care that the paste doesn't burn. Add a little water – enough almost to cover but not quite. Bring to a boil, then turn down the heat and simmer for 10 to 15 minutes. Pass through a fine sieve and keep to the side.

Take the tail of the lobster and split it in half lengthwise through the shell. Cut each half into pieces, about ⅝ to ¾ inch. We leave the shell on because it gives a little more shape to the dish than if you just serve the lobster meat, and it will easily come out of the shell as you eat it, but, if you prefer, you can remove the shell at this stage.

Put a pan of water on to boil and when it does, put the claws in for about 30 seconds. Remove and cool. With the back of a knife, crush the claws and pick out the meat. Set aside (if you are not making the sauce right away, store in the fridge).

Bring a large pan of water to a boil for the linguine.

Blanch the fresh tomatoes, skin, quarter and deseed (see page 304). Then cut each quarter in half, so you have 8 pieces.

Heat half the olive oil in a large sauté pan. Because you want to cook the garlic (so that it is digestible) but not burn it (or it will be bitter), it is a good idea to tilt the pan a little, so the oil flows to one spot, and put in your garlic so it can cook in this depth of oil. That way it will be less likely to burn. Add the chile and cook gently for a few minutes, until the garlic starts to color.

Add the chopped lobster, including the claw meat, and cook for about 30 seconds, tossing the pieces around. Season.

Add the white wine, allow the alcohol to evaporate and turn off the heat. Add the fresh tomatoes and the tomato passata, with a ladleful of stock.

Meanwhile, cook the linguine in the salted boiling water for about a minute less than the time suggested on the package. Drain and add to the sauce, with the rest of the oil.

Toss thoroughly for about a minute to let the pasta finish cooking and allow the starch to thicken the sauce (if you need to loosen it slightly, add a bit more stock). You will see that, after a minute or so, the starch that comes out of the linguine will help the sauce cling to the pasta, so that when you serve it the linguine will stay coated with the sauce.

Sprinkle the parsley over and serve immediately.

Linguine agli scampi

Linguine with langoustine

You can make a variation of the lobster dish on page 310 using langoustines or large crayfish (make sure they are absolutely fresh or live, in which case kill them in exactly the same way as for lobster) or, if you don't want to make stock, you can do this quicker version.

Start by splitting 24 langoustines in two completely, from head (between the eyes) to tail. Then get a sauté pan big enough to give all the langoustines space to touch the bottom without crowding, so they can sear quickly; otherwise they will release their juices and boil in them rather than pan-fry (if you don't have a big enough pan, cook them in two batches).

Sauté 3 finely chopped garlic cloves gently in around 2 tablespoons of extra virgin olive oil for a few minutes until the garlic starts to color (but don't let it burn or it will taste bitter), then add a finely chopped and deseeded chile pepper. Add the langoustines, flesh side down, and cook for 1 minute, crushing the heads at the same time, to release their juices. Season, add half a glass of dry white wine, allow the alcohol to evaporate, then add 4 tomatoes that have been peeled, deseeded and cut into 8, together with 2 tablespoons of tomato passata, and turn off the heat. Remove the langoustines and, if you like, take off the heads and claws and keep them for a garnish.

Meanwhile, cook and drain the pasta as for the previous recipe, and finish in exactly the same way, adding another 2 tablespoons of extra virgin olive oil to the sauce, finishing with chopped parsley and garnishing, if you like, with the langoustine heads and/or claws.

Linguine alle vongole

Linguine with clams

The magic of clams is that wherever you are when you eat them, they evoke the flavor of the sea. I would never trust anybody who served me pasta with clams without the shells, though, as I want to see for myself that they are fresh. For this dish, we usually use the tender carpet-shell clams with the lined and patterned shells, which the French call palourdes. We sometimes also use striped venus clams, which are typical in Chioggia near Venezia.

The clams should be fresh and alive. Put them in a bowl and wash them under cold running water for a few minutes. Then add a handful of salt, to re-create their natural environment, so that they will breathe and filter the water, releasing any sand they have inside their shells. Discard any that are open, as these will be dead. Sometimes there is too much sand to come out into the water, and the weight of it can keep the shell of a dead clam closed. To be sure, drop each clam into a bowl, and if the clam is dead the impact should make the shell open.

Heat around 2 tablespoons of extra virgin olive oil in a large sauté pan, add 3 finely chopped garlic cloves and cook gently for a few minutes until it starts to color (but don't let it burn or it will taste bitter). Then add a deseeded and finely chopped chile pepper and 2¼ pounds of clams (prepared as above) and cook for 30 seconds. Add a wineglass of dry white wine and cover the pan with a lid, to allow the clams to steam open (about 1 to 1½ minutes). Throw away any clams that haven't opened. Leave around a quarter of the clams in their shells, but scrape out the rest and discard the shells. Taste and season if necessary – though you shouldn't need any salt.

Meanwhile, cook and drain the pasta as for the recipe for linguine with lobster (see page 313) and finish in exactly the same way, adding another 2 tablespoons of extra virgin olive oil to the sauce, together with the reserved clams (shelled and unshelled), and finish with chopped parsley.

Linguine alla bottarga

Linguine with bottarga

I love bottarga, though I had never even tasted it until I met Mauro, the owner of Olivo, who comes from Cagliari in the south of Sardegna, where they traditionally serve pasta simply with bottarga, butter or oil, and pepper. (Just melt most of the bottarga in the butter or olive oil and a little water, then finish off the spaghetti in it, and grate some more bottarga over the top.) Mauro would never eat it done with chile pepper and garlic, as in the recipe below, which is the favorite way in Sicilia, but one of the waiters who came from there used to make it this way for the staff when Mauro wasn't around. Funny, isn't it, how, even from one side of an island to the other, Italians will always disagree about how to use an ingredient. The first time I tried the combination of linguine with bottarga, chile pepper and garlic, I loved it. You can use either the bottarga made from the roe of the gray mullet or that made from tuna roe (see page 114). Personally I think the tuna roe works best with the chile and garlic. Again, this is a very simple dish to make, relying on a few intense flavors.

You just need to grate around 3½ ounces of bottarga, then start cooking the linguine in a large pan of salted boiling water – use a little less salt than usual as the bottarga has a rich, fishy flavor that shouldn't need any extra seasoning. When the pasta has been cooking for about 4 minutes, heat around 2 tablespoons of extra virgin olive oil in a large sauté pan, add 3 finely chopped garlic cloves and a deseeded and finely chopped chile, and cook gently for a couple of minutes. Turn off the heat just before the garlic starts to color (but don't let it burn or it will taste bitter). By now the pasta should have had 5 to 6 minutes' cooking and be al dente (with this dish I think it is extra-important that the spaghetti be al dente, because the slight "crunchiness" works very well with the richness of the bottarga). Drain it, reserving the cooking water, and add to the pan containing the garlic and chile, together with 1 tablespoon of the bottarga and a handful of chopped parsley. Add a ladleful of the reserved pasta cooking water and another 2 tablespoons of extra virgin olive oil. Toss thoroughly for about a minute or so, until the sauce clings to the pasta, loosening it with a little more cooking water if necessary, then serve with the rest of the grated bottarga sprinkled over the top.

Linguine con sardine e finocchietto selvatico

Linguine with sardine and wild fennel

We are talking about the feathery, anise-flavored herb here – not the bulbous vegetable (Florence fennel). In Italy, it grows wild by the roadside, and is traditionally used in this dish, which comes from the south; and in Toscana, it is served with pork (sprinkled with the dried flowers). If you can't find it, you could use the fronds from the top of the fennel bulbs, but the flavor will be different and not as long-lasting.

Soak 2 tablespoons of golden raisins in warm water for about half an hour so that they plump up. Then roughly chop 12 medium-sized fresh sardine fillets and blanch, peel and deseed 4 good-quality tomatoes (see page 304) and cut each into eighths. Spread 2 tablespoons of pine nuts on a baking tray and put in an oven preheated to 350°F very briefly, just long enough to turn them golden. Remove from the tray and set aside. Heat around 2 tablespoons of extra virgin olive oil in a large sauté pan, add 3 finely chopped garlic cloves and cook gently for a few minutes until they start to color (don't let the garlic burn or it will taste bitter), then add the chopped sardines and cook for 1 minute. Season, add half a glass of dry white wine and allow the alcohol to evaporate. Put in the tomato, pine nuts, drained golden raisins and 2 tablespoons tomato passata, and turn off the heat.

Meanwhile, cook and drain the pasta as described on page 313 and add to the sauce, with another 2 tablespoons of extra virgin olive oil. Toss in 2 tablespoons of chopped wild fennel and a handful of finely chopped parsley and serve.

Peperoncini

Chiles

People are often surprised to find chiles in Italian cooking – but they arrived in Italy back in the sixteenth century, probably via Mexico or Spain. In the south of Italy, especially, you find chiles in everything from salami and sausages to soups and pasta sauces – though one of the most famous Italian chiles is the *diavolicchio* (little devil) of Abruzzo. There, in the summer, you will see strings of the bright red peppers hanging over doorways and from balconies so that they can dry in the sun.

Spaghetti with some dried chile pepper, garlic and olive oil, and sometimes parsley and sautéed bread crumbs, is such a brilliant, quick thing to do when friends come around – it's the kind of thing we cook up after a football match.

In Calabria they make the famous fiery salami *'nduja* (so spicy that in our family only Plaxy and Jack can eat it). Because the heat and antimicrobial qualities of the chiles help the curing of the meat, they can use less salt when they make the salami, which is why it is so spreadable (the more salt you use, the more you draw out the moisture). Some *'nduja* melted in a pan with a little olive oil and garlic and some fresh tomato makes a fantastic sauce for pasta.

Each September in Calabria they hold the *Sagra del Peperoncino*, with every restaurant serving chiles, and the *pasticceria* making cakes, pastries and biscuits spiced with chiles – you can even find it in ice cream. In the north, we have traditionally been more wary of spices – a peppery olive oil used to be too much for most people – but now you find chiles being used all over Italy, though away from the south it is often more for flavor than heat.

Different varieties of chiles have different intensities of heat, but mostly the smallest are the hottest – and the concentration of heat is in the seeds and inner membrane, so remove these unless you like real fieriness. After cutting up chiles, wash your hands in cold water, then with soap, and never touch your eyes or sensitive parts of the body immediately after handling them, or they will burn and sting.

Orecchiette alle cime di rapa e peperoncino

Orecchiette with broccoli rabe and chile pepper

Orecchiette come from Puglia, where they are traditionally handmade using only flour, water and olive oil. The joke is that everyone in Puglia has big, bent thumbs from pressing them into the little ear shapes that give them their name.

Broccoli rabe is in season from around September to January; it forms little florets like broccoli in October – which is the time to use it, otherwise the leaves are a little too bitter and fibrous. The florets have a sweet flavor and a texture that also makes the sauce creamier. At other times of the year, though, or if you can't find broccoli rabe, use broccoli instead. Cut off the florets, leaving a couple of inches of stalk, and blanch them, then chop and sauté them in the same way as for the broccoli rabe in the recipe. You can use the water you blanched them in to cook the pasta afterward (don't do this if you are using the broccoli rabe, though, as they will make the water bitter and this will flavor the pasta).

Remember that the chiles you need for this recipe should be quite long, and not very hot – we are not talking about Thai food here. (If you like a little extra heat, though, you can leave in the seeds.)

3 small bunches of broccoli rabe
    tops (cime di rapa)
5 tablespoons
    extra virgin olive oil
2 garlic cloves, thinly sliced
2 medium red chiles, deseeded
    (leave the seeds in if
    you want more heat)
    and thinly sliced
14 ounces dried orecchiette
2 anchovy fillets
salt and pepper

Take the leaves and florets of the broccoli rabe from their stalks and blanch them in boiling salted water for about a minute, just to take away some of their bitterness. Drain and squeeze to remove the excess water. Chop very fine.

Warm half the olive oil in a large sauté pan, add the garlic and chiles, and gently cook them without allowing them to color (don't let the garlic burn or it will taste bitter). Then add the broccoli rabe and toss around. Add another tablespoon of olive oil.

Meanwhile, bring a large pan of water to a boil, salt it, put in the orecchiette and cook for about a minute less than the time suggested on the package until al dente.

While the pasta is cooking, ladle out a little of the cooking water and add to the pan containing the broccoli rabe. Then turn down the heat and add the anchovies as well. Let them dissolve without frying them, stirring all the time. Taste and season if necessary – remember that the anchovies will add their own saltiness.

When the pasta is cooked, drain, reserving the cooking water, and add the pasta to the pan containing the sauce. Toss for 2 to 3 minutes, so the turnip tops cook and begin to cling to the pasta.

Add the rest of the olive oil, toss well to coat and serve.

Orecchiette con piselli, pancetta e tartufo nero

Orecchiette with peas, pancetta and black truffle

1 tablespoon plus 1¼ teaspoons
    butter
3½ ounces pancetta,
    thinly sliced and
    cut into thin strips
8 tablespoons raw peas
    (preferably fresh)
14 ounces dried orecchiette
1 tablespoon grated Parmesan
1 ounce fresh black truffle
salt and pepper

Melt half the butter in a large sauté pan, add the pancetta and cook for a couple of minutes just to release some of the fat, but without allowing it to color. Then add the peas and toss around for a couple of minutes.

Add a couple of ladlefuls of cold water, cover the pan with a lid, and cook slowly for 3 to 4 minutes until the peas are tender enough to crush.

Bring a large pan of water to a boil, salt it, put in the pasta, and cook for about 1 minute less than the time suggested on the package.

While the pasta is cooking, start to crush the peas with a wooden spoon or spatula, so that they resemble "mushy peas." If they seem too thick, take a little of the cooking water from the pan of pasta and add to the peas. Season.

Drain the pasta, reserving the cooking water, and add the pasta to the pan containing the peas. Toss around for a couple of minutes, then add the rest of the butter, and keep on stirring. The pea "sauce" should start to thicken, so you might need to add a little more cooking water to loosen it.

Add the grated Parmesan, toss well and then, at the last minute, grate the truffle over the top. Toss again and serve.

Malloreddus al pomodoro e ricotta salata

Sardinian-style pasta with tomato and ricotta salata

Malloreddus are little dried Sardinian gnocchi, made from durum wheat semolina with saffron mixed into the dough, which you can find in Italian delicatessens. They look a little like small ridged caterpillars – traditionally the ridges come from pressing the pieces by hand against straw baskets. These pasta shapes are often served with a ragù made with tomatoes and local sausage *(malloreddus alla campidanese)*. We serve them with tomatoes and ricotta salata. It is important not to season the sauce with salt until the end, and to taste it first, as the cheese has a strong and salty flavor.

Blanch the fresh tomatoes, skin, quarter and deseed (see page 304).

Heat a tablespoon of the oil in a saucepan and add the onion. Sweat it until soft but not colored, about 5 minutes.

Add the canned tomatoes and simmer for another 15 to 20 minutes.

Bring a large pan of water to a boil, salt it, put in the malloreddus and cook for 8 to 12 minutes (check the instructions on the package as a guide – cook for about 1 minute less than they say), until al dente.

While the pasta is cooking, heat half the remaining oil in a sauté pan, add the garlic and cook without allowing it to color for a few minutes (don't let it burn or it will taste bitter). Add the fresh tomatoes, cook for a minute or so and then add the tomato sauce.

Drain the pasta, reserving the cooking water, then add the pasta to the sauce and toss around for a couple of minutes until the sauce becomes "creamy."

Grate half the ricotta salata into the pan and toss again for a couple of minutes. Taste, season as necessary and serve with the rest of the cheese grated on top.

4 tomatoes
5 tablespoons olive oil
1 onion, finely chopped
one 15-ounce can of
       chopped tomatoes
14 ounces malloreddus
2 garlic cloves, chopped
1¾–2 ounces ricotta salata
salt and pepper

Homemade walnut paste

You need around 2 pounds of walnuts for this. It's best to use fresh nuts around the end of October, as they will be less bitter than older ones, and because their flesh is softer it will be easier to make the paste.

Buy them in their shells (once they are shelled, they turn bitter quickly). Crack them, keeping them as intact as possible, so they will be easier to toast evenly and to peel. Put them on a tray and toast them in the oven at about 340°F for about 4 to 5 minutes until golden. Then, while they are still warm, wrap them in a cloth and rub the bundle to pull off as much of the skins as possible. You can then peel off any remaining skin with a small knife. Leave to cool.

In the meantime, crush 2 garlic cloves in a mortar, add the walnuts and pound into a smooth paste, then stir in 2 or 3 tablespoons of olive oil – just enough to make a thick paste. If you are not using it all right away, you can keep it in a sterilized jar covered with at least a finger depth of extra virgin olive oil – it should keep for around 4 weeks.

We use this paste in all kinds of fish and pasta dishes.

Garganelli in salsa di noci

Tubular pasta with walnut sauce

You can make this and the following recipes with penne if you prefer. We make our own fresh garganelli. If you do this, or if you can find good fresh garganelli in an Italian delicatessen, you need to cook the pasta for 2 or 3 minutes only. You can make your own walnut paste (see above), but you need a lot of patience to peel all the nuts – so it might be easier to buy a good-quality paste.

14 ounces garganelli
2 tomatoes
    (the best you can find)
4 tablespoons walnut paste
5 tablespoons
    extra virgin olive oil
2 tablespoons grated Parmesan
5 sage leaves, finely chopped
sprig of rosemary,
    leaves finely chopped
salt and pepper

Get a large pan of salted boiling water ready for the pasta.

Blanch the fresh tomatoes, skin, quarter and deseed (see page 304).

Cook the garganelli in the salted boiling water for about a minute less than the time suggested on the package.

While the pasta is cooking, put the walnut paste into a large sauté pan or frying pan with 3 tablespoons of the oil and heat gently so that the paste melts but doesn't fry. Season if necessary. Sometimes you will find that the walnut paste may break up a little if you overheat it; if this happens, stir in a little hot water to bring it back together.

Drain the pasta, reserving some of the cooking water, add the pasta to the pan of sauce, and toss well. If you feel the sauce needs loosening slightly, add a little of the cooking water from the pasta.

Add the tomatoes to the pan, together with the Parmesan, chopped herbs and the rest of the oil. Toss well and serve.

Garganelli pesto e pomodoro

Tubular pasta with tomato and pesto sauce

This relies on a very few, very good ingredients and, like so many pasta dishes that use fresh tomatoes, is best in summer, when the tomatoes are really, really ripe and the basil is plentiful. Usually, though, even when you are using the best fresh tomatoes you can find, you will still need some good-quality canned tomatoes to make some extra sauce.

If you like, add a little chopped chile pepper to the sauce – just add it to the garlic before you put in the tomato. Or, if you prefer a more creamy sauce, add a dash of cream before you put the pasta into the sauce.

Sometimes we make a variation of this using just fresh and sun-dried tomatoes. We heat the oil, add the garlic, and when it starts to color add 6 fresh tomatoes – again, the best you can find – blanched, skinned, deseeded and each cut into eighths. Cook them until the tomatoes start to become squashed, then add some sun-dried tomatoes and cook for another 2 to 3 minutes, before finishing the pasta in the same way. Because the sun-dried tomatoes are quite strongly flavored – and sometimes salted – it is best to taste and season the sauce at the end.

To make the sauce, first blanch, skin and deseed 2 of the best-quality tomatoes you can find, and cut each one into eighths (see page 304). Heat 2 tablespoons of extra virgin olive oil in a large sauté pan and cook 2 finely chopped garlic cloves very gently until they start to color (don't let the garlic burn or it will taste bitter).

Add a can of chopped tomatoes, together with the fresh tomatoes, and cook for 10 to 15 minutes until you have quite a thick sauce. Toward the end of that time, cook the garganelli in a large pan of salted boiling water for about a minute less than the time suggested on the package.

When the sauce is ready, turn off the heat, season and add 2 heaped tablespoons of Pesto (page 309). Drain the pasta, reserving some of the cooking water, and add the pasta to the sauce, together with

2 more tablespoons of extra virgin olive oil. Toss well and, if necessary, loosen the sauce with a little of the reserved pasta cooking water. Add 2 tablespoons of freshly grated Parmesan and serve.

Garganelli con triglia e olive nere

Tubular pasta with red mullet and black olives

This is a little more complicated than the last few recipes, but worthwhile because it is quite impressive. Although you can buy the mullet already filleted, it is better to buy whole ones from a fishmonger and ask him to fillet them for you, as the dish will have a more intense flavor if you ask for the bones to use for the stock, and for the liver, which is crushed and mixed with butter and beaten into the pasta right at the end.

1 tablespoon plus 1¼ teaspoons
    unsalted butter
3 tablespoons black olives,
    such as Taggiasche
4 small fillets or 2 large fillets
    of red mullet (ask your
    fishmonger to give you
    the bones and the liver)
14 ounces garganelli
4 tomatoes
4 tablespoons
    extra virgin olive oil
2 garlic cloves, finely chopped
½ wineglass of white wine
4 tablespoons tomato passata
handful of parsley, finely
    chopped, reserving the
    stalks for the stock
salt and pepper

    For the stock:
1 tablespoon olive oil
½ carrot, cut into chunks
½ onion, cut into chunks
1 celery stalk, cut into chunks
1 bay leaf
2 black peppercorns
½ wineglass of white wine
½ tablespoon tomato paste

First take the butter out of the fridge to let it soften. Pit the olives.

To make the stock, heat the olive oil in a pan. Add the vegetables, bay leaf, peppercorns and reserved parsley stalks. Sweat for a couple of minutes to soften but not color. Add the fish bones and continue to cook until these start to stick to the pan. Add the wine and cook until the alcohol has evaporated completely. Add the tomato paste and continue cooking over a low heat for another 2 minutes or so, taking care that the paste doesn't burn. Add a little water – enough almost to cover, but not quite. Bring to the boil, turn down the heat and simmer for 10 to 15 minutes. Pass through a fine sieve and keep to one side.

Put the butter in a bowl. Crush the mullet liver, preferably using a pestle and mortar or the back of a knife. Then mix with the butter – it should be a nice pink color.

Slice the red mullet into strips and keep at room temperature.

Get a large pan of boiling salted water ready for the pasta.

Blanch the fresh tomatoes, skin, quarter and deseed (see page 304).

Heat half the olive oil in a large sauté pan. Put in the garlic and cook it gently for a few minutes until it starts to color (don't let it burn or it will taste bitter).

Add the red mullet and cook for 1 to 2 minutes until the fish starts to stick to the pan. Keep scraping it, and it will crumble.

Add the white wine, then the fresh tomato, olives and stock. Finally, add the tomato passata and cook for another 2 to 3 minutes.

Meanwhile, cook the pasta in the salted boiling water for about a minute less than the time suggested on the package (usually 5 to 6 minutes).

Drain the pasta well (it needs to be quite dry to take up the liver butter), reserving some of the cooking water, and add the pasta to the sauce with the rest of the olive oil.

Just before serving, beat in the liver butter with a wooden spoon, and, if necessary, you can add a little cooking water to loosen things. Finish with the chopped parsley.

Fresh egg pasta

In most small towns in Italy, you have the *pastificio* – the shop that specializes in making only pasta, and often it is of amazing quality. In some places, the local restaurants don't even bother to make their own fresh pasta, they just ask the pasta maker at the pastificio to do it for them. In America, you often find Italian specialty shops making their own, which can be good, and of course you can buy it in the supermarkets, but most commercial fresh pasta is made with water added to the dough, so that it can be extruded through the machines more easily. If you start with such a soft dough, and then leave it for a day or so, it will be even softer. Then, when you cook it, it will have less "bite" than I like from a good pasta.

When you make egg pasta at home, though, in around half an hour you can have something that has real personality and you have the satisfaction of knowing all the ingredients that went into it. You know you chose the best flour, the best and freshest eggs … you are not at the mercy of companies that only want to make a profit. And while rolling out pasta was once a laborious process that you had to do with an enormous rolling pin, every kitchen shop now sells little machines that will roll the pasta for you and cut it into various widths, if, for example, you want to make tagliatelle.

I can't promise that the first time you make fresh pasta it will be absolutely perfect; not because I don't have complete confidence in the recipe – this is the one we use every single day in the restaurant – but because the conditions in every kitchen are different, and the heat and humidity can affect the way the dough comes together. I am completely at ease making pasta in my own kitchen, but if you say to me, "Okay, you have to go to Scotland, buy your ingredients and make pasta for a hundred people in a strange kitchen," I will be a bit scared, because I don't know the quality of the flour or the eggs, and I don't know the temperature and humidity.

You need a few trial runs to get it absolutely right, but if you fail the first time, what is the worst that can happen? A few eggs and a bag of flour end up in the bin. I promise you, once you get the feel of it, it will seem like therapy, not a job.

Even though making pasta is a pretty straightforward thing, everyone in Italy has his own idea about how to do it, how many eggs to use, whether to put in a drop of olive oil, or add some water. And then there are regional differences: in Emilia-Romagna, for example, they like to use more whole eggs – one for every 100g (¾ cup) of flour – whereas we prefer to use a mixture of whole eggs and egg yolks.

In the kitchen, we typically use 6 whole eggs and 4 egg yolks to 1 kilo (7 cups) of flour, but you can make egg pasta with a much higher concentration of eggs. The more you add, the "crispier" (more brittle) the pasta becomes. We sometimes make a pasta with zucchini and bottarga (see page 346) in which we use 32 eggs to 500g (3½ cups) of flour. The greatest number of eggs I have ever used to a kilo of flour was when I was working at Le Laurent in Paris, where the consultant chef was Joël Robuchon. One day he came by for lunch and asked who I was. "So, you can make pasta – why don't you do some for me?" he said (this was at a time when Italian food was still a big mystery and the chefs in the kitchen had very little idea how to make fresh pasta or a proper risotto). The chef told me that Robuchon was looking for a clever garnish for some fish dishes, something special, and so I started to work with the dough, adding more and more eggs, and eventually I came up with an amazingly rich dough that had 52 egg yolks to a kilo of flour and was incredibly elastic.

The way I like to make fresh egg pasta is to make the dough quite "tight," which means about 10 minutes of hard work, as the mixture will feel quite stiff and unyielding. As soon as the dough comes together, we stop working it, because we know it will loosen and soften as it rests. One of the reasons we make our dough this way is that, at the restaurant, we make a lot of filled pasta like ravioli and, while you can get away with pasta that is a bit overelastic if you are going to cut it into strips, like pappardelle, you need it to be firmer for filled pasta. This is because if the dough is too soft and elastic, it will stretch when you roll it, but then pull back again while you are making the ravioli, leaving the pasta too thick around the edges.

After we have made the pasta, we let it rest and it will soften up and become just the way we want it. In the restaurant, we usually leave it in the fridge for 24 hours, because we roll it through big pasta machines. At home, though, if you are using a small domestic machine, you only need to let it rest for an hour, covered with a damp cloth, and it will be ready to work with.

Making the pasta

All over the world, there are different grades of flour, but most Italians use 00 (doppio zero) for fresh pasta, because it has small, fine particles that will give you a smooth dough. The flour may be made from durum wheat or a combination of various strains of wheat; it varies according to manufacturers, and every household in Italy will buy the flour they swear is the *only* one to use, just as they believe completely in a particular brand of dried pasta.

You can either make egg pasta in the traditional fashion, by hand – which is the best and most enjoyable way – or use a food processor that has a dough hook. If you are finding it hard work to bring the dough together in the kneading, which can happen sometimes if the kitchen is hot, don't just take a jug of water and start adding it; instead wet your hands a little and keep working the dough until you begin to get some humidity into it, and then it will come together.

When you make egg pasta, much of the "bite" comes from the protein in the eggs, which also contain lecithin. This is a natural emulsifier that gives a malleability and elasticity to the pasta, allowing you to twist it and bend it. Also, as you knead the dough, you help to stretch the gluten in the flour, strengthening and making it more elastic. However, if you keep on kneading and kneading, and really overdo it, you can break the strands, which is why it is better to stop kneading the moment the dough comes together, then let the dough relax for an hour.

We use Italian eggs, which have very rich orange, almost red, yolks, because the hens eat grass and vegetation in spring and summer, and corn in the winter. So, when the pasta is made, it is a lovely golden color. If you are able to buy fresh eggs, preferably organic, from a farm where the hens can wander around freely and eat vegetation, rather than being penned into cages on a diet of formulated feed, you will find the yolks have a similar rich color and their flavor and quality will be much higher.

Makes about 1⅓ pounds
3½ cups 00 (doppio zero) flour
3 large eggs, plus 2 extra
(large) egg yolks
(all at room temperature)
pinch of salt

Preferably make the pasta by hand – especially if you are making a relatively small quantity like this, which will be difficult for a food processor to mix well. Sieve the flour into a clean bowl, then turn it out into a mound on a clean surface and make a well in the middle (in Italy we call this the *fontana di farina*, "fountain of flour"). Sprinkle the salt into the well, and then crack in the eggs.

Have a bowl of water on one side so you can wet your hands, to help bring the dough together if it is being stubborn toward the end of kneading. To begin, break up the yolks with the fingertips of one hand, and then begin to move your fingers in a circular motion, gradually incorporating the flour, until you have worked in enough to start bringing it together in a ball. Then you can start to work the ball of dough by pushing it with the heel of your hand, then folding the

top back on itself, turning it a little clockwise, and repeating, again and again, for about 10 minutes, wetting your hands if it helps, until the dough is springy but still feels quite firm and difficult to work. (If you are using a food processor, sieve the flour into the bowl, add the salt, then start the machine, and slowly add the egg yolks, followed by the whole eggs. Keep the motor running slowly, or it will heat up the pasta too much and also "beat" rather than mix. Once the dough has come together, take it out and put it on a clean work surface.)

Don't worry that the dough feels hard; after it has relaxed for a while it will be perfect. Divide the dough into 2 balls, wrap each in a damp cloth and allow to rest for about 1 hour before use.

Rolling the pasta

Roll the first ball of dough with a rolling pin (keep the other covered with the damp cloth) until it is about ½ inch thick and will go through the pasta machine comfortably (if it is too thick, the pasta machine will have to use so much force to make it go through that it will damage the machine and squeeze out too much moisture in the process, so the pasta will be dry). There isn't an exact number of times you will need to feed the pasta through the machine – each time you make it, it might be slightly different (and not every pasta machine has the same number of settings), but use the next few steps as a guide and, after a while, you will get the hang of rolling the pasta and feel your own way.

Put the machine on the first (thickest) setting to start with, then feed the piece of pasta through the machine, turning the handle with one hand and supporting the dough as it comes through with the other. Then change to the second setting, and put it through again. Repeat another 2 to 3 times, taking the setting down one step each time. Don't worry if the pasta appears slightly streaky; this should disappear as you continue rolling it.

Next, fold the strip of pasta back on itself, put the machine back on the first setting and put the pasta through. Repeat 3 to 4 more times, again taking the setting down one each time, and you will see that the pasta begins to take on a sheen. As it begins to get longer, you will find that you have to pull it very gently, so that it doesn't begin to pleat. You shouldn't need to dust it with flour, unless you feel it is too soft and likely to stick and stretch too much.

Now you need to cut your strip in half. Put one half under cover of the damp cloth, then fold the length of the other strip into three, bringing one end in and the other over the top of that, so that the pasta is the same width as the machine. Roll it with the rolling pin, so it is no more than ¼ inch thick, then put the machine back on the first setting and feed the pasta through – this time across

the width not lengthwise. The idea of changing direction is to put equal elasticity and strength throughout the pasta. Keep feeding it through this way, taking it down two or three settings as you go.

Finally, fold the pasta back on itself, then put the machine back on the first setting, and take it down again through the settings until it is about ⅝ inch thick. By now the pasta should be nice and shiny, with no lines in it, and you are ready to cut it into strips (either by hand or using a cutter attachment on your machine), or use it to make filled pasta. It is best to use each sheet as soon as it is ready, before starting to roll the rest of your dough.

Egg pasta: long

Fettuccine ("flat long ribbons") – Also called *trenette*, or *piccage* in the Ligurian dialect, these are narrower than tagliatelle, but are often used in similar recipes, depending on the region (fettuccine originally hails from Roma, tagliatelle from Bologna). Like tagliatelle, fettuccine is usually sold wound into nests. Its rough porous surface is designed to grip creamy or rich sauces, often incorporating vegetables like eggplant, mushroom, etc. The famous *fettuccine alfredo*, in which the pasta is tossed in a sauce made with cream, cheese and butter, was invented in Alfredo's restaurant in Roma, while the traditional dish of "straw and hay" *(paglia e fieno)* is made with both green spinach fettuccine and egg fettuccine.

Pappardelle ("fat ribbons") – These are the widest of the pasta strips, about ¾ inch wide. In Bologna, they are also called *larghissime*, meaning "very wide," and are traditionally served with a rich ragù of game, such as hare or pigeon, sometimes chicken livers, and porcini.

Pizzocheri – This comes from Valtellina in Lombardia and is made with no eggs and a mixture of plain and buckwheat flour. It also gives its name to the most famous dish of the region, which is made with cabbage, potatoes, onions and Bitto cheese.

Tagliatelle (the word means "little cuts") – The pasta strips should be ⅜ inch wide. Tagliatelle has quite a noble, elegant tradition, and is held in such reverence in Bologna, where it originates, that there is a strand of tagliatelle cast in gold at the Chamber of Commerce there. Tagliatelle is best eaten with ragù, especially of game, and with rich creamy sauces or porcini. We also serve it with marinated sardines (see page 342). According to the great early Italian food writer Pellegrino Artusi, the people of Bologna used to say that "bills should be short and tagliatelle long." Fresh tagliatelle is best made at home, unless you have a good Italian deli near you where they make it themselves. Rather than buying house-brand supermarket packages of fresh tagliatelle, I would buy dried.

Tagliolini – These are narrow ribbons, about 1/16 inch wide, that are used in soups or sometimes with a light sauce. We often serve them with chicory or zucchini and bottarga (see page 346).

Egg pasta: short

Garganelli – Most tubular pasta is dried, but this one can also be made by hand, with egg pasta, which is cut into rectangles against a grooved stick, or comb, called a *pettine*. It is best with sauces like pesto and tomato, or walnuts. We also use it with fish, such as mackerel, and olives.

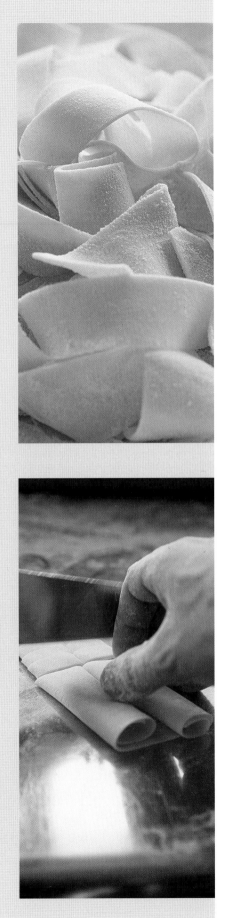

Egg pasta: flat

Cannelloni – Rectangular sheets of pasta, stuffed with ricotta, vegetables or meat, and rolled up, then baked.

Lasagne – Large sheets, which are blanched briefly – in some regions just wetted with water – then layered up with meat and/or seafood or vegetables and béchamel sauce and baked. If I didn't make my own fresh lasagne, I would buy dried rather than the commercial fresh lasagne sold in the supermarkets.

Egg pasta: filled

Agnolotti – This is what we call them in Piemonte, but they are also called raviolini ("small ravioli"). They are usually square but can be round, and are traditionally filled with meat, cheese, etc.

Anolini – Typical of Emilia-Romagna, these are half-moon-shaped. The stuffing is put in the center of the disks of pasta; then they are folded and pinched together to seal. Traditionally, they are stuffed with meat and served in stock; alternatively, they can be cooked, drained and served simply with butter and grated Parmesan.

Cappelletti ("little hats") – Similar to anolini, but this time you take your half-moon shapes (usually the pasta is filled with ricotta) and bring the ends together around your little finger to form a shape like a three-cornered hat. There is a larger version, called cappellacci, which are shaped around your ring finger.

Malfatti – These are similar again to anolini; however, the tip of the triangle is folded down and then sealed on top of the pasta parcel.

Ravioli – The most famous square filled pasta, details of which are recorded as far back as the fourteenth century, stuffed with pork or cheese. They usually have fluted edges, unlike tordelli (also called tortelli), in which the edges are left plain. Nowadays they are used to hold every filling you can think of, from mushrooms to game to seafood.

Tortellini – Small filled pasta that are twisted to look like belly buttons – supposedly the inspiration for these was the belly button of Venus – they are a speciality of Bologna and are usually stuffed with cheese and prosciutto or mortadella, served with cream sauce or in broth, traditionally on New Year's Eve.

Tortelloni – Large stuffed pasta, usually filled with spinach and ricotta, or Swiss chard, and tossed in butter and grated Parmesan.

Pappardelle alle fave e rucola

Pappardelle with fava beans and arugula

I really think of this dish as my own – it is based on a traditional pasta but has a twist that comes from ideas I had when I was working in Paris, and has been perfected at Locanda. I love it; but it is a dish that has to be made in springtime, when the young fava beans are in season and are beautifully sweet. For the puree, though, we use frozen fava beans, because the chlorophyll content is higher, as they are frozen as soon as they are picked – with fresh ones, the puree tends to darken almost to black, and looks off-putting, rather than staying nice and bright green.

1 recipe quantity of fresh egg
    pasta dough (page 330)
flour for dusting
2 handfuls of shelled fava beans
2 tablespoons grated
    Pecorino Sardo
2 small bunches of arugula,
    plus one extra for garnish
salt and pepper

For the butter sauce:
1 cup butter
1 shallot, finely chopped
2 black peppercorns
⅓ cup plus 1 tablespoon
    white wine
2 tablespoons heavy cream

For the fava bean puree:
2 tablespoons olive oil
1 white onion, finely chopped
11 ounces (about 1½ cups)
    frozen fava beans,
    defrosted, blanched
    and peeled
7 tablespoons cold unsalted
    butter, cut into small cubes

First make the pappardelle by rolling the pasta through the machine as described on page 332. Work with one strip of pasta at a time. If it is dry or frilly at the edges, trim with a sharp knife. Then, using your rolling pin as a straight edge, cut the pasta across into strips ¾ to 1 inch wide.

Dust a tray with flour. Then, with a spatula, lift up the strips 3 or 4 at a time and lay them on the tray. Dust again with flour, cover with a damp cloth and leave aside to rest while you prepare the sauce and pure.

Cut all but two pats of the butter for the sauce into small cubes and keep in the fridge.

To make the puree, heat the olive oil in a pan, add the onion and cook for 4 to 5 minutes without allowing it to color. Add the frozen fava beans and cook with the onion for another 4 to 5 minutes.

Slowly add some water, a ladleful at a time, until the vegetables are covered. Bring to a boil, then turn down the heat, put on the lid and leave to cook slowly (adding more water if necessary) until the beans are soft (about 20 to 25 minutes). At this point, continue cooking, without adding any extra water, until you have a very firm mixture.

While still hot, puree with a hand blender or a food processor, adding the butter cubes as you go (if the puree gets too dry, add a little water – the finished consistency should be like mushy peas). Transfer to a small saucepan, check the seasoning and keep warm, covered with plastic wrap to stop a skin from forming on the top.

Make the butter sauce: melt one pat of butter in a pan, add the shallots and sweat them for 2 to 3 minutes with the peppercorns, then add the wine and reduce that by three-quarters. Add the cream and reduce for another 2 minutes or so. Take off the heat and keep to the side.

Bring a large pan of salted water to the boil, put in the fava beans and blanch them for 2 to 3 minutes, then drain and refresh under cold running water. Peel off the outer skins of the beans.

Melt the other pat of butter in a sauté pan, and add the fava beans. Season lightly and turn off the heat.

Put the pan containing the wine reduction back on the heat, bring back up to a boil, then slowly whisk in the cold butter cubes. While you are whisking in the cold butter, turn up the temperature slightly to keep it from splitting, but once it is all incorporated turn it down again for the same reason. Pass through a fine sieve into a warm container and keep in a warm place.

Bring a large pan of water to the boil, add salt, put in the pappardelle and cook for a couple of minutes, keeping it moving all the time until al dente (checking after a minute). Drain, reserving the cooking water.

Put the pan containing the beans back on a low heat, and add the pasta, with a little of its cooking water. Toss, add the pecorino, some pepper, the 2 bunches of arugula and 3 or 4 ladlefuls of the butter sauce. Toss a little more for 1 to 2 minutes, adding a little more cooking water if necessary to loosen.

While you are tossing the pasta, warm up the puree, then spread a little on each of the plates, and top with the pasta. Garnish with a little more fresh arugula.

Pappardelle ai fegatini di pollo e salvia

Pappardelle with chicken liver and sage

In autumn we shave some black truffle over the pasta just before serving.

1 recipe quantity of fresh egg
    pasta dough (page 330)
5¾ ounces chicken livers
    (about 6)
2 tablespoons vegetable oil
1 shallot, finely chopped
4 tablespoons brandy
1 glass of white wine
2 tablespoons heavy cream
1 cup butter, plus 2 extra pats
10 sage leaves
2 tablespoons freshly grated
    Parmesan cheese
salt and pepper

First roll the dough through the machine as described on page 332, and then cut as in the recipe on page 338.

In the center of each of the chicken livers is a white filament, so cut around this and keep it to the side, as you will need it to make the butter sauce. Chop the livers coarsely.

Put a large pan of water on to boil for the pasta.

In a separate saucepan, heat half the vegetable oil and add the reserved chicken liver trimmings. Make sure all the pieces are spread out over the pan, so they all touch the bottom. Leave on a high heat for about 2 minutes – the pieces should stick to the base of the pan, so gently scrape them off with a spatula and flip them over. Let them stick to the pan again, then scrape them off again, so they won't burn. Turn down the heat and squash the pieces in the pan until you have a paste. Add the shallot, toss for another couple of minutes, then turn up the heat, add 2 tablespoons of brandy and carefully flame.

Add the white wine and cream, and reduce for 2 to 3 minutes or so. Turn the heat down to low.

Cut the 1 cup of butter into cubes, and slowly whisk it in. While you are doing so turn up the temperature slightly to keep the sauce from splitting, but once it is all incorporated turn the heat down again for the same reason. Pass the sauce through a fine sieve and keep warm.

In a sauté pan, heat the rest of the vegetable oil, add the chicken livers, season and turn over. Turn down the heat, add the rest of the brandy, carefully flame again and season again. Add the 2 extra pats of butter, then put in the sage leaves and let the butter foam.

Put your pasta in the salted boiling water for a couple of minutes (checking after a minute), until al dente.

Drain, reserving some of the cooking water. Add a little of this to the pan containing the chicken livers, then put in the pasta and toss. Add the reserved liver butter sauce, taking care not to heat too much or the butter will split. Add the Parmesan, a little more cooking water, if necessary, and serve.

Pappardelle ai porcini

Pappardelle with porcini

If you can't find any porcini (ceps), or they are out of season, you can still make this with other wild mushrooms – but not button mushrooms (as they don't have enough flavor) or trompettes (as they are too dark and bitter).

1 recipe quantity of fresh egg
    pasta dough (page 330)
7 tablespoons butter
2 garlic cloves, finely chopped
½ pound (8 ounces) porcini,
    sliced
½ glass of white wine
small bunch of chives,
    cut into short lengths
handful of parsley,
    coarsely chopped
2 tablespoons freshly grated
    Parmesan (optional)
salt and pepper

First roll the dough through the machine as described on page 332, and then cut as in the recipe on page 338.

Heat half the butter in a sauté pan, add the chopped garlic and cook gently without allowing it to color. Add the mushrooms and stew them gently without frying. Season and add the white wine. Cover with a lid and cook for a couple of minutes.

Put a large pan of water on to boil for the pasta. Salt it, put in your pasta and cook for a couple of minutes (checking after a minute), until al dente.

Drain, reserving some of the cooking water. Add the pappardelle to the pan containing the mushrooms. Toss for a minute, add the rest of the butter and stir in. Add the chives and parsley, with some more cooking water if needed, and serve with Parmesan if you like.

Tagliatelle alle sarde in saor

Tagliatelle with marinated sardines

Although there is a famous Sicilian pasta dish made with sardines, golden raisins and wild fennel or fennel seeds, this is a variation on a Sardinian starter of just the marinated sardines, no pasta.

We felt it needed some other element to turn it into a dish that we could serve in the restaurant, and I think the sweet and sour flavors work really well with the tagliatelle.

It is also a dish that owes something to the way my grandmother prepared sardines for us – she would fry them first and then put them under a warm marinade.

Some pastas work because they have a homogeneous sauce, but this is a good example of one in which every mouthful is different. As you turn the tagliatelle with your fork, the sauce coats it, but you also spear pieces of melting sardines and golden raisins, and different flavors and textures jump out at you.

Make the pasta and roll the dough through the machine as described on page 332. Work with one strip of pasta at a time. If it is dry or frilly at the edges, trim with a sharp knife. Then cut the pasta strip into lengths roughly 8 inches long. Attach the tagliatelle cutter to your pasta machine and put the strips through one at a time.

Put the oil, herbs, juniper berries, peppercorns and cloves into a deep saucepan over a low heat, turn up the heat and let the flavors gently infuse the oil. When the herbs begin to fry very gently, add the sliced onion, season with salt and cook very gently, without frying, for about 20 minutes, until the onion is soft but not dark and the volume has reduced right down and is covered by the oil.

Meanwhile scale the sardines, clean them and fillet them (see page 94). Season the fillets and dust lightly with flour.

Heat the vegetable oil in a deep fryer or pan (no more than one-third full). To test whether it is hot enough, put in a little flour and, if it fries, then the oil is ready. Put 2 or 3 sardine fillets at a time on a skimmer or metal sieve and dip into the oil for 1 minute. They shouldn't color and should be rare inside – they will continue cooking in the warm marinade. Drain on paper towels to soak up the excess oil.

Turn up the heat under the pan containing the onions and slowly, slowly add the vinegar. Turn the heat off and add the golden raisins.

Put 2 or 3 tablespoonfuls of this mixture into a deep dish. Place the sardines on top and cover with the rest of the mixture. Leave to cool and then cover with plastic wrap. Leave in a cool place (preferably not the fridge) to marinate for 2 to 3 hours. (You can marinate them overnight, but in that case put them in the fridge and bring up to room temperature when you are ready to use them.)

Put a large pan of water on to boil for the pasta.

Take the herbs and cloves out of the marinade. Then, with a slotted spoon, transfer the sardine mixture to a large sauté pan. Place on low heat and let everything warm through. At the same time, using a spoon, gently smash some of the sardines and onions.

Put the pasta into the salted boiling water and cook for a couple of minutes until al dente (check after a minute). Drain, reserving some of the cooking water.

Add the pasta to the pan containing the sardines and toss for a minute or so, adding a little oil from the marinated sardines (go gently, as you don't want the pasta to be too oily). Also add a little of the reserved cooking water, if necessary, to loosen the sauce, and serve.

1 recipe quantity of fresh egg
    pasta dough (page 330)
⅔ cup olive oil
1 bay leaf
sprig of rosemary
2 juniper berries
3 black peppercorns
2 cloves
8 white onions, thinly sliced
10 medium-sized sardines
about 2 tablespoons flour
vegetable oil for deep-frying
5 tablespoons
    white wine vinegar
2 tablespoons golden raisins,
    soaked in water for
    about 30 minutes
salt and pepper

Tagliatelle di castagne ai funghi selvatici

Chestnut tagliatelle with wild mushrooms

This is a pasta that has its roots in necessity. After the Second World War there was a big shortage of flour, so chestnut flour was used to bulk up whatever wheat flour there was available. Because it has no gluten, you need the mixture of the two flours, as you couldn't use chestnut flour alone. The sweetness of the chestnuts really comes through, which is why we use wild mushrooms in this dish, because they often grow underneath the chestnut trees in the woods, so the flavors seem to have a natural affinity.

2¾ cups 00 (doppio zero) flour
¾ cup chestnut flour
1 tablespoon
     extra virgin olive oil
15 egg yolks
pinch of salt

     For the wild
     mushroom sauce:
11 ounces (about 2 cups)
     mixed wild mushrooms
7 tablespoons butter,
     cut into small cubes
2 garlic cloves
½ wineglass of white wine
handful of parsley, chopped
small bunch of chives, cut into
     short lengths
⅓ cup freshly grated Parmesan
     (optional)
salt and pepper

If you are making the pasta by hand, sieve the two flours together in a bowl, then turn out into a mound on a clean surface, and make a well in the middle. Pour in the oil, add the salt and the egg yolks, and slowly start to bring in the flour with the edge of your hand, so that the flour becomes absorbed. If you are using a food processor, sieve the flours into the bowl, add the olive oil and the salt, then start the machine and slowly add the egg yolks. Keep the motor running slowly, or it will heat up the pasta too much and also "beat" rather than mix.

When the mixture starts to come together in a dough, if you are using a food processor, switch off the machine, take out the dough and put it on a clean work surface. Work the dough with your hands, kneading for about 5 minutes. The dough will be much softer than normal egg pasta dough, and darker in color, thanks to the chestnut flour. If it feels too soft, though, add a little more flour as you are kneading.

Divide the dough into two balls, wrap in plastic wrap and keep in the fridge until you are ready to use (it will keep for 2 to 3 days).

Put the dough through the pasta machine as described on page 330. Then, if the strip of pasta is dry or frilly at the edges, trim with a sharp knife. Cut the pasta strip into lengths roughly 8 inches long. Adjust your pasta machine to the tagliatelle setting and put the strips through one at a time.

Make the mushroom sauce: pick through the mushrooms, brushing out any grains of sand or earth. Trim the stalks and tear the mushrooms lengthwise into halves, quarters or eighths, leaving the stalks attached, so that the pieces are all roughly the same size.

Heat half the butter in a large sauté pan, add the garlic and cook for a minute without allowing it to color. Add the mushrooms and cook for 2 more minutes, then pour in the wine and let the alcohol evaporate. Season and take off the heat.

Bring a large pan of water to a boil for the pasta, then salt it, put in the tagliatelle and cook for a couple of minutes until al dente (checking after a minute). Drain well (so that the mushroom mixture clings well to the pasta), reserving some of the cooking water.

Add the pasta to the pan containing the mushrooms and toss together, stirring in the rest of the butter. Then add the chopped parsley and chives. Now you can add a little of the cooking water from the pasta to loosen, if necessary, and serve with Parmesan if you like.

Tagliolini alle zucchine e bottarga

Tagliolini with zucchini and bottarga

You can use the egg pasta dough on page 330 for this, though at Locanda I like to have a more "crunchy" pasta here, which we make in the same way as the basic egg pasta dough, but we use 1¾ cups semolina flour and 1¾ cups 00 (doppio zero) flour mixed together and lots of egg yolks – 16 (no whole eggs this time). Because we use Italian eggs, which tend to have very deep-colored, red-gold yolks, the pasta is a lovely yellow color, which looks good with the zucchini. If your egg yolks are pale, you can add a pinch of turmeric if you like, to deepen the color. You need a tagliolini cutter for your pasta machine for this. If you can't find any bottarga, you can toss some anchovy fillets through the pasta when you combine it with the sauce (see picture).

1 recipe quantity of fresh egg
    pasta dough (page 330, or
    try the variation above)
6 zucchini
up to ½ cup extra virgin olive oil
2 garlic cloves, chopped
½ wineglass of white wine
4 anchovy fillets
3 tablespoons tomato passata
4 tomatoes, quartered
1½ ounces tuna or
    gra y mullet bottarga
handful of chopped parsley
salt and pepper

To make the tagliolini, follow the instructions for rolling the dough on page 332, then, using the tagliolini cutter, put the pasta through the machine again, so that you have strips of pasta just a little wider than spaghetti.

Cut the outer green layer only of the zucchini into strips the same width as the tagliolini, preferably using a mandoline grater.

Put the strips into a colander, season with salt and leave for 10 to 15 minutes in a warm place, so that they lose some of their moisture and become soft, like the pasta.

Heat half the oil in a large sauté pan, add the garlic and fry gently, until soft but not colored. Shake the zucchini to remove excess water, and add to the pan. Stir for a minute or so on a high heat, then add the white wine and allow the alcohol to evaporate. Add the anchovies and let them "melt," without frying them, then add the tomato passata and the fresh tomatoes, and cook for another minute or so, then take off the heat. Season lightly.

Bring a large pan of water to a boil for the pasta, add salt and put in the tagliolini, stirring to prevent sticking. Cook for a couple of minutes until al dente, then drain, reserving some of the cooking water.

While the pasta is cooking, grate the bottarga (not too thick).

Add the drained pasta to the pan containing the sauce, toss and use a fork to mix the pasta and zucchini together, so that it looks like two different colors of tagliolini. Gently add the remaining olive oil, incorporating everything together. Add some of the cooking water from the pasta, if necessary, to loosen, followed by the chopped parsley, and serve with the grated bottarga sprinkled on top.

Tagliolini con cicoria

Tagliolini with chicory

1 recipe quantity of fresh egg
     pasta dough (page 330)
small head of chicory
5 tablespoons
     extra virgin olive oil
2 garlic cloves, finely chopped
½ wineglass of dry white wine
4 anchovy fillets
2 tablespoons grated
     pecorino cheese
salt and pepper

Roll the pasta dough as described on page 332, then make the tagliolini as in the previous recipe.

Bring a large pan of salted water to the boil for the chicory. Cut off the base of the chicory, so that the leaves come away, then wash them carefully. Put the chicory in the boiling water and blanch for about a minute, to take away the excess bitterness. Drain.

Lay the leaves on a cutting board and flatten them. Cut each leaf in half across the width (so each half is more or less the same length as the tagliolini), then cut into thin strips, so that they look similar to the tagliolini.

Heat half the oil in a large sauté pan, add the garlic and cook gently until soft without allowing to color. Add the strips of chicory and cook, stirring, for a couple of minutes. Add the white wine and let the alcohol evaporate. Put in the anchovies and let them dissolve without frying. Taste and season as necessary.

Bring another large pan of water to the boil for the pasta. Salt it and put in the tagliolini, stirring to prevent it from sticking. Cook for a couple of minutes, until al dente. Drain, reserving some of the cooking water.

Add the drained pasta to the pan containing the sauce, toss and use a fork to mix the pasta and chicory together, so that it looks like two different colors of tagliolini. Gently add the rest of the olive oil, incorporating everything together. Add some of the cooking water from the pasta if necessary to loosen, then add the grated pecorino and serve.

Pasta with ragù

Ragù – traditional meat sauce – is, as I said in the introduction to this chapter, best with fresh egg pasta, especially tagliatelle or pappardelle, but not with spaghetti, which is too thin to hold the chunks of meat. You can also serve it with short pasta, such as penne or farfalle; in fact, when the meat is minced (as in the case of beef and pork), it works better with these pastas, and also with fusilli. When you make ragù with wild boar or game, which is cooked on the bone to retain the flavor, and then flaked, the meat has a different consistency that will coat long pasta, such as pappardelle or tagliatelle, better. Sometimes, too, we use ragù as a filling for ravioli.

Each region of Italy has its favorite ragù; sometimes you will even find a mixture of veal, pork and beef all in one sauce. In Toscana, where my sous chef Federico comes from, they like to add chicken liver to pork or beef ragù. At Locanda we vary the ragù according to the season; so sometimes it might be venison or kid (baby goat) – which we get just after Christmas. We make ragù with baby goat in a similar way to wild boar (see page 351) but we don't marinate the meat first. At other times it might be hare, pork, veal or lamb. The beauty of making it at home is that you can cook up a big quantity, then divide it into portions and freeze it, ready to heat through when you want it. Cook the pasta, reserving the cooking water, as usual, then toss the pasta in the pan of ragù, adding a little of the cooking water if necessary to help the sauce cling to the pasta. Stir in a couple of pats of butter, and if you like, add some grated pecorino or Parmesan.

Sometimes I make a very quick and simple sausage and tomato ragù, which the kids love. I chop up some good pork sausages, sauté them in a pan with some garlic cloves – no onions – add a can of good tomatoes and maybe some chopped fresh ones, bring to a boil, then turn down the heat and simmer for about 40 minutes until it is good and thick.

Because it makes sense to make ragù in large quantities, I have broken with the pattern of the rest of the book and given recipes that should make enough to feed eight people, or four for two different meals. If you want to make only enough for four at one sitting, just reduce the quantities.

Ragù alla bolognese

This is the most famous Italian ragù, which I love with gnocchi.

In the restaurant we cook this in the oven in big pans at about 250°F so it just simmers, for about the same length of time as if you cooked it on the stove – if you have a big enough oven and big enough pans, you can do the same.

Makes enough for 8
4 pounds minced beef,
    preferably neck
5 tablespoons olive oil
2 carrots, finely chopped
1 celery stalk, finely chopped
2 onions, finely chopped
sprig of rosemary and sprig
    of sage, tied together for
    a bouquet garni
2 garlic cloves
up to 1 bottle of red wine
1 tablespoon tomato paste
32 ounces (4 cups)
    tomato passata
salt and pepper

To serve:
pasta, preferably pappardelle
    (page 338), tagliatelle or
    short pasta
freshly grated pecorino cheese

Take the meat out of the fridge and lay it on a tray and let it come to room temperature, so that it will sear rather than steam when it goes into the pan.

Heat the oil in a wide-bottomed saucepan, add the vegetables, herbs and whole garlic cloves, and sweat over a high heat for 5 to 8 minutes without allowing it to color (you will need to keep stirring).

Season the meat with salt and pepper and add to the pan of vegetables, making sure that the meat is covering the base of the pan. Leave for about 5 to 6 minutes, so that the meat seals underneath and heats through completely, before you start stirring (otherwise it will ooze protein and liquid and it will steam rather than sear). Take care, though, that the vegetables don't burn – add a little more oil, if necessary, to stop this happening.

Stir the meat and vegetables every few minutes for about 10 to 12 minutes, until the meat starts to stick to the bottom of the pan. At this point, the meat is ready to take the wine.

Add the wine and let it reduce right down to virtually nothing, then add the tomato paste and cook for a couple of minutes, stirring all the time.

Add the passata with 4 cups of water. Bring to the boil, then turn down to a simmer and cook for about 1½ hours, adding a little extra water if necessary from time to time, until you have a thick sauce.

When you are ready to serve the ragù, cook your pasta (preferably pappardelle, tagliatelle or short pasta) and drain, reserving the cooking water. Add the pasta to the ragù and toss well, adding some of the cooking water, if necessary, to loosen the sauce. Serve with freshly grated pecorino.

Ragù di maiale

Pork ragù

This is done in exactly the same way as the ragù alla bolognese (above), but with finely diced meat rather than minced. I also like to add a little milk just after the water has been added and the heat has been turned down to a simmer, to give the ragù a good color and creaminess, and to draw out a little of the acidity from the tomato paste. Serve it in the same way as the ragù alla bolognese, with Parmesan grated over (Parmesan goes better with pork than pecorino).

Ragù di cervo

Venison ragù

Again, this is made in the same way as the ragù alla bolognese (see page 349), but instead of the bouquet garni we add finely chopped rosemary and sage (a sprig of each) to the vegetables, and lots of cloves and juniper berries (about ¼ cup of each). We usually serve it in the same way, but instead of pecorino, we grate over a cheese from Piemonte, called Sola, which is made from goat's and cow's milk.

Ragù di cinghiale

Wild boar ragù

The meat needs to be marinated for a day or two first. We like to cook the meat on the bone for extra flavor, and we add an extra carrot for sweetness.

A few days ahead, put the boar into a large bowl with all the marinade ingredients, cover with plastic wrap and leave in the fridge for at least a day, preferably two. Before you make the ragù, bring the wild boar out of the fridge and let it come back to room temperature. Lift it from the marinade and pat dry. Strain the marinade through a fine sieve.

Heat the olive oil in a large, wide-bottomed pan. Add the vegetables, herbs and garlic, and sweat over a medium heat for about 5 to 6 minutes without allowing it to color.

At the same time, in a separate sauté pan, heat the sunflower or vegetable oil, until smoking hot. Season the wild boar on both sides, put into the pan and cook for 3 or 4 minutes, until slightly crusty on one side, then turn it over and repeat on the other side.

Lift the wild boar from the pan and add to the vegetables. Cook for about 5 to 8 minutes, then add the tomato paste and passata. Cook for a couple more minutes, then add the strained marinade. Bring to the boil, turn the heat down to a simmer and skim off any impurities on the surface. Cook for about 1½ hours, until the meat comes off the bone (if using) and flakes easily. It will be quite stringy but should be tender. Check the seasoning and adjust if necessary.

When you are ready to serve the ragù, cook your pasta (preferably pappardelle or tagliatelle) and drain, reserving the cooking water. Add the pasta to the ragù and toss well, adding some of the cooking water, if necessary, to loosen the sauce. Add a little extra virgin olive oil just before serving.

Makes enough for 8
4 pounds wild boar shoulder (preferably on the bone), cut into pieces about 3¼–4 inches long
5 tablespoons extra virgin olive oil
2 carrots, finely chopped
1 celery stalk, finely chopped
2 onions, finely chopped
sprig of rosemary and sprig of sage, tied together
2 garlic cloves
2 to 3 tablespoons sunflower or vegetable oil
2 tablespoons tomato paste
2 cups tomato passata
salt and pepper

For the marinade:
1 bottle of red wine
2 juniper berries
2 black peppercorns
1 bay leaf
1 small carrot, coarsely chopped
1 small celery stalk, coarsely chopped
1 onion, coarsely chopped
sprig of rosemary

Pasta al forno

Baked pasta

"Great dishes, much misunderstood"

Kids will cry in Italy if you give them *lasagne al forno* that doesn't stand up straight on the plate. If it falls over, they say: "What's wrong? It's all floppy!" Lasagne – which involves thin pasta sheets layered with meat ragù or vegetables, and usually cheese – is clearly the best-known baked *pasta al forno*, a generic term for anything in which pasta of any shape is combined with sauce and then baked in the oven. It is also a dish that is much misunderstood.

The classic *lasagne alla bolognese*, which everybody knows, is meant to be a sturdy, quite dry pasta dish, with a little bit of meat ragù and besciamella (béchamel) sauce in it, not sheets of pasta floating in minced beef and lots of sauce, which will boil up in the oven, so the whole thing comes out moist and soft. That is completely contrary to its spirit. In a true lasagne all the elements come together as one, with a top that crisps up until it is beautifully, cracklingly burnt.

In Britain, when I look at the lasagne that is served everywhere from highway cafés to pubs, or the ready-made versions you can buy in supermarkets, what I see is not lasagne but a version of shepherd's pie, only made with pasta instead of potato, which is all wrong. It is a classic case of Italian tradition colliding with another culture's way of eating meat. Supermarkets have sometimes asked me to develop a lasagne for them, but when I say, "Why do you have to put so much meat in it?" the answer is always "If you don't, people will think they aren't getting a good deal."

In Italy, since the 1960s – just as everywhere in the world – lasagne has become popular all over the country. At one time, though, you had lasagne only on Sunday, at home or in a restaurant. Often in the country, before every house had a modern oven, the women of the village used to take their assembled dishes of lasagne to the bakery and, when the morning's bread had been made, all the dishes would be baked in the big ovens, ready for their owners to collect them and take them home, wrapped in cloths, for the family lunch. Even if you didn't want to make your own dish, you would never buy a ready-made lasagne in a supermarket, because either the local deli would make their own, or you would go to your local restaurant on a Saturday or Sunday, give them your baking dish, and say, "Can you make me enough lasagne for six?" So, while they were making their own lasagne, they would also make some for you, in your own dish, ready to take home and bake yourself.

The women would also know that one of the great secrets of lasagne is to assemble it or have it made for you a day in advance, because a

night's resting lets the pasta and sauces really gel together, so all the elements will properly cook as one. Franco Taruschio always used to say that it was better still if you cooked your lasagne the day before, then put it in the oven for a second baking before serving (in a bain-marie to keep it from drying out). Like a good stew, heating, cooling down, resting, then reheating seems to enhance the flavor.

Think of *pasta al forno* as a dish that can really help you if you have lots of people to feed, because all the work is done in advance. You can have your lasagne in the fridge, ready to bake or baked once already, and say to yourself, "Fantastic, all I have to do is buy some salami to eat first, and maybe some cheese and fruit for afterward, and everyone is going to be full and happy." When we do big parties at Locanda, we often make three different lasagne: one with spinach and ricotta for vegetarians, one classic one, and an extra-special one with porcini. On one occasion, we cooked for friends who were throwing a party at one of London's art galleries. We brought in big ovens with enormous dishes that fitted the oven exactly, and we had perfect hot food in abundance for 450 people standing around and eating in complete ease.

When we make lasagne, we use our own fresh pasta (though at home, because Margherita is allergic to eggs, we often use dried durum wheat pasta). We roll it out very thin, cut it into sheets (for 4 you would need around 12 to 16), then blanch them, 2 or 3 at a time, for a minute or two in plenty of boiling water, moving around the pieces so that they don't stick together. Then we drop them into cold water to stop them cooking any more, take them out and lay them on cloths to dry, before beginning to build the lasagne. Some people say you can make lasagne without blanching the pasta – and it is true they do it this way in some traditional recipes; in others they merely wet the pasta in bowls of cold water. In these dishes, though, you have to be sure that the rest of your ingredients are going to provide plenty of moisture, so that the whole thing doesn't dry out and the pasta doesn't begin to flake and break.

We have ready our ragù alla bolognese (see page 349) and besciamella (béchamel sauce, see page 129, but omit the cheese). First we spread just a thin ladleful of ragù over the dish, then a ladleful of besciamella, again spread thin like a layer of jam on bread. Next goes another layer of pasta and so on, finishing with besciamella and lots of grated Parmesan that will crisp up in the oven (we put it in at 375°F for 30 to 40 minutes). If you want to make the dish more luxurious, you can sprinkle some grated Parmesan over each layer of besciamella, together with a few pieces of mozzarella and a couple of pats of butter.

Not only lasagne…

The classic *lasagne alla bolognese* may be the one that everyone knows best outside Italy, however, from the north to the south of the country, every region uses different ingredients and has its own traditions of *pasta al forno*.

In the south, you find a great use of eggplant – sometimes instead of besciamella, because it provides the same kind of moisture you need to make the dish meld together. In Sicilia, they make an elaborate dish with tubular pasta, spicy sausage and eggs, baked inside a case made with slices of eggplant. Coming up toward Calabria, they often use spicy sausage, mozzarella and ricotta. In Napoli, during carnival time before Lent, you find the traditional lasagne di Carnevale, made with things like ricotta, eggs, spinach and meatballs *(polpettine)*. Once upon a time, when meat was expensive, finding a meatball in such a dish would have been like discovering a golden nugget.

One of the most renowned baked pasta dishes is *vincisgrassi*, which is traditional in the Marche region and uses layered sheet pasta with cured ham and porcini. Some say it was created by a local chef for an Austrian general, Prince Windischgrätz, who was commander of the Austrian forces stationed in Marche during the Napoleonic wars in 1799. As always, though, there is a dispute about this, because something similar, called "princisgras," is mentioned earlier in 1784 in a famous book by Antonio Nebbia called *Il Cuoco Maceratese*, which was one of the first to champion Italian dishes, such as pasta, over French influences. Marche is a region that is divided: half is by the sea and half in the mountains, where you have plenty of butter, hams, cured meat, mushrooms and truffles. Franco Taruschio, who comes from Marche, made a famous *vincisgrassi* during his time at the Walnut Tree near Abergavenny, using the wild mushrooms from the local woods. Sometimes in mountain areas the pasta is replaced by polenta, which is layered in the same way and known as *polenta cuncia* – the polenta has great absorbency, so we are talking about a very heavy, thick, warming food.

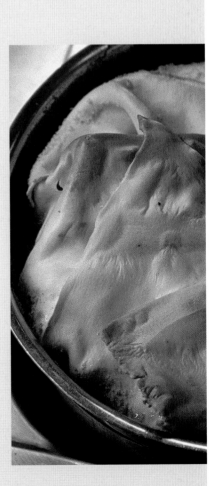

And then there is *timballo* (or timpani, as it is called in the south), the subject of the brilliant 1996 movie *Big Night*, the "horn of plenty" of Italian cooking – a rich, lavish dish that has been embedded in our culture of celebration since Renaissance times, when it would be served by the great chefs at court banquets in Napoli. It is baked in a round mold, often lined with big, long tubular ziti (traditional at weddings), tagliatelle or tagliolini, and sometimes it is encased in pastry. Everything you have goes into the timballo. It is a fantastic thing; the panettone of pasta. When *Big Night* opened in London there was a big party at Locanda – and so we made timballi encased in sheet pasta and inside a mix of short pasta and meatballs. One of Italy's most famous modern chefs, Alfonso Iaccarino, of the restaurant Don Alfonso 1890 at Sant'Agata sui Due Golfi, near Napoli, made everyone smile at the cleverness of his variation, which uses a mold lined first with bread crumbs, then with peeled, roasted yellow peppers, and filled with bucatini (big, fat tubular pasta), tossed in garlic, tomatoes, olives, capers, basil and mozzarella, then wound around and around.

There is a newer Italian-French style of pasta that resembles *pasta al forno* but in fact never goes into the oven, which we call *gratinata* – something that came into fashion in the sixties and seventies. It is very much a "restaurant" sort of thing; the sheet pasta is cooked as the order comes in, layered up with its sauce inside a pastry ring, then "glazed" with béchamel, which is flashed under a grill before the dish goes out to the customer. It works especially well with seafood, which is difficult in a pasta dish baked in the traditional way, because the fish would be seriously overcooked; this way the whole dish becomes lighter, and you can work on it to make it look beautiful. It is a concept most exploited by the Cipriani family of the Cipriani restaurants and Harry's Bar in Venezia, and it is a brilliant idea. I enjoy doing it myself sometimes in the restaurant, but it has no real basis in Italian tradition.

Fazzoletti alla purea di legumi e basilico

Layered pasta with spring vegetables and basil puree

This is a quite new way to serve pasta, in the style that the Milanese chef Gualtiero Marchesi has made famous. It is a little like a lasagne, except that it isn't baked – the pasta and sauce are just built up on the plate before serving. In the restaurant, we add parsley leaves to the pasta for the last rolling through the machine, to make it look attractive, and add an extra flavor. When the pasta has gone through once on 0.5, we scatter it with whole flat parsley leaves, then fold it in two and put it through again, so that the leaves are pressed into the pasta. In spring, in addition to asparagus, we also add some blanched fava beans, peas or snow peas to this recipe but at other times of the year you can leave them out. Sometimes we also add some sautéed morels or other mushrooms.

Finely chop one eggplant and one zucchini, and cut the rest into large dice. Put the eggplant and zucchini in separate colanders or sieves, sprinkle with salt and leave for at least a couple of hours, but preferably overnight, so that you draw out as much of the water as possible, and also any bitterness.

Put the pasta dough through the machine following the instructions on page 332 (if you like, put it through once more, scattered with parsley leaves as described above). Trim the edges of your pasta if they are dry or frilly. Cut each strip of pasta in half lengthwise, then cut each piece in half, so that you have 16 squares. Lay the pasta squares on a floured tray and put in the fridge until you need them.

Put a large shallow ovenproof dish into a barely warm oven – you will need this to keep the pasta warm later.

Melt half the butter in a medium saucepan, add the shallots and cook for 6 to 7 minutes until soft but not colored.

While the shallots are cooking, put the milk and basil into a blender and liquefy, as if you were making a basil milk shake. Set aside.

Bring a large pot of water to a boil for the pasta.

Take the finely chopped eggplant from the colander and squeeze very well in your hands to remove the remaining moisture, and add to the pan of shallots. Cook quickly on a high heat, stirring all the time. After 4 to 5 minutes, add the peppers and keep cooking quickly and stirring.

2 medium-sized eggplants
2 zucchini
1 recipe quantity of fresh egg
    pasta dough (page 330)
about 7 tablespoons
    unsalted butter
1 banana shallot or 2 regular
    shallots, finely chopped
2 cups plus 2 tablespoons milk
handful of basil leaves
½ red pepper, deseeded
    and finely chopped
½ yellow pepper, deseeded
    and finely chopped
1½ tablespoons flour
vegetable oil for deep-frying
8 asparagus spears
3 tablespoons
    extra virgin olive oil
about 7 to 8 tablespoons
    freshly grated Parmesan
salt and pepper

After about 6 to 7 minutes, squeeze the finely chopped zucchini in the same way as the eggplant, add it to the pan and lightly season (go easy as you have already seasoned the eggplant and zucchini with salt). Cook for another 3 to 5 minutes, still stirring.

Add the flour and cook for a couple of minutes, still stirring, then add the basil mixture, a little at a time, stirring as you go. Bring to a boil, then turn down the heat and simmer for about 5 minutes, still stirring, until the sauce begins to thicken – like a green vegetable béchamel. Turn off the heat and cover with a lid, plastic wrap or foil to stop a skin from forming.

Meanwhile heat the vegetable oil in a deep fryer or deep saucepan (don't fill any more than one-third full). To test whether it is hot enough, sprinkle in a little flour and if it sizzles it is ready. Take the diced eggplant and zucchini in your hands and squeeze well, to get rid of a little more moisture. Fry separately in batches for about 2 minutes, so that they turn slightly crisp (be careful, as any remaining moisture may cause the oil to foam up). Drain on paper towels.

Tie the asparagus with string and stand in a tall pan of boiling salted water, keeping the tips above the water so they will steam gently, for about 4 to 6 minutes depending on thickness. Untie them, wrap in a wet cloth and keep on one side.

Put the rest of the butter in a small saucepan over low heat so that it begins to melt and then foam, while you are finishing everything off. Keep an eye on it and, if you feel that it is bubbling too much, add another pat or two of butter and turn off the heat.

Put the pasta into the salted boiling water for a couple of minutes until just soft (slightly beyond al dente). Drain, reserving a little of the cooking water.

Drizzle the olive oil into the ovenproof dish you have been keeping warm, add a little of the cooking water, then put in the pasta, moving it around so each square is covered in water and oil to keep the pieces from sticking to each other.

Have 4 warmed plates ready and start to build up your "lasagne." Put a tablespoon of sauce in the middle of each plate, sprinkle with some Parmesan (for each plate you are going to need 5 layers of Parmesan, so use just a little at a time). Add a layer of pasta, then more sauce, Parmesan, pasta, etc., finishing with a layer of pasta and a final sprinkling of Parmesan. Add some of the reserved deep fried zucchini and eggplant to each plate along with 2 asparagus spears. Spoon some of the foaming butter over the top and serve.

Filled pasta

In general, the filled pasta of the north tends to involve meat, whereas in the south and around the coast you are more likely to find stuffings of vegetables or seafood. Of course there are exceptions, and one of my favorites is a typical filled pasta from Lombardia, made with pumpkin and amaretti cookies (see page 366). In Lombardia we even have a kind of sweet filled pasta, a tortelli, dusted with sugar, which is one of the many specialties we make for the feast of San Giuseppe.

Each region also tends to have its preference for a particular shape of pasta, which they believe works best with the filling, but you can substitute any you like in the recipes that follow.

When you make filled pasta, one of the most important things is not to try to make too many all at once, or they will become dry and start to crack. Work with only one strip of pasta at a time, keeping the rest of the pasta dough wrapped in a damp cloth until you are ready for it.

The relationship between the pasta and its stuffing is important – you don't want too much floppy pasta around the edges, but take equal care not to overstuff them, or they might "explode" when you cook them.

Filled pasta is wonderful for freezing. Put a tray into the freezer, then make your ravioli, bring out your tray, put the ravioli on it, making sure they are completely separate from one another, put them into the freezer for 10 minutes, then turn them over, and then when they are hard, put them into a freezer bag. Then, when you are ready to cook them, you can do so from frozen.

The best thing of all is to have some cubes of homemade stock in the freezer (see page 264). Then, when you come home at night, you can just put some in a pan, and, when the stock is boiling, put in your frozen ravioli, bring the stock back up to a boil, and cook for a few minutes until the pasta is just soft and you have *ravioli in brodo;* a fantastic plate of pasta soup.

Ravioli di patate e menta con peperoni

Potato and mint ravioli with pepper sauce

In the restaurant, we often also make these using a slightly different shape of pasta pocket, called malfatti (see page 336).

2 red peppers
2 tablespoons
    extra virgin olive oil
12 ounces (¾ pound)
    new potatoes
1 stick plus 2 tablespoons
    butter, diced
sprig of rosemary
¾ cup freshly grated Parmesan
1 recipe quantity of fresh egg
    pasta dough (page 330)
1 egg, beaten, to brush on
    the pasta
about 40 mint leaves
sprig of sage
salt and pepper

Preheat the oven to 340°F and, when hot, put in the whole peppers drizzled with the olive oil and roast for about 15 minutes, turning them every 5 minutes, until soft but not black. Take them out, put into a bowl, cover with plastic wrap and let them steam for about 10 minutes, so that you can take the skins off easily.

While the peppers are in the oven, make the filling for the pasta. Boil the potatoes in their skins for about half an hour, then peel while still warm and put into a food processor and process.

In a small pan, melt 7 tablespoons of butter with the rosemary, so that the flavor infuses and the butter starts to color.

Slowly add the butter to the potatoes and continue to process until smooth. Add half the Parmesan and season to taste. Transfer to a bowl, cover with plastic wrap and leave to cool.

Next make the sauce: skin the peppers, deseed and chop them, then put them into the (clean) food processor and process until smooth. Transfer to a small saucepan and set aside.

Make the pasta dough in the usual way (see page 330) and put through the machine (see page 332). Mark the halfway point of your first strip of pasta and brush one half with beaten egg, then place little mounds of filling (each about a teaspoonful) two abreast on the half brushed with egg, leaving a space of about 1¼ to 1½ inches between each mound. You should have enough to make around 10 from each strip.

Put a mint leaf on top of each mound of filling. Fold the other half of the pasta over the top, carefully matching the long edges down one side and pressing them together, then doing the same on the other side. Gently press down around each raviolo (don't worry if you compress the filling a little as you go).

Using a fluted ring cutter about ½ inch bigger in circumference than the filling, cut out each raviolo and discard the trimmings. Seal each one and press out any air trapped inside, by taking each raviolo and carefully, with your thumbs, pinching around the outside. If you hold each raviolo up to the light, you can see where the filling is, and whether you have smoothed out all the air pockets. Repeat with the rest of the pasta.

Bring a large pan of water to a boil.

Put the pan containing the peppers back on the heat to warm through, with a tablespoon of the remaining butter, stirring it in.

Melt the rest of the butter with the sage in a large sauté pan.

While the butter is melting, put the ravioli into the salted boiling water and cook for 3 to 4 minutes, then drain them using a slotted spoon or a skimmer and transfer to the pan containing the butter and sage. Toss gently for a minute or so.

Spoon some pepper puree on each of your plates, then arrange the ravioli on top, sprinkle with the rest of the Parmesan, spoon the rest of the butter and sage over the top and serve.

Ravioli di erbe con salsa di noci

Herb ravioli with walnut sauce

This is a springtime dish, when the herbs are in season – you can use borage or young nettles as well, if you like. You can buy the walnut paste from Italian delicatessens, but make sure it is good quality. It's best to make the filling at least half a day before you need it.

4½ ounces Swiss chard leaves
2 large bunches of parsley leaves, plus a handful to garnish
2 large bunches of basil leaves
2–3 sprigs of rosemary
bunch of sage leaves
⅓ cup extra virgin olive oil
11 ounces fresh spinach
3½ ounces young nettle leaves (optional)
2 ounces borage leaves (optional)
12 ounces (about 1⅓ cups) ricotta
¼ nutmeg, freshly grated
1 tablespoon grated Parmesan
2 eggs
1 tablespoon bread crumbs
2 tomatoes
1 recipe quantity of fresh egg pasta dough (page 330)
4 tablespoons Walnut paste (see page 322)
5¼ tablespoons butter
salt and pepper

Add the herbs to the chard leaves, reserving one of the bunches of parsley for garnish.

In a separate pan, warm the olive oil, add the herbs and chard leaves and the spinach, together with the young nettle and borage leaves if using them. Gently "stew" without frying for 4 to 5 minutes until soft (you are softening, rather than cooking, as you want everything to stay green). Drain in a colander and weight everything down for about half a day to lose as much of the excess moisture as possible.

Put the contents of the colander into a food processor and process to a smooth paste, then transfer to a fine sieve and leave to drain for another 10 minutes or so.

Put the ricotta into a bowl, add the drained herbs and leaves, season and add the nutmeg, Parmesan, one of the eggs and the bread crumbs. Taste and adjust the seasoning, if necessary, then put into the fridge until needed.

Put the tomatoes into a large pan of boiling water for 10 seconds. Skin, quarter and deseed (see page 304), then cut into about ½-inch dice. Set aside while you make the ravioli.

Make the pasta dough in the usual way (see page 330) and put through the machine (see page 332). Make the ravioli as described in the previous recipe, omitting the mint leaves.

At the same time, in a separate pan warm the walnut paste with a little of the boiling water.

Heat the butter gently in two separate sauté pans, and add another tablespoon of the boiling water to each.

Add salt to the boiling water, put in the ravioli and cook for 3 to 4 minutes, then drain them using a slotted spoon or a skimmer and transfer to the pans containing the butter and water. Toss gently for a minute or so, then add the diced tomato and chopped reserved parsley.

Spoon some walnut sauce onto each of your plates, arrange the ravioli on top and serve.

Ravioli di patate e funghi selvatici

New potato ravioli with wild mushrooms

This is a variation on the recipe for Potato and mint ravioli (see page 360) – without the mint.

We use about ¾ pound mixed wild mushrooms, like *finferle* (chanterelles), porcini (ceps), *fungo ostrica* (oyster mushrooms), *steccherino dorato* (pied de mouton), whatever is in season. Then we cook them gently in butter, using one or two flat sauté pans, with 2 chopped garlic cloves for a couple of minutes. We add a glass of white wine, season with salt and pepper, and let the alcohol evaporate.

We have some chopped parsley and chives ready, make and fill the ravioli, omitting the mint, then cook. We drain the ravioli, add them to the pan of mushrooms and cook for a minute or so, with a couple of extra pats of butter. Check the seasoning, add the parsley and chives and a couple of tablespoons of freshly grated Parmesan, and some cooking water if necessary to loosen, and serve.

Tordelli di cipolla rossa e salsa al Chianti

Red onion tortelli with Chianti sauce

Tortelli are similar to ravioli, except that they have a plain – rather than fluted – edge.

2 tablespoons
    extra virgin olive oil
8 large red onions, thinly sliced
3 tablespoons grated Parmesan
2 tablespoons
    fresh bread crumbs
2 eggs
1 recipe quantity egg pasta
    dough (see page 330)
4¼ tablespoons unsalted butter
8 sage leaves
1 recipe quantity Chianti sauce
    (see page 497)
2¾ ounces ricotta salata
salt and pepper

Heat the olive oil in a pan, add the onions and cook very gently without allowing them to color, for about 30 minutes. Season and transfer to a colander or a sieve, and leave to drain (either overnight or for several hours – or, if you want to use them sooner, put a weight on top of the onions to force out the moisture more quickly).

When the onions have drained and are cold, put them into a bowl, add the Parmesan, bread crumbs and one of the eggs, and check and adjust the seasoning (remember, the Parmesan will be salty).

Make the pasta dough as described on page 330 and put through the machine (see page 332). Make the tortelli as for the ravioli on page 360, using a plain ring cutter or glass instead of the fluted ring, and omitting the mint leaves.

Bring a large pan of water to a boil for the pasta.

Melt the butter in a large sauté pan, then add the sage and, when the butter begins to foam, add the Chianti sauce.

Put the tortelli into the boiling water and cook for 3 to 4 minutes, then drain them using a slotted spoon or a skimmer and transfer to the pan containing the sauce. Toss gently for a minute or so and serve. Grate the ricotta salata on top.

Tordelli di zucca agli amaretti

Tortelli with pumpkin and amaretti

As always, throughout the different regions of Italy, recipes for filled pasta with pumpkin vary – sometimes they are spiced with ginger, sometimes nutmeg. In Mantova, in Emilia-Romagna, they tend to add a mustard fruit *(mostarda di frutta)* to the filling. Federico, my sous chef, is from Toscana and there they like the pumpkin completely plain. In my region, Lombardia, we like to add amaretti cookies, and when we have truffles, we sometimes shave some over the tortelli before serving. Pumpkins are in season from the middle of October until January, and one of the best varieties we have found is the ironbark. Because pumpkin flesh contains a lot of water, you need to dry it out before making the filling. When we make this at the restaurant, we start a day ahead, wrapping the processed, cooked pumpkin flesh in a clean cloth, then hanging it in the big walk-in fridge to drain away the excess moisture. You can do a similar thing at home, but if you want to make the recipe in more of a hurry, you can cook out the moisture in the pan. However, it will take 15 to 30 minutes, depending on how wet the pumpkin is, and you will have to keep stirring it all the time.

about 2 pounds pumpkin flesh
    (you will need a 5½- to
    6-pound pumpkin or
    2 butternut squash)
3 tablespoons
    extra virgin olive oil
1 white onion, thinly sliced
6 tablespoons freshly
    grated Parmesan
4 tablespoons crushed
    amaretti cookies
1 tablespoon bread crumbs
2 eggs
pinch of freshly grated nutmeg
1 recipe quantity of fresh egg
    pasta dough (page 330)
5¼ tablespoons butter
6 sage leaves
1 tablespoon Amaretto liqueur
salt and pepper

Preheat the oven to 390°F. Cut the pumpkin into chunks, put them on a tray, skin side down, add half a wineglass of water, cover and seal with foil. Put in the oven for about 1 to 1½ hours, depending on the size of the chunks – until they are soft enough for your finger to press easily into the flesh.

While the pumpkin is cooking, heat the oil in a saucepan, add the onion and cook gently without allowing to color for 10 to 15 minutes. Turn off the heat and cover with a lid.

When the pumpkin is cooked, scrape the flesh from the skin and add to the onion. Turn on the heat again and cook for another 10 minutes so that the pumpkin begins to lose some of its moisture. If you are going to hang up the pumpkin flesh to drain (see above), remove from the pan, put into a blender and blend until smooth, then season. If you are not going to drain it like this, continue cooking over a low heat for another 15 to 30 minutes, until the mixture has dried out. If it is still too moist, put it into a clean cloth and squeeze out as much moisture as you can.

Transfer the pumpkin mixture to a mixing bowl, add half the Parmesan, half the crushed amaretti cookies, the bread crumbs, one of the eggs and grated nutmeg. Mix everything together, check and adjust the seasoning again, if necessary, and put to one side.

Make the pasta dough (see page 330) and put through the machine (see page 332). Make the tortelli as for the ravioli on page 360, using a plain rather than fluted cutter, and omitting the mint leaves.

Bring a large pan of water to the boil for the pasta.

You need two large sauté pans – melt half the butter in each with half of the sage.

Put the tortelli into the pan of salted boiling water and cook for about 3 minutes, then drain and put half into each of the two sauté pans for a minute or so, basting them with the butter until it coats them. If the butter begins to turn too brown, add a few more pats of butter to bring the temperature down.

Take 2 tablespoons of the remaining grated Parmesan and sprinkle a little over each of your plates, followed by the rest of the crushed amaretti cookies, and then put the tortelli on top. Sprinkle with the rest of the Parmesan.

Pour the sage butter from one pan to the other, then tip the pan toward you so that all the butter collects at the front of the pan and pour in the Amaretto (if you just pour it straight in, it may flame and burn the butter). Stir in quickly and pour over the tortelli.

Tordelli di melanzane e mozzarella

Eggplant and mozzarella tortelli

For the filling for these tortelli, preheat the oven to 430°F and halve 5 eggplants lengthwise, put them, skin side down, on your work surface, and with a sharp knife score the flesh diagonally one way (quite deeply), then the other way, to make a diamond pattern. Slice 4 garlic cloves quite thick and slot the pieces into the cuts at random – about 2 pieces per half of eggplant. Push some leaves of rosemary into the slots, then put the halves of eggplant back together, so that you now have 5 "whole" ones, and wrap in foil. Put on a tray and cook in the preheated oven for 25 to 30 minutes (they need to be well cooked – if you push your finger against them, it should make a dent).

While they are cooking, dice 14 ounces mozzarella and put into a colander to drain. When the eggplants are cooked, take off the foil, remove the garlic and rosemary, spoon out the flesh, put into a colander and leave to cool and drain, then chop finely.

Heat 2 tablespoons of extra virgin olive oil in a saucepan, chop a bunch of spring onions and add those, then cook gently for a few minutes. Add the eggplant and a tablespoon of tomato paste, and cook for another minute or so. If you feel the eggplants are still too wet, continue cooking a little longer until they lose their moisture. Season, remove from the pan, and leave to cool completely.

Make the tortelli in the same way as for the recipe on page 360, topping each mound of eggplant filling with a cube of mozzarella. Before you cook the tortelli, make a simple sauce by putting about ⅓ cup of extra virgin olive oil in a sauté pan with 2 tablespoons of chopped parsley and 3 peeled, quartered and deseeded tomatoes – but don't heat it up until you have cooked the tortelli. When the tortelli are ready, transfer them to the pan of sauce, then turn on the heat and add a couple of spoonfuls of the cooking water, so that the oil doesn't fry, but everything just warms through and the tortelli don't stick to the pan. Toss gently for a minute or so and then serve.

Malfatti di ricotta, melanzane e noci

Ricotta pockets with eggplant and walnuts

Malfatti are yet another variation of filled pasta, in which you make a triangle and then fold down the tip and seal it. Because this is a very simple pasta, it relies heavily on the quality of the three ingredients – ricotta, eggplant and walnuts. So it is best to buy whole walnuts in season.

If you want to make an even simpler, classic ricotta filling, just mix 14 ounces (about 1⅔ cups) of ricotta with ½ cup of cooked spinach (about ½ pound (8 ounces) raw), 3 tablespoons of grated Parmesan and an egg, then season with salt and freshly ground black pepper and a pinch of nutmeg.

4 tablespoons shelled walnuts,
    or equivalent in whole nuts
2 eggplants (the round, pale
    ones if possible)
2 tablespoons
    extra virgin olive oil
1 onion, finely chopped
one 15-ounce can of
    chopped tomatoes
12 ounces (about 1⅓ cups)
    ricotta cheese
vegetable oil for deep-frying
pinch of freshly grated nutmeg
2 eggs
6 tablespoons freshly
    grated Parmesan
1 recipe quantity of fresh egg
    pasta dough (page 330)
5¼ tablespoons unsalted butter
around 5 fresh basil leaves
salt and pepper

If you are using whole walnuts, crack them, trying to keep them as intact as possible. Put them on a tray and toast them in the oven at about 340°F for about 4 to 5 minutes until they are golden. While still warm, wrap them in a cloth and rub them to pull off the skins. Then, while the nuts are still warm, peel off whatever is left of the skins with a small knife. Chop the nuts.

Cut the eggplant into about ¾-inch dice, put in a colander, season with salt and set aside to drain in a warm place.

Heat the olive oil in a saucepan and add the onions. Cook gently without allowing to color for about 4 to 5 minutes, then add the tomatoes and cook until the excess juice has evaporated and the consistency is quite thick (10 to 20 minutes, depending on the size of your pan). Take off the heat.

While the tomatoes are cooking, put the ricotta into a colander to allow any excess moisture to drain.

Heat the vegetable oil in a deep fryer or deep saucepan (don't fill any more than one-third full because, however much you drain the eggplant, it will still be wet and might cause the oil to foam up). To test whether it is hot enough, sprinkle in a little flour and if it sizzles it is ready.

Take the pieces of eggplant in your hands and squeeze well, to get rid of a little more moisture, and then fry in two separate batches, for about 2 minutes each, so that they turn slightly crisp (this is important, as you don't want soft, greasy eggplant inside your pasta parcels). Drain on paper towels.

Put the ricotta in a bowl, add the walnuts, eggplant, nutmeg, one of the eggs and 4 tablespoons of Parmesan, and mix well. Check and adjust the seasoning, if necessary.

Make the pasta dough as described on page 330 and put through the machine (see page 332). Beat the remaining egg and use it to brush each pasta strip, then place little mounds of filling two abreast along the length of the strip, leaving a space of about 1½ inches between each mound. Then cut down the center of the strip so that you have two long strips (about 3 inches wide) with mounds of filling at intervals. Then cut these across into squares of 3 × 3 inches.

Working with one square of pasta at a time, take one corner and bring it over the top of the filling to the opposite corner, pressing down the edges and moving your fingers inward toward the filling to push out any trapped air. Brush the tip of the triangle with a little more beaten egg, then fold it back toward the center and press down to seal.

Bring a large pan of water to the boil for the pasta. You need two large sauté pans – melt half the butter in each.

Put the malfatti into the pan of salted boiling water and cook for about 3 minutes, drain and divide between the two sauté pans. Gently cook until golden. If the butter begins to turn too brown, add a few more pats of butter to bring the temperature down.

While the malfatti are browning in the pans, put the pan of tomato sauce back on the heat. Tear the basil leaves and add them, heat through and check and adjust the seasoning, if necessary.

Spoon half of the tomato sauce into the middle of the plates, arrange the malfatti around the edge, sprinkle with the rest of the Parmesan and spoon the rest of the tomato sauce into the center, between the malfatti.

Melanzane

Eggplants

"As strange as bananas"

I could happily talk about eggplants for hours. They are so beautiful, aren't they? But weird – as strange as bananas are compared to other fruits, with their meaty texture and skins that can be glossy and purple-black or every shade of violet and indigo, marbled or streaked with creamy white; even white and green; they can be pure white and egg-shaped or bigger and round. Originally from India, where they were grown more than 5,000 years ago, they arrived in Italy as a result of trade with the Arabs in the thirteenth century through the influence of the Jewish communities – Pellegrino Artusi talks about them as "Jewish food."

At first they were treated with great suspicion – people thought they would poison you (it is true that they belong to the nightshade family) or drive you insane. In fact, the Italian word for them, *melanzana*, comes from the Latin *mala insane*, "apple of madness." Eventually, though, the fact that they grow well in a dry climate and in not very fertile ground made them a great food for everyone.

What makes eggplants special is that when you first put them into your mouth they have quite a neutral taste, followed by a distinctive, slightly bitter back flavor, and a texture that soaks up the flavor of other ingredients, especially tomato, the acidity of which really brings out the flavor of the eggplant.

Good eggplants have smooth skins and feel firm to the touch, but not too heavy, as this shows they are full of seeds and good only to make eggplant "caviar" (see page 456). Unlike most fruits, the larger the eggplant, the stronger the flavor will be, because the bitterness, which is what we tend to recognize as the characteristic flavor, becomes more developed as the fruit grows.

Choose medium-sized eggplants that will have a good flavor but are not so huge and overblown that they will be particularly bitter and their texture too spongy.

It is important to use them in season, which in the Mediterranean is from June to October. I think eggplants raised hydroponically in a greenhouse are a crime – what is the point of having a fruit that looks perfectly pear-shaped and shiny but hasn't enjoyed any sun and has just become puffed up and spongy and flavorless?

I don't know why the eggplant should be so associated with the south, since it's an ingredient that you rarely eat cold or in salads in hot weather; it feels more at home in stews, or pasta, or with tomato sauce. The most famous eggplant dish is *pasta alla Norma*, made with tomato sauce and basil – which sounds very basic, but with the best tomato sauce, and the right eggplant, it tastes amazing.

If you go into a traditional bar in Palermo, you will find big slices of eggplant, fried in bread crumbs or flour and used as a base for mozzarella or other antipasti, which you have with your aperitif. Around Napoli they like to cook eggplant in water and vinegar, maybe with some garlic, herbs and salt, then squeeze and drain them, cut them into stringy strips, and keep them under oil. Again, they serve these in bars. My wife, Plaxy, calls them "worms," because they look quite unappealing, nothing about them says "eat me" – but they are great with a drink, and maybe some olives (see page 85).

In Maiori, on the Amalfi coast, eggplant is even eaten as a dessert *(melanzane al cioccolato)*. Slices of eggplant are fried, dipped in egg and flour, fried again, dipped in chocolate sauce and layered in a dish with nuts, crushed amaretti cookies, and sometimes candied fruit, then chilled.

The only eggplant dish I ever saw my grandmother make was *melanzana alla Parmigiana*, which they say originated in Calabria, but of course the people of Campania, Sicilia, Sardegna and Puglia all claim it as their dish too. It is literally a lasagne made not with pasta but with seasoned and fried eggplant, similar to the Greek moussaka. My brother, Roberto, and I used to steal as many slices of eggplant as we could before they ever made it into the oven, because they tasted so good.

Because melanzana alla Parmigiana was at one time one of the things that my daughter, Margherita, wasn't allergic to, we often made it for her and used the actual eggplant as a container, so she could take it to school. I thought it was a brilliant thing to do, but she complained, "Why can't I have lunch that looks like everyone else's?"

Eggplant is the most important ingredient in caponata (see page 58) – one of my favorite things to have for a barbecue or to pack when you are traveling. When Plaxy and I are driving with the kids in Italy, I have my Swiss army knife in my pocket and we buy some salami and bread and cheese and pack a jar of caponata, and stop off and eat in a field for the best kind of picnic. No hampers or tables and chairs, no plates, just caponata piled up on bread, with pieces of salami to eat with your fingers.

People say you don't need to salt eggplants before using them, because modern strains are not as bitter as they used to be, but I still prefer to salt them and let them drain slowly, preferably overnight, to draw out excess moisture. At the Laurent in Paris, we used to salt them this way, cut them into strips, season them with lemon juice and a little more salt, and steam them. Because they had first been drained of excess moisture, they kept their shape. Then we layered the strips with peppers, zucchini, and langoustine to make a terrine – the thought of which would cause most Italians to throw their hands in the air – eggplant and fish, not a popular combination where I come from, but I thought it was an excellent idea.

Ravioli di gamberi

Prawn ravioli

It is best to use fresh prawns – you need big tiger prawns – but you can use ones that have been previously frozen. They must be very cold and dry before they go into the food processor; otherwise the action of the motor will warm them up and they will start to cook, and if they are too wet the mixture will be too watery, so when you add the cream it will split. The mussels in this dish just flavor the sauce, you don't actually eat them – but you can keep them, mix them with some parsley and serve them before the ravioli, as a small antipasto.

1 tablespoon parsley leaves
14 ounces peeled tiger prawns,
    cold and dry (see above),
    plus 4 extra prawns,
    cut into 3, for garnish
    (optional)
¼ cup cooked spinach
½ teaspoon paprika
2 tablespoons heavy cream
1 recipe quantity of fresh egg
    pasta dough (page 330)
1 egg, beaten, to brush on
    the pasta
8 basil leaves
1 teaspoon salt

For the sauce:
2 garlic cloves, finely chopped
⅓ cup plus 1 tablespoon
    extra virgin olive oil
1¼ pounds fresh mussels,
    cleaned carefully in salty
    water (see page 167)
1 wineglass of white wine
1 tablespoon tomato passata
zucchini blossoms (optional),
    to garnish (slice any
    attached fruit fine)

Chop the garlic for the sauce and mix with 2 teaspoons of olive oil. When you are ready to start, lift out the garlic and set aside.

Put the parsley into a food processor and process until chopped, then quickly add the prawns, process again and add the reserved garlic-infused oil, followed by the spinach, paprika and salt. Finally, while the motor is still running, slowly add the cream. The whole process shouldn't take more than 2 minutes, so that you don't start to "cook" the prawns with the heat from the motor. Put the mixture into a container and keep in the fridge until ready to use.

To make the sauce, put another tablespoon of the olive oil into a saucepan and add the reserved garlic. Cook for a few minutes, without allowing it to color, then add the mussels and cover with a lid. Cook for a couple of minutes, then add the white wine and cook for a further minute or two, to let the alcohol evaporate. Take off the heat and keep on the side – that way, if there is any trace of sand left from the mussels, it will sink to the bottom.

Make the pasta dough as described on page 330 and roll through the machine (see page 332). Make the ravioli (see page 360), omitting the mint leaves.

Lift the mussels out of their pan, trying not to disturb the cooking liquid too much (if you like, sprinkle them with a handful of chopped parsley and serve before the ravioli). Tilt the pan slightly and carefully spoon out the liquid, making sure you don't scoop up any of the gritty sediment.

Bring a large pan of water to the boil, salt it, and cook the ravioli for 2 to 3 minutes.

While the ravioli are cooking, put the mussel liquid into a large sauté pan (better still, divide it between two pans), add the tomato passata and warm slowly. Add the extra prawns and zucchini blossoms (if using). Add the rest of the olive oil and let that warm through.

Drain the ravioli using a slotted spoon or a skimmer and transfer to the pan or pans containing the mussel liquid and tomato. Toss gently for a minute or so.

Tear the basil leaves, add to the pan or pans and serve (if you feel the sauce is too soupy, arrange the ravioli on your plates, then quickly turn up the heat under the pan or pans and reduce the sauce a little).

Ravioli all'osso buco

Veal shank ravioli

This is the kind of ravioli I love to make. For me this is a great example of calling on traditional pasta-making techniques to upgrade a peasant dish such as *osso buco* into something quite sophisticated, which people love to eat. Choose veal shanks from the middle part of the leg, which is the meatiest. You will probably have quite a bit of sauce left over from cooking the osso buco – which you could just use with some pasta tossed through it another day (it will keep for about 4 days in the fridge).

3 tablespoons
    extra virgin olive oil
1 onion, cut into ½-inch dice
1 celery stalk, cut into ½-inch dice
1 carrot, cut into ½-inch dice
4 veal shanks,
    each 1¼ inches thick
1 tablespoon flour
2 tablespoons vegetable oil
2¼ cups white wine
1 tablespoon tomato paste
8 cups veal stock (see page 266)
3–4 saffron threads
1 bouquet garni (a sprig each of
    rosemary and sage and a
    bay leaf, tied together)
3 tablespoons freshly
    grated Parmesan
2 eggs
1 tablespoon bread crumbs
½ recipe quantity egg pasta
    dough (page 330)
4 tablespoons unsalted butter
sprig of rosemary
salt and pepper

Preheat the oven to around 390°F. Heat the olive oil in a pan that will transfer to the oven and is large enough to hold all the veal shanks. Add the vegetables, cover and cook gently for about 10 minutes, until soft but not colored.

Season the shanks and then dust with flour, very lightly – as if you were seasoning them. Shake to remove the excess flour.

Heat a large sauté pan until it smokes, then add the vegetable oil and put in the shanks. Cook quickly until golden, then turn over and cook until golden on the other side (this will also help to seal in the marrow in the bone).

Remove the shanks, add them to the pan of vegetables, then turn the heat down under the sauté pan, add the wine and reduce for a minute or so, scraping the bottom of the pan as it cooks, so that all the pieces of shank are incorporated. Take off the heat and keep to one side.

Let the shanks cook with the vegetables, covered, for about 3 to 4 minutes. Add the wine reduction from the other pan and reduce further until there is no liquid left.

Add the tomato paste, cook for another minute or so, taking care nothing burns, then add the stock and saffron threads and bring to a boil. Skim, then turn down the heat and simmer for 5 to 10 minutes.

Add the bouquet garni, transfer the pan to the oven and leave for about an hour. Check every 10 minutes to ensure that it isn't boiling too fast – otherwise the meat will toughen and dry out. You want it to braise gently, i.e., a few bubbles should be breaking the surface.

When the meat is cooked, take it out of the oven, let it cool a little, but while still warm discard the bouquet garni and remove the shanks and half the vegetables. Keep on the side.

If you have a hand blender, blend the contents of the pan to break up the vegetables so that they will thicken the sauce (otherwise, mash them roughly with the back of a spoon). Pass through a fine sieve and keep on the side.

Strip the cooked meat from the central bone and push out the marrow. Discard the bone. Put the meat, marrow and reserved vegetables into a food processor and process to a rough paste.

Transfer to a bowl, add the Parmesan, one of the eggs and the bread crumbs, and mix. If you feel the mixture is too wet, add an extra tablespoon of bread crumbs. Season if necessary and keep in the fridge until you are ready to use.

Make the pasta dough as described on page 330 and roll through the machine (see page 332). To make the ravioli follow the directions on page 360, omitting the mint leaves.

Bring a large pan of water to a boil for the pasta, and salt it.

Melt the butter with the rosemary in a large sauté pan and, when the butter begins to foam, add about 2 to 3 ladlefuls of the sauce (you can keep the rest to serve with pasta another time).

Put the ravioli into the boiling water and cook for 3 to 4 minutes, then drain using a slotted spoon or a skimmer and transfer to the pan containing the sauce. Toss gently for a minute or so and serve.

Ravioli di coda di manzo

Oxtail ravioli

This variation on the recipe on the previous page goes way back, to a time when I was talking to Marco Pierre White about how great oxtail is, but how difficult it is to get people to try it in restaurants, because their perception of it is as something too robust and difficult to eat. He used to make little ballotines of oxtail in caul fat. He said: "Why don't you try wrapping it up?" So I came up with these ravioli, which are a perfect vehicle for people to enjoy all the fantastic flavors in a way that is easy for them to cope with.

Choose the thickest part of the oxtail. To make the filling, cut the oxtail into 4 or 5 pieces, rinse it, put it in a large pot, cover with cold water and bring to the boil, then skim, drain and set aside. Put 3 tablespoons extra virgin olive oil in another pan big enough to hold the oxtail, with 4 chopped garlic cloves, 2 carrots and 2 banana shallots (or 4 small ones), all cut into large dice, and cook gently for about 10 minutes. Then add a bouquet garni, made with a sprig of rosemary and a small bunch of sage, 2½ ounces pork belly and the oxtail. Cook gently for 5 to 6 minutes, then add 1½ cups dry white wine and continue to cook until the wine evaporates.

Next add 3 tablespoons tomato paste and 4 cups of chicken stock, bring to the boil, skim, then turn down the heat and simmer for 45 to 60 minutes, until the meat falls apart. Separate the meat and vegetables into two different bowls. Pass the remaining cooking liquid through a fine sieve into a clean pan, put back on the heat, and simmer until it thickens to a sauce-like consistency.

Flake the oxtail meat with your fingers, breaking the meat down as much as possible and discarding the bones and any fatty parts (don't chop with a knife or you will lose the nice "stringiness"). Mix in half of the reserved vegetables, put into a food processor and process to a coarse paste. Add ¼ cup grated Parmesan cheese, taste and season, then add one egg and mix – the mixture should come together easily in soft balls, but if it seems too dry, mix in a little of the sauce. Make up and cook the ravioli as on the previous page, adding the sauce to the pan containing the butter and rosemary, along with the remaining vegetables. Toss gently for a minute or so, and serve.

Ravioli di fagiano

Pheasant ravioli

The pheasant season starts in October. If you live in the country, and you find yourself being given a couple of pheasants, a very nice way to prepare them is to take off the legs, roast them and use the meat to make ravioli as a starter. Then roast the breasts separately for the main course – keep them quite rare, so they are nice and juicy (you could also make a stock with the carcasses, then reduce it down to make a little sauce) – that way you make a big deal about celebrating the birds in an entire meal. In the restaurant, however, we tend to use breast meat for the ravioli.

Preheat the oven to 425°F, then cut 4 breasts in half and season them on the skin side. Heat an ovenproof sauté pan until it smokes, put in a tablespoon or so of vegetable oil and add the pheasant, skin side down. Cook it quickly until the skin turns golden, then add ½ cup finely chopped pancetta and 1 finely chopped banana shallot (or 2 ordinary shallots), turn the pheasant over and continue to cook for a couple more minutes.

Add a wineglass of dry white wine and cook for a minute or so to let the alcohol evaporate. Transfer the pan to the preheated oven for 2 to 3 minutes, until the meat is cooked through, but not overcooked, as it will continue to cook as it cools down and you don't want it to end up too dry. Let everything cool a little, but while still warm put into a food processor and process until you have a coarse paste.

Spoon a little of the mixture at a time onto a cutting board, and run over it with a spatula or table knife, just to feel whether any shot is left in – if so, remove it (if you are really worried, you can also pass it through a very fine sieve).

Put the mixture into a bowl, add 2 tablespoons of grated Parmesan cheese and an egg, and season if necessary. Slowly mix in 4 tablespoons heavy cream and put into the fridge until it is cold. Then you can take small quantities, roll them with your hands into balls (you should have enough mixture for about 32) and place on a tray or large plate, ready to make and cook the ravioli in the same way as for the osso buco recipe (see page 374).

Finish off simply with the melted butter and rosemary, an herb that has a special affinity with pheasant.

Strozzapreti alle tre cipolle

Pasta twists with onion

Strozzapreti – or "priest stranglers" – are so called because a greedy priest is supposed to have eaten too many and choked to death. They are egg-free, made only with flour, oil and water. For this sauce, we use red or white *cipollotti*, which are similar to scallions but a little stronger in flavor. If you can't find them, just use scallions – preferably ones with large bulbs.

This sort of pasta is also good with a very simple tomato sauce with basil or arugula (see Potato dumplings with tomato and arugula, page 390), or you could make the tomato sauce and, instead of adding arugula, mix in 2 tablespoons of pesto. It is a pasta that needs quite a thick sauce but not a ragù (i.e., a meat sauce), because the pasta won't grip the chunky pieces of meat as well as egg pasta does.

3½ cups 00 (doppio zero) flour
¾ cup plus 2 tablespoons
    warm water
1 tablespoon
    extra virgin olive oil
pinch of salt

For the sauce:
3 tablespoons olive oil
1 garlic clove, finely chopped
1 red and 1 white onion,
    thinly sliced
6 cipollotti or scallions, thinly
    sliced, plus a little extra,
    to garnish
2 tablespoons tomato passata
2 tomatoes
¾ cup good-quality canned
    chopped tomatoes
1 small bunch of chives,
    cut into batons
1 tablespoon freshly
    grated Parmesan
salt and pepper

Follow the method for the basic fresh egg pasta described on page 330, but add the warm water in place of the eggs. Knead in the same way, but instead of allowing it to rest, put it through the pasta machine immediately (see page 332).

Cut each strip of pasta into 2 lengthwise, then cut each length into 3 pieces across the width. Working with one strip at a time and using a rolling pin or a clean plastic ruler, cut across the width into strips ¼–½ inch wide. Take a thin spatula or a long blunt knife and press it down gently on one end of each strip, then twist and pull it away from you, so that the pasta twists roughly. Don't try to be too perfect about it: the pasta should be rough and rustic; the idea is just that the dents in the pasta will hold the sauce better. Repeat until all the pasta is used.

Blanch the fresh tomatoes, skin, quarter and deseed (see page 304).

To make the sauce, heat half the olive oil in a sauté pan, add the garlic and start to cook it gently without allowing it to color. Add the onions, season, cover with a lid and let them stew gently until they soften and cook without coloring. Add the cipollotti or scallions, season and cook briefly (so they stay crunchy). Add the passata together with the fresh and canned tomatoes and cook for 5 minutes.

Bring a large pan of salted water to a boil for the pasta. Put in the strozzapreti, let them rise to the top, leave for a minute or two more, then drain, reserving some of the cooking water.

Put the pasta into the pan containing the sauce and toss. Cook for another 2 to 3 minutes, then add the chives, with the rest of the olive oil. Check and adjust the seasoning, if necessary. Add the Parmesan and serve, topped, if you like, with a little sliced onion.

Spaghetti alla chitarra con polpettine di tonno

Handmade spaghetti with balls of tuna

This style of spaghetti, which is square rather than round, also known as *tonnarelli*, originates in Abruzzo and gets its name from the implement that is traditionally used to make it – the *chitarra*, which means "guitar." The dough is the same as we use for strozzapreti, but with the addition of saffron threads to give it its particular color.

You can make a version at home by putting the dough through the pasta machine on the tagliolini setting or cutting it by hand. As with the strozzapreti dough, it is important that, instead of resting it in the fridge, you work it right away, while it is still at room temperature. If you don't want to make the pasta yourself, you can do this recipe with dried spaghetti.

This is a typical dish from Puglia, which at first might seem to go against the idea of spaghetti and meatballs not working well together – despite the dish made up in America. However, the balls of tuna are very fragile, so when you spear them with your fork they are crushed and fall apart.

If you like, you can cook some mussels as we do for prawn ravioli on page 372 (you can serve them as a starter), then add their juice to

the sauce, after you have added the wine, along with the tomato and passata.

Add the saffron or turmeric to the warm water and stir around. Follow the method for the egg pasta described on page 330, but add the water in place of the eggs. Knead in the same way, but instead of allowing the dough to rest, roll it through the machine immediately (see page 332).

If you have a tagliolini attachment for your machine, put the pasta through again using this; otherwise cut it by hand.

To do this, first cut your strip of pasta into lengths of about 6 inches (probably about three lengths). Working with one strip at a time, and using a clean plastic ruler as a guide, cut strips lengthwise about ⅛ inch wide (make them a little wider if you find it difficult). Repeat until all the pasta is used, dusting the pasta with flour if you feel it is getting too sticky.

Chop the tuna very fine and squash it a little with the flat side of a knife. Put it into a mixing bowl, season and add the egg yolk. Mix well, then take a little at a time and roll into small balls about ¾ inch in diameter.

Put a large pan of water on to boil for the pasta.

Heat half the oil in a sauté pan, add the garlic and fry gently until soft but not colored, then add the tuna balls and turn them gently, so that they are sealed all around – don't worry if some of them break up.

When the tuna balls have changed color completely from pink to gray, add the white wine, let it reduce until it has almost evaporated, add the quartered tomato and the passata, and cook for a couple of minutes. Season.

Put the pasta into the salted boiling water and keep stirring, as it will tend to stick together. Cook for about 2 to 3 minutes, then drain, reserving the cooking water.

Add the pasta to the pan containing the tuna, then chop the parsley leaves and scatter in.

Toss everything together, add the rest of the olive oil and keep stirring for another minute or so, adding a little of the reserved cooking water to loosen if necessary. If you are using fresh pasta, you will need this, as it will suck in more liquid than egg pasta – and don't worry if the sauce seems slightly more soupy than usual when you serve it, as the pasta will absorb it very quickly, even on the plate.

pinch of saffron threads or
    ground turmeric
¾ cup plus 2 tablespoons
    warm water
3½ cups 00 (doppio zero) flour
1 tablespoon
    extra virgin olive oil

For the polpettine:
7 ounces fresh tuna
1 egg yolk
4 tablespoons
    extra virgin olive oil
2 garlic cloves, thinly sliced
½ wineglass of white wine
2 tomatoes, blanched, skinned
    and quartered
3 tablespoons tomato passata
handful of parsley leaves
salt and pepper

Potato gnocchi

One of my favorite dishes in the world is gnocchi with ragù alla bolognese (see page 349). Potato gnocchi is a very northern thing (around Italy, gnocchi can also be made from pumpkin, or spinach and ricotta, semolina or polenta). While in the center of Italy they had wheat practically growing in the back garden with which to make flour for pasta, in the north, rice and potatoes were the staples; so if you wanted to make pasta, you made the flour go further by adding potato. In the north, they also say that the starchy water from cooking gnocchi (or rice) is very good for you. When I was young, if my brother, Roberto, or I was ill, especially with an upset stomach, my grandmother used to give us some to drink, with a little sugar.

For gnocchi, you need very starchy potatoes. We use the Piacentine, which we get from Italy, but in this country look for the Italian Spunta, if you can find them. Of the widely available varieties, Desiree is the best. Because you are going to boil them whole, you also need to choose potatoes that are all the same size, so that they will be cooked at the same time.

It is worth putting the oven on at 225°F before you start, so that if the potato skins split during cooking and they absorb a little too much water, you can put them into the oven briefly to dry them out – not too long, though, or they will become crusty and stick to the oven tray. If you overcook the potatoes, though, they will definitely be too wet, so forget about it and have steak and mashed potatoes for dinner instead, because if you want potato gnocchi that tastes of potatoes, you have to have really dry ones. Of course, you can compensate by adding more and more flour to the dough – but then it will taste only of flour. As much flour as you put in, the potatoes will just absorb, so start with three-quarters of the flour, and only add the rest if you need to, just use as much as it takes to bring the dough together.

Two things are particularly important: don't let the dough get cold or the finished gnocchi will become chewy, and work it as little as possible. If you keep on working it, it will become softer and, again, you will find yourself adding more flour, until eventually you will have dumplings that, when they are cooked, you could throw against the wall and they would bounce back at you, whereas the idea is that they should be so light they melt in your mouth.

This is an easy quantity to handle quickly without the gnocchi getting too cold but, if you are doubling or tripling the quantity, have some foil ready so that you can work with some of the dough and keep the rest warm, wrapped in the foil. If you do double the quantity, you don't need to double the eggs – just use one large egg – if you are tripling it, use two small ones (otherwise, too much egg will make the dough hard).

Potato gnocchi dough

It is quite difficult to work with small quantities of dough, so it is better to make a larger amount, then lay the finished gnocchi on a tray and put them into the freezer. When the gnocchi are hard, you can put them into a freezer bag and keep them for when you need them.

Makes about 2½ pounds
2¼ pounds very
    starchy potatoes
    (see page 384)
2 small eggs, lightly beaten
about 2¼ cups all-purpose flour
    (you may not need all of
    this, or you might need
    a little more)
pinch of salt

Have all your ingredients ready, because it is very important to work with the gnocchi dough while the potato is still hot.

Leave the potatoes whole, still in their skins. Cover with cold water and bring to a boil, then turn down the heat and simmer until soft (about 45 minutes to 1 hour, depending on the size). Put the potatoes into a warm oven (see the introduction on the previous page).

While the potatoes are still hot, peel them and put them through a fine sieve. Put them in a bowl or on your work surface, make a well in the center, then add the egg, a pinch of salt, and about three-quarters of the flour. Mix well and, as soon as the dough comes together, stop, adding the rest of the flour only if you really feel that you need it. It will still feel soft, but don't worry – the eggs will firm it up.

Dust your work surface lightly with flour, then take your dough and flatten it down with the palms of your hands into a rough square about ⅝ inch thick.

With a knife, cut the dough into strips about ⅝ inch wide – so you have "square" cigars. Dusting your hands with flour all the time, roll each piece lightly until it is cylindrical.

Take two or three cylinders at a time, lay them next to each other, then, cutting through them all at the same time, trim off the ends and cut the rest into pieces (½ to ⅝ inch in width). Repeat with the rest of the cylinders, until you have lots of little nuggets of dough.

Lightly dusting with flour all the time, take a fork (or gnocchi paddle, if you have one) and push each piece of dough onto the prongs, so that it rolls itself up and is marked with lines – they don't have to be perfect; it is nice when they look rustic and hand-made, not made by machines. However, they should all be the same size, if not the same shape, so that they will all cook evenly. As you make each one, roll it on a tray dusted with flour.

Now they are ready to cook. You really need to cook them as quickly as possible, but if you need to keep them for an hour or so, make sure you dust the gnocchi again with flour, keeping them separate from each other on the tray, and every 10 minutes or so shake the tray a little, to move them around.

Gnocchi di patate al pepe nero e salsa al caprino

Potato gnocchi with black pepper and goat cheese sauce

When we have black truffles, we do a variation on this without adding any black pepper to the gnocchi dough, and using a slightly strong, more mature goat cheese (Robiolina di Capra, which comes from Piemonte) – about 4¼ ounces – and just 2 tablespoons of milk. We add some diced vegetables to the cheese sauce (2 tablespoons each of carrot, celery and onion, seasoned and stewed gently in 1½ tablespoons of unsalted butter for 10 minutes or so, until they are just soft but have a little bite). Then, when we put in the chives, we add some freshly grated Parmesan (about ¼ cup), and finish with some grated black truffle over the top.

½ recipe quantity of
　　potato gnocchi dough
　　(see previous page)
about 2 teaspoons freshly
　　ground black pepper,
　　plus extra to taste
3 tablespoons milk
about 5⅔ ounces soft goat
　　cheese, broken into pieces
small bunch of chives, half of
　　them chopped and the rest
　　cut into matchsticks
2 tablespoons freshly grated
　　Parmesan (optional)

Follow the recipe for potato gnocchi dough as on the previous page, but mix the 2 teaspoons of freshly ground black pepper into the flour before you add it. Shape into gnocchi.

Warm the milk in a sauté pan, add the goat cheese and let it melt gently to form a thick sauce. Grind in black pepper to taste.

Bring a large pan of salted water to the boil, put in the gnocchi and keep stirring until they rise to the surface (a minute or so), then lift them out carefully with a slotted spoon or a skimmer and put them into the sauce.

Sprinkle in the chopped chives and toss the gnocchi around very carefully, just to coat them in the sauce. Add the Parmesan and a little of the cooking water, if you think the sauce needs loosening, but don't leave the gnocchi in the sauce any longer than about a minute, or they will start to break up.

Serve garnished with the matchsticks of chives.

Gnocchi di patate pomodoro e rucola

Potato gnocchi with tomato and arugula

½ recipe quantity of
  potato gnocchi dough
  (see page 386)
4 tablespoons
  extra virgin olive oil
2 garlic cloves, chopped
16 cherry tomatoes, halved
2 tablespoons Tomato sauce
  (see page 302)
2 handfuls of arugula, coarsely
  chopped into large pieces
2 tablespoons freshly grated
  Parmesan, plus a few
  shavings for garnish
  (optional)
salt and pepper

Make the potato gnocchi as described on page 386.

In a sauté pan, heat the oil, then add the garlic and cook gently, without allowing to color, for a minute or so. Add the cherry tomatoes and cook gently with the garlic for a couple of minutes, then season. Add the tomato sauce and cook for another couple of minutes, until the tomatoes squash into the sauce.

Bring a large pan of water to a boil, salt it and put in the gnocchi. Keep stirring until they rise to the surface (a minute or so), then lift out carefully with a slotted spoon or a skimmer and put them into the sauce.

Add the chopped arugula and Parmesan, toss the gnocchi in the sauce very briefly to coat, adding a little of the cooking water if you think the sauce needs loosening – but don't leave the gnocchi on the heat for longer than a minute, or they will start to break up.

Serve with a few shavings of Parmesan over the top if you like.

Gnocchi di patate al pesto

Potato gnocchi with pesto

½ recipe quantity of
  potato gnocchi dough
  (see page 386)
handful of green beans
1 large potato, cut into about
  ½-inch dice
pat of unsalted butter
6–7 tablespoons Pesto
  (see page 309)
2 tablespoons freshly
  grated Parmesan
salt and pepper

Make the potato gnocchi as described on page 386.

Blanch the beans in boiling salted water for 2 to 3 minutes until just soft. Split them in half lengthwise – if you pull on either side of the beans, they will come apart at their "seams."

Put the diced potato in a small pan of cold water with the butter. Bring to the boil, turn down the heat and simmer until just beginning to soften. Take off the heat and leave in the cooking water to finish cooking and soften a little more.

Bring a large pan of water to a boil, salt it and put in the gnocchi. Keep stirring until they rise to the surface (a minute or so).

While the gnocchi are cooking, lift the potatoes out of their water with a slotted spoon and put into a sauté pan, together with the pesto and the beans, over the very lowest possible heat (if necessary, hold the pan above the burner, so that the pesto only slightly warms and keeps its flavor and color).

Lift the gnocchi out of the cooking water carefully, using a slotted spoon or skimmer, and put them into the pesto.

Add the Parmesan and toss the gnocchi in the sauce very briefly to coat, adding a little of the cooking water if you think the sauce needs loosening – but don't leave the gnocchi on the heat for longer than a minute, or they will start to break up. Season if necessary and serve.

Gnocchi di patate ai funghi porcini

Potato gnocchi with porcini

You can this with mixed wild mushrooms or fresh morels, if you like.

½ recipe quantity
    potato gnocchi dough
    (see page 386)
1 stick unsalted butter, diced
3 garlic cloves, chopped
6 ounces (about ⅓ pound)
    porcini, cleaned and sliced
½ wineglass of white wine
handful of parsley, chopped
⅓ cup freshly grated Parmesan
bunch of chives, cut into batons
salt and pepper

Make the potato gnocchi as described on page 386.

In a sauté pan, melt half the butter, then add the garlic and cook gently, without allowing to color, for a minute or so.

Add the mushrooms and a little more butter if necessary. Season and gently "stew" the mushrooms without frying, or they will turn bitter.

Add the wine, turn up the heat and let the alcohol evaporate. Turn off the heat.

Get a large pan of boiling water ready, salt it and put in the gnocchi. Keep stirring until they rise to the surface (a minute or so).

While the gnocchi are cooking, put the pan containing the mushrooms back over a low heat, add the parsley, then lift the gnocchi carefully from the cooking water with a slotted spoon or a skimmer and put them into the pan containing the mushrooms.

Add the rest of the butter and toss the gnocchi around to coat. Add the Parmesan and chives. Don't leave the gnocchi in the sauce for longer than a minute or so, or they will start to break up. Just before serving, if you need to loosen the sauce slightly, add a little of the cooking water from the gnocchi.

Gnocchi di patate con carciofi e Murazzano

Potato gnocchi with artichokes and Murazzano cheese

Murazzano is a Piemonte cheese made with a mixture of goat's milk and cow's milk, which works very well with the artichoke. If you can't find it, you can use Parmesan instead.

Prepare the artichokes as described on page 70. Make the potato gnocchi as described on page 386.

When you are ready to cook the gnocchi, slice the artichokes thinly.

In a sauté pan, heat the olive oil, then add the garlic and cook gently without allowing it to color for a minute or so.

Add the artichokes and fry gently for 2 to 3 minutes. Season and add the white wine. Let the alcohol evaporate and turn off the heat.

Get a large pan of boiling water ready, salt it and put in the gnocchi. Keep stirring until they rise to the surface (a minute or so).

While the gnocchi are cooking, put the pan containing the artichokes back over a low heat, then lift the gnocchi carefully from the cooking water with a slotted spoon or a skimmer and put them into the pan with the artichokes. Add the butter and toss the gnocchi around to coat. Add the chives and parsley. Don't leave the gnocchi in the sauce for longer than a minute or so, or they will start to break up.

Just before serving, if you need to loosen the sauce slightly, add a little of the cooking water from the gnocchi. Serve with the grated Murazzano or Parmesan sprinkled over the top.

5 baby artichokes
½ recipe quantity
    potato gnocchi dough
    (see page 386)
3 tablespoons
    extra virgin olive oil
3 garlic cloves, chopped
½ wineglass of white wine
4¼ tablespoons unsalted butter,
    cut into small cubes
bunch of chives, cut into batons
handful of parsley, chopped
⅔ cup freshly grated Murazzano
    cheese or Parmesan
salt and pepper

Gnocchetti di funghi al burro e salvia e tartufo nero

Small mushroom dumplings with butter, sage and truffles

This recipe uses mushroom paste to flavor the gnocchi – you will find it in good delicatessens. If your paste is very moist, you need to add another egg to the gnocchi mixture, to help it bind. When you make your dough, it will look much softer than usual.

½ recipe quantity
  potato gnocchi dough
  (see page 386)
2 tablespoons good-quality
  mushroom paste
5 tablespoons grated
  Parmesan cheese
⅓ cup unsalted butter
10 sage leaves
1¾ ounces black truffle
salt and pepper

Make the potato gnocchi as described on page 386, but add the mushroom paste along with the flour, egg and salt. Taste the mushroom paste before you start, and if it is quite bland, add a little extra salt to the mixture.

Get your serving plates ready. Take half the grated Parmesan and sprinkle some on each plate. Keep on the side. Have a large pan of boiling water ready to cook the gnocchi.

Put the butter and sage into a sauté pan and, as soon as the butter starts to bubble, season it lightly and turn down the heat.

At this point, salt the boiling water and put the gnocchi into it. Keep stirring until they rise to the surface (a minute or so).

While the gnocchi are cooking, keep an eye on the butter – it should slowly be starting to color, and by the time the gnocchi are ready, it should be golden (if it is cooking too fast, take it off the heat).

Lift the gnocchi from their cooking water carefully with a slotted spoon or a skimmer, taking care to drain them completely, then place them on top of the Parmesan on your serving plates.

Sprinkle the rest of the Parmesan over each serving. Finally, spoon some of the foaming golden butter and sage leaves over the top. Finish with grated black truffle and serve immediately.

Paris

Everything I have done in my life is reflected in my food, though it is hard for me to say exactly what I took from my time studying French cooking at the Savoy and in Paris. Some ideas are obvious – purees, for example. In Italy, these are things you do only for kids. I don't think a kitchen in Italy would present *branzino* (sea bass) the way we do at Locanda – in an herb and tomato crust with Vernaccia sauce and an artichoke puree underneath. The French idea of stocks and sauces is also more refined and elaborate than you would find in most kitchens in Italy, where stocks are usually made in a lighter way, purely from bones and vegetables simmered in water. At Locanda, we make stock as the French do, roasting the bones and vegetables before they go into the stockpot, and then skimming the stock constantly. If we want to make a sauce for meat or game, we will reduce the stock down further, often with wine, in a way that is foreign to traditional Italian cooking. Or we might use a sauce like beurre fondue, something I didn't know existed before I left Italy. Mostly, though, what I took from the whole French experience was the emphasis on precision and attention to detail.

In Italy, we have a saying that translates roughly as "Either the king is from Spain, or the king is from France, as long as we have something to eat, who cares?" In other words, Italians tend to be more relaxed and spontaneous when they cook, not so pedantic and governed by rules. The Italian way is to see what ingredients you have each day and then do the best you can with them, which is contrary to the elaborate à la carte menu typical of a Michelin-star French restaurant, which relies on very precise mise-en-place. At Locanda, I like to think we have the best of both worlds: the essential flavors, simplicity and spontaneity of Italian cooking, refined sometimes with a little bit of French technique and presentation, and a lot of serious preparation.

When I arrived at the Laurent in Paris, Nouvelle Cuisine was over, and there was a new way of looking at food, with more respect for ingredients. I was amazed at the uncompromising demands of the chef. We bought fifty lobsters every day, and each one had to be weighed, because it must be a kilo exactly or it was sent back. We measured the artichokes one by one, and if they weren't the right size, they went back... there were thermometers to measure oven temperatures precisely, and stopwatches to monitor cooking times. Even if you were roasting a chicken, it had to be basted every six minutes, exactly. I had never seen anything like that before.

I was twenty-seven, I had been sous chef at the Savoy, my head was full of ideas and recipes, and I was already thinking I would have my own restaurant one day. So I didn't think I was going to start again as a commis, from zero – but that is how it was. There were chefs-de-partie there who were twenty, and I was the oldest, and at the bottom. The head chef was a guy named Jacques Rolancy, and I liked him. He was a great character – tough but very fair, though of course I was the butt of jokes from most of the boys in the kitchen. They thought I was the lowest of the low: an Italian who had been working in England, learning French cooking from *Les Rosbifs*. It made me laugh because I knew the Escoffier repertoire inside out – I used to sit in the pub with the boys from the Savoy, and we would talk for hours about classic French dishes and how they could be reinterpreted and worked on.

The exception was the senior sous chef at the Laurent, Daniel Fradin, who helped me out, fed me, invited me to his home at Christmas, and generally kept me alive. One of the happier memories I have of Paris is the annual bike race in which chefs from restaurants all over Paris compete against each other around an amazing racetrack outside the city. Daniel's wife made a beautiful picnic and we had a wonderful day. Of course for most of us, it was a bit of fun, but there were chefs taking part who were unbelievably serious, who trained every day. The Ritz was so competitive that there was always a keen rider in its kitchen brigade, who would be given special time off to train.

Back at the Laurent, when Joël Robuchon came by he asked me to make him some pasta, and so we began to work on ideas, gradually introducing some polenta and risotto to the menu, including the pasta dough with 52 egg yolks, which was almost "crispy." We used it as a garnish for fillet of sole and champagne sauce, or with lobster – the head, tail, claws, everything. When I was at the Savoy I had absorbed everything, but I had never cooked a dish of my own. Now I started to see that I could combine the things I knew as an Italian with what I saw in Paris, to present food in a different way.

The French chefs in the kitchen were still quite ignorant of Italian cooking. Olive oil was starting to appear in French kitchens, where traditionally you would cook with butter, and Alain Ducasse, with his Mediterranean approach to cooking, was hitting the food world hard. But, to most of the boys, an eggplant was just an eggplant; whereas I had known since I was a child watching my grandmother that every eggplant is different and that each one is right for a particular dish. One might be good for caponata – eggplant, cooked with other vegetables, pine nuts and raisins, with an *agrodolce* (sweet-and-sour) dressing. Another might be too wet, too seedy, so it would be better for making eggplant caviar (the seedy pulp from baked eggplant). So I was the golden boy for a while, which made some of them jealous, and they tried to put me down even more, watching for my mistakes. If I didn't make one, they made one for me.

Then one day I walked into the kitchen and Jacques Rolancy was gone. I was destroyed, because in his place was a new guy, who was completely crazy and when things went wrong, he blamed everyone around him. It became a very political kitchen – which is something I hate. I had no respect for him, and so we clashed and, after one particularly big row, I left. I went home to my seventh-floor apartment. What was I going to do now? Then the phone rang and it was my friend Daniel at

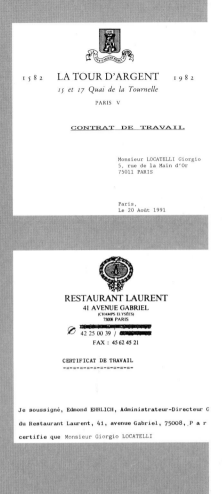

1582   LA TOUR D'ARGENT   1982
15 et 17 Quai de la Tournelle
PARIS V

CONTRAT DE TRAVAIL

Monsieur LOCATELLI Giorgio
5, rue de la Main d'Or
75011 PARIS

Paris,
Le 20 Août 1991

RESTAURANT LAURENT
41 AVENUE GABRIEL
(CHAMPS ELYSÉES)
75008 PARIS
42 25 00 39 /
FAX : 45 62 45 21

CERTIFICAT DE TRAVAIL
-=-=-=-=-=-=-=-=-=-=-=-

Je soussigné, Edmond EHRLICH, Administrateur-Directeur G
du Restaurant Laurent, 41, avenue Gabriel, 75008, P a r
certifie que Monsieur Giorgio LOCATELLI

the Laurent, telling me that if I went across town to La Tour d'Argent there was a job there for me. La Tour d'Argent is one of Paris's most famous restaurants, in the grand theatrical tradition of classical French *gastronomie*. It was an enormous place near Notre Dame, with a sixth-floor roof garden that looked out over the Seine. The restaurant had been in the same family since 1910, had three Michelin stars and was famous for its *canard à la presse*.

Somehow I didn't feel quite comfortable with the idea of working there, and as it turned out, I was right to be wary. The chef was an enormous guy and nice enough. He called me *Le Petit Italien*, and he was interested in Italian food, so I worked on some dishes with him. But the sous chef and all the commis were French and, as at the Laurent, they hated me. They would do petty things like put ingredients in my wastebasket and then complain to the chef that "L'Italien" was wasting food. Worse, for someone who had been brought up to anticipate the pleasure of food from the start of every day, there was no satisfaction, no excitement in the cooking – it was just a technical exercise. No love, no passion. I cooked 140 ducks a day for the famous specialty but never had the chance to taste the finished dish.

The restaurant was split into many levels – the pastry was on the fourth floor – and I saw how divisive it could be when everyone is detached from one another. And we worked so hard – really, really hard, from seven-thirty in the morning to one o'clock the next morning, six days a week, for a pittance. Three-quarters of my wage went to rent, and I would have to decide whether to take the bus to work or walk and keep back enough money to buy cigarettes.

Sometimes when I was feeling homesick on my day off, or even at two or three in the morning, after my shift had finished, I would stop off at a Thai restaurant in the Bastille, where I knew the chef, and even after the doors were closed to the customers he would invite me in through the kitchen at the back and cook coconut rice for me, steamed inside lotus leaves. The taste was fantastic and if I closed my eyes, I got the same warm feeling as I did when I used to go home to my grandmother after work and she would give me a big bowl of hot risotto. In the whole of my time in Paris, that rice was one of my favorite things.

Pesce

Fish

"I still remember my surprise at being offered such an unlikely combination as fish and broccoli in a restaurant in Bologna, where dishes outside the traditional, yet excellent, range of local cooking are viewed with suspicion."

Anna Del Conte, *Entertaining all'Italiana*

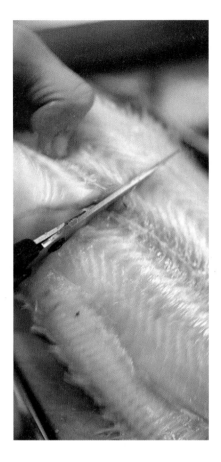

Italian people tend to cook and eat in a very purist way – almost ferociously so sometimes. If you order fish in a traditional restaurant in Italy, that is exactly what you get – no vegetables, not even any salad leaves, just fish, usually whole, with its head on, and a piece of lemon. And I have to admit that some of the best meals I have had in my life have been that simple, just concentrated on one or two brilliant flavors. What is most important is not what you serve with the fish but its quality and how well you cook it.

Almost everywhere in Italy has access to fish: three-quarters of our regions have their own coastlines, and the rest have lakes and rivers. Even if fresh fish wasn't readily available, there would always be cod that had been preserved either by salting at sea and then drying (*baccalà*), or by air-drying (*stoccafisso* or stockfish).

Italians also love sushi, perhaps because in certain areas, especially Puglia, Abruzzo and Marche, we have our own tradition of raw fish dishes. You go to a little restaurant in Puglia and they might bring you some raw prawns, just chopped in half with a lemon to squeeze on top; or there might be raw fish marinated in lemon juice or vinegar. And, at La Madonnina del Pescatore near Ancona, Moreno Cedroni has made famous his *"susci and sushi"* (he wrote the book of the same name) – an Italian take on the Japanese way with raw fish and rice.

I would like to say that we should eat fish as much as possible, because it is such a light healthy food, but we all know the damage we are doing to our seas with our greed for fish. We used to think we could go on taking what we wanted and the fish would just multiply and replenish themselves forever, but now we know that isn't true. Seventy-five percent of the world's fish stocks are either exhausted or overfished – cod and haddock are in real danger of extinction in the Atlantic – and it is a scandal that the enormous trawlers that rake the seabed, and destroy ecosystems in the process, pull in so much fish that is wasted because it is too small. Surely everything that comes up in the net should reach the market – not be chucked back into the water, dead?

I don't think that farmed fish are the answer either. The biggest industry for farmed fish is salmon, which affects us very little at Locanda, as salmon is not a fish Italians traditionally cook (although smoked salmon has now become very popular for the Christmas lunch) – but what are these farmed fish eating? Mostly feed made from small fish – which only plunders the oceans even more. And what chemicals are being put into the water to control disease? It has become fashionable to create salmon farms in rough

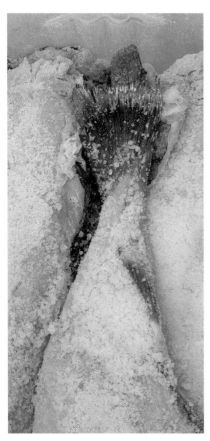

waters around the coast, so that the fish develop firm flesh from swimming against the tides, but when they are situated in the mouths of salmon rivers, do they pollute the wild fish on their way to the sea, or even escape and mate with them, creating weird unnatural hybrids?

If we aren't going to rob the sea of its treasure forever, perhaps we have to learn to enjoy different varieties of fish – and to ask hard questions about whether it comes from sustainable sources, and how it was fished.

What kind of fish?

In Italy, we have a rather different tradition of sea fishing from that in the UK and the States. Instead of big trawlers staying out at sea for weeks, catching big fish that are destined to be cut up, Italian fleets tend to be smaller, spending less time out at sea, and often specializing in small "blue" fish, like sardines and mackerel, which I consider extremely valuable for our health, because they are rich in omega-3 oils. They are also so quick and easy to cook, perhaps wrapped in prosciutto and quickly fried in a pan with some red wine and vinegar whisked in to make a warm vinaigrette.

The fish come in from two seas, the cold, deeper waters of the Mediterranean and the warmer, shallower waters of the Adriatic, but even from coastline to coastline, though the species may be the same, the habitat changes, and with it the nature and quality of the fish – and also, confusingly, the name. In Italy, the same fish can have twenty-five different names. At Locanda, the boys in the kitchen are all the time coming into the office saying, "What is the English for this or that?" and looking things up in books so they can learn the words for the menus, and, when it comes to fish, there is a big, noisy "discussion," because we cannot even agree a common name in Italian, let alone English.

You must remember that in Italy it is only relatively recently that ingredients have moved around the country, rather than staying localized. Now when I go to the Milano fish market the choice of fish from all over Italy is amazing, but at one time you ate only what was caught on your stretch of coastline, or the freshwater fish from the nearest lake or river.

In our house in Corgeno, we always had fish on Fridays, and often two or three more times during the week, but I only rarely saw anything other than the freshwater fish from Lago Comabbio, below my uncle's hotel, La Cinzianella, or from nearby Lago Varese or Maggiore. The exceptions were the occasional mackerel from the Ligurian coast, the red prawns that came from San Remo once a week, and the salted cod *(baccalà)*, bought in slabs, soaked in water or milk, and then cooked slightly differently in every region and village. In Lombardia, it was often cooked *"in umido"* – stewed with onions and tomatoes and served with polenta. Around Liguria, it was traditional to cook it with spinach, or fry it and serve it with a

sauce made with garlic and bread crumbs; in Firenze it was first pan-fried and then stewed in tomato sauce; in Roma battered and deep-fried.

The lakes around Corgeno are deep, with a continuous force of water pushing through them from the rivers and glaciers in the mountains: perfect for the likes of eel, carp, pike, perch and the *lavarello* (which, just down the road around Lago Maggiore, is called *coregone*, or white-fish). This fish belongs to the salmon and trout family, and for many generations it was a staple for local families. It is a beautiful, distinctive fish with a white belly, silver sides and a back that is sometimes olive-green. Because it eats insect larvae and crustaceans instead of feeding from the muddy bottom of the lake, it has white, tasty flesh.

As with sea fish, however, stocks are suffering. Not, for once, from over-fishing, but because pollution – which has now been tackled – and more recently the warming of the planet are taking their toll. The waters of the lake are not as cold as they once were, so the habitat is changing, and not as many eggs are being produced, so there is a big regeneration process going on now, to restore the stocks of fish to the levels they were at when I was little. They were then so plentiful, you could put down a rod and you would catch something almost immediately.

Eel from the lake is traditionally stewed, usually with tomatoes, and in the spring with peas. Then there is pike (there is an old saying: "*carne de lusso carne de musso,*" which means that the flesh of the pike is a little like donkey meat) and also carp. These three are the predators, the sharks lurking and feeding in the murky slime at the bottom of the lake, and, to varying degrees, they can have a flavor that is "muddy" – not un-pleasant, but just different from sea fish, and needing robust ingredients, such as onions and vinegar, to help their flavor. I read about a Chinese emperor who was so in love with one kind of freshwater fish – probably carp – from a particular region that he constructed a series of ponds all the way to his palace at the Forbidden City, so that the live fish could be transferred from one pond to another until they reached him. Maybe I am not that dedicated, but still I would love to get the English excited about freshwater fish, especially perch – my favorite – which, like the lavarello, eats insects and fish larvae, rather than other fish, and so doesn't have such a muddy taste as carp or pike. Perch are native to England's lakes and rivers – but how often do you see them in fish markets or restaurants?

Freshwater fish like perch tend to have softer flesh than sea fish. To turn that defect into an asset, we would usually fry it, so that you would have a crispy contrast on the outside. Often we would make a *carpione*, which is similar to a *scabeccio*, in that the fried fish is marinated in vinegar and oil with garlic and herbs, but it is usually served cold. Once the fish was under the marinade, it could be kept for 4 to 5 days, and the taste became even better as the time went on.

Another favorite local dish that I remember so well is perch with al-monds. The almonds would be picked during the summer and dried in the sun, so that in September, when the perch is at its best, they would be ready. First you crushed your almonds, then filleted the fish and dipped the fillets in a batter made by first mixing egg yolks and flour, then whisking in the egg whites – and maybe a little beer – and some salt and pepper. The battered fish would be pan-fried in sunflower or vegetable oil, so that it was softer than the quite hard, crunchy batter that characterizes English fish and chips – which I love. While the fish was frying, you heated a little of the very white local butter in a pan, and then added some sage leaves and the almonds, let the butter bubble and froth until it just turned golden, then poured it over the battered fish. The nutty sweetness of the almonds infused the butter, and the flavors were brilliant. It sounds simple, I know, but it is one of those dishes that stays in your mind.

Despite my love of these kinds of fish, at Locanda I have to respect the fact that when people want to eat fish, they expect to see the varieties that are considered a bit more elegant, or fashionable: like turbot, sea bass and sole. Even so, when we cook them we draw upon the bread crumb and herb or tomato crusts, the olives, and the walnut pastes that my chefs all recognize from their mothers' and grandmothers' kitchens.

The smell of the sea

The perfect time to cook fish is within a few hours of its being caught, when the rigor mortis has disappeared but if you touch it, the flesh will spring back and your fingers will leave no dent. Always buy fish that smells only of the sea – it should never, ever smell fishy, as this means that it is old. Really fresh fish is lightly covered in clear slime (not opaque slime, which also shows that it is old), will be vivid red under the gills and have bright, shiny eyes.

At home, I love to bake big fish whole in the oven, but in restaurants, you have always to think in terms of individual portions – and we are the generation of the fillet, aren't we? Twenty years ago, you ordered fish in a restaurant and it came with its skin and bones and head – the only thing you had filleted was smoked salmon. Now no one wants to see any bones, which is a great, great pity, because the bone – which imparts its milky gelatinous juices into the flesh of the fish as it cooks – has a great influence on flavor and texture. We have people in the restaurant saying, "I can't eat turbot unless it is off the bone," but if you cook a rich heroic fish like turbot without the bone, it loses its magic. So we say, "Okay, we'll cook it on the bone, then take it off for you," and they really notice the difference in flavor.

If you do want fillets, I would always say that instead of buying them in packages in the supermarket, you should try to buy the whole fish and take them off the bone yourself – or ask your fishmonger to do it for you – assuming you are lucky enough still to have a fishmonger – and ask him to give you the trimmings to make fish stock (see page 267).

A note on cooking fish

Whereas meat can be quite forgiving if you overcook it a little, fish punishes you if you take your eye off it. If you are cooking fillets or steaks, the best way is to use a nonstick pan – almost essential in every restaurant kitchen these days. There is no point in talking about how long to cook a piece of fish, because it depends on its thickness – the trick is to know how to recognize when the fish is ready.

Heating up oil in a pan can be dangerous if you take your eyes off it, so heat the dry pan first, then you can put in a thin film of oil and, as it hits the hot pan, it will come up to temperature right away. You do need the oil to be really hot, because we are talking here about some aggressive cooking to crisp up the skin quickly – don't be afraid of a bit of smoke.

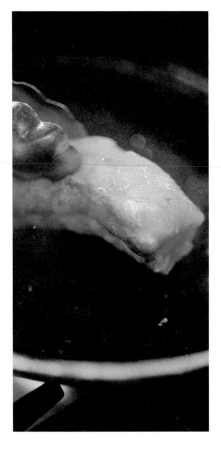

Season the fish well, just before it goes into the pan. The salt will draw out a little moisture, helping the fish to crisp better (but if you season it too early, it will dry out the flesh). Then get your pan good and hot, put in the oil and, when you put in the fish, skin side down always, leave it where it is while the skin becomes really golden and crisp. Don't be tempted to fiddle with it because, if you move it or try to turn it too early, you will leave the skin behind.

While the skin is crisping up, watch the flesh. As the heat travels upward through the fish, you can see that it turns from translucent to white and opaque. Keep watching and, as soon as it has turned opaque almost all the way up the thickness of the fish (by now the skin should also be crisp), flip it over, then immediately take the pan off the heat, and it is ready. Sometimes, especially if we are cooking fish in a bread crumb crust that we want to be really crunchy, we start the cooking on the stove, then transfer the fish (still in its pan) to a very hot oven – as in the sea bass recipe on page 408. In this case, to compensate for the extra few minutes of cooking time in the oven, we would flip the fish over earlier – when it has turned opaque about *halfway* up its thickness.

Parsley, sage, rosemary – but not thyme

When my grandmother cooked fish, she would go out into the garden with the scissors and cut everything that grew there: sage, parsley, rosemary, chervil, wild garlic, the whole lot … her idea was that if an herb was growing next to the lake in which the fish was growing, all the flavors would naturally work together. I like the notion that what grows together goes together and I don't think you should get fussy about what herbs go best with what fish.

I remember once, while on holiday, seeing a chef chop up parsley, sage, rosemary and garlic, packing the mixture on top of some oysters, topping them with bread crumbs, and putting them under the grill, then finishing with a grating of lemon zest. I thought, "Rosemary and sage? Surely they are reminiscent of red meat, not oysters?" And yet the combination was fantastic. The only herb I wouldn't use is thyme or lemon thyme. For some reason, I just don't like the flavor of thyme with fish.

The herb I probably love most is parsley – and when I say a handful of parsley, I mean a good, big handful. Ask my wife, Plaxy. Whenever she is cooking, I always seem to be telling her, "Put in some parsley," then I see her chopping some puny little sprigs, and I say, "No! No! I mean *really* put parsley in! *Masses.*"

Branzino alla Vernaccia in crosta di pomodoro

Sea bass with tomato crust and Vernaccia wine

For this dish, we use Vernaccia wine from San Gimignano, the quite dry, fresh and spicy wine that was favored at the royal court in Toscana during Renaissance times. It is a very simple recipe that relies on perfect fish with crispy skin and flesh that is just cooked through. You can really use any fish you like, other than flatfish like sole, but if you are using sea bass, try to find wild fish, which are bigger and taste better. The sea bass we get are really big, weighing about 5 to 10 pounds each, and they give us fillets about ⅝ inch thick, which we can cut into portions. You are more likely to find smaller fish, but try to find the thickest fillets possible, because they are harder to overcook. With thinner fillets, by the time the skin crisps up the flesh is already in danger of being overdone.

2 tomatoes
3 tablespoons diced green olives
1 tablespoon sun-dried tomatoes
2 tablespoons bread crumbs
4 thick sea bass fillets
    (see above), each about
    7 ounces
juice of 1 lemon
3 tablespoons extra virgin
    olive oil
⅔ cup Vernaccia, or other spicy
    dry white wine
3 tablespoons fish stock
2 tablespoons chopped parsley
salt and pepper

For the artichoke puree:
2 large globe artichokes
2 tablespoons olive oil
1 white onion, thinly sliced
⅔ cup white wine
3 tablespoons heavy cream
3 pats of butter

Blanch the tomatoes, skin, quarter and deseed (see page 304), then cut into dice about the same size as the olive dice.

Put the sun-dried tomatoes into a food processor, process them quickly, then add the bread crumbs and whiz again until the tomato is absorbed into the bread crumbs and it looks a bit like a crumble mixture. Spoon out onto a tray and flatten down. Leave in a warm place in the kitchen for an hour or so to dry out.

Preheat the oven to 390°F and take your sea bass out of the fridge so that it can come to room temperature. Squeeze the lemon juice, put half to one side and add the rest to a bowl of water. Have this ready before you start preparing the artichokes for the puree.

To make the puree, snap off the artichoke stalks and discard them. With a small paring knife, starting at the base of each artichoke, trim off all the green leaves and put the artichoke into the bowl of water with lemon juice while you remove the leaves from the next one. Repeat with the remaining artichokes. Using the same paring knife, begin to trim away the white leaves from each artichoke until you are left only with a few tender ones surrounding the heart. Put back into the bowl of water and continue to trim the other artichokes, putting them into the water as soon as they are ready, so that they don't discolor. Cut each artichoke heart in half, scoop out the hairy chokes and discard them. Leave the remaining hearts in the bowl of water until you need them.

Heat a saucepan, add the olive oil and then the sliced onion. Cook for about 10 minutes until the onion is soft but not colored. Thinly slice the artichoke hearts, add them to the onion and cook for another 5 minutes, then add the white wine. Allow the alcohol to evaporate completely (about 15 to 20 minutes) and then add 1 cup water. Continue to cook for another 20 minutes or so, until the

artichokes are soft and all the water has disappeared – keep an eye on the pan and stir as the water evaporates, to avoid the artichokes catching fire and burning.

Transfer the contents of the pan containing the artichokes to a food processor and puree until smooth.

Put the cream in a pan and boil it to reduce it by half. Add the artichoke puree and let it cook for a few minutes. The resulting puree should be soft but firm enough for the sea bass to sit on top; if you feel that it is too wet, let it cook a little longer to dry it out. When it is ready, season to taste, cover and keep to one side.

Take an ovenproof nonstick frying pan big enough to fit all the fillets comfortably and get it hot on the burner. (If you don't have a big enough pan, you will need to cook the fillets in two batches.) Lightly season the fish on the skin side, put a tablespoon of olive oil into the pan (it will heat up instantly) and add the fillets, skin side down. As the heat goes through the fish, it will turn from translucent to white and opaque.

As soon as the fillet has turned white halfway up the fillet, turn it over (the skin should now be crisp and golden) and sprinkle with the dried bread crumb and tomato mixture. Pour the wine into the pan (around, not over the fish) and transfer to the oven for a couple of minutes. The bread crumbs will crisp up and become darker in color.

Take the pan from the oven and lift the fish onto a warm plate. Put the pan back on the heat, add the olives and fish stock, and bubble up so that it reduces by half. Then put the sea bass back into the sauce, crust upward, for a minute or so to heat through.

At the same time, put the artichoke puree back on the heat to warm through. Stir in the butter and, when the puree is hot, spoon it onto your plates and put the fish on top.

To the pan in which the fish has been cooked, add the reserved lemon juice, the rest of the olive oil and the parsley, then spoon this mixture around the fish and serve.

Branzino in crosta di sale e erbe

Sea bass in sea salt and herbs

Baking inside a crust of salt is one of the oldest ways of cooking fish, which has become fashionable all over again. Originally it would have been done by simply sprinkling a layer of sea salt in a dish, laying the whole fish on top, then burying it with more salt and perhaps some herbs, and sprinkling the salt with water, so that it stuck together and formed a crust. The idea is that, as the fish cooks, the salt flavors the flesh but also forms a barrier against the heat, so all the juices stay inside. In the restaurant we do this more elegant version, using a more sophisticated crust, which is more like a dough, made with salt, flour and egg whites, which can be easily molded and becomes rock-hard in the oven. It is important that the fillets of sea bass are all the same thickness, rather than, say, two thick ones and two thin tail ones, so that they all cook for the same length of time.

At home, though, it is lovely to do this with a whole fish (scaled and cleaned) – stuff the cavity with some fresh herbs, and allow around 20 minutes baking time for a fish of about 4 pounds (test to see if it is ready, as in the recipe below).

You need a lot of egg white for this recipe, but don't waste the yolks – you can use them to make pasta (one of the reasons we dreamed up this way of making the crust is that we always have lots of egg whites left over after we have made our pasta).

If you happen to have any aged balsamic vinegar (see page 46) – which is very expensive but beautiful – then, instead of the dressing, just pour a little around the fish, with some good olive oil.

Preheat the oven as high as it will go.

Blanch the spinach leaves in boiling salted water for the briefest time (5 to 10 seconds only), then drain and squeeze out the excess water.

Mix the herbs together. Either put the sea salt into a food processor and crack it a little, then add the herbs and process until the herbs are very finely chopped, or do this by hand.

If you have a food processor, put the flour, egg whites and the salt and herb mixture into it, and process to a green dough. Otherwise, mix the flour and the salt and herb mixture well in a mixing bowl, then transfer to a clean work surface, pile up like a small mountain (which we call a *fontana* or fountain) and make a well in the middle. Beat the egg whites lightly in a bowl, then pour them into the well in the flour. Put in your hand and slowly and gently turn it, working in a little of the flour mix at a time, so that the egg white is absorbed gradually and forms a dough.

Knead the dough for 3 to 4 minutes. If it feels too hard as you work it, wet your hands with a little water, which should help to loosen it. The dough needs to be firm and elastic enough to enclose the fish without breaking but not too loose; otherwise when it cooks it will release too much moisture, and the fish won't cook properly. Wrap the dough in plastic wrap and keep to one side.

4 handfuls of spinach
5 ounces basil, trimmed
5 ounces parsley, trimmed
1 ounce rosemary leaves
1 ounce sage leaves
4 cups sea salt
5¼ cups all-purpose flour
⅔ cup egg whites
    (about 6–8 eggs),
    plus 1 yolk for brushing
4 sea bass fillets, each about
    7 ounces, of a consistent
    thickness, i.e., with no
    thinner tail parts
2 pats of butter
1 tablespoon olive oil
salt and pepper

For the balsamic dressing:
8 tablespoons good
    balsamic vinegar
1 teaspoon honey
about 1 tablespoon sugar
juice of ½ lemon
½ tablespoon olive oil
2 drops of Worcestershire sauce

Make the balsamic dressing: put the balsamic vinegar in a bowl, add the honey and sugar, and leave in a warm place (but not on the stove), so that the honey and sugar can dissolve into the vinegar. When they have, add the lemon juice, olive oil and Worcestershire sauce. Taste and, if you think it is too sharp, add a little more sugar to taste. Keep to one side.

Roll the dough out to about ⅛ inch thick. You need to cut this into 8 rough squares of dough – 4 to go beneath the fillets (make these about ¾ inch bigger all round than the fish) and another 4 to go over the top of each fillet to enclose them completely (these top squares will need to be about 1¼ inches bigger all around than the fish). Each fillet will be slightly different, so use them as a guide when you are cutting out your dough.

Lay out the 4 squares of dough that will go underneath the fish and place a fillet on top of each, skin side facing upward, then brush the edges with beaten egg yolk and put the top square on top. Seal tightly and trim the edges neatly. Make sure there are no holes in the dough; if there are any, take a piece of the dough trimmings, wet it with water and use it to patch the hole. Brush with more egg.

Line a flat ovenproof tray with baking paper, put the sea bass "parcels" on it and place in the preheated oven. The length of cooking time will depend entirely on the thickness of the fish, so start testing after about 7 minutes (but bear in mind you might need up to 10 minutes or so more). Take one of the sea bass out – the crust will now be golden and hard – and, with a sharp knife, cut around three sides, so you can lift up the crust like a lid, and check the fish inside. Press your finger against the fillet: if it is soft, then it is ready; if the flesh of the fish is resistant, replace the "lid" and put back in the oven. Test again after a couple of minutes or so.

When the sea bass is ready, take it out of the oven and leave it in its crust, while you warm up the spinach in a saucepan with the butter and the olive oil. Season with salt and pepper. Arrange in the middle of your plates.

With a knife, cut the crusts all the way round and lift off the tops. With a spatula, lift out the fish and put them on top of the spinach. Finish with the balsamic dressing and serve.

Branzino al basilico

Sea bass with basil potato puree

The rich flavor of sea bass marries really well with basil and potatoes. When you make potato puree, it is important to use the right potato – you want ones that are not too starchy. As always, we cook them with the skin on to keep in all the flavor. Once the water comes to the boil, we turn down the heat and let them cook very slowly. This will keep the skins from splitting, and stop water getting inside, which will spoil the floury texture. The potatoes are ready when a sharp knife goes through them easily. If they fall apart, they are overcooked. When they are ready, you need to work quickly – have the milk ready and warm, peel the potatoes as soon as they are just cool enough to handle, and put them through a very fine sieve right away (it does need to be very fine, so that you get a smooth puree). Return them to the hot pan and make sure once they are pureed that they are kept hot. If you lose the heat, the puree will lose flavor and become grainy in texture.

2 large bunches of basil,
    trimmed
7 tablespoons unsalted butter,
    softened
2 large red potatoes, preferably
    Desiree, unpeeled
⅓ cup plus 1 tablespoon milk
4 teaspoons sunflower or
    vegetable oil
4 sea bass fillets,
    each about 7 ounces
3 tablespoons
    extra virgin olive oil
salt and pepper

Put the basil leaves in a food processor and chop them, then add the butter and process to a bright green paste. Spoon into a container and leave in the fridge until you need it.

Put the whole unpeeled potatoes in a pan of cold salted water. Bring to the boil, then turn down the heat to a simmer and cook until soft (about an hour, depending on the size).

When the potatoes are nearly cooked, warm up the milk in a pan – don't let it boil, just heat it through, so that it won't bring down the temperature of the potatoes when you add it to them.

Peel the potatoes when cool enough to handle and, while still hot, put through a fine sieve. Add the milk and season. Keep in a warm place.

Meanwhile, heat two nonstick pans and divide the sunflower or vegetable oil between them.

Season the fish fillets and put them into the pans, skin side down. Gently press the fish down, so that the skin is all in contact with the pan, and cook until it turns golden and crisp, and you can see the flesh gradually turning white and opaque almost to the top. Turn the fillets over and turn off the heat.

Cut the basil butter into cubes. Put the potato puree back on the heat and beat in the cubes of basil butter.

Spoon some of the potato puree into the middle of each of your serving plates. Lift the fish out of the pan, place on top of the puree, drizzle each fillet with olive oil and serve.

Trancio di tonno alla griglia

Chargrilled tuna

You can also do this with swordfish *(pesce spada)*, which is actually
more typical in Italy. Ask your fishmonger to give you quite large steaks,
not cut from the tail, as you need them to be about 3¼ to 4 inches in size
and around ⅝ to ¾ inch thick. This a recipe that is best in the summer,
when the tomatoes are good – look for the juiciest, sweetest ones you
can find. Whenever we are serving a salad of arugula and tomatoes, we
season the tomatoes separately, as they need more salt and vinegar.

Get a griddle pan or grill smoking-hot. Meanwhile, take the fish
out of the fridge and let it come to room temperature.

Cut the tomatoes in half if small, quarters if large. Put into a bowl,
season well with salt and pepper and toss with the vinegar.

Season the fish steaks and sprinkle with parsley. Cook the steaks 2
at a time for about 2 minutes on one side, then turn them over and
give them another couple of minutes on the other side for fish that
is still rare in the middle (cook for longer if you don't like it like
this). Keep warm while you cook the other steaks.

While the fish steaks are cooking, season the arugula with salt and
pepper and dress with Giorgio's vinaigrette.

Arrange the tomatoes on the plates, the rocket on top and place the
fish steaks on top of that. Finish each steak with a little extra virgin
olive oil and serve with a lemon quarter.

4 tuna or swordfish steaks,
    each about 7 ounces
around 24 cherry tomatoes,
    or 5 large tomatoes
3 tablespoons white wine vine-
    gar
2 tablespoons chopped parsley
4 handfuls of arugula
3 tablespoons Giorgio's
    vinaigrette (see page 51)
3 tablespoons
    extra virgin olive oil
1 lemon, cut into quarters
salt and pepper

Limone

Lemons

"You have to smell them all"

When we are out shopping, my wife, Plaxy, always says, "Why does it take you two hours to buy three lemons?" "Well," I say, "because there are so many lemons, and there must be some that are good, some not so good; so you have to smell them all." For me the leaves tell the tale. The fresher the leaf, the less time the lemon has been off the tree. Look for lemons that are unwaxed and have a lively-looking skin. A good lemon feels firm when you squeeze it. My favorites are the really thick-skinned ones, whose juice seems to have a slightly less aggressive flavor.

Lemons are so important in Italian cooking – we use their zest and juice in everything from fish dishes to salads, stews, and desserts. Around the country you will find risotti flavored with the zest and juice, and pasta tossed with lemon juice, butter, cream and Parmesan. But we are not talking about just any old lemons – they have to be big and scented, and full of powerfully flavored juice that has a slight sweetness, taking the edge off the acidity. So, if you squeeze them over cooked fish, the flavor is less harsh, and if you use them in a marinade, they don't "cook" the flesh too quickly.

The lemons I love best are from either Sorrento or Sicilia, where we go on vacation sometimes in the summer and where every house seems to have a lemon tree. You see the old men picking boxes of lemons in the morning when the sun comes up, then driving them in their three-wheelers to the local bar; and the scent that rises up from the fruit is fantastic. Order a fish in a café or restaurant, and they don't just give you a slice of lemon, or a quarter, they give you a whole lemon to squeeze over it.

From Sorrento, we get the beautiful Femminello lemons, which are the ones that are used for the local limoncello liqueur, made by infusing the lemon peel in alcohol. Since 2000, Sorrento lemons have achieved Protected Geographical Indication (PGI) status, which specifies that they can be grown only in the Sorrento peninsula, or on Capri, and they must weigh at least 3 ounces. They are planted in straight lines on terraced slopes going down to the sea and sheltered under *pagliarelle* (straw mats) that are attached to chestnut poles, to protect against the salty sea air and help the fruit to ripen evenly.

The lemons grow all year round, but are at their best between May and the end of October. During the peak times for picking you see everyone running around like monkeys, with bags of lemons on their backs, picking from miles and miles of terraces covered in bright yellow perfumed fruit; it is quite beautiful to see.

Nasello in scabeccio

Steamed hake with parsley and garlic

Hake, also known as whiting, is such a lovely fish, but it isn't used as much as it should be. You can do this dish either with fillets or, if the hake is quite small, ask your fishmonger to cut steaks – across the fish – and serve it on the bone. You really need a mandoline for this, so you can slice the fennel very, very fine. As the hot *scabeccio* is put on top of the fennel, it cooks some of the slices slightly, softening them. It is this contrast with the lovely crunch and freshness of the rest of the fennel that makes it come alive and sing out above the other flavors.

Preheat the oven to 390°F. Prepare 4 pieces of foil, each twice the length of the pieces of fish. Cut one of the lemons in half and squeeze some juice over each piece of foil. Place the fish toward one end of each piece of foil and season. Drizzle each with 2 teaspoons of the olive oil. Fold the remaining foil over the top and fold the edges over to seal all the way round, so you have 4 foil parcels. Make sure the fish is sealed in properly and there are no holes in the foil; otherwise the steam will be lost and the fish won't cook properly.

Slice the fennel very, very thin and put the slices into a bowl. Mix the juice of the other lemon with the remaining oil and use to dress the fennel. Season.

Put the fish parcels in the oven. Depending on the size, you will need to cook them for between 4 and 8 minutes. Check the largest fillet (they will inevitably be slightly different sizes) by testing with your finger: the flesh should still be soft and moist – don't worry if you think it is slightly undercooked, as the hot sauce you are going to pour over it will finish cooking it on the plates.

While the fish is cooking, make the scabeccio: heat a small pan, add the olive oil and the garlic, and let it fry gently. When it starts to color, add the parsley – be careful, as the water in the parsley may cause the oil to spit a little. Leave for a minute or so to bring the oil back up to temperature, then, very slowly, add the vinegar and then the sugar. It will bubble up and evaporate a little, leaving its flavor without the sharp smell.

By now the fish should be ready. Take it from the oven but don't open the parcels immediately.

Arrange the fennel salad in the middle of your plates. Open the parcels and lift out the fish with a spatula. Place on top of the fennel. Spoon the juices over the top, followed by the sauce, and serve.

4 hake fillets or steaks
    (see above), each
    about 7 ounces
2 lemons
4 tablespoons
    extra virgin olive oil
2 small fennel bulbs
salt and pepper

For the scabeccio:
8 tablespoons
    extra virgin olive oil
2 garlic cloves, thinly sliced
handful of parsley leaves
8 tablespoons
    white wine vinegar
pinch of sugar

Sgombro alla griglia con crosta di erbe

Chargrilled mackerel with herb crust

Mackerel is another fantastic but underrated fish, which is marvelous cooked inside a crispy herb crust that protects the fish, keeping it moist and trapping in all the delicate flavors. You can do this with mackerel fillets, too, in the same way, but leave out the stuffing and cook the fillets, skin side first, for 2 to 3 minutes depending on the thickness, then turn over for a further 2 to 3 minutes.

4 tomatoes
⅓ cup plus 1 tablespoon olive oil
4 white onions,
　　cut into about ½-inch dice
3 tablespoons
　　white wine vinegar
4 tablespoons salted capers
　　(preferably baby ones),
　　rinsed
4 medium-sized mackerel,
　　gutted
4 sprigs of rosemary
4 garlic cloves
4 handfuls of
　　mixed salad greens
4 tablespoons Giorgio's
　　vinaigrette (see page 51)
salt and pepper

　　For the herb crust:
small bunch of parsley, trimmed
small bunch of rosemary,
　　trimmed
bunch of basil, trimmed
bunch of sage
1 scant cup bread crumbs
3 tablespoons olive oil

Blanch the tomatoes, skin, quarter and deseed (see page 304), then cut into ¾-inch dice.

Get a griddle pan or grill smoking hot.

To make the herb crust, put the herbs into a food processor with the bread crumbs and a little of the olive oil, and process. Then slowly add the rest of the oil until you have a quite oily paste. Transfer to a large tray or plate.

Put 2 tablespoons of the olive oil into a pan, add the onions, cover and cook gently for about 10 minutes, until they become translucent but not colored. Add the vinegar and cook for another 2 to 3 minutes. Add the capers and set aside.

Season the fish lightly inside and stuff each one with the rosemary sprigs and garlic cloves (crush them lightly first). Season the outside of the fish. Brush another 2 tablespoons of the remaining oil over the fish, then roll it in the herb and bread crumb mixture, making sure it clings well.

You should be able to cook 4 fish at the same time. Place them on the hot griddle pan or grill and cook for about 4 to 5 minutes on one side (depending on the size) so that it marks well but doesn't burn (turn down the heat if necessary). Turn over and cook for another 4 to 5 minutes.

While the fish is cooking, put the salad leaves in a bowl, season and toss with the vinaigrette.

Put the pan with the onions back on the heat to warm through. Check and adjust the seasoning, if necessary. Stir in the diced tomato.

Divide this mixture between 4 plates and arrange the salad on one side of each. Lay the fish on top of the onions and drizzle the remaining olive oil over.

Anguilla

Eel

I wish I could entice more people to eat eel. The Romans loved it and it often appears on the menus of Renaissance banquets. In Italy, there are two ways to cook it: braised slowly (though I never saw eels in jelly before I came to London), or cooked hard over a high heat. I love it chargrilled in an herb and bread crumb crust, or the way Vincenzo Borgonzolo cooked it for me one night after service had finished at Al San Vincenzo. He tossed it in flour, then pan-fried it and squeezed lots of lemon juice over it. Before I tasted it, I would never have believed that lemon would be good with eel; the two seem to be such opposite flavors, but the lemon seems to grab hold of the oiliness of the eel, and change its character completely so that it melts in your mouth, and the flavor is brilliant. If you gave that dish to 20 people, probably only a few would recognize it as eel. Such a simple, perfect piece of cooking.

I later discovered that this dish has its roots in some of the old recipes collated by Artusi, the great nineteenth-century Italian food writer, who reckoned that medium-sized eels can be cooked on the grill without skinning (which is necessary for large ones), as the skin "when seasoned with lemon juice at the moment of serving, is not unpleasant to the taste when you suck on it." Often the eel is threaded on skewers, in-

terspersed with sage or bay leaves and pieces of bread, and then put on the grill for 10 minutes or so until the eel is cooked through and the bread toasted. Then it is served, again with lemon juice squeezed over.

In my region of Lombardia, it is stewed with tomatoes and, sometimes, peas. Peas are also a favorite in eel recipes from around Venezia. Elsewhere, it is typically stewed in wine. According to Artusi, in Firenze they marinated the eel in oil and salt and pepper, then rolled it in bread crumbs and cooked it with garlic, sage and seasoned oil in a cast-iron pot, "with fire above and below." Then, when it started to brown, they added a little water to the pan.

Many of the recipes come from the lagoons of the Valli di Comacchio in the Po delta, in the northeast of Italy, where the best eels are reckoned to come from. Here they tell beautiful stories about the dark stormy nights of *la calata* "the descent," when in November and December the eels leave the fresh water in which they have spent most of their lives and head out to the Sargasso Sea to spawn. The fishermen built intricate traps in a series of linked basins, called *lavorieri*, to catch them at this time, when they have changed color from yellow or brown to silver and would be at their fattest, ready to take on the long journey. Then when the young "glass eels" or elvers returned from the sea in January and February to make *la montata*, the ascent into the marshes and rivers, they would be caught again in the *lavorieri*, and the salt water would have enhanced their flavor. During the brief season, bands of eel workers would arrive in Comacchio and stay in special very basic houses, called *casoni*, from where they sent the live eels in boats to Venezia, or fried them, marinated them in oil and vinegar and packed them in big barrels.

Everywhere you go in Comacchio today there are shops selling live eels, or eels that have been smoked, or fried and then marinated in the traditional fashion, and they are on every menu in every restaurant, maybe salted, or with cabbage or in *brodetto* or risotto. Artusi reports an old recipe from this region that he tried for eel "stew" or *umido* (which means "humidity") that I particularly like the idea of. You take a couple of pounds of medium-sized eels, with the skin on, and cut them into segments, but leave them connected together by a strip of flesh. Then you coarsely chop three onions, a celery stalk, and a carrot and some parsley, and parboil them in about two glasses of water with the peel of half a lemon and some salt and pepper. Then you take an ovenproof pot and put in a layer of eel, followed by a layer of vegetables (discard the lemon at this point), then another layer of eel, and a final layer of vegetables, and top with their cooking water. You cover it tightly with a lid and let it cook very slowly in the oven (Artusi buried his pot of eels in ashes and coals in front of a wood fire) so that the eel gives up its own juices, shaking and turning the pot, but not stirring or you will break up the eel. When the pieces of eel start to pull apart and are almost cooked, you add a generous tablespoonful of strong vinegar mixed with a touch of tomato paste, taste and season generously if necessary. Bring it to the boil for a little longer, to finish off cooking the eel, and that is it; you take it off the heat and serve it with warm bread.

Trancio di merluzzo con lenticchie

Cod with lentils

I made this for the first time in Olivo. Tony Allan, who supplied our fish, brought me some cod, which I cooked in a pan, and I happened to have some lentils there for another dish. I put the two together, and thought the flavors were amazing; and the flakiness of the really fresh cod worked so well with the flouriness of the lentils. In Italian cooking you find some stews of fish with lentils, but they are longer-cooked, whereas part of the pleasure of this dish comes from the crispy skin of the pan-fried cod. Cod is one of the most overfished fish, so buy it only from genuinely sustainable sources, and preferably line-caught rather than landed by trawler.

Prepare the lentils: soak them in water for half an hour, then drain. While they soak, finely chop the vegetables.

Heat half the olive oil in a pan and add the chopped vegetables and the piece of pancetta. Cook for 5 to 10 minutes, until the vegetables are soft but not colored. It is important that the vegetables be soft, so that they release all their sweetness, flavor and moisture into the lentils.

Add the lentils together with the herbs, all tied together, and cook for 5 minutes, stirring until everything is well mixed and the lentils start to stick to the bottom of the pan. Don't season at this point, as salt will make the lentils harden.

Add around 4 cups of stock (to cover the lentils by about a finger) and keep the rest hot on the burner in case you need it. Bring the contents of the lentil pan to a boil, turn down the heat and simmer for 45 minutes until the lentils are soft, adding more stock if they begin to get dry. Remove the pancetta and keep the lentils on one side, but keep the stock hot in case you need to loosen the lentils before serving.

Put the 2 handfuls of parsley into a food processor with the olive oil and process as quickly as possible until you have a bright green sauce.

Season the fish. If you have two large nonstick frying pans, heat them at the same time and divide the sunflower or vegetable oil between them. When it is just beginning to smoke, put in the fish, skin side down, and keep pressing down and checking underneath – the skin should turn crispy and golden brown. You will see the flesh beginning to turn opaque. When it has turned white almost all the way through, turn it over. Divide the butter between the two pans.

While the butter is foaming, put the pan of lentils back on the heat – the lentils need to be the consistency of a risotto, not "soupy," or they will be too loose after you add the butter; so, if necessary, drain off a little of the liquid. Add the parsley and stir in the butter. If, on the

2 handfuls of parsley
⅓ cup plus 1 tablespoon
    extra virgin olive oil
4 large cod fillets (from the
    center of the fish), each
    about 8 ounces (½ pound)
3 tablespoons sunflower or
    vegetable oil
3½ tablespoons butter,
    cut into small cubes
a few rosemary leaves to garnish
salt and pepper

    For the lentils:
1⅓ cups green lentils (preferably
    lenticchie di Castelluccio)
1 white onion
1 carrot
1 celery stalk
1 small leek
4 tablespoons
    extra virgin olive oil
3½-ounce piece of
    unsmoked pancetta
sprig of rosemary
small bunch of sage
2 bay leaves
6 cups vegetable stock
    (see page 268)
handful of parsley, chopped
3½ tablespoons butter,
    cut into small cubes

other hand, the lentils are not loose enough, you can add a little of the reserved hot stock. Check the seasoning and adjust if necessary.

Spoon the lentils onto the plates, with the parsley sauce on the side. Tilt each pan containing the fish toward you so that the buttery juices collect in one spot, then spoon this over the top of the fish. Lift the fish out and serve on top of the lentils.

San Pietro con patate e olive

Fillet of John Dory with potato and olives

This is a favorite dish that we have been cooking for many years. John Dory has a kind of metallic taste that I like, which amazingly comes through the flavors of the crispy potatoes, the wine and olives. We use Cerignola olives for this – the giant green ones from Puglia – but any large olives are good. Just remember that, if they are salted, you need to wash them well before you use them, or the salt will affect the flavor of the dish. I love to make this with Jersey Royal potatoes when they come into season, because they are so light and less floury than many other varieties.

16 new potatoes (whole and scrubbed but unpeeled)
around 20 very big green olives, with pits
3 tablespoons extra virgin olive oil, plus more to serve
1 wineglass of dry white wine
about 5 tablespoons Fish stock (see page 267)
2 tablespoons sunflower or vegetable oil
4 skinless John Dory fillets, each about 6–7 ounces
2 tablespoons chopped parsley
1 lemon
salt and pepper

Cook the potatoes in salted water from cold for about 15 to 20 minutes until slightly undercooked. Take off the heat, drain and, when cool enough to handle, peel. Cut the potatoes in half and keep to one side.

With a knife, take the flesh off the olive pits and set aside.

Heat half the olive oil in a large sauté pan, then put in the potatoes and cook until nice and golden and crusty – don't worry if they break up a little. Add the olives and toss for a minute or so. Add the white wine and allow to evaporate, then add the fish stock and cook for a minute or so more. Season and turn off the heat.

If you have two nonstick pans, get these hot at the same time. While they are heating, season the fish. Divide the sunflower or vegetable oil between the two pans – it will get hot immediately. Put in the fillets (if you can tell on which side the skin has been, this should be facing upward – if not, don't worry). Cook on one side until golden underneath – you will see the heat going upward through the fish, turning it opaque. When it is opaque almost to the top, flip the fish over, then turn off the heat and leave to rest for a minute or so.

While the fish cooks, turn the heat on again under the pan of potatoes and cook for a minute or so, until the mixture is quite soupy. Add the parsley, spoon on to the plates, and serve the fish on top. Drizzle with extra virgin olive oil and a squeeze of lemon juice.

Coda di rospo in salsa di noci e agrodolce di capperi

Monkfish with walnut and agrodolce

Monkfish needs to be treated more like a beefsteak than some of the more delicate fish – partly because the flesh is firm and dense and "meaty," and partly because it contains more moisture than other fish. So you need to sauté it quite aggressively at first on both sides, then turn the heat down to let it cook through gently. The fish should be nice and golden after 3 to 4 minutes (if it doesn't color much, it isn't absolutely fresh). You can buy good walnut paste in Italian delicatessens, or make it (see page 322).

You need only around 1½ tablespoons of the *agrodolce* sauce, but it is easier to blend a larger quantity. Any you don't need you can keep in the fridge for several weeks and use with roast fish or meat (remember, though, that it is quite sweet, so it is good to offset it with something a little bitter, like chicory or endive or Swiss chard).

2 tablespoons walnut paste
2 tablespoons white wine
　　vinegar
4 tablespoons
　　extra virgin olive oil
2 Swiss chard stalks with leaves
2 tablespoons vegetable or
　　sunflower oil
4 monkfish tails, each about
　　8 ounces (½ pound)
4 tablespoons Giorgio's
　　vinaigrette (see page 51)
12 caper berries
2 handfuls of arugula
salt and pepper

　　For the agrodolce sauce:
5 tablespoons white wine
　　vinegar
⅓ cup sugar
3½ ounces (about ¾ cup) capers
　　in brine, drained, washed
　　and dried
⅓ cup plus 1 tablespoon
　　extra virgin olive oil

Make the agrodolce sauce by putting the vinegar and sugar in a small pan and letting it bubble up and reduce to a clear syrup.

Hand-blend the capers, very slowly adding the syrup (as if making a mayonnaise), then blend in the oil (again very slowly, so that the sauce doesn't split) until creamy. Transfer to a small pan and keep on a very low heat, without boiling, for about 15 to 20 minutes, until any excess liquid disappears and the sauce is very thick. Leave to cool.

Mix 1½ tablespoons of the agrodolce sauce with the walnut paste, then slowly mix in the vinegar and half the olive oil. The sauce will become paler. Keep warm.

Separate the chard stalks from the leaves. Cut the stalk across into batons about ¼ inch wide. Blanch these in boiling salted water for a couple of minutes, lift them out with a slotted spoon and keep on one side. Then put the whole leaves into the water and blanch for a minute or so. Drain and squeeze the leaves, then chop coarsely. Put the stalks and leaves in a bowl, mix together and keep on one side.

Put a nonstick pan (or two, if necessary) on to heat. Add the vegetable or sunflower oil. Season the fish, put in the pans and cook quickly for 3 to 4 minutes on each side (depending on the size), then turn the heat down, and let the fish relax for a couple of minutes.

Season the chard and toss with half the vinaigrette. Mix the caper berries with the rocket, season and toss with the rest of the vinaigrette.

Spoon the reserved sauce onto the plates, arrange the chard on top, then the fish on top of that. Spoon the pan juices over, drizzle with the rest of the olive oil and finish with the arugula and caper berry salad.

Trancio di rombo ai funghi porcini con purè di patate

Roasted turbot (or brill) with porcini and potato puree

My granddad would turn in his grave if he knew I cooked mushrooms with fish. He would never ever have put them in the same dish, but there is something about the two flavors, brought together with parsley, that I have to say is weird, traditionally, but works very well, because of the richness and sweetness of the turbot (or its cousin, brill – this is one dish I wouldn't do with a "poor" fish). You need to make it when the porcini are abundant, so you can choose ones with large caps *(cappella)*. The trick is they go in right at the end, so when the dish arrives at the table, you smell them first.

2 large red potatoes (preferably Desiree), scrubbed but unpeeled
14 ounces fresh porcini (ceps), sliced very thinly
7 tablespoons unsalted butter
2 garlic cloves, chopped
½ wineglass of white wine
⅓ cup plus 1 tablespoon milk
2 tablespoons sunflower or vegetable oil
4 turbot or brill steaks on the bone, each about 7 ounces
handful of chopped parsley
salt and pepper

Put the whole unpeeled potatoes in a pan of cold salted water. Bring to a boil, then turn down the heat to a simmer and cook until soft (about 30 minutes to an hour, depending on the size). While the potatoes are cooking, brush, clean and slice the porcini (see page 239).

Melt 2 tablespoons of the butter in a sauté pan, add the garlic and cook without allowing it to color for a minute or so. Add the mushrooms and gently toss without frying. Add the white wine and let the alcohol evaporate. Season, then turn down the heat, cover with a lid and let the mushrooms stew gently for a couple of minutes. Take off the heat and keep on one side.

When the potatoes are nearly cooked, warm the milk in a pan.

Peel the potatoes as soon as they are cool enough to handle, and push through a very fine sieve. Put back into the pan and beat in half the remaining butter and the warm milk (you should have a very smooth puree). Season with salt only. Keep warm (cover the pan with plastic wrap to stop the potato from becoming dry and crusty on the top).

Meanwhile, heat 2 nonstick pans if you have them and divide the sunflower or vegetable oil between them. Season the fish and put into the pan, skin side down. Cook until the skin turns golden and crunchy, and you can see the flesh has turned from translucent to white and opaque almost to the top. Turn over and turn off the heat.

Return the pan of potato puree to the heat. Warm through and then beat in the remaining butter.

Put the pan containing the mushrooms back on the heat, and heat through. Stir in the parsley.

Spoon some of the potato puree into the center of each of your serving plates, arrange the mushrooms around it and place the fish on top.

Sogliola arrosto con patate, fagiolini e pesto

Roast Dover sole with potatoes, beans and pesto sauce

Sole isn't big in Italy, but the Dover sole you can buy in the U.S. is a beautiful fish that deserves everything good that has been written about it. This is a late spring/summer dish, which is the time when the Dover sole are at their best. The mixed vegetables are held together in a "sauce" that is made using just potatoes and onions cooked together and pureed in a blender. The cooking of the vegetables may seem a bit time-consuming – we cook each one separately, drain them and refresh under cold water before putting the next vegetable into the cooking water – but each vegetable will taste much better and keep its bright color.

You don't need to include all of the vegetables; you can vary them, according to what you have – just fresh peas, if you like, in season. The important thing is that if you use fava beans, cook them last. If you were to put them in first, they would turn the cooking water dark green and any delicate vegetables that followed, like peas, would darken too.

Peel the potatoes and cut 2 into ½-inch dice. Put into a pan of salted water, bring to a boil, then turn down to a simmer for a minute or so, turn off the heat, cover with a lid and leave to finish cooking.	3 medium potatoes 5 tablespoons olive oil 1 white onion, chopped 4 tablespoons fresh peas 4 snow peas

Peel the potatoes and cut 2 into ½-inch dice. Put into a pan of salted water, bring to a boil, then turn down to a simmer for a minute or so, turn off the heat, cover with a lid and leave to finish cooking.

In a separate pan, heat a tablespoon of olive oil, add the onion and cook gently for about 5 minutes, without allowing it to color.

Roughly slice the third potato and add to the onion. Cook for a couple of minutes. Add water to cover and cook until the potato breaks up.

Bring another pan of salted water to a boil, put in the peas and let them cook for a minute or so, lift out with a slotted spoon and refresh under cold running water, then transfer to a dish or plate. Next, put the snow peas into the cooking water and repeat the cooking, draining and refreshing process. Keep these separate from the peas. Do the same thing with the long green beans, and finally the fava beans (these need to be last, or they will turn the water dark green, see above).

Put the onion and potato mixture into a blender and blend until you have a thick "sauce," the consistency of a milk shake.

Split the green beans lengthwise, and slice the snow peas. Drain the potato dice, add to the beans and snow peas, then add the peas, fava beans and cranberry or cannellini beans. Season and mix lightly.

Heat 2 nonstick oval pans if you have them and divide the vegetable or sunflower oil between the two. Season the fish and put 2 in

3 medium potatoes
5 tablespoons olive oil
1 white onion, chopped
4 tablespoons fresh peas
4 snow peas
12 long green beans
4 tablespoons fresh fava beans
4 tablespoons cooked cranberry
    or cannellini beans
    (see page 183 for how
    to cook the beans)
3 tablespoons vegetable or
    sunflower oil
4 Dover sole, each about
    1 pound, heads and skin
    removed, and trimmed
4 squash flowers (if available)
4 tablespoons Pesto
    (see page 309)
salt and pepper

each pan. Cook gently for about 6 minutes on one side until golden, then turn and cook for another 6 to 8 minutes. If you press with your thumb the fillets should start to pull apart.

While the fish are cooking, put the mixed vegetables into a saucepan, add the potato "sauce" and warm everything up. Season.

Spoon this mixture into the middle of your plates. If you have any zucchini blossoms, arrange these around the outside, place the fish on top of the potato and vegetable "sauce," spoon some of the remaining olive oil over each piece of fish, and drizzle the pesto around.

Orata al balsamico

Pan-fried sea bream with balsamic vinegar

I love this dish. I'm very proud to have stolen the outline of the idea from a dish created by Jacques Rolancy at Le Laurent in Paris, which he based on something he had seen done by the great French chef Alain Chapel. In Paris the dish was overcomplicated, with quenelles of tapenade and shaped tomatoes and potatoes, but the combination of the flavors of fish, spinach, tapenade and balsamic vinegar was a fantastic one. When we opened Zafferano, I remembered it and started to work on the idea, putting in some crunchy chives and radish, some spinach, and a dressing made with balsamic vinegar. I only occasionally put balsamic vinegar with fish, because it has such an intense flavor, but here it is softened by honey and lemon, and we use a light Ligurian olive oil, as you don't want one that is too strong and peppery. Over the years we have played around with this dish so much, but now I think we couldn't get it any better. I am very wary of saying that I "created" anything in the kitchen – but this dish I do now consider to be "mine."

Blanch the spinach in boiling salted water for 10 seconds – virtually just in and out – so that you keep the flavor, color and texture. Drain, squeeze out as much water as possible and set aside.

Slice the radishes and then cut the slices into matchsticks roughly the same size as the chives. Mix with the chives and keep on one side.

Season the fish on both sides. Heat 2 nonstick pans if you have them and put half the sunflower or vegetable oil into each. Add the fish, skin side down. When you put the fish in, it will arch upward from the first contact with the heat. Leave it for a minute or so to warm through, then slowly press the flesh down, from the tail end upward, so that all the skin is in contact with the pan and crisps up evenly. You will see some excess fat coming out of the fish between the flesh and the skin – so blot this up with some paper towels to help the skin to crisp up even more.

As the heat travels upward through the flesh, you will see it starts to turn white and opaque. When it is white almost to the top (probably only after about 2½ minutes in all), turn it over and then quickly take it out of the pan. Transfer to a warm tray or plate, flesh side down.

While the fish is cooking, put the spinach in a pan with the butter and warm through. Season and stir in the olive oil.

Spread the skin of the fish with the olive paste. Divide the spinach among 4 plates and spoon the balsamic dressing over. Place the fish on top. Season the radishes and chives and mix in the sesame oil. Arrange on top of the fish and serve.

4 handfuls of spinach
5 large radishes
small bunch of chives,
    cut into batons
4 sea bream fillets, each about
    ½ pound, cleaned and
    pin bones removed
4 teaspoons sunflower or
    vegetable oil
2 tablespoons unsalted butter
2 tablespoons
    extra virgin olive oil
4 teaspoons black olive paste
    (tapenade)
4 tablespoons Balsamic dressing
    (see page 411)
1 tablespoon sesame oil
salt and pepper

Trancio di rombo liscio all'acquapazza

Roast brill with green olives and cherry tomatoes

Acquapazza means "crazy water" – which is the way they describe the thin, watery sauce with tomatoes and olives in Napoli, where the dish comes from. I suppose the name is derived from the way the fishermen used to cook the fish on the shore, by taking a bit of water from the sea, crushing in a few tomatoes (you needed no salt, because it was already there in the seawater), boiling it up over a fire, then putting in the fish.

We make this dish with *scarola*, a crunchy Italian winter lettuce with a yellow heart – romaine lettuce is a good substitute. Usually in the restaurant we cook the brill on the bone – so if you can, ask your fishmonger to cut it into steaks, with the bone in, rather than fillets. If he has any extra brill bones, you can also make a very simple fish stock to use for the sauce, by putting them in a pan with some halved onion, chunks of carrot, celery, a handful of parsley stalks, a bay leaf and some peppercorns. Put in enough water to cover, bring to the boil, then turn down to a simmer, cook for 20 minutes and strain. If you don't have the bones, or the time, just use water.

12 giant green olives, preferably
      Cerignola, with the pits
4 teaspoons sunflower or
      vegetable oil
4 skinless fillets of brill
      (or steaks, see above),
      each about ½ pound
1 wineglass of white wine
8 cherry tomatoes, halved
1 tablespoon tomato passata
2 garlic cloves, crushed
1 head romaine lettuce,
      separated into leaves
5 tablespoons
      extra virgin olive oil
juice of 1 lemon
handful of chopped parsley
salt and pepper

Pit the olives, and cut them in half.

Heat 2 nonstick pans if you have them and divide the sunflower or vegetable oil between them. Season the fish and put into the pans. Fry on one side quite fast, so that they become nice and golden underneath (this will take about 3 minutes for fillets, about 6 if you are using steaks). Turn them over and immediately lift the fish out of the pans. Keep warm.

Divide the white wine between the two sauté pans and allow the alcohol to evaporate. Add half the tomatoes, then the passata and olives and a garlic clove to each pan and gently squash a couple of the tomato pieces. Add a ladleful of water (or, if you have made any fish stock as above, add this instead).

Let the sauce reduce for a minute or so, then put in the fish and gently heat it through.

Blanch the lettuce leaves in boiling salted water for 10 seconds – virtually just in and out – so that you keep the flavor, color and texture. Drain and toss the lettuce in a couple of tablespoons of the olive oil.

Arrange some lettuce in the middle of each of your serving plates. Lift the fish from the sauce and place on top. Mix together the 2 pans of sauce, add the lemon juice, parsley, and the remaining olive oil. Mix in and spoon over the fish.

Filetti di passera al basilico con patate e olive

Plaice with basil, potatoes and olives

Plaice is a fish I never saw in Italy, and here it seems very underrated – the ugly sister of the likes of sole – but it is fantastic when it is properly cooked. The problem with plaice is that because it is thin it is easily overcooked. Often people fry it in butter to crisp it up, but the butter burns, and everything tastes horrible. By cooking it in an herb crust you can turn the disadvantage of its thinness into a virtue, because you can get the crispiness without burning it, and the fish stays moist and protected inside. For the crust, we took some of the ingredients of pesto – including Parmesan, which goes against the rule of serving cheese and fish – and mixed them with some ciabatta, soaked in water, and bread crumbs. (In Italy, from north to south, everyone has bread crumbs in the kitchen – see page 436.)

2 bunches of basil, trimmed
bunch of parsley, trimmed
1 garlic clove
½ cup extra virgin olive oil
2 slices (4½ x 3¼ x ¾") ciabatta,
    crust removed and
    soaked in water
1 tablespoon bread crumbs
1 tablespoon freshly
    grated Parmesan
8 new potatoes, unpeeled
4 tablespoons tomato passata
8 skinless plaice fillets,
    each about 5 ounces
12 black olives, preferably
    Tagiasche; buy them pit
    in, then take out the pit
4 teaspoons sunflower or
    vegetable oil
salt and pepper

Keeping back a few leaves, put the basil into a food processor with the parsley leaves, garlic and 4 teaspoons of the olive oil. Process until the herbs and garlic are chopped, but not too fine.

Squeeze the excess water from the bread and add to the herbs and oil. Add the bread crumbs and Parmesan and continue to process until you have a bright green paste. Put into the fridge until needed.

Put the unpeeled potatoes into cold salted water, bring to the boil, turn down the heat and cook until just tender (about 15 to 20 minutes), then drain.

Put the tomato passata into a small pan, season and add 2 tablespoons of the remaining olive oil. Leave over a low heat to reduce and thicken to a sauce-like consistency.

Peel the potatoes and cut in half.

On a clean work surface, lay out the plaice fillets and cut each one across in half. With a small table knife or spatula, spread each fillet with some herb paste, leaving a border all the way around the edge about ¼ inch wide. Cover with plastic wrap to avoid the crust darkening.

Heat a nonstick pan, put in a tablespoon of the remaining olive oil, add the potatoes and cook them until golden all over. Add the olives and toss for a minute or two – don't let the olives get too dry. Turn off the heat.

Heat 2 more nonstick pans to medium-hot and divide the sunflower or vegetable oil between them. Lift each piece of fish and put it into the pan, crust side down. Season the flesh and let the fish cook until the crust becomes slightly golden and the borders of fish around it become completely golden.

Turn on the heat under the potatoes and olives. Add the reserved basil to the pan containing the tomato sauce.

When the fish has become white and opaque almost to the top, turn it over, then immediately take the pan off the heat.

Spoon the potatoes and olives onto each of your serving plates and drizzle the tomato sauce around. Lift the fish out of the pan, place on top of the potatoes and drizzle the rest of the olive oil over. Serve.

Pangrattato

Bread crumbs

"No one throws away bread"

From the north to the south of Italy, everyone uses bread crumbs. There is always bread in the house – no one eats a meal without it, and no one throws away bread, ever. My grandmother always had leftover bread drying by the oven. She would grate it (before the time of food processors) and store the crumbs in separate jars: one for fine crumbs, which would be used as a binder in *polpette* (meatballs), and one for thick crumbs, which might be mixed with herbs to make a crust in which to bake fish. Some bread crumbs she would put into the oven until they dried out but barely colored. These are the ones she would use to coat pieces of veal to make *Scaloppina Milanese*, and the toasted crumbs would add a nutty flavor and extra crunch.

Bread is our thickener: big chunks in soups, thick crumbs in stews, finer ones in sauces. We rarely use flour as a thickener in the way that other countries do (for example, in France they would make a roux with flour and butter; in Asia they might use corn flour). The only time I remember my grandmother doing something similar was when she browned some flour in the oven to thicken onion soup, which no doubt owed something to the classic French soup.

In the south of Italy, especially around Calabria, if they made pasta with olive oil, garlic, chile pepper and tomato, and it was too expensive to grate cheese over the top, they used bread crumbs.

We also use torn bread with the crust taken off, which we call *mollica*. It might be soaked in milk, wine, water or vinegar, according to the dish. In Toscana they make panzanella, with (unsalted) Tuscan bread that is a few days old. At its simplest, the bread is torn up and mixed with chopped tomatoes, onions and basil (though sometimes people will add some capers, or chopped cucumber, peppers or celery), tossed in vinaigrette, then left overnight in the fridge, so that all the flavors develop. We serve it with chargrilled sardines (see page 438).

Filetti di passera con castelfranco finocchi e bagna càôda

Roast fillet of plaice with fennel and anchovy sauce

This is a very light dish but with a very full flavor. Normally, I prefer not to buy anchovies in oil because, unless you are sure of the quality, they can sit around too long and become rancid. Traditionally in Piemonte, however, they use them for this dish, so just try to buy good-quality ones. Alternatively, buy salted anchovies, soak them, pat dry and put them under oil yourself. In winter we use Castelfranco, a type of radicchio that looks like a yellow rose with red spots (see page 468), but you can use arugula instead.

Lay each plaice fillet between 2 sheets of plastic wrap and, with a meat pounder or rolling pin, very gently pound to make the fish thin enough to roll. Remove the plastic wrap, then carefully roll up each fillet into a cylinder, trim each end, and secure with a cocktail stick.

Cut the fennel bulbs in half lengthwise, then slice lengthwise again, fairly thickly – each slice should be around ¼ inch thick.

Heat a tablespoon of the olive oil, crush one of the garlic cloves and add to the pan, with the fennel. Cover with a lid, and stew gently for about 5 to 6 minutes, adding a little water if necessary. The fennel should be cooked but still slightly crunchy. Turn off the heat and leave to cool in the cooking liquid.

While the fennel is cooking, put the milk into a small pan with the rest of the garlic, bring to the boil, turn down to a simmer, and cook until the garlic is completely smashed (about 10 minutes).

While the garlic is cooking, put the anchovies into a small bowl over the top of the pan and stir to "dissolve" them – it will only take a few minutes. Push through a fine sieve.

When the garlic is cooked, hand-blend it with a little of the cooking milk. Add the anchovies and 2 tablespoons of the remaining olive oil.

Heat 2 nonstick pans and divide the sunflower oil between them. Season the fish rolls and put into the pans, each roll standing on its end. Cook for 2 minutes until the bases turn golden, then turn each roll over on to the other end, and cook for another 2 minutes. Turn the heat down and leave to rest for a minute or so in the pan, to cook through.

While the fish is resting, toss the Castelfranco or arugula with a mixture of lemon juice, the remaining olive oil and salt and pepper. Arrange in the middle of your serving plates with the fennel around it. Drizzle with the anchovy sauce, then place the fish on top of the salad.

8 skinless plaice fillets,
    each about 5 ounces
2 fennel bulbs
4 tablespoons
    extra virgin olive oil
3 garlic cloves
3 tablespoons milk
10 anchovy fillets in oil
4 teaspoons sunflower oil
1 head of Castelfranco radicchio
    (see above) or a large bunch
    of arugula
juice of 1 lemon
salt and pepper

Sardine con panzanella

Sardines with bread salad

Panzanella is a very old Tuscan tradition – a salad made with leftover bread, which would be unsalted, in the local style. It is a summer dish, which you would make when tomatoes and basil were good and plentiful. If you want to make it the day before you eat it, the flavors will have longer to infuse and it will taste even better.

When you cook the sardines, it is very important to get your griddle pan really hot; otherwise the sardines will stick and you won't be able to turn them without breaking them up.

12 large sardines
5 tablespoons
    extra virgin olive oil

For the panzanella:
7 ounces (about 7 slices
    $4\frac{1}{2} \times 3\frac{1}{4} \times \frac{3}{4}$") stale
    Tuscan bread or ciabatta,
    without crusts, torn up
4 tablespoons
    white wine vinegar
3 tomatoes on the vine
1 large red onion,
    cut into $\frac{3}{4}$-inch dice
big bunch of basil
5 tablespoons
    extra virgin olive oil
salt and pepper

First, get a griddle pan smoking hot; otherwise the sardines won't release their fat and will stick to the pan.

To make the panzanella: soak the bread in the vinegar. Take the tomatoes from the vine, dice and add to the bread, together with the chopped onion. Tear the basil and add that too. Add the olive oil and season with salt and pepper. Stir together and set aside.

Scale and fillet the sardines (see page 94).

When all the sardines are prepared, season, brush with a little of the olive oil and put in the hot griddle, 6 at a time. Let them get crusty on one side (about 3 minutes), then turn over and do the same on the other side (about 2 minutes).

While the sardines are cooking, spoon some of the panzanella on each serving plate, then put the sardines on top, drizzle with the remaining olive oil and serve.

Paella on a motorcycle…

My last year in Paris was traumatic, an experience I have virtually blanked out of my memory. At the Tour d'Argent, we were expected to give everything, but got nothing back. At the end of service, even on Christmas Day, I would sit on a trash can eating two sausages, while people in the restaurant were paying half of what I earned for a portion of spinach à la crème. It felt so unjust. I told myself that my own restaurant wouldn't be this way. Your staff has to have quality in their lives. It is the people who make the restaurant, and if they are miserable, you have a miserable restaurant. After nearly a year, I woke up one morning and said: "That's enough."

I handed in my notice and, at first, the chef wouldn't accept it. He gave me such a hard time about wanting to leave I felt even more pressured, but I told myself, "If you don't want to work there, don't do it, they can't come hunting for you…" So I left and went back to Italy, totally depressed and unwell. I didn't even know if I wanted to cook anymore. I was smoking a lot and barely eating. I weighed nothing, and I was coughing all the time.

My mother took me to the doctor, and she and my grandmother were so worried about me, they thought I was going to die. But I got back on my feet, put on some weight, borrowed some money from my brother and took off with my good friend Mario on our motorcycles to travel around Morocco and Spain. Mario was a big guy and he loved food, so eating and drinking were our priorities. His father was a wealthy man, and he saw our trip as a last chance for two young guys to have some fun before knuckling down to proper work, and so he kept sending us money.

We had a brilliant time, lost in a completely different world, totally free, just us, our bikes and the clothes on our backs. We were reinventing ourselves every day in a different place, stopping wherever we wanted, usually where we were drawn to somewhere selling simple and inspiring food. On the way home we stopped in Barcelona – what a place! We met some girls and stayed on…so in the end the month we were supposed to be away had turned into nearly three.

When we arrived back in Italy my father said, "What are you going to do now?" and I didn't know. I felt totally out of the restaurant world, but I had regained what I had lost: the pure pleasure of simple, good food. Everything to do with cooking in that last year in Paris had been so impersonal, technical, so designed, so perfectly finished, yet I didn't remember one thing that I had eaten that had exploded in my mouth, that had made me say, "This is fantastic." It is something that happens to most chefs at some time in their lives: you spend so much time working with food that you become completely numb to the humble joy of eating it. You feel just like a machine. Now my senses were full of tagines and spices and tapas, but, most important, I had rediscovered the simple fact that you don't need a dining room filled with chandeliers – you can eat a great paella sitting on the back of a motorcycle and feel that the world is a wonderful place. But the summer was over and I was twenty-eight, no longer a boy, and there was pressure on me to get a job – in the north of Italy, remember, everyone works. I thought, "Now I must be able to do my own thing – but what? How?" When I look back, I think that so much that happens in your life is about luck; so much is about making your own luck, and sometimes everything comes together in a moment that is quite magical.

On this particular day, my cousin Stefano and I had been to Varese to buy a copy of the cookbook *Le Ricette Regionali Italiane* by Anna Gosetti della Salda, one of my favorite books, which sits alongside Artusi on my bookshelf at Locanda. Then we bought a big box of marrons glacés and ate them all on the way back in the car, while Stefano drove and I read him some of the recipes from the book. We started making up a menu for the restaurant I was going to have one day. For so long I had been writing menus in French; now I began to think of the kind of Italian food I would cook if I had my own place, and we got more and more excited about birds wrapped up in pancetta, served with polenta, all kinds of things… the menu is still there where I wrote it, on the front page of the book.

When we got back to Corgeno, we said to my grandmother, "Listen to this …," and as we started to read the menu, the phone rang. It was a friend from London, Mark Armstrong, whose mother was Italian. He told me a guy we knew, Mauro, was planning an Italian restaurant called Olivo, and he needed a chef. So I called Mauro and when he told me his ideas my only questions were "Where can I stay? And can I cook *my* kind of food?"

"…there was plenty of banter between butcher and customer… then it was down to business, as the meat was ordered bit by bit. First the lamb.
'Five chops.'
The five chops were carefully cut, laid out on the paper, shown to the *signora*, and then wrapped.
'Anything else?'
'Oh, I'll have four kidneys.'
The lady and the butcher went through the ritual again.
'Anything else?'
'Do you have any *spezzatino*?'
'Of course, *signora*. How much?'
She conferred with her husband.
'*Tre etti e mezzo*. No, make that half a kilo.'
And so on and so on for twenty minutes."

Matthew Fort, *Eating Up Italy*

One day a friend of our son, Jack, was at our house and I roasted a chicken. When I took it out of the oven, he looked at it and said, "What's that?" He had never seen a whole chicken before. He told me that he ate chicken all the time at home, but his mother always bought chicken breasts in a package from the supermarket. He was 14 years old, and yet somehow in his mind he had never made the connection between the pictures he had seen of chickens in farmyards and what he had been eating. You bought a package of chicken, a box of cookies, a bag of chips – what was the difference? He ate the roast bird and he loved it, but it was quite a shock to him to discover: "My God, I've been eating an animal for nearly fourteen years!"

I find it incredible that we teach our kids to speak French and German, and how to do algebra, but we don't teach them where our food comes from. So many barriers are put between the animal and the product that appears on the refrigerated shelves in the supermarket, so that what you have is a feeling of guilt-free food. To me that is wrong. I believe that kids should know that an animal has been killed in order to feed us, because that is the way we learn respect for the animals, and for the food we have. When my brother and I were growing up in Corgeno, we saw my granddad choose the rabbit to be killed, and we watched him do it, just as we saw the cow being shot once a week. Yes, there was blood, but we never looked on what we saw as anything bad, because we knew the love our granddad had for those rabbits while they were alive, and we knew that they were killed to feed our whole family. And when the vet came to supervize the shooting of the cow, we knew that everyone in Corgeno would have meat because of that animal.

Whenever I am out in the country with the kids, and my daughter, Margherita, sees a duck or a goose, she will say, "Oh, nice duck, nice goose…" and I will say, "Yes, nice and plump – that would feed three or four people really well," and I am only half joking, because it is important that the kids remember this is the way we survive.

Save the butchers

If we want to have a proper connection with our meat, we have to do everything we can to keep the tradition of good butcher shops alive. And I mean butchers of quality, not the ones who can't tell you where their beef or chickens come from, or who are just trying to compete with the supermarkets by cutting their prices. In Italy, butcher shops mostly still do well, because people are concerned about traceability. Just as a tomato isn't just a tomato to an Italian, we are also very choosy about the meat we eat. When I go shopping at home with my father, it takes hours, while he goes to this butcher for one particular piece of meat, somewhere else for another, because he thinks they source it or look after it better. Of course, he also knows everyone by name; so there must be a big conversation while the meat is being prepared and wrapped up in little paper parcels.

Even in places where supermarkets have killed off the local shops, what they often do is reemploy the butchers to run the supermarket meat counters, so you still have someone there who understands about the meat, someone with knowledge, so you can build up a relationship. Sometimes I think people feel more secure in a supermarket where the meat is portioned up with price tags, so they know how much their bill will be, but if you get to know your butcher, you can say: "This is how much I want to spend and who I am cooking for – what do you suggest?"

In Britain, the disasters of BSE, etc., have surely proved that everybody has to take responsibility all the way along the chain. Nobody must cut corners. Think about it: if you rear an animal in its natural habitat, with its natural feed, and slaughter it locally and carefully, you should have no problem. But in the name of profit and speed what do we do? We rear our animals intensively, we pump water into them to plump them up and fetch a better price, we inject them with antibiotics, not caring that if we ingest so many our bodies may become so exposed to them that one day, when we are sick and the doctor says, "Take antibiotics," they won't do anything for us.

When we compare prices of meat, we have to consider not why something seems expensive, but why its equivalent can be so cheap. How is it possible to rear a chicken properly, kill it, take off its feathers, hang it, etc., and then charge only a few dollars for it? It isn't possible; really, it isn't. Short cuts must be taken at the expense of the animals and the quality of the meat.

We have become so used to seeing bright red beef in vacuum packs in the supermarket that we are apparently suspicious of anything that looks dark. However, the meat is bright red because it has gone from the abattoir to the refrigerator as quickly as possible, as it is considered too expensive and time-consuming to hang it in the traditional way, so that it matures properly and its own natural enzymes work on the proteins and break them down. This is the process that makes the meat more

tender and improves the flavor – and turns the flesh dark red in the process. And I wonder how many people would buy processed meat if they knew that it had been mechanically processed – jet-washed out of carcasses of meat that have been intensively farmed.

At Locanda, we avoid the mainstream markets and buy only from suppliers we know and trust, many of whom have become family friends over the years. Often we buy directly from the farmers or producers themselves – our guinea fowl comes from a farm I discovered while out riding my motorcycle in the country one Sunday. It might not always give the kitchen the same continuity – if there are not enough guinea fowl one day then there are not enough, that's that. But we have always written our menus according to whatever we have that is special each day; and this intimate relationship with producers gives me total confidence in the sourcing of every piece of meat I serve.

We all have to get used to the idea of quality, not quantity. It is better to have meat only once a week, and make sure it is fantastic meat, than to fill ourselves up every day with cheap, carelessly reared meat. In Italy, of course, we are far more used to the idea of having meat only one day, then maybe pasta with tomato sauce another day, or risotto with saffron, or Parmesan or vegetables. Even many of our pasta dishes that involve meat, such as lasagne, use only a small percentage of meat – this is a pasta dish made with meat, not the other way around.

I come from a rural culture that embraces the idea of stretching a little meat a long way, so I can't understand why anyone would buy a package of chicken breasts that are good for one meal only, when you can cook a whole chicken, eat some, then use the rest in a risotto, to make a filling for ravioli, or soup, and keep the carcass for stock. It seems to me that everything sold in supermarkets is geared to giving people nice tidy fridges, but that isn't what good food is about. It is about fridges full of good things to eat, and that includes leftovers, little pots of this and that, which can be brought out again for the next meal.

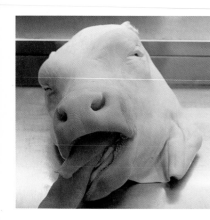

Nose to tail

When people think about Mediterranean food, they tend to envisage an abundance of fish, olive oil and vegetables. In Italy, though, despite the fact that a large proportion of the people either lived on the coast, or beside a lake, and had easy access to fish, many of the regional dishes that have been passed down are made with meat. When I first started researching old recipes, I was amazed to find that even in Campania, around Napoli, there were probably 200 recipes with pork, compared to 100 using fish.

Even in poor rural areas, there would usually be the chance to keep a few chickens or a pig, which would be made use of from nose to tail. Once the animal was killed, unless 200 people were coming to eat, you had to make it last, so curing became important, which is why there are hundreds of traditional hams, cured meats and boiling sausages, such as *cotechino* – made with pork rind, meat and fat, and flavored with cinnamon and cloves – and *zampone*, in which a similar mixture is stuffed into the skin of pig's feet. Everywhere you find recipes that use offal, or "variety meats," often in fillings for tortellini or ravioli, so that nothing from brains *(cervello)* to sweetbreads *(animelle)* and liver *(fegato)* would be wasted.

A traditional dish of Torino is the *finanziera*, made with all sorts of different pieces of chicken offal cooked in brodo; and then you have *fritto misto* (mixed fried morsels), which people in Britain sometimes think involves only seafood – and it can, if you are in a coastal area, but really it depends on where you are, and what is the local produce. A true rustic fritto misto can involve fried pig's feet, brains, sweetbreads and liver, as well as rabbit or chicken. Il grande fritto misto of Bologna is an extravaganza that also includes the likes of mortadella and skewers of pork, topped with *crema fritta* (fritters of sweet custard – see page 470).

I really like to cook offal – even if I hardly sell any in the restaurant. Maybe I couldn't get away with il grande fritto misto at Locanda, but we make a beautiful dish with sweetbreads (see page 495) and one with calves' brains (see page 494), which Italians consider a big delicacy because of their delicate flavor and creamy texture. In Milano, one of the traditional ways to serve them is fried (cervello fritto alla Milanese), while in the south, in Napoli, they bake them with olives, capers, bread crumbs and olive oil.

Long and slow

In many ways, the dishes that are most representative of Italian regional cooking are the stews, often made without much sophistication, using small quantities of humble cuts of meat. In the mountain regions, this would be sheep or goat, and in the flatter lands of the north, veal or beef (you couldn't farm cows in the Appenninei or the mountains of Liguria, or they would kill themselves falling down the steep slopes). Whatever meat there was would be stretched and supplemented by other local ingredients, and cooked slowly while everyone was at work in the fields or factories and the children were at school.

If you look at many of the old recipes from the north, where cattle were the big working animals, it is also clear that only when the beast had spent its life giving you milk and calves would it be slaughtered for food. A young animal gives meat with a fresh flavor, and its flesh has elasticity, so you can grill it quickly, whereas a slice of beef from an older animal that has been giving milk for ten years and worked all its life is going to need long cooking in order to achieve a similar tenderness.

A good stew is based on flavor exchange: the liquid, vegetables and herbs flavor the meat, and at the same time the juices of the meat flavor the liquid. It is very satisfying to stew a shank of beef that has been marinated for 24 hours in wine with some celery, carrot, onion or leek, cracked peppercorns, cloves and juniper berries, bay, and maybe even some cinnamon bark. After 24 hours, the process is simple. You separate everything into three elements: meat, vegetables and marinade. Then you pass the meat through some seasoned flour (about 1⅓ cups for every 2 pounds of meat), making sure it is well dredged, sauté a little pancetta or lardo in an ovenproof casserole, add the meat and brown it. Take out the meat, put in the vegetables, brown them briefly, return the meat to the pan, filter in the wine through a fine sieve, and put the casserole into a low oven for about 4 hours so all the flavors come together. In Lombardia, after about 2½ hours of cooking, it is traditional to put in some roughly chopped potatoes (skin on if you like), which will cook slowly in the thick sauce.

At home in Corgeno, though veal was much more usual at our table (along with pork, chicken and rabbit), my grandmother would often make beef stews in this way. I was so used to well-done beef that had been cooked very slowly that when I began cooking at Il Passatore and they put me in charge of the grill, I used to get complaints that the steaks were overcooked.

In Britain and America, despite the heritage of stews and casseroles, people seem less interested in these kinds of dishes, because everyone has been sold the idea of chops or steaks that can be quickly cooked. But if you invited me to your house and put a big pot of braised meat and vegetables on the table, I would be very happy. Yes, these dishes involve a bit of work in advance, but once they are in the oven, you are free to relax, sit with your friends, have a drink, and not worry about the cooking. And if you make enough to feed everyone three or four times over, you can freeze some for later.

Vitello
Veal

In Lombardia and Piemonte, veal *(vitello)* was traditionally a specialty. I never saw steak tartare when I was younger, but we would often have a dish of raw veal *(carne cruda)*. The raw meat would be very finely chopped, using two knives, then dressed in a little extra virgin olive oil, with black pepper, maybe some lemon juice, sometimes a touch of anchovy or some shavings of Parmesan or truffle – but never chiles or Tabasco. Our family used to go to a local restaurant where this was the specialty, followed by tortelli with ricotta and spinach, and then the local freshwater fish, lavarello.

Lombardia is also famous for its veal dishes, such as osso buco, costoletta alla Milanese (chops), *piccata* (floured veal medallions, fried in butter with various sauces) and *vitello tonnato*, in which the veal is covered with a sauce made from tuna, anchovies, capers, cream and lemon. This is the dish my grandmother used to make to eat cold when we went on a special Tuesday each year to the sanctuary at Madonna di Oropa, in Biella in Piemonte, where the Madonna was supposed to perform miracles.

Each year my grandmother would ask for something and make a promise that if it happened she would be back again the next year. So, on this special day, the whole family would go to the church and take a big picnic. It was very different from the spontaneous eating outside that we were used to for half the months of the year. My dad would bring tables and chairs, and often a portable barbecue. One time we had a whole cured leg of goat, and always grissini, salami, lots of antipasti and my grandmother's vitello tonnato. She would layer up the slices of cooked veal, with sauce in between each layer, pour the last of the sauce over the top, and then pack it into a container, so that every slice you took was enveloped in sauce – so beautiful.

Another dish from Milano is *messicani* (meaning "Mexicans," probably because they look like tacos), in which the slices of veal are wrapped around a mixture of sausage, Parmesan, eggs and nutmeg, secured with skewers and sautéed in butter, with sage and a little Marsala – you often see it served with risotto alla Milanese. In Liguria they are known for pan-roasted veal with sage and white wine, or *tomaxelle*, veal rolled around a filling of mushrooms, pine nuts, eggs and bread crumbs, and cooked in tomato sauce. In Emilia-Romagna, veal is often cooked in milk. At one time in Italy you would rarely find veal anywhere further south than Emilia – with the exception of Roma, where they do their famous *saltimbocca*, the flavors of which are supposed to "leap in the mouth," which is what the name means. Saltimbocca are simply thin slices of veal and prosciutto, rolled up with a sage leaf, skewered and pan-fried.

For some time now, veal has been out of fashion, particularly in Britain and America, because of concerns about the welfare of veal calves, kept alone in cramped "crates" (illegal in Britain and America, soon to be outlawed by the EU) or in "group housing" in small uncomfortable pens. However, the true mountain veal calves of the north of Italy are allowed to wander free all their lives, and many people are going back to rearing it, thanks particularly to support from the Slow Food movement. Mountain veal are lovely small animals, with a beautiful gray, silvery mantle. I remember, as a child, picking up the calves and playing with them. Because they are free, and have a normal diet rather than a milk-based feed, they have a muscle structure that is firmer than the Dutch veal people have come to know, and the meat is pink rather than white and more flavorsome – closer in taste to beef. Also, it contains much less water, so it doesn't shrink when you cook it.

La Chianina

Along with veal chops, the most famous prime cut of Italian meat is the massive Florentine steak, bistecca alla Fiorentina, which must be at least two finger-widths thick and weigh at least 800g (28 ounces), and is traditionally chargrilled (Artusi insisted they should never be dressed with oil before cooking, or they would "taste like snuffed candles" and be "nauseating").

The very best bistecche use Chianina beef. We can't talk about Italian meat without mentioning the huge, beautiful porcelain-white Chianina, one of the oldest – and biggest – breeds of cattle in the world (the most famous bull weighed 1.7 tons), which take their name from the Chiana Valley in Toscana. These are the strong working cattle used by the Romans, written about in their poems and carved in sculptures. When you go to museums in Italy, you will see the Chianina in paintings. They were lost for a while, when people turned to other breeds, but then rediscovered in a big way in the eighties and, along with the Romagnola and the Marchigiana, other breeds of white cattle, they are now raised specifically for their meat, and come under the collective name of Vitellone Bianco dell'Appennino Centrale, which have been given Indicazione Geografica Protetta (protected status) by the EU. The Chianina has a fantastic flavor and an exceptional marbling of fat, almost comparable to the famous Japanese Kobe beef.

The hunt

Personally, I don't enjoy hunting – unless it is for porcini or truffles – but for most Italians, especially in my native Lombardia, the culture of hunting for game is very strong. People travel over the world to hunt and no one feels ashamed to have the heads of animals stuck on their walls as trophies. In the mountains above Corgeno, the locals are so crazy for the hunt they shoot everything they see – especially little birds (some so tiny you could eat the bones), or larger ones like quail, which we would stew and serve with mounds of soft polenta.

I may not enjoy the ritual of hunting, but I love to cook and eat game birds. When we had a few pheasants, my grandmother would hang them and then we would have an entire meal from them. The legs would be cooked slowly and the meat shredded as a filling for ravioli, the breasts would be taken off and roasted for the main meal, and the carcass boiled up to make the soup that would start the feast.

When my granddad shot hare, we would marinate it and cook it in a rich red wine sauce. My brother, Roberto, and I used to be beaters for my granddad when he went out with his gun, and there is a famous story in our family about the day Granddad shot me accidentally, when I was only eight or nine. He was eighty-two at the time, and he put me on his back and ran all the way home – what a hero. I'll never forget his face when he got me into the house, and had to listen to me scream as my grandmother took out the pieces of shot with a pair of tweezers. The pain is not from the pellets but from the heat of them, which burns into your skin. I still have the marks on my thigh today. When my grandmother had finished, she turned to my granddad and said, "Now you go and tell Giuseppina and Ferruccio [my parents] that you shot Giorgio!" This is how to make a big man look small. After that she went to the carpenter and asked him to cut the barrels off the gun, but of course he couldn't cut the iron, so he sawed away half of the wood, which left a gun like the ones gangsters use.

It was left in the garage for about twenty years, until one day, after my granddad had died, my dad found it again, and thought it would be nice to put Granddad's gun back together. He called a friend for advice, and he told him that he had to register the gun again, because after all those years the licence would be lost. So my dad, in his innocence, walked into the *carabinieri* (the police station), carrying the sawed-off shotgun – and the moment they saw him, they put him up against the wall. Fortunately, the *maresciallo* (marshal) knew my father, who is one of the most honest people in the world. The idea of him going around with a gun, robbing people, is hilarious. So it was all sorted out, and eventually the gun was restored without my father ending up in jail.

One of the reasons I love game birds is that, unlike so much of the meat we eat nowadays, it is bursting with its own natural flavor, which means you must do as little as possible with it – a game bird roasted simply with a little rosemary is a fantastic thing.

In Corgeno and the villages around, the time of the hunt is another excuse to have a festival (at other times it might be to celebrate the harvest of the peaches, strawberries, asparagus, pumpkins…). It is a chance to have a big meal outside, with wine from the cooperative, and music and dancing, and everyone is involved; no matter who they are, the wealthiest or the poorest, people will bring or cook whatever is their specialty: maybe a salame, or a pasta, or a tart, and then there will be a big spit roast, perhaps a wild boar, or whatever birds have been shot, or a goat kid, marinated in lemon and oil, garlic, rosemary and a little sugar, so that the sugar and lemon caramelize on the skin as it cooks.

A note about cooking meat

Always bring the meat out of the fridge for an hour or so before cooking, to bring it up to room temperature, otherwise it will take longer than you expect to cook. This is especially important if you are quickly sautéing chops or steaks – the outside will sear and brown but underneath the surface the meat will still be cold and will take much longer to cook.

Season your meat just before cooking. Salt has great extraction properties, so if you salt the meat too early, it will start to sweat and its juices will leach out, whereas you want the meat to seal quickly as it starts cooking, keeping in all the moisture and juices.

When you are cooking meat in a frying pan or on a ridged grill pan, as we do in many of the recipes that follow, the same rule applies as for seafood – if you overcrowd the pan, it will lose heat and the meat will steam rather than sear. So it is better to cook one or two breasts of chicken, lamb, pork or veal chops, or veal or beef steaks at a time, if necessary. Before you start, preheat the oven to low (about 255°F – no higher or the meat will end up like the sole of your shoe) and put each piece of meat into the oven as you cook it.

With big joints of meat and whole birds, resting after cooking is especially important, to relax the meat again and let the juices flow through it. If I have roasted a chicken, I rest it with the breast down, so that this part of the bird becomes tender and moist. Even smaller cuts of meat that have been sautéed or grilled are better with a few minutes' resting.

Agnello primaverile alla griglia con peperonata e melanzane

Chargrilled lamb with peppers and eggplant puree

When I was growing up, I never saw spring lamb, but I have come to love its sweet flavor. Like so many of the recipes in our kitchen, this uses ingredients that all come into season together. There is a bit of French technique in use here. If I were making this in a purely Italian way, I would probably cook the eggplant and peppers together, but we have separated them, to concentrate the flavors (this way of cooking and pureeing eggplants, so that the seeds look a little like fish eggs, is also known as "eggplant caviar"). Beyond that, there are no tricks; the flavor comes simply from the freshness and quality of the ingredients.

2 eggplants (pale egg-shaped
　　ones if you can find them)
2 garlic cloves
sprig of rosemary
about ⅔ cup
　　extra virgin olive oil
1 onion, cut into
　　about ¾-inch dice
1 red pepper, deseeded and cut
　　into about ¾-inch dice
1 yellow pepper, deseeded and
　　cut into about ¾-inch dice
3 spring onions
1 tablespoon tomato paste
small bunch of basil
1 tablespoon tomato passata
4 lamb fillets,
　　each about 6 ounces
8 tablespoons Lamb sauce
　　(see page 497)
2 handfuls of mixed greens
2 tablespoons Giorgio's
　　vinaigrette (see page 51)
salt and pepper

Preheat the oven to 425°F. Halve the eggplants lengthwise, then place them on a work surface, skin side down. Using a sharp knife, score the flesh quite deeply at an angle one way and then the other way, to give a diamond pattern. Slice the garlic quite thick and slot the pieces into the cuts in the eggplants at random – about 2 pieces per half of eggplant. Push some leaves of rosemary into some of the other slots. Put the halves of eggplant back together, so that you now have 2 "whole" ones again, and wrap in foil. Put on a baking tray and put in the oven for 25 to 30 minutes (the eggplants need to be well cooked – if you push your finger against them, it should make a dent).

While the eggplants are cooking, heat a saucepan, add 2 tablespoons of the olive oil, then put in the onions and cook gently for about 5 minutes, without allowing them to color. Add the peppers, season and cover with a lid. Cook for about 10 to 15 minutes, checking every now and again. The peppers should be just soft, neither mushy nor crunchy. Take the pan off the heat and keep to one side.

When the eggplants are cooked, remove the foil, then take out the garlic and rosemary. Spoon out the eggplant flesh into a colander and leave to cool and drain. When cool, chop it fine.

Heat 2 more tablespoons of the oil in a saucepan, add the spring onions and cook gently for a few minutes, then add the chopped eggplant flesh and the tomato paste, and cook for about 5 minutes. If you feel the eggplants are still too wet, continue cooking a little longer until they lose their moisture. Season.

While the eggplants are cooking, put the pan containing the peppers back on the heat. Add the basil and tomato passata, and simmer to let any excess liquid evaporate (take care not to overcook

the peppers – if they start to get soft, just strain off the excess liquid instead). Stir in 2 tablespoons of olive oil.

While that is simmering, heat a griddle pan until smoking. Season the lamb and brush with a little of the olive oil. Put the lamb on the griddle pan and cook for about 2 minutes on each side, depending on the thickness (this will give pink meat, so cook longer if you prefer). Take off the heat and keep warm.

Warm up the lamb sauce in a small pan. Season the salad leaves and toss with the vinaigrette.

Spoon the eggplant puree onto one side of the warmed plates, put the peppers in the middle, and the salad on the other side.

Slice the lamb, if you like, or leave the fillets whole, and place on top of the peppers. Spoon 2 tablespoons of lamb sauce per person over the meat, and finally drizzle a tablespoon of extra virgin olive oil over.

Stufato di agnello con peperoni

Lamb stew with peppers

When we buy lamb at Locanda, it is the whole animal, so we find ourselves with many different cuts, such as neck, which are perfect for stews. This is a great stew to make at home – you just have to remember that the meat needs to be marinated for a day in advance. I really like to marinate meat, which is something that has been done for hundreds of years, originally to preserve the meat and cover any odors if it was past its best. Of course, this is no longer the point; the idea is to tenderize the meat and add flavor before cooking. You can serve this with mashed potato instead of polenta if you prefer.

The day before, mix all the marinade ingredients together. Put the pieces of lamb into a bowl, cover with the marinade and keep in the fridge overnight.

Next day, drain the meat from the marinade. Pass the marinade through a fine sieve and set aside. Put the meat on a tray or large plate and season. Put the flour on another plate and use to dust the meat. Shake off any excess flour.

Heat a large saucepan until really hot. The pan needs to be big enough to hold all the meat at once, letting it all come into contact with the base so that it sizzles and forms a crust, rather than steaming (if necessary, use two smaller pans). Add the sunflower or vegetable oil, put in the lamb and cook quickly, until the meat is golden brown and crusty, then turn over and let the other side become golden and crusty as well. Turn the heat down and lift out the meat – keep it on a warm plate.

Add the chopped onion to the pan, stirring and scraping to pick up all the crusty pieces of protein that will be clinging to the base. Cook for about 5 minutes – the onions will color a little – adding an extra spoonful of oil if necessary (the pieces of meat left in the pan will tend to suck up all the oil). Add the strained marinade and reduce right down for about 10 to 15 minutes. Skim off any impurities (scum) that come to the surface, and continue to boil until you have a rich dark sauce.

Put the lamb into the sauce and stir to coat for a couple of minutes. Add the stock, bring back to a boil, skim again and then turn down the heat to a simmer for about 1 hour.

While the meat is simmering, make the polenta: put the milk and cream into a pan and bring to the boil. Whisk in the polenta and cook on a high heat for about 5 minutes until it thickens. Turn down the heat and cook for around 30 minutes, stirring every 5 minutes, until the polenta has the consistency of porridge.

8 lamb fillets,
    each about 3 ounces
about ⅓ cup all-purpose flour
about 3 tablespoons sunflower
    or vegetable oil
2 onions, finely chopped
6 cups Lamb stock
    (see page 267)
salt and pepper

For the marinade:
1 bottle of red wine
1 carrot
1 onion
1 celery stalk
1 bay leaf
2 juniper berries
2 black peppercorns
sprig of rosemary

For the polenta:
3⅓ cups milk
¾ cup plus 2 tablespoons
    double cream
⅔ cup polenta

For the peppers:
2 tablespoons
    extra virgin olive oil
1 onion, cut into
    about ¾-inch dice
1 red pepper, deseeded and cut
    into about ¾-inch dice
1 yellow pepper, deseeded and
    cut into about ¾-inch dice

While the polenta is cooking, prepare the peppers: heat a saucepan, add the olive oil, then put in the diced onion and cook gently for about 5 minutes, without allowing it to color. Add the peppers, season and cover with a lid. Cook for about 10 to 15 minutes, checking every now and again. The peppers should be just soft, neither mushy nor crunchy. Take off the heat.

When the meat is cooked, it will be soft and will flake to the touch. Lift it out with a slotted spoon, taking care not to remove too many onions at the same time.

Put the remaining sauce through a fine sieve and then back on the heat. Reduce until it has a coating consistency. Taste and adjust the seasoning, if necessary. Add the meat, bring back to the boil, then turn down to a simmer.

Season the polenta and put the pan containing the peppers back on the heat to heat through.

Spoon the polenta into the middle of warm serving plates, arrange the peppers around that, then spoon the meat on top of the polenta. Finish with the sauce, just before serving.

Polenta

I remember reading a story once in which a family from Abruzzo in central Italy met up with a family from the north, and the two mothers had a massive "discussion" about what to do with polenta. The woman from Abruzzo accused the other of making terrible slush that she wouldn't give to her pigs. Instead, she boasted about the fantastic yellow bread she made from polenta, which was traditional in her region.

In Lombardia, our loose polenta – I prefer to call it "loose" rather than slushy – is traditionally a staple of our diet. In the old days in some of the poorest areas of the north, you would take a piece of cured fat (*lardo*) from the pig and have it in the middle of the table, cook some polenta and then everyone would just touch their polenta to the lardo to flavor it, because that was all that they had.

During the Second World War, polenta was what everyone lived on. You grew corn to feed the animals, and to grind for polenta. The way it would typically be eaten would be with cheese and sautéed porcini that had been gathered from the woods in the mountains. Sometimes we serve a small portion this way as a starter in the restaurant. The polenta is cooked and left to set, so that it can be cut into slices, topped with slices of Taleggio cheese, and grilled so that the cheese melts. It makes me smile to see people tucking into such a dish at lunchtime in London, when it is something born out of keeping yourself warm after a day on the mountains, when it is twelve below zero.

In our house in Italy, Sunday is the day when we often make a whole meal around polenta. It is a big ritual, with my dad in charge. He is famous for his outdoor cooking – big barbecues with fish, prawns, baby chickens flattened out – and then on cooler days, the deep yellow polenta that he makes in a traditional *paiolo*, a massive copper pot, on the wood-fired stove my granddad built in the garden. (My granddad was someone who really couldn't stay in the house for very long, so he made a little wooden structure, with a table and chairs, so everyone could eat outside.) What is special about the polenta cooked this way is that the burning wood gives it a particular smoky flavor, which stays in your consciousness, like that of a truffle.

The polenta pot also seems to send out a signal to friends and family, who all mysteriously show up, so we end up with a big noisy gathering that goes on for hours, starting with the salami and bread and red wine that we share while the polenta is cooking.

Even after I have watched my dad make polenta so many times, it is still considered that I am only serving my apprenticeship. For 40 minutes, he is there in his big apron, tending the pot, folding and stirring with the big curved wooden stirrer that my granddad also made, making sure that the polenta bubbles slowly, like a volcano – erupting every now and then. Our family dog sits waiting for the little pieces to fly out of the pot.

She knows to wait a little – as they will be scalding hot – before she eats them up.

When the polenta is finally ready, my dad turns it out with great ceremony like an enormous cake onto a big white cloth. Then my mom will bring out the big ragù she will have made to eat with it. Often it is the typical meat sauce of our region, which we call *bruscitt*, made with beef coarsely chopped into small pieces, red wine and fennel seeds. These were traditionally put into the pot in a little muslin bag, so that they flavored the dish, but didn't go into it, because it was considered such seeds on your plate were like *mangià da buricu* – donkey food. When everyone has been given some, the cloth is pulled over the top of the polenta to keep it warm. At the end of the meal, it is sliced and served again, this time with creamy Gorgonzola, which melts into it, and then we must use up the "shirt" – the polenta that sticks to the side of the pot. You fill the pot with water, bring it to the boil, and it pulls away this fantastic crust, which we eat with sugar sprinkled over it.

If there is still polenta left over, it will be cut into slices and baked, fried, or layered up like a lasagne, with ragù and besciamella, and baked in the oven, to make polenta pasticciata. As always, nothing is wasted.

Traditionally, in Italy the emphasis has been on polenta with a little meat, whereas these days, in a restaurant, it must be the other way round, so at Locanda we think of our polenta as much more of an accompaniment. The ratio of polenta to liquid that we use is lower, and whereas my dad uses water, we use milk and cream, so that the finished polenta is much softer. I first began to make it in this way when I was cooking at La Tour d'Argent in Paris, where they wanted something with the flavor of polenta that would taste creamy and look elegant on the plate – crème de mais is what they called it.

Sometimes we also use the more subtle-flavoured polenta bianca, the white strain of polenta from Venezia, which is typical with fish. One of the ways I like to serve it is with a little stew of *seppia* (cuttlefish), tomatoes and peas.

Filetto di manzo, spugnole e patate

Beef chop with morels and potatoes

1 pound (4 sticks) butter
2 large red potatoes,
    preferably Desiree
sprig of rosemary
4 beef chops,
    each about 7 ounces,
    at room temperature
2 tablespoons vegetable oil
2 garlic cloves, chopped
11 ounces morels,
    rinsed and halved
½ wineglass of dry white wine
1 tablespoon chopped parsley
about 8 tablespoons Chianti
    sauce (see page 497)
salt and pepper

Preheat the oven to 475°F.

First make some clarified butter: put 1 pound of the butter into a tall, small-based pan and let it melt. Once completely melted, it will separate into two layers: buttermilk solids underneath and the clear, golden butter on top. Gently spoon this off and discard the rest.

Peel the potatoes and cut them into matchstick pieces, preferably using a mandoline grater. Put into a colander and season with salt, then squeeze gently for a couple of minutes, so that the salt is absorbed and they start to lose excess water.

Sprinkle on the rosemary and leave for 10 minutes more, until the potatoes have lost most of their moisture and have begun to darken in color.

Season the chops.

Squeeze out any excess water remaining in the potatoes. Add a ladleful of clarified butter and massage in with your hands. Heat a nonstick sauté pan, add another ladleful of clarified butter, put in the potatoes and press down into a rösti-like "cake." Keep cooking on a medium heat until the cake is golden underneath, then turn it over and cook until golden on the other side. Drain off any excess clarified butter, then turn off the heat.

While the potatoes are cooking, heat a frying pan, add the vegetable oil and slowly fry the chops for about 5 minutes on each side, until they start to color, then roll to the sides of the pan for a minute or so until they are colored all around. Take the pan off the heat and leave the meat to rest for 5 to 10 minutes.

Heat another pan, add half the remaining unclarified butter and chopped garlic, and cook without coloring for a few minutes. Add the morels and sauté for a couple of minutes. Then add the white wine, cover and let the liquid evaporate. Check the seasoning and adjust if necessary. Add the parsley and stir in the remaining unclarified butter.

While the morels are cooking, transfer the rösti and chops to the oven to heat through.

Heat the Chianti sauce through in a pan. Cut the rösti into 4 portions and arrange on the serving plates with the mushrooms. Serve the beef on top, with the sauce poured around.

Sottofiletto di manzo alla griglia con radicchio trevisano tardivo e polenta

Chargrilled beef sirloin with trevisano radicchio and polenta

This dish uses the most prized – and expensive – of the red radicchio, which is in season for a few months only (see the following page) and has a wonderful, very special flavor that is both sweet and bitter, but not as bitter as many of its relations'.

It is a very simple dish, based on Italian cooking at its best – just a few brilliant flavors coming together on a plate. Try to buy sirloin that has been well hung and has a good marbling of fat through it to keep it moist. And remember to take the meat out of the fridge an hour before cooking.

Preheat the oven to 425°F.

In a large pan, bring the milk and cream to the boil. Whisk in the polenta and cook on high heat for about 5 minutes until it thickens. Turn down the heat and cook for around 30 minutes, stirring every 5 minutes, until the polenta has the consistency of porridge.

While the polenta is cooking, heat a griddle pan. Cut each radicchio head lengthwise into quarters (or into halves if they are small), season with salt and pepper, brush with a little of the olive oil and fry until they color (about 4 to 5 minutes), turning them regularly. Take the radicchio out of the pan and put into a roasting tray. Turn the heat down under the griddle pan.

When the polenta is nearly cooked, season the meat, brush with a little more olive oil and sprinkle with the rosemary. Turn the heat up under the griddle pan and put the steaks on it. Cook for a couple of minutes on each side (depending on the thickness) for medium-rare meat; more if you prefer. Because you have brought the meat up to room temperature before cooking, it will cook very quickly – so keep an eye on it, to make sure it is cooked as you like it.

While the meat is cooking, put the radicchio into the oven.

When the meat is just ready, quickly spoon the polenta onto warmed plates, arrange the radicchio alongside it and put the steak in the middle. Drizzle with the rest of the olive oil.

3⅓ cups milk
¾ cup plus 2 tablespoons heavy cream
⅔ cup polenta
2 heads of trevisano radicchio
about ⅓ cup plus 1 tablespoon extra virgin olive oil
4 sirloin steaks, each about 7 ounces
sprig of rosemary, finely chopped
salt and pepper

Radicchio/cicoria

Radicchio/cicoria

Chicory/endive

The chicory family is a big, beautiful one that includes puntarelle from Roma, but the most fantastic and famous varieties are the red radicchio family from the Veneto, where a big fair is held every year to celebrate the crop. As far back as Roman times, Pliny the Elder wrote about radicchio, praising it for helping to purify the blood and stop insomnia. The main varieties are called after towns in the region and include the Castelfranco, which looks very different from its cousins. It is round and pretty, like a rose, with variegated creamy leaves that are speckled from pink to deep red. Then there is the Verona, which has quite full-shaped heads of bright red leaves with white ribs. The round Choggia's leaves look similar, but it is more like a red cabbage in shape; it is cultivated all year long, but has a less concentrated flavor than other varieties.

The most famous and oldest variety is the Treviso, with its long pointed leaves, which now has protected PGI status so it can be cultivated only in Treviso and a few towns outside Venezia and Padova, and should be labeled Consorzio Radicchio di Treviso. Treviso comes in two varieties: the early plant is called *precoce*, but the best, because of its more pronounced bitter-sweetness, is the late radicchio, the *tardivo*, which is also known as the "winter flower" and is in season from Christmas to Easter. You can recognize it immediately, because the heads look like tall chef's hats, with their trimmed roots below the heads of long closed leaves, and their strong white ribs.

What is so special about the "winter flower" is the unique and intricate way in which it is harvested and its roots "blanched" in circulating spring water (a process called *imbianchimento*), which brings on crisp new bright red shoots. Everyone who grows radicchio in the Veneto has a well of spring water for the task. The plants start out green, then begin to turn a mottled red. After the first November frosts, the radicchio stops growing, its leaves turn brighter red, then tighten up and close. This is the time when the heads must be harvested quickly before more frost can damage them.

Whole families will be out in the fields at this moment, cutting them, then packing them in covered baskets in special sheds where they can be kept quite dark, while their roots are immersed in the constantly moving spring water. After around ten days, the radicchio begins to sprout new hearts of bright, wine-red, crisp leaves, with white ribs. When the new heads are mature (and a minimum weight of 3½ ounces), the plants are left to dry on sand or straw, and the outer leaves peeled away, to leave the fantastic red hearts.

Traditionally, radicchio was either eaten raw with lemon juice or vinegar and oil, or drizzled with hot pork fat and vinegar, as part of the antipasto. It might also be lightly griddled, with a sprinkling of salt and olive oil, and served with local sausage and polenta; with veal, chicken or beef; or put into pasta or risotto, along with local Montasio cheese.

Because it is such a beautiful leaf, chefs are endlessly fascinated by radicchio and, particularly in its native Veneto, you will find it used in every way, in every course, even desserts. Often you will find the shredded or whole leaves cooked in honey, and sometimes liqueur, or caramelized in sugar and served with poached fruit, baked in tarts with ricotta and crème pâtissière or mixed with mascarpone and ricotta and used to stuff cannoli (a biscuit mixture that is rolled up in tubes as it comes from the oven, hot and malleable). Radicchio is also typically conserved in brine, vinegar or a mixture of oil and vinegar, or made into a compote with orange juice and sugar. It is even used to flavor grappa.

Filetto di cervo, porcini e crema fritta

Loin of venison, porcini and fried pastry cream

We wanted to give an extra sweetness to the dish, so we added crema fritta, a typical thing in Mantova (similar to the custard fritters used in Bologna to top fritto misto). It is just crème pâtissière – the custard for desserts – except that it is very, very thick, so when it cools down properly (make it a couple of hours in advance), it becomes solid enough to be pan-fried. I know the combination of meat and fried custard might sound strange, but it is brilliant. When you are ready to serve, cut the crema into shapes, dust in bread crumbs and quickly pan-fry in a little butter until golden.

If you don't want to make the red wine sauce, add a little of the marinade to the pan after you have cooked the meat, bubble it up to thicken, scraping the pieces of meat from the bottom, and whisk in a pat of butter. We serve this with a salad of shredded radicchio, dressed with vinaigrette.

1¾ pounds lean loin of venison
2 tablespoons vegetable or
     sunflower oil
¾ cup plus 1 tablespoon butter
2 garlic cloves, chopped
11 ounces dried porcini (ceps)
     (see page 239 for
     preparation)
½ wineglass of dry white wine
1 tablespoon of chopped parsley
8 tablespoons Red wine sauce
     (see page 497)
salt and pepper

For the marinade:
4 cups red wine
1 white onion, roughly chopped
1 carrot, roughly chopped
1 celery stalk, roughly chopped
1 bay leaf
1 sprig of rosemary
4 juniper berries
2 black peppercorns
2 garlic cloves

For the crema fritta:
5 egg yolks
¼ cup sugar
⅔ cup flour
1 heaping tablespoon cornstarch
2 cups plus 1 tablespoon milk
3–4 tablespoons dry bread crumbs

Put the venison into a container with all the marinade ingredients and leave to marinate for a couple of days in the fridge. (If you like the flavor of juniper and want to intensify it, crush 2 of the berries first – but remember, it has a very strong taste.)

A couple of hours before you need it, take the venison out of the fridge and pat it dry or wrap in a cloth. Discard the marinade.

Preheat the oven to 475°F.

To make the crema: in a bowl mix the egg yolks with the sugar, flour and cornstarch. Bring the milk to the boil, then take off the heat immediately and beat into the egg mixture. Pour into a clean pan and cook for about 5 minutes, until the custard becomes very thick. Pour it into a tray, to come to a depth of about ½ inch, and leave to cool completely. (Incidentally, we also use this custard as a stuffing for pasta – though with a little less flour, so that it is softer.)

When the custard is cold and set, cut into whatever shapes you like and dust in the bread crumbs.

Heat an ovenproof frying pan and add the vegetable or sunflower oil. Put in the meat and cook for about 5 minutes on each side, then transfer to the oven for about 7 minutes (this will still be pink inside – if you prefer it better done, leave it in there a little longer). Bring out of the oven and leave to rest for about 5 minutes.

Meanwhile, heat a saucepan. Add half the butter and the chopped garlic. Add the mushrooms and sauté until soft. Add the white wine and cook until it evaporates. Season, add the parsley and set aside.

Heat the rest of the butter in a small frying pan. It needs to be hot so the crema fritta turns golden quickly (but be careful not to burn it) – otherwise it will start to melt.

Heat the red wine sauce in a separate pan.

Put the venison on a cutting board and slice it as thickly as you like. Arrange some mushrooms on each of 4 warmed plates, with the slices of meat on top and the crema fritta on the side. Pour the sauce around.

Costoletta di vitello con carciofi e patate novelle

Veal chop with artichokes and new potatoes

This is best done with veal stock, but if you don't have any made, use chicken or vegetable stock instead. If you prefer, you can use pork chops. Wrap each one in 2 slices of pancetta, then put into the oven for at least 6 minutes, or until the juices run clear when you pierce the meat.

8 new potatoes
8 baby artichokes
⅓ cup white wine
⅓ cup white wine vinegar
1 tablespoon sea salt
2 tablespoons sunflower or
    vegetable oil
4 large veal chops
4 tablespoons
    extra virgin olive oil
1 garlic clove, chopped
½ wineglass of white wine
¾ cup Veal stock (see page 266),
    or use vegetable or
    chicken stock
2 tablespoons unsalted butter,
    plus a little more for
    dotting the chops
handful of chopped parsley
salt and pepper

Preheat the oven to 465°F.

Cook the potatoes whole and unpeeled in salted water for about 15 to 20 minutes, until slightly undercooked. Take off the heat, leave to cool down in the cooking water and then drain and peel. Cut in half and keep to one side.

Clean the artichokes as described on page 70. Blanch them in the white wine, with the white wine vinegar, ⅓ cup water and the sea salt for 4 to 6 minutes, until tender but still slightly crunchy. Drain and leave to cool.

Get a large sauté pan (that will transfer to the oven) medium hot on the burner. Put in the sunflower or vegetable oil, season the veal and put the chops in the pan. Sauté until golden on all sides (a couple of minutes on each), making sure you keep the heat up inside the pan; otherwise the meat will steam rather than sear. Take them out of the pan and keep in a warm place.

In the pan in which you have seared the veal, heat 2 tablespoons of the olive oil, then put in the garlic and potatoes and cook until the potatoes are golden and crusty – don't worry if they break up a little. Add the artichokes and toss around for a couple of minutes until heated through. Add the wine, and allow the alcohol to evaporate. Add the stock and boil for 3 to 4 minutes. Season and turn the heat down.

Dot the chops with butter and put in the oven for about 2 to 3 minutes.

Meanwhile, add the 2 tablespoons butter to the potatoes – the mixture should now be quite soupy. Add the chopped parsley, spoon onto your warmed plates and drizzle with the remaining extra virgin olive oil.

Take the chops from the oven, place on top and serve.

Scaloppine

"The 'fish fingers' of my mother's generation"

One of the most typical things cooked all over Italy is *scaloppine*. You go to your butcher and ask for these thin slices of meat (it could be pork, beef or veal), which are cut against the grain, then the butcher will beat them even more thin with little meat pounders. You take them home and cook them quickly in a sauté pan, and finish them off in a sauce, with whatever you have – maybe some wine, tomatoes or lemon juice.

Scaloppine were the "fish fingers" of my mother's generation; something that became especially popular in the sixties, when women started to work more and needed something quick to cook, because scaloppine meant that you could have dinner on the table in 15 minutes. My mother used to sauté some artichokes first, dust the scaloppine in flour and sauté them, then add a little wine and cream. Sometimes she used to make scaloppina alla Milanese with breaded veal – baby versions of costoletta alla Milanese – and my brother, Roberto, and I would have competitions to see who could eat the most. Now Roberto's children eat the same thing.

One of the most typical ways with scaloppine is "al limone," with lemon and white wine, which you can easily make a version of yourself by buying a thin piece of veal, pork or beef and pounding it until it is about ¼ inch thick. Flour it, then put it into a very hot pan with a little oil (it is best to use vegetable oil, which you can heat almost to the point of smoking), and cook it through quickly on each side. Then, if you like, you can add a pat of butter – it is best to do this at the end as, if you use butter from the beginning, it is easy to burn it.

When meat is done, take it out and let it rest for a moment while you work sauce in the pan. Add some wine, let it reduce down, then add lemon juice, reduce it some more and season. Now you can turn off the heat and put meat back into the sauce – be careful not to let it boil or the meat will become tough – heat it through, and that is it.

Paillard di pollo con spinaci

Chargrilled chicken breast with spinach

This is a very simple thing to do – our equivalent of scaloppine, which just relies on fantastic-quality meat. Instead of the spinach, you could serve the chicken with broccoli, potatoes…whatever you like.

If you prefer, you can substitute chicken breasts for baby chickens, or even use poussins, opened out (we call them *galletti*). In Italy, there is a tradition of doing this with a brick on top to keep the flesh flat, which helps them to cook evenly and keep their shape. We call this *pollo al mattone* (*mattone* means "brick"). Start them off skin side down, for 5 to 7 minutes or more, depending on the size.

Halfway through cooking, once the skin has been marked by the grill, turn the birds 45 degrees, so that the marks form a diamond pattern. Then turn them skin side up and repeat until they are cooked through. This is a great thing to do on the barbecue. It was a favorite of my father's when we were growing up – he used to marinate the chicken first in olive oil, lemon juice, flakes of dried chile pepper and, later, an ingredient I introduced him to – Worcestershire sauce.

We also do this recipe when we find good veal, or you could use sirloin steaks. Ask your butcher to slice 4 steaks about ¾ inch thick, from the top side. When you pound out the veal, don't do so between sheets of plastic wrap, as you do with chicken. Chicken is quite a soft meat, so it needs this protection, otherwise it would disintegrate, but veal is a more solid meat, so you need to break up the fibers and tenderize it a bit more, which you won't be able to do through the protective plastic wrap.

Put the steaks on the griddle, and cook in the same way as for the baby poussin, but try to cook it only quite rare, unless you really don't like rare meat – i.e., turn it as it marks, then, once you have the diamond pattern, turn it over onto the other side right away. We often serve chargrilled veal with a salad of arugula and tomato, or a pesto made with arugula, and some oven-dried tomatoes.

4 boneless chicken breasts
with the skin
4 handfuls of spinach
½ cup extra virgin olive oil
handful of chopped parsley
1½ tablespoons butter
1 lemon
salt and pepper

You want to start off with chicken breasts that are equal in thickness all the way through. To do this, take off the skin and lay the breast on a cutting board (with the side that had the skin on downward). Lift up the fillet and lay it down on the other side of the breast. Then with a sharp knife, make an incision down the opposite side of the breast to the fillet, starting at the top (the thickest part) and working down, so that you can open this part of the breast outward, like a book.

Put each breast in between pieces of plastic wrap and, with a meat pounder, flatten very gently (as the meat is fragile) to about ¼ inch thick.

Blanch the spinach in boiling salted water for 5 seconds, drain and refresh under cold running water, then squeeze out the excess moisture.

Heat a griddle pan until smoking. Lay the chicken breasts on a large plate or tray, brush with a tablespoon of the olive oil, season and sprinkle with half the parsley. Turn them over and brush the other side with another tablespoon of olive oil, season and sprinkle with the rest of the parsley.

Put the chicken breasts, one or two at a time, on the griddle pan. Cook on one side until you see the heat has come almost all the way through, turning the flesh white, then turn over and cook for another 30 seconds or so (if you are cooking in batches, keep the cooked breasts in the oven).

While the chicken is cooking, put the spinach in a saucepan with the butter and 3 tablespoons of olive oil, and warm up gently without frying.

Cut the lemon into quarters and put on your warmed plates. Spoon the spinach onto the plates and place the breasts to one side, then drizzle with the remaining olive oil and serve.

Pollastra bollita al tartufo nero di norcia, vegetali bolliti e salsa verde

Poached chicken stuffed with black truffle, with boiled vegetables and salsa verde

If you are making this for 2 people, buy a whole chicken, take the breasts off and use the carcass to make the stock (see page 264). You could either roast the legs for another recipe, or do as we do at Locanda and use the leg meat to make some tortellini (see page 190, substituting the chicken leg meat for the breast meat). However, if you just have chicken breasts and you have some chicken stock already made, you can do this simpler version.

The dish, complete with tortellini, was the idea of one of my chefs, Marco Torri, who based it on the way of cooking chicken for *bollito misto* (just one of a selection of boiled meats) – which is a crazy thing to do at home unless you happen to have about eighteen people coming for dinner. At the restaurant we cook the chicken breasts *sous vide*, which is a method developed in France and pioneered in the UK by the Roux brothers, in which ingredients are hermetically sealed in a pouch and then poached very gently, so that all the cooking juices stay inside. Since you need a special machine to make the pouches, you obviously can't do this at home, but if you wrap the chicken in plastic wrap, it helps to protect the chicken and keep it moist and tender. Or, of course, you can just poach it in the traditional way.

4 chicken breasts
small black truffle, thinly sliced
¾ cup plus 2 tablespoons
      chicken stock (see page 264)
1 carrot, sliced
1 celery stalk, chopped
8 baby new potatoes
Chicken tortellini
      (see page 190, optional)
Salsa verde (see page 132),
      to serve
salt and pepper

Insert a sharp knife under the skin of each chicken breast and make a pocket. Slide in some slices of black truffle.

Season the chicken breasts and wrap them in plastic wrap. Bring a pan of water to the boil, put in the chicken, reduce the heat and simmer for 12 to 15 minutes until cooked (check that the juices run clear when you pierce the thickest part of the meat).

In the meantime, bring the chicken stock to the boil in a separate pan, add the carrot, celery and new potatoes, and cook until tender. If using tortellini, add these to the pan for the last 4 to 5 minutes.

Slice the chicken and arrange in large soup plates. Lift out the tortellini, if using, from the pan, add to the plates and then ladle out the vegetables and stock. Serve with the salsa verde on the side.

Filetti di maiale con cavolo nero e fagioli

Pork chops with black cabbage and cannellini beans

I never saw cavolo nero, black cabbage or Tuscan kale, which is a native of Toscana, until I came to London. The cabbage doesn't look black at all when it is raw – it is a dark green color – but once it has been cooked properly (for around 40 minutes) it turns completely black – don't listen to anyone who suggests just blanching cavolo nero briefly, because such short cooking doesn't bring out the full flavor or soften the bitterness.

If you want to save time, you can cook the beans – and even the cavolo nero – the day before; it won't affect the flavor. In fact, many people would say that both beans and black cabbage taste even better a day after cooking.

Sometimes, when chestnuts are in season, from late September to the beginning of December, we use them instead of the cannellini beans. We take about 16 to 20 chestnuts in their shells and make an incision in each shell. Then we lay them on a sheet of foil on a baking tray, pour on 3 tablespoons of water, close up the foil to make a parcel and cook in an oven preheated to 425°F for around half an hour, so that the chestnuts steam inside the parcel. Then we take them out, wrap them in a clean cloth and leave them to cool down for 5 to 10 minutes, until they are cool enough to touch. We peel them – if some break up, it doesn't matter – then we warm them up in a pan with a little butter and water, so that some of the chestnuts break up and they become creamy.

First cook the beans, with the garlic, celery, sage and half the olive oil, as described on page 183. Leave to cool in the cooking water.

While the beans are cooking, chop 4 slices of the pancetta and put into a large dry saucepan with the onion. Cook with the lid on for about 10 minutes, until the pancetta slowly crisps up and the onion softens without coloring, then add the rest of the olive oil.

Pull the cavolo nero leaves from the base of the stalk. (Unless the leaves are covered in earth, don't wash them.)

When the onions are soft, add the cavolo nero to the pan, cover and "stew" gently for about 40 minutes until the cabbage is completely black.

While the beans and cabbage cook, heat the oven to 465°F.

Get a large sauté pan (that will transfer to the oven) medium-hot on the burner. Add the sunflower or vegetable oil, season the pork chops and put into the pan. Sauté until golden on all sides (a cou-

1¾ cups fresh cannellini beans, or ¾ cup dried cannellini beans soaked in cold water for 24 hours
3 garlic cloves
1 celery stalk
small bunch of sage
4 tablespoons olive oil
10 thin slices of pancetta
1 onion, chopped
2 heads of cavolo nero
2 tablespoons sunflower or vegetable oil
3 large pork chops
8 tablespoons Pork sauce (see page 497)
salt and pepper

ple of minutes on each), making sure you keep the heat up inside the pan; otherwise the meat will steam rather than sear.

Meanwhile, lift the beans from their cooking water into a separate pan. Add a couple of ladlefuls or so of the cooking water – just enough to cover the beans (the water will be quite glutenous). Warm up the beans and season generously with pepper and normally with salt.

Transfer the pork to the oven for a couple of minutes, then take out and leave in the pan for about 5 minutes to let the meat rest.

Heat the sauce. Season the cavolo nero and put the pork back into the oven for 2 to 3 minutes to heat through.

Arrange some cavolo nero on warmed plates, spoon the beans around and drizzle with the rest of the olive oil. Take the pork out of the oven and slice at an angle into chunks about 1¼ to 1½ inches thick. Arrange on top of the cavolo nero, pour the sauce over and serve.

Filetto di maiale con crosta di mostarda e borlotti

Pork chops with mustard crust and borlotti beans

The crust here, which is made with *mostarda di Cremona* (see page 482), gives a nice crunch to the meat and protects its interior texture. If you are using dried beans, first soak them for 12 hours in cold water out of the fridge (see page 183). If you can't find cime di rapa (broccoli rabe), you could use broccoli.

First cook the beans with the whole garlic cloves, celery, sage and 2 tablespoons of the olive oil, as described on page 183, then leave them to cool in the cooking water.

Preheat the oven to 465°F. If you have a separate grill, preheat that too.

To make the crust, put the mustard fruits into a food processor and process until chopped, then add the bread crumbs and finally the butter. Everything should come together in a paste. Chill in the freezer for about 10 to 15 minutes.

Meanwhile, take the leaves of the broccoli rabe from their stalks and blanch them in boiling salted water for about a minute, to take away some of their bitterness. Drain and squeeze to remove the excess water. Chop the leaves very fine.

Take the mustard fruit mixture from the fridge. Lay a sheet of parchment paper on your work surface. Spoon the mixture on top, then put another sheet of parchment paper on top and roll over it with a rolling pin, until the mixture has flattened out into a sheet of paste just a few millimeters thick. Put back into the freezer.

Cut each pork chop in half across the width, then flatten each piece to a thickness of about 2 inches and wrap each one with strips of pancetta.

Heat a large ovenproof sauté pan until medium-hot. Put in the sunflower or vegetable oil, season the pork and put it into the pan. Sauté until golden on both sides (a couple of minutes on each), making sure you keep the heat up inside the pan; otherwise the meat will steam rather than sear. You may need to cook the pork in two batches (just keep the first batch on the side while you sauté the rest).

Put the chops into the oven (if you have cooked them separately, put them back together in one pan) for about 3 minutes. Take out of the oven and leave to rest.

1¾ cups fresh borlotti (cranberry) beans, or ¾ cup dried borlotti beans soaked in cold water for 24 hours
3 whole garlic cloves and 1 garlic clove, chopped
1 celery stalk
1 small bunch of sage
⅓ cup extra virgin olive oil
⅓ cup mustard fruits
½ cup bread crumbs
2 tablespoons butter, softened
2 bunches of broccoli rabe (cime di rapa)
4 pork chops
8 thin slices of pancetta
2 tablespoons sunflower or vegetable oil
1 green chile pepper, deseeded and chopped
2 tablespoons tomato passata
handful of chopped parsley
salt and pepper

Take the crust from the fridge and, working very fast (as it will soften up almost immediately), cut out 8 square or round pieces, roughly the same size and shape as each piece of pork. Put back into the freezer for a few minutes to harden again.

Lift each sheet of crust with a fish slice and place on top of each piece of pork, then put into the oven for about 4 to 5 minutes.

Put 3 tablespoons of the olive oil into a sauté pan, add the chopped garlic and chile, and fry for a few minutes until the garlic starts to color (but don't let it burn or it will taste bitter). Add the broccoli rabe and season. Toss around for a couple of minutes and turn the heat down.

Take the pork out of the oven and put under the broiler (if you have a combined oven-grill, turn on your grill to high and, as soon as it is hot, put the pork underneath). Grill until the crust becomes light golden (take care not to let it burn).

Meanwhile, lift the beans from their cooking water and put in a separate pan. Add a ladle or two of the cooking water and the tomato passata (the beans should be quite soupy). Warm through and then season with salt and generously with pepper.

Stir in the chopped parsley and spoon the beans onto warmed plates. Drizzle with the rest of the olive oil, then place the broccoli rabe on top. Take the pork from under the grill and arrange on top of the broccoli rabe.

Mostarda di Cremona

Mustard fruits

Mostarda di Cremona is the typical hot and sweet "mustard fruit" of Lombardia, traditionally eaten with boiled meats. It is made up of pieces of candied fruit, mixed with honey, white wine syrup, mustard and spices. Elsewhere in Italy you will find different versions: mostarda di Vicenza is made with apples, pears, quince and lemon, and in Sicilia they make a mostarda with grape juice, almonds, golden raisins and pine nuts, which is dried in the sun. Mostarda di Cremona is, however, the most famous.

In Italy if you go to markets or delicatessens they will have mostarda in big jars or pots, and you can choose the fruits you want (sometimes they will be whole, or cut into big chunks), so that you have a good mix of colors, flavors and textures, and then chop them down to the size you want before serving. My absolute favorite are the cherries – the boys have to stop me from eating them all in the kitchen, otherwise there would never be any in the mostarda that we serve in the restaurant. Cherries, pears and then apricots – those are my favorite mustard fruits. A fresh pear, some pear in mustard syrup, and Parmesan is a fabulous thing to eat; and a mixture of fruits is lovely with a fatty cheese like Taleggio.

If you buy mostarda di Cremona in jars, as opposed to loose, look for straight-sided jars, rather than ones with necks, or you can break the chunks of fruit as you lift them out. Make sure the fruit that is left in the jar stays underneath the syrup, and then it will keep for a long time, no problem. I would usually let the fruits sit in a colander for a while if you are just serving them as an accompaniment, to let some of the sweet syrup drain off, and bring out the flavor of the fruits more.

You can make your own, if you can find mustard essence – you need only the tiniest drop, so a small bottle will last you all your life. Be very careful when you use it – never smell it when you open the bottle (it will usually have a dropper to dispense the essence). It is so pungent, it is as if someone has put a lighted match up your nose, and it will cause real pain. If you can't find the essence, you can make a version using mustard seeds.

To make mostarda, choose your fruits, according to season: cherries, pears, apricots, apples, quince, small oranges, figs, plums. They need to be slightly firm and underripe. Make a syrup by putting equal quantities of sugar and of white wine and water into a large pan, bringing it to a boil, then simmering until it reduces and becomes thick (for around 4 pounds of fruit use 2½ cups sugar, 1 cup wine and 1 cup water). Wash the fruit, peel and core where necessary, and cut into large chunks. Add a drop of mustard essence (check the instructions on the bottle) to the syrup and stir. Put the different fruits in according to how hard they are and their size: for example, a hard pear will need longer in the syrup than a cherry. When the last fruit is in, bring the syrup back up to the boil, take off the heat and pack into hot, sterilized jars, making sure that the fruit is covered by the syrup.

Fegato di vitello al balsamico

Calves' liver with balsamic vinegar

I think of this as one of *my* dishes, with a sauce that is based on French rather than Italian technique, but with flavors that are truly Italian. You don't need to use the best-quality balsamic vinegar for cooking. In fact, if you use an expensive vinegar that has been aged, and therefore has a higher concentration of sugar, it might catch fire and burn while you are reducing the sauce.

small bunch of Swiss chard
2 tablespoons
    extra virgin olive oil
1 tablespoon sunflower or
    vegetable oil
8 pieces of calves' liver, each
    about 2½ ounces
6 tablespoons butter
1 cup balsamic vinegar
3 tablespoons pine nuts, toasted
3 tablespoons golden raisins,
    soaked in warm water
salt and pepper

Preheat the oven to 425°F.

Remove the leaves from the chard stalks. Blanch the stalks in boiling, salted water until just tender (about 3 to 4 minutes), drain and pat dry (this is important as you are going to put them into oil later). Put the leaves into the water for about a minute, drain and pat dry. Cut the stalks into thin batons.

Put the chard leaves and stalks into a pan with the olive oil. Turn the heat to low and gently warm these up.

Heat an ovenproof sauté pan until medium-hot, then add the sunflower or vegetable oil and put in the liver. Seal until crusty on both sides, taking care not to get the pan too hot or the liver might burn. Season.

Turn down the heat, add half the butter and put the pan into the oven for a minute or so, depending on the thickness and how you like your liver cooked (in the restaurant, we serve it medium-rare).

Take out of the oven, lift the liver out onto a warm plate, drain off the butter, add the balsamic vinegar to the pan and reduce by half, or until you have a syrupy consistency. Beat in the rest of the butter, add the pine nuts and drained golden raisins, then turn the heat down and put the liver back in.

Spoon the chard onto your warmed plates, place the liver on top and drizzle with the sauce.

Rognone di vitello con lenticchie e carciofi

Veal kidney with lentils and artichoke

This is one of my favorite dishes – the artichoke and lentils seem to give a new dimension to the kidneys, which are wonderful things and so underrated. If the kidneys smell a little strong, soak them in cold running water for a couple of hours before you use them. The seasoning here is very important. Don't season the kidneys before they go into the pan, or they will start to sweat and they won't caramelize on the outside when they are in the pan.

Occasionally, for a change, we serve kidneys cooked in this way with potato puree and porcini cooked as in the recipe for Roasted turbot (see page 428). When porcini are out of season, we might substitute red onions. Just cut 2 into 6 pieces each, stew them in a little olive oil until soft, about 10 to 15 minutes, then add about 4 tablespoons of white wine vinegar just before serving.

Soak the lentils in water for half an hour.

While they are soaking, finely chop the carrot, onion, celery and leek. Heat the olive oil in a pan and add the chopped vegetables and the piece of pancetta. Cook for 5 to 10 minutes until the vegetables are soft but not colored. It is important that the vegetables be soft, so that they release all their sweetness, flavor and moisture into the lentils.

Add the drained lentils and the bouquet garni, and cook for 5 minutes, stirring, until everything is well mixed and the lentils start to stick to the bottom of the pan. Don't season at this point, as salt will make the lentils harden.

Add enough vegetable stock to cover the lentils by a finger (keep the rest hot on the burner in case you need more), bring to the boil, then turn down the heat and simmer for 45 minutes until the lentils are soft, adding a little more stock if they begin to dry out. Remove the pancetta and set the lentils aside.

While the lentils are cooking, prepare the artichokes as described on page 70 and cut each heart into 6 pieces. Blanch these in the white wine and white wine vinegar, with ⅓ cup water and 1 tablespoon of sea salt, for 3 to 4 minutes, until tender but still slightly crunchy. Drain and leave to cool.

Heat a large sauté pan (or preferably two, so that the kidneys aren't overcrowded). Put in the sunflower or vegetable oil and add the kidneys, spreading them around so that they all touch the pan. Season, let them get crusty and golden on one side, turn them over and repeat on the other side.

2 globe artichokes
⅓ cup plus 1 tablespoon
    white wine
⅓ cup plus 1 tablespoon
    white wine vinegar
2 tablespoons sunflower or
    vegetable oil
1½ pounds veal kidneys, cleaned
    (see above), fat removed and
    sliced about ½ inch thick
wineglass of white wine
⅓ cup plus 1 tablespoon Chicken
    stock (see page 264)
3 tablespoons butter
handful of chopped parsley
salt and pepper

For the lentils:
1 cup lentils, preferably
    lenticchie di Castelluccio
1 small carrot
1 small onion
1 stalk celery
1 small leek
3 tablespoons olive oil
3½-ounce piece of pancetta
small bouquet garni (sprig of
    rosemary, small bunch of
    sage and 2 bay leaves, all
    tied together)
about 6 cups Vegetable stock
    (see page 268)
1½ tablespoons butter

While they are cooking, put the lentils back on low heat to warm through and drive off any excess liquid. Beat in the butter.

Lift the kidneys out of the pan and put in a sieve to drain off any excess liquid (you want the kidneys to be quite dry when they go back into the sauce; otherwise they will become tough).

Add the wine to the pan in which you sautéed the kidneys, and let it bubble up, scraping the bits from the bottom of the pan.

Add the artichokes and the chicken stock. Reduce the liquid by half, put back the kidneys and toss to heat them through. Beat in the butter, and you should have a creamy sauce. Add the chopped parsley and turn the heat down.

Spoon the lentils onto warmed plates, and spoon the kidneys and artichokes on top.

Anatra con broccoli

Duck breast with broccoli

If you can find broccoli rabe (cime de rapa), you could use it instead of broccoli for a change. Sometimes we do a variation with balsamic vinegar (about ⅓ cup) instead of Worcestershire sauce. We add the balsamic vinegar to the pan in the same way, let it reduce by half, then, instead of adding olive oil, we put in a couple of pats of butter, beat them in and continue with the recipe. Rather than the broccoli, we serve it with a mixed salad, dressed with Balsamic vinaigrette (see page 52). We also sauté the spelt with around 1 tablespoon of golden raisins and 1 tablespoon of toasted pine nuts.

4 duck breasts
4 tablespoons spelt (see page 184)
⅔ cup extra virgin olive oil
2 heads of broccoli, separated
   into florets
2 tablespoons
   Worcestershire sauce
2 garlic cloves, sliced
1 red chile, deseeded and sliced
salt and pepper

Bring the duck breasts out of the fridge an hour before you want to cook them.

Soak the spelt in cold water for 20 minutes, then drain. Preheat the oven to 425°F.

Bring a pan of water to the boil (no salt, as this will make the spelt harden), put in the spelt and cook for 15 minutes. Drain and tip on to a tray or large plate. Sprinkle with 2 tablespoons of the olive oil and toss around to coat the grains and keep them separate. Move them around every couple of minutes, so they don't stick together.

Blanch the broccoli in boiling salted water for about a minute or so, just to soften it. Drain and set aside.

Season the duck. Heat an ovenproof sauté pan to medium-hot, then put in the duck, skin side down (you don't need any oil, as the fat in the skin will melt), and cook until the skin turns golden. Turn over, cook for 1 minute, then turn down the heat. Take the duck out of the pan and keep in a warm place.

Drain the fat from the pan, add the Worcestershire sauce and 3 tablespoons of the remaining olive oil. Stir to emulsify and turn off the heat.

Heat a sauté pan, add the remaining olive oil, followed by the garlic and chile, and cook without allowing to color for a few minutes. Add the broccoli and sauté without allowing it to color, until just soft. Season.

In a separate pan, fry the spelt without any extra oil until slightly crisp (drain off any excess oil as you go). Season.

Put the duck into a roasting tray and put it in the oven for about 2 to 3 minutes, depending on whether you like it pink inside or more well done.

Spoon the spelt into the middle of warmed plates, and arrange the broccoli around it, with the oil from the pan. Take the duck out of the oven and slice it if you like, then place on top of the spelt and finish with the sauce.

Pernice con lenticchie e purè di patate

Partridge with lentils and potato puree

In Italy, we have both the red-legged and gray-legged varieties of partridge, as well as a special kind of red-legged one that you find only in Sardegna. However, the most common type are the gray ones – which are also farmed – but the red are the tastiest, so try to find them if you can.

Bring the partridges out of the fridge well ahead, so that they can come up to room temperature before cooking. Soak the lentils in water for half an hour.

Chop the vegetables finely. Heat half the olive oil in a pan and add the chopped vegetables and the pancetta. Cook for 5 to 10 minutes, until the vegetables are soft but not colored. It is important that the vegetables be soft, so that they release all their sweetness, flavor and moisture into the lentils.

Add the lentils and the herbs, tied together, and cook for 5 minutes, stirring, until everything is well mixed and the lentils start to stick to the bottom of the pan. Don't season at this point, as salt will make the lentils harden. Add 4 cups of stock (keep the rest

4 red-legged partridges,
    cleaned and trussed
1 cup green lentils (preferably
    lenticchie di Castelluccio)
1 white onion
1 carrot
1 celery stalk
1 small leek
4 tablespoons
    extra virgin olive oil
3½-ounce piece of unsmoked
    pancetta, sliced
sprig of rosemary
small bunch of sage
2 bay leaves
6 cups Chicken stock
    (see page 264) or Vegetable
    stock (see page 268)
2 large red potatoes,
    preferably Desiree
2 tablespoons sunflower or
    vegetable oil
⅓ cup milk
½ cup (1 stick) butter
4 tablespoons Partridge
    or Chicken sauce
    (see page 497)
handful of chopped parsley
salt and pepper

hot on the burner), bring to a boil, then turn down the heat and simmer for 45 minutes, until the lentils are soft and there is very little liquid left in the pan.

Remove the pancetta and keep the lentils on the side (keep the pan covered, to keep them from drying out).

While the lentils are simmering, cook the potatoes whole and in their skins in salted boiling water for about 45 minutes, depending on size.

Preheat the oven to 500°F.

Heat a large sauté pan (that will transfer to the oven) and add the sunflower or vegetable oil. Season the partridges and put them in the pan, first on one leg for about 3 to 3½ minutes, then on the other leg for another 3 to 3½ minutes. Next, turn the birds on their breasts for 4 minutes, then prop them up against the edge of the pan so that they are standing on their neck ends for another minute. Turn them onto their backs, turn off the heat and leave them to rest.

When the potatoes are nearly cooked, warm the milk in a pan. When the potatoes are ready, peel while still hot and pass through a very fine sieve. Put back into the pan and beat in a third of the butter and the warm milk (this should give a very smooth puree). Season with salt only and keep warm (if you cover the pan with plastic wrap it will keep the potato from becoming dry and crusty on the top).

Put the partridges into the oven for about 4 minutes and put the sauce into a small pan to warm through.

At the same time, return the pan of potato puree to the heat. Warm through and then beat in half the remaining butter.

Also at the same time, put the pan of lentils back on the heat and warm through. Make sure they are not too soupy; they should be risotto consistency (if necessary, drain off a little liquid), then beat in the rest of the butter, stirring all the time, to make sure they don't stick. If you need to loosen them at this point, you can add a little of the reserved stock. Stir in the parsley.

Spoon the lentils into the middle of your warmed plates, then spoon the puree around as you like. Take the partridges from the oven, remove the strings and place on top of the lentils.

Piccione, tartufo nero e purè d'aglio

Roast pigeon, black truffle and garlic puree

Because garlic is quite pungent, you need to soften the flavor slightly and make it more digestible, so we usually take out and discard the central shoot of the garlic, which is the strongest part and is usually tinged green at the top (it may be green all the way through, if it is spring garlic). Then we blanch the remaining garlic twice in boiling water.

Bring a pan of water to a boil, put in the garlic, leave it for a minute then remove with a slotted spoon and drain. Bring a pan of fresh water to a boil, put in the garlic for another minute, then drain again.

Pour the milk into a small pan and add the blanched garlic. Bring to a simmer for around 20 minutes, until the garlic is completely soft, then add the cream and keep on cooking for about 3 to 4 minutes. Take off the heat. With a hand blender, whiz the garlic to a creamy puree. Cover with plastic wrap.

Preheat the oven to 500°F.

Blanch the spinach in boiling salted water for 5 seconds (literally in and out), drain, refresh under cold running water, drain again and squeeze out excess water.

Put the spinach in a pan, add the olive oil and butter, and set aside (not on the heat at this stage).

Heat a large sauté pan (that will transfer to the oven) and add the sunflower or vegetable oil. Season the pigeons and put into the pan, first on one leg, for about 3 to 3½ minutes, then on the other leg for another 3 to 3½ minutes. Turn them on their breasts for 4 minutes, then prop them up against the edge of the pan, so that they are standing on their neck ends for another minute. Finally, turn them on their backs, turn off the heat and leave to rest for 5 to 8 minutes.

Meanwhile, put the sauce into a small pan and warm through. At the same time, put the pan containing the spinach over a low heat to warm through and season. Also put the pan of garlic puree back on the heat to warm through and season with salt only.

Put the pigeon back into the oven for 3 to 4 minutes to heat through.

Spoon the spinach into the center of your warmed plates, then spoon the garlic puree around. Take the pigeon from the oven, remove the string from the pigeons and place one on top of each mound of spinach. Finish off with the sauce, and either grate or slice the black truffle over the top.

10 garlic cloves, peeled
    and split in half
½ cup milk
3 tablespoons heavy cream
4 handfuls of spinach
3 tablespoons
    extra virgin olive oil
2 tablespoons unsalted butter
2 tablespoons sunflower or
    vegetable oil
4 oven-ready squab pigeon
4 tablespoons Pigeon or Chicken
    sauce (see page 497)
¾ ounce (about 2 inches around)
    black truffle
salt and pepper

Cervello

Brains

I know that many people feel nervous about brains – because either they make them feel squeamish or the BSE crisis has made them scared. If we look back into history, though, we can see that a very large proportion of the world's population has been eating things like this for thousands of years. I really believe we should eat everything from an animal; it doesn't make sense to eat only fillets and steaks, which make up only a small percentage. In Italy, just as I feel salumi represent the traditional food of the people, so too do the recipes for brains, kidneys and feet, since the prime cuts were for the rich people only. A dish of fried brains says more to me about Italian food than something like *tournedos rossini*, which is only the grand idea of a composer, not at all reflective of what the rest of the people ate.

Brains are very popular in northern Italy, to the point that people used to say that if you ate them, they would make you clever. That's what my grandmother used to say to my brother, Roberto, all the time, when he complained that they were soft and he didn't like the texture – even though she used to keep them in the oven until we came home, so they were really, really crispy on the outside. I always loved them; I thought the sweetness was fantastic, and I liked the quite weird way they were crispy and then so soft inside you didn't need to chew; they just disappeared in your mouth – a bit like arancini, the fried balls of risotto.

At Locanda, we don't often put brains on the menu, because not many people order them, but we have regular customers who love them, and we will always cook them for them, as a special. We serve them cooked in two ways, deep-fried and pan-fried, on either side of a big square plate (cervello fritto e al saltimbocca). To prepare the brains, you have to wash them gently under water, so that you can take the skin off. The ones that are going to be deep-fried are first passed through some flour, beaten egg and fine bread crumbs before they go into the hot oil. Next to them we usually serve a little salad and a very strong salsa verde (see page 132) made with more capers than usual.

We experimented for some time to find another, more unusual way of cooking the brains to serve alongside the deep-fried ones, and eventually came up with the idea of rolling them, like a cigar, inside a slice of prosciutto. Then we sauté them in a nonstick pan with just a film of oil, and a little butter towards the end, and serve them on a bed of stewed leeks, with a sharp Marsala sauce over the top. It is a dish that looks and tastes fantastic.

Animelle di vitello in agrodolce

Veal sweetbreads with sweet-and-sour sauce

Veal sweetbreads – we use the thymus gland of the calf rather than the pancreas – have a very delicate flavor, and so they are usually coated in flour, as here, or sometimes bread-crumbed, then fried and paired with a piquant sauce; or sometimes they are used in stuffings. In Roma, they are mixed with peas and used to stuff baby artichokes, which are then fried.

Some butchers sell sweetbreads with their protective, quite gelatinous membrane taken off, but mostly it will still be on, so the sweetbreads must be peeled. To do this, put them in a bowl under cold running water for around half an hour and the membrane should then come away easily.

Sometimes, instead of breaking up the sweetbreads, we cook them whole. We put a sage leaf on top of each one and wrap them in prosciutto, then sauté them. When the prosciutto is golden all round, we turn the heat down for 3 to 4 minutes, then take the pan off the heat and leave them to rest for 5 minutes before transferring to the oven for 3 to 4 minutes. When the sweetbreads are cooked through (i.e., springy to the touch), we serve them with chopped leeks cooked in butter until they are soft, and, when white truffles are in season, we grate these over the top of the sweetbreads.

Blanch the spinach in boiling salted water for 5 seconds, refresh under cold running water, drain and squeeze out the excess water. Put into a pan with half the butter and half the olive oil.

Blanch the whole carrots for a couple of minutes in boiling salted water, drain and leave to cool naturally, then cut at an angle into slices about ½ inch thick.

Preheat the oven to 480°F.

Crush the garlic with the back of a knife and put into a pan with the rest of oil, the bay leaf and the sliced carrots. Place over very low heat, cover with a lid and gently stew for about 10 to 12 minutes, until the carrots are soft. Take off the heat.

If the sweetbreads are still whole, gently break them apart (they will fall into pieces naturally). Season and dust with flour. Heat a large sauté pan (that will transfer to the oven), add the sunflower or vegetable oil and put in the pieces of sweetbread. Cook until golden on all sides, turn the heat down, leave for a minute, then transfer to the oven for about 3 minutes until cooked through. When they are ready, if you press them with your finger they should be springy, like a sponge cake.

While the sweetbreads are cooking, put the pan containing the spinach on to the heat to warm through, and season. Then put the pan containing the carrots back on the heat to warm through.

4 handfuls of spinach
1½ tablespoons unsalted butter
⅓ cup extra virgin olive oil
4 large carrots
1 garlic clove
1 bay leaf
4 veal sweetbreads, each about
    ¼ pound, peeled and
    washed (see above)
1 tablespoon all-purpose flour
2 tablespoons sunflower or
    vegetable oil
8 tablespoons Veal sauce
    (see page 497)
Agrodolce di capperi
    (see page 426)
salt and pepper

Take the sweetbreads out of the oven and let the pan cool down slightly, put it on the burner, pour in the sauce and heat through. Toss the sweetbreads in the sauce to coat. Take off the heat and carefully beat in the remaining butter, taking care not to smash the sweetbreads.

Spoon the spinach into the middle of your warmed plates and arrange the carrots around. Lift out the sweetbreads and spoon on top of the spinach. Then pour the veal sauce over the top. Finish with a tablespoon of agrodolce sauce over each plate.

Basic sauce for meat

This is a very simple all-purpose sauce that you can make plenty of and freeze in ice cube trays. Once the cubes are frozen, you can transfer them to labeled freezer bags, and you can then put them into a pan and heat them through without having to defrost them first. Using this basic method, you can make a sauce to go with all kinds of meat – chicken, beef, veal, pork, etc. – just vary the trimmings you use (see below). If you want a red-wine-based sauce, just add 1⅔ cups Chianti or other red wine at the stage shown in the method. When we make a partridge sauce, we add 1 cup white wine and, if we want to make an olive sauce, we add 20 good pitted black olives, just before putting in the vegetables. For a duck sauce, we leave out the vegetables, but add 2 or 3 extra cloves of garlic. Just be sure to have a big enough pan for all the trimmings to come into contact with the base, so that they seal rather than boil at the beginning of cooking.

Heat the pan to medium-hot, then put in the oil.

Just before it starts to smoke, put the trimmings into the pan a few at a time, making sure they all touch the bottom of the pan. Leave these to roast without touching them for 2 to 3 minutes, until they start to become golden underneath. Turn them until they are golden and caramelized on all sides, another 5 to 10 minutes. (If adding olives, do it now.)

Add the carrot, garlic and herbs, and leave to roast for another 2 to 3 minutes, then add the shallots and roast for another couple of minutes.

Turn down the heat, add the butter and let it foam without burning. (If adding wine, add it now and let it reduce until some of the alcohol has evaporated.)

Add the flour and tomato paste, turn up the heat again, and cook for a minute or so, until the temperature of the pan comes up again.

Add the stock, scraping the bottom of the pan with a wooden spoon. Bring to a boil, skim, turn down the heat and cook for about half an hour.

Pass through a fine sieve and reduce until you have a sauce consistency.

Makes about 3–4 cups

2–3 tablespoons sunflower or vegetable oil

1 pound meat trimmings (chicken, veal, pork, lamb, beef, venison, duck, pigeon, partridge), cut into roughly 1½-inch dice, at room temperature

1 carrot, diced into roughly the same size as the meat (make sure the dice are the same size so they cook evenly)

2 garlic cloves

1 sprig of rosemary

1 bay leaf

1 shallot, diced

1½–2 tablespoons butter

1 teaspoon flour

1 tablespoon tomato paste

6 cups good stock (chicken, veal, etc., depending on your meat; see page 264)

London to stay

When we moved house in London, I found a battered old red tartan bag in the attic that I had forgotten about for years. There were my diplomas and certificates; my first pay stub as a sous chef from the Savoy, and a banqueting menu dated on my birthday; a reference saying I had a courteous and gentle manner, and my contract at Le Tour d'Argent, along with a menu I kept after a visit to the famous restaurant Alain Chapel. There were photographs of the Wheelers Fish restaurant that would eventually become Zafferano, our first menu there; and the book I kept at Olivo, the restaurant I returned to London to help open. Everything is listed meticulously in that book: the design of the kitchen, how many covers we did every day, what we ordered.

The style I have now was born at Olivo. Part of me was still locked into the chic restaurants I had been cooking in for the last five years, but Mauro, who had formed a business partnership with a Frenchman, Jean-Louis, knew what he wanted. Olivo was a lovely little place. I helped sand the floors and paint the walls blue; we had no tablecloths and everything was very simple, just four of us in the kitchen – myself, Michaele and Andy who came with me later to Zafferano, and John, who is now cooking in Australia – and three in the restaurant. For the first time I was in charge of everything, from choosing what kind of coffee we served to the style of glasses and coffee cups, and there was no time to be scared.

The *London Evening Standard* restaurant critic Fay Maschler came in early on and wrote a very good article about us, and we won a lot of respect. We were always full – we did sixty covers at lunch and again at dinner – and I learned how to balance the menu to suit the people and keep the price down, at the same time as seeking out the best-quality ingredients. Mauro had a great palate and really understood food. He was from Sardegna, so he introduced me to the dishes of his region and ingredients like bottarga, and we worked on the menus and tasted everything together. It was a good collaboration. Mauro made me see that I must be involved in everything that happened in the dining room as well as the kitchen, that a dish is finished only when the plate is back in the kitchen and everyone is happy.

I lived in an apartment above the restaurant, and I did little else but work. I literally had my wages stashed under the mattress, because I didn't have time to open a bank account. But on the occasional time off, or when we were finished in the kitchen at night, I hooked up with the old crowd from my time in Soho. Fergus Henderson was now cooking at the French House, Peter Gordon was at Green Street; and another old friend, Dan Lepard, who had been photographing fashion for *Vogue*, was now working as a baker and pastry chef.

On one of these nights, I met Plaxy, my wife. She was a friend of a friend I had shared a house with in my nomadic days before leaving for Paris, and I had actually met her once before, with her partner, the father of

Jack. This night, after a party at the Institute of Contemporary Arts, a crowd of us went to Fred's, a late-night club where there was always a drink waiting for us. I still see the guy who ran it sometimes, and I feel so guilty because I must owe him so much money! Without him, most of us wouldn't have had a social life. This night a guy who waited tables at L'Escargot was celebrating qualifying for his pilot's licence. Plaxy was a friend of his – she also worked at L'Escargot – and I remember walking in and seeing her there looking gorgeous. I didn't waste any time. "So, what's the deal here, are you still with this guy…?" I asked her. The answer was no, and when we started seeing each other I very quickly realized that this woman was not just important to me but good for me.

My big sadness was that, while I was at Olivo, my grandmother, who had been such a big influence in my life, died of cancer at the great age of 104. Even at the end, she was still worrying about me. One of the last things she said to my mum and dad was, "I trust you to look after Giorgio." She was an amazing woman, and when she was buried, hundreds of people came from miles around Corgeno for the funeral.

In London, Marco Pierre White had opened the Canteen in Chelsea Harbour, with Michael Caine and Claudio Pulze, and everyone was talking about it. Marco was truly "rock and roll," and the Canteen was such a glamorous place, always buzzing. One lunchtime Tony Allan, a former chef who had started Cutty's, supplying seafood to restaurants, organized a big party of chefs to eat at the Canteen. They were mostly guys who worked in hotels, who arrived in smart suits and ties. Then I showed up, unshaved, with my hair all over the place, in ripped jeans, a pair of Timberland boots with no laces in them, a T-shirt, a beautiful Italian jacket I had, and a dark red scarf that wound around and around, with beads on the end. At the reception, Fatima, who later worked with me at Zafferano, looked at me and said: "If you are here for an interview you have to go around the back." It was the first time I met Claudio Pulze. Afterward he used to tell people about that moment, when suddenly the door swung open and in came this skinny six-foot guy with a wild look and a ten-foot-long scarf, and he thought, "It's Dr. Who!" I always joke that of course I look like a giant to Claudio, who is only about three and a half feet tall!

Claudio was at the bar with Marco, and Tony introduced me as "the Italian Marco Pierre White," which to me was the best compliment. Marco looked me all over and said, "You need a haircut." "So do you," I told him. I think he liked the fact that I wasn't defensive or intimidated by him. I went back to work after lunch, and Marco and Claudio came in to eat that night. After that, they came in regularly. Marco was always surrounded by lots of people. Sometimes Michael Caine would be with him, and Gordon Ramsay, who had worked in Marco's kitchen at Harveys and had been cooking in Paris. Now he was back working at La Tante Claire with Pierre Koffmann. Claudio had formed a company called A–Z with two other directors, and they were about to open Aubergine, with Gordon in charge of the kitchen.

Olivo continued to get fantastic reviews. Critically and financially, we were a success, and maybe I was getting too full of myself, but increasingly I wanted more freedom to try different things, and there were massive fights with Jean-Louis over the running of the business. Then one day, I was crossing the road outside and Claudio was waiting for me in his car. He said, "Why don't we do a restaurant together …?" Of course I was flattered. This was the guy who worked with Marco Pierre White and I thought, "Why couldn't I have a really smart, serious Italian restaurant?" Plaxy and I talked about it, and we decided, "Okay, we'll look around for a place…"

On a Saturday morning, when Olivo was closed, we often went to eat breakfast at the Fifth Floor at Harvey Nichols, and on our way one time, we passed the site of Wheelers Fish restaurant, standing empty. It seemed perfect, and I kept cycling over to look at it. Eventually I told Claudio, "I've found a fantastic place," and the site for Zafferano was settled.

At Olivo, Mauro had smelled for some time that things weren't right and that I wanted to leave, and though I think he would have done anything to keep me there, he was caught between me and Jean-Louis. Eventually there was a big row with Jean-Louis and in the heat of the moment I packed my stuff and moved out. It was sad the way it ended, but I am very proud of having worked at Olivo and what we achieved there.

While we were waiting for Zafferano to be ready, at the suggestion of Marco Pierre White, I helped open the Red Pepper in St. John's Wood with Bijan Behzadi. He had the first of the new generation of wood-burning ovens to be used in London, and I talked to a pizza chef I knew in Italy, who helped us to set it up. The pizzas were fabulous, on another planet for London, so different from anything anyone else was doing. We used fresh toppings of buffalo mozzarella, and prosciutto and arugula and basil… and we charged relatively nothing for them. As well as the pizza, we made pasta and gnocchi, and changed the menu every day. Often there was a line to get in, but what was special was that the local people all came, and everyone enjoyed themselves. It was a proper neighborhood restaurant. Plaxy worked with me, front of house, and we lived next door to the restaurant. Even now, if I walk down Formosa Street, it is like being in

Corgeno – people still open their windows or poke their heads out of shop doorways and say, "Hey Giorgio, how are you doing?"

As the Red Pepper became more and more talked about, I began to feel more sure of myself, and when we finally opened Zafferano in 1995, everything came together. I felt I had a clean drawing board on which I could pull together all my experiences: my grandmother's food, the more refined techniques of Paris and the Savoy, the gutsy cooking at Olivo, the conviviality of the Red Pepper.

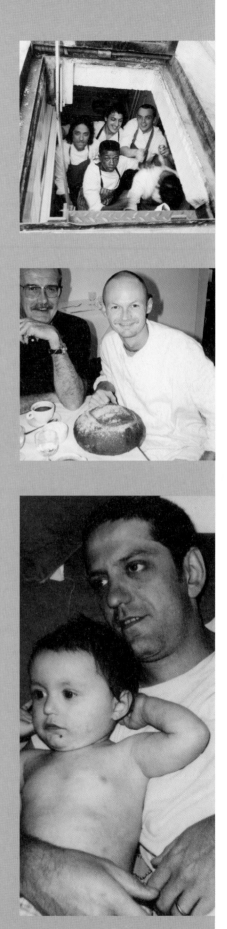

We had the resources to reach as high as we could go, and I felt mature enough to take the responsibility on my shoulders. With friends around me in the kitchen I could communicate with and trust, chefs like Michaele from Olivo, and eventually Federico Sali, who is now my sous chef at Locanda, and a good friend – I felt like a god in my own kitchen.

At Olivo, the dishes we cooked had been very straightforward, typically Italian, with not much garnish or decoration. Now we had license to be adventurous. We kept the structure of the Italian meal: antipasto, soup, pasta and risotto, then fish or meat and dessert. We used Italian ingredients and researched dishes not only from my own region of Lombardia, but from all around Italy –then we reworked and reinterpreted them. Instead of the desserts we had made at Olivo – mostly cakes or tarts and desserts in a glass – we worked on more serious, elaborate dishes and my friend and baker Dan Lepard came in to run the pastry section and develop breads for the restaurant.

After two months we were a success and for the first time I was being written about as a serious chef, as was Gordon Ramsay at Aubergine. Both of us had Marco Pierre White to thank for the massive attention we drew. Marco had raised the game. He generated superstardom, and made people understand that chefs were living people with personalities, not caricatures with big mustaches, or robots working unseen behind closed kitchen doors. Gordon and I were on a very important learning curve. We were in the fast lane, and everyone, especially the media, seemed to be watching, wanting to photograph us, write about us, print our recipes...We used to act as if we knew how successful we would be, but I used to go home sometimes and think, "This is crazy..." Two years after we opened, we were awarded a Michelin star. People said to me, "If you were French you would have had a star two years earlier," but despite the fact that the Mediterranean diet was popular and people were taking Italian food far more seriously, Michelin still had its own ideas about Italian cooking.

Sometimes in the midst of everything, things happen that put your whole life in perspective. In 1996, our daughter, Margherita, was born, with eczema so severe she almost died, and, as we later discovered, an extreme allergy to around 600 foods, including nuts, egg white and especially tomatoes and fish. If she came near me when I had been cooking fish, her face would redden and swell up, so I had to shower before I

could even touch her. Sometimes they kept her in hospital for weeks, and while Plaxy stayed with her, I would take Jack to school in the mornings, then pick him up in the afternoon and bring him to Zafferano, where he would do his homework.

We had our first encounter with anaphylaxis (an extreme reaction to food, which causes the throat to swell, and can be fatal) when Margherita was one and we had borrowed a friend's house for a vacation in the south of France. We had been told that the sun would be good for her skin. She had eaten a tiny piece of smoked salmon and was playing with Jack when suddenly he came rushing in saying that Margherita's face had gone "all funny." Her face and her lips were swollen and she couldn't breathe properly. It was Sunday and we were in the middle of nowhere. We just scooped her up and headed off down the mountain road, with Plaxy still in her bikini. Incredibly, a fire engine was coming down the road and we stopped it to ask the guys the way to the nearest hospital, but not only did they give us directions, they took us, getting us there just in time. Margherita was given an adrenaline injection, and she recovered immediately. Now everywhere we go we carry an injection kit and we have to be aware of the terrible possibility that if we don't know what is in her food, we could lose her. So we make up special meals for her to take to school, and we eat out only at places where I can trust the chef totally, without question.

Chefs can sometimes be dismissive of people with food allergies. They don't always understand the dangers; they think someone is just being faddish about something they have probably spent all day preparing – but when you have run down the road with your baby daughter in your arms, not knowing whether she will live or die, then you understand. In my kitchen, every chef is aware of the problem of allergies and the precautions you have to take, and they are brilliant when Margherita comes into Locanda – which she loves to do. But it is hard to think that when I am getting excited about a beautiful tomato or a perfect egg pasta, she might never know what I am talking about.

In all I spent seven years at Zafferano, and I opened up two great pizza restaurants, Spiga and Spighetta, but once again, there were problems. First Claudio split with A–Z, then Gordon, and finally I left too. It was time for Plaxy and me to stand on our own feet. I knew what I wanted to call our restaurant, before we even decided on the site in Seymour Street, in the Churchill Hotel. In Italy, a *locanda* is a kind of inn, or truck stop with rooms, serving good food, where the drivers meet on their travels. There was a locanda near Corgeno, where I used to help out sometimes and listen to the guys talk. One driver, I remember, used to carry locally grown feed for racehorses to Toscana. On the way back, he would stop in Mantova or Parma and buy a load of Parmesan wheels. My uncle used to buy a couple, and help him cut up the rest, which he would sell to everyone in the village. The idea of the journeys had always appealed to the free spirit in me, and I liked the respect for good local produce, and the conviviality of the truck stop. Locanda Locatelli seemed like the right name.

Dolci

Desserts

"Into your last glass of white wine after luncheon slice a peeled yellow peach. Leave it a minute or two. Eat the peach and then drink the wine."

Elizabeth David, *Italian Food*, 1954

The rhythm of a traditional Italian meal, with its risotto or pasta course, has enough carbohydrate highs without needing anything elaborate to follow, so the typical Italian dessert repertoire tends to be more humble than that of other cultures. Actually, I love English desserts like sticky toffee pudding and bread and butter pudding, but not after an Italian meal. Then all I really want is fruit, which in Italy is considered noble enough to be a dessert in itself.

Of course, every region has its cakes and pastries, but these are things we eat out, perhaps in the afternoon at the café or *pasticceria* (pastry shop), or keep for Sundays with all the family, or for special celebrations. Because we never miss the chance of a feast or a carnival, for every harvest or saint's day or important occasion in the church calendar there will be something special – *torta* (cake), *frittelle* (fritters), *biscotti* (cookies), or a sweet such as *torrone* (nougat). Maybe it is just that Italians feel guilty about eating a dessert as well as three other courses, so we justify our favorite things by associating them with saints.

Perhaps the biggest festival of eating and drinking is the *Panarda* held in Abruzzo, most famously in the village of Villavallelonga. On the feast of Sant'Antonio Abbate (*abbate* means "abbot"), on January 17, an incredible parade of anything from 30 to 50 dishes goes on all night, finishing up with pastries like *fiadoni*, little envelopes filled with fruit and ricotta. One of the legends – as ever, Italians can never agree on such things – is that a local woman went to draw some water, and when she came home, she found that a wolf had picked up her baby in his mouth. So she prayed for help from Saint Anthony. He was the founder of monasticism, a hermit who was supposed to be a great naturalist and protector of animals, and so the people of Villavallelonga would pray to him to help protect them against wolves. When the wolf let go of the baby, she made a big feast to say thank you to the saint.

Italians are not ashamed to buy their desserts, so on Sunday mornings the family will go to church and on the way home stop off at a pastry shop like my uncle's in Gallarate to buy a cake to take home and have after lunch. Going out for a pastry or an ice cream is also a social thing, so in the summer everyone might sit down and have a meal together in the evening, then go out for a walk and end up at the *gelateria* for an ice cream and a coffee. In America, the tradition is that the ice cream trucks come around and play tunes that appeal to the kids, but in Italy, it has always been considered a grown-up, civilized thing to go out for an ice cream. Sometimes the men will go to the bar or a social club, but the clever places are the ones that combine the bar and the gelateria, so everyone is happy.

Fruit

At home, my father never finishes a meal without an apple, or whatever fruit is in season. Even if he goes out to a restaurant, that is what he asks for. In our house in Corgeno there is always a big fruit bowl in the kitchen and, if you were to come over for dinner, dessert might be just black and green grapes, in a bowl filled with water and ice. Though there is a school of thought that fruit at the end of the day creates too much acidity in the stomach, my family have all lived long lives eating fruit after dinner.

If you look at old menus and books, it is clear that fruit has always been significant in our religion and culture. We don't talk about forbidden cakes, do we? The Romans were crazy about exotic fruits and brought them in from all over the world, so we have them to thank for cherries (though some people think they were already known in Italy), for peaches (which originated in China and were brought to Italy from Iran, or Persia as it was then) and for figs. Figs are so important in our history that the story is that Romulus and Remus, the legendary founders of Roma, were nursed by a she-wolf under a fig tree, which was later considered to be sacred. There is also an idea that the forbidden fruit in the Garden of Eden was originally a fig, and that much later the Catholic Church changed the story, because apples represented the evil fruit of the Romans who, like the druids before them, celebrated their pagan rituals and festivals by getting high on cider. I like to think of figs as the fruits of Paradise, and I like to serve them as simply as possible – perhaps just with some Mint sorbet (see page 560) and some fresh mint leaves.

In Italy, because we love fruit so much, we have a great respect for its seasonality and locality. When you go to the market, the fruit there will have been grown in orchards and fields nearby, and because it is picked ripe, it must be sold by the end of the day, or it is wasted. You see the people touching and smelling everything, because a peach isn't just a peach, a cherry isn't just a cherry. If you have ever tasted and smelled a peach at that perfect point of ripeness, straight from the tree, you will understand that such a fruit is something beautiful, not just a commodity that can be grown anywhere in the world to the perfect size, shape, color and degree of fake ripeness that the supermarket demands. Fruit shouldn't be harvested underripe, then kept chilled while it is transported so that it still has a "shelf life" of many more days, but never ripens to the same extent. What sort of mind games are being played with us, when we see these fruits that look ready but are hard enough to play tennis with?

Every fruit has a place in the year that seems to make sense, and that can be appreciated and looked forward to. When I was little everyone had vines, so there would be grapes in the autumn, and each year we would go to visit a friend of my granddad near Asti, famous for its Moscato Bianco (white Muscat) grapes, to have a big lunch and celebrate the start of the harvest. In the north, there is also a big production of pears, and there

would be a special dispensation during the apple and pear harvest when the secondary school would close for a week, so everyone could help. I love pears – particularly small ones – possibly even more than peaches, especially the way you can fry them very fast with some sugar and they will be crunchy and colored on the outside, and on the inside soft but granular, in their peculiar way. And I love the way pears work as generously when you add them to a savory dish as in a dessert. There is a famous saying in Italy, *"Al contadino non far sapere quanto è buono il formaggio con le pere,"* which translates roughly as: "Never tell the farmer how good a pear is with cheese" (or he will charge you more). And it is true: a hard, rich, salty cheese is perfect with a sweet pear after a meal – Parmesan in the north, pecorino farther south. Or it can be a meal in itself. I remember when I was little, seeing people going skiing, and instead of sandwiches, they would take a pear and a piece of Parmesan to eat up on the slopes.

Sometimes we also picked the fruit of the wild apple trees, which we called *ranetta* (little frogs) because their skins were so rough, like sandpaper. My grandmother would make them into *frutta cotta* (jam) for a *crostata*, a very thin, crispy base of pastry with the jam spread over it, or she would cook them with a little sugar and water to make a "fruit cheese" or paste, to eat with Parmesan after dinner. When the first oranges came in from Sicilia, you would see people filling big baskets at the markets, and when the cherries and peaches came into season there would be more excitement. In the summer, too, you would see guys selling pieces of watermelon in the street (in the country, they would often keep the melons cool in the river) because, when you are in the blistering sunshine, it is the right time to eat something so refreshing – not imported from South America and packed in baskets at Christmastime.

What relatively few recipes there are for fruit desserts throughout Italy are usually simple transformations incorporating local ingredients but preserving the shape and essence of the fruit, such as *pere cotte al vino* (pears poached in wine, see page 524), traditional in Piemonte, or *pesche ripiene*, peaches stuffed with almonds (and/or amaretti biscuits). Two of my favorite fruit desserts are actually French: Poire Belle Hélène, which I eat whenever I go to Paris in a café near l'Opéra, where they do it brilliantly – hot chocolate sauce, ice cream, pear … fantastic; and Peach Melba (see page 528), the most famous of all peach recipes. Both of them have a connection with opera. Poire Belle Hélène was supposed to have been created in Paris to celebrate the opening of the operetta by Offenbach about Helen of Troy, *La Belle Hélène*; and Peach Melba was created by the famous chef Auguste Escoffier in honor of the opera singer Dame Nellie Melba.

In Italy, the tradition of preserving seasonal food also applies to fruit. Especially in the south, where there is a massive production of citrus fruits, much of it goes into candied fruits and peel, a major ingredient in pastries and desserts. It must have been amazing 100 years ago to eat oranges, lemons and cherries in winter. If you go to shops in Sicilia, they have mountains of candied fruit in glass containers on the counter, which they scoop out for you. Sometimes they are whole, so you cut them up yourself.

Torte e pasticceria

Cakes and pastries

Many of our celebratory cakes like *panettone* (our famous Christmas cake from Milano), *pandoro* (the Venetian answer to panettone) and *panforte* from Toscana travel all over the world and are considered "Italian"; other cakes are only famous locally – perhaps made in a particular village café or bar. In Varese in Lombardia, there is a bakery where they make a brilliant *torta di Varese:* a French-style *sablé* with nuts in it. Not far away in Gallarate, at the Bar Bianchi, they make their own specialty, *torta del Bianchi*, which is made with hazelnuts, almonds, eggs and flour, a little like frangipane, but very moist and crumbling at the same time. There are hundreds of different recipes, which might be as humble as *pan tramvai* (raisin bread, see page 158) or as elaborate as *torta alla Milanese*, a traditional pie filled with something like old-style English mincemeat: minced roast or stewed beef or veal, mixed with sugar, butter, chocolate, pine nuts, golden raisins and candied fruit.

Even though these days northern and southern Italians have moved around the country and are all mixed up, our cakes and pastries still reflect the way that, as with all Italian food, ideas varied from region to region, depending on local ingredients and influences. In the northeast, especially around Milano, Torino and Venezia, which are so close to the borders of Austria and Germany, you have a great excitement over patisserie, which you eat with coffee or hot chocolate in more bohemian Viennese- or Parisian-style cafés. Whereas in the south, around Palermo and Napoli, they also have fantastic pastries, but they have their place in the more multicultural bars: perhaps just one or two local pastries made in their own kitchens.

In the north you can see the mark of French and mid-European patisserie in the use of locally produced cream and butter, and puff pastry *(pasta sfoglia)*. To make puff pastry successfully it needs to be kept cold, so in the days before refrigeration was available to everyone you would find this kind of rich pastry only in the north. In the hotter south, pastry made with pork fat (lard) was more normal. In Trentino–Alto Adige and Friuli–Venezia-Giulia, close to the border with Austria, strudel is a typical thing, and at Easter time in Friuli they make a strudel called *presnitz*, stuffed with candied fruit and spices. In 1891, in *Science in the Kitchen and the Art of Eating Well*, Pellegrino Artusi included a recipe for strudel, warning Italians in other regions, "Do not be alarmed if this dessert seems to you to be a strange concoction, or if it looks like some ugly creature such as a giant leech or a shapeless snake after you cook it; you will like the way it tastes."

In the north, in addition to cream and butter, you see a great use of chestnuts (see page 576) and chestnut flour. Chestnuts were an important staple for people during the war, and typical desserts are *castagnoli con crema* (fritters filled with chestnut cream), *castagnaccio* (a cake

made with chestnut flour, often with golden raisins, walnuts and pine nuts added, and sometimes topped with rosemary) and *torta di pasta alle castagne* (pasta made with chestnut flour, cooked in a syrup and pressed and set hard into a solid cake, which is very, very good). Since "light" is not a word we use often in the north, you find all kinds of *torte di tagliatelle*, and also *torte di riso* (rice cakes), which reflect our love affair with rice.

Further north, in the Valle d'Aosta, they are famous for *montebianco*, named after the highest mountain of the Alps: chestnuts cooked with milk, sugar and vanilla, then puréed, flavored with rum, piled up to look like a mountain, and chilled. Before serving, the "mountain" is smothered in whipped cream to look like a snowy peak. In Piemonte, they are also known for *pannacotta*, which literally means "cooked cream," and another important dessert is the *bonèt*, which is made with amaretti cookies, eggs, sugar, cream, cocoa and rum in a bain-marie, and served cold. One story is that it is called *bonèt* because the bain-marie it is made in looks like a hat; other people say that because it was served at the end of a meal, it was called after the hat your friends would put on to go home afterward. Or, I think, because of the local French influence, it could be that it just means the "very good" dessert. Tiramisù (see page 554), which means literally "pick-me-up," is one of our most loved northern desserts, though it isn't a traditional recipe at all. It is supposed to have been invented by a restaurateur in Treviso in Veneto in the sixties.

After such excitement over patisserie in the north, as you work down the regions, traditionally desserts become a little boring. Toscana, for example, a region that has produced some of the great classics of Italian cooking, and contributed so much to shaping the idea of Italian food all over the world, is quite poor on desserts. And what there is, like the medieval *panforte*, tends to be visually a little on the brown side, like the distinctive colors of the land around.

In Abruzzo, they go for cakes like the *parrozzo*, made with almonds and covered with chocolate. Its name, which comes from *pan rozzo*, the local round country bread, was given to it by the poet D'Annunzio, who was a friend of the cake maker who created it. Then, when you reach the south, what amazes me about the desserts is that, though you might expect them to be refreshing because of the heat, apart from the *gelati* (ice cream) and *sorbetti* (sorbets), in fact they are very sugary and rich, often filled with ricotta (which replaces the mascarpone of the north), candied fruits and nuts. In Napoli you find the Easter *pastiera*, an elaborate tart of sweet pastry *(pasta frolla)* spread with ricotta, candied fruits and spices, topped with a lattice of more pastry and baked (see page 548). Napoli is also the home of rum baba, which is supposed to have been created by King Stanislao Leszczynsky of Poland, who was the father-in-law of Louis XV of France. While he was exiled in Lorraine, he used to soak stale *kugelhupf,* the local cake, in rum, and he called his concoction the Ali Baba, because he loved to read *The Ara-*

bian Nights. When the house of Bourbon took over Napoli, the dessert came too, but just became known as baba.

Sardegna is famous for its honey desserts, and you can see the influence of the Arab invasion in regions like Calabria and Sicilia, where candied fruit figures in many of the local desserts, such as *cannoli* (see page 545), the famous pastry tubes (made with pork fat) flavored with cocoa, then fried and filled with sweetened ricotta, candied peel, pistachio nuts and pieces of chocolate. Or *cassata*, a complicated cake made again with ricotta, vanilla, chocolate and candied peel, covered with almond paste and decorated with more candied fruit. *Cassata gelata* is an iced dessert with similar flavors, which we used to make at Zafferano.

In the south they also play a lot with sweet-and-sour flavors, so you might find desserts made with eggplants and chocolate. In Sicilia, they have their own typical pastries, such as *sfogliatelle*, sheets of puff pastry, again made with lard, which are rolled up, then shaped around a filling of cooked semolina, ricotta and candied fruits, so that when they are baked they look like clamshells. Like many of our traditional pastries, they were initially made by monks and nuns. Apparently, sfogliatelle were first made in the eighteenth century for guests at the monastery of Croce di Lucca, but they were made famous much later by an innkeeper, Pasquale Pintauro, who prepared them fresh throughout the day, and they were so good, people lined up for them all the way down the streets.

Sicilians also make spectacular use of sculpted almond paste or marzipan *(pasta reale)*. They are crazy about it. When you go into the pastry shops, you find dramatic, kitsch displays of marzipan shapes, which make you want to laugh sometimes. When we go on vacation to Sicilia, even in the villages in the middle of nowhere – so remote and hot, that if there is a puff of wind, the dry branches go rolling down the street as if in a spaghetti western – you can have three coffees in the morning at three different pastry shops, and each shop will be full of different elaborate creations.

Frittelle

Frittelle – fritters, which are more often sweet than savory – are something we have in common from the north to the south of Italy. My grandmother never made cakes, but she would make *chiacchiere*, which were fried pieces of sweet lard pastry. Usually she made them when we had fish to fry for dinner. She would put a big pot of clean oil on the stove first, and cook the chiacchiere, and then afterward put the fish into the same oil. At one time not everybody had ovens, so frittelle were easy to make, especially for many people in the village square, or at stalls on city streets for festivals or at *carnevale*. Personally, though I don't think deep-fried food is generally a good idea, these things are so pleasurable, you just have to forget about what is good for you for a little while.

Festival time

Every village, town or city has its *festa* or *sagra*. The *festa* is a saint's day or a national holiday, whereas the *sagra* is dedicated to an ingredient, or celebrates a local harvest, such as the *Sagra del Miele* (honey festival) in Sardegna, the Lazio strawberry festival in June, or the *Sagra del Dolci Eoliani* (festival of typical Aeolian island sweets). At this last, the *pasticceria* are full of things like *piparelli*, made with honey, almonds, vanilla and spice, for dipping into the local Malvasia wine; and *nacatuli*, which are pasta parcels with a filling made with almonds, vanilla, cinnamon and tangerine juice. When I was young, I remember all the stalls being set up in the villages dedicated to different ways to cook and eat whatever ingredient was being celebrated, whether it was pumpkin or honey. In small communities, the festivities would often be around the church; and there would be music and dancing.

Often the *feste* celebrate very local historical events or saints. Since every saint seems to have his own frittelle, and virtually every day of the year is a different saint's day, you can imagine how many different frittelle are made all over Italy. Some festivals are celebrated throughout Italy – though, even so, each community will have its own particular cakes, fritters, sweets and biscuits. *Carnevale*, for example, begins on January 17 and ends on Ash Wednesday, and all the kids have parties at school, so this is a time when the mothers all make special frittelle and they are all looking at each others', thinking, "mine is better than yours." In Lombardia, we celebrate with special chiacchiere di carnevale, sweet fritters, flavored with Marsala and dusted with sugar; while in Venezia they have *galani*, flavored again with Marsala or grappa, but made in the shape of a bow.

On March 19 Italians celebrate the Feast of San Giuseppe (St. Joseph), which is our Father's Day, and, if you were in Bologna, the *pasticceria* would be full of *ravioli di San Giuseppe*, fried sweet pastries filled with jam or almond paste; in Napoli you would find *zeppole di San Giuseppe*, cream-filled rings of dough, which are fried for you on the streets and decorated with flowers and branches, and in Sicilia, *sfingi di San Giuseppe*, shells of puff pastry filled with ricotta and lemon and orange zest.

In Lombardia, on October 4, we celebrate the feast of St. Francis of Assisi, who looked after the animals, with *mostaccioli*, a special cake made with almonds, honey, sugar, spices, vanilla and sometimes orange peel. They say this cake is the only earthly food that St. Francis loved, and he is supposed to have asked for it on his deathbed. At Easter time we have our own special Easter cake, *colomba pasquale*, which is similar to *panettone* but made in the shape of a dove, covered with sugar crystals and almonds. Sometimes we serve it a bit like the French *pain perdu* (French toast), sliced and fried in butter, with ice cream. One of the things I remember most when I was growing up was the *pan dei morti*, a soft, dry kind of bread, made dark with chocolate, I suppose to signify death, which we eat on *Il Giorno dei Morti* (the Day of the Dead) on November 2. This is the day when everyone goes to the cemetery to lay flowers on the graves of family and friends; then we remember them and celebrate their lives with big feasts and parties. In other regions they have *fave dei morti*, biscuits made in the shape of black fava beans, which, according to Pellegrino Artusi, were offered to the Fates, Pluto and Persephone, at the gates of Hell, because the beans were believed to contain the souls of the dead.

November 11 is another significant day, the Feast of St. Martino, which marks the end of the season of harvesting and preserving for the winter months, and also the first tasting of the new season's wine, *vino novello*, which is often celebrated in festivals along with roasted chestnuts. St. Martino is said to be the protector of drunks, since he cut his cape in half and gave one half to a drunken man on a freezing night, and special biscuits are made to different recipes all over the country. Some of the most interesting are the Venetian biscuits, which are shaped like the saint on horseback.

Christmas, of course, is one of the biggest times for all kinds of traditional sweets, featuring local ingredients. Napoli is famous for its festive *struffoli* – fried dough balls dipped in a syrup of honey, spices and candied peel, then piled up all together in the shape of a wreath, and sprinkled with *diavolilli*, colored candied almonds. In Liguria, they make fried ravioli, stuffed with marrow, candied pumpkin and citrus peels; in Basilicata, sweet *panzerotti*, which are sweet ravioli filled with pureed chickpeas, chocolate and cinnamon; and in Sardegna their fried ravioli are filled with fresh pecorino and covered with honey.

Biscotti

The other things Italians have a big love affair with are *biscotti* (biscuits or cookies) – the word comes from the Medieval Latin *biscotus*, meaning "twice cooked." I sometimes wonder when do we eat all these cookies? We must have hundreds of different recipes around the country. In the north, many biscuits became fashionable as Torino was a big center of commerce (and later in the nineteenth century, the capital of all Italy), so in the afternoons the merchants would break for tea or hot chocolate.

At the Venier pastry and coffee shop in Torino you can still see big cabinets filled with little cookies made by the chef Luciano to traditional Piedmontese and Campagnola recipes.

In Toscana, it is a custom to dip almond *cantucci* biscotti into the sweet wine, vin santo, and all over Italy, biscuits like *savoiardi* (ladyfingers) will be served with ice cream or creamy desserts. In any one region, you might have 25 different biscotti recipes, which, like those for our cakes, are mostly all variations on the same ingredients – nuts (almonds or hazelnuts), sugar and golden raisins. These range from the famous almond macaroons, *amaretti*, from my region of Lombardia, to *ricciarelli*, the typical almond and honey cookie of Siena, flavored with orange zest, spicy *spezzatini* or *pepatelli*, made with black pepper, both typical of Toscana, *baci di dama* (lady's kisses), to which chocolate is added, and Umbrian *pinoccate*, cookies made with pine nuts.

Pellegrino Artusi even includes a recipe for cookies for "birthing mothers" that were supposed to be eaten with a spoon and were made with sugar, vanilla sugar, cocoa powder, butter and egg yolks. The recipe was given to him by a lady from Conegliano, and she considered the results "nourishing and delicate, just the thing for restoring the strength of women who have grown weak bringing a baby into the world."

Then there is a big fight with the French over who invented *savoiardi* (savoyarde) biscotti – these are the sponge fingers often served with ice cream and traditionally used in tiramisù. The French say they created them in Yenne in the Savoy region, but in Italy people say they were first made in Torino in around 1348 for Amadeus VI of Savoy, who was called Il Conte Verde, the Green Count, because he and his ensign always wore green. Since Torino first came under the control of the French house of Savoy in the thirteenth century, who really knows who influenced whom?

The art of the pastry chef

At Locanda, it is hard to put a simple fruit salad on the menu, or the kind of typical tarts or cakes we used to make at Olivo, because most people who come to eat consider a more complex dessert to be a highlight of a restaurant meal. And, anyway, Plaxy wouldn't allow me to have a dessert menu without at least one chocolate dish on it. On the other hand, especially at lunchtime, we find that people want something light and easy to digest, and then, like Italians, they lean toward fruit, as long as it is presented in an interesting way, with some extra elements and different textures. So what we do is follow the same philosophy as for the rest of the kitchen, and take another look at the typical regional cakes, cookies, ice creams and combinations of fruit that all Italians know and understand, then rework them, give them a new twist, or bring together four or five different ideas on one plate; so we keep the spirit of Italian desserts, but with respect for the different appetites of our customers.

Every major restaurant kitchen has a pastry chef who is in charge of his own section, and concentrates only on the desserts. While I don't like to see complicated presentation in our starters and main courses, I feel that you have to let pastry chefs spread their wings and fly. Antonio Carluccio once said to me that when you get to the dessert course at Locanda it is almost like going to another restaurant – but I am happy with that, because it means our desserts are a talking point.

Pastry chefs are a different breed from the rest of us in the kitchen. When you are working at the stoves, of course you do as much of the preparation as possible in advance, but when someone orders a piece of fish, you must cook it for them then and there, and it is all about speed, immediacy and spontaneity – no two fish are ever exactly the same; there is always an edge of unpredictability. And if you overwork and fuss over the garnishes and sauces, it is an obstacle to the quality of the finished dish, which gets confused and colder the more you meddle with it.

When you work on the pastry section, though, it is exactly the opposite. Everything is about thinking, planning, weighing, measuring and preparing, quietly and meticulously, so that all the elements look – as well as taste – beautiful, and only need to be assembled at the last moment. And once you have designed a dish the way you want it, that is it – you can repeat it again and again, and it should always be perfect.

Personally, I never liked working on the pastry section much; I am too impatient. I like to work with handfuls of parsley, not spend my time weighing out every crystal of sugar or every gram of cream – which is what you must do to ensure that the chemistry works. Of course I have my ideas and my opinions, and I taste everything and sometimes, when the boys on the pastry get too carried away, I tell them that all that chocolate and vanilla must have gone to their brains and made them crazy. But we are lucky in that we have had two brilliantly creative pastry chefs at Locanda, who have given a real sense of excitement to what we do. In the

beginning, it was Damian Allsop, who was in charge of the pastry and who first came up with all sorts of dramatic desserts. Then he went off to work with the Italian chocolate maker Amedei, and Ivan Icra took over. Ivan is Catalan, from Barcelona, which is a hotbed of new ideas in cooking, and especially desserts. In Barcelona, one of the most talked-about restaurants is Espai Sucre (sugar space), where the whole menu is devoted to desserts. Ivan is one of a new wave of pastry chefs who is excited and influenced by the brilliant Spanish chef Ferran Adrià at El Bulli, with his way of questioning and deconstructing dishes, and building up different textures with jellies and foams – which are easy to do at home; you just need the kind of chargeable siphon you can buy for whipping cream.

Of course, Catalunya is culturally quite close to Italy, because it was once a principality of Aragon, and the Aragonese invaded northern Italy in the fifteenth century. In Alghero, the northern city of Sardegna, which was part of the Catalan kingdom for more than 400 years, many people still speak Catalan, and you find Catalan food in the restaurants. We share a love of many of the same ingredients, like tomatoes and almonds, and we all treasure our special dishes for festival days – so our ideas are very much in sympathy. Though, of course, that doesn't stop the constant Catalan versus Italian banter that goes on in the kitchen.

As always, though, what we do in the restaurant and what I would do at home are two different things. At home, I wouldn't make a cake and ice cream and cookies, and a foam and a sauce, all for one dessert. I also think it is important that, if you have cooked a meal for six people, you don't kill yourself over the pudding; so unless you are feeling ambitious or you really, really love making desserts, you don't need to do all the elements that we bring together at the restaurant. Maybe just make a cake or a tart, or poach some peaches or pears, and, if you like, you can buy some good ice cream to serve alongside. Or just make an ice cream, and perhaps a cookie. It's up to you.

Sorbetto di melone, fragole selvatiche, salsa all'arancio

Wild strawberries with melon sorbet and orange sauce

1 pint wild strawberries

For the orange sauce:
1 cup fresh orange juice
1/3 cup superfine sugar

To serve:
Melon sorbet (see page 560)

When wild strawberries are in season, we serve them with melon sorbet and orange sauce. To make the sauce, simmer the fresh orange juice with the superfine sugar, until you have a spooning consistency, then leave to cool. Arrange the wild strawberries in the center of your plates. Put a scoop of melon sorbet on top of the strawberries and spoon some of the orange sauce around. If you like, you can garnish the sorbet with Melon crisps (see page 581).

Lasagne di fragole e mango

Strawberry and mango lasagne

This is a lovely fresh dessert that might sound complicated but is actually very straightforward – and the advantage is that you make it the day before you want to serve it. We first made it by chance, really. We have some friends who have a farm near Mumbai in India, and we always give them some seeds of things like arugula to experiment with and, in return, when they visit us they bring us some fruit. One year they came over with about five boxes of mangoes – what were we going to do with them? At the time, we were searching for different ways of serving fruit for the lunchtime menu, and so we came up with this idea of a "fruit lasagne" – layers of fruit, which are pressed. We serve it with a scoop of vanilla ice cream (or sometimes Amaretto ice cream; see page 564) on top of a square of caramel sponge (though if you like, you could substitute a sweet cookie). For this recipe, you need two plastic containers of the same size, roughly 6 × 4½ inches and about 2½ inches deep.

The day before you want to serve the lasagne, peel the mangoes and slice very thin. Wash, hull and dry the strawberries and slice them lengthwise, just slightly thicker than the mangoes. Keep the trimmings from around the mango stones and blend these with a hand blender to make a smooth puree. Keep in the fridge.

Line one of the two containers with plastic wrap, enough to come over the sides.

Line the base with about a fifth of the mango slices, making sure there are no gaps between the pieces (when it is turned out, this will be the top layer of your "lasagne"). Next, make a layer of strawberries, using about a quarter of the slices. Repeat the layering three more times and finish with a layer of mango slices.

Cover with a large sheet of plastic wrap – again big enough to overhang the sides. Have a flat plate or tray ready that is big enough to put the containers on top of one another, and fit into the fridge. Put the second container on top of the first, hold firmly and flip the two containers over together onto the tray. Put a weight on top (a milk bottle or some cans will do). The idea is that the excess juices from the fruit will drain out onto the tray, so cut away the excess plastic wrap, so that it doesn't get in the way. Put in the fridge for 12 hours.

To make the sponge, first make a caramel, see page 522.

Preheat the oven to 300°F, grease a rectangular baking dish with butter and dust it with flour.

Whisk the caramel with the rest of the sponge ingredients until you have a smooth mixture. Pour the mixture into the prepared baking

4 ripe mangoes
14 ounces (about 2½ cups)
    strawberries

    For the caramel sponge:
1¼ cups tin of condensed milk
⅔ cup (3 large eggs) beaten eggs
¾ cup flour
1 heaping teaspoon
    baking powder
½ cup butter
2 tablespoons golden syrup
pinch of mixed spices, such as
    ground cinnamon, cloves,
    star anise (optional)
a little flour and butter for
    preparing the baking dish

    To serve:
Vanilla ice cream (see page 561)
4 Candied vanilla beans
    (optional, see page 583)

dish and bake for 25 minutes, until springy to the touch and a sharp knife inserted in the center comes out dry (if it is moist, keep the sponge in the oven for a little longer).

Turn the sponge out on to a cooling rack and leave to cool, then cut into squares.

When ready to serve the lasagne, take off the weights and remove it from the fridge. Turn the two containers back over together and remove the top one. Put a chopping board over the top of the remaining container and, holding it firmly, turn both board and container over together, so that you turn out the lasagne on to the board. Trim the edges if necessary, cut it into 4 and place a square on each of 4 plates.

If you have a kitchen blowtorch, dust the top of each slab of lasagne with sugar and glaze it quickly with the torch.

Scoop some ice cream on top of each square of sponge, spoon the reserved mango puree around and garnish with strips of candied vanilla pod, if using them.

Dulce de leche caramel

For this kind of caramel, which we use in lots of desserts, we have a trick that is famous in South America and used in things like banoffee pie.

All we do is put a can of condensed milk into a pan of boiling water and let it simmer away for about 3 to 3½ hours, topping up with more water if necessary.

The sugar in the milk caramelizes and when you take out the can (carefully) and open it, you will find a thick, dark toffee, known as *dulce de leche*, which is much more dense than you could easily make with whipping cream and sugar – and much easier.

The toffee makes a wonderful "glue," if for example we want to stick a cookie or a piece of pineapple to a plate, so that it doesn't slide when the waiter carries it – such considerations are very important in a restaurant!

Pere cotte al vino rosso e bianco

Poached pears in red and white wine

We had a big pear tree in our garden in Corgeno and, in the season, we had pears coming out of our ears, so my grandmother often used to poach them in wine. We add some spices and, when we serve them, we go to town a bit, building up different flavors and textures to set off the fruit, with various sorbets and ice creams and cookies. However, you can serve the pears very simply with vanilla ice cream, and, if you like, some sweet biscuits, such as Sablé (see page 578).

4 medium-sized ripe pears
1¼ cups white wine
½ cup superfine sugar
2 cloves
2 cardamom pods
1¼ cups red wine
1 cinnamon stick
1 star anise

To serve (optional):
Vanilla ice cream and cookies,
     such as sablé (to make
     your own, see pages 561
     and 578)

Or:
8 Frangipane wafers, in rounds
     (see page 575)
4 Frangipane wafers, twisted
     into balls (see page 575)
Mascarpone ice cream
     (see page 562)
Cinnamon ice cream
     (see page 569)

Peel the pears and cut them in half, remove the cores, then cut each half lengthwise into thirds.

Put half the pear pieces in a pan with the white wine, half the sugar, the cloves and cardamom pods. Put the rest of the pear pieces in another pan with the red wine, the rest of the sugar, the cinnamon and star anise.

Heat both pans very, very slowly on as low a heat as possible for around 10 minutes – the wine shouldn't even reach a simmer, as you want to cook the pears through, without their falling apart. When the wine begins to get hot, test the pears with a sharp knife. If it slides into the pears easily, they are ready. Take off the heat and leave to cool.

Lift out the pears (keeping them separate), then boil up each liquid separately (to 250°F, if you have a thermometer) and reduce to a thick syrup – remembering that it will thicken more when it is cold. To check if it is the right consistency, put a spoonful on top of a piece of marble or a cold plate – within seconds it will be cold. If it is watery, it needs to be boiled for a little longer, but if it spreads a little but holds its shape, it is ready.

Serve 3 pieces of each type of poached pear in each bowl, with vanilla ice cream, drizzled with the two different colored syrups, and cookies. Or, if you want to be more elaborate, arrange the two pears separately on plates, drizzled with their respective sauces, together with 2 rounds of frangipane wafers on each plate. Top one cookie with mascarpone ice cream, the other with cinnamon ice cream, and garnish with frangipane wafers.

Pere cotte e crude con zabaione a moscato

Muscat zabaglione with confit and fresh pears

If possible, use organic, free-range eggs (we use Italian eggs, the yolks of which are very deep orange-yellow); and try to find really juicy pears. The ones we use are Italian Forelle, which are very beautiful, small and juicy, with a fantastic yellow and crimson skin.

4 pears
¾ cup plus 1 tablespoon
    Moscato wine
superfine sugar, for dusting
¼ pound puff pastry

For the zabaglione:
8 egg yolks
¾ cup Moscato wine
3¼ tablespoons superfine sugar

Preheat the oven to 250°F.

To make the confit, cut two of the pears into dice (about ¼ inch) and put in a pan with the Muscat wine. Cook very slowly until the pear is soft. Leave to cool.

Dust a work surface with superfine sugar and roll out the pastry as thin as you can, sprinkling with more sugar as you go, then cut it into strips about ¼ inch wide (you need 2 or 3 per person), and twist them like loose corkscrews.

Lay the strips of pastry on a baking sheet and put into the oven for 4 to 6 minutes, or until golden. Leave to cool.

Peel the remaining pears, slice them very thin, preferably on a mandoline grater, and keep to one side.

To make the zabaglione, bring a pan of water to a boil and turn down the heat. Put the egg yolks, Muscat wine and sugar into a round-bottomed bowl, start to whisk a little, then put the bowl over the pan of water and continue whisking until you can form a figure eight with the mixture that will hold for a few moments.

Lift the confit pears into a fine sieve and drain off the juice (you could chill it and serve it as a drink, mixed with Prosecco).

Arrange some of the drained pear dice in each of four bowls, then spoon some zabaglione on top. Arrange the slices of fresh pear around the outside, and crisscross the strips of puff pastry over the top.

Pesche

Peaches

"Such beautiful, sensual fruits, aren't they?"

All Italians grow up with a love of peaches, which arrived from China in Roman times via Persia (now Iran), and we have a great respect for their seasonality and locality: the relationship of a particular variety to its native climate and territory. Most of the fruit on sale is grown locally, and the variety among peaches is amazing. The white peaches of the north are probably the most famous. These are the ones we bake stuffed with amaretti, and that are used in the Bellini, the famous drink "invented" in Harry's Bar in Venezia. (I am sure someone, somewhere made such a drink before – how could you not put two such marvelous ingredients together?)

Nothing compares to a peach plucked straight from the tree – they're such beautiful, sensual fruits, aren't they? I love to take the kids to pick them, and see them growing in their natural surroundings. Near Corgeno, next to Lake Monate, there is a consortium that grows Pesche del Lago di Monate: very small trees, hundreds of years old, with each tree giving around 25 to 30 peaches – gorgeous, juicy yellow ones with a quite firm texture, which you can buy from stalls on the roadside.

One of the best peach desserts I have ever eaten was not in Italy at all but Anton Edelmann's peach melba at the Savoy. It is a dish that generally has a bad reputation in England, since it is often made with canned fruit and ice cream, but the version at the Savoy, served inside a caramel cage, was a complex, perfectly balanced mix of crunch and gorgeous fruit. There they made it with white peaches, but I love to do it with the Pesche del Lago di Monate, because the slight crunch of the peaches is fantastic with the softness of the ice cream. First, you make a tuile basket for each person (see page 574) and some raspberry sauce. For four people you need to puree 10½ ounces (about 1⅓ pints) raspberries in a blender, add 2 teaspoons lemon juice and 4¼ tablespoons confectioner's sugar, and put the sauce through a fine sieve. Set aside while you poach 4 whole peaches in sugar syrup for about a minute, or until the skin comes off easily, then peel them, let them cool, cut in half and remove the pits. Now you need to make your caramel cage. Mix 1¼ cups superfine sugar with ⅓ cup plus 1 tablespoon water and 1½ teaspoons corn syrup in a pan, and put it on high heat. Brush the sides of the pan with water regularly to prevent the sugars from crystallizing, and cook to "hard crack" stage (300°F on a candy thermometer). Leave to cool until the syrup becomes thick.

Oil the outside of the bowl of a 4-inch-diameter ladle and lay it (round side facing upward) on your work surface. Dip 2 forks into the syrup and pull fine threads of it over the ladle in opposite directions to give a lattice effect. Finish with a thin line of syrup around the edge of the ladle to form the base of the cage. As soon as the syrup cools, carefully remove the cage from the ladle and keep it somewhere cool and dry. Repeat for 3 more cages.

To serve, pour a little of the raspberry sauce onto 4 plates, place a tuile basket in the center, scoop in some vanilla ice cream, top with a peach half, then spoon over a little more sauce. Carefully put a sugar cage over the top.

Spun sugar might seem a bit "eighties" now, but I have never thought of this dessert as at all pretentious, and I have never found a better way to serve peaches. All of us in the kitchen at the Savoy were so in love with this dessert – we were always trying to get the pastry cooks to let us have one. When I was in Paris and came back to London for a visit, I went to the Savoy to eat, and when they asked what I wanted, I said, "I don't care, as long as I have a peach melba."

Pesche sciroppate, semifreddo di menta e gelatina d'Amaretto

Poached peaches with fresh mint nougat glace and Amaretto jelly

To make the molds for the nougat glace we use clear PVC tape (6cm wide), which you can buy in specialty kitchen shops. We roll it into cylinders about 1¼ inches in diameter, secure with tape, then put these inside small pastry cutters of the same size to hold them steady. Alternatively, you could use 4 flexible molds around 2½ inches tall and 1¼ inches in diameter – or even use a deep ice cube tray and give everyone 3 cubes each.

3 firm but ripe peaches
1¾ cups superfine sugar
½ cinnamon stick
1 star anise
8 mint leaves, to garnish

For the nougat glace:
¾ cup plus 1 tablespoon
    whipping cream
1 bunch (about 1 ounce)
    fresh mint
whites of 3 large eggs
¼ cup superfine sugar

For the Amaretto jelly:
1½ ounces water
2g gelatine leaves, soaked in wa-
    ter and squeezed
3 tablespoons plus 1 tablespoon
    Amaretto liqueur

For the ginger custard:
¼ cup egg yolks
    (from about 3 large eggs)
¼ teaspoon ground ginger
2½ tablespoons superfine sugar
½ cup milk
½ cup whipping cream

The day before you want to make this dessert, put the whipping cream for the nougat glace into a pan with the fresh mint and heat until it starts to steam (175°F if you have a thermometer). Take off the heat, allow to cool and put in the fridge for a day to let the flavor infuse.

Take the cream and mint mixture from the fridge and pass through a fine sieve, pressing the mint leaves down to extract the maximum flavor. Put into a mixer and whip until it makes firm peaks, then transfer to a bowl.

Clean the bowl of the mixer thoroughly, then put in the egg whites and whisk until they start to foam and white bubbles appear around the bowl. Very slowly, add the sugar, whisking continually until the mixture makes stiff peaks. Stop the machine and carefully fold in the reserved mint cream, keeping as much air inside the mixture as possible. Spoon the mixture into the molds (as described above), smoothing the top. Put into the freezer for at least 4 hours.

To poach the peaches, cut them in half, leaving the skin on, and remove the pits, then cut each into 4 segments. Put the sugar, cinnamon and star anise into a pan with 2 cups water, add the peach pieces and heat very, very slowly on as low a heat as possible for around 10 minutes – the wine shouldn't even reach a simmer, as you want to cook the fruit through without its falling apart. When the wine begins to get hot, test the peaches with a sharp knife. If it slides into the flesh easily, they are ready. Take off the heat and leave to cool.

To make the Amaretto jelly, warm the water in a pan and melt the gelatin into it. Stir in the Amaretto and pour into a bowl. Put into the fridge for around an hour to set.

To make the ginger custard, put the egg yolks, ginger and sugar into a bowl with 1¾ tablespoons of the milk. Put the rest of the milk and cream in a pan on the burner, and when almost boiling add the egg yolk mixture and cook (at 185°F if you have a thermometer) until thick enough to coat the back of a wooden spoon.

It should leave a clean mark if you run your finger across it. If not, cook it a little longer. Take off the heat and leave to cool. Lay a piece of plastic wrap over the surface to stop a skin from forming and put into the fridge until you need it.

To serve, spoon some custard on to each of 4 plates, take your cylinders of nougat glace from the freezer and arrange 2 per person on top of the custard. Put a mint leaf on top of each – it will stick to the cream. Lift the peaches from their juice, and arrange alongside, together with scoops of the Amaretto jelly.

Macedonia di nespole e sanguinelle, gelatina di violetta
e schiuma allo yogurt

Blood orange and fresh loquat salad with violet jelly and yogurt foam

This is a fresh, colorful salad of fruit that is easy to make – you just need a half-liter (2-cup) siphon (the kind used for whipping cream) to make the foam.

8 fresh loquats, peeled and put
    into a bowl of water with
    a few drops of lemon juice,
    to keep the color
8 blood oranges, peeled and
    separated into segments

For the violet jelly:
2 tablespoons plus 1 teaspoon
    superfine sugar
½ cup plus 1 tablesoon water
violet coloring, optional
violet essence, to taste
2g gelatine leaves

For the yogurt foam:
⅓ cup whipping cream
scant ½ cup superfine sugar
1 gelatin leaf, soaked in water
345g plain yogurt
0.5-liter (2-cup) siphon,
    plus 1 charge

To make the violet jelly, put the sugar in a pan with the water and bring to the boil. Take off the heat and add the coloring, if using.

When cold, add the violet essence to taste. Put a little of the mixture into a pan and heat gently. Add the gelatin, let it dissolve, then add to the rest of mixture and stir. Pour into a deep container and put into the fridge for 1 to 2 hours until set.

To make the foam, put the cream and sugar in a pan and heat until the sugar has dissolved. Take off the heat and add the gelatin. When it has dissolved, add to the yogurt and mix together. Pass through a fine sieve, and put into the siphon. Charge and put into the fridge for 2 hours.

Serve in deep plates or bowls: arrange the loquats and blood orange segments around the outside, with a square of jelly in the center and the foam on top.

Catalan cream foam with berries

I don't want to give this an Italian name, because it is a dish that arrived with Ivan and is based on a recipe by Albert Adrià, brother of Ferran Adrià of El Bulli, who runs the restaurant's famous laboratory in Barcelona. For me, a chef who is trying to impress, and be creative, will always be happiest when he works with ideas and ingredients that he understands – just as when you cook at home, you are always most comfortable when you cook something you know for friends rather than trying something new for the first time. So, of course, the idea of reinventing the famous crème Catalan dessert was quite natural; and we are very proud of it, because what was quite a thick creamy dessert is now transformed into something light and frothy, yet the essence and the recognizable taste are still there. And, you know, in reality I could call this a Milanese cream foam, because the ingredients, the flavor, the creaminess, everything about it chimes with the spirit of Lombardia.

1 pint mixed berries
(strawberries, raspberries,
blueberries, etc.)
8 tuile biscuits (to make your
own, see page 574)
Crème Catalan ice cream
(see page 561)

For the Catalan cream
foam:
¾ cup whipping cream
¾ cup milk
½ vanilla bean
½ cinnamon stick
peel of ½ orange
peel of ½ lemon
yolks from 4 large eggs
2 heaping teaspoons cornstarch
¼ cup superfine sugar,
plus extra to caramelize
0.5-liter (2-cup) siphon,
plus 1 charge

First make the Catalan cream foam: put the cream and milk in a pan with the vanilla bean, cinnamon stick and the orange and lemon peel. Bring to a boil. Take from the heat and leave for 30 minutes to infuse. Pass through a fine sieve.

Put the egg yolks, cornstarch and sugar into a bowl and whisk together, then add ¼ cup of the milk and cream mixture, and whisk again.

Have a large bowl of iced water ready. Put the rest of the cream and milk mixture back on the burner and, when it is almost boiling, add the egg yolk mixture and whisk very quickly.

When you see the first bubbles appearing (if you have a thermometer this will be 185°F), take from the heat quickly and put the base of the pan into the ice water to cool it down as quickly as possible.

Before it is completely cold, blend with a hand blender until completely smooth, then put into the fridge until cold. Pass through a fine sieve and then into the siphon. Charge it, and then put the siphon into the fridge for 2 hours.

To serve, arrange some berries on each plate, then the ice cream and foam on top, and some tuile biscuits on the side, which you can use like spoons for the foam. Sprinkle the foam with superfine sugar and use a blowtorch to caramelize it quickly.

Sorbetto di menta, frutta della passione e schiuma di cocco

Mint sorbet, passion fruit jelly and coconut foam

This is a quite soft jelly that we layer up with the sorbet and foam in a martini glass. Together the three flavors are unbelievable; very different, something you really have to taste for yourself – though some people, I know, don't like the flavor of real coconut. I have had people tell me that it reminds them of soap or body lotion. I am so against the idea of soaps and shampoos and even household cleaners being made to smell of fruit – because it is so misleading, especially for kids. They think of apple as the aroma of a shampoo, instead of the real thing. I say only food should smell of food.

First make the jelly. To make the syrup, put the water in a pan with the sugar, bring to a boil, stirring to ensure all the sugar is dissolved, and then take off the heat and leave to cool. Mix the passion fruit juice and syrup together in a bowl. Warm 3 tablespoons of the mixture in a small pan. Remove from the heat, add the gelatin leaves and stir until dissolved. Add to the rest of the juice and syrup mixture, and stir well. Chill in the fridge for 2 hours until set.

To make the foam, warm 3 tablespoons of the coconut puree in a pan, then take off the heat, add the gelatin leaves and stir to dissolve. Add to the rest of the coconut puree. Put through a fine sieve.

Spoon the mixture into the siphon, charge it and put into the fridge for 2 hours.

Just before you want to use it, take the jelly from the fridge and break it up with a spoon.

To serve, put a scoop of sorbet into the bottom of a martini glass (or similar) and press down to make a neat layer. Add a spoonful of the broken-up jelly, then shake the siphon and squirt some coconut foam on top. Do this gently, to keep it from mixing with the jelly – the idea is to keep the three different-colored layers of sorbet, jelly and foam separate.

4 scoops of mint sorbet (to
    make your own, see page
    560)

For the passion fruit jelly:
¼ cup water
⅔ cup superfine sugar
1¼ cups passion fruit juice
4g gelatin leaves, soaked in cold
    water and squeezed

For the coconut foam:
2 cups frozen coconut puree
6g gelatin leaves, soaked in cold
    water and squeezed
0.5-litre (2-cup)siphon,
    plus 1 charge

Pasta frolla

Sweet pastry

This is a very good, easy pastry that isn't difficult to work with and won't break if you roll it. We use it to line a nonstick tart pan and bake it "blind," i.e., empty, so that it can cook a little and crisp up before you add a wet topping of fruit, frangipane, etc. We use ovenproof plastic wrap, filled with rice, dried peas or beans to weight it down, rather than baking paper, as it is tricky to keep this touching the pastry everywhere and keep it completely flat, whereas plastic wrap immediately sticks to it. Make sure you leave enough overlapping the edges to lift it out easily. Six minutes at 340°F is enough to start setting the pastry, then you can take out the plastic wrap and weights and return the tart case to the oven for about 15 minutes, until just golden, or whatever is required for your recipe. Make sure you preheat your oven for a good half hour before you start. It is easier to make double or even triple the quantity you need, as a larger volume will mix better, and you can freeze what you don't use immediately.

**Makes enough for two
11-inch tarts or eight
4-inch tarts**
1 cup butter
1 cup confectioner's sugar
2 eggs
3 cups plus 2 tablespoons flour

With the paddle attachment on the mixer, blend the butter until soft. Add the sugar and continue to mix until the mixture turns pale. Add the eggs one by one, and when they are incorporated, add the flour. Continue to mix until all the flour is incorporated. Divide into 2 balls.

Torta di ciliege

Cherry tart

When the cherry season is over, you can make this with fresh red plums. You can also make one large 11-inch tart if you prefer.

Makes four 4-inch tarts
½ recipe quantity Sweet pastry
2½ cups fresh cherries (or
plums), halved and pitted
about 2 tablespoons
superfine sugar

For the frangipane:
7 tablespoons butter
½ cup superfine sugar
2 eggs
1 cup ground almonds
(or hazelnuts)
3½ teaspoons flour

Roll out the pastry and use it to line four 4-inch nonstick tart tins. Then put the tins in the fridge for 2 hours to keep the pastry from shrinking in the oven.

Toward the end of that time, preheat the oven to 340°F. Line the chilled pastry cases with plastic wrap, fill with rice or dried peas or beans and bake blind for 4 minutes. Take out the weights, remove the plastic wrap, and put back into the oven for around 5 minutes (7 to 10 for a large tart), until baked but only very lightly colored (the base should feel firm when you touch it). Take out and turn the oven up to 180°C.

To make the frangipane, put the butter into a mixer with a paddle attachment and mix until soft. Add the sugar and continue mixing

until the mixture turns pale. Add the eggs one by one until all are incorporated. Turn the speed to low and add the ground almonds and flour. Mix well, then turn the speed up to maximum for 1 to 2 minutes, no more, to incorporate some air, which will make the frangipane a little lighter and fluffier in texture (the mixture will turn paler and expand in volume a little).

Spread the frangipane over the tarts and arrange the cherries (or plums) cut side down over the top. Press the fruit down gently until it is completely embedded in the frangipane mixture.

Put back into the oven for about 12 minutes (15 to 20 for a larger one), during which time the frangipane will rise and turn golden. Halfway through the cooking time, sprinkle with the superfine sugar and return to the oven – some of the sugar will melt and caramelize, and give the tarts a rustic look.

Serve at room temperature.

Torta di pesche all'amaretto

Peach and amaretto tart

Peaches and amaretti biscuits are a classic match that you will find in different variations all over Italy. The amaretto cream is really frangipane, with the addition of what, in the north of Italy, we talk about as bitter almonds (see page 576), but are actually bitter apricot kernels. They come not from the apricots we have in the fruit bowl but from immature fruit that looks very like almonds and are cultivated specifically for their kernels. You can buy them in specialty stores and health food shops.

Makes four 4-inch tarts
½ recipe quantity Sweet pastry
(see page 536)
1 cup crushed amaretti cookies
10 small peaches

For the amaretto cream:
1¼ cups bitter apricot kernels
1 cup plus 2 tablespoons butter
1¾ cups superfine sugar
5 eggs
2 tablespoons plus 2 teaspoons
flour, plus more for dusting
1½ cups ground almonds

Preheat the oven to 340°F.

To make the amaretto cream, put the bitter apricot kernels into a food processor and grind to a powder. Put the butter in the bowl of an electric mixer with a paddle attachment and soften it. Add the sugar and mix for a minute or so until the mixture turns pale. Add the eggs one by one, mixing each one in well before adding the next. Switch off the machine and, with a spatula, scrape around the edges of the bowl until all the mixture is incorporated.

Mix together the flour, ground almonds and bitter apricot kernels, and stir into the butter mixture. Mix at a slow speed until everything is incorporated, then turn the speed up to maximum for 2 minutes to incorporate air. You will see that the mixture turns paler and expands in volume a little.

Roll out the pastry on a floured surface and use it to line four 4-inch nonstick tart tins, or one 11-inch one. Line the pastry shell with plastic wrap, weight with rice or dried peas or beans, and bake blind for 4 minutes. Take out the weights, remove the plastic wrap, and cook for 5 more minutes (7 to 10 minutes for a larger one), until lightly colored around the edges. Turn up the oven to 355°F.

Spoon the amaretto cream into the pastry cases in a layer about ¼ inch thick, smooth with a spatula and sprinkle the crushed amaretti cookies over the top. Halve the peaches and take out the pits. Arrange them alternately, one cut side up, then one cut side down, in a ring around each tart, and press down slightly into the cream.

Put into the oven and bake for about 12 minutes (or 15 to 20 for a larger one), until the amaretto cream is golden and has puffed up around the peaches.

Serve at room temperature.

Torta di mele

Apple tart

This is a very thin and crispy tart, so thin we could almost call it pizza di mele – and have a bit of a game with words and serve it alongside the fruit lasagne (see page 521). It is the kind of French-influenced Milanese tart with a "wow factor" that we used to make at Olivo in the mornings, so it would look as though we had a pastry chef, when there were only three of us in the kitchen. You can make one big one or four individual ones. I find it is better to use a conventional oven rather than a convection oven, as you want the heat to be concentrated on the bottom of the pastry rather than circulating around it, so it crisps up quickly and uniformly. In summer, we also make this with halved cherries. Serve it with vanilla ice cream.

Makes four 4-inch tarts or one 11-inch tart
½ pound puff pastry
8 Granny Smith apples
about 2 tablespoons superfine sugar

For the pastry cream:
⅓ cup superfine sugar
½ cup cornstarch
yolks from 6 large eggs
13½ ounces milk
⅓ cup plus 1 tablespoon whipping cream
1 cinnamon stick
peel of 1 lemon (in a strip)

To serve:
Vanilla ice cream (optional, to make your own see page 561)

Preheat the oven to 355°F.

To make the pastry cream, whisk the sugar, cornstarch and egg yolks together in a bowl until pale. Put the milk and cream in a pan with the cinnamon stick and lemon peel. Bring to a boil, then immediately take off the heat and leave to stand for 20 minutes for the flavors to infuse.

Slowly whisk the milk mixture into the sugar and egg mixture. Return to the heat, and when you see the first bubble, remove from the heat. Take out the cinnamon stick and lemon peel, and pass the mixture through a fine sieve.

Roll out the pastry into 4 circles of 4-inch diameter, or 1 of 11-inch diameter, and around ⅛ inch thick. Prick all over with a fork. Spread with pastry cream.

Halve the apples and remove their cores. Slice them about ¹⁄₁₆ inch thick (if the apples are just slightly thinner than the pastry, they should both cook properly in the same time). Arrange them in concentric circles, skin side up, embedding them well into the pastry cream – if they stick out they are likely to burn.

Put into the oven for about 20 to 30 minutes (another 5 minutes or so for a larger one), until the pastry is golden and crisp. Halfway through baking time, sprinkle with the superfine sugar, which will melt and caramelize a little to give the tarts a nice sheen – if the apples appear to be cooking too quickly, add a little extra sugar, as this will act as a barrier to the heat.

Serve at room temperature, with ice cream if you like.

Torta di limone e mascarpone

Lemon and mascarpone tart

Because the lemon and mascarpone mixture for this is quite liquid when it is first mixed, we completely cook the pastry case first, then turn the oven down, so that the topping can set without the pastry cooking further.

Preheat the oven to 340°F. Roll out the pastry and line an 11-inch nonstick tart tin with it. Line with ovenproof plastic wrap, fill with rice or dried peas or beans and bake blind for 4 minutes. Take out the weights, remove the plastic wrap and cook for around 10 to 12 minutes, until golden – the color you want it to be at the end.

Take out of the oven, brush the pastry all over with the beaten egg yolks and return to the oven for another 2 minutes. This forms a skin, so that even if there are tiny holes in the pastry, the topping won't seep through and burn.

Turn the oven down to 230°F. The pastry is now cooked, so all you need to do is set the topping.

To make the topping, mix together the mascarpone, cream, milk, lemon juice and sugar in a bowl. Whisk the egg yolks separately, then add to the mascarpone mixture and incorporate quickly with a hand blender.

Spoon into the pastry and put into the oven for 20 to 25 minutes until the center is set but still the slightest bit wobbly. Leave to cool, during which time the topping will firm up.

To finish, dust the top with the confectioner's sugar and caramelize it with a blowtorch. Serve at room temperature.

Serves 6–8
½ recipe quantity of
　　Sweet pastry (see page 536)
2 egg yolks, beaten
confectioner's sugar, to finish

For the filling:
1⅓ cups mascarpone cheese
¼ cup whipping cream
¼ cup milk
⅓ cup plus 1 tablespoon
　　lemon juice
½ cup superfine sugar
½ cup egg yolks
　　(from about 7 large eggs)

Ricotta

A true cheese is made with the milk of a cow, goat or sheep, but ricotta is made with the by-product of cheese making, whey. The story is that a long time ago, a shepherd left a pot on the fire with some whey in it after he had heated the milk to separate the curds from the whey to make a primitive cheese. When he returned, he found that the whey had been "recooked," which is what ricotta means, and formed into lumps that tasted sweet.

These days ricotta is still made in a similar fashion, with the whey left over from making cheese such as provolone being reheated to a temperature of around 185°F. This causes the proteins to separate from the whey and rise to the surface in little lumps, which are skimmed off and left in rush baskets to drain. This is *ricotta fresca* (fresh ricotta), which is pure white, looks a little like cottage cheese, and is sold in tubs all over Italy but is traditional in southern cakes and desserts, such as Cannoli (see page 545) and the Easter tart, Pastiera Napoletana (see page 548) – where it takes the place of the mascarpone or cream of the north. *Ricotta fresca* is also fantastic in salads, or for mixing with herbs or spinach to fill ravioli.

Most of the ricotta we have in the north, where the production centers around Piemonte, is made with whey from cow's milk and is very creamy, but it can also be made with the whey from sheep's milk, which can have a much stronger flavor that isn't really suitable for desserts, though it can also be quite mild *(gentile)*. The most famous is *ricotta romana*, which traditionally comes only from the Agro Romano area of Lazio but has become a generic name for most ricotta – even cheese made with cow's milk.

The curds can also be dry-salted and pressed, then matured in the curing room, so that the ricotta is semi-hard *(ricotta salata)* and can be grated over savory dishes such as the Sicilian *maccheroni alla Norma*, pasta with tomato, eggplant and basil. When it is aged more, it is called *stagionata*, and becomes more pungent and yellow in color, with a slightly *piccante* flavor. Dry-salted ricotta is also smoked *(ricotta affumicata)* by shutting it in a room where an aromatic fire is burning. In the north, beech wood is often used; in Abruzzo and Molise, where they make ricotta with the whey from pecorino production, they like juniper wood *(ricotta al fumo di ginepro)*, and in Sardegna, herbs *(ricotta mustia)*. I sometimes use smoked ricotta in a salad with baby onions in balsamic vinegar (see page 82). In Sicilia they do something different again, called *ricotta infornata*: sea salt is added to the whey, and when the cheese has drained, it is sprinkled with black pepper and baked in a stone oven for about half an hour.

Once when I was in Sicilia with the family, as if in a re-creation of the rustic origins of ricotta, we got talking to a shepherd, who made some ricotta from sheep's milk for us for lunch over a fire in a field, using a wooden stirrer, and we ate it while it was still warm, or at least Plaxy and I did. As I say, sheep's milk can be very strong. I thought it was quite incredible, I loved it, but the kids wouldn't eat it, because they said it tasted too much of the animal. Jack still says it was the worst cheese he ever ate in his life.

Torta di ricotta

Ricotta tart

I think this is the nicest of all the tarts and cakes we make in the restaurant. On the Amalfi coast in Campania (and also in Sicilia), they produce the *cedro* (citron), a bigger relative of the lemon that has a thick, nubby, aromatic zest, which is used to make candied peel. You can buy citron confit ready-made from Italian delicatessens – and sometimes, in season, the whole fruit, so you can make your own, as we do in the restaurant. The inspirational Patricia Michelson has them at her treasure trove of a shop and café, La Fromagerie in Marylebone (and Highbury) in London; or you could try Italian delis and also Jewish grocers and delis, as the particular variety of citron known as the *etrog* has a great significance in Jewish culture. Of course, you can make confit from normal lemons, but they won't have quite such a distinctive flavor.

The way we do our confit is to make holes all over the skin of the *cedri* with a skewer, then put the whole fruits into a big pan with enough sugar syrup to cover. We then cook them very slowly over a gentle heat for about 4 hours (make the syrup using a ratio of 70 percent sugar to water, i.e., just under ¾ cup sugar for 1 cup of water). When the pan comes off the heat, we lay some parchment paper over the top of the *cedri* and place something heavy, such as another saucepan, on top to keep the

fruit pressed down under the syrup. They stay like this for 5 to 6 hours, then we check that they are ready by taking one and cutting it in half. The flesh should be completely soft and the pith a uniform dark yellow. At this point, you can put the *cedri* into a sterilized jar (use disposable kitchen gloves to handle them, so you don't transfer any bacteria into the jar) and cover with the syrup. That way they will keep for up to a year.

When you want to use the *cedri*, carefully cut off the peel (discarding the flesh) and cut it into strips. It will have a texture almost like marmalade, and the most fantastic rich flavor, which is beautiful with this ricotta tart.

When cherries are in season, we make this tart in the same way but substitute 1½ cups of fresh cherries, pitted and halved, for the citron – you don't need any garnish.

Preheat the oven to 340°F.

Roll out the pastry and use it to line a 10-inch square tart tin. Line the pastry shell with ovenproof plastic wrap, fill with rice or dried peas or beans and bake blind for 5 minutes. Take out the weights, remove the plastic wrap and cook for 5 more minutes, until lightly colored around the edges. Turn down the oven to 300°F.

Put the ricotta, eggs and extra yolks, honey, cinnamon, Marsala and sugar into a bowl and whisk everything together, then chop the citron or lemon confit and mix that in.

Make the meringue by whisking the egg whites until you can make a trace with the whisk. Add the sugar very slowly until the mixture is firm and forming stiff peaks.

Take one-third of the meringue and fold it into the ricotta mixture, then fold in the rest very lightly.

Spread the mixture over the pastry base and cook for 15 to 20 minutes until golden. Allow to cool to room temperature to serve, and garnish with more thinly sliced citron or lemon confit if you like.

Serves 6–8
½ recipe quantity Sweet pastry
    (see page 536)
1⅓ cups fresh ricotta cheese
2 eggs, plus 2 extra egg yolks
2 tablespoons plus 2 teaspoons
    honey
1 teaspoon ground cinnamon
1 tablespoon plus 1¼ teaspoons
    Marsala
2 tablespoons plus 2 teaspoons
    caster sugar
1 cup citron or lemon confit
    (see above), plus more for
    garnish (optional)

For the meringue:
⅓ cup egg whites
    (from about 2 large eggs)
2 tablespoons plus 2 teaspoons
    caster sugar

Cannoli di ricotta

Traditionally, *cannoli* are made with *strutto* – snow-white pork fat that has a clean, quite neutral flavor – but you can use duck fat instead, or lard. You need a clean metal (¾-inch diameter) tube for this – it must be metal, as it has to go into hot oil. We serve this with Amaretto ice cream (see page 564) and Frangipane wafers twisted into corkscrew shapes (see page 575), and make a lighter lemon confit than in the previous recipe.

1⅓ cups plus 2 tablespoons flour
1 tablespoon plus 2 teaspoons sugar
2 tablespoons plus 2 teaspoons
     strutto, duck fat or lard
1 egg, plus a little more beaten
     egg for sealing the cannoli
3 tablespoons Muscat wine
vegetable oil, for deep-frying

For the lemon confit
(optional):
1 lemon
1½ cups water
1¼ cups superfine sugar

For the vanilla syrup:
⅓ cup plus 1 tablespoon water
½ cup sugar
1 vanilla bean

For the filling:
1 cup ricotta cheese
4¼ tablespoons candied lemon
     peel, diced small
4¼ tablespoons candied orange
     peel, diced small
⅓ ounce dark chocolate (70
     percent cocoa solids), cut in
     a similar size to the peel
5 roasted hazelnuts, cut in
     a similar size to the peel
¼ cup superfine sugar
¼ cup whipping cream

For the chocolate sauce
(optional):
¼ cup water
2 heaping tablespoons sugar
2 tablespoons plus 1 teaspoon
     cocoa powder
⅓ cup plus 1 tablespoon
     whipping cream

To serve:
confectiner's sugar, for dusting
4 scoops of ice cream,
     preferably Amaretto
4 Frangipane wafers or cookies
     of your choice

Make the lemon confit a few hours ahead: peel the lemon (making sure not to include the bitter white pith) and cut the peel into julienne strips. Have ready a bowl of ice water. Bring a pan of water to a boil, then put in the strips of peel and blanch for 30 to 60 seconds. Lift out with a slotted spoon and plunge into the iced water. Discard the water in the pan, pour in some fresh boiling water and put in the peel to blanch again – just for 5 seconds this time, then lift out and put into the cold water again. This process will take out some of the bitterness.

Put 1½ cups water into a pan with 1¼ cups superfine sugar and heat. When the sugar is dissolved, add the blanched lemon and cook gently for 10 minutes until soft. Take off the heat and cool.

Make the cannoli a few hours ahead. To make the vanilla syrup, put ⅓ cup plus 1 tablespoon water in a pan with the sugar and vanilla bean, bring to a boil, stirring to dissolve the sugar, then take off the heat. Put the flour, sugar and fat into a mixer with a dough hook and mix for 2 minutes on medium until it resembles bread crumbs. Add the egg and mix some more, then add 2¼ teaspoons of vanilla syrup and the Muscat wine, and mix into a dough. Wrap in plastic and let rest for a few hours in the fridge.

When ready to use, roll out the dough as thin as possible and cut into 12 squares, about 2¾ × 2¾ inches. Wrap one square around the tube (see previous page) and seal with a little beaten egg.

Heat some vegetable oil in a deep-fat fryer or a large pan (no more than one-third full) and, with the help of a fish slice or skimmer, carefully lower the tube into the hot oil and fry until the cannolo turns golden brown. Lift out carefully with the fish slice or skimmer and drain on paper towels. When it has cooled just enough for you to touch it, slide the cannolo off the metal cylinder, and wrap the next square around it. Deep-fry as before. Repeat until all the cannoli are done.

Make the filling by mixing all the ingredients together.

To make the chocolate sauce, put the ¼ cup water and the sugar in a pan, bring to a boil, then add the cocoa powder. Bring back to a boil, add the cream, bring back to a boil again, then reduce the heat and cook slowly until the sauce is thick, dark and shiny. To test when it is ready, spoon a little onto a cold surface. It should keep its shape and set. Take the sauce off the heat and leave to cool – but don't put it in the fridge, or it will lose its shine and become too hard.

Spoon the filling into a piping bag, and fill the cannoli. Dust with confectioner's sugar. Arrange two small mounds of lemon confit on each plate (you could pack a small pastry cutter with the confit, to make a neat circle). Place a cannolo on one mound of confit, and a ball of ice cream on the other. Dot the chocolate sauce around. Top the ice cream with a Frangipane wafer or other cookie.

Pastiera Napoletana

Easter tart

This is the traditional tart made in Napoli for the Easter festivities, and was originally made with grains of wheat, but is sometimes now made with pearl barley (soaked overnight and cooked according to instructions). The combination of ingredients may seem strange, but they are associated with ancient Roman celebrations of the rite of spring: flowers, eggs for new life, ricotta from the sheep, wheat and flour from the land – though the tart as we know it today is said to have been created, like so many of our sweet dishes, by a nun in a local convent. One of the many legends associated with the dish involves a mermaid called Partenope. One of the best stories is that she lived in the Gulf of Napoli, and to celebrate the arrival of spring each year she would come and sing to the inhabitants. One year, to say thank you for her songs, they offered her local gifts: ricotta, flour, eggs, wheat, perfumed orange flowers and spices. She was so delighted, she took them to her kingdom under the sea, where the gods mixed them together into a cake.

Serves 8–10
a little melted butter
1 pound (approximately
⅔ recipe quantity) Sweet
pastry (see page 536)
confectioner's sugar to dust

For the filling:
¾ cup wheat grains (bulgur)
1 cup milk
pared peel from ½ lemon, left
whole, the rest grated
2 pinches of ground cinnamon
½ cup superfine sugar
pinch of salt
1 cup fresh ricotta cheese
4 teaspoons orange flower water
⅓ cup candied citron (or lemon)
peel and candied orange
peel, chopped
3 eggs, separated

Put the wheat in a pan, cover with water (no salt) and boil for 20 minutes. Leave to cool in its own water, then drain in a sieve.

Bring the milk to a boil in a pan. Then add the drained wheat, the piece of lemon peel, 1 pinch of cinnamon, a tablespoon of the superfine sugar and the salt. Cook really slowly until all the milk has been absorbed (around an hour). Take the lemon peel out and spread the mixture on a plate to cool.

Put the ricotta into a sieve to drain off its liquid. Mix it with the rest of the sugar, the grated lemon zest, another pinch of cinnamon, the orange flower water and the candied fruit. Add the egg yolks a little at a time, mixing in well. Stir in the cooled wheat mixture.

Whip 2 of the egg whites until stiff, and incorporate into the mixture.

Brush a 13-inch round (2 inches deep) tart tin with melted butter. Divide the pastry into 2 balls, one slightly bigger than the other. Roll out the larger piece and use to line the tart tin. Spoon in the wheat mixture and trim the pastry around the rim of the tin. Leave to rest in the fridge for about 30 minutes.

Preheat the oven to 355°F. Roll out the other ball of pastry and cut into strips. Lay these over the top of the tart to make a lattice design, sealing well at the outer edges. Bake for about an hour until colored, then turn down the heat to 250°F, and bake until a skewer inserted into the center of the filling comes out clean (around 10 minutes). Cool inside the tin and dust with confectioner's sugar.

Rusumada

When I was a kid and waiting for the school bus in the morning, I used to see the farmers go into the local bar, where the guys would make a tonic with red wine and egg yolks, which was supposed to give you strength, and which now reminds me of Vov, the liqueur made with egg yolks and Marsala, which you drink after a coffee when you are skiing. The barman would warm up the red wine like milk, with the steam from the coffee machine, then put some sugar in a cappuccino cup, add the egg yolks, whip them up until they were almost white, and then pour in the hot wine. The drink was called *rusumada* and when I was writing this, I called my mum to ask her what it meant. Of course, there were big discussions with whoever was around, but nobody really knew where the word came from. The best we could think of was that it comes from *riesumare*, which means "to take a body out of the ground," i.e., exhume it, because it is a drink that is supposed to revive you when you feel dead on your feet. It was especially popular in the times when Mussolini decided he must increase the export of tea and coffee, so only the rich people could afford what was left – the rest of the people boiled up orzo (barley) instead of coffee, and instead of tea we had *carcade*, which was made from the red calyx and fruit of a particular hibiscus plant. But if you kept chickens and were lucky enough to have eggs, you could take one down to the bar, and they would make you rusumada.

If you add the whisked egg whites to the rusumada it makes a good dessert, very similar to zabaglione, which, like Vov, is made with egg yolks and Marsala wine (or Muscat wine in Asti) – and which the French say they invented and named after St. Pascal Baylon, one of the many patron saints of cooks. In Italy, of course we say *we* invented it. One story is that it was invented by Bartolomeo Scappi, the personal cook of Pope Pius V, who wrote an enormous cooking manual containing five books, called *Opera*, in 1570. Others say it was an invention of the court of the Medici in Florence. Then again, the great Italian food writer Anna Del Conte has a different theory. Anna is an amazing fount of knowledge about all of our food, its history, and the way each region does things differently. When I started out in London and needed to know how to explain my dishes correctly in English, I used to phone Anna up, because she has lived in this country since the fifties, and she would always put me right. According to her, zabaglione is said to have been invented when the chef of Duke Carlo Emanuele I of Savoy accidentally poured some fortified wine into an egg custard in the seventeenth century. How often we have mistakes to thank for the best things.

Mix the egg yolks with the sugar and whisk until almost white.

In a separate bowl, whisk the egg whites, then gently fold into the yolk mixture and whisk in the wine.

Serve with a spoon and with cookies, if you like.

6 very fresh eggs, separated
6 tablespoons superfine sugar
2–3 tablespoons red wine, such
    as Barbera or Barbaresco

Zuppa di pomodoro dolce, gelatina di balsamica e sorbetto al basilico

Sweet tomato soup, balsamic jelly and basil sorbet

When Italian people come into the restaurant they are not sure about this at first – but when you coax them into tasting it, it is amazing to see the way they react, because when the tomatoes are at their perfect moment of sweetness, you experience a real intensity of sugar, and the aroma is so fresh, it is as though you were walking into a garden full of tomato vines. Because the tomatoes have to be so good, we might have this on the menu only five or six times a year. You need very ripe tomatoes, left on the vine so they can dry out a little to concentrate the sugar. On warm days, you could even put them on the window ledge in the sun for a few hours. The ideal scenario is to have tomatoes so sweet that you don't need any sugar syrup at all, because the more complex you make the soup, the more you lose the amazing freshness. However, if the tomatoes are not as sweet as you would like, have a little syrup ready.

We serve the soup with a sablé biscuit (see page 578) "stuck" to the bottom of a shallow soup dish with toffee, topped with Basil sorbet (see page 560), which rises up above the soup and is garnished with Candied basil leaves (page 581). The slightly salty biscuit intensifies the sweetness of the soup.

14 ounces (about 1¾ cups) very sweet cherry tomatoes (see above), such as Pachino from Sicilia or San Marzano
about 5 fresh mint leaves
about 2 tablespoons syrup (made with a tablespoon of water boiled with a tablespoon of sugar, then taken off the heat)

For the balsamic jelly:
2 teaspoons balsamic vinegar
1 tablespoon plus 2 teaspoons sugar
3g gelatin leaves, soaked in water and squeezed

To serve:
toffee made with a can of condensed milk (see page 522)
4 Salted special sablé biscuits (see page 578)
Basil sorbet (see page 560)
8 Candied basil leaves, for garnish (see page 581, optional)

Prepare both soup and jelly a few hours ahead. To make the soup, put the tomatoes in a blender and blend until they are completely liquid, adding the mint halfway through. Pass through a fine sieve and chill in the fridge for about 3 hours. The juice will separate – the bubbles that you introduced during the blending will cause any small particles of tomato to rise, so you can spoon them off and discard them.

Taste the soup and, if necessary, stir in a little syrup. Go gently, because the soup should taste tomato-sweet, not sugar-sweet. Put back in the fridge until ready to serve.

To make the jelly, put the balsamic vinegar and sugar in a pan and bring to a boil. Allow to bubble and reduce by about two-thirds (to around ⅓ cup). Take off the heat and mix in the gelatin leaves until they dissolve. Pour into a shallow dish, leave to cool and then put into the fridge for around 2 hours until set. When set firmly, cut into 16 pieces.

To serve, put a little toffee into the base of each of 4 deep soup plates and stick a salted sablé biscuit on top. Pour the soup around, so that it comes just to the top of the biscuit, and add 4 cubes of jelly to each soup. Scoop out 4 balls of Basil sorbet and place on top of the biscuits. If you like, finish by sticking 2 candied basil leaves into each ball of ice cream.

Soufflé di riso carnaroli al limone

Carnaroli rice and lemon soufflé

The rice of the northern Lomellina region and the big Sorrento lemons from the southern Amalfi coast (see page 416) brought together in a soufflé – for me this is an incredible dessert. We use carnaroli rice because it becomes very creamy but retains its shape and bite. Technically, of course, we could make a more perfect, symmetrically risen soufflé in a ramekin dish, but the flavor that infuses into the rice when you cook the soufflé inside the halved lemons is just beautiful – this is really one of those dishes that people go mad for whenever it is on the menu. If you can't find Sorrento lemons, look for big, thick-skinned ones that are all the same size, so that the soufflés cook for a similar length of time – or, if you like, you can use oranges.

Serves 6
1 cup plus 2 tablespoons
    carnaroli rice
8½ cups milk
½ vanilla bean, split lengthwise
1 tablespoon plus 2 teaspoons
    orange juice
¼ cup superfine sugar
¼ cup unsalted butter
3 large similar-sized lemons
    (preferably Sorrento)
    or oranges
½ cup cornstarch
3 gelatin leaves, soaked in water
    and squeezed

For the meringue:
1 cup egg whites
    (from 7–8 large eggs)
1 scant cup superfine sugar

Put a tray into the fridge so that it gets really cold. Preheat the oven to 390°F.

Put ⅓ cup plus 1 tablespoon of the rice into a pan with half the milk, bring to a boil, then turn down to a simmer and "overcook," i.e., until the rice is really soft. Blend the rice and milk with an immersion blender until smooth, and pass through a fine sieve. Set aside.

Put the rest of the milk in a pan, add the vanilla bean, scraping in the seeds, and bring to a boil. Add the remaining rice and this time cook until it is al dente (just firm to the bite). Drain through a fine sieve, take out the vanilla bean and spread the rice out on the tray you have chilled in the fridge – this will stop it from cooking any more. Leave in a cool place (though not in the fridge) so that it cools as quickly as possible.

Warm the orange juice and sugar in a pan. When the sugar has dissolved, take off the heat, add the butter, and whisk until it is properly incorporated. Leave this at room temperature while you prepare your lemons or oranges.

Trim each end of the fruit until flat, then cut in half across the width. Scoop out all the flesh with a spoon and discard it, leaving you with 6 fruit "ramekins." Put in the fridge for 30 minutes to an hour.

Brush the inside and rims of the fruit with the orange juice mixture, making sure every bit is completely covered – this is to make sure that the inside, and particularly the rims, are completely sealed and smooth, so that the soufflé doesn't catch as it rises. Lay upside down on a tray lined with a sheet of parchment paper and put back in the fridge for about 5 minutes, so that any excess syrup can drain off, then turn them upright again and leave in the fridge until you need them.

With a knife, chop through the cooled rice grains to produce finer pieces and put into a bowl.

Put the reserved rice "milk" back on the heat, keeping back about 4 tablespoons. Mix this with the cornstarch. When the rice mixture comes to the boil, add the cornstarch mixture, stirring all the time, and simmer for about a minute to cook out the flavor of the flour. Take off the heat and add the gelatine. When the gelatine has dissolved, pour the mixture over the rice grains, stirring all the time, as the mixture will now be very thick.

To make the meringue, put the egg whites into a mixer and whisk until you can make a trace with the whisk. Add the sugar very slowly, until you can form firm peaks. Very carefully and lightly, begin to fold the meringue into the rice mixture – incorporate a third of it first and fold it in completely, then, again, but very lightly, fold in the rest. It is important not to overwork the mixture, as you are trying to trap as much air into it as possible, to enable the soufflé to rise.

The easiest way to fill your fruit containers evenly is to spoon the mixture into a piping bag with a large hole and pipe it in to about ¼ inch below the rim. Alternatively, you can just spoon it in. Put the soufflés into the oven for around 8 minutes until they are puffed up and golden. Don't open the oven door before then.

Tiramisù with banana and licorice ice cream

Tiramisù is the dessert that most people associate with Italy; perhaps because it is made with coffee, which is considered a very Italian thing. However, a real tiramisù at the end of the meal is a killer – very heavy to digest. It is made all over the country, but it is one of those dishes that you have when all the family comes together for a long convivial lunch and so much food that you think you will never eat it, but the meal takes so many hours that at the end you are feeling hungry again. In London, however, I felt it was too heavy, so we experimented with a lighter version.

8 Savoiardi (ladyfingers)
just enough espresso coffee
    to soak the ladyfingers –
    a little over ⅓ cup
1½ bananas

For the mascarpone mousse:
¾ cup whipping cream
1 large whole egg,
    plus yolks of 3 large eggs
¼ cup sugar
2 tablespoons Grand Marnier
2g gelatine leaves, soaked in water and squeezed
¾ cup mascarpone cheese

For the Frangipane wafer:
25g ground almonds
2 tablespoons plus
    1 teaspoon flour
⅓ cup confectioner's sugar
scant ¼ cup melted butter
2⅔ tablespoons egg whites
1 teaspoon Amaretto liqueur

For the chocolate sauce:
3½ tablespoons water
2 heaping tablespoons sugar
2 tablespoons good
    cocoa powder,
    plus more for sprinkling
⅓ cup plus 1 tablespoon
    whipping cream

To serve:
Licorice ice cream (see page 566)

Preheat the oven to 320°F.

To make the mascarpone mousse, first whip the cream until it forms stiff peaks and put into the fridge. Put the eggs, extra egg yolks and sugar into a mixer and mix until pale and tripled in volume.

Heat the Grand Marnier gently in a pan, add the gelatin and let it dissolve. Take off the heat and mix in the mascarpone. With a spatula, fold in the chilled cream mixture a little at a time and return to the fridge.

Make the Frangipane wafer mixture as described on page 575. Line a baking tray with waxed paper and spread the mixture thinly in 4 rectangles, each roughly 8 x 3½ inches, leaving a good space between each one. Put in the oven for about 4 minutes until light golden, then take out one at a time and roll around a tall, square bottle to make a "tower." Seal the "seam" by pressing the bottle down on to your work surface, then slide the "tower" off quickly and stand it on its end.

To make the chocolate sauce, put 3 tablespoons of the water and the sugar in a pan and bring to a boil, then add the cocoa powder. Bring back to the boil, add the cream, bring back to a boil again, then reduce the heat and cook slowly until the sauce becomes thick, dark and shiny. To test when it is ready, spoon a little onto a cold surface; it should keep its shape and set. Take the sauce off the heat and leave to cool – but don't put it in the fridge, or it will lose its shine and become too hard.

Dip the ladyfingers in the espresso just long enough for them to turn pale coffee color. Peel the bananas and cut them into small dice.

To serve, dot the chocolate sauce around the 4 plates, put a cylinder of frangipane wafer upright in the center of each one, then start to layer up the tiramisù inside: first some of the soaked ladyfingers, then a layer of banana, then some of the mascarpone mousse. Repeat this layering three times, finishing with mousse, then sprinkle the top with cocoa powder. Serve with the ice cream. We make 4 small quenelles of this and balance one on the edge of each cylinder.

Gelati e sorbetti

Ice creams and sorbets

The Italians are one hundred percent the inventors of ice cream as we know it today (a frozen confection made with milk and/or cream and often egg yolks). Definitely. No contest. But who actually made the first ice cream? As always with Italians, in every region there is somebody who makes a claim, and everybody reckons they have the answer. One of the best-known stories is that it was a Sicilian from Palermo, named Francesco Procopio dei Coltelli, who set up Le Procope in Paris in 1686, serving ice cream in cups with stems to fashionable Parisians. Some people dispute this, saying that it was only sorbet (frozen fruit syrup or pulp) that he served. Others say that ice cream was already known for over a century before, when Catherine di Medici taught her pastry chefs how to make it at the French court when she married Henry II in 1533. This too, though, is the subject of a big debate. Certainly, by 1775, when the first book dedicated to frozen confectionery, *De'sorbetti*, by Filippo Baldini, was published in Napoli, it had a chapter on "milky sorbets," so some kind of ice cream as we know it was being made by then.

Of course, the use of ice, and the idea of mixing it with flavored liquids or fruits, goes back to ancient times. The Romans dug out pits, which they insulated with straw, then packed in ice and snow and covered it with more straw, to keep throughout the summer. In my home village of Corgeno you can still find the place near the *palazzo* where they built a whole refrigerated room, like an igloo, in which they stored ice from the lake in winter, which would be used for the whole community.

The Chinese are supposed to have been the first to discover that ice could be mixed with salt, which lowered its temperature to below freezing point, so that you could freeze liquids. As always there is a story about Marco Polo – that he saw the Chinese freezing syrups in vessels buried in a mixture of salt and ice, and brought the idea home, but like most Marco Polo stories it is probably a myth.

Others say that as far back as A.D. 64, the Roman emperor Nero used to send slaves to collect snow and ice from the Appennine mountains, to mix with fruit and honey; or that the Arabs brought the idea of storing ice and snow and mixing it with fruit pulp to Sicilia – they called such drinks sherbet, which became sorbetto (sorbet).

In Napoli, you still find places where they make the most pure and primitive kind of granita (which we think of as frozen juice or coffee, crushed into thin flakes) by literally chipping shards of ice from a big block and adding a squeeze of Sorrento lemon or citrus juice, or some pureed fruit. They are better than anything for quenching your thirst, but in the searing heat of the summer you have to be careful not to eat them too quickly, because you feel the coldness so strongly inside your body that you almost pass out.

The science of ice cream

These days anyone can make ice cream at home, thanks to all kinds of home ice cream machines. Choose a big one with a powerful motor and a small cylinder, if possible, as the idea is to churn the mixture as little as is needed to bring it all together. Even if you don't have a machine, of course you can put the ice cream into a container, put it into the freezer, and stir it with a fork every 20 minutes during the first 2 hours, so that you break up any crystals, and it will still be much more flavorful and wholesome than any commercial oversweetened ice cream.

At Locanda, however, we are always in search of perfection. Also, we can't make ice cream every single day in every flavor, so we have perfected a formula that means that two weeks later when we take the ice cream out of the freezer it is still beautifully soft, with no crystallization. In order to achieve this, we use different sugars with different properties of sweetness and "nonfreezing power." Sugars don't freeze, but they have different levels of resistance to freezing, so by playing around with the ratio of sugars, you can alter the freezing point of your mixture, and therefore control the texture, as well as the sweetness.

In addition to sucrose, which is the sugar that everybody knows, extracted from cane or beet, we use invert sugar, which is made by heating sucrose and water with sodium bicarbonate. This sugar has anticrystallizing properties and helps make ice cream softer, especially when it has a high solid content, for example, chocolate or nuts. We also use dextrose, which is extracted from maize during a process in which the starch (a chain of glucose molecules) is broken down until only pure glucose is left. Because of its mild sweetening power, it allows fresh flavors to come through strongly. Also, we use some dextrose that still contains starch. This is glucose syrup, which, in its powdered form (easier to use in ice cream making), is known as atomized glucose, and works a bit like cornstarch, in that it has the power to thicken an ice cream mixture. In addition to whole milk and heavy cream, we also use some powdered milk (with 0 percent fat) to give a more pronounced milk flavor. Some of the recipes include eggs, which contain lecithin, a natural emulsifier; in others, we sometimes use a stabilizer made from natural ingredients (such as plants, including algae) to make sure the ice cream keeps its ultrasoftness and smoothness – but there is no need for this at home.

The lead is being taken in this technological field by an Italian, Angelo Corvitto, who has lived in Spain for many years – as you can imagine, Ivan, our pastry chef, likes to say that he had to go to Spain to learn how to make ice cream properly. Corvitto has devised a complex computer-based program for commercial ice cream makers. Ivan has studied all the new techniques, and then modified the ideas to suit our idea of what a fantastic ice cream should be about.

The recipes here have all been adapted to work in home ice cream makers, and, if you prefer, instead of using the different sugars, you can simply add up the total amount of sugar each recipe calls for, then make this up using one-third dextrose, which is easily available, and two-thirds superfine sugar.

Each recipe follows the same basic method, but the ratio of ingredients varies with each one, in order to achieve the best possible consistency and flavor. For someone like me, who likes to work with handfuls of this and that (which is, after all, the Italian way), it can seem pedantic to have to weigh out quantities so minutely – in the kitchen Ivan measures everything down to 1 or 2 grams, though for the recipes here we have rounded the amounts for American kitchens. But this is one area of the kitchen where we have to forget about spontaneity, because accuracy really makes a difference. That is why we have given the quantities for the ice cream recipes in grams and ounces – if you weigh your milk, sugar, etc., it is far more precise than trying to judge the level in a measuring cup. You also need to use a candy thermometer, so that you can measure the temperature at the crucial stages of the recipes.

Points to remember

Once you have heated the mixture, you must take it off the heat, cool it down and get it into the fridge as quickly as you can. This is because there is a critical point between 59°F and 113°F, at which it is easy for bacteria to reproduce. The best way to cool it down quickly is to put the base of the pan into a bowl of ice, and keep stirring as it cools down. Make sure it goes into the fridge within 30 minutes of coming off the heat.

Also, it is important that your mixture spend 6 to 12 hours in the fridge before you churn it, because during this time not only do all the flavors come together but the water in the mixture spreads all the way through it and amalgamates with the fat, so the ice cream will be smoother and lighter and the water won't crystallize.

A note about the sugars

Where a recipe calls for different sugars, such as invert sugar or atomized sugar, if you like, you can instead just add up the total quantity of sugar, and use one-third dextrose and two-thirds superfine sugar.

Makes 1kg
(about 2½ quarts)
745g (25.19 fluid ounces) melon juice (puree the melon in a food processor, or put through a juicer, then strain it through a fine sieve)
180g (6.35 ounces) dextrose
20g (.71 ounce) superfine sugar
5g (.18 ounce) sorbet stabilizer (optional)
50g (1.76 fluid ounces) lemon juice

Sorbetto di melone

Melon sorbet

Put 200g (6¾ fluid ounces) of the juice into a pan, add the dextrose, mix with a hand blender and bring to 104°F (40°C). Whisk in the sugars and stabilizer, if using. Bring up to 185°F (85°C), then take off the heat and cool as quickly as you can, so that you don't encourage bacteria.

When the mixture is cold, mix in the rest of the melon juice and the lemon juice. Put into the fridge for 6 to 12 hours. Put into an ice cream maker and churn according to instructions.

Makes 1kg
(about 2½ quarts)
605g (20.46 fluid ounces) water
20g (.71 ounce) fresh mint leaves, chopped
50g (1.76 ounces) atomized glucose
155g (5.47 ounces) dextrose
110g (3.88 ounces) superfine sugar
5g (.18 ounce) sorbet stabilizer (optional)
50g (1.76 fluid ounces) lemon juice

Sorbetto di menta

Mint sorbet

With a hand blender, mix the water with the mint and atomized glucose, if using, and the dextrose until smooth. Put into a pan and bring to 104°F (40°C). Whisk in the sugar and stabilizer, if using. Bring up to 185°F (85°C), take off the heat and cool as quickly as you can, so that you don't encourage bacteria.

When the mixture is cold, use a hand blender to mix in the lemon juice. Put into the fridge for 6 to 12 hours. Put into an ice cream maker and churn according to instructions.

Makes 1kg
(about 2½ quarts)
625g (21.13 fluid ounces) water
10g (.35 ounce) chopped basil leaves
50g (1.76 ounces) atomized glucose
160g (5.64 ounces) dextrose
110g (3.88 ounces) superfine sugar
5g (.18 ounce) sorbet stabilizer (optional)
50g (1.76 fluid ounces) lemon juice

Sorbetto di basilico

Basil sorbet

With a hand blender, mix the water with the basil and atomized glucose, if using, and the dextrose until smooth. Put into a pan and bring to 104°F (40°C). Whisk in the sugar and stabilizer, if using. Bring up to 185°F (85°C), take off the heat, and cool as quickly as you can, so you don't encourage bacteria.

When the mixture is cold, use a hand blender to mix in the lemon juice. Put into the fridge for 6 to 12 hours. Put into an ice cream maker and churn according to instructions.

Gelato alla vaniglia

Vanilla ice cream

With a hand blender, mix the milk, cream, powdered milk and dextrose until smooth. Put into a pan and bring to 104°F (40°C).

Whisk in the sugars and egg yolks, and put in the vanilla beans (halved) and scrape in the seeds. Bring up to 185°F (85°C), take off the heat and cool as quickly as you can, so that you don't encourage bacteria. Put into the fridge for 6 to 12 hours. Remove the vanilla beans.

Put into an ice cream maker and churn according to instructions.

Makes 1kg
(about 2½ quarts)
545g (18.43 fluid ounces)
    whole milk
85g (2.87 fluid ounces)
    whipping cream
50g (1.76 ounces) powdered milk
170g (6 ounces) dextrose
40g (1.41 ounces) superfine sugar
10g (.35 ounce) invert sugar
100g (3.38 fluid ounces) egg yolks
2 vanilla beans

Gelato al latte

Milk ice cream

With a hand blender, mix the milk, cream, milk powder and dextrose until smooth. Put into a pan and bring to 104°F (40°C). Whisk in the sugars and stabilizer, if using.

Bring up to 185°F (85°C), then take off the heat and cool as quickly as you can, so that you don't encourage bacteria. Put into the fridge for 6 to 12 hours.

Put into an ice cream maker and churn according to instructions.

Makes about 1kg
(about 2½ quarts)
565g (19.1 fluid ounces)
    whole milk
170g (5.75 fluid ounces)
    whipping cream
40g (1.41 ounces) powdered milk
135g (4.76 ounces) dextrose
50g (1.76 ounces) superfine sugar
25g (.88 ounce) invert sugar
5g (.18 ounce) ice cream
    stabilizer (optional)

Gelato di crema Catalana

Crème Catalan ice cream

First make the caramel: put the sugar into a pan and heat slowly until it turns to a golden caramel. Pour onto a sheet of waxed paper. Leave to set and then smash into small pieces.

With a hand blender, mix the milk, cream, milk powder and dextrose until smooth. Put into a pan and bring to 104°F (40°C).

Whisk in the sugars and egg yolks, then add the citrus peel, cinnamon stick and vanilla bean (halved) and scrape in the seeds. Bring up to 185°F (85°C) and take off the heat. Cool as quickly as you can, so that you don't encourage bacteria. Put into the fridge for 6 to 12 hours.

Put through a fine sieve, then into an ice cream maker and churn according to instructions.

Mix in the pieces of caramel and serve.

Makes 1kg
(about 2½ quarts)
545g (18.43 fluid ounces)
    whole milk
85g (2.87 fluid ounces)
    whipping cream
50g (1.76 ounces) powdered milk
150g (5.29 ounces) dextrose
50g (1.76 ounces) superfine sugar
20g (.71 ounce) invert sugar
100g (3.38 fluid ounces) egg yolks
strip of lemon peel
strip of orange peel
1 cinnamon stick
1 vanilla bean

For the caramel:
100g (3.53 ounces) superfine
    sugar

Makes about 1kg
(2½ quarts)
265g (8.96 fluid ounces)
   whole milk
160g (5.41 fluid ounces)
   whipping cream
40g (1.41 ounces) powdered milk
145g (5.11 ounces) dextrose
50g (1.76 ounces) superfine sugar
25g (.88 ounces) invert sugar
5g (.18 ounce) ice cream
   stabilizer (optional)
300g (10.71 ounces)
   mascarpone cheese

Gelato al mascarpone

Mascarpone ice cream

I think people are a bit confused by mascarpone and mozzarella – but before you say, "Well, you couldn't make an ice cream with mozzarella," we did: with olive oil and Parmesan too, and it was fantastic; but so is this ice cream made with mascarpone, our famous gorgeously creamy "cheese" from Lombardia, which is used in desserts and savory dishes. In fact, like ricotta, it isn't a true cheese at all but is made in a similar way to yogurt, with cream from cows fed on a special diet of grasses, herbs and flowers. The cream is heated, then citric, tartaric or acetic acid is added and it is allowed to rest and separate, before being drained through cloth. Some say the name comes from the word *mascarpa*, which means the whey of an aged cheese *(stracchino)*; or perhaps from *mascarpia*, which is the local dialect word for "ricotta," its close relation. Others say that, since the Spanish ruled in Lombardia in the sixteenth and seventeenth centuries, the name comes from the Spanish expression *"mas que bueno,"* which means "more than good."

With a hand blender, mix the milk, cream, powdered milk and dextrose until smooth. Put into a pan and bring to 104°F (40°C). Whisk in the sugars and stabilizer, if using.

Bring up to 185°F (85°C), then take off the heat, and cool as quickly as you can, so that you don't encourage bacteria.

When the mixture is cold, mix in the mascarpone. Put into the fridge for 6 to 12 hours.

Put into an ice cream maker and churn according to instructions.

Makes 1kg
(about 2½ quarts)
615g (8.96 fluid ounces)
   whole milk
125g (4.23 fluid ounces)
   whipping cream
40g (1.41 ounces) powdered milk
160g (5.64 ounces) dextrose
40g (1.41 ounces) fresh
   lemon thyme leaves
25g (.88 ounce) superfine sugar
25g (.88 ounce) invert sugar
5g (.18 ounce) ice cream
   stabilizer (optional)

Gelato al timo limonato

Lemon thyme ice cream

With a hand blender, mix the milk, cream, milk powder and dextrose until smooth. Add the lemon thyme. Put into a pan and bring to 104°F (40°C). Whisk in the sugars and stabilizer, if using.

Bring up to 185°F (85°C), take off the heat, pass through a fine sieve, and then cool as quickly as you can, so that you don't encourage bacteria. Put into the fridge for 6 to 12 hours.

Put into an ice cream maker, and churn according to instructions.

Makes about 1kg
(about 2½ quarts)
430g (14.54 fluid ounces)
whole milk
95g (3.35 fluid ounces)
whipping cream
55g (1.94 ounces) powdered milk
145g (5.11 ounces) dextrose
80g (2.82 ounces) superfine sugar
100g (3.38 fluid ounces) egg yolks
90g (3.04 fluid ounces)
Amaretto liqueur
100g (3.53 ounces)
crushed amaretti cookies

Gelato all'Amaretto

Amaretto ice cream

With a hand blender, mix the milk, cream, powdered milk and dextrose until smooth. Put into a pan and bring to 104°F (40°C). Whisk in the sugar and egg yolks.

Bring up to 185°F (85°C), take off the heat, and cool as quickly as you can, so that you don't encourage bacteria.

When the mixture is cold, mix in the Amaretto with the hand blender. Put into the fridge for 6 to 12 hours.

Put into an ice cream maker and churn according to instructions. Stir in the crushed amaretti cookies before serving.

Makes 1kg
(about 2½ quarts)
515g (17.41 fluid ounces)
whole milk
115g (3.89 fluid ounces)
whipping cream
35g (1.23 ounces) powdered milk
70g (2.47 ounces) dextrose
30g (1.06 ounces) superfine sugar
20g (.71 ounce) invert sugar
90g (3.04 fluid ounces) egg yolks
120g (4.06 fluid ounces)
Mirto (myrtle liqueur)

For the myrtle sauce:
100ml (3.38 fluid ounces)
Mirto (myrtle liqueur)
30g (1.06 ounces) dextrose

Gelato al mirto

Myrtle ice cream

Mirto is the name not only for myrtle in Italy but for the liqueur made from the myrtle berry, which is traditional in Sardegna. (There is also a dryer white Mirto, made with the leaves.) You should be able to find it in specialty liquor stores or Italian importers, or you could replace it with black currant liqueur.

With a hand blender, mix the milk, cream, powdered milk and dextrose until smooth. Put into a pan and bring to 104°F (40°C). Whisk in the sugars and egg yolks.

Bring up to 185°F (85°C), take off the heat, then cool as quickly as you can, so that you don't encourage bacteria.

When the mixture is cold, mix in the Mirto. Put into the fridge for 6 to 12 hours.

Meanwhile, make the myrtle sauce. Put the liqueur and dextrose in a pan, bring to a boil and let it reduce to the consistency of caramel.

Put the ice cream mixture into an ice cream maker and churn according to instructions.

Serve the ice cream with some of the myrtle sauce drizzled over the top.

Gelato al Limoncello

Limoncello ice cream

Limoncello is the famous liqueur made with Sorrento lemons.

With a hand blender, mix the milk, cream, powdered milk and dextrose until smooth.

Put into a pan and bring to 104°F (40°C). Whisk in the sugars and egg yolks. Bring up to 185°F (85°C), take off the heat, then cool as quickly as you can, so that you don't encourage bacteria.

When the mixture is cold, mix in the Limoncello and lemon juice. Put into the fridge for 6 to 12 hours.

Put into an ice cream maker and churn according to instructions.

Makes about 1kg
(2½ quarts)
545g (18.43 fluid ounces) whole milk
95g (3.35 fluid ounces) whipping cream
35g (1.23 ounces) powdered milk
70g (2.47 ounces) dextrose
50g (1.76 ounces) superfine sugar
20g (.71 ounce) invert sugar
90g (3.04 fluid ounces) egg yolks
110g (3.72 fluid ounces) Limoncello liqueur
20g (.68 fluid ounce) lemon juice

Gelato al tartufo e miele

Truffle honey ice cream

Truffle honey (honey with slivers of white truffles) is a specialty of Toscana, which you can find in delicatessens.

With a hand blender, mix the milk, cream, powdered milk and dextrose until smooth. Put into a pan and bring to 104°F (40°C). Whisk in the sugar and egg yolks, then add the honeys.

Bring up to 185°F (85°C), take off the heat, then cool as quickly as you can, so that you don't encourage bacteria. Put into the fridge for 6 to 12 hours.

Put into an ice cream maker and churn according to instructions.

Makes about 1kg
(2½ quarts)
535g (18.09 fluid ounces) whole milk
85g (2.87 fluid ounces) whipping cream
50g (1.76 ounces) powdered milk
45g (1.59 ounces) dextrose
20g (.71 ounce) sugar
120g (4.06 fluid ounces) egg yolks
105g (3.05 fluid ounces) honey
40g (1.41 fluid ounces) truffle honey

Makes about 1kg
(2½ quarts)
315g (10.65 fluid ounces)
whole milk
195g (6.59 fluid ounces)
whipping cream
60g (2.12 ounces) powdered milk
140g (4.94 ounces) dextrose
60g (2.12 ounces) superfine sugar
25g (.88 ounce) invert sugar
5g (.18 ounce) ice cream
stabilizer (optional)
200g (6.76 fluid ounces)
espresso

Gelato al caffè

Coffee ice cream

We serve this with Milk wafers (see page 578).

With a hand blender, mix the milk, cream, powdered milk and dextrose until smooth. Put into a pan and bring to 104°F (40°C). Whisk in the sugars and stabilizer, if using. Bring up to 185°F (85°C), take off the heat, then cool as quickly as you can, so that you don't encourage bacteria.

When the mixture is cold, mix in the espresso. Put into the fridge for 6 to 12 hours.

Put into an ice cream maker and churn according to instructions.

Makes 1kg
(about 2½ quarts)
575g (19.44 fluid ounces)
whole milk
170g (5.75 fluid ounces)
whipping cream
40g (1.41 ounces) powdered milk
150g (5.29 ounces) dextrose
45g (1.59 ounces)
licorice root powder
30g (1.06 ounces) superfine sugar
25g (.88 ounce) invert sugar
5g (.18 ounce) ice cream
stabilizer (optional)

Gelato alla liquirizia

Licorice ice cream

True licorice root is a forgotten thing in this country. I love it. The real thing looks and smells beautiful and it is so pure-tasting – sweet yet not sweet – so different from the shiny black stuff you see in candy stores shaped into shoelaces and so on, which is made by cooking the root until it forms a black syrup, sweetening it with sugar and adding starch. We buy our licorice from the Amarelli family in Calabria, whose great plantations of licorice plants are about 600 years old and are grown on big stones, so the roots hit them and turn upward and can be harvested easily. When I was little, I used to see the old men sitting outside in the afternoons, chatting and chewing on pieces of licorice root, and I read in an Italian newspaper that since Italy introduced a smoking ban in public places, people have been rushing to buy licorice sticks to put in their mouths as a substitute.

With a hand blender, mix the milk, cream, powdered milk, dextrose and licorice until smooth. Put into a pan and bring to 104°F (40°C). Whisk in the sugars and stabilizer, if using. Bring up to 185°F (85°C), take off the heat, pass through a fine sieve, then cool as quickly as you can, so that you don't encourage bacteria. Put into the fridge for 6 to 12 hours.

Put into an ice cream maker and churn according to instructions.

Makes about 1kg
(2½ quarts)
255g (8.62 fluid ounces)
    whole milk
60g (2.12 ounces) powdered milk
140g (4.94 ounces) dextrose
300g (10.14 fluid ounces) water
10g (.35 ounce) superfine sugar
100g (3.53 ounces) invert sugar
5g (.18 ounce) ice cream
    stabilizer (optional)
20g (.68 fluid ounce) egg yolks
100g (3.53 ounces) hazelnut
    paste (see above)

Gelato alle nocciole

Hazelnut ice cream

You can buy ready-made hazelnut paste (praline) or make your own by putting 50g (1.76 ounces) roasted hazelnuts into a food processor with 50g (1.76 ounces) superfine sugar and blending to a paste.

With a hand blender, mix the milk, powdered milk and dextrose with the water until smooth. Put into a pan and bring to 104°F (40°C). Whisk in the sugars, stabilizer, if using, egg yolks and hazelnut paste. Bring up to 185°F (85°C), take off the heat, then cool as quickly as you can, so that you don't encourage bacteria.

When the mixture is cold, put into the fridge for 6 to 12 hours.

Put into an ice cream maker and churn according to instructions.

Makes 1kg
(about 2½ quarts)
200g (7.05 ounces)
    pistachio nuts
320g (10.82 fluid ounces)
    whole milk
60g (2.12 ounces) powdered milk
140g (4.94 ounces) dextrose
340g (11.99 ounces) water
60g (2.12 ounces) superfine sugar
25g (.88 ounce) invert sugar
5g (.18 ounce) ice cream
    stabilizer (optional)
40g (1.35 fluid ounces) egg yolks

Gelato al pistacchio

Pistachio ice cream

Preheat the oven to 320°F. Put half the nuts on a baking tray and let them dry out and roast a little in the oven for about 5 minutes. Take out, allow to cool, chop and keep to one side.

Put the rest of the nuts into a food processor and whiz until they become oily. Keep this paste to one side.

With a hand blender, mix the milk, powdered milk and dextrose with the water until smooth. Put into a pan and bring to 104°F (40°C). Whisk in the sugars, stabilizer, if using, egg yolks and pistachio paste. Bring up to 185°F (85°C), take off the heat, then cool as quickly as you can, so that you don't encourage bacteria.

When the mixture is cold, put into the fridge for 6 to 12 hours.

Put into an ice cream maker and churn according to instructions.

Sprinkle with the chopped pistachio nuts before serving.

Gelato al tè

Marco Polo tea ice cream

Marco Polo tea is quite spicy and floral, but you could make this with any tea you find that has a fantastic flavor and aroma, perhaps a fruit tea or chai. Something quite potent, like mango – you don't want anything too delicate, as freezing has the effect of closing down flavor a little, and too subtle a tea might get lost. Good-quality green tea is also very good and refreshing.

With a hand blender, mix the milk, cream, powdered milk and dextrose until smooth. Put into a pan and bring to 104°F (40°C). Whisk in the sugars and stabilizer, if using.

Bring up to 185°F (85°C), then take off the heat. Add the tea leaves and cool as quickly as you can, so that you don't encourage bacteria. Put into the fridge for 6 to 12 hours.

Pass through a fine sieve, then put into an ice cream maker and churn according to instructions.

Makes about 1kg
(2½ quarts)
565g (19.1 fluid ounces) whole milk
170g (5.75 fluid ounces) whipping cream
40g (1.41 ounces) powdered milk
135g (4.76 ounces) dextrose
50g (1.76 ounces) superfine sugar
25g (.88 ounce) invert sugar
5g (.18 ounce) ice cream stabilizer (optional)
40g (1.41 ounces) Marco Polo (or similar) tea leaves

Gelato alla cannella

Cinnamon ice cream

With a hand blender, mix the milk, cream, powdered milk and dextrose until smooth. Put into a pan and bring to 104°F (40°C). Whisk in the sugars, stabilizer, if using, and cinnamon. Bring up to 185°F (85°C), take off the heat, then cool as quickly as you can, so that you don't encourage bacteria. Put into the fridge for 6 to 12 hours.

Put into an ice cream maker and churn according to instructions.

Makes 1kg
(about 2½ quarts)
520g (17.58 fluid ounces) whole milk
190g (6.42 fluid ounces) whipping cream
60g (2.12 ounces) powdered milk
140g (4.94 ounces) dextrose
60g (2.12 ounces) superfine sugar
25g (.88 ounce) invert sugar
5g (.18 ounce) ice cream stabilizer (optional)
10g (1.41 ounces) ground cinnamon

Gelato al panettone

Panettone ice cream

This is something we make in the restaurant at Christmastime – and it is a fantastic thing to do with leftover panettone at home, using the Vanilla ice cream recipe on page 561.

All you do is tear the panettone into shreds, then, the day before, soak them in the milk you are going to use for the ice cream. Pass through a fine sieve, reserving the panettone. Make the vanilla ice cream as usual, but when it has been churned add the pieces of reserved panettone. The sweet, spicy-citrus slivers of panettone give the ice cream a fascinating flavor.

Panettone

"Bread was what most people still ate at Christmastime, but panettone was what they dreamed of eating."

When my cousins at the bakery in Gallarate begin the production of panettone in the weeks before Christmas, the smell in the morning when you walk into the bakery is the best, really the best. The dough is put into the molds, and then into the proofers, so the mixture rises up almost to the top, like a mushroom. Then, after they come out of the oven – 150 or so at a time – they are lifted up on massive ladders, so that they can cool slowly upside down – this is what "stretches" the warm cake and gives it its characteristic dome shape.

The only things that we can say for sure about panettone – our Italian Christmas cake that is really more like a bread – is that it was invented in Lombardia and most probably in Milano, since this was the rich capital, where the wealthy people built their houses away from the malaria of the rice fields. The rest is the subject of myth and legend.

One story is that there was a young nobleman from Milano, named Ughetto degli Antellari, who fell in love with a baker's daughter named Toni, and to impress her father, he blustered his way into the bakery kitchen, pretending to be an apprentice, and made a huge, sumptuous bread shaped like a dome, using an abundance of rich ingredients like eggs, butter and fruit. He called it Pan de Toni (Toni's bread) and it became all the rage.

In another version of the story, it was the baker who was named Toni. Then again, other people say that panettone was first created by a kitchen boy called Toni, at the court of the Duke of Milano, Ludovico il Moro. He is supposed to have come to the rescue when the cook ruined the Christmas dessert, by improvising a sweet bread with leftover dough and fruit, which the duke loved so much, he ordered it to be brought to him for breakfast, lunch and dinner. In yet another tale, the nobleman Ughetto turns into a nun named Sister Ughetta, who added fruit to the usual bread and made a cross in the top for Christmas.

The less romantic idea is that panettone evolved from a dark country bread that was typical in Lombardia back in the tenth or eleventh century. On Christmas night, the ritual was that the family poured red wine and juniper onto burning logs in the fireplace, and then distributed the loaf. In medieval times, as white flour became more popular and ingredients such as butter and eggs, raisins, sugar and candied fruit became more available to the wealthier people, the recipe changed and became more elaborate. I like to imagine that in the early days of its evolution, bread was what most people still ate at Christmastime, but panettone was what they dreamed of eating.

I love panettone. It is such a fantastic present to give at Christmastime, in a big box with a ribbon. But it must be a good panettone. These days you can buy all sorts of variations: made with champagne creams, chocolate and coffee, but for me the traditional recipe is the best. A good panettone seems quite firm when you first open it, but as soon as it comes to room temperature, the fantastic aromas and flavors of vanilla and fruit open out, and when you bite into it, it becomes soft and buttery. I find the best ones usually come simply wrapped. The more flutes and frills and excess packaging that you have, the more you suspect that the money has been diverted away from the ingredients for the cake.

Because there is now such a big market for panettone all over the world, the big-brand companies make the cakes on a large scale, often putting in added flavorings and preservatives so that the cake will last for a long time, whereas the panettone that comes from the smaller, family bakeries, like the Gnocchi Bakery of my cousins, is made only one month before Christmas, so that the cake matures at just the right time, and it contains no preservatives, because it is meant to be eaten only during the Christmas and New Year festivities.

For a panettone of this quality, you need to pay a bit more money. Look at the ingredients: butter, fruit, etc. – it is impossible to produce a 2-pound cake cheaply, unless you are using inferior produce. I would use cheaper ones only to make bread pudding. I don't know who started making such a traditional English dessert with panettone, but I remember we did it at Olivo, and it was very fashionable.

At home in Corgeno, the local tradition was that every family would buy two or three panettone at Christmastime. Not all of them would be sweet. You also find salted panettone (or *pandoro* in Venezia), which you cut crosswise and then layer up with ham and cheese, and maybe some smoked salmon, which is popular in Italy at Christmas. Then you cut slices, so that, a bit like a club sandwich, each mouthful tastes different. This is what you would make to share with friends on Christmas morning, when they come to your house for the first drink; and you also see it done in bars over the holidays, for everybody to eat with a glass of wine.

Always we would keep one sweet panettone until the third of February, the feast day of St. Biago (protector of the throat). Then everyone would take their cake to the church and the priest would bless it. By now the panettone would be quite dry, so naturally you had to have a drink to go with it – or perhaps some Muscat to dip the panettone into. So that was how we celebrated the day of St. Biago: with panettone and Muscat.

Amaretti cookies

Perhaps the most famous Italian macaroons all over the world are amaretti. I was even given them at the end of a meal in Tokyo. The name *amaretti* means "little bitter ones" because traditionally bitter almonds (see page 576) are used to make them. For me, they are essential. Without them, the cookies would be too sweet. With them, the flavor of the sweet almonds is enhanced, and you get the full, characteristic, intensely almondy taste that everyone loves. However, like salami, amaretti are one of the cultural expressions of the people that really show the tastes of a particular region, because the recipe and style change with the territory.

Even though we are talking about the same basic ingredients – eggs, sugar, almonds (or hazelnuts), sometimes bitter almonds, and flour – you would be amazed at the differences you can create by varying the ratio. There must be 200 recipes all over Italy, though they are originally from the north.

The biscuits most people know are amaretti di Saronno, from Lombardia, which are the hard, crunchy ones, usually made commercially and wrapped in papers, which travel well around the world. But there are also beautiful soft amaretti, which my uncle makes in his bakery in Gallarate. In this area, the cows graze on the flat land, so milk and butter are plentiful, and both ingredients are used in the amaretti instead of egg white, which is what gives the macaroons their special softness. If you happen to live in a community that raises lots of chickens, you might use more eggs, and in areas where hazelnuts are plentiful, they are used instead of almonds, or there will be a mixture of both nuts.

Sometimes you might even add walnuts, if these are abundant. At some bakeries, the almonds might be crushed still in their skins, so the biscuits become more golden brown. It is the usual regional and local Italian story: little differences everywhere you go, and everybody protesting that their way is the best.

At Locanda, we make two batches of fresh soft amaretti cookies every day, following a recipe similar to the one my uncle uses in Gallarate, using both almonds and hazelnuts. Because the mixture needs to rest and dry out a little for 12 hours before baking, we pipe out one batch first thing in the morning, ready for dinner, and then every evening we make more, which we leave to dry overnight, ready to be baked in the morning and served for lunch. Before the amaretti are baked, we crush them a little with our fingers to give the characteristic bumpy shape that in northern Italy we call *"brutti ma buoni"* – ugly but good. Such a beautiful name, isn't it? It could apply to so many foods – and people. It makes me laugh sometimes when someone says, "How lovely!," when they don't know about this name, or that the shape they like so much is the result of being squashed.

The biscuits that we don't use we leave to dry out further, and then smash them up and use them in a Peach and amaretto tart (see page 538) or Amaretto ice cream (see page 564).

Makes about 35 amaretti
20 roasted hazelnuts
1 scant cup blanched almonds
1 cup apricot kernels
2½ cups superfine sugar
½ cup egg whites
    (from 3–4 large eggs)
confectioner's sugar for dusting

Crush the nuts and apricot kernels to fine crumbs in a food processor. Add the sugar and egg whites and process until the mixture all comes together. Spoon the mixture into a pastry bag.

Line 1 or 2 baking sheets with waxed paper and pipe the mixture into rounds on them, spacing them out well. Dust liberally with confectioner's sugar. Leave for 12 hours so that the mixture can dry out slightly. After this time, they will have formed a "skin." Pinch the biscuits lightly with the fingers to break this and give a bumpy appearance.

A good half hour or so before you are ready to bake the cookies, preheat the oven to 355°F, then bake them for 11 minutes until light golden.

Almond tuiles

Makes about 12 tuiles
⅔ cup confectioner's sugar
1 tablespoon plus 1¼ teaspoons
    all-purpose flour
1 tablespoon plus 2 teaspoons
    melted butter
¼ cup egg whites
    (from 1–2 large eggs)
1⅓ cups chopped almonds

Preheat the oven to 330°F.

Line a baking sheet with waxed paper. Put the confectioner's sugar and flour into a food processor and blend. Add the melted butter and the egg whites, and blend again to a paste. Spoon into a pastry bag.

Pipe or spread the mixture quite thin on the paper into any shapes you like, leaving generous space between each biscuit. Scatter some chopped almonds on top of each one.

Bake for about 4 minutes, until golden. To make baskets, form them inside a ramekin while still warm.

Hazelnut tuiles

Makes about 12 tuiles
⅓ cup flour
¼ cup ground hazelnuts
1 tablespoon plus 1 teaspoon
    dextrose
¼ cup water
⅓ cup plus 1 tablespoon
    superfine sugar
3 tablespoons plus 1½ teaspoons
    butter

Preheat the oven to 330°F.

Mix the flour and ground hazelnuts together. Put the dextrose, water and sugar into a pan. Bring to the boil, then take off the heat and whisk in the butter. When it has melted, whisk in the flour and nuts until smooth (it is a good idea to use a hand blender). Put into the fridge until cold.

Line a baking sheet with waxed paper. Either spoon the mixture into a piping bag and pipe into strips of about 6 inches, or spread with a spoon.

Bake for about 5 minutes until light golden – the mixture will flatten out into biscuit shapes.

Frangipane wafers

If you like, you can twist or roll each biscuit into another shape, such as a "cigar," while still warm (see specific recipes, such as the Cannoli di ricotta on page 545 or the Tiramisù on page 554 for ideas). Other variations include using a pastry bag with a very small opening to pipe the mixture onto the waxed paper in thin strips, making hairpin-like shapes. When they come out of the oven and are still warm, twist them into balls. Alternatively, you can brush the mixture onto the waxed paper in whatever shapes you like, using a pastry brush, and the biscuits will come out looking like lace. The thinner the mixture, the less time it needs in the oven, so keep an eye on it, and take it out as soon as it turns pale gold.

Put the ground almonds, flour and sugar into a food processor and blend. Add the melted butter and blend again.

When well incorporated, add the egg whites, blend again and, when they are incorporated, add the Amaretto and blend again. Leave to cool. If you want to pipe the biscuits, put the mixture into a pastry bag, then put the bag into the fridge for about 30 minutes.

Preheat the oven to 330°F. Line a baking sheet with waxed paper.

Spread or pipe the mixture quite thin into whatever shapes you like (or whatever a specific recipe calls for), leaving a good space between each one.

Bake for about 4 minutes until golden.

Makes about 12 wafers, depending on shape
¼ cup ground almonds
1 tablespoon plus 1¼ teaspoons flour
⅓ cup confectioner's sugar
3 tablespoons plus 1 teaspoon melted butter
2 tablespoons plus 2 teaspoons egg whites
1–1¼ teaspoons Amaretto liqueur

Hazelnut wafers

Preheat the oven to 330°F.

Line a baking tray with waxed paper.

Mix the confectioner's sugar and flour together in a bowl. Add the milk and mix with a spatula until you have a thick paste. Brush the paste on to the waxed paper in long crisp shapes (or whatever shapes you like). Sprinkle each one with chopped hazelnuts.

Bake for about 4 to 5 minutes. The mixture will bubble up and look quite transparent, then turn pale gold.

Makes about 15 wafers
⅓ cup plus 1 tablespoon sugar
1 tablespoon plus 1¼ teaspoons flour
1 tablespoon plus 1¼ teaspoons milk
a few hazelnuts, chopped

Mandorle, nocciole, noci e castagne

Almonds, hazelnuts, walnuts and chestnuts

The French may talk about their *pâte d'amande* (almond paste) for pastries, but it was the Italians who showed them how to use almonds via Catherine de' Medici. In Italy, the production of nuts is incredible; everywhere you see people growing, selling or buying them, and they appear all over the country in desserts, cakes, biscuits, *torrone* (nougat, made with egg white, sugar and nuts), in Amaretto liqueur, or just candied, like the sugared almonds *(confetti)* that are typical of Abruzzo.

Even in the north, I never saw anyone pay for almonds, hazelnuts or walnuts. Everyone has a tree in the garden, and, around the time of picking, the atmosphere is so intense with the scent that we have to keep my daughter, Margherita, away, or she will have an allergic reaction. When I was growing up, in November there would be huge cloths laid out in the courtyards in Corgeno, where everyone spread out the nuts to dry in the sun.

The almonds everyone grows are sweet, but there is a second type, the bitter almond, that contains prussic acid – a deadly poison. When the almonds are heat-treated and processed, they become safe. In Italy, we tend to use the crushed kernels of a specially grown apricot instead (these are also heat-treated before they are sold, and can be toxic in very high doses) – though we still call them "bitter almonds." The crushed kernels are often used together with sweet almonds in confectionery to boost the flavor.

Further up in the mountains around our house in Corgeno, there would be only hazelnuts. Almonds cannot survive if the temperature goes to zero, so if there is a frost, the nuts can be lost, whereas hazelnuts thrive on cold. The harder it is in winter, the better the fruit next year, my granddad used to say. The best hazelnuts in the world, for size and flavor, are the *tonda gentile*, "round and tender," nuts from the Langhe area of Piemonte, home of Barolo wine, with its Alpine territory and very cold winters.

In the north, chestnuts are also very important, and in Cuneo in Piemonte there is a big chestnut festival each October, which lasts for five days. In the time of Mussolini, the partisans hiding in the mountains would probably have died without chestnuts. They grow in the woods all along the spine of the Appennines, and there are over fifty different varieties. In Lombardia and Piemonte, we use the nuts to make chestnut flour or we cook and puree them in everything from desserts to savory dishes and stuffings.

The most prized chestnut is the *marrone*, which is big and light brown inside a spiky shell, and has a thin skin, so that you can peel it easily. This is the chestnut that is made into the famous marrons glacés, candied chestnuts, which I absolutely love. In the lead-up to Christmas, if I am in Milano, I buy the cracked ones in the jar and by the time the plane lands in London I've eaten them all, so I feel sick by the time I arrive. I know what is going to happen, but I can't help myself – I do it every time.

Special sablé biscuits

Makes about 15–20
200g butter
2¾ cups plus 2 tablespoons flour
½ teaspoon baking powder
¾ cup cornstarch
1¼ cups confectioner's sugar
2 egg yolks
pinch of salt

Half an hour before you need it, take the butter out of the fridge.

Mix the flour, baking powder, salt and corn starch in a bowl.

Put the butter into a mixer with a paddle attachment and mix. When soft, add the confectioner's sugar and keep mixing until the mixture turns pale. Add the egg yolks and mix in briefly. Add the flour mixture and continue to mix until it is almost incorporated.

Spread the mixture in a flat tray, about ¾ inch deep, and leave in the fridge for about 5 hours until the mixture sets.

A good half hour before you are ready to bake, preheat the oven to 340°F and line a baking sheet with waxed paper. With a cookie cutter about 1 inch in diameter, cut the mixture out into round biscuits and arrange on the lined baking sheet.

Bake the biscuits for 13 minutes, until golden and slightly puffed. Leave to cool (if you like, while they're still warm, you can use the same cutter to neaten and trim the biscuits into more perfect rounds).

Salted special sablé biscuits

Similar to the biscuits above but a little saltier, these work well with something sweet, such as the Sweet tomato soup on page 550, as the salt contrasts with – and helps intensify – the sweetness of the tomatoes.

Makes about 10
7 tablespoons butter,
    at room temperature
¼ cup milk
1¼ cups plus 2 tablespoons flour
½ teaspoon baking powder
1 teaspoon salt

Put the butter into a mixer with a paddle attachment and work until soft. Add the milk slowly and, when it is fully incorporated, add the flour, baking powder and salt, a little at a time.

When everything is all mixed in, spread the mixture in a flat tray, as above, leave to set and bake in the same way.

Biscotti al latte

Milk wafers

These are the best cookies. I love them. The flavor is fantastic and, when they are warm, you can shape them any way you like. If you want to spoil your kids, make them into ice cream cones (you can make up lots of them and keep them in an airtight container). That is what we do on Sundays, when families come into the restaurant and we take the kids into the kitchen to choose their ice cream, which we scoop into the cones for them to hold in their hands. We also serve the wafers with coffee ice cream, as they really accentuate the flavor of the coffee.

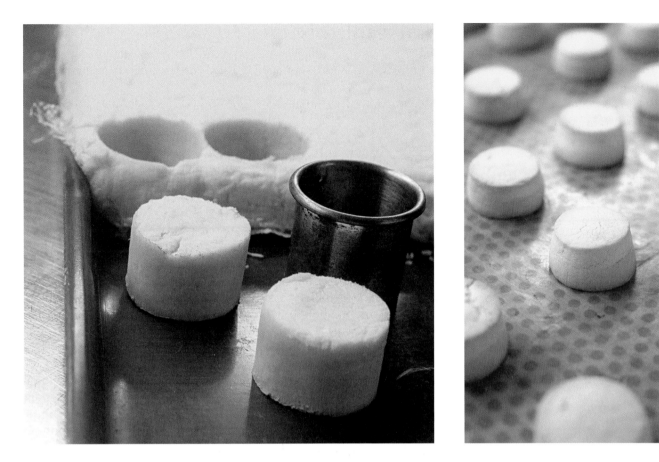

Makes 30 cones
or small wafers
1¼ cups powdered milk
2 tablespoons plus 2 teaspoons
sugar
½ cup plus 2 tablespoons
egg whites
(from 4–5 large eggs)
⅓ cup plus 2 tablespoons
melted butter
pinch of salt

Mix the powdered milk, sugar and salt together, then whisk in the egg whites and melted butter, and put into the fridge for 12 hours.

Preheat the oven to 340°F.

Line a baking sheet with waxed paper. You can either spoon the mixture into small mounds and spread it, using a palette knife or rubber spatula, into whatever shape you like, or do as we do and make the biscuits into cones. From the center of a sheet of waxed paper we measure 5½ inches vertically. From this point we measure 3½ inches at a right angle, and make a mark. Then we go back to the original point, measure 1½ inches horizontally, and make a second mark. Then we join the two marks together to make a geometric shape approximately 5½ x 3½ x 6 x 1½ inches. We cut this out of the paper and discard it, lay the template firmly on top of a lined baking sheet and spread some of the mixture over the top, then lift off the template. Repeat with the rest of the mixture – you will probably need to do this in a few batches, depending on how many baking sheets you have.

Bake for about 5 minutes, until the biscuits begin to color.

When they come out of the oven, while still warm, starting with the corner where the 5½-inch side meets the 3½-inch side, roll into a cone shape. Gently lay the cones on a tray to cool.

Lemon thyme caramel wafers

Makes about 20 wafers,
depending on shape
½ cup corn syrup
250g sugar fondant
1 ounce lemon thyme,
chopped
very fine

Heat the glucose and fondant in the pan until it starts to look golden (if you have a candy thermometer this should be 316°F, just below caramel, which forms at 325°F).

Have ready a baking sheet lined with waxed paper. Take the pan off the heat and pour the syrup over the paper. Sprinkle with the chopped lemon thyme. Put another sheet of waxed paper over the top and roll with a rolling pin until you have a flat layer about ¼ inch thick. Leave until completely cold, then break into pieces. You can store them in an airtight container until you need them.

When you want to use them, preheat the oven to 310°F. Take however many pieces you need, put them on a baking sheet lined with waxed paper, spaced well apart, and put into the oven, until just soft, like butter.

Take out of the oven and cover with waxed paper, then roll out each wafer again until really thin and transparent. Leave to cool.

Le guarnizioni

Garnishes

Slice some fruit thin or take a few herbs such as basil, dip in syrup, let them dry out and crisp up in a cool oven, and you have an impressive decoration for anything from ice cream to a tart.

Apple crisps

If you make these crisps more than a few hours before you need them, keep them in an airtight container until you are ready to use them (but don't keep them for more than a day). They should stay crisp; but, if not, you can put them back into the oven again – though they won't be quite as crisp as the first time.

Put the sugar in a pan with the water and heat until the sugar dissolves. Take off the heat and leave to cool. Mix in the lemon juice.

Slice the apple (skin on) as thin as possible, preferably using a mandoline grater. Put the slices into the syrup and leave for an hour.

Preheat the oven to 125°F or 140°F (if you have a gas oven, have it as low as it will go). Line a baking sheet with waxed paper.

Lift the apple slices from the syrup, shaking off the excess, and lay them on the prepared baking sheet. Put in the oven for about 3 hours, until completely dry and crisp, but not colored.

Take out and leave to cool down on top of the oven, or nearby, to maintain the crispness.

Makes about 10 crisps
3 tablespoons plus 1 teaspoon
  sugar
4 tablespoons water
juice of ½ lemon
1 Granny Smith apple

Variations

Melon Crisps (makes 4): Make in the same way, but use 4 very, very thin slices of very cold honeydew melon instead of the apple.

Blood Orange Crisps (makes 4): Make in the same way, but increase the quantity of sugar to 4 tablespoons plus 2 teaspoons, and use 4 thin slices of blood orange.

Candied Basil (makes 8): Make in the same way, but use ½ cup sugar and ⅓ cup plus 1 tablespoon water, and let it cool before you put in the basil. Shake off the excess syrup before laying them on your lined baking tray. They will need around 4 hours until they become crisp.

Candied mint

Preheat the oven to 285°F.

Whisk the egg whites with the salt and pass through a fine sieve. Dip the mint leaves into the mixture, shake off the excess, and lay on a sheet of waxed paper.

Dust with the confectioner's sugar and put into the oven for about 20 minutes, checking regularly, until the egg white starts to bubble up and color very slightly. To check whether the leaves are ready, take one out and leave to cool slightly. If it is crunchy, it is ready; if not, discard that one and give the others 5 minutes more, then take another one out and check again. If still not ready, give the remaining leaves another 5 minutes. Hopefully, you should end up with 8 to 10 perfectly crunchy leaves.

Makes 8–10
3 tablespoons plus 1½ teaspoons
    egg whites
10 mint leaves
2 tablespoons plus ½ teaspoon
    sugar
pinch of salt

Candied vanilla beans

For some desserts we make at the restaurant, such as the poached pears served with ice cream on page 524, we candy the vanilla beans, then chop them in a food processor until they turn into a powder, which we dust over the ice cream.

Preheat the oven to about 125°–140°F.

Cut the vanilla beans into thin strips lengthwise.

Put the sugar and water in a pan and heat until the sugar dissolves. Put in the strips of vanilla bean, bring the syrup to a boil, then turn down the heat and simmer very slowly for 30 minutes.

Line a baking sheet with waxed paper.

Take the vanilla strips out of the syrup, shaking off the excess, lay them on the tray and put in the oven until they have become completely dry, about 5 hours. To check whether they are ready, take out a strip, leave it to get cold, then break it. It should snap very easily; if not, leave the strips in the oven a little longer.

4 vanilla beans
¾ cup plus 2 tablespoons water
⅔ cup sugar

Cioccolato

Chocolate

In Italy, we see chocolate in a very different way than they do in England or America. We don't have newsstands full of thousands of different candy bars to pick up and eat as a snack. Of course, we like chocolate, but you are more likely to see it used to cover almonds and sold in the *pasticceria* or a specialty *cioccolateria*, or used in desserts or even savory dishes, such as Caponata (see page 59). I have to confess, though, that I loved the *gianduia* bars we used to have at home in Corgeno – Gianduia was a famous marionette who loved food, wine and girls, and was the King of the Torino carnival. The bars were made with chocolate and almond liqueur and hazelnuts, and I used to steal them from the kitchen and stuff them in my pockets. Then they would melt, so I had to wash them out to hide the evidence, and walk around with wet trousers.

The idea of mixing toasted hazelnut paste and chocolate was made famous in 1865 by a Torino chocolate maker, Michele Prochet, who created the city's specialty, *gianduiotto* chocolates wrapped in gold papers, to celebrate the carnival season, shaping them like the hat worn by the Gianduia character. The idea was born out of scarcity – the Napoleonic Wars meant that the chocolate makers of Torino couldn't get enough cocoa beans, so Prochet made the chocolate go further by adding the local Tonda Gentile hazelnuts. But Piemonte is probably most famous for Nutella, which was created in the forties by another genius, Pietro Ferrero (of Ferrero Rocher), in Alba. Chocolate was scarce again during the war, so he added the local hazelnuts to make a paste, which he called Pasta Gianduia, and wrapped it in foil, so that it could be sliced and eaten on a piece of bread. Eventually, in the sixties, it became even more spreadable – *supercrema* – and was sold in a jar and renamed Nutella.

Sometimes at Locanda we make a chocolate fondant with a filling of a chocolate and hazelnut liqueur called Bicerin di Gianduiotto (see page 594), which is now being exported and reminds me of those flavors. Bicerin is another famous Torinese speciality, a drink that has been made for centuries and that you will find in most bars. As always, there is a big debate about who makes it the best way – but it contains layers of chocolate, milk and sugar heated together, hot coffee and whipped cream, and the most famous bar to drink it in is Al Bicerin in Piazza della Consolata.

Real, pure chocolate is a world apart from the sweetened bars the British and Americans love so much. The big, multinational chocolate companies put their money into cultivating high-yield varietals of beans such as Forestero in West Africa, which can be produced on a massive scale. Then they either buy cocoa "mass" or "liquor," or they blend beans from different countries to a recipe that means their chocolate always tastes the same. However, there are a growing number of small, serious chocolate makers who are excited about showing off the individual characteristics of different varieties, grown in particular geographical conditions, which can be compared to the way we think of coffee beans in the same way as the single "crus" of the wine world. Often they look to the ancient plantations of South America, and particularly the Criollo bean, which is difficult to grow and produces only enough for around 2 percent of the world's cocoa production. You can see a great similarity between the production of great chocolate and that of great wine. Sara Jayne-Stanes, a director of the Academy of Culinary Arts and an expert on chocolate, talks about roundness and aftertaste, and length in the mouth, and describes the flavors of individual chocolates in terms of ripe red fruits and plums, wood, tobacco, tea, spice, leather and earth, just as a wine taster might. According to her, the cocoa bean has more than 400 distinct aromas and 300 different tastes.

One of our most popular desserts at Locanda is a tasting plate using two different styles of chocolate from the house of Amedei in Pontedera, near Pisa, which we use in many different ways, from parfait to foam to nougat: the idea is to create different textures to show off the different properties of the chocolate.

Most of the chocolate we use at Locanda is made by Alessio Tessieri and his sister Cecilia, the master chocolate makers at Amedei, and we work with them developing ideas and sending our pastry chefs out to Italy to learn about how to use the chocolate – because these are people who, like us, are truly in love with what they do.

The story of Alessio and Cecilia is fantastic. When they took over a small praline business, they wanted to buy some wonderful chocolate to coat the pralines. So Alessio went to Lyon, to the head office of Valrhona, the famous French chocolatiers, to see if they could buy their chocolate, and they were told "no" – because Italy was not ready to accept chocolate of this quality. You can imagine how Alessio felt – but it made him more determined to find his own chocolate, and the goal was the famous Criollo cocoa beans from Chuao in Venezuela, which at the time were sold, via middlemen, only to a few chocolatiers such as Valrhona.

This is cocoa that is being grown on the edge of nowhere, beyond mountains and rain forests, where the people of the little town of Chuao are descended from the slaves brought over by the Spanish conquistadors in the seventeenth century, but the cocoa is considered to be very, very complex and sophisticated, and in the hands of Amedei, it produces chocolate that has a fantastically powerful, rich and fruity flavor.

Trading cocoa is often a dirty, corrupt business, in which poor farmers have traditionally been squeezed by the big players, who decide how much their beans are worth – and what else can they do but sell? So Alessio offered to pay the farmers directly, giving them a higher price, taking on their debts and committing himself to increasing the productivity of the plantation, in return for exclusive rights to the Chuao plantation. It was quite something to pull off, and not only that, but he also managed to gain exclusive rights to the even rarer Porcelana beans, which are grown near the border with Colombia, and which make a very delicate chocolate, often described as having notes of roast almonds. The production is so limited that each box is numbered. They also make selections of chocolate from Venezuela, Madagascar, Jamaica, Trinidad, Ecuador and Grenada, as well as Toscano Black, which is their special, rich, spicy blend of Criollo and Trinitario (a cross between Criollo and Forestero) and which we use alongside the Chuao in our desserts.

What is special about Alessio and Cecilia is that they watch over and control every stage of production, right from the processing, fermentation and drying (which is done in the country of origin) to the roasting and grinding, which is done back in Pisa in their old granite mill. To make the chocolate so smooth, each granule is no more than 15 microns, compared to the standard for the chocolate industry of 30 microns. Apparently, the human mouth is able to detect granules only over 18 microns, which shows you how particular they are about every detail. Not only have they made Italy famous for chocolate but they produce it in a way that supports and looks after the people who grow the beans.

Note: When you melt chocolate, either do it gently in a bowl over a pan of barely simmering water (don't let the bowl touch the water), or put it in the microwave, using the defrost setting. Don't put it straight into a pan over direct heat, let any boiling water come in contact with it, or use the microwave on full power as you might burn the cocoa, which will give the chocolate a bitter edge and cause it to "seize," i.e., turn thick and gritty.

Chocolate parfait and foam

This is part of our Amedei Tasting Plate, but it is fantastic to serve on its own, with or without the chocolate foam. For the foam, you need a 0.5-liter (2-cup) siphon. Of course, you can use any good chocolate (at least 70 percent cocoa solids), but we use Toscano Black for the foam because it has a deep, strong flavor that holds up well in the foam, gives you a big hit in the mouth, and then fades; whereas the Chuao, which we use for the parfait, has a rich and more persistent flavor that works well with the egg whites and cream, is able to come through strongly despite the coldness of the parfait (cold can dull flavors) and lasts longer in the mouth. I love this parfait, which we make using a meringue in which the sugar is heated with the egg whites before whipping (sometimes called Swiss meringue), but is very straightforward to do. Even if you don't want to add the foam, you can just make the parfait, keep it in the freezer and then slice it and serve it with some cream.

1 cup whipping cream
6 ounces Amedei Chuao or
    Valrhona chocolate (at least
    70 percent cocoa solids)
$\frac{1}{3}$ cup egg whites
$\frac{1}{3}$ cup superfine sugar
2 tablespoons plus 1$\frac{1}{2}$ teaspoons
    dextrose

For the chocolate foam:
8 ounces Amedei Toscano or
    Valrhona chocolate (at least
    70 percent cocoa solids)
1 tablespoon plus 2$\frac{1}{2}$ teaspoons
    sugar
1 cup plus 1 tablespoon
    still mineral water

Whisk the cream until it is firm and holds in peaks. Put into the fridge.

Melt the chocolate in the microwave on defrost, or very gently in a bowl over a pan of barely simmering water (make sure the base of the bowl isn't actually in contact with the water). Set aside.

Put the egg whites and sugars in a separate bowl over the simmering water, whisking all the time, until the sugar has melted and the mixture is hot to the touch (122°F if you have a candy thermometer). Take off the heat and continue to whisk (use an electric mixer if you like) until the meringue is cold and firm, and will stand up in peaks.

With a spatula, begin to fold the meringue into the chocolate. Mix in one-third first, then the rest, then add the cream. Fold that in lightly, trapping as much air into the mixture as possible.

Line a metal or plastic tray with plastic wrap, spoon in the mixture, smooth with a spatula and freeze for at least 3 hours until firm.

To make the foam, first melt the chocolate in the same way as above. Put the sugar and mineral water into a pan and bring to the boil. Take off the heat and whisk in the melted chocolate, a little at a time, like making mayonnaise; otherwise the mixture might split.

Take off the heat and pass through a fine sieve, then into the soda siphon. Close up and charge with the gas, while the liquid is still hot. Shake and put into the fridge for about 2 hours until cold. Keep cold until the moment you want to serve it; otherwise it will collapse.

When ready to serve, turn out the parfait, remove the plastic wrap and cut it into slices. Serve with the foam squirted alongside.

Torta al cioccolato e mandorle

Chocolate and almond tart

This tart has a fantastic sheen from the chocolate glaze, which we pour over it while it is still warm. Then we sprinkle it with *grué de cacao* – chopped or ground "nibs" (raw cocoa beans without their shells), which are very chocolatey and bitter tasting.

Serves 6–8

½ recipe quantity of Sweet
    pastry (see page 536)
14 ounces good dark chocolate
    (at least 70 percent cocoa
    solids), finely chopped
1 scant cup whipping cream
1 egg plus 1 extra egg yolk
¾ cup milk
11 toasted almonds (or roasted
    hazelnuts), chopped

For the glaze:

½ cup superfine sugar
¼ cup water
1¾ ounces good dark chocolate
    (at least 70 percent cocoa
    solids), finely chopped
1 tablespoon corn syrup
¼ cup good cocoa powder
2 tablespoons plus ½ teaspoon
    whipping cream

To finish:

grué de cacao
    (optional, see above)
cocoa powder, to dust

Preheat the oven to 345°F.

Roll out the pastry and use to line a 11-inch nonstick tart tin. Line with ovenproof plastic wrap, fill with rice or dried peas or beans and bake blind for 4 minutes. Remove the weights and plastic wrap, and return to the oven for around 7 to 10 minutes, until cooked but only very lightly colored (the base should feel firm when you touch it). Take out and turn the oven down to 285°F.

Melt the chocolate (either gently in a bowl over a pan of simmering water, or on the defrost setting of the microwave).

Put the cream in a pan and, when it comes to a boil, remove from the heat and add to the chocolate, mixing well.

In a separate bowl, whisk the egg, extra egg yolk and the milk, then add to the bowl of chocolate cream. Stir in the chopped nuts.

Spoon the mixture into the pastry and put back into the oven for 6 to 7 minutes, until the sides are set but the center moves a bit if you gently shake the tin (don't touch the topping or you will leave marks). The mixture will set as it cools, so if you leave it in the oven until it is completely firm, by the time it is cool it will be dry.

Allow to cool slightly, remove from the tin and put on a serving plate.

To make the glaze, first make a syrup, by putting the sugar into a pan with the water and heating until the sugar dissolves. Take off the heat and leave to cool. Put the chopped chocolate into a bowl. Put the syrup and corn syrup in a pan with 1 tablespoon plus 2 teaspoons water and bring to a boil. Add the cocoa powder, carefully, a sprinkle at a time, or it will spit, and bring back to the boil. Take off the heat and pour over the chopped chocolate, stirring until it is melted. Add the cream and mix well, then pass through a fine sieve to make sure it is completely smooth.

While the tart is still warm, spread the glaze over the top with a palette knife or rubber spatula to form a dark, shiny surface and leave to cool completely. Sprinkle with grué de cacao (if using) and dust with cocoa powder.

Zuppa di cioccolato e yogurt

White chocolate and yogurt soup

Here the sablé biscuit is really just to raise the ice cream, which sits in the soup – you can either make the cookie as described on page 578, or buy some good ones, or something similar – and the caramel, which we make with condensed milk, helps to stick the biscuit to the base of the serving bowl to prevent it from sliding around when the waiter carries it.

Sometimes, for a change, we make a milk chocolate soup, rather than white chocolate. We melt 6¾ ounces good milk chocolate (at least 70 percent cocoa solids), then put 3¼ ounces whipping cream in a pan with 3¼ ounces milk and bring to a boil, take off the heat and then gradually whisk into the melted chocolate, finally whisking in ½ cup water at room temperature. We cool it and leave overnight or for 12 hours in the fridge. Instead of the orange and passion fruit jelly, we make a jelly with caramelized honey. We use 3 tablespoons plus 1½ teaspoons white clover honey, which we heat to 325°F, then take off the heat and very slowly and carefully whisk in ⅓ cup hot water, taking care not to let it splash and burn the skin. Then we squeeze out 2g gelatin leaves that have been soaked in water and add them to the honey, and leave it to cool and set in the fridge – again overnight or for 12 hours. We serve the soup in the same way, substituting a Hazelnut wafer (see page 575) for the sablé biscuit, and Hazelnut ice cream (see page 568) for the Pistachio ice cream.

Make the toffee using a can of condensed milk (see page 522).

To make the soup, melt the chocolate in the microwave on the defrost setting or in a bowl set over a pan of barely simmering water. Don't let the base of the bowl touch the water.

Combine the cream and milk in a pan, and bring to a boil. Remove from the heat.

Pour the mixture in a slow stream onto the chocolate, whisking continuously (as you would for mayonnaise), until it is all incorporated. You need to do this slowly so the mixture emulsifies properly.

Leave to cool, then mix in the yogurt. Leave in the fridge for at least 3 hours, and until 10 minutes before serving.

To make the jelly, reduce the orange juice down to 2 tablespoons. Cool, put in a bowl and add the passion fruit juice and sugar to taste.

Heat a tablespoon of the juice mixture in a pan, then add the squeezed gelatin leaves and stir until dissolved. Take off the heat and stir into the rest of the juice mixture. Put in the fridge for at least 30 minutes until set.

3¾ ounces white chocolate
1 cup whipping cream
5 tablespoons plus 1 teaspoon
    milk
⅓ cup plus 1 tablespoon yogurt

For the orange and passion
    fruit jelly:
¼ cup orange juice
1 tablespoon plus 2¼ teaspoons
    passion fruit juice
sugar to taste
2g gelatin leaves, soaked in
    water and squeezed

To serve:
one 14-ounce can condensed
    milk, for the toffee
4 sablé biscuits, bought
    (or make your own as
    described on page 578)
Pistachio ice cream (page 568)
4 Apple crisps (page 581)

When ready to serve, put a little toffee in the center of each of 4 soup plates, with a biscuit on top.

Take the chocolate mixture from the fridge and froth with a hand blender, to give a bubbly, cappuccino effect. Spoon the soup into the plates, just up to the level of the biscuit – don't pour it over the top or the ice cream won't stick to the biscuit.

Scoop a ball of ice cream on top of each biscuit. With a teaspoon, scoop out 16 small pieces of jelly (you want only little pieces, as the jelly is quite sharp and acidic, to cut through the creaminess of the chocolate). Arrange 4 pieces, like jewels, around each plate. If you like, top each ball of ice cream with an Apple crisp (see page 581).

Saffron and chocolate fondant

⅓ cup plus 1 teaspoon
    all-purpose flour
½ heaping teaspoon
    baking powder
3½ teaspoons cocoa powder
3½ ounces dark chocolate (at
    least 70 percent cocoa solids)
7 tablespoons unsalted butter,
    softened
2 large eggs
⅓ cup superfine sugar

For the chocolate sauce:
25g superfine sugar
2 tablespoons plus 1 teaspoon
    cocoa powder
⅓ cup plus 1 tablespoon
    whipping cream

For the saffron filling:
5 tablespoons milk
1¾ teaspoons cornstarch
5 tablespoons whipping cream
generous pinch saffron threads
1½ ounces white chocolate,
    chopped

To serve (optional):
Milk ice cream (see page 561)
4 Hazelnut tuiles (see page 574)

The idea of these chocolate fondants is that, when you cook them, the creamy center stays cold. We serve them with Milk ice cream, garnished with a Hazelnut tuile – but you can use vanilla ice cream and a cookie of your choice, or just serve the fondants as they are. You can make them up to four days in advance, and have them in the fridge, ready to go.

To make the sauce: bring 3 tablespoons plus 1½ teaspoons water and the sugar to a boil in a pan. Whisk in the cocoa powder very slowly – just a sprinkle at a time – so that it doesn't spit. When it is all incorporated and boiling again, add the cream, bring back to a boil and then turn the heat down and reduce for 5 to 10 minutes very slowly, whisking occasionally, until you have a thick sauce. To check it is the right consistency, spread a spoonful onto a plate; it should hold its shape and look dark and shiny.

To make the saffron filling, mix a little of the milk with the cornstarch to make a paste. Mix the rest of the milk with the cream and the saffron in a pan. When almost boiling, add the cornstarch. Bring to a boil. Boil for 1 to 2 minutes to cook out the starchy flavor.

Take off the heat and add the white chocolate. Whisk until the chocolate has melted. Pour into a container, to make a layer ¾ inch deep. Put in the freezer.

When it is solid, take a pastry cutter 4 inches in diameter and cut out 4 cylinders. Put back into the freezer.

To make the fondant, mix the flour, baking powder and cocoa powder together, and pass through a fine sieve.

Put the chocolate in a bowl set over a pan of barely simmering water (don't let the base touch the water) until the chocolate melts. Take off the heat and stir in the softened butter.

Beat the eggs and sugar together until pale, then mix into the chocolate mixture with a spatula.

Slowly fold in the flour and cocoa powder until they are incorporated.

Take 4 pastry rings, 2½ inches deep and 2 inches in diameter, and lay them on a sheet. Grease them with butter, then line them with buttered parchment paper, to come about ¾ inch above the rim. Pipe in the mixture to halfway up each ring, then put one of the disks of saffron filling that you have been keeping in the freezer on top. Press down (the cold will set the walls of the fondant around it) and pipe the rest of the mixture over the top, up to three-quarters of the height of the ring. Don't fill it any higher, as it will rise in the oven. Keep in the fridge for 2 hours until the fondant is completely cold and solid (by now the filling will have defrosted and be liquid).

Preheat the oven to 355°F and put in the fondants for 9 minutes until they have risen and taken a little color.

While the fondants are in the oven, have your plates ready, decorated with some chocolate sauce. If you like, at the last minute you can add a scoop of ice cream and decorate that with a hazelnut tuile. Loosen the fondants from their rings, remove and put one on each plate. Serve immediately.

Variation

Sometimes we serve them with a filling made with basil rather than saffron.

The day before, we put 1¾ ounces basil into a pan with the milk, then warm it up to infuse the flavors, leave it to cool down, pass it through a fine sieve and put it into the fridge. Then we make the filling in exactly the same way, omitting the saffron.

In addition to the milk ice cream, we make a little green apple compote to go with it. We peel ½ green apple slices and cut them into small cubes, then put 2 tablespoons sugar and 1½ teaspoons into a pan, and heat to make a light golden caramel, then we add a teaspoon of lemon juice and the apple, and cook it slowly until the apple is soft. Then we cool it and put it into the fridge to chill before serving.

Chocolate fondant with Bicerin di Gianduiotto

This is a very straightforward dessert that uses a different technique that has become a classic. You simply make your chocolate mixture with a low ratio of flour to chocolate and, in this case, the Bicerin di Gianduiotto liqueur that is famous in Torino (see page 584) and is now available online.

The cleverness of desserts like this is that they are "self-saucing" — when they are in the oven the center remains liquid and will ooze out when you put your spoon into the fondant.

Make the fondant in the same way as for the previous recipe, but using ¾ cup flour. Sieve with the ½ heaping teaspoon baking powder and 3½ teaspoons cocoa powder and set aside.

Melt 2⅛ ounces dark chocolate (at least 70 percent cocoa solids) and mix it with 7 tablespoons softened butter, together with ¾ cup plus 2 tablespoons Bicerin di Gianduiotto.

Beat 2 large eggs with ⅓ cup superfine sugar until the mixture becomes pale, incorporate this into the chocolate mix using a spatula, and finally fold in the flour and cocoa.

Grease 4 pastry rings, lay them on a baking tray, spoon in the mixture, and bake in an oven preheated to 390°F for 7 minutes. Lift out with a spatula and slide off the rings to serve.

Sformato d'arancia e cioccolato, pannacotta all'acqua di rose

Orange and chocolate sformato sponge with rosewater pannacotta

We make this with what everyone in the kitchen now calls Margherita's chocolate sponge — it is the one we make for my daughter that doesn't contain eggs, as she is allergic to them.

The chocolate sponge is layered with caramelized blood orange segments, and topped with rosewater pannacotta. We also serve it with lemon thyme ice cream.

It is difficult to make small quantities of sponge, so you will end up with more than you need for this dessert, but it is so good, I am sure it won't be wasted.

We use a little white wine vinegar in the mixture, which might sound odd, but its acidity helps to relax the protein in the flour, with the result that the sponge becomes lighter.

Preheat the oven to 340°F and butter and flour a 6-inch square cake pan.

Make the sponge by sieving the dry ingredients in a bowl, combining all the liquid ingredients, and mix the two until smooth.

Pour the mixture into the prepared pan and bake for 18 minutes, until a skewer inserted into the center comes out clean. Leave to cool in the pan. Then, when cold, transfer to the freezer for an hour to firm up the sponge and make it easier to cut.

Use a 2½-inch diameter pastry cutter to cut out 4 disks from the sponge, then carefully cut each disk horizontally to give 4 thin rounds from each one. Keep the discs in the fridge until you need them.

To make the pannacotta, warm the milk in a pan with the vanilla bean (scraping in the seeds) and add the sugar. When it has dissolved, add the gelatin. Heat gently until hot to the touch (if you have a candy thermometer this will be 150°F), let cool a little (to 113°F), then add the rosewater (if the mixture is too hot, the alcohol will evaporate, and the flavor will disappear with it). Pour into a bowl, cool as quickly as possible, remove the vanilla bean and put in the fridge until set.

To prepare the blood orange segments, segment the blood oranges, spread out on a tray or plate that will go in the fridge, and set aside. Discard the pith and squeeze what is left of the oranges to extract as much juice as you can. Make this up to 2 cups plus 2 tablespoons with fresh orange juice. Mix the sugar with the pectin (mixing them will stop the mixture from turning lumpy when you add them to the juice). Heat the orange juice in a pan, and, when it is just smoking (150°F), add the sugar and pectin, whisk in and bring to a boil for just 1 minute. Pour over the orange segments and leave on a counter to cool.

To make the chocolate glaze, put the sugar in a pan with 3 tablespoons plus 1½ teaspoons water and heat until the sugar dissolves. Take off the heat and leave the syrup to cool. Put into a pan with the corn syrup and 5¼ teaspoons water and heat. When it starts to boil, add the cocoa powder very slowly, just a sprinkle at a time to prevent it from spitting and splashing. Bring back to the boil, then take off the heat. Add the chopped chocolate, let it melt, then add the cream. Pass through a fine sieve and leave to cool.

To serve, place a clean 2½-inch diameter pastry cutter in the center of each of 4 plates. Put a disk of chocolate sponge in the bottom of each, then spoon in some of the orange segments, add another disk of sponge, and some more orange, then repeat, ending with sponge. Carefully slide off the pastry cutters, spoon on some glaze and serve with a scoop of pannacotta. Garnish with a lemon thyme caramel wafer (optional). If you like, you can arrange a blood orange crisp alongside, and top with a scoop of lemon thyme ice cream.

butter for the cake pan
1½ cups plus 1 tablespoon flour,
　　plus more for the cake pan
3 scant tablespoons
　　cocoa powder
½ heaping teaspoon
　　baking powder
½ heaping teaspoon
　　bicarbonate of soda
¾ cup superfine sugar
⅓ cup vegetable oil
⅔ cup water
¼ cup white wine vinegar

For the rosewater
　　pannacotta:
⅓ cup plus 1 tablespoon milk
½ vanilla bean, split lengthwise
1 heaping tablespoon
　　superfine sugar
2g gelatin leaves, soaked in
　　water and squeezed
2 teaspoons rosewater

For the blood
　　orange segments:
8 blood oranges
fresh orange juice (blood orange
　　juice if you can find it)
⅓ cup superfine sugar
1 heaping tablespoon pectin

For the chocolate glaze:
½ cup superfine sugar
⅓ cup water
2¼ teaspoons corn syrup
¼ cup cocoa powder
1¾ ounces chocolate
　　(70 percent cocoa solids),
　　finely chopped
2 tablespoons plus ½ teaspoon
　　whipping cream

To serve (optional):
4 Lemon thyme caramel wafers
　　(see page 580)
4 Blood orange crisps
　　(see page 581)
Lemon thyme ice cream
　　(see page 562)

Frittelle di cioccolato e banana

Chocolate and banana beignets

Life would be miserable without beignets, which is just a fancy way of describing doughnuts; there is nothing better. You need to put them in the freezer (in ice cube trays) for several hours or overnight to harden before you fry them, but you can make large amounts and then cook them from frozen any time you like. We sometimes serve the beignets with a milk wafer cone (see page 578) filled with coffee ice cream (see page 566).

Makes around 20
small beignets
1 small (6-inch) peeled banana
2½ teaspoons superfine sugar
⅓ cup plus 1 tablespoon milk
7 tablespoons unsalted butter
100g (3.53 ounces) all-purpose
flour
3 eggs
around 40 (about 3½ ounces)
plain chocolate pastilles
(55 percent cocoa solids)

To serve (optional):
4 Milk crisp cones (see page 578)
Coffee ice cream (see page 566)

In a blender, puree the bananas with the sugar. Put the milk and butter in a pan and bring to the boil. Add the banana puree, bring back to a boil, then add the flour and fold in. The mixture will come together like a dough. Cook for a minute, then put into a mixer with a paddle attachment and, while still hot, add the eggs slowly, one at a time, until they are all incorporated.

With a pastry bag, pipe the mixture into soft flexible ice cube trays, filling each compartment three-quarters full. Press 2 pastilles of chocolate into the middle of each one. Make sure that the chocolate is completely surrounded by dough, as the mixture is going to be deep-fried and, if the chocolate isn't encased inside, it will disappear into the oil. Pipe a little more dough on top to bring the level up to the top of the tray. You should have enough mixture for about 22 beignets – you need a couple of extra to use as testers, to see whether they are ready when you deep-fry them. Cover with plastic wrap and put in the freezer for several hours or overnight until hard.

Heat some oil in a deep-fat fryer to 340°F or use a pan (no more than one-third full). Check the temperature by putting in a beignet. After 5 minutes, take it out and cut it in half. The chocolate should have begun to melt and the dough will be cooked. If it is too golden on the outside, and not cooked inside, lower the heat a little.

Fry your beignets in batches, for 5 minutes each. Drain them briefly on paper towels, then arrange about 5 on each plate. Serve, if you like, with the cones and ice cream.

Formaggi

Cheese

Like salami, the regional cheeses we have in Italy tell a story about the way many people were living until the beginning of the last century. In some of the most remote places, particularly in the north, very little has changed: shepherds still spend part of the year in the mountains, tending a few cows, sheep or goats, with only spartan places to sleep and eat. Mountain communities have traditionally been poor in terms of money but rich in tradition and values. Cheese was bartered for other foods, paid as rent to landlords, and of course cheese is what everyone ate. There is a cheese called Bitto, from my region of Lombardia, the oldest cheese in Italy, made with cow's milk, something that was introduced by the Celts. Bitto is a big, solid block of cheese, and the name means "forever" in the Celtic language. The idea was that you gave people this cheese, they could put it in their bag and travel through the mountains, and it would last "forever."

All over the world there has been a big revival of interest in artisan produce, and in many regions, traditional cheeses are protected by vigorous consorzio, who give the PDO stamp only to high-quality cheesemakers following particular criteria in a designated region. At the same time, though, for many families who have been making cheeses in a small way for generations, it has been hard to keep going in the face of EU regulations and demands for modern equipment, so it is very important that we continue to support them or their traditions will be lost. We buy our cheeses from Marco Vineis, who has a fantastic shop called Gastronomica next to Borough Market in London. Marco used to work in a bank to satisfy his parents, but the moment he could break free, he started his little business, indulging his love of cheese (he also sells wonderful salumi, bread – including my favorite, the rosetta panini – mustard fruits, etc.). He jokes that he talks about cheese so much he has no friends. He knows everything about the cheeses, the animals, what they eat, and the old stories about how each one came to be made in the first place. Whether they are true, who knows, but as he says, "Why spoil a romantic story with reality?"

Marco, who, like me, is from the north of Italy, has established links with small cheesemakers in the mountains, some of whom we have come to know well, and we believe that by having their beautiful cheeses on our board at Locanda we are not only giving people a taste of something a little different but helping to regenerate the economy of the mountains. There are supposed to be more than 400 cheeses in Italy, but in reality, there are many more. For example, in Piemonte alone there are 100 valleys, each with its own version of the traditional Toma cheese (very similar to the cheese made on the French side of the border, Tomme de Savoie). It is funny to think that if you were to walk into Gastronomica you could taste more Italian cheeses than most Italians have ever tasted, because if you go to a cheese shop in Torino or Toscana, you will find only what is made locally.

These are just a selection of the cheeses we have at any one time at Locanda, along with Ovinfort (see page 69) and Castelmagno (see page 244).

Caprino Lo Puy

These are beautiful little creamy goat cheeses, made by a family who live in an old church they are protecting from falling into ruin, high up where eagles fly, overlooking a valley. They have 52 goats and all the cheeses are made with their own milk, in shapes from pyramids to rounds, matured at a slightly different rate, so they have different characters.

Formaggio di Fossa

These are not "easy" cheeses, but they are fascinating and I love them. They are made in Romagna and their name comes from the way they are matured, in underground pits near the river Rubicon. In the Middle Ages they dug out lines of wells at the side of the river in order to contain the water when the river rose too high, and to stop it from flooding the local villages. Much later, when the course of the river had changed, the partisans used them as underground cellars to hide cheese and grain from invading armies. These days they are lined with straw and fitted with wooden shelves and used to mature fresh sheep's milk cheeses inside cloth bags. Once the cheeses are inside, covers are put over the top. Traditionally the cheeses went in at the end of August and came out on St. Catherine's day, November 24. Now the cheeses are so popular it is much more of a continual process. Even so, you can imagine the smell as the covers are removed after several months, because inside all the pungent aromas from the cheeses have been building up like a bomb, but the cheeses themselves are quite light and crumbly, and according to the time spent in the fosse, have an aroma that develops as you eat: a mix of pure animal, autumn woodland, mushrooms and truffles...all my favorite things.

Gorgonzola

This is one of our most famous Lombardia cheeses. At one time in England everyone knew it as Dolcelatte, which is actually the name of a manufacturer of sweet, young Gorgonzola, matured for only 20 days, which we call dolce, as opposed to mature Gorgonzola, matured for 90 days, and known as piccante. There is a story that the first Gorgonzola was actually a Stracchino (the pure white soft cheese of Lombardia), which an innkeeper left for a few weeks in the kitchen, then realized it had become blue with mold. It tasted good, so it began to be made in this way.

Gran Sardo

This is one of the newer style of cheeses that they are beginning to make in Sardegna, from sheep's milk. In this region they have one of the highest populations of sheep in Italy – over 7 million – and the milk is usually used to make Pecorino Romano, much of which is exported to America to put on top of pizza. But now they are beginning to experiment with slightly different styles, and this one is more like a Parmesan.

Nostrano Val di Fassa

This is a very distinctive cheese, very strong-smelling, and different from most Italian cheeses as it is made up in the Dolomites in the Tyrolean region, close to Trentino–Alto Adige, so in character it is quite close to an Austrian or Swiss cheese. During the maturation, the cheeses are washed regularly with a solution of water and salt, which softens their quite pungent smell. The cheese is fantastic on its own with a glass of wine, or it can be melted over polenta, or in a sauce for gnocchi.

Pecorino di Pienza

Pienza is a small town in Toscana, close to Siena, that is famous for pecorino, and if you go there it is like stepping back 2,000 years in time. The pure sheep's milk cheeses are produced from December to September, then there are a couple of months when the sheep need more milk to feed their lambs, so at this time a little cow's milk is added to the cheese. The very young, fresh cheese is a creamy color, then when it is semi-mature, at around 40 days, the rind is painted with oil that has been colored with tomato and, when it is more mature, painted with oil colored with black olives.

Piave

Produced in Veneto, in the valley of the Piave river, which is famous for a battle the Italians won against the Austrians during the First World War, the cheese has the consistency of Parmigiano-Reggiano, but it is younger and has a slightly different flavor, a little like Montasio. It is good shaved over bresaola as well as for eating as it is. When it has been "medium" aged, it is called *mezzana*, but the best is the stravecchio, the aged cheese.

Sola

Sometimes called Sora, the cheese is made with a mixture of raw cow's and goat's milk, and is roughly square and a little flat. Some say the name was given because the cheese looks like the sole of a shoe, others that the cheeses are this shape because they used to stack them like slabs of stone. According to another story, the shepherds would bring the cheeses down from the mountains by donkey, bumping along in saddlebags, so by the time they reached the bottom they had become flat and square.

This life

We have a saying in Italy, "The cobbler always has holes in his shoes." Chefs are always hungry because we are so busy cooking for other people, if we're not careful, we forget to feed ourselves. So we have beans on toast in front of the television at two o'clock in the morning, when we have finally locked up the kitchen for the night and crept home, long after people with normal lives are in bed. But we think about food all the time, we cook for our friends and families and eat out on our time off, and we dream about food and agonize and argue about it... a new way to prepare something that makes you crazy because you didn't know about it before, a fish so beautiful it brings tears to your eyes...

I like to see people excited about food, awake, switched on to the possibilities every time a box of fantastic ingredients comes into the kitchen. If you look at chefs who are really successful, they have all had some experience of life outside the kitchen too – music or football or motorcycles or art... they are not the ones who come in to work, do their job quietly all day, then get the number 147 bus straight home.

I became a chef in the first place because in my uncle's kitchen at La Cinzianella the chefs were not only more colorful but more independent than anyone else who worked there. My dad always said to me, "Don't be a waiter – be a chef, then you can cook your food and go home; you have only to relate to your ingredients; not the customers." It was true. At ten o'clock the kitchen was winding down, but outside in the restaurant the people were still there and the waiters had to be saints because, you know, Italians will sit talking for hours on end, and they keep on asking for a bit of this, a glass of that; and the waiting staff had to pander to them. And in the back Auntie Luisa and Cousin Maurizio would be having an argument, because everyone was tired and just waiting to go home.

Later in life, I realized that you can have the kind of detachment my father talked about only when you are younger and without the responsibilities of your own restaurant. When you have your own place, you can do everything right all evening in the kitchen, but outside in the restaurant it only takes the credit card machine to tell some guy he can't pay his bill, he gets angry, and the evening is spoiled. But when you have your own place, you are also in control of your own destiny, and that is worth everything.

Kitchens have their own unique microclimate and they can be hard places, extreme. But it isn't true, as people who have read Anthony Bourdain's book *Kitchen Confidential* might think, that kitchens are all full of crazy people, high on drugs or drink, getting mad at each other. Sometimes, though, you do have chefs with massive personalities who like to transmit their power and their ego all the time, and it's a terrible shame when you see them bullying and putting people down in front of everyone. I really believe that a kitchen, even if it is tough sometimes, should be fair. These days, we love to hand out awards and make big stars out of chefs, but it isn't right that one guy should get all the credit and the glory, because it is the *team* that does the job. You teach young chefs, of course, you get your kitchen to work in a certain way, and you check and taste everything, but everyone is important and none of us ever stops learning. Guys like Federico Sali, my sous chef, who is from Toscana, and our Catalan pastry chef, Ivan Icra, bring with them the ideas of their own regions, or the knowledge of a particular ingredient, and they influence what you do.

There are people who say you shouldn't show your recipes to new guys in the kitchen until you trust them not to steal them and take them to the next kitchen, but for me cooking is about sharing. You eat in someone's restaurant, and you see something that gives you an idea; you sit around talking shop with other chefs; sometimes you learn from raw kids who are just starting out. You can do something for twenty years and you can't see it in any other way, then an eighteen-year-old comes in fresh to the restaurant world, and says, "Why don't you do it like this?" and the moment he says it, you think, "What an idiot I am; why did I never see that before?"

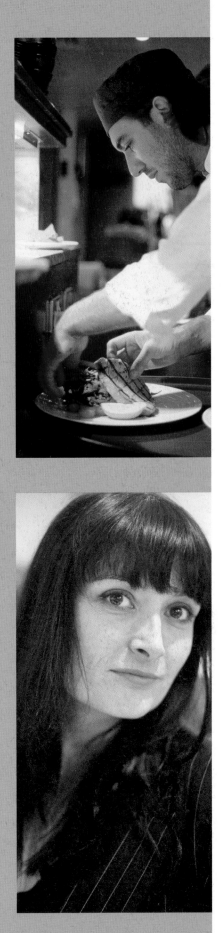

Every kitchen has its own rhythm. In the morning, when you are preparing, everyone is relaxed; there is a lot of banter and jokes. Then there are the two moments in the day when the people come in for lunch and dinner, and you kick off. Suddenly you have to get everybody's attention focused, quick, ready to go, because you all have to react and work for each other.

In the old hotel style of cooking, everything was put on a plate and sat there with a cloche on top, waiting for the rest of the dishes to be done. In the modern way, each dish comes together at the last minute, and each table's orders must be ready at the same time. You have to shout across the noise of the kitchen, so the person who is sautéing the fish is ready at exactly the same time as the one who is making the sauce, and the one who is doing the salad or making the pasta for someone else at the same table. So, like the build-up to a goal, we are talking about the collaboration of four or five people, and precision and timing are of the essence. You are sweating, out of breath, trying to keep your concentration, and if one person is asleep, or being too cocky, then the work of everyone else can be ruined.

You go through nightmares sometimes, because none of the customers has appeared when they are supposed to, then you have four tables that arrive together, and you can't go out and say, "Sorry; some of you will have to wait half an hour more." Everybody's food has to go out *now*, and you have to get it right. It doesn't matter how many times you cooked it previously and it was fantastic every time, because the people in the restaurant are going to judge you only on the dish *they* eat at *that* time.

At Locanda, just as I always promised myself we would be, we are one team. Everybody. Everyone eats together, holds meetings together, and tastes and discusses every new dish, so whenever a customer says, "What should I eat?," all the staff really know what they are talking about.

Sadly, we recently lost a treasured chef at Locanda, Mario Bonaccorsi, who had been with us since the days at Zafferano and was in his sixties when he

died just before this book was published. Mario was from Toscana, like Federico, and was like a father figure to us all. A real character, he had done so many things in his life and been a playboy in his time, and his stories were brilliant. Even after he was supposed to have retired, he missed the kitchen so much that he still insisted on coming in to do the butchering and he always helped us to teach the young boys. Mario was extraordinary in that he knew so much about the history of Italian cooking and ingredients; and he would always prepare the meals for the staff – because neither he, nor I, wanted them to be like cobblers with holes in their shoes.

I've seen chefs in kitchens get nothing but cornflakes for lunch, or a piece of white bread with a bit of cheese on top to put under the grill. Or they live on burgers, because that is all they can find when they finish work late, or they don't earn enough to eat out in restaurants. But if you get used to that flat, universal flavor of burgers, how are you ever going to come to really love and understand food? You can't describe a flavor or a texture. You have to experience it. I learned that sitting outside La Tour d'Argent in Paris on a trash can, eating sausages, while the customers tucked into the three-star Michelin dishes I had helped prepare but never tasted.

With success, your life changes. There are times when I think a little wistfully about Corgeno, about La Cinzianella with its view over the lake. Sometimes I go into the kitchen at Locanda on a Sunday, when the restaurant is closed and it is so, so quiet, and I think back to the country rhythm I grew up with. Everyone was so much less stressed. What was the occasional argument between Auntie Luisa and Cousin Maurizio? During the week, trade would be gentle, and then busy on the weekends, and in the autumn and winter it would be especially quiet. On Tuesdays, La Cinzianella would be closed, and my grandmother would cook her special meal for the whole family at our house at the top of the hill; and every summer, everyone would go on vacation and simply shut the restaurant for two weeks.

When we changed the menu for the month at La Cinzianella, we would do it on a Wednesday and have two gentle days to test and perfect the new dishes before the restaurant became busy on Friday. At Locanda, the menu evolves all the time; and if we decide on a new dish in the morning, because some fantastic prawns or mushrooms or artichokes have come into the kitchen, at lunchtime 80 people will try it, and another 120 at dinner.

When we go on vacation as a family to Sicilia, we stay in a tiny village, where there is a little restaurant called Da Vittorio. Vittorio, who is originally from the north of Italy, does all the cooking – and there is no menu. You just go in and he gives you whatever he has that is best – usually fish straight from the boats, and his own Limoncello. If he has enough people, and he doesn't want to work anymore he will just say, "Shut the gates." What a life – tempting? Not really, because the truth is, being still for too long is something I have never been good at, and when I look at what we have, Plaxy and I, and Margherita and Jack, it is fantastic.

I think of myself as an Italian who cooked in France but came of age in London. This is where I 'grew up' as a cook. Olivo was what I did in my twenties, Zafferano in my thirties; and now at Locanda, this is me at forty. One of my few regrets is that my granddad and my grandmother didn't live long enough to see me and my family here at Locanda. One of the best presents I could have had would have been for them to come here, just for one day, for one meal, to see what we do.

We are in this business, like my uncle at La Cinzianella, to serve people. If I didn't love welcoming everyone to Locanda, cooking for them, trying to see that they have a good time, I might as well get a job as an executive chef in a factory producing pies. I could go to work at nine, come back at four, and have an easy life, and earn roughly the same amount of money. But here, at Locanda, you enter into people's lives, and they enter yours.

This is what is exciting about we do; it is an important thing, which makes you feel very, very good. I tell the boys in the kitchen this all the time: it isn't just the food, it is about conviviality, sharing, about giving something special, the best you can give. Of course, there are people who will eat here tomorrow, in another restaurant the next day, somewhere else the next, and only want to cross Locanda Locatelli off their restaurant list. But for every one of those, there is someone who has become a friend, and someone else who might pass you in the street and not remember your name, but they remember a dish, a meal, an occasion, or a moment that they will treasure for the rest of their lives. Really for the rest of their lives.

Also by Giorgio Locatelli
Tony & Giorgio (with Tony Allen)

MADE IN ITALY. Copyright © 2007 by
Giorgio Locatelli. Photographs © 2006 by
Dan Lepard. All rights reserved. Printed in
Italy. No part of this book may be used or re-
produced in any manner whatsoever without
written permission except in the case of brief
quotations embodied in critical articles and
reviews. For information, address Harper-
Collins Publishers, 10 East 53rd Street,
New York, NY 10022.

HarperCollins books may be purchased for
educational, business, or sales promotional
use. For information, please write: Special
Markets Department, HarperCollins Publishers, 10 East 53rd Street, New York, NY
10022.

Quotes from: Pellegrino Artusi, *Science in the
Kitchen and the Art of Eating Well* (Marsilio,
1997); Elizabeth David, *Italian Food* (Pen-
guin, 1989); Anna Del Conte, *Entertaining
All'Italiana* (Transworld, 1991); Matthew
Fort, *Eating Up Italy* (Fourth Estate, 2004).

Originally published in Great Britain in a
different form in 2006 by Fourth Estate,
an imprint of HarperCollins Publishers.

FIRST U.S. EDITION PUBLISHED 2007.

*Designed by William Hall and Nicholas
Barba / www.williamhall.co.uk*

Library of Congress Cataloging-in-
Publication Data is available upon request.

ISBN: 978-0-06-135149-5
ISBN-10: 0-06-135149-0
07   08   09   10   11   HCUK/LEGO
10 9 8 7 6 5 4 3 2 1

Acknowledgments

This book is dedicated to Plaxy, my wife and alter
ego, to Jack, my son, whom I have watched grow
into a man, who has eaten every single thing that
was put in front of him with enthusiasm (even if it
was still moving); and my beautiful daughter,
Margherita "Dita," who hasn't been able to eat very
much at all, but has accepted her condition with
extraordinary courage, humor and good grace.

To my mum, Giuseppina, and dad, Ferruccio,
my brother, Roberto, my cousins, the Gnocchis,
in Corgeno and Gallarate; and everyone else
who knows me in Italy. To my *nonno* Mario
Caletti and *nonna*, Vincenzina Tamborini: I
wish you could have seen this book. My love of
food and life comes from both of you.

Thanks to everyone who has contributed to the
book, starting with Sheila Keating, who wove
everything I wanted to say together with great
understanding, and eventually had to shut me
up, or this book would have ended up as ten vol-
umes. To Dan Lepard for his creative input. Not
only for his great pictures, but his priest-like
quality of soaking up stress. Whenever my brain
was fogged up during the pressure of preparing
so much food for photography, he would say
"don't worry" and somehow I would stop worrying. Well done, William Hall, who valiantly led
and saw us through the complicated design
process. Special thanks to Federico Sali, who has
grown up with me over the past eight years, and
shares the same philosophy of food and cooking.
The success we have at Locanda is as much his as
it is ours; Federico Turri, who gives us the fantastic bread that is so important to the restaurant, on
a daily basis (Amen!) and is like my little brother;
Ivan Icra Salicru for being *the* man in the pastry
section; and Mario Bonaccorsi for being a father
figure to us all and bringing a real sense of family
to the kitchen. We will never forget you. A big
thank-you to everyone at Fourth Estate, especially Louise Haines, for commissioning the book
in the first place, supporting us all the way, and
having faith that we would eventually finish it;
and to Silvia Crompton and Michelle Kane for all
their hard work; many thanks too, to Lewis Es-
son and Jane Middleton for their diligent editing.

To Andy Needham; who in the face of adversity is still a loyal friend, Calogero "Rino" Bono, Alessandro Bottazzi, Alessandro Bay, Fabiano Righetti, Marco Torri, Roberto "Samurai" Fiumi, Lorenzo Preti, Elena Reygadas Castillo, Max Sali, Flavio Crisostomi, Roberto Veneruzzo and Chike. To Aline, who knows more about everyone who works in the restaurant than I do; all the girls on reception, the Dream Team; all the men and women who have worked in the restaurant, serving food, clearing glasses, keeping focused; Clem "Padre" Arricale and The Legendary Danny Murphy and Dr. Kalina for looking after la famiglia, at home and at work.

All of us in the food world owe a debt to the encyclopedic knowledge of writers such as Anna Del Conte and Alan Davidson, and to the work done by the Slow Food movement. Anyone who wants to know more about the brilliant diversity of Italian cheeses should check out their book on the subject, which has become one of our kitchen "bibles." The traditional cooking celebrated in *La Scienza in Cucina e l'Arte di Mangiar Bene* (Science in the Kitchen and the Art of Eating Well) by Pellegrino Artusi and *Le Ricette Regionali Italiane* by Anna Gosetti della Salda are at the heart of everything we do at Locanda, and I recommend them to anyone interested in Italian cooking. Thanks too, to Sheila's son Liam's classics teacher, Paul Stubbings, for getting stuck into some tricky ancient Latin for us. And from Dan, thanks to Delfina at Pietro Romanengo for the beautiful mostarda and frutta candita, and Michael Feldman, Toni and Raffaela Vitiello for their help on the photography. Thanks, too, Roberta Bradanini McEvoy.

A special mention must go to Franco and Anne Taruschio for being such great role models, Roy Ackerman for being a friend and diplomatic gentleman at all times; to Valerio Daros and Tarcisio Mauro, for being my rocks, and Marco Arrigo for his passion, honesty and sense of humor. To Mara and Clive Exton for being loving and welcoming from day one; Matthew Fort for believing in me; Paul Simonon and Damien Hirst for their wonderful paintings that hang in the restaurant. To Gavin and Gwen, Chico and Roberta, David Dawson and Lucian, Maureen Mills, Antonia and her lovely children. Also Gary, Antigone, and Keith. To David Buxton, who makes numbers bearable; Magimix, Porcelana and Illy Caffè and all our loyal suppliers, especially Marco at Gastronomica, Alivini, Ciborio, Green Landscape Nursery, KelticSeafare, Machiavelli, Vincenzo, Trustmeat, Foodhouse, Salvo, Ben's Fish, Almeida, Chef's Connection, Yorkshire Game, Heritage Prime, Secrett's Farm, Brindisa, Italbrokers, La Credenza, Bruno Giorgi, Portland Shellfish, Luca Castraberte and Montalcino.

Finally, to everyone who made me feel that, even though I was Made in Italy, England is my home.

You can order a range of Italian food and wines from:

Machiavelli
www.machiavellifood.com
Portobello Food
www.portobellofood.com
Savoria
www.savoria.co.uk (delivery nationwide)
Vincenzo
www.vincenzoltd.co.uk

Cheese, salumi and other produce:
Gastronomica
www.gastronomica.co.uk
La Fromagerie
www.lafromagerie.co.uk

Fish: *KelticSeafare*
www.kelticseafare.com

Game: *Yorkshire Game*
www.yorkshiregame.co.uk

Meat: *Heritage Prime*
www.heritageprime.co.uk
(organic, biodynamic beef, lamb and pork)

Vegetables: *Secrett's Farm*
www.secretts.co.uk

Miscellaneous: *Brindisa*
www.brindisa.com
(especially for anchovies and saffron)

FREE PUBLIC LIBRARY UNION, NEW JERSEY

3 9549 00399 2261